Contents

Chapter 7: Mainstream Media   191

Chapter 8: Heath and Health Care   220

Chapter 9: Schooling and Post-Secondary Education   244

Chapter 10: Work, Working, and the Workplace   275

PART 4: THE CHALLENGE OF DIVERSITY   297

Chapter 11: "Indian" Problems/Aboriginal Solutions   300

Chapter 12: Immigration and Multiculturalism   326

Preface

The aftermath of September 11th made it abundantly clear: The world we inhabit is riddled with contradictions both terrifying and destructive, yet immune to quick-fix solutions. Unparalleled global prosperity stands astride the poles of poverty and powerlessness; a commitment to equity clashes with the reality of grave injustices; and a growing endorsement of human rights is betrayed by spasms of butchery so barbaric in intensity as to question the very nature of human nature. Automation and labour-saving technology confer benefits, yet simultaneously inflict costs that compel many to work harder than ever or lose their jobs. An emergent respect for diversity is compromised by the demands of an evolving global monoculture that embraces the "McDonaldized" adage of "one size fits all." (Ritzer, 2000). Politicized minorities have soared on the wings of multicultural initiatives; the less fortunate remain locked in cycles of deprivation or despair. Nationalist movements have empowered some, destroyed others, while ushering in a topsy-turvy world order of challenge and change. The pull of globalization in defining a new map of the world cannot be denied; nevertheless, the push of nation-states and cultural values could well re-emerge as determining forces in the 21st century (Gaffield, 2003). Of particular worry is the environment. In the space of a century, our perceptions of nature have evolved from a foe to be vanquished, to a beleaguered friend in desperate need of protection from pollution and profit. Yet we appear incapable of slowing down this assault on the environment—with horrifying consequences for human survival (Paehlke, 2003).

The list could go on, but the point should be abundantly clear: So ensnared are societies by the crosswinds of competing dynamics that many people are reeling from the "new normal." The interplay of the progressive with the regressive has created a social world of baffling paradoxes. The "good" intersects with the "bad" to create an "in-between" that is "either-or" or "both-and" depending on the context or criteria. This interpenetration of the good with the bad has proven perplexing. The panic that crept into our consciousness when two planes crashed—kamikaze style—into the World Trade Towers has yet to subside. The aftermath of "9/11" not only revealed our vulnerabilities but also magnified the consequences of any mistakes; the complexities of a cooperative coexistence in a deeply divided world were also exposed. What values will govern the global age? A market society and global economy in which the quest for short-term profits is proving incapable of responding to human needs and the environmental crisis? Or a citizen-driven democracy, including an interventionist government on behalf of genuine national interests rather than transnational investment (Klein, 2002)? Choices will invariably inflict discomfort and dismay because, whatever the options, a sense of loss or restriction is inevitable (Pal and Weaver, 2003).

Perhaps a kind of cautious optimism is in order. On the plus side is an unshakable optimism that human ingenuity can solve all problems. No challenge is insurmountable in a world where everything is doable with a bit of "spit" and "polish." On the minus side is the paranoia that if things can go wrong, they will. No matter how much energy and expense is expended, there is always too much conflict or injustice but too little tolerance or cooperation. Public confidence is further shaken by the fact that solutions to problems remain as elusive as ever, while the unintended consequences of even well-intentioned actions may prove calamitous. Even more madness is feared as we confront yet uncharted realms—no more so than in Canada where the prospect of living together differently in a multicultural and multinational society without maligning national and vested interests is proving much more challenging than anticipated.

Canada clearly exudes an astonishing array of physical resources and social resourcefulness. It remains the envy of many because of its knack in forging unity from the strands of diversity without sacrificing national prosperity or human rights in the process. Many admire the "Canadian Way" in empowering Canadians with the resiliency (an ability to respond to stresses that differ from the usual) to absorb internal shocks while defusing external threats. Yet for all its munificence, this "adventure called Canada" is pervaded by problems, ranging from the deplorable state of aboriginal reserves and violation of indigenous people's rights, to the national disgrace of poverty, homelessness, the persistence and pervasiveness of racism, and a creaky criminal justice system that many regard as criminally unjust in its own right. Relative abundance and affluence notwithstanding, Canadians are experiencing bewilderment in coming to terms with new realities. Fears persist that the pursuit of material wealth may subvert the very things people are searching for: namely, contentment, security, and peace of mind. And worries about Canada's survival are constant because of nationalistic pressures. In their quest for self-determining autonomy, both aboriginal peoples and the Québécois are challenging the very notion of "what Canada is for," in effect, prompting critics to question the future of Canada as "our home and 'Native' land."

Which interpretation of Canada is more accurate—problem-free or problem-plagued? Any response will have to tiptoe around a series of contradictions. One arm of the UN has designated Canada as one of the world's best places to live, while another agency has lambasted Canadians for their human rights record (Seiler, 2003). If Canada is as progressive and egalitarian as many contend, why do Canadians continue to tolerate glaring extremes of poverty and affluence, mistreatment of aboriginal peoples, gender inequities, and hostilities toward immigrants? Alternatively, if Canada is the "mother of all evils," as some insist, how do we explain its prosperity and popularity? A sense of perspective is critical: Compared to its past, Canada has come a long way; in contrast with the human rights records of other countries, Canada is indeed a beacon of enlightenment. But in comparison with the ideals that Canadians have defined for themselves, principles have yet to match practice. Perspective is everything: Canada may not be a perfect society; nevertheless, it may well be one of the least imperfect of societies, given its commitment to equality (in principle, if not always in practice); endorsement of diversity as a virtue rather than a vice; a relatively high threshold for negotiation and compromise as a way of muddling through problems; and a commitment to inclusiveness despite mounting costs and carping criticism.

In light of such effusive praise—some deserved, some not; some earned, some bequeathed—Canadians have much to be grateful for. Even the idea of nit-picking over Canada's flaws may strike the reader as morbidly cynical in a land of such bounty. But however bountiful and beautiful, Canada is rife with social problems, and the fourth edition of *Social Problems in Canada* capitalizes on this mismatch between reality and espoused ideals by exploring those gaps that continue to perplex, provoke, and punish. A sociological perspective is applied to a host of social problems with respect to prevailing conditions, evolving constructions, ongoing controversies, and challenges to Canadian society at interpersonal, institutional, national, and global levels. Reference to social problems as conditions examines the antecedent causes of social problems, proposed cures, characteristics, and inadvertent consequences of problem-solving initiatives. Analyzing social problems as social constructions provides another insight. Particular attention is directed at public reactions to problematic conditions, together with political responses to the claims-making activities of aggrieved groups. Controversies that embroil Canadians are addressed as well, including those that threaten national unity or subvert the Canada-building process. Finally, emphasis remains riveted on those groups, movements, and initiatives that challenge those values, structures, and institutions which generate social problems.

Two themes undergird this edition of *Social Problems in Canada*. First and foremost is the commitment to improve our understanding of Canadian society by examining it through the prism of social problems. This edition's focus on the social dimensions of social problems promises to cast a fresh perspective on inconsistencies and injustices that compromise Canada's international standing. Controversial issues are examined from several perspectives as well, not only because it is unfair to impose a single point of view on a captive audience, but also because each perspective imparts a distinctive spin in the framing of both problems and solutions (Henslin, 2000). The sociological task should engage with competing views on what makes a social problem, how and why this makes a difference, and what should be done to right the wrong. Second, there is a commitment to explore the concept of social problems through the prism of Canadian society. Social problems are better understood when grounded in the realities of a Canada that is changing and diverse as well as connected and confused. Employing this two-way lens secures a coherent framework for what might otherwise look like a random collection of social issues and conditions.

There are several things this book is not. The book does not unscroll as a shopping list of social problems in Canada, with a one-size–fits-all formula for quick-fix solutions. Nor does it offer a scathing polemic that mercilessly castigates Canada for fouling its nest. Ethical issues about the morality of certain actions (from human cloning to capital punishment) are generally avoided, as is a moralizing about good or evil. Instead of prejudging who is right or wrong in applying appropriate solutions to problems, the focus is on theorizing social problems and claims to solutions by making explicit ("problematizing") the criteria for analysis, measurement, and assessment. All sides of an issue are approached as fairly and objectively as possible, while clearly specifying the underlying assumptions and implications of each perspective. The objective is to look behind and beneath Canada's social problems without bogging down in convoluted argument or paralyzing detail. Emphasis is on "problematizing" (making transparent) the process by which some conditions get to be defined as social problems (how, why, and by whom), debated in the public sphere, and acted on by way of policies and politics. In taking a sociologically informed approach for making transparent those social problems that many routinely take for granted, the intent is not to indoctrinate by telling readers what to think but what to think *about* in a critically informed manner. The challenge lies in going "against the grain,"—to be counterintuitive, so to speak—by interrogating the conventional without lapsing into a kind of "paralysis by analysis."

The fourth edition of *Social Problems in Canada* subscribes to the well-worn adage of "continuity in change." With respect to changes, the book continues the ongoing process of revision, updates, and improvements in content and style. Canada and Canadians are experiencing such dizzying changes that new editions can barely keep up with the latest without risking datedness. A new chapter entitled "Health and Health Care" has been introduced in response to growing concerns that not all is "healthy" in Canada. The triple whammy of SARS, BSE (human variant of mad cow), and West Nile Virus (with monkey-pox looming) is just the latest reminder of how the environment controls us, rather than the reverse (DiManno, 2003). Several chapters have merged in response to editorial decisions: "Social Inequality and Poverty" have been compressed into a single chapter as have "Globalization and Global Problems." A diversity dimension is incorporated throughout to acknowledge how political responses to differences are proving both a solution and a problem. In terms of pedagogical changes, each chapter contains a single case study with corresponding discussion questions, as well as "Did You Know?" boxes for additional information. Added improvements include the addition of discussion (or essay) questions in addition to several weblinks at the end of each chapter.

With regard to continuity, the book continues to explore the conditions, controversies, and constructions that challenge Canadian society. Social problems are analyzed around four distinct yet mutually related levels of reality: (a) interpersonal; (b) institutional; (c) societal; and (d) global. To get at the structural roots of social problems, the themes of "causes," "characteristics," "consequences," and "cures" are prominently featured throughout. Attention is also aimed at how interest groups interact with the political sector to construct conditions that are defined as socially problematic. True, a macrosociological orientation prevails; nonetheless, this book never loses sight of human agency in shaping definitions, responses, and outcomes. The overall thrust is thus sociological: Both structure (including the "determinism" of the market) and agency (including culture, creativity, and "free will") are rejected as exclusive explanatory frameworks since neither model can capture the complexity of human social life (Gaffield, 2003). Finally, the organization of the text remains largely unchanged from the previous edition, as indicated below.

1. The first part of *Social Problems in Canada* theorizes the concept of social problems by utilizing the insights and perspectives of sociology. The first chapter draws attention to how sociologists apply the concept of social problems. Particular attention is directed at deconstructing both the "problem" and the "social" in the expression "social problems."

2. The second part begins with the notion that social inequality is not only a problem in its own right but also an important source of Canada's social problems. Growing inequities, far from being accidental or inconsequential, threaten to undermine the very freedoms and benefits promised by economic development and a market economy (Kawachi and Kennedy, 2002). Patterns of inequality are analyzed with respect to class, race, aboriginality, ethnicity, and gender. Analyzed as well are proposals for solutions that entail a rethinking of both inequality and equality.

3. The third part explores the concept of institutions in crisis. The costs associated with the criminal justice system including policing, prisons, and courts are examined from a social problem perspective. References to mass media (including newscasting, TV programming, advertising, movie-making, and the Internet) as a social problem should come as no surprise, given the oft-stated relationship between media consumption and antisocial behaviour, especially among young males. The issue of health and health care are discussed as a social problem as well, including coverage of ageing and demography. Also discussed are challenges to traditional family structures; changes to the workplace and the concept of work and working; and the crisis in schooling and education, especially at the post-secondary level.

4. The fourth part delves into the promises and perils of engaging diversity at societal levels. Canada may appear to be tottering on the edge because of ethnic brinkmanship; nevertheless, its precedent-breaking models for living together differently may prove Canada's most enduring legacy. Canada's perpetual quest for national unity is situated within the context of aboriginal people's demands for self-determining autonomy. The chapter on immigration and multiculturalism demonstrates the challenges in forging a cooperative coexistence.

5. The fifth and final part deals with the problems of Canada's evolving relationship to a new global order. With globalization as the dynamic animating this era, the chapter addresses an array of global problems pertaining to the environment, population, ethnic nationalism, global monoculture, and poverty and urbanization. Canada's complicity in reinforcing a global apartheid that segregates the rich from the poor is implicated within the politics of foreign aid and development.

The fourth edition of *Social Problems in Canada* does not pretend to do more than it can deliver. Social problems are too complex and too inextricably embedded within the social fabric of society to yield pat answers, offer quick-fix solutions, or convey false optimism. What the book does deliver are timely and relevant questions for stimulating critical reflection, informed debate, and focused action. If just one reader is inspired to make Canada a better place in which to live by acting upon these questions, this edition will have done its job.

SUPPLEMENTS

A Test Item File is available to faculty members who adopt this book. The Test Item File contains multiple choice, true or false, and essay questions for each chapter in the text.

ACKNOWLEDGMENTS

I would like to thank the following reviewers: Jeannette Auger, Acadia University; Steve Dumas, University of Lethbridge; and Thomas Groulx, St. Clair College for their insightful comments. I would also like to thank the team at Pearson Education, which includes developmental editor Jennifer Murray and production editor Richard di Santo. Special thanks to copy editor Nancy Carroll whose skills and commitment will never be underappreciated.

part one

Conceptualizing Social Problems

Whatever else it may be or aspire to be, Canada is a land of contradictions. The interplay of history, geography, and demography has conspired to create a series of paradoxes that invariably create social problems in need of solutions. To one side, Canada is under pressure to address the concerns, claims, and aspirations of its major ethnicities, namely, French, English, and aboriginal, and to do so in a manner consistent with an official multiculturalism, the provisions of the 1982 Constitution Act, and the values embraced by The Charter of Rights and Freedoms. To the other side, Canada must be constantly on guard to protect, preserve, and promote its unity, identity, and integrity in the face of both internal and external pressures. On the one hand, Canada has implemented a number of initiatives to remove discrimination while improving the inclusiveness of historically disadvantaged groups such as aboriginal peoples, women, visible minorities, the poor and disempowered, and people with disabilities. On the other hand, the struggle for equality has faltered in the face of entrenched interests, systemic barriers, hidden agendas, and a constitutional order that privileges "pale-male" interests at the expense of others' interests. For some, Canada is one of the best places in the world to live because of its commitment to freedom, opportunity, participation, and equality. For others, these commitments are not worth the paper they are printed on, and living in Canada has proven an exercise in futility and frustration. Not surprisingly, problems for some Canadians are solutions for others, while solutions in some cases have proven problematic for many.

Canadians are perplexed and provoked by the enormity of these contradictions and challenges. So too are sociologists who must live with the rather awkward realization that the worse things get, the more appealing is their discipline. Central to any sociological debate about social problems and claims to solutions are the following questions that provide a framework for analysis:

- What are social problems? What distinguishes a social problem from an ordinary problem? Does everything "bad" that happens in society automatically qualify as a social problem regardless of intent or impact? Or should we only include problems that attract a public response?

- Are social problems "out there" or "in here"? Or are they somewhere "in between" the external and the internal? Do social problems exist in their own right, or are they an attribute or label that is applied after the fact because of context, criteria, or consequences? Should social problems be conceptualized as a thing or a process?

- What is the relationship between the personal and the social? To what extent can intensely personal incidents that involve individuals as victims or perpetrators be defined as social problems? Are personal troubles reflective of more fundamental problems related to structures, values, and change? Does a focus on the broader context gloss over the role of individual agency in defining and solving problems?

- What about solutions? Do solutions exist for every social problem? What is it about problems that preclude solutions? How do sociologists cope with the challenge of matching solutions to problems? How do we account for the quintessential North American belief that there is a solution for every problem, and that's the end of it? Is this a healthy outlook or does such an optimistic mindset cripple our efforts for meaningful solutions, while setting us up for failure?

This section explores many of the theoretical issues that inform a sociological analysis of social problems. The world we inhabit is riddled with moral dilemmas (Lee, 2003): crime, violence, discrimination, poverty and inequality, environmental pollution and deterioration, sexism, institutions in crisis, and global apartheid. These problems are routinely dealt with by magazines, newspapers, and television talk shows; nevertheless, media treatment often obscures rather than clarifies because of a focus on the superficial, flamboyant, and confrontational (Ritzer, 2002). By contrast a sociological analysis provides a holistic analysis that explores root causes and connections. A sociologically informed approach points to the possibility of solutions by allowing us to go "behind" and "beneath" the problems. To be sure, sociologists tend to disagree over the most basic issues, including: (a) what constitutes a social problem, who says so, and why; (b) the magnitude and scale of social problems; (c) the preferred methods of analysis; (d) proposed solutions; and (e) what (if any) solutions are possible. Still, some consensus can be discerned. Most sociologists would probably subscribe to the following sociological "jingle": The personal is the social; the social is constructed; the constructed is contextual; and the contextual is personal. That is to say, there is nothing natural or normal about the world we live in except as a social convention, which is created by those who define situations as best they can under the circumstances and who interact accordingly. Yes, we make choices but our choices are societally determined within broader contexts that are not necessarily of our choosing or making. Additional commonalities can be found as well. Sociologists emphasize the social dimensions of human behaviour rather than the biological or psychological to explain causes, consequences, and cures. Individual actions that create social problems are not necessarily dismissed as a sign of personal weakness or moral degeneracy. Rather a person's identity, experiences, and opportunities are thought to reflect his or her social location in society—with respect to gender, race, social class, age, sexual orientation, and so on (also Mooney et al., 2004).

This focus on the social and cultural improves our understanding of social problems. It has also proven critical in advancing solutions by framing how social problems are defined. Framing remains a key means for processing information, in part by mobilizing preferred meanings on a mass scale through control of the agenda, vocabulary, and boundaries of the debate (Rohlinger, 2002). The framing of social problems in terms of *conditions* (causes, characteristics, consequences, and cures) and *constructions* (claims-making activities) secures a conceptual framework for analysis and assessment. In shifting attention from either objective reality or subjective conditions, a constructional analysis emphasizes a people's collective reaction to troublesome conditions (Best, 2001; Blumer, 1971).The distinctive way in which social problems are framed for debate and solution should never be underestimated: The framing experience not only shapes public policies and social services; more importantly, it also influences how people make sense of themselves and others in constructing a world where solutions do not always match problems, and vice versa, to the dismay of many (Loseke, 2003).

chapter one

Problematizing
Social Problems

FRAMING THE PROBLEM

Both Canada and the United States have been racked by a spate of incidents that have triggered what media experts call a "moral panic." Moral panics arise when an "incident" is so shocking that its sensationalization by the media becomes the starting point for prolonged debates over problems and solutions. Take the United States: The events of September 11th continue to reverberate with a resonance that speaks of American anger and anxieties. A fierce determination to avenge the deaths of nearly 4000 in the World Trade Towers has prompted a national dialogue. What "problems" could have caused the tragedy? Complacency and lax security? Arab nationalism? A pervasive anti-Americanism? What about solutions? Should the United States do nothing? Improve internal security? Bomb everything in sight that opposes American interests?

Canadians too have had to confront their demons. The emergence of Severe Acute Respiratory Syndrome (SARS), a virus that eventually claimed the lives of 44 Toronto area residents, including two nurses in the line of duty, while crippling the local economy, is just the latest in a long list of problems to confront Canada. Additional social problems include ongoing confrontations with aboriginal peoples over competing rights, national unity crises that repeatedly push Canada to the brink, persistent levels of poverty and homelessness that mock our collective self image as a progressive society, isolated acts of violence that never cease to shock when innocent victims are involved, and incidents of racism, including allegations of police racial profiling. Even seemingly progressive moves toward inclusiveness, such as recognition of same-sex marriage, may be criticized as a sign that Canada has abandoned its moral moorings. The perception of a troubled Canada was poignantly articulated by the father of Jason Lang, a young Albertan gunned down at school, who told a news conference: "May God have mercy on this broken society and all the hurting people in it … that a lot of things have to change in our society, lots of things need to be healed" (*National Post*, 30 April, 1999: A-10).

Reaction to each of these events produces intense introspection about the health of contemporary Canada. The verdict is mixed: Yes, this "adventure called Canada" may yet prove the quintessential 21st century country (Greenspon, 2003), a shining example of how to forge a distinctive third way—as glowingly explained by Britain's *The Spectator*:

> Indeed, Britons should look to Canada for an example of civilized 21st century living. There they will find a state that is unafraid of preserving its sovereignty in the face of enormous pressures to integrate with its gigantic neighbour … a society which combines prosperity and opportunity for the individual with socialized medicine, a successful system of public education …. Canada really is the best place in the world; a fact repeatedly endorsed by that bete noire of the American Right, the United Nations (Robinson, 2003: A-18).

Others have been no less stinting in their kudos: Canada is about as close to "utopia" as humanly possible (Heath, 2001) and, if not perfect, certainly the least imperfect country in the world. No wonder, then, a Mexican ambassador to Canada once complimented Canada as "a solution in search of a problem."

Yet fears are mounting that not all is well. The rules, roles, and relationships that once governed Canada are becoming unstuck, particularly among young Canadians who are defying both labels and conventions—and doing so without mainstream ("adult") approval (Anderssen and Valpy, 2003; Handa, 2003). For example, in surveys that ask people what makes them proud of Canada, an age divide is quickly apparent. General responses include Canada's peacekeeping or high ranking by the UN; for those in their twenties, the focus is on Canada's commitments to multiculturalism, tolerance, bilingualism, and The Charter of Rights and Freedoms (Mendelsohn, 2003). Other social cleavages, including the rural–urban divide, are no less important in defining—and dividing—Canada between the Old and New. The changing nature of Canada raises an important question: What kind of society do Canadians want: One in which all decisions are filtered through a materialistic lens, that emphasizes "having" as more important than "being," that measures the worth of people on the basis of wealth or appearances, that treats other people as commodities for instant gratification, and that reinforces a myth of personal happiness without social responsibility (Klein, 2002)? Or should we promote a Canada that endorses civilized ways of living together differently—as a community of communities—without forsaking its commitment to unity, identity, and prosperity?

This chapter explores many of the theoretical issues that inform a sociological analysis of social problems. The concept of social problems is neither self-evident nor reflective of common sense. There is nothing natural or normal about social problems in the sense of inevitability. Rather, social problems are social constructions that reflect definitions of the world by those with the power to impose their agendas and interests. Two major questions are central to any theorizing of social problems: What is meant by the "problem" in social problems? And what is so "social" (or should it be "antisocial") about social problems? A sociologically informed approach enables us to deconstruct these questions by going "behind" and looking "beneath." It also provides a look at why solving social problems remains an elusive goal. The chapter begins by defining social problems, followed by a look at the contested notion of "social" and "problem," in each case asking what makes a problem "social" and what makes the social a "problem." Particularly relevant is the distinction between "constructionists" and "conditionalists" in defining the subject matter for analysis. The major sociological perspectives of functionalism, conflict, and interactionism are offered as alternative frameworks for explaining human behaviour and the social condition. An extended study of suicide as a social problem rather than a personal problem demonstrates the value of a sociologically informed analysis. This study also demonstrates the key insight of sociology: That our location in society in terms of gender, race, class, or age will profoundly shape our experiences and opportunities—making it even more critical to connect the individual with society through the social. The chapter concludes by discussing how proposed solutions to social problems have proven a problem in their own right. This lack of consensus, commitment, or concern has complicated the prospect of living together in a diverse and changing Canada.

Praise for Canada as a solution in search of a problem should not be accepted uncritically. If Canada is such a solution, how do we explain the proliferation of problems? Conversely, if Canada is such a problem, how do we account for its remarkably high standard of living, both material and social? A sense of perspective is helpful. There is a possibility that Canada has actually set itself up for "failure." Social problems may be a "normal" and necessary component of a Canada because of our commitment to ideals that may be humanly impossible to achieve. The implausibly ideal standards that Canadians have established for themselves may create an awareness of situations as social problems that other jurisdictions might dismiss as "normal" or "inevitable." For example, Canada may define as a social problem (and illegal as well) discrimination on the basis of sexual orientation; other jurisdictions may prefer to see homosexuality as a problem to be ruthlessly suppressed. To the extent that Canada is a society with many social problems as a consequence of its decision to establish higher standards of justice, equality, and fairness, a rethinking is in order: We should not judge Canada by the number of social problems; rather, judgement should be based on Canada's willingness to address these problems as part of its commitment to a just and inclusive society.

DEFINING (ANTI-) SOCIAL PROBLEMS

Defining social problems is not as simple as it seems. Definitions of social problems are as varied and numerous as they are confusing and contradictory. Much of this definitional disarray reflects the nature of the definition process: That is, things or events can be defined in terms of what they look like; what they are supposed to do; and what they actually do. For example, Canada's official multiculturalism can be defined: (a) in descriptive terms that reflect its ethno-cultural diversity; (b) prescriptively, with respect to ideals for living together with our differences; or (c) proscriptively, as government policy for securing consensus and control. None of these definitions of multiculturalism is more correct than the next. Nor is there such a thing as a right or wrong definition. After all, each casts light on certain aspects of multiculturalism that others prefer to ignore. Rather than reflecting an accurate appraisal of reality, definitions are best evaluated for their utility as explanatory tools for understanding social reality. And the best definitions tend to incorporate as many dimensions as possible; for example, a comprehensive understanding of multiculturalism would include the descriptive, prescriptive, and proscriptive.

A similar line of reasoning applies to social problems where the proliferation of definitions provides both insight and confusion. Definitions can be divided into two major streams, condition-based (both subjectivists and objectivists), and construction-based. The earliest definitions emphasized social problems as conditions that posed a threat to (a) society; (b) the prevailing social order; and (c) existing institutional structures. One of the earliest definitions by Fuller and Myers (1941) explained social problems as a condition perceived by a significant number of people as a harmful departure from some cherished norm. Sociology as a discipline originated in the study of social problems that accompanied the decline of the traditional order, followed by its transition into a modern social order. Sociologists were preoccupied with social stability as the norm, and defined social problems as conditions of deviance created by defective socialization and social misfits who challenged the normative basis of society (Coleman and Cressey, 1984; Bolaria, 2000). Any behaviour at odds with conventional rules, roles, and relationships was deemed pathological (dysfunctional), and in need of solution if a functioning society was to survive. The notion of social problems as conditions persists. But, whereas social problems were once framed as conditions of dysfunction or deviance, the current focus is on those relatively normal conditions (from structures and institutional frameworks to cultural values) that induce problems (Bolaria, 2000).

Definitions of social problems as conditions vary along subjective or objective dimensions. For subjectivists, social problems come into existence only when a condition is defined as problematic by a critical mass of people. No matter how contemptible or destructive a particular situation, few conditions are inherently problematic until defined as such by some interest group. Conditions that are defined as disruptive or harmful may be deemed as social problems, as are conditions that reflect a gap between our ideals and reality. True, conditions may be real regardless of peoples' awareness or intent; however, they only become social problems when defined as such. What is then defined as problematic will vary from one time period to another, and is relative to particular cultural contexts. For example, smoking in public was once regarded as acceptable—even sophisticated and health inducing. At present, smoking in public is widely despised as a serious health problem and legally banned in many public areas, although smoking in private remains a personal choice.

Other condition-based definitions emphasize the objective dimensions of social problems. Objective definitions approach conditions as external realities that inflict harmful effects ("problems") irrespective of public awareness of what is going on (Green, 1994). Problems include those conditions that contradict core values at the heart of Canada's constitutional order or conditions that violate fundamental individual and human rights—regardless of recognition or reaction. For example, capitalist exploitation is a social problem, whether the exploited are aware of it or not. In fact, one might argue that the whole point of class exploitation is to construct ideas and ideals that conceal the source of inequities ("false consciousness"). In short, both subjectivists and objectivists differ in emphasis; nevertheless, they share a common commitment by focusing on conditions as the primary field of study. These problematized conditions are then analyzed in terms of "causes," "characteristics," "consequences," and "cures."

Other definitions embrace a <u>constructionist orientation</u>. A constructionist orientation has transformed this field by approaching social problems not as inherently unjust and objectively immoral, but as an <u>interpretative process, including those politics by which</u> problems were defined as <u>social problems and then acted upon by way of claims-making</u> <u>activities that challenged, resisted, and transformed</u>. The focus is not on people's perception of harmful conditions per se but on <u>how people *react* to these harmful conditions</u> through <u>social movements</u> that challenge those conditions defined as harmful or disruptive. Political reaction (both negative and positive) to these claims-making activities is also included in a constructionalist focus. As noted by Blumer (1971) and others (Gusfield, 1996) certain conditions become a social problem of interest to sociologists only when defined as such by some sector of society, then elicits an organized response by way of mobilized resistance or reaction through collective action or public policy. Questions of relevance to constructionists include: Why are some conditions rather than others the target of claims-making actions? How are individuals mobilized to resist and challenge these socially defined conditions? In what ways are problems publicized and drawn to the attention of central authorities? To what extent will authorities devote attention or expend resources to ignore, deflect, modify, or respond to the claims-making activities of aggrieved groups? What happens when social problems are perceived as inadequately addressed by the claims-making group?

On the surface, there is not much to distinguish a subjectivist (conditions) approach from a constructionist approach. Both endorse the notion of social problems as rooted in subjective awareness, socially constructed, and situationally defined. Problematic conditions are neither normal nor inevitable, according to both positions, but reflect definitions that are socially created by individuals making meaningful choices in contexts that are not necessarily of their making. What distinguishes the two approaches is the concept of claims-making. Subjectivists are concerned with the *conditions* that become defined as a social problem; who says, why, and on what grounds; and to a lesser extent on what is proposed as a solution, by whom, with what tactics, and with what kind of outcomes. By contrast, constructionist approaches tend to focus on the *processes* by which some conditions rather than others are acted upon; how power is exercised in shaping agendas; what measures are invoked to draw public and political attention; to what extent official responses prove satisfactory; and what is involved in repriming the process if political responses prove inadequate. Constructionists perceive conditions as largely irrelevant: The true focus of study are the claims-making activities of groups who articulate grievances and make claims in reaction to some perceived conditions, whether real or imagined (Kitsuse and Spector, 1987). For conditionalists, then, conditions represent the source of study; for constructionists, claims-making is central. Without a reactive-interactive component, constructionists argue, problems are not social problems.

Which definition "works" for this edition of *Social Problems*? A definition is endorsed that combines both conditionalist and constructionist approaches, namely, social problems as conditions that are harmful or are deemed wrong, persistent, and widespread (rather than a single person), the conditions are changeable, and pressure is exerted to change these antisocial conditions (Loseke, 2003). Put simply, social problems are conditions that are harmful or defined as disruptive and acted upon accordingly through protest or politics. More generally, social problems are defined as those conditions that are defined by a critical mass of people to be harmful to society or its members, together with the process by which these "problematized" conditions are collectively challenged by way of claims-making activity. This definition is not without flaws. For example, how do we operationalize and provide measurable values to terms such as "critical mass"? References to "harmful" are equally vague, given the difficulties of operationalizing this term for purposes of measurement.

Still, the value of this definition is two-fold: First, it acknowledges that social problems may reflect objective conditions in society. But social problems only become sociologically relevant when challenged by those with the resources and resourcefulness to do something about them. Yes, objective conditions that harm or disrupt may be real and powerful, but to study these types of conditions does not distinguish sociology from other approaches. This idea that conditions become sociologically relevant only when acted upon by claims-making individuals imparts a distinctively sociological spin to the study of social problems. Second, the definition also concedes the importance of process; that is, conditions called social problems become sociologically relevant when the social kicks in by way of protest, collective action, or government policy.

WHAT'S THE "PROBLEM" IN SOCIAL PROBLEMS?

What kind of problems are sociologists attracted to? Under what circumstances are conditions defined as problematic? By whom? What for? On what grounds? Answers to these questions are more elusive than many might imagine. Part of the difficulty arises from the fact that most problems are not self-evident.

Did You Know?

How is inequality a social problem? Does the very existence of material differences between individuals indicate a problem? Take income inequality: Should a university professor earn more money than the cleaning staff at the university? More than the prime minister of Canada? More than professional hockey players? Who says so, and why? And on what criteria can such an assessment be made? Or how about death by trauma? Is suicide, which claims nearly 4000 Canadians a year, a social problem? Should car accidents that claim nearly 2000 lives in Canada each year be regarded as a social problem? Are the 550 homicides per year in Canada a social problem? What about the 14 people killed in two spectacular avalanches in the winter of 2002 in western Canada? Or the horrific death of ten-year-old Holly Jones of Toronto? Or life expectancy: A girl born in Canada in the year 2000 can expect to live to age 82; a boy born in 2000 has a life expectancy of 76.7. Should the 5.3 year gap be considered a social problem or simply a fact of life reflecting a male inclination toward riskier choices?

Part of the problem also reflects the nature of social problems. Social problems do not exist as discrete and readily labelled categories for analysis or assessment. Cross-cultural studies confirm the near lack of universally defined conditions as problematic, in effect reinforcing the relative and socially constructed nature of social problems. For instance, crime may be widely condemned as a problem except among those whose livelihood depends on proceeds from criminal activity or with jobs in the criminal justice system. Moreover, the tendency to confuse laws with problems must be tempered by the relativities of a specific context. In some Malaysian countries, crimes punishable by fines include chewing gum, spitting on sidewalks, or driving around with less than half a tank of gas. Such actions would not be regarded as criminal or even problematic in many North American jurisdictions. Similarly, acts of deviance involving widely accepted norms may or may not be seen as a problem if context is taken into account. For example, speeding on a highway is illegal, yet many act as if such actions were normal and acceptable rather than problematic. By contrast, any excessive speed or reckless driving around a school zone may be harshly deplored and vigorously punished.

Of particular note is the perception that problems themselves are relative to time and place, with the result that what once was defined as a problem may now be seen as normal. Consider gay rights in Canada (Philp, 2003). The rapid emergence of gay rights is the most striking example of Canada's growing tolerance. A generation ago, homosexuality was defined as a mental illness, gay sex was a crime, equality rights for gays and lesbians had yet to be contemplated, sexual orientation was grounds for discrimination, gay pride parades didn't exist, and the idea of same-sex marriage seemed like a contradiction in terms. A generation later, gay rights are taken as a birthright, at least by younger Canadians, and more cautiously by those 55 years and older (Philp, 2003). Gay households are counted in the census, same-sex relationships have the same benefits and rights as heterosexual common law relations, including fertility clinics and progressive adoption agencies that create the possibility for alternative families. And, in June 2003, the Ontario Court of Appeal ruled in favour of legalizing same-sex marriages—a move heralded by some as the cutting edge of a New Canada, and by others as an abandonment of this country's moral compass in a morass of political correctness.

What was historically considered normal may now be re-evaluated as problems. For example, the spanking of children by parents or guardians once was regarded as obligatory and good ("spare the rod, spoil the child"). To not spank was scorned as a sign of parental irresponsibility that would inevitably lead to greater personal and social problems. Today spanking is increasingly defined as a problem in its own right, a gross violation of children's human rights and a recipe for problems in later life. Or take domestic abuse. Domestic abuse was rarely seen as a social problem when a patriarchal society openly privileged men as "kings of their castles" and dependents as their "property." Changes in society have shattered this sexism; domestic abuse is against the law and dealt with accordingly. Similarly, a raft of new social problems have entered into public awareness in recent years, including smoking, drinking and driving, suntanning, fur-wearing, meat-eating, homelessness, obesity, and the emergent troika of "road rage," "air rage," and "work rage." In short, problems come and go because of changes in the social environment— including people's evolving perceptions, definitions, and assessment of those situations once personal, now public; once tolerable, now deviant; once normal, now anti-social; and once a solution, now a problem. The lesson should be clear: Problems by nature are not inherent to society but reflect violations of shifting community values and norms resulting from rapid social change, institutional changes, and contrasting subcultures.

Even the word "problem" is problematic. For most, the term "problem" conjures up something that is devalued or disruptive, a departure from the norm or the usual or natural.

However, there is nothing unusual or unnatural about the persistence and pervasiveness of social problems. To the contrary, social problems are an inevitable and recurrent feature of a society that is complex, changing, and diverse. Confrontation, conflict, and contradiction are inevitable under these circumstances, given the existence of diverse publics with divergent agendas over who gets what. Social problems are also known to arise from normal decision-making processes that may create negative consequences. Or problems arise from well-meaning actions that are rooted in miscalculation or incorrect assumptions, but which may have the effect of creating new problems or intensifying existing ones. The same values that induce pro-social behaviour (for example, competitive individualism) can also elicit anti-social activity, depending on the context, or when taken to extremes. Put baldly, social problems are a normal component of society, and the frequency of social problems is no less a departure from the norm than the prevalence of consensus or regulation. No one should be surprised by this admission. In a postmodern world of diversity and change, with its uncertainty and confusion, a problem-free society is a contradiction in terms.

For the most part, then, problems are difficult to define or defend in a world that has largely abandoned absolute standards of right or good. In the postmodernist world of the millennium—where everything is sharply challenged—the rules, roles, and relationships that once secured the moorings of a predictable society have been cut adrift because of defiance toward convention or authority, with the result that some virtues are now seen as vices and vice versa. One person's definition of a problem may be another's solution. What some define as social problems are regarded as normal and desirable conditions for others, depending on one's preferred vision of society. For those who believe society is fundamentally sound, the problem is with individuals who don't fit; for those who see society as fundamentally unfair, the system (not individuals) is the problem.

Sociologists continue to dwell on the "problem" in social problems. At the heart of sociological interest are debates over the ontological status of problems. Three scenarios prevail: (1) Do problems really exist as objective conditions that fall outside public or political awareness? (2) Or do social problems reflect objective conditions that are perceived as problems by a significant number of people because they are disruptive, harmful, or diminishing the quality of life by exposing gaps between ideals and reality? (3) Or are problems properly viewed not as conditions—real or perceived—but as constructions involving people doing something about the conditions around them? Conditionalists (objectivists/subjectivists) and constructionists have radically different views of the "problem" in social problems (Best, 1989). For objectivists, the problem is the condition; for subjectivists, problems are perceived conditions; for constructionists, the problem is properly situated around collective reactions to unacceptable conditions.

Also evolving over time are differences in conceptualizing social problems. Sociologists themselves have experienced a shift in how problems are discussed, the type of questions asked, the manner in which responses are framed, and the kind of answers that are permissible. Each of these narratives about social problems corresponds with sociological perspectives on society—namely, functionalism, conflict, and interactionism. Functionalists interpret society as a complex system of interrelated parts, with each part contributing to stability and order. Society is envisaged as fundamentally sound; anything that detracts from the moral consensus at the core of a sound society is, by definition, a social problem. Social problems are thus seen as aberrations in a normally functioning society. Social problems arise from rapid social change and corresponding culture lag. They also reflect the fact that different groups have different values, agendas, and demands; that socialization is imperfect, and that institutions do not necessarily do what they were intended to do.

Conflict theorists also interpret society as a site of inequality involving competition over scarce resources. According to conflict theorists, society is essentially "exploitative"; therefore, anything that perpetuates this inequality is a social problem. Conversely, practices and developments that challenge the system are defined as solutions. Those in positions of power and wealth possess the resources to define social problems as those conditions or activities that disrupt the prevailing status quo. Rather than an aberration from the norm, conflict theorists define social problems as intrinsic to the structure, organization, and process of society. For example, social problems are inescapable in those societies organized around the capitalist principles of profit, competitive individualism, and class conflict. Contradiction, confrontation, and conflict are integral to the very functioning of a system devoted to exploitation and oppression, even though considerable effort is expended in conveying the impression of social order and inter-group harmony.

Interactionist perspectives on society tend to reject the inevitability of social problems, preferring instead to see this dimension of social reality as constructed and contested. Society is neither good nor bad; it just is, and it is up to the sociologists to discover how people go about defining situations as a problem. Rather than focusing on objective conditions as the source of problems, the emphasis is on people's reactions to these conditions. For interactionists, especially symbolic interactionists, there is no such thing as external human reality (or conditions) that is independent of human experience or logically prior to everyday existence. Social reality is an ongoing human accomplishment, constructed by human actors who symbolically define conditions, assign meanings, and act accordingly. Similarly, social problems are constructed through meaningful interaction, insofar as people define situations as problematic and act upon their decisions in seeking a solution. Interactionist perspectives are less interested in what is right or wrong, much less in what is moral or immoral in the ethical sense, except as perceived as such by the public. Their interest revolves around people's perception of right or wrong, how these perceptions undergo change, and how agencies are enlisted to remove these disruptions.

This analysis of perspectives exposes the logic behind a "problem" definition. Problems are defined as such when reality runs afoul of a preferred vision of society. If society is envisaged as tolerant and open, anything that detracts from this ideal—prejudice or racism—will be defined as a problem. For example, social inequality is generally regarded as a social problem. But this was not always the case. Historically, inequality was deemed to be necessary, inevitable, and normal—either because of human nature or the divine right of nobility. In some parts of the world this perception is still the case, including those sectors of Canada who see inequality as critical to prosperity; conversely, equity efforts to eliminate inequality are deemed a problem rather than a solution. Functionalists, for example, may not define inequality as a problem unless something unfair interferes with the process of sorting out who gets what. For many sociologists, however, inequality is defined as a problem because its presence is contrary to the ideals of a fair and just society. In other words, the gap between the ideal (egalitarian) and reality (unequal) is what generates the social problem known as inequality. Similarly, the gap between an author's vision of an ideal society and the reality "out there" provides a rationale that justifies the inclusion of certain social problems, and not others. For example, the inclusion of a social inequality chapter implies that equality is the preferred state of affairs while inequality is framed as a social problem.

WHAT'S SO "SOCIAL" ABOUT SOCIAL PROBLEMS?

Problems exist everywhere. They vary in scale from the trivial to the cataclysmic, from the intensely personal to the remote and abstract, and from the local to the global. Such a span raises the question: What is distinctive about social problems? Is there a subject matter that can be labelled "social problems," or does the study of social problems simply refer to a distinctive way of looking at the world around us? What distinguishes social problems from other problems in society? How do personal problems differ from social problems? Why are anti-social activities called "social" problems? Why don't we call social problems anti-social problems to reinforce their negative and harmful impact on society? Framing the problem socially is critical for a sociological analysis. Instead of asking why people are poor or live in poverty, sociologists might well ask: What is it about society that creates poor people, then punishes their presence? Why is it that the poor rather than the affluent are defined as a social problem? Why are individuals rather than institutions and government policies blamed for being poor? A closer look at the "social" of social problems casts light on the distinctiveness of sociology compared to other disciplines.

What, then, do we mean by the "social" in social problems? A useful point of contrast begins with the concept of personal problems. A problem is defined as personal when the individual serves as the centre of analysis, assessment, reform, and outcome. Both the source of and solution to the problem are thought to reside within the person. Two variants of a personal problem include: First, personal problems are the result of biology or inherited characteristics. Problems are attributed to flaws in the bio-genetic hard-wiring of a person, thus contributing to antisocial behaviour that the person has little control over. In some cases, the problem is seen as a pathology ("sickness"), or is defined as a disease. Second, problems are "psychologized" by pointing to personality flaws, repressed impulses, and interruptions in the maturational process. By emphasizing unresolved conflicts in early childhood, these psychological explanations tend to focus on the individual as primarily responsible for behavioural outcomes. Faulty early socialization is also seen as a contributing factor. Each of these individualistic types of explanations shares a common attribute: They tend to blame the individual for social problems. They also emphasize the precipitating or immediate causes of problems, thus failing to see the wider social context in which problems germinate. Not surprisingly, such solutions focus on changing the person by addressing symptoms rather than root causes.

How relevant is the distinction between private (personal) troubles and social problems (Mills, 1967)? For sociologists, the answer lies in the notion that the personal is the social. If one person is unemployed because of sloppy work habits, according to C. Wright Mills, this personal problem is of marginal interest to sociologists. If, however, thousands are unemployed because of corporate decisions or government policy, the situation qualifies as a social ("public") problem. Sociologists are rarely interested in the suicide of one person, although the social context that contributed to the suicide may prove relevant, but the nearly 4000 suicides that occur in Canada each year are an entirely different story. This is not to suggest a lack of sociological interest in the problems of individuals. On the contrary, sociologists may be interested in studying what it is about society and culture that encourages problems to be personalized rather than approached within the broader context in which individuals think and act. In that sense, all personal problems are potentially social problems because of the social dimension inherent in all human actions. This willingness to tackle problems as part of the "big picture" imparts a distinctive sociological spin to the study of social problems.

What, then, is meant by the "social" in social problems? According to many sociologists, a problem is social and amenable to sociological analysis if it meets four criteria: (a) origin; (b) definition; (c) impact; and (d) treatment.

- First, a problem is seen as social in origin when it is perceived to originate in a society or a social context (including values, institutions, and structures) rather than in the individual by way of biology or psychology. Of course, no one is dismissing biology as irrelevant to a study of human problems. The interplay between genes and society may create social problems related to violence. Nevertheless, the genetic can only make sense when situated within the broader context.

- Second, a problem is social in definition when defined as such by some sector of society. This sector is prone to define something as a social problem when they find their interests compromised, privileges challenged, and values and visions in conflict with others. This raises the question of why some inequities are defined as problems, and others not.

- Third, a problem is social in treatment when the proposed solution to the problem is achievable by and through human agency. On the assumption that problems created by human action can be undone by social activity, a problem qualifying as social must have the potential to be corrected or controlled by way of collective action or institutional reform.

- Fourth, a problem is social when a certain condition exerts a negative impact on society or harms segments thereof. Social problems consist of those actions or omissions that have the intent or effect of undermining the social fabric of society, in part, by eroding the trust and predictability that underpins human existence. People become so demoralized that they are unable to take control of their lives, make meaningful choices, or withstand negative pressures from the outside. A social breakdown can be defined and measured by conventional indicators like higher rates of violence, child neglect and abuse, and substance abuse—so disruptive that customary norms of behaviour are displaced or diverge sharply from those prevailing in similar communities (Shkilnyk, 1985).

In short, the "social" in social problems emphasizes the social dimensions of human reality, namely, structural arrangements, cultural values, and situational circumstances. The social also draws attention to how the relationship between social problems and society is constructed, challenged, and transformed. Admittedly, not all problems are social; nor are they all amenable to analysis by sociologists. Only those problems qualify that originate in human interaction, exert a negative impact on society, are defined through intergroup dynamics, and respond to collective treatment. For sociologists, social problems are properly approached by looking past the individual, even though the problem itself may entail individual choices and actions. Choices and actions do not occur in a social vacuum, but within political and economic contexts that are not necessarily of a person's making. No one should be surprised, then, that social problems resist solutions if solutions are "individualized": that is, reduced to the level of individual behaviour modification. In some cases, such misguided initiatives may even aggravate the situation by drawing attention away from the root causes, while channelling resources into inappropriate ciphers.

The Sociological Imagination: Re-imagining Suicide

Sociologists have long displayed an interest in social problems. According to Rubington and Weinberg (1995), sociology as a discipline originated to explain and solve breakdowns of traditional society at the end of the 19th century. Particular attention was directed at isolating disruptions to the social order caused by the misdeeds of maligned individuals, thus obscuring the broader social context in which these problems originate and flourish (Henslin, 1994; Bolaria, 2000). Yet few misconceptions are more dangerous than a belief in social problems as the handiwork of the intrinsically deranged. Social problems are not necessarily caused by evil or sick individuals who explode in random antisocial rampages. Rather than fixating on the moral depravities of individuals, a sociology of social problems acknowledges the social dimensions of antisocial behaviour with respect to causes, consequences, characteristics, and cures. It is within this broader context of social structures and cultural values that people are mobilized to promote or resist changes to the status quo. In other words, by linking the society to individuals by way of the social, sociologists embrace a social and cultural context as explanatory variables in the study of social problems.

Few actions can be regarded as intensely personal as the decision to take one's life. A common-sense view sees suicide as a pathological disorder of the very rich or poor, the eccentric and creative, the elderly, or the physically or mentally disabled. Suicides in the past were often associated with a variety of disturbed states of mind. References proliferated about possible causes, including death wishes, imbalances in the superego, depression, sublimated aggression, and bottled-up frustration. Much of our understanding of suicide continues to reflect an inclination to individualize social reality. Genetic explanations continue to be popular, including recent references to a gene "mutation" as a possible cause (Evenson, 2000). These interpretations may reflect a need for direct and simple explanations. However valid they may be in explaining individual cases, such interpretations cannot account for patterns of suicide over time, rates of suicide between and within groups, and constancy in both patterns and rates across time and space.

These concerns deserve a sociological airing at a time when controversy rages over the ethics of assisted suicide, the self-destruction among aboriginal youth, a growing crisis in youth suicide, and concern over copycat suicides. And while a sociological analysis may seem cold and heartless in its analytical rigour, sociologists are only too aware that suicide is a painful and perplexing tragedy that has inflicted the lives of many Canadians and continues to exert a relentless toll—both directly and indirectly (Langlois and Morrison, 2002). But it is precisely a careful analysis of this problem that may lead to solutions for reducing the loss of lives. Such insight can't come a moment too soon, since people routinely misperceive the magnitude of suicide as a health and social problem despite it claiming more lives per year in Canada than the combination of car and pedestrian accidents, AIDs, and homicides (Fenlon, 2002).

The Legacy of Durkheim: The Personal As Social, the Social As Personal

Emile Durkheim, a pioneering figure in early sociology, advocated a novel approach to understanding suicide. Durkheim was one of the first scholars to call himself a sociologist, and an understanding of his work cannot ignore a lifelong devotion to establishing sociology as a distinct and respectable discipline. In 1897, Durkheim proposed the then provocative idea that suicides are essentially social rather than personal problems. Durkheim's contemporaries had linked suicide with mental illness, inherited tendencies, and general unhappiness. But Durkheim rejected this reductionism because of its excessive reliance on the individual in isolation from the group or society. Individuals may see themselves as exercising choice and free will, yet their behaviours are often socially shaped, including highly personal acts such as suicide (Macionis and Plummer, 2002). His conclusions were anchored in the observation that patterns and rates of suicide were relatively constant between and within groups. Some groups were more likely than others to commit suicide: Men committed suicide more frequently than women, the rich more than the poor, the elderly more than the young, Protestants more than Catholics, Catholics more than Jews, and the single more than the married. Durkheim also observed a certain constancy in these rates over time, thus ruling out the effect of periodic fluctuations and historical accidents.

Durkheim argued that social factors accounted for patterned group differences. Rates and patterns of suicide varied with the degree of social solidarity across society and within groups. Two important social bonds proved key indicators of solidarity: regulation and integration. Put simply, Durkheim argued that suicide rates were most likely among those who found themselves in contexts that were excessively overregulated or underregulated. Anomic suicides were caused by a lack of social regulation (divorces) while fatalistic suicides reflected too much regulation (honour suicides). Problematic, too, were contents of too much or not enough integration. Suicides were marked in contexts of low integration (Protestants) while altruistic suicides resulted from too much integration (suicide bombers) (Macionis and Plummer, 2002). Suicides also occurred in contexts of disruptive change which could erode the normative attachments underlying integration or regulation. Thus, suicides were less likely among those individuals who were insulated from such stresses because of a stable marriage, involvement in cohesive groups and community life, high levels of religious devotion, and identification with normative value systems. Conversely, suicides were most likely in contexts that lacked attachment, leaving individuals more socially isolated and less integrated. From this Durkheim surmised that the solution to the problem lay in creating a society that reflected a working balance between agency (individual freedom) and structure (social constraints).

Contemporary Trends in Suicide

How valid are Durkheim's assertions regarding suicide and its relation to society? Do his observations stand the test of time, or are they culturally bound by that era's intellectual constraints in the same way many see Freudian theories as culturally circumscribed? Can the growing rate of suicide in Canada and the United States be attributable to patterns of integration, regulation, or attachment? Or does the increase reflect a greater willingness to report deaths as suicide, in addition to changing definitions and burdens of proof? Can a single explanation possibly cover the entire spectrum of suicidal behaviour?

Suicide as the "act of deliberately killing oneself" is a global phenomenon. It is sanctioned in some societies as a face-saving device, but reviled in others as unnatural or morally repugnant (Edgerton, 1976). Worldwide rates are punishing: According to the World Health Organization, suicide remains the greatest single cause of death around the globe in 2000. Of the 1.6 million people killed by acts of violence, suicides claimed 815 000; homicides claimed 520 000, and group conflicts at 310 000 claimed the rest. The highest suicide rates were found in Eastern Europe, with Lithuania, Belarus, and Estonia leading the pack, while men aged between 15 and 44 accounted for just under one-third of the tally (Laurance, 2002). Yet caution must be exercised when interpreting the available data. As Mark Twain once quipped, "There are lies, damned lies, and statistics." Statistics are never as objective and reliable a source of information as many believe. Selectivity and bias are inherent in all aspects of research, from data collection to interpretation. The field of suicide is no exception. Both data collection and cross-national comparisons lack consistency, reflect subjectivity, are subject to second-guessing, and resist verification. Cross-national differences may reflect changes in the way suicide is defined, catalogued, and reported. Even Canadian data are suspect. A death is certified as a suicide by medical or legal authorities only when a victim's intent is known. Without a suicide note or other corroborating evidence, it is a coroner who ultimately determines whether death resulted from an accident, or unnatural causes, or stemmed from a self-inflicted injury with intent to cause death (Douglas, 1967; Windspeaker, 1995). Evidence to date suggests a conservative bias in suicide rates: An underreporting of suicide remains a perennial concern because of the stigma associated with self-killing. Coroners are pressured to mislabel suicides as "accidents" to ease the trauma and stigma for family and relatives, to comply with religious observances that reject the legitimacy of suicide, and to circumvent insurance companies that withhold payment for what, prior to 1972, was defined as an illegal act. (At present, it is illegal only to aid and abet someone in committing the act).

Did You Know?

How do rates in Canada compare globally? With a rate of 14 per 100 000 of population in 1998, Canada stands in the middle of 22 Western industrial countries. This figure has remained relatively constant since rates peaked in 1983 at 18 per 100 000. Raw numbers are relatively consistent with percentage ratios. In 1997, 3,941 Canadians committed suicide or 11.3 per 100 000 of total population; this figure had declined to 3 605 in the year 2000. By comparison, the suicide rate in Greece stood at three per 100 000, in England and Wales at 6.4 per 100 000 and the United States at 10.5 per 100 000. Australia and Ireland have rates similar to Canada. At the opposite are countries such as Finland with a rate of 21 per 100 000 in 1996. These statistics are useful for putting Canada into a broader global perspective. However, they must be interpreted with caution as methods of death certification and rate assessment can vary. For example, Canada's rate of 14 per 100 000 reflects a database of Canadians ten years and older—a statistic that makes sense since those under ten years rarely commit suicide and including them in the sample creates a distortion. Those jurisdictions that include all ages as a basis for assessment will yield a lower ("crude") rate of suicides per 100 000.

Canada's national rate of suicide conceals group variations. In general, suicide rates vary by gender, age, region, and ethnicity. Some groups may be considered high risk because they have higher than average suicide rates compared to the general population. Groups at high risk include older White males, young men, gays, individuals with mental disabilities, inner-city minorities, those prone to substance abuse, the unemployed, divorced, and widowed. The most common means of suicide in 1998 was suffocation (hanging) (39 percent), poisoning (overdoses and exhaust inhalation) (26 percent) and firearms (22 percent) (Langlois and Morrison, 2002). In addition, many Canadians who try to commit suicide do not die in the attempt (according to World Health Organization, about 20 attempts for every death), with the result that 23 000 hospitalizations in 1998/99 were related to suicide and self-inflicted injuries (Langlois and Morrison, 2002).

Age differences influence patterns of suicide. Men between the ages of 20 and 59 have the highest rates at between 24.7 and 26.3 per 100 000 of population ten years of age and over. The combination of work pressures, family problems, financial difficulties, spiralling complications, and dashed expectations may account for this rate. The suicide rate for women is relatively constant, ranging from 7.2 per 100 000 for those 45 to 59 years of age, to 4.9 per 100 000 for women 20 to 29 years. Men over 75 have a rate of 24.5 per 100 000 (Langlois and Morrison, 2002). Elderly males are prone to suicide because of disconnection from social routines and meaningful interaction in a society where worth is equated with youth, strength, beauty, productivity, and the ability to work. It is interesting to note that senior citizens in other cultures are less prone to suicide because of greater acceptance of elders as valued repositories of traditional wisdom.

Among adolescents, suicide routinely ranks among the first three causes of death (Leenaars et al., 2001). The high suicide rates for young men are particularly disturbing, given the squandered potential. Those between 15 and 19 committed suicide at a rate of just over 18.2 per 100 000 population in 1998, nearly double the rate in 1971 (Statistics Canada, Suicide Information and Education Centre, cited in the *Toronto Star*, 10 October, 1999). How do we account for this upsurge, especially among men? Sociologically speaking, quadrupling of rates for men since the 1950s may reflect reality gaps between cultural norms and social changes. The persistent circulation of masculine images and macho expectations serves as a breeding ground for failure because of continual testing (and teasing) over symbols and standards of masculinity that few can hope to achieve. But males continue to be conditioned to emulate strong, silent types without gratuitous displays of inner emotions (except anger) and dependency. Efforts to escape from this rigid stereotyping because of culture changes continue to be dismissed as a sign of weakness rather than a show of strength. The loss of control is also a contributing factor. Suicide is likely to occur following the breakup of a relationship, an inability to take control of a situation, or a lack of perspective about personal failure. Taking one's life becomes a viable option when one is confronted by deep disappointment or conformist pressure. Young men believe they have little recourse except to self-destruct by resorting to one final act of defiance in defence of (or rejection of) male norms about masculinity (Crook, 2003).

Gender differences are readily apparent. Men commit suicide more frequently than women. In 1998, the rate for Canadian males ten years and older was 23 per 100 000, compared to six per 100 000 for females. Women, however, are more likely to attempt suicide (possibly up to ten times the rate for men). This is reflected in hospitalization rates: In 1998/99 the hospitalization rate for attempted suicide was 108 per 100 000 women aged ten years or older, including a rate of 221 per 100 000 girls between the ages of 15 and 19, compared to 70 per 100 000 for the general population (Langlois and Morrison, 2002). Suicide remains the leading cause of death by trauma for men, including Ontario men causing 29 percent of trauma deaths, followed by car crashes at 27 percent and falls at 22 percent. By contrast, injury deaths for women in Ontario put suicide third at 12 percent, well behind falls at 48 percent and crashes at 25 percent (Fenlon, 2002). No less gender-related are the instruments of choice. Men tend to rely on guns and suffocation although between 1979 and 1998, the proportion of men who committed suicide with firearms declined from 41 percent to 26 percent, while death by suffocation rose to 40 percent. By contrast, women prefer to employ non-disfiguring techniques such as poisoning, which accounted for 41 percent and suffocation which increased from 19 percent to 34 percent between 1979 and 1998. Firearms were used in only 7 percent of the cases. The choice of instrument may explain the disproportional number of male suicides compared with women. Even the reasons behind suicide may be gendered. Suicide may provide an escape from a difficult situation for men; for example, the suicide rate for divorced men in Canada is 41.2 per 100 000 of population. Women may resort to suicide as a belated call for assistance (Langlois and Morrison, 2002). Conflict over the role young women are expected to play in society—independent and career oriented or family and domestic oriented—may drive many to contemplate suicide (Blackwell, 2002).

Suicide rates also vary by region in Canada. Historically, the highest rates of suicide follow a pattern from east to west, from south to north. Since 1993, however, Quebec has had the highest provincial rate at 21 deaths per 100 000 of population aged ten years and older. Alberta also had a higher than average rate, while Newfoundland, Ontario, and BC reported rates below the national average. The territories have considerably higher rates than the national average, including the Yukon at 26 per 100 000 (five deaths) and the Northwest Territories at 56 per 100 000 or 35 deaths. Urban differences are evident as well; according to Statistics Canada, Edmonton had the highest rate of suicide at 15.5 per 100 000 of population, followed by Montreal at 14.6 and Charlottetown at 14.1. Mississauga had the lowest rate at 6.4 per 100 000 (*National Post* 19 October, 2002). Interestingly, Quebec had a much lower hospitalization rate of attempted suicides at 49 per 100 000 of those ten years and older, while the rates in the Yukon and Northwest Territories were much higher at 169 and 219 per 100 000. Keep in mind that both suicide and hospitalization rates in Canada's North are based on relatively small numbers that can inflate the ratio or fluctuate substantially from year to year (Langlois and Morrison, 2002).

Minority groups also reflect a variable pattern. Of the various groups in Canada, few have experienced as much distress as the First Nations, whose suicide rates outpace the national norm by a wide margin. Aboriginal men commit suicide at the rate of 56.3 per 100 000, quadruple the national rate for males in general; while the rates for young men between 15 and 19 years of age on certain reserves stands at six to eight times the national average, with the highest rate among Inuit, followed by Dene. That figure makes this age group one of the most suicide-prone in the entire world. A lethal combination of risk factors that are systemic to the life experiences of aboriginal communities may account for the alarmingly high rates; namely, rapid social change, identity confusion, rising expectations (versus stalled reality), alcohol and drug abuse, family violence, poverty, and lack of opportunity (up to 95 percent unemployment in some areas). Personal factors appear equally important, spanning the range from alienation and boredom to frustration, poor self-image, self-hatred, and hopelessness from being caught between two cultures (Shkilnyk, 1985; Windspeaker, 1995). Refusal of governments to deal squarely with the problem has contributed to difficulties, according to the Report of the Royal Commission on Aboriginal Peoples (1996). In addition, some aboriginal leaders have been reluctant to press for solutions, partly from shame and embarrassment, and partly for fear of distracting from their political agenda related to land claims settlement or inherent self-government. Aboriginal initiatives to establish institutional structures for expressing inherent rights to self-determining autonomy over land, identity, and political voice offer the best opportunity for healing and renewal (Mercredi and Turpel, 1993; Maaka and Fleras, 2004).

Putting the Personal Back into the Social

Sociology begins with the Durkheimian assumption that the personal is social, the social is constructed, the constructed is contextual, and the contextual is personal. Sociologists prefer to deal with rates and patterns as subject matter, rather than the isolated and random. Instead of precipitating triggers, the focus is on root causes within the framework of structures, values, and institutions. By contrast, precipitating causes point to immediate factors that may inspire a suicidal impulse, such as alcohol and drug abuse, coupled with anxiety, helplessness, and depression (Leenaars et al., 2001). True, approximately 90 percent of those who commit suicide are thought to suffer from depression, another mental illness, or substance abuse disorder (Langlois and Morrison, 2002). Yet even these personalized factors occur within a broader social context with the result that sociologists are more interested in the underlying ("root") causes that may lead to dependency or alienation.

Suicides are not a random occurrence based on personal whims or rash decisions. Suicide rates are relatively constant, endemic to certain groups or areas rather than others, and more likely to occur during periods of rapid social change and cultural upheaval. A sociological approach does not deny the existence of free will; few would be bold enough to reject the possibility of individual choice or personal responsibility. Choices are never made in a moral vacuum, but within a social context in which alternatives and options are culturally defined and constrained by the demands of the situation. Nor does sociology posit a direct causal relationship between suicide and society. Society does not "determine" behaviour; nor does it "cause" suicides. Rather, it provides the context that increases the probability of making poor choices, especially for high-risk or vulnerable groups. The importance of the inter-subjective should dismiss popular misconceptions of sociology as a discipline that studies why people don't have any choices to make. Finally, no one can confidently predict who will commit suicide. Sociological or statistical data can only yield estimates ("probabilities") that apply to groups or categories of persons. But specific cases may elude the power of statistics to predict with accuracy. Individuals bring their own unique characteristics to each situation. However, individuals also live out their lives within a shared framework of social institutions and cultural conventions that constitute the basis of society. The intersection of the personal with the social may expand our level of analysis, but it also complicates the solving of social problems.

SOLVING SOCIAL PROBLEMS

The chief cause of problems are solutions.

—Eric Severeid

Sociology as a discipline originated around a commitment to solve the problems of rapidly changing societies at the turn of the 20th century. Exploring solutions to these problems remains integral to the sociology of social problems. Yet the link between problems and solutions is extremely tenuous. Solutions were designed to address problems as defined and understood at the time. As the problem definition changed, so too did the proposed solutions, at least in theory, if not always in practice (Walker, 1999). But with growing awareness of the complexity of social problems, the possibility of solutions has grown increasingly remote. For too long, people have been asking the wrong questions, and finding inappropriate answers, suggesting that if we don't have the answers ("solutions"), perhaps we need to rethink the question ("problems"). Or as Albert Einstein once said, "You cannot solve the problems of the present with the solutions that produced them." Not surprisingly, the optimism associated with sociology's reformist tradition has gradually diminished. The contemporary sociology of social problems has tended to be characterized instead by an "almost paralyzing pessimism" (Scarpitti and Cylke Jr., 1995: x). Sadly, perhaps, this pessimism about solving social problems is well founded: The persistence of problems in search of solutions is matched only by the proliferation of solutions that rarely connect with the problems they are meant to solve.

Defining a social problem is critical in framing the solution. Solutions will vary with the theoretical perspective employed: Functionalists tend to see social problems as the result of individuals who fail to fit into the system. The solution is to improve fit by modifying the individual through attitude change or behaviour modification. Conflict theories tend to root social problems in an exploitative social system. The solution is in transforming core institutions to create a more humane, just, and equitable system. Interactionists tend to see problems as social conventions created through meaningful interaction. Thus each perspective blames the problem on someone or something. Solutions lie in eliminating or changing whatever is blamed. Historically, the causes of social problems and the preferred way of solving them have reflected four patterns: blaming the victim; blaming the enemy; blaming the institution; and blaming the system (Elias, 1986).

Blaming the Victim   With "blaming the victim" explanations, individuals are at fault. Those who constitute the problem are seen as responsible for their condition in which they find themselves because of attributes that contribute to their marginalization or oppression. For example, the poor are seen as responsible for their poverty because of psychological dispositions, cultural deprivation, faulty socialization, or circumstances of their own making. Solutions to problems that blame the victim involve changing the person rather than addressing the broader context.

Blaming the Enemy   This category of explanation attributes blame to some non-mainstream group. Immigrants, for example, may be blamed for taking jobs from "real" Canadians, thus adding to this country's unemployment woes. By pitting one group of

Canadians against another, the blame shifts from "us" to "them." Such labelling detracts from the possibility of looking at the broader picture of power, profit, and privilege as a primary source of the problem (Davis, 1998). The scapegoating of certain groups as the cause of Canada's social problems (for example, youth) also oversimplifies an often complex situation. Solutions to problems created by the enemy are based on removing the offending group.

Blaming the Institution   Blaming institutions acknowledges that social problems are located within institutional arrangements as they apply to access, treatment, rewards, and external relations. Institutions are criticized for discriminatory barriers that either have the intent or the effect of denying, excluding, or exploiting others on the basis of race, ethnicity, gender, class, sexual preference, ability, or age. As we shall see, institutions such as media or policing are often targetted as sites that wilfully or inadvertently deny or exclude both workers and customers who do not fit a mainstream profile (Henry et al., 1999). Solutions to institutional failures range from the minimal, such as improved training or removal of discriminatory barriers, to transformative strategies that overhaul the entire structure.

Blaming the System   Blaming the system looks at society as the source of social problems. Social problems stem from cultural values and the political ideals associated with a particular type of society. The problems are often seen as systemic; that is, the rules, roles, and relationships that constitute society are not openly discriminatory or exploitative, but their very arrangement is likely to have that effect on vulnerable groups. For example, in a patriarchal society, sexism and misogyny are perceived as the logical outcome of androcentrism; that is, the idea of interpreting reality from a male point of view as normal and necessary, and assuming that others will or want to do so. Marxists also like to blame the capitalist system as the ultimate cause of oppression or exploitation. Solutions follow accordingly: if the system is to blame, the focus of change must be structural.

Who to blame? Are individuals entirely to blame for what they do regardless of the social context? Such an indictment seems excessively harsh, for as Parenti (1978) shrewdly observed, "blaming the poor for being poor while ignoring the system of power, privilege, and wealth that creates poverty, is a little bit like blaming the corpse for its murder." Should the system take the blame but at the risk of removing individual responsibility? Or must people take ownership of their actions without ignoring how certain contexts can make some choices more likely than others? The next case study on Employment Equity explores this notion of agency versus structure in the cause–cure debate. It also reveals the importance of defining problems in framing a solution consistent with the problem definition.

CASE 1-1	**Employment Equity: Quick-Fix Solution Or Sure-Fire Problem?**

Canada is widely proclaimed as an egalitarian society in which commitment to inclusiveness is globally admired. Yet commitment has proven one thing, implementation another. Consider disparities that punish Canada's historically disadvantaged: Women in full-time employment continue to earn less than men; visible minorities may comprise nearly 14 percent of Canada's pop-

(continued on next page)

ulation but as a rule tend to have less income, experience more poverty, and are excluded from full involvement; aboriginal peoples remain at the bottom of every socioeconomic indicator; and individuals with disabilities remain marginalized in terms of societal partic- ipation. How do we account for these disparities? Are members of these cate- gories to blame for not trying hard enough? Is the problem rooted in the prejudice associated with the different "isms" in society (namely, racism, sex- ism, ableism, ethnocentrism, classism)? To what extent is the problem systemic, (i.e., embedded in the institutional structures and normal functioning of society)? As this chapter has made clear, how the problem is defined greatly influences the proposed solution that is proposed. Failure to frame issues appropriately creates solutions that con- vey the illusion of change but with little to show for the effort. Worse still, mis- guided solutions may intensify the exist- ing problem or create collateral damage.

Canada's response to these unequal relations is a proactive program known as "employment equity." Introduced in 1986 and expanded in 1996, the Employment Equity Act is based on the principle that marginalized individuals are not entirely responsible for the problem of inequality. Solutions must focus on changing the institutional structures related to hiring, recruitment, reward, and promotion if the cycle of inequality is to be broken. This sounds straightforward enough, yet few issues have elicited as much admiration or hostility as the Employment Equity Act.

- For some, employment equity is a problem rather than solution since it only deals with symptoms rather than root causes of inequality. Critics attack the Act as a cosmetic solution to structural problems—little more than a public relations exercise that fails to challenge the foundational principles of unequal distribution. As a solution, it leaves everything to be desired since the true source of the problem—the system—remains untouched.

- For others, employment equity is to be resisted as a violation of core values in a liberal-democratic capitalist system. Employment equity is criticized as a violation of (a) the principle of equality; (b) the liberal commitment to individual self- sufficiency; and (c) the corporate right to conduct business as they see fit. According to critics, an individual's worth should not be determined by race and ethnicity, and policies that view individuals primarily as members of minority groups go against the grain of Canadian values. Besides, it is argued, the prospect of establishing preferences on the basis of race or gender is just as racist as old-fashioned racism—it is just as unfair to give minorities preferential treatment as it is to discriminate against them. True equality cannot possibly arise from a politically cor- rect stance of treating people differ- ently, but from treating all people the same regardless of who they are.

- For still others, employment equity makes good business sense by expanding the pool of qualified candidates from which to recruit and reward. Rather than violating the merit principle, the commitment to remove all discriminatory barriers reinforces the principle of meritocracy to ensure that everyone is judged on merits rather than on race or gender. As the Samuel Report (1997) noted: What the public service needs is not

(continued on next page)

quotas for visible minorities but a removal of barriers to make sure that real merit is rewarded and recognized."

- For still yet others, there is no problem with the principle or philosophy behind employment equity. Rather, Canada's responses to the equity challenge—the Employment Equity Act—is deemed a problem. Consider a May 2003 posting for a $99 700-a-year civil service job for a communications official with the Federal Fisheries Department in Vancouver that was open only to non-Whites. This kind of dogmatic application of a "restricted competition" not only makes a mockery of employment equity, according to a comment in the May 30th issue of *The Globe and Mail*, but also proves a lightening rod for resentment and backlash.

Not surprisingly, reaction to employment equity has varied from the supportive to the dismissive. Responses appear to depend on how the problem of disadvantage is defined, how issues are framed in terms of causes and cures, and whether equity engineering is the solution.

A key distinction is required from the outset: Employment equity as a formal government policy and employment equity as a principle or philosophy. Employment equity as a policy constitutes a legislated program with a formal set of practices to achieve government goals. The policy is aimed at proactively assisting minorities who, through no fault of their own, have been marginalized from full and equal workplace participation. According to the Employment Equity Act of 1986, the goal is to:

> ... achieve equality in the workplace so that no person shall be denied employment opportunities or benefits for rea-

sons unrelated to ability ... by giving effect to the principle that employment equity means nothing more than treating persons in the same way but also requires special measures and the accommodation of differences.

Instead of passively responding to complaints of discrimination, the Act sets out to remedy the effects of past discrimination by identifying and eliminating discriminatory barriers in the workplace. Provisions of the Employment Equity Act apply to all federally regulated employers (with 100 or more employees), public sector companies, and crown corporations. In 1996, the Act was revised to include the federal public service. These employers were obligated to publish annual reports on the composition of their workforce, with particular reference to the number and type of jobs performed by women, visible minorities, people with disabilities ("differently able"), and aboriginal peoples. Minorities would be hired and promoted in numbers commensurate with their ratio in the general workforce. Federal contractors with at least 100 employees also had to comply. Each had to sign a certificate of commitment to comply with equity provisions ("contract compliance"), if they wanted to bid on government goods or services contracts worth $200 000 or more. All organizations were expected to file an annual report outlining their progress.

As a philosophy or principle, employment equity is about institutional inclusion. It is based on the inclusiveness principle that all persons, regardless of who they are or aren't, should be treated equally within the workforce. That is, each person should be recruited, hired, promoted, trained, and rewarded on the basis of merit and cre-

(continued on next page)

dentials—assuming he or she is qualified on the basis of job-related skills for available positions. The goal is to ensure equitable representation of designated groups throughout all occupational and income levels at numbers consistent with their percentage in the regional workforce (Jain and Hackett, 1989). Three premises prevail:

> First, employment equity is concerned with moving over and making space. Instead of compelling minorities to do all the adjusting, institutions are expected to accommodate minority women and men by way of concessions, preferences, and reforms. Minorities are not the problem, according to employment equity; institutions are—because of discrimination—both deliberate and systemic. Without discriminatory employment barriers (following this line of logic), minority women and men would be distributed relatively equally along all occupational and income levels in accordance with population numbers (allowing, of course, for individual and cultural pressures, which may restrict occupational choices).

> Second, employment equity is premised on the belief that, left to their own, organizations will tend to reproduce themselves unless an outside force is applied to interrupt the circularity of like hiring like. For example, audits indicate biases in hiring; managers often tailor requirements to match candidates, thus ensuring they hire the person they had in mind, i.e., a relative or someone they previously knew (Gordon, 2003). Temporary colour-conscious intervention may be required to break the vicious cycle of exclusion.

> Third, employment equity is predicated on the premise that minorities are unduly handicapped when applying the principles of equal opportunity and merit-based hiring. Treating everyone alike by judging them on similar standards conspires against those whose

experiences, interests, and concerns do not correspond with the "pale-male stream." Such an outlook contradicts those who argue that differences and disadvantage must be taken into account if true equality is to be achieved. Treating everyone the same in an unequal situation—especially in contexts where some have the advantage of a head start—is likely to preserve the status quo rather than to bring about substantive change.

Employment equity has triggered an avalanche of reaction, both supportive and dismissive. Is employment equity a solution to the problem of ethnic inequality? Or does it create more problems than existed in the first place (Fleras, 2001)? To what extent does employment equity help to right historical wrongs by "reversing" discrimination? Or is it really an exercise in political correctness that advocates *reverse* discrimination—despite good intentions? Reaction to employment equity varies according to one's political stance. Some see employment equity as more of a problem than a solution. As a so-called solution it creates more problems than it solves, while intensifying existing problems by generating more grievance, division, discrimination, and political correctness (Loney, 1998).

Discriminating against the advantaged to improve opportunities for the historically disadvantaged has had the effect of treating some people unjustly in seeking a more just world (Editorial, *Guardian Weekly*, July 2–9, 2003). Others disagree. Rather than seeing employment equity as reverse discrimination, they see it as reversing discrimination through removal of discriminatory barriers (Fish, 1993). The removal of discriminatory barriers is intended to expand the pool of qualified, but formerly excluded, applicants

(continued on next page)

in the competition for employment rather than to explicitly exclude the "pale-male stream." In a world of globalization, businesses need skills that can only be obtained through exposure to widely diverse peoples, cultures, and viewpoints. In the final analysis, the "reversing of discrimination" is intended to create a workplace culture, both inclusive and equitable, as well as prosperous and connected.

Case Study Questions

1 Distinguish between employment equity as an official Canadian policy and as a principle. Does Canada's Employment Equity Act reflect and reinforce the principles of employment equity?

2 Does a commitment to the principle of employment equity or the Employment Equity Act contribute to or detract from the principle of meritocracy? Can the two rights be reconciled?

The Politics of Solutions

What can we infer from this discussion on the politics of solutions? First, quick-fix solutions tend to ignore the complexity of problems, both in terms of history and culture. The complexity of social problems has many sources, including the enduring or emergent nature of many social problems, divergent interests of different publics, the problem of definitions, and the tendency to individualize problems (Dunn and Waller, 2000). Second, solutions tend to emphasize either *agency* (blaming individuals for misfortune by focusing on immediate causes such as wrong choices, bad attitudes, addiction, and so on) or "structure" (blaming the system and absolving individuals of responsibility for actions and reforms). Failure to acknowledge the interplay between agency and structure in creating problems undermines the effectiveness of solutions. Third, many solutions fail to take into account the interconnectedness of the world we live in, with the result that many solutions to problems often trigger unintended consequences. Elements exist only in relation to others, often in ambiguous or contradictory ways, so that changes in one area will affect other areas because of this interconnection. Fourth, solutions may be implemented for the best of intentions, but may trigger unintended effects that aggravate the original condition or create a host of new problems. Social reality is too complex and too interconnected to allow us to confidently predict outcomes or to control outcomes (Jackson, 1992). Fifth, solutions may never get going because the problem is inappropriately defined. Or the solutions may never get off the starting block because the political will is lacking to implement any reforms except, perhaps, as exercises in public relations or appeasement. Too much of what passes for solutions is not really intended to solve anything, except to convey the impression of change or improvement. Sixth, solutions are rarely intended to get at the root of the problem, given the costs, difficulties, and resistance of vested interests. Symptoms are dealt with but not the root causes.

Proposed solutions may become entangled in a struggle between equally valid but competing rights. Consider the recent onset of whale-hunting among some aboriginal nations along the Pacific coast (Martiniuk, 1999). The conflict of interest between animal rights activists and aboriginal peoples may be impossible to resolve. At the core of this conflict are competing values over the hunting of whales and other endangered species. For animal rights activists, animals have rights, and it is immoral to use or exploit them as a means to an end except to hunt for subsistence or survival. For aboriginal peoples, they have rights too as a "nation" with self-determining rights to define what is right or acceptable for them. Whale-hunting is endorsed as a traditional cultural practice that must be resuscitated for reviving threatened aboriginal identities. Besides, aboriginal leaders argue, hunting whales is an aboriginal right reaffirmed in treaties, and outsiders have no right to dictate what aboriginal peoples can or cannot do. A similar conflict of interest is revealed in the recent decision by the Supreme Court of Canada to allow aboriginal peoples in Atlantic Canada to fish and hunt for subsistence or moderate livelihood without a licence all year round. For some, this right is just; for others, it is unjust to confer rights on some, but not on others (Coates, 2000). In both cases, the issue is not between right versus wrong. Rather it is between two equally valid if seemingly opposed rights that appear impervious to compromise, thus complicating any possibility of an easy problem definition or quick-fix solution.

It is possible that some problems are destined to persist and prevail. The idea that some problems cannot be solved to everyone's satisfaction in a liberal-democratic society is off-putting to those who believe everything is solvable with sufficient resources and resourcefulness. Yet not every social problem can be solved regardless of data or determination. In cases where problems are part of a society's structure, history, and identity, solutions may have the opposite effect of producing new and more damaging imbalances. For example, crime is usually perceived as a social problem; the criminal justice system is endorsed as one solution to this problem. Will prisons ever solve the problem of crime? Will more police? Harsher sentences? It is hard to imagine a society that could eliminate all crime without trampling on basic democratic and human-rights principles. A certain degree of criminal activity is inevitable because people differ in their degree of commitment to conformity or deviance, depending on the situation in which they find themselves. Imbalances of power, privilege, and profit in contemporary society intensify the potential for more criminality. In a competitive society in which demand is meant to exceed supply, the gap between expectations and achievements encourages people to rely on illegal shortcuts to achieve the culturally prescribed "good life." Mix in youthful defiance and rebelliousness toward authority, convention, and tradition and the prospect of a crime-free society begins to fade. Finally some social problems may be better left unsolved. Take the case of Quebec and the question of national unity. It has always been assumed that there is a problem here, and that rational efforts must be directed at blocking Quebec's threat to separate. However, as suggested by David Cameron, a University of Toronto political scientist, it is also possible that this problem cannot be fixed, despite costly and sometimes risky ventures to do so, in which the cumulative impact may have the effect of keeping the problem festering in the foreground. Rather than framing it as a problem to be solved, the relationship between Quebec and Canada should be seen as "a tension to be accommodated, an arrangement to be lived with, a practical situation which is not perfect but eminently tolerable." (Gwyn, 10 June, 1998). In short, doing nothing may be the best.

Finally, the problem-solution link is increasingly challenged by the existence of many publics in Canada, each with their own definition of problem and proposed solutions. This should come as no surprise: Many have claimed that what we know depends on where we stand or who we are. This postmodernist position reinforces the sociological axiom: Where we are socially located in society with respect to race, class, or gender will profoundly influence our experiences, identities, and opportunities. And nowhere is this more true than between those who endorse an Old Canada and those who are constructing a New Canada. Recent surveys confirm what many have long suspected: There is an age divide with respect to what Canadians define as problems, differences in proposed solutions, and marked variation in anticipated outcomes for the future of Canada (Valpy and Anderssen, 2003; Mendelsohn, 2003 a,b). What historically have been defined as problems are now dismissed by the twentysomethings as unimportant or redefined as solutions; in turn, tried and true solutions that worked in the past are deemed irrelevant or counterproductive. The "hot button" issues of today such as same-sex marriages are dismissed as the dying gasp of Old Canada raging against the new (Mendelsohn, 2003a). This generation is rewriting the future of Canada, by posing a challenge to conventional wisdom in the workplace, orthodox government social policies, and traditional cultural norms related to social relationships and social institutions such as marriage and family (Valpy and Anderssen, 2003). This generation also exhibits a world of astonishingly high expectations that often puts them at odds with mainstream decision-makers who appear out of touch, but who still retain the levers of power (Mendelsohn, 2003b). Key issues include (Mendelsohn, 2003 a,b; Adams, 2003):

- In building a diverse and tolerant society, young Canadians are recreating a new multiracial, multicultural, boundary-free ethnic, post-national society of Canadians linked not by blood, race, history, or religion but by a set of ideas and principles (Starowicz, 2003). The old symbols of Canadian identity—from the Canadian Pacific Railroad (CPR) to the Canadian Broadcasting Corporation (CBC) that are tied to institutions or maintained by the federal government—are no longer seen as salient for Canada's survival. The new Canadian identity is about commitment to values that make them proud, including multiculturalism, individual rights, egalitarianism, environmental sustainability, social liberalism, and nonviolent solutions to problems.

- The twentysomething generation differs from other generations in value orientations. Their values of tolerance, diversity, and social justice not only distinguish us from Americans but also redirect attention from those old debates that historically have posed problems for Canadian unity, identity, and prosperity. While most Canadians take their ethnicity as an important marker of personal identity, ethnicity is not seen as grounds for exclusion, entitlement, or engagement. What prevails instead is described as a "mobile paradoxical space" in which people of mixed backgrounds can inhabit their paradoxes by inventing and reinventing their identities to fit environments (Wiwa, 2003).

- A new ethnicity—Canadian—may be emerging. Canadians are increasingly incorporating internationalism into their identity. They are more engaged with the world than ever before, embracing trade and globalization as keys to national prosperity and imploring other countries to share Canadian values.

- Young Canadians tend to trust the courts more than the political process. The fact that only 21 percent of first-time voters cast a ballot in the 2000 election is not necessarily a sign of apathy, but a disengagement with the political world that is perceived as irrelevant, out of touch, and self-serving. While politicians waffle and pontificate, then complain about the judiciary usurping their parliamentary power, the courts have taken their responsibilities seriously by promoting decisions that reflect new interests, realities, and priorities.

- Tolerance and egalitarianism are the new norm and moral principle. Battles over family structure or sexual orientation are seen as stale as debates over desegregation and civil rights. Deference toward the past has been replaced with a political culture that accepts new ways of doing things, such as the reality of dual working parents, and that society has to accommodate this new reality.

• Neither the market nor the government can solve the big problems of homelessness or aboriginal poverty. Programs that empower individual Canadians to make the most of their opportunities, while freeing them to make their own choices is the new norm.

In short, the New Canada differs from the Old Canada in outlooks, discourses, and outcomes. The New Canada is challenging the Old to move beyond old dualisms, to think outside the box, and to discard solutions that worked well in the 19th and 20th centuries. This deep dissatisfaction with "but this is how things are done around here" did not spring up suddenly. Rather the shift capitalized on values from the preceding generation, gathered momentum from evolving cultural climates regarding right and wrong, and drew inspiration from an infusion of new immigrants. Of course, this assessment does not apply to all young Canadians. Many continue to uphold parental values or reject both traditional and postmodern norms. Nor is there any proof that the projections of a preselected focus group of high achievers are representative of Canadians at large or will practice what they preach. A gender divide can be discerned as well. For example, as Mendelsohn (2003b) points out, young women's values tend toward the social, men's toward the economic. A Rashomon effect appears to be in effect: Women continue to see discrimination in the workplace; men think the glass ceiling is shattered. Inconsistencies are evident elsewhere: The claims of aboriginal peoples and the Quebecois for special status rather than equal status does not fit comfortably with the cultural ideology of individual rights and equal opportunity. The limit to Canadian tolerance wavers over special treatment to assist the disadvantaged or to right historical wrongs (Bricker and Greenspon, 2001: 319). These differing perceptions will remain a tension in the new Canada, and governments will have to be conscious of these different priorities to ensure a balanced policy agenda. But as this generation moves into positions of power and authority, their values will prove pivotal in shaping the contours of a new Canada. These values will also generate a host of new problems as challenging as the "old."

DISCUSSION QUESTIONS

1 Indicate how the concept of claims-making distinguishes the conditionalists from the constructionists in defining social problems.

2 Compare how functionalists and conflict theorists approach the concept of social problems.

3 What is meant by the "social" in social problems?

4 Explain how the seemingly personal act of suicide may be interpreted and analyzed as a social problem, thereby reinforcing the notion that the personal is indeed the social. Use the findings of Durkheim in your answer.

5 Demonstrate why social problems are so difficult to solve.

 ## WEBLINKS

A social problems index for Canada.   **www.cpa-apc.org**

Sociology: social problems papers.   **www.dissertationstation.com**

Centre for Research and Information in Canada.   **www.cric.ca**

part two

The Structures of Inequality

The study of inequality and its relationship to society is inseparable from the socio-logical enterprise. Sociology is concerned with studying society as a network of relations in the broadest sense of the term—from the interpersonal to the international. In that most human relations are unequal in terms of power or privilege, the focus is on analyzing how these inequities are constructed, expressed, and maintained, in addition to how they are challenged and transformed by way of government policy, institutional reform, and organized protest. Sociologists have long endorsed the study of social inequality, despite clear differences in research traditions and theoretical orientations. The discipline itself originated at the turn of the century in an attempt to fathom the social dislocations associated with urban-industrial transformations. Early disciplinary work also focused on how to ameliorate dysfunctional social conditions. Some of the earliest concerns centred around questions of inequality: "Why does inequality persist in the distribution of wealth and power? Where do its causes lie? How and why is inequality structured over time and place? What are the ideological supports that justify inequality? Can inequality be eliminated without depriving society of its potential for creativity and change? What exactly would a perfectly equal society look like?"

Contemporary sociologists are no less preoccupied with the concept of inequality. Sociological interest extends to defining it, exploring its genesis, evolution, expression, magnitude and scope, and examining its consequences for society. But while sociologists have been successful in isolating the concept of inequality for study and analysis, they have been far less successful in defining its causes, characteristics, impact, and solu-tions. And only recently have they begun to consider how patterns of stratification—class, race and ethnicity, gender, and regional location—generate overlapping and intersecting patterns of inequality that amplifiy the challenge of living together.

Nevertheless, concerns are increasingly focused around the following equality issues: (a) why and when is inequality a social problem; (b) who says so, why, and on what grounds; (c) how is this social problem manifested; (d) what, if anything, can be done to eliminate gaping disparities; and (e) what are the impact and implications of inequality for society as a whole and individuals in particular? Disagreements over inequality are not so much about its existence per se; after all, some degree of inequality is inevitable and even necessary. Rather the focus is on patterns of inequality that (1) are unjustified and based on irrelevant characteristics; (2) persist over time or space; (3) are entrenched within institutional structures; (4) are supported by ideological beliefs; (5) are rooted in the exploitation of others and restrictive of their life chances; and (6) are unresponsive to treatment. That each of these questions about social inequality continues to baffle and infuriate sociologists is testimony to the elusiveness of this concept. To assist in sorting through these dilemmas, while providing an introduction to issues in this section, the following questions are posed to provide insights into the magnitude and nature of inequality in Canada:

- Can we explain—and justify— the fact that some Canadians, especially sports stars, entertainers, and high flying CEOs earn millions each year while thousands of Canadians earn less than poverty wages and others live in utter destitution?

- Can we justify that men on average earn more than women, that Whites tend to outearn visible minorities, that the Canadian-born usually earn more than the foreign born, and that those who live in major urban areas outperform those who live in regional hinterlands?

- Does class still matter? While many would agree that a person's family background makes a difference, the relevance of social class in shaping experiences, opportunities, and identities is largely underestimated.

- Why do many women encounter a glass ceiling in scaling the corporate ladder of success: Is it because of sexist attitudes? Gendered discrimination? The paradox of double shifts in juggling the demands of home and career with minimal support from partners and bosses? The penalty for working in a patriarchal system that inadvertently rewards men, not women?

- Minority women and men continue to be denied, excluded, or exploited despite the commitments of Canada's official multiculturalism, Charter of Rights and Freedoms, and anti-hate/employment equity initiatives. How does the pervasiveness of prejudice, discrimination, and racism help to account for this disparity between ideals and reality?

- Aboriginal peoples in Canada remain the poorest of the poor. Are they largely responsible for the so-called "Indian Problem" or should we look to the broader social, political, and historical context?

- Some regions in Canada experience less economic success than others. For example, Atlantic Canada has received billions of dollars in transfers from the federal government to assist the economy. Yet major problems persist. Why?

- Are patterns of social inequality the fault of individuals or the result of structural arrangements beyond their control? Is it better to approach individuals as responsible for their decisions and choices, or to acknowledge that people's options are restricted by the social conditions in which they find themselves?

- Should we look for quick-fix solutions or substantial reform? Are employment equity initiatives the best way of addressing income differences or does this type of social engineering create more problems than solutions?

Answers to these questions are not readily available. Nor is there much agreement on answers over the causes of inequality, its characteristics and consequences, and proposed cures. Yet answers are critical if we are to solve the problem of inequality—assuming, of course, that inequality is a social problem amenable to solution. This section on inequality does not promise to simplify either defining the problem or proposing workable solutions. Nevertheless, the very act of formulating the right kind of questions, while applying different perspectives to responses, yields insight into the centrality of inequality as a major social problem in Canada.

chapter two

Inequality and Poverty

FRAMING THE PROBLEM

Canadians possess a reputation at home and abroad as a "kind and compassionate" people. Many believe the jarring extremes of conspicuous wealth and abject poverty that define the United States do not apply to Canada. Canada is perceived instead as a remarkably egalitarian society, with only moderate differences in wealth, status, or power. This portrayal of Canada as relatively egalitarian is arguably true in a relative sense. Compared to the magnitude of inequities and racial oppression elsewhere, Canada is a remarkably open and pluralist society with a powerful commitment to equal opportunity and full participation, regardless of a person's nationality or race. Enlightened government intervention has ensured almost universal access to basic physical necessities of food, clothing, and shelter, even though a few may lack some of the creature comforts that others take for granted. Even Canadian seniors are healthier and wealthier because of increased government transfers and benefits. Evidence of Canada's seemingly progressive status is bolstered by UN quality of life surveys that consistently rank it near the top of the global heap.

But not everyone is convinced by this benign portrayal. On closer inspection, Canada's reputation as egalitarian is tarnished by gaping levels of inequality that expose glaring inequities between the "haves" and the "have-nots." Canada is not more just, equal, or fair, but increasingly meaner, greedier, and less caring (Lauziere, 2003).

Pyramids of privilege exist that elevate Whites, males, the middle-class, middle-aged, and the able-bodied to the top of the heap; others are less fortunate. Those who stray outside the script for success confront the possibility of economic dislocation, powerlessness, social ostracism, inadequate levels of service delivery, and threats to a cherished identity. Employment equity initiatives, notwithstanding, women in full-time employment—with the possible exception of single, university-educated women—earn less than men in the ongoing struggle to walk up the down-escalator of corporate success. Minorities continue to be marginalized because of income inequalities and opportunity barriers not altogether different than those first exposed by the eminent Canadian scholar John Porter in his classic, *The Vertical Mosaic* (1965). The inception of official multiculturalism and The Charter of Rights and Freedoms has not appreciably altered this arrangement. The fact that aboriginal incomes hover well below half of the national average, with a standard of living comparable to that of many developing world countries, is surely a scathing indictment of Canada's priorities and self-delusions (Maaka and Fleras, 2004).

Let's not beat around the bush. All the deeply ingrained myths about this country cannot disguise the obvious: Canada remains a stratified society where people are denied, excluded, or exploited—often through little fault of their own. In reminding us that a society that condones unfettered affluence yet tolerates grinding poverty must confront its contradictions, Buzz Hargrove and Wayne Skene (1999: 13) reinforce the paradoxes that abound in Canada: "Canada in the late 1990s is a strange place. We pride ourselves on being a society committed to equality and compassion, yet we're living through a period of unparalleled inequality and bitterness." Consider the conundrums: To one side, we have the seemingly inflated salaries of professional sports stars and the exponential number of millionaires (the number of millionaires in Canada rose by 15 000 to 180 000 in 2002 even as the number dropped by 100 000 to 2 million in the United States (Thorpe, 2003). To the other side are nearly 1.5 million children who live below Canada's so-called poverty line, while 778 000 Canadians had to rely on food banks in March of 2003. The proliferation of million-dollar homes in Toronto and Mississauga continues to astonish, while thousands of homeless are without a roof over their heads. Yes, a few have prospered because of a corporate-driven global economy; for example, the median salary of CEOs in Canada rose to $1.52 million in 2002, an increase of 8.3 percent over the previous year (McFarland, 2003), yet the average worker's wages have barely budged, with the result that median household income held at about $55 000 between 1990 and 2000 (Canadian Council of Social Development, 2003). Nor is there much relief in sight as the safety net continues to be shredded. Put candidly, Canada is a land of contradiction. It may be one of the luckiest countries in the world, yet it is hardly immune to the harsh realities of inequality (Frizzell and Pammett, 1996). Admittedly, few would go so far as to downgrade Canada to the level of a northern "apartheid." Nevertheless, inequality is deeply entrenched in Canada, and its pervasiveness and persistence in a land of plenty is deemed a major social problem—not only in contradicting our ideals but in generating many additional problems.

Most Canadians are only superficially acquainted with these gaping realities, despite constant reminders that not all is well in our "kinder, gentler society." But no one should underestimate the damage that inequalities can inflict on Canada's social fabric and national cohesion. Expanding economic gaps have had the effect of partitioning Canada into three layers. One is growing more prosperous and powerful, the second is being squeezed by stagnant incomes, and the third appears to be spiralling downward into destitution and despair because of socially toxic environments that delay, deter, and punish (Covell and Howe, 2001; also Fischer et al., 1998). Inequality is not only about economic privilege or material distribution. People's lives are deeply affected by economic insecurity because of disruptions to their emotional well-being, physical health, and relationship to others (Grab, 1999). Those at the bottom are more likely to suffer from poor health or to be denied access to proper medical attention; to endure lower educational levels and revolving cycles of poverty; to reside in substandard housing; to jeopardize prospects for career advancement; and to be punished more harshly by the justice system. The consequences are foreboding: The juxtaposition of extreme wealth with grinding poverty creates the potential for frustration and rage—and conflict. Or in the words of the prominent American sociologists, Jonathan H. Turner (2000: 62), "Inequality is a tension-generating dynamo; it sets into motion individual misery and social pathologies, such as high crime rates, unstable families, dependence on drugs, domestic and civil violence, and ethnic and racial conflicts, which become difficult to contain."

This chapter addresses the concept of inequality as a persistent yet contested social problem in Canada. The chapter focuses on the process by which patterns of inequality are created, expressed, and maintained in addition to being challenged and transformed by way of policy, protest, and politics. Inequality as condition is analyzed and assessed at the level of causes, cures, characteristics, and consequences. Notions of inequality as "natural" or "normal" because of human nature, culture, or psychology are rejected in favour of sociological explanations rooted in public policies, social structure, and human behaviour. Four key premises prevail: (1) patterns of inequality are socially constructed rather than inherent or inevitable in society; (2) inequality is amenable to sociological analysis because of measurable rates that persist over time; (3) patterns of inequality are not randomly distributed but structured around the statistically significant variables of race, ethnicity, gender, class, and regional location; and (4) equality is preferable and attainable even if few can agree on what this means or how to achieve it. Particular attention is directed at poverty as the definitive expression of inequality in Canada. The politics of defining poverty—what it is, and how much of it there is—are matched in complexity and controversy by debates over solving the "poverty problem." Proposed solutions to the inequality problem are shown to vary with differing notions of equality.

It's been said that the familiar and routine are often the most difficult to explain (Grab, 2002). Such a warning is applicable to Canada: Why is there so much inequality in a country with (a) one of the world's highest standards of living; (b) a national commitment to equality; and (c) a host of government programs to alleviate economic stress? But obvious questions rarely produce simple or straightforward answers, prompting sociologists to probe beneath the superficial of everyday life to uncover structural constraints (Bennett and Watson, 2002). The concept of inequality has also proven a difficult problem to define, explain, and solve: Is inequality good or bad? Inevitable or constructed? Attitudinal or structural? Permanent or transitory (Grab, 2002)? To be sure, the notion that our life chances are socially conditioned and structurally constrained is not a popular sell in Canada. Canadians tend to be in denial about inequality in Canada (Allahar, 1998). They are rarely encouraged to think of their own experiences in those terms unless someone has to explain why they didn't get the job or promotion (Kraybill, 2002). Many believe that the removal of discriminatory barriers has transformed Canada into an equal society of free choice and equal opportunity. But inequality in Canada is not simply the result of market imperfections that responds to cosmetic reform. Inequities in wealth and power appear to be chronic and persistent over time, firmly embedded within the structures of a capitalist society, and resistant to even carefully crafted solutions. Even the ideal of equality has proven elusive in both principle and practice. What do we mean by equality, on what grounds do we justify its forms, its attainability in a competitive economy, and how will we know when we have it? It is precisely this enigma between the ideals of equality (however defined) and the reality of inequality (however measured) that prods sociologists into analyzing this most baffling of social problems.

PROBLEMATIZING INEQUALITY

The study of social problems is loosely organized around two major perspectives. The first begins with the existence of social problems and attempts to go "behind" to explain how and why these conditions exist. The second starts by acknowledging how concern over conditions become the basis for organized social action by claims-making individuals (Gray, 2001). This line of thinking applies to the concept of inequality. As conditions or constructions, social problems such as inequality are inherently ambiguous concepts that defy commonly accepted definitions (Liddiard, 2001). However true such a claim, defining a problem is more than an analytical exercise. Definitions are critical in shaping responses; after all, decisions-makers are inclined to act on the basis of how a problem is defined, how public issues are framed, and how solutions are identified (Spector and Kitsuse, 1979; also Holstein and Miller, 2003).

In general, inequality is about entitlements: that is, who gets what, how, and why? It reflects a condition and a process in which preferential access to the good things in life is not randomly distributed but patterned around those human differences that are devalued for purposes of entitlement—or rejection (Fleras, 2001). For various reasons related to race, class, disability, sexuality, or gender, certain individuals are precluded from access to wealth, power, and status. Of course, neither race nor disability are in themselves a problem. But those who are disabled or racialized are perceived as problematic or confront a variety of problems because of their devalued and vulnerable status (Dunn and Waller, 2000). These inequities are socially constructed: That is, there is nothing natural or normal about social inequality—despite concerted efforts by vested interests to make it appear so. Rather, unequal relations represent conventions designed by individuals who make meaningful choices albeit in wider contexts not necessarily of their making. These inequities are also socially constructed because access to social rewards is patterned around relations of power. Those who are advantaged because of birth or achievement tend to be rewarded in a cyclical process that reinforces that hoary cliché about the "rich getting richer."

Reference to social inequality as a social problem encompasses three dimensions: objective conditions, ideological supports, and social reforms (Curtis et al., 2004). First, reference to objective conditions invariably culminates in questions about causes of inequality, its expressions, magnitude, and scale. Social scientists have argued that perfect equality is a contradiction in terms. No human society is "equal" in the sense that everyone has identical access to valued resources (Turner, 2000). Both simple and complex societies are stratified by the universals of age or gender. Yet only agricultural–industrial societies can produce the extremes of structured inequality that stratifies individuals and groups into different layers according to occupation, income, wealth, class, and race or ethnicity. In acknowledging that all human societies are unequal and stratified to some extent, stratification can be conceptualized in two ways. It can refer to the unequal allocation of scarce resources among different groups or households; it can refer also to the unequal distribution of people in relation to scarce resources such as income or educational levels. This division of society into unequal horizontal layers is known as strata. A society is said to be stratified when categories of individuals who differ because of their appearance or location, are ranked along a hierarchy of ascending and descending order with respect to varying amounts of power, privilege, and wealth (Barrett, 1994). The interplay of these hierarchically ranked strata comprises the condition of inequality in society.

Second, attention to ideological supports emphasizes how ideas and ideals are used to justify the realities of inequality, regardless of how measured or conceived (Case, 2000). Ideology can be defined in political terms as a relatively consistent set of ideas and ideals that justifies an unequal status quo. The role of ideology is two-fold: first, to conceal the conditions that secure the dominant group's dominance; second, to subordinate non-dominant groups by co-opting them into the status quo (Gray, 2001). Those in positions of power and privilege have a vested interest in framing inequality as natural and normal, beneficial and fair. A host of self-serving myth-conceptions continue to colour people's perception of inequality, thus camouflaging its most pernicious effects. These include:

- Canada is a classless society with everyone bunched into the middle.
- Hard work equates with success.
- People who are poor have only themselves to blame.
- Individuals are judged and rewarded only on the basis of merit.
- As a land of equal opportunity, Canada embraces high levels of social mobility.
- Inequality is natural and normal, and there isn't much we can—or should—do about it.

Third, social reforms consist of both formal and informal strategies for challenging inequality, including state-intervention policies such as employment equity (see the Case Study in Chapter 1). Also evident is the proliferation of organized resistance and protest groups among the historically disadvantaged—women, racial minorities, gays and lesbians, people with disabilities, and the poor and the homeless.

References to inequality within the context of condition, ideology, and reform poses an awkward question. Inequality itself is not self evident as a social problem. When and how is inequality a social problem? Who says so, and why? Are all differences because of income a problem? For example, should university professors earn more than the support staff? How much more? Should a full professor earn more than a lecturer? On what grounds? Should tenured professors earn more than contract faculty (Rajagopal, 2003)? Consider as well the following range of income differences:

- Shania Twain can earn up to $70 million per year, including endorsements.
- David O'Brien, CEO, Fairmont Hotels and Resorts, earned $35 million, including $900 000 in salary, $3.9 million in bonuses, and $30 million in other.
- The average salary in professional baseball now stands at US$2.6 million, up 136 percent between 1993 and 2003, just behind the NBA at $4.9 million, up 279 percent since 1993, but ahead of the NHL at $1.8 million, up 213 percent since 1993, and the NFL at $1.3 million, up 71 percent since 1993 (all figures from *Maclean's* Magazine, 3 November, 2003)

- Larry Walker of the Colorado Rockies earns CDN$17.8 million per year while Paul Kariya earned CDN$14.8 million annually when he played for Anaheim Mighty Ducks.
- Paul Martin, Canada's prime minister, earns about $260 000 (of course, there are additional perks). By contrast, Bill ("Microsoft") Gates is worth about $46 billion, while the total wealth of Warren Buffet ("Berkeley-Hathaway") amounts to a whopping $36 billion.
- University professors earn between $40 000 and $150 000 with an average of about $90 000.
- Parking lot attendants earn around $21 000 per year.
- Those with minimum-wage jobs in Ontario earn just over $14 000. Babysitters, nannies, and parent helpers earn about this amount.

Several questions come to mind. How do we account for these income differences? Who or what is responsible? Are they justified? On what grounds? Is there any justification why some should earn millions while others must get by on a minimum-wage salary? Is there a rationale to explain why sports figures and entertainers earn much more than those entrusted to care for our most important resources—children? Why is the office of prime minister—arguably the most important position in Canada—relatively poorly paid in comparison to high flying stars? Can these discrepancies be defined as a social problem in a society that strives for better? Or are they consistent with the principles of supply and demand in a merit-based market economy? As we shall see, answers to these questions depend on our perception of what society should be.

EXPRESSIONS OF INEQUALITY

Imagine a society of perfect equality! Picture a social setting in which individuals are exempt from extremes of privilege, wealth, or power. Scarce resources and unearned privileges would be distributed in relatively equal fashion. "From each according to their ability, and to each according to their need," as Karl Marx once proclaimed of his communist Utopia. Individuals, of course, would not be clones of one another; rather, differences would be accepted and taken into account when necessary. This egalitarian ethos would apply as well to groups within society. Intergroup conflict would diminish gradually over time with the elimination of class competition over scarce resources, while exclusiveness and denial would become things of the past with the removal of discriminatory barriers.

Does this scenario sound too good to be true? It probably is—at least outside of some utopian fantasy. There is no historical evidence of a society that maintained perfect equality among its members. All known societies are characterized by inequalities, with the most privileged enjoying a disproportionate share of the total wealth, power, and prestige (Turner, 2000). Even the simplest hunting and foraging communities reflect a social hierarchy. A commitment to egalitarian principles may have ensured relatively open access to the basic necessities for individual survival, but it did little to diminish the status of those with age, strength, or gender on their side. Contemporary attempts to create equal societies—such as the kibbutz in Israel or the Hutterite communities in North America—have also fallen short of their utopian ideals, despite being more egalitarian in material terms than surrounding communities. Moreover, there is little evidence to suggest that most of us would enjoy a perfectly equal society—however that might be defined. For many, it is not the principle of inequality that rankles or rubs. Rather, problems arise when the *degree* of inequality becomes grotesquely disproportional, institutionalized, and embedded within the structure of society, rendered permanent and persistent, reflects illegal attainment, inflicts harm or deprivation, and resists solutions.

Patterns of inequality are not randomly distributed, as far as sociologists are concerned. Unequal access to scarce resources is patterned around and expressed through certain groups because of defining characteristics, including: (a) social class, with its basis in material wealth; (b) race (inequality due to visibility); (c) ethnicity (inequality because of cultural differences); (d) gender (inequality based on perceived sex differences); and (e) region (inequality reflecting geographical location). The concepts of race, gender, ethnicity, location, and class may be treated as analytically distinct dimensions of inequality. Nevertheless, each is thought to combine with other dimensions to generate overlapping hierarchies of subordination that intersect with one another in mutually reinforcing ways (Stasiulis, 2000).

Social Class

Debates over inequality initially focused on the concept of social class. Lack of consensus over its nature and characteristics did little to blunt debate over causes, consequences, and cures (Curtis et al., 2004). But concern is mounting that class as an explanatory framework is less valid than in the past because of changes to society. New forms of inequality have replaced the old, although new patterns and expressions of inequality do not necessarily imply the death of old forms (Lemel and Noll, 2003). Class boundaries are becoming less visible and meaningful in everyday life, while individual life styles and consumption patterns are increasingly influenced by the identity politics of age, gender, race, ethnicity, and sexual orientation. But challenging the total explanatory power of class relations is not the same as rejecting the notion that class relations are largely unequal relations. Our family background in terms of property, power, and prestige continue to influence what we do, who we are, and how others relate to us—that is, our identities, experiences, and opportunities—regardless of our level of awareness or consent.

Public aversion to the "c" word remains unabated despite its contested status among academics. References to class are dismissed as feudalistic remnants whose only relevance applies to European countries with their inherited aristocracy. Canadians reject the notion of Canada as a graded hierarchy of social classes. Contrast this Canadian indifference to Britain where class has long served as a social category for assessing social distinctions, a marker of identity, a device for evaluating the worth of individuals and an indicator of a person's thoughts and behaviour. Even more contested in Canada is the notion that classes might have an impact on people's lives and life-chances. To be sure, several exceptions to this casual indifference can be gleaned. For instance, class may be tolerated when defined as material rewards involving layered rankings of people because of prestigious occupations or high incomes. Class may also make sense when applied to lifestyle differences in relation to wealth or poverty. And class may be accepted in the sense of family background and breeding. Those with privileged backgrounds are more likely to succeed; others will probably falter. But many are skeptical of situating class within an economic framework around the ownership and control of productive property.

Academics, too, have begun to challenge the primacy of class as a key explanatory variable. They argue that rapid changes in society have delegitimized the class concept to the point of irrelevance for studying inequality; that divisions based on race or gender are not reducible to class, even if closely related; and that reference to class cannot possibly capture the diversity of social experiences at the heart of contemporary society (Gillespie, 1996). Class consciousness is rapidly fading: In a society such as the United States that purports to be classless, vast income disparities do not automatically translate into self-conscious classes with corresponding inequalities. Class lines have blurred as well because of a commodity culture. A person's class status could at one time be judged by appearance. But in a world where brands such as Nike or Abercrombie and Fitch are available to rich and poor alike, these distinctions are no longer reliable. Moreover, with the proliferation of identity politics because of shifts in power and culture, the inversion of class within fashion is no less evident. Many of the latest fashions by top designers originate among poor kids on the street. Designers co-opt the "cool" look of the urban poor and sell it to the rich.

But many sociologists disagree with dismissing class as a framework for explaining inequality. They take exception to the notion of individuals as atomistic actors, preferring, instead, to situate people within a broader context in which they share common interests related to ownership of property, the kind of work they do, and preferential access to scarce resources. Yet class is much more than a classification of people based on similar amounts of property, power, or prestige. Rather, class counts in accounting for identities, experiences, and outcomes; after all, a person's family background may be the single most important factor in influencing who gets what. Consider how people in higher income brackets tend to be healthier, live longer, get better medical treatment or protection from the law, and generally have more opportunities. Sociologists are also unhappy with the depoliticization of inequality into lifestyle statements (Grab, 1999). Classes in Canada are real in terms of their impact. They are a key determinant of work, wealth, income, and education; they also "count" as key variables for explaining inequality, whether people are aware or not; and they help shape how individuals think, experience, and relate to others—and how others, in turn, relate to them.

Definitions of class predictably vary: In general, class is defined as a category of persons with similar family backgrounds with respect to wealth, power, and prestige. More specifically, classes are defined as groups of individuals who share a common relationship to scarce and valued resources. For Marxists, classes are inseparable from ownership to the means of productive property. Class structure revolves around three core categories. The first is a group of individuals who own productive property, the second consists of workers who survive through the sale of their labour, and a third incorporates a residual class of professionals, small business owners, administrators, and wage-earners with some certifiable credentials and power to control others. By contrast, functionalists define classes as sets of occupations with a similar level of prestige and income. A popular approach is to divide the population into deciles (tenths) based on income levels. Median income (halfway point between extremes) after adjustment for inflation stood at $55 016 in the year 2000, compared to $54 560 in 1990 (Statistics Canada, 2003). The top tenth earned $185 070 annually, an increase of 14.6 percent in 1990, thus accounting for 28 percent of all Canadian income, up from 26 percent of its share in 1990. By contrast, the bottom tenth earned $10 341—a figure largely unchanged from the $10 260 in 1990, reflecting a 2 percent share of national income totals.

To be sure, an emphasis on income may be misleading in defining class, since the possession of wealth or assets is a more reliable measurement of inequality (Oliver and

Shapiro, 1995). Income refers to a flow of money over time; wealth is a stock of assets owned at a particular time. Income is what people earn from work or receive as government transfers; wealth is what people own (from stocks and bonds to home ownership) and signifies command over those financial resources that a household has inherited or accumulated over a lifetime with which to create opportunities, secure a desired status, or pass status on to children. Not surprisingly, there is more inequality in wealth than income. According to Statistics Canada, the richest fifth in Canada owned 39 percent of the income in 1998, while the poorest fifth owned 7 percent. By contrast the richest fifth owned 63.8 percent of Canada's wealth in 1999 compared to the poorest fifth whose ownership totalled a measly 0.06 percent! Between 1984 and 1999, the richest fifth became more asset rich with a net worth that increased 39 percent to $403 500. The poorest fifth saw a decline to minus $-600 during that same period of time. Clearly, then, focusing on wealth rather than income casts new light on an old problem (Nares, 2003).

To what extent are social classes a problem? For many, the central issue is not the existence of class inequities per se. Problems arise when the gap between the "have" classes and the "have-not" classes undermines the potential for social stability and cohesion. Inequality becomes a problem because of barriers that inhibit the qualified from switching classes. This ability to change one's position in the social hierarchy is called "social mobility." Canada is often perceived to be a relatively open society, a perception honed by constant references to Canada as a land of limitless opportunity. But social mobility is not nearly as extensive as myth making implies. Few societies—Canada included—can afford unrestricted movement up and down the class ladder without destabilizing the social order. As might be expected, rates of mobility can increase during periods of economic expansion and technological growth. Yet a rags-to-riches type of mobility is rare; nevertheless, the fact that it occasionally happens seems sufficient to substantiate people's faith in the virtues of an open system. The end result? Canadians live in a society where social mobility is highly valued in principle, if not always implemented in practice.

Race

Canada may claim to be a multicultural society. In theory, no one is denied the right to full and equal participation because of their visibility (Fleras, 2002). In reality, Canada is informed by a high degree of inequality that rewards certain groups because of what they do but penalizes others because of who they are. Visible minorities do not share equally in the creation or distribution of wealth, power, or social status (Breton, 1998). Canada is characterized instead by layers of inequality divided along the lines of aboriginality, race, and ethnicity. Rather than an equitable arrangement, racial and ethnic groups are sorted out unequally around a "mosaic" of raised (dominant) and lowered (subordinate) tiles (Tepper, 1988). The fact that many minorities occupy the lower rungs of the socio-economic ladder does not auger well for Canada's future.

Even a cursory inspection of Canada's race relations record reveals a history of inequality (Henry et al., 1999; Satzewich, 1998). In the past, immigrants were frequently imported as a source of cheap menial labour, either to assist in the process of society-building (for example, Chinese for the construction of the railway) or to provide manual skills for labour-starved industries such as the garment trade (Bolaria and Li, 1988). Once in Canada, many became convenient targets for abuse or exploitation. Immigrants of colour could be fired with impunity, especially during periods of economic stagnation. Promotions, of course, were entirely out of the question. Political or civil rights were routinely trampled on without many channels for redress. And no one took minorities seriously in making a positive contribution to Canadian society.

The situation at present is significantly improved. Blatant forms of discrimination are neither tolerated nor legal. Canada's diversity is touted as a strength rather than a liability, with vast potential to improve Canada's competitive edge in a global economy. Nevertheless, both native-born and foreign-born minorities continue to be shunted into marginal employment ghettos from which escape or advancement is difficult. On average, racialized workers earned 16.3 percent less than other workers in 1999, according to a study by the Canadian Labour Congress, an increase from the 15 percent gap in 1996, in part because of fewer work weeks and lower pay (Galt, 2002). Several other studies clearly indicate that new immigrants are significantly worse off financially than earlier new Canadians (Kunz et al., 2001). Temporary workers are especially vulnerable: Immigrant labourers from the Caribbean are brought to Canada for seasonal employment, primarily in those agricultural fields that mainstream Canadians shun. Domestic workers (nannies) from the Philippines are taken advantage of by middle-class families who should know better. Working conditions for domestic workers are reported to be among the worst of any occupation in denying fundamental worker's rights (Stasiulis and Bakan, 1997). For Black urban youth, relations with the police border on the criminal (Cryderman, O'Toole, and Fleras, 1998). Indo-Pakistani Canadians continue to experience widespread dislike and resentment, judging by national attitude surveys (Berry, 1993).

Improvements notwithstanding, national studies continue to expound what many "intuitively" know: Canadians are not on equal footing when it comes to sorting out the "goodies." Inequality remains a fact of life in Canadian society—at least judging by income differences (Lian and Matthews, 1998; Galabuzi, 2001). Canada's labour force may be increasingly diverse, yet visible minorities continue to experience difficulties in securing employment consistent with their educational qualifications or foreign-trained credentials. An important study by Jean Lock Kunz and associates (2001) for the Canadian Race Relations Foundation demonstrated the scope of the disparities that exists between Whites (or non-racialized groups) and visible minorities ("racialized groups") with regard to income, education, and employment. The table below demonstrates average earnings by visibility, place of birth, and gender in 1996 (Fleras and Elliott, 2003).

TABLE 2.1	Earnings by Gender and Visibility in 1996		
	Male	Female	Total
Visible minority (CB)	$42 433	$35 519	$38 582
Visible minority (FB)	$35 329	$27 075	$31 829
Whites (CB)	$43 456	$31 150	$38 529
Whites (FB)	$46 457	$31 627	$40 854
Aboriginal Peoples	$32 369	$26 361	$29 290

Adapted from Kunz et al., 2001
Note: full-time, full-year earnings for those aged 25 to 64
CB – Canadian Born, FB – Foreign Born

The table clearly demonstrates the salience of visibility, immigrant status, and gender in determining income outcomes. Men outearn women, foreign-born visible minorities earn less than Canadian-born visible minorities, and aboriginal peoples remain most disadvantaged. Visible minorities (especially the foreign-born) perform more poorly than Whites with regard to employment, income, and access to professional/managerial jobs (Kunz et al., 2001). They also have a higher rate of unemployment, a lower average income, and are more likely to be poor than White—despite having higher education levels (Galabuzi, 2001; Kazemipur and Halli, 2001; Pendakur, 2000). Poverty looms as a major problem: In the report entitled, "Ethno-Racial Inequality in the city of Toronto: An Analysis of the 1996 Census," Michael Ornstein found that, while 14 percent of European families live below the low income cut-off line, the rate for aboriginal peoples is 32.1 percent, 35 percent for South Asians, and 45 percent for Blacks, Arabs, and West Asians. For some racialized minorities, the figures are much higher, including a staggering 90 percent for Ghanians and Afghans at 80 percent. These differences are tied to race, Ornstein concludes, in part because of (a) inequities built into the social structure; (b) continued job discrimination; and (c) government policies that prioritize balancing budgets by slashing welfare and employment equity programs (see also Chapter 11). Workplace bias, racial discrimination, and labour market discrimination are rarely openly expressed but tend to be subtle or systemic.

Gender

Many acknowledge that women and men are penalized because of class. But women are doubly disadvantaged because of membership in a historically devalued category: gender. Unlike men, women face sexist barriers that arise from their gender status in a predominantly patriarchical society. Patriarchy can be defined as the organization of society—from foundational principles to normative standards—that systemically reflect, reinforce, and advance male agendas at the expense of female priorities. To be sure, there are signs that the patriarchy is eroding. The past decade has proven a period of remarkable gains for women in the job market. More women than ever are working, average earnings are up, and the jobs tend to be more senior and skilled. While men have seen their earnings stagnate from the 1990s onward, average earnings for women have edged upwards, although the adjustment has stalled in recent years. The income gap between women and men closes further if comparisons are restricted only to full-time workers, and nearly vanishes if comparing unmarried, university-educated women with male equivalents.

Other signs indicate that little has changed except the optics. Women in full-time employment continue to earn less than men (although age and marital status are key variables), with negligible improvement since the mid-1990s. The average annual earnings for full-time workers in Canada in 2001 for all educational levels stood at $49 198 for men, $34 642 for women. For those with university degrees, according to Statistics Canada (MacQueen, 2003), the gap remained proportionately the same, with men earning $71 957, women $48 257. Women remain underrepresented on corporate boards and in executive suites (Flavelle, 2003). Few women hold the titles of president, CEO or chair; most are still confined to the pink-collar ghettoes of administration or support roles (MacIvor, 2003). Finally, women continue to be saddled with the bulk of unpaid domestic work, thus reinforcing the career-sapping burden of the double shift.

Minority women experience gender differently from mainstream women because of racism and race (Ng, 2000). Gender intersects with race to create interlocking patterns of inequality that mutually reinforce existing inequities while generating new ones. Women as a group may be united in a common experience of patriarchy; nevertheless, their experience varies because minority women are positioned differently to White patriarchy. Each expression of subordination is differently influenced by the social location of women of colour, immigrant women, and aboriginal women (Hurtado, 1996; Gillespie, 1996). For women of colour, for example, their experiences and exclusions are socially and institutionally structured in ways that are different from mainstream women and men (Elabor-Idemudia, 2000). As Hurtado (1996) observes, while women of colour are largely excluded from the corridors of power, mainstream women are largely concerned with projecting private sphere issues into the public realm (such as unequal division of household labour, media double standards, daycare in the workplace, and glass ceilings). By contrast, women of colour focus on public issues related to female job ghettos (sex, child rearing, and domestic labour), racism, and healthy children. Sisters, yes, but differently privileged (see Chapter 4).

Minority women also confront racial discrimination since race intensifies the marginality associated with gender and class (Macklin, 2000). Those who are socially devalued in two or more hierarchies are susceptible to patterns of discrimination that increase the risks of being left out of the loop (Stasiulis, 2000). After all, to be poor in a society that values wealth is to live with shame. To be poor and different—and a woman—is triply jeopardizing. Even strategies for change differ. In contrast with White women, women of colour are not in a position to distance themselves from the men of their group since neither can exist without the other in the struggle against oppression (Jahnke, 1997). For aboriginal women, the situation is even more complex—given the dynamics of working together to advance indigenous rights to self-determining autonomy while warding off patriarchal pressures within their communities (Monture-Angus, 2003).

Ethnicity

Ethnicity has proven a key variable in shaping unequal outcomes. Ethnicity-based inequities are generated in two ways. First, ethnic groups may be singled out as inferior or irrelevant, then dismissed or disparaged accordingly (Berry et al., 1993). Ethnicity is thought to interfere with the attainment of equality in Canada by precluding individuals from full and equal participation. Second, ethnic groups may possess cultural values at odds with those of the dominant stream. Endorsement of these values, such as obligations to kin or deference to tradition, may prove a barrier in the competition for scarce resources.

The ethnicity factor may be experienced differently by women and men. Minority women are subtly, yet profoundly undermined by ethnicity. Women in many ethnic communities are expected to know their place and do as they are told. Actions that do not conform to tradition or male values may be criticized as a betrayal or dishonour. For the sake of appearances, many women of colour are expected to defer to the authority of tradition and community. Such passivity and submissiveness may foster the facade of unity and cohesion; it may also inhibit the expression of skills necessary for women to excel in society at large. Assertiveness or freedom can lead to conflict when challenging the privilege of tradition-bound males. Minority women remain the "hushed-over" victims of violence. This violence results from cultural traditions that (a) normalize male abuse of women; (b) naturalize battery as a male right and a rite of passage for both women and men; (c) discourage public disclosure of abusive patterns because of family honour or community pride; and (d) foreclose access to help or escape. The family may be widely regarded as a bastion of privacy that shuns or punishes those who refuse to shield unpleasant issues from the public (Buckley, 1996). This indictment is not to suggest that domestic violence is more prevalent in minority or immigrant communities. Its effects on women may exert a different impact because of ethnicity. Options for escape or recourse may be few and far between when incidents of domestic abuse intersect with the realities of loneliness, dependency, homesickness, lack of knowledge of English or access to services, and the threat of social ostracism (Leckie, 1995; Easteal, 1996).

Regions

Some people have remarked that Canada is a country in search of a reason. Others have declared the absurdity of this country's very existence as a society. Consider the challenges of domesticating this sprawling land mass along an east-west axis when the natural pull is north-south, with eventual absorption into the United States (Hiller, 2000). These musings can be interpreted in different ways. Central to each level of interpretation is the importance of regional difference (Nurse, 2003). The existence of regions gives rise to the politics of regionalism because of grievances, in part generated by federal commitment to extend the principles of justice and equality to all parts of Canada (Wein, 1993). According to the principle of equalization and federal transfers, unchecked market forces create regional deficiencies. Only a major redistribution of resources by the government can correct these market failures (Corcoran, 1996). The reality of regionalism is further entrenched by the logic of a federal system in which provincial governments compete with each other in advancing sectoral interests. Not surprisingly, with the exception of PEI, all of Canada's provinces do more trade with the United States than between themselves because of punishing interprovincial tariffs. In that sense, regionalism is a structural problem rather than one of personalities or history.

Canada's regional differences are not merely geographic or demographic curiosities. Regions are also characterized by inequities because of housing, health, education, and resources (Swan and Serjak, 1993). Periods of high unemployment and debilitating levels of dependency on government assistance are two additional dimensions. Yet regional inequalities have revealed an astonishing tenacity, despite federal efforts to standardize access to services and goods (Economic Council of Canada, 1977). Government intervention has proven double-edged (Gherson, 1997). Short term benefits have contributed unwittingly to local economic decline while reinforcing patterns of dependency (Corcoran, 1996). Income support without more comprehensive measures pertaining to harvesting, conservation, and professionalization of a diminishing fishing industry has proven a waste of public money (Millen, 1998). The intractable nature of this inequality has given rise to regionally based alienation and social protests (Sinclair, 1991).

Regional inequalities are a chronic and complex social problem rarely amenable to solution by rote formula. The challenge for federal government policy points to the creation of sustainable regional development. But how does one go about neutralizing the deleterious effects of poor location and resource depletion, the flight of foreign capital, imbalances in free trade created by continentalism, and continued federal cutbacks across the board? The fact that regional inequities remain as entrenched as ever is a sad indictment of the prob-lem–solution mismatch. The lack of results confirms the inadequacy of reforms that con-centrate on internal changes rather than external forces. Nor is there much hope for substantial change without incorporating the structural into a program of comprehensive renewal (Sinclair, 1991). The intractability of regional social problems has prompted the government to pare away transfer payments, regional freight subsidies, regional develop-mental funds, and retraining programs (such as the $1.9 billion Atlantic groundfish pack-age, which attempted to wean the Atlantic provinces from their dependency on fishing) (Gherson, 1997). Political expediences loom large when government initiatives emphasize voter appeal rather than problem solving. Still, there is always hope: According to a *Globe and Mail* survey of provinces (Little, 1999), Newfoundland was judged to have the "hottest" provincial economy on the basis of seven economic indicators.

POVERTY AS INEQUALITY

The year 1989 proved to be an interesting year. Many welcomed the dismantling of the Berlin Wall for symbolizing the collapse of a system whose commitment to engineered equality ran roughshod over individual freedoms (Mayor, 1999). But a freewheeling glob-alization with its privileging of market freedom over social equality is proving no less dis-ruptive. In 1989, another event transpired of somewhat less international significance but one that has perplexed and provoked Canadians since then. In that year, an all-party House of Commons resolution promised to eliminate poverty among Canadian children by the year 2000. With the vast resources and resourcefulness at Canada's disposal, the challenge seemed achievable.

But rhetoric is one thing; reality has proven yet another. With just over 18 percent of all children (or about 1.5 million) living below the low-income cut-off ("poverty") line—a 58 percent jump or some 400 000 children since 1989—Canada appears to be moving in the opposite direction (also Rowlingson, 2001). While a growing number of millionaires in Canada are making a killing, poverty is literally killing Innu children in Labrador and northern Quebec (Samson, 2003). The child poverty rate in Toronto is a staggering 39 per-cent, including a large percentage of children of recent immigrants. In contrast with a well-established system that provides income and assistance for the elderly, Canada appears to have abandoned those in early childhood, without realizing the detrimental, long-term effects of such indifference. After all, if children are an investment in the future, down-wardly poor children are a poor investment (Rowlingson, 2001: 112). To the surprise of many, Canada attained the dubious distinction of having the industrial world's second highest rate of child poverty in 1997, second only to the United States. Even more startling was the realization that, contrary to popular belief, the proportion of Canadians in concen-trated urban poverty may be higher in Canada than in the United States—a proportion that has increased markedly in the last 20 years (DeKeseredy et al., 2003). Put candidly, the report card on Canada's war against poverty is nothing short of scandalous, especially with the economy firing on all cylinders.

The polarization between wealth and poverty is commonly regarded as a major social problem (Townsend, 2002: 3). As expressed by Ann Golden, the author of a major report on poverty and homelessness, "A healthy society is one where everyone feels included. Poverty shuts people out. And if large numbers of people don't feel they are part of the mainstream, social cohesion begins to break down." In other words, poverty is not just about the lack of basic necessities, but also about the exclusion and deprivation that affects people's sense of self and relationships to others (DeGroot-Maggetti, 2002). Poverty and an exclusionary labour market are key contributors to urban crime—not poverty in the absolute sense but a relative poverty that is experienced as unfair by those who turn to crime as a solution to the problem of individual discontent (DeKeseredy et al., 2003). Yet there remains little agreement over the magnitude and scope of poverty in Canada. What precisely do we mean by poverty? Who defines it, why, and on what grounds? What does it mean to be poor in a relatively affluent society? Does being poor mean not having enough to eat or not eating out? Does poverty mean the same in sub-Saharan Africa as it does Southern Ontario? Should there be a distinction between the optimistic poor versus the downward poor? Where exactly do we draw the line between poverty and inequality? Between poverty and destitution? Who is to blame for being poor? Is poverty the result of social injustice and structural impediments, or, should blame reflect personal deficiencies such as laziness or parental neglect? Is homelessness an expression or cause of poverty?

Answers to the above questions are more vital than ever. Just as a chain is only as strong as its weakest link, so too does Canada's unity and strength depend on its commitment to assist those most vulnerable. But while policy solutions follow from how the problem of poverty is defined and analyzed, a preoccupation with definitions can be double-edged: The politics of definition can be controlling in their own right. A "paralysis by analysis" may erode the spirit of activism for motivating decision-makers and political wills into direct action. Energy is dissipated in endless academic debate over the parameters of the problems rather than practical solutions. Worse still, relief may be denied to the truly destitute who, for one reason or another, become lost in the definitional shuffle.

Several assumptions underpin this section: First, references to poverty are essentially a social construct rather than anything objective about reality. As a social problem, poverty is social in origins, defined as such by sectors of Canada, subject to correction by way of resources and political will, and exerts a punishing impact on individuals and society at large. To the extent that those with power can enforce their definitions by controlling the terms of the debate and proposed solutions, the politics of poverty will become even more intense. Second, technically speaking, it is affluence rather than poverty that should be the problem under consideration. After all, the poor are not the problem per se. Blame must be shared with the structures of society that are organized to enrich some while impoverishing others (Isbister, 2003). Poverty is the symptom of the affluence and greed that increasingly dominate public debate in Canada, thus reinforcing the marginalization and impoverishment of the have-nots. Third, too heavy a reliance on the economic dimensions of poverty overlooks a key factor: For many, poverty is not only about money but also about powerlessness (Shkilnyk, 1985). Without power, the poor are robbed of control over their lives and are often unable to participate fully in contemporary society.

The Politics of Poverty

By almost any measure, Canada is surfing the crest of a buoyant economy (Weber, 2003). Indictors are pointing to often dramatic improvements in virtually every aspect of Canada's economic well-being. In 2002, the Canadian economy posted growth of 3.3 percent while creating a record 560 000 jobs, compared with economic growth in the United States of

2.4 percent and a loss of one million jobs. Corporate profits are at record levels while business investments are booming, from construction of new plants to installation of equipment—each indicative of business confidence in a robust economy. Real incomes for ordinary Canadians are rising following years of stagnation. The torrid pace of housing starts and new car sales reflects how pent-up consumer demand is finally fuelling this economic surge.

Yet not all Canadians are benefitting from these bullish good times. The conventional optimism that poverty can be diminished through the trickle down effect of economic growth is losing its lustre (Townsend, 2002). Rather than randomly distributed, poverty is increasingly concentrated among five high risk groups, namely, female-headed, lone-parent households, families headed by a person with a disability, young adults between 18 and 24 years of age, unattached individuals, and elderly women on their own (Fawcett, 1999; Policy Research Initiative,1999). Children are particularly vulnerable because of debilitating long-term effects, culminating in costly adult problems and expensive social services (Hunter, 2003). Chronic levels of poverty among aboriginal peoples are deemed an "overriding concern," according to the newly elected Grand Chief of the AFN, Phil Fontaine (Girard, 2003), a "plague" with an "enormous cost" that remains resistant to quick-fix solutions. Poverty is also higher among recent immigrants who are finding it more difficult to break into the labour market or to achieve comparable levels of earnings as immigrants of a generation ago (Kazemipur and Halli, 2000; see Chapter 12 in this text). Finally a growing number of working families who earn minimum wage are not making a living wage. Do the math yourself: How does a household of four cope when the wage earner earns $14 248 a year at $6.85/h (just raised to $7.15)—especially when the average annual rent in Toronto of $10 440 exceeds the income of the poorest 10 percent of families ($9600), yet construction of affordable housing is largely non-existent while the lifting of rent controls has resulted in rents going through the roof (Editorial, *Toronto Star*, 17 May, 2003). Regardless of the math or distribution, poverty is an embarrassing blot on a Canada that aspires to lead by example.

How much poverty is there in Canada? International studies are inconsistent because of different measures that are used. According to a UNICEF annual survey that defines a household as poor if its disposable income is less than half that country's overall median income, 16 percent of Canada's children are poor, compared to 26.6 percent of children in the Russian federation, 26.3 percent in the United States, 21.3 percent in the UK, and 17.1 percent in Australia. But another UN study concluded that only 6 percent of Canadians are living in poverty, less than half the proportion in the United States, and about one-third the rate claimed by some indicators in Canada (Beauchesne, 1999). This gives Canada one of the lowest poverty levels among major industrial countries, just behind Norway (3 percent) and Finland, Japan, and Luxembourg at 4 percent, but ahead of the United States (14 percent) and Britain (13 percent). Ireland, at 37 percent, and Spain, at 21 percent, were the highest. These figures are based on the proportion of people who live on less than the equivalent of US$14.40 per day, adjusted to reflect the purchasing power in each country. In Canada, this works out to about $20 dollars per day or less than $8000 per year per person, a figure that many dismiss as miserly and unrealistic.

Still others believe that living standards in Canada have improved to the point where poverty is of marginal significance. Compared with the past, according to Christopher Sarlo, an economist at Nipissing University in North Bay, rates of poverty have sharply declined, from one in three Canadians in 1951 to only one in 20 by the late 1970s, a figure that has since remained constant. Unlike developing world countries, Canada has virtually no poverty if measured by the presence of a destitute underclass living in squalor. The poor, it is proclaimed, are better off than before because of social security supports. Those defined as poor in Canada are appreciably better off than even the affluent in some developing world countries. Nobody in Canada needs to starve to death on the streets. Only a handful are forced by circumstances to live out in the open. Few are denied access to health care and welfare services, although some individuals may fall in between bureaucratic cracks. What is defined as poverty is simply a case of inequality in which some are more deprived compared to others.

There is yet another side to the poverty story that defines Canada. Compared to its utopian ideals, Canada falls short of its self-appointed benchmark as a happy balance between too rich or too poor. Canada may bask in the limelight as one of the best places to live, but too much self-congratulation breeds indifference or complacency. While there is general agreement that poverty exists and is a problem, there is much less consensus on how to frame the issue in terms of causes or cures. There is even less consensus over the magnitude and scale of the poverty as a social problem. Box 2–1 provides a snapshot look at the scope of poverty in Canada.

Poverty Facts and Figures

- What constitutes poverty in Canada? The most frequent measure is the low income cut-off line which adjusts for family size and location. For a family of four in Vancouver, any household earning less than $34 572 before tax would be regarded as living in "straitened circumstances" (poor). For a family of four in a medium-size city like Kitchener, Waterloo, the figure is $29 653. For a family of four in rural areas, the figure is $23 892.

- What percentage of children in Canada are thought to be poor? 18.4 percent. This figure is largely unchanged from a decade ago. A Statistics Canada Low Income Measure (LIM or half the median income measure) puts the number of poor children in Canada at 26 percent (or 1 851 400), including a third of Toronto children under the age of 18 (Carey, 2003).

- Other figures disagree: According to one study, only 786 000 or 11.4 percent of children lived in families with incomes below the low-income cut-off line in 2001, down from 16.7 percent in 1996, and the best rate since Statistics Canada started tracking poverty in 1980 (Watson, 2003). The number of low income families with children has declined as well, from 15.8 percent in 1996 to 11.4 percent in 2000, in part because of the federal National Child Benefit program (Lawton, 2003).

- Regional and provincial differences are clearly evident. In the year 2000, according to the report, *Child Poverty Persists, Time to Invest in Children and Families,* nearly 390 000 children in Ontario or 14 percent were defined as poor in the year 2000, an increase of 41 percent over the decade.

- Low income (poverty) rates vary with immigration status. The low income rates for children where neither parent is an immigrant is 15.5 percent. The rate for children whose immigrant parents have been in Canada for ten years or more is 15 percent. The rate for children whose parents have been in Canada for less than ten years is 32.7 percent (Statistics Canada, 2003). In 2000, 39 percent of children

(continued on next page)

whose parents immigrated to Canada during the 1990s were living in poverty (Chic and Fraser, 2003; Canadian Council of Social Development, 2003).

- What about the working poor? According to Statistics Canada (2003), almost 1.5 million, or 17 percent of Canada's full-time workers, earned $20 000 or less in 2000. The proportion increases to 41 percent if part-time work is included. This figure falls below the low-income cut-off line for both rural and urban areas. The national average full-time wage is $43 231. By contrast, 4.2 percent or 360 000 workers earned $100 000 or more in 2000.

- Housing or food? A single person living in Toronto is eligible for a welfare benefit of $520 a month; the average rent for a bachelor flat in the city is $733 a month. A lone parent with two children may receive a benefit of $1086 a month. The average for a two-bedroom apartment in Toronto is $1055. That leaves all of $31 for food and necessities (Goar, 2003; Mascoll, 2003).

- While poverty continues to bite deeper, corporate profits set a record in 2003 by jumping 15 percent to $168.3 billion (*National Post*, February 26, 2004).

- Welfare equals poverty. According to the National Council on Welfare, the poverty line for an urban family of four in Ontario is $36 235. This family is entitled to welfare that amounts to $18 000 or 51 percent of the poverty line. Most people on social assistance are not frauds or freeloaders but individuals who have lost a job, left a spouse, or contracted an illness.

- Disability means poverty. A single person on Ontario's disability income plan receives about $930 a month—a total that is worth about $100 less in spending power than it was worth in 1995. The Tory government is promising a monthly increase to about $975—hardly a bonanza when factoring in the cost of living (Henderson, 2003).

- For seniors who were not institutionalized, the low-income rate based on before-tax income declined from 20.4 percent in 1990 to 16.8 percent in 2000—continuing a downward trend that has seen the number of "poor" seniors reduced by a half over the past two decades.

- The income gap between census families continues to expand. The lowest tenth of families earned $10 341 in the year 2000, while the highest decile had an average income of $185 070. The biggest gap was in Toronto where the lowest tenth had an average annual income of $9571 compared to $261 042 for the highest tenth (Statistics Canada, 2003). In Nunavut, the lowest ten percent of families averaged $6100 while those at the top end of the scale averaged $151 400.

- As recently as 1980, food banks were unheard of in Canada; by March of 1999, there were 698 food banks and some 2000 agencies operating an emergency food distribution program for nearly 800 000 Canadians per month, up sharply over the previous year (Lawton, 2003). Twenty-eight Canadian universities and colleges have food banks, including thirteen post-secondary institutions in Ontario.

- In the United States, poverty is officially defined as economic deprivation based on specific income thresholds for families of different sizes. In 1997, the threshold for a family of three (one adult and two children) was set at $12 931. The average poor family of this size may also receive up to $6329 in government transfers and welfare payments, according to the March 1999 issue of *UNESCO Courier*.

Facts and figures do not tell the whole story: what about the human and social costs? How long can people be deprived without suffering long-term damage to their self-worth and ability to cope? Poverty wears people down by making it painfully difficult to be productive or positive. Up to one child in five faces a higher than average risk of poor physical and mental health, higher infant mortality rates, and higher rates of delinquency and dropping out of school. Children's ability to learn is affected by poverty-related hunger, violence, illness, domestic problems, and deprivation. According to the National Longititudinal Survey of Children and Youth by Statistics Canada and Human Resources (*The Globe and Mail*, 24 November, 1999), children who live in poverty are less ready to learn when they enter school, are more likely to live in dysfunctional families, exhibit behavioural problems such as aggression or depression, and reflect academic lapses such as failing a grade or becoming easily distracted. They also are subject to substance abuse. That poverty exists—and hurts—is certainly beyond doubt. Still, it is one thing to ponder the magnitude and scope of the problem. It may be quite another to define and implement solutions that are workable, necessary, and fair.

Defining Poverty: Absolute Or Relative

It has been said that problems can't be solved unless properly identified. Problems need to be defined in terms of causes and scale if there is any hope of finding solutions. Poverty is one of those unsolved problems about which people cannot even agree on a workable definition, let alone take steps on a clear solution. Without a definition, it is impossible to determine the nature and scale of poverty in Canada. And the lack of a clear definition leads to puerile debates in which people literally talk past each other because of wildly different reference points.

Defining poverty as a social problem is not as simple as it looks. On what grounds is poverty defined—as something absolute and measurable, or as something relative to the context? Is poverty about subsistence needs or about inclusiveness through participation? In what way does definition influence the calculation of the number of poor in Canada? To date, there are no objective measures for quantifying the number of poor because there is no consensus regarding definition. For example, poverty may be defined as "unacceptable hardship" that is, conditions that create a sense of deprivation but that could be reduced or eliminated if society were organized differently (Dennison, 2001). Other definitions disagree. Not unexpectedly, governments in Canada reject the term "poverty" on the grounds of inadequate consensus, preferring instead to depoliticize the issue by relying on references such as "straitened circumstances," "low-income cut-off line," and "substantially worse off than average." This conceptual void has prompted a proliferation of definitions, with each having its own bias, subjective assumptions, and emotional language. Depending on which measure is employed, the results can lead to high or low measures of poverty. Yet poverty is more than a statistical "bean counting" exercise. The poor are people with needs and rights, not just a problem in need of a solution. In other words, how poverty is defined is a reflection of who we are as a society and the kind of society we aspire to (Bauman, 1999).

Most definitions of poverty fall into one of two categories: absolute versus relative. These categories usually coincide with poverty definitions that are needs-oriented (subsistence needs) versus inclusiveness-based (participation). One side of the debate defines poverty in absolute terms reflecting a chronic absence of the fundamental necessities of life ("needs") pertaining to food, shelter, and clothing. Absolute measures look at what it takes to survive in Canada by examining a basket of goods for physical survival—a position endorsed by the Fraser Institute. The "Basic Needs Measure" excludes non-essentials such as books, toys, haircuts, dental services, and school supplies. The food budget is restricted to basic subsistence; for example, no tea or coffee are included (Shillington, 1999). Health items are not included in the basket on the grounds that the poor should use emergency facilities or free community clinics (Chwialkowska, 1999).

Public criticism of this mean-spirited approach has prompted a less tight-fisted definition. The federal government now endorses the concept of a "Market Basket Measure" that defines poverty around access to a particular basket of goods. Broader than subsistence, but narrower than full inclusiveness in definition, it draws the poverty line at those families who cannot afford a set shopping basket of ingredients perceived as necessary for a minimum standard of living (Mascoll and Carey, 2003). According to Market Basket Measure, a reference family of four requires a basket of goods worth $27 343 to live for a year which breaks down into $5778 for food, $2992 for clothing and footwear, $11 399 for shelter, $2316 for transportation, and $5558 for incidentals. A rural Ontario family would need $25 117 a year, including access to a five-year-old Chevy Cavalier with insurance and 1500L of gas—in lieu of public transportation. A family in Montreal is entitled to a market basket totalling $22 441 because of lower housing costs. This measure acknowledges that children should not feel excluded from society by being denied the things that many kids take for granted, like school trips and Internet access.

Poverty can be defined in relative terms: that is, poverty varies over time and place. Poverty is a kind of relationship since people tend to think of themselves as poor only if others are rich and a person's poverty is compared with someone else's affluence (Isbister, 2003). In a society in which virtually everyone has access to the necessities of life, poverty cannot be about subsistence or survival. Poverty is measured in terms of how people compare to commonly accepted standards of living. Rather than a checklist of items, the focus is on how people compare with the rest of society, particularly in terms of their ability to participate and be involved. Statistics Canada has historically used two relative measures. A Low Income Measure (LIM) draws the line at half the median income of the average Canadian family. The more popular "low-income cut-off" line (LICO) compares the spending on necessities by low-income families with the spending of typical families. Statistics Canada (2003) has consistently emphasized that LICO is not a measure of poverty but a yardstick that simply identifies those who are substantially worse off than the average. "Poverty" is defined as implicit in any household that spends more than 55 percent of its income on food, shelter, or clothing. This figure is based on what an average family in 1986 spent on the basic necessities of food, shelter, and clothing (36.2 percent) plus an additional (and largely arbitrary) 20 percent (Watson, 1996). This "poverty" measure also takes into account the size of the family and distinguishes between rural and urban families.

The debate is clearly polarized: Relative measures define people as poor if they have much less than most in the community; by contrast, absolute measures don't take into account how anyone else is doing (Mascoll and Carey, 2003). While some believe poverty should be defined in relative terms that measure people's level of community involvement, others prefer a more absolute measure that focuses on an inability to purchase the basic necessities of food, shelter, and clothing (Mascoll, 2003). Yet this distinction between absolute or relative may be overstated; after all, reference to basic needs rests on a value judgement about which needs are more important relative to the capacity and commitment of society to do something about it (Pyatt, 2003).

Absolute and relative indices of poverty differ in emphasizing a restrictiveness or inclusiveness. Restrictive definitions of poverty often convey a sense of destitution—those who we normally think of as the poor such as the bedraggled in appearance, perpetually hungry, and homeless. According to this "basic level of subsistence" scenario, poverty-stricken individuals should be given sufficient necessities to ensure they do not sicken and die, become a public nuisance, or impose an unnecessary burden on society. By contrast, inclusiveness definitions tend to be associated with more progressive entitlements. The emphasis is not simply on staving off disease or starvation but on being able to participate equally and fully in society. The inability to make choices is at the heart of relative poverty, since a family below the poverty line is restrained in the kind of choices it makes because of material shortages and social insecurities (Isbister, 2003). Not surprisingly, poor families are encouraged to invest in themselves as the first step in taking control of their destiny (Nares, 2003).

Inclusiveness definitions acknowledge the importance of community involvement as central to poverty. Poverty for children is more than basic survival: What is at stake is the capacity to participate fully as equals in community life, with enough money to go on school trips or to register for organized sports. As Steve Kerstetter, director of the National Council of Welfare writes (1999: A-19) in denying that poverty lines are about being one calorie away from starvation: "… If they were, we could provide every poor person with a giant bag of oatmeal, a gunny sack, and a cot in the flophouses, and feel we had done our job as a compassionate and fairminded people. In reality, poverty lines are about a minimum standard of living in one of the richest countries of the world. They should mark a standard that allows a person to participate in society, not merely to go on breathing." In other words, references to poverty reflect values about a preferred vision of society (DeGroot-Maggetti, 1999): Are we comfortable with bulging gaps between the rich and poor in society? Can we live with the idea of homelessness in a climate that punishes the roofless? Do we believe in a society where poor children are deprived of the competitive edge to success, thus perpetuating the poverty cycle? Is there a place for food banks in a society that produces an annual food surplus?

The Art of Defining Problems Away

The combination of hunger, homelessness, and hardship is transforming Canada into a land of poverty amid plenty (Goar, 1998). Those who prefer to dwell on the positive argue that average family incomes have risen, most houses come equipped with "all mod cons," few are starving in the streets, and no one is denied basic health care. Those who dote on the downside point to rising rates of poverty in addition to a UN committee rebuke of Canada for tolerating poverty and a dramatic increase in food banks. Both pictures of Canada are true in the sense that a glass is neither half full nor half empty but both half full and half empty regardless of optics.

Not unexpectedly, there has been a backlash in sorting through this confusion. In his controversial publication, *Poverty in Canada*, Christopher Sarlo refutes the notion that those who live below the poverty line are actually poor. Poverty lines are arbitrarily constructed, with income cut-offs providing much more than required for survival. Much of what passes for official poverty, Sarlo contended, confuses being poor with inequality and lack of access to middle-class amenities. It simply indicates that some are doing less well than others. For Sarlo, true poverty is rare when measured in terms of "stomach stretching" starvation or a roofless homelessness. To claim that 3 to 5 million Canadians are living in poverty is dismissed as largely a fabrication, according to critics, concocted by welfare advocacy and lobby groups for self-serving purposes. Moreover, measures such as the low-income cut-off point are designed to ensure a constant supply of poor regardless of improvements in the economy. For example, the Canadian Council of Social Development defines any family that makes less than half the median income of Canadian households as poor. This kind of relative measure casts doubt on whether poverty can ever be completely eliminated; after all, even a doubling of incomes across the board would not disturb the ratio of poor to rich. Such a sliding scale not only makes it difficult to measure progress on the poverty front, it also reinforces the counter-intuitive notion that Canada has more poor people now than in the past.

The political nature of these number games should be self-evident. Those whose livelihood depends on the presence of the poor have a vested interest in inflating poverty figures. Others would like nothing better than to reduce the number of official poor in Canada for self-serving reasons. The current figures are so grossly inflated, they contend, that the government invariably looks derelict in meeting its responsibilities. Conversely, a reduction in absolute numbers may reflect a wider government strategy for putting a positive spin on its social programs. Put candidly, the government has been accused of trying to define the poor out of existence. The net result is a gradual demonization of the poor as a freeloading burden on Canadian taxpayers. And no one has endured a greater hardening of the attitude arteries than the most conspicuous of the poor, the homeless.

CASE 2-1	Homelessness: Poverty in the Streets

Poverty as a social problem can be expressed in different ways. In recent years, the profile of the homeless as a major poverty problem has grown rapidly, in the process revealing certain difficulties in defining the problem and proposing solutions. The prospect of the homeless creating shanty towns under bridges and viaducts akin to those in squalid overseas slums seems strangely incongruous in a society that has so much going for it. Small wonder, then, the concept of homelessness elicits a strong visceral response: To some, homelessness is an indictment of Canadian society; to others its existence is an affront to hardworking Canadians everywhere (Ibbitson, 1999).

Many Canadians were startled to learn that homelessness was a far more pervasive social problem than they had imagined. Homelessness was not restricted simply to jobless "bums" who thought nothing of gulping down a couple bottles of cheap "plonk" before noon. It went beyond a bunch of spoilt but rebellious teens who preferred a life on the streets to the pampered confines of mom and dad. Even more shocking was the realization that homelessness was not always a lifestyle choice, but a default option because of necessity or

(continued on next page)

duress. Homelessness now included the "deserving poor"—people who, through little fault of their own, found themselves in dire straits. With shelter costs rapidly rising in major centres, the emergence of the working poor (those whose minimum wage cannot possibly cover the bare essentials) has evolved into a distinctive feature of Canada's poverty landscape.

A moment's consideration suggests a crisis in the making. The number of poor has increased in recent years, yet access to reliable housing has shrivelled up to the point where children are now forced to live in hostels or in substandard private dwellings. The federal government stopped building social housing in 1992; Ontario's provincial government got out of funding subsidized housing in 1994. The Ontario government's decision to cut welfare rates, including the shelter allowance by 21.6 percent, has compounded the problem. With government lifting the lid on rents by suspending rent control on vacant apartments, the combination of fewer subsidized apartments and escalating rents on private rentals has proven a surefire recipe for homelessness. True, subsidized housing is back on the government's agenda, but the delayed reaction means the government will have trouble coping with current demand, let alone addressing a backlog because of government inactivity.

Homelessness is a social problem in the same way that poverty is deemed a social problem. Both poverty and homelessness are social in origin, definition, impact, and treatment. Moreover, neither poverty nor homelessness can be regarded as good for individual health. Compared to men in the general population, young homeless men between the ages of 18 and 24 in Toronto are eight times more likely to die as a result of accidents, poisonings, or overdoses (Tobin, 1999). Most of the homeless in an Ottawa-based survey reported physical and mental health problems, with 60 percent having a diagnosable mental illness, mainly depression (Picard, 2000). The fastest growing group of homeless people are those under 18 years of age and families (usually headed by a single mother) with young children (Valpy, 1999). Yet children who are homeless are prone to behaviour that precludes integration into society. Life is lonely on the streets: Two-thirds of homeless people have less than four people in their social circle, including family, and often their only friends are other homeless people (Picard, 2000). This collapse of a social network from failure to foster a positive self-esteem may magnify major social problems later in life.

References to homelessness and poverty remain hotly contested. Just as a lack of definition precludes any reliable measure of poverty, so too is there no agreement over defining homelessness. Is it living without a home? No fixed address? Rooflessness? (Liddiard, 2001). As well, there is no consensus among experts as to the causes of homelessness. For some, it is about the lack of affordable housing and removal of rent controls (Gillespie, 2003); for others, it is about lack of government support for those with mental health problems, substance abuse, and abusive relations; for still others, there are too many causes for a single explanatory framework (Fiorito, 2003). Yet without a good grasp of causality, as Liddiard points out, the problem of homelessness loses its "resolvability." Worse still, quick-fix gimmicks may be introduced that evade the basic challenges by hiding behind the problem rather

(continued on next page)

than addressing it (Quaid, 2002). The usual factors are often cited, including both root and immediate causes: poverty; inadequate affordable housing; greedy landlords; a not-in-my-backyard-mentality, which makes it difficult to establish shelters for the needy; declining incomes; soaring rents; slashed social spending; mental illness; immigration and refugee adjustments; substance abuse; a lifestyle statement; or domestic abuse. Even defining who qualifies as homeless is not without its quirks. The term itself may include runaways, aboriginal peoples in the streets, psychiatric patients, families on waiting lists for shelters, drug addicts, panhandlers, and those who simply like to live "on the edge" (Henslin, 2000).

How many homeless people are there in Canada? According to data compiled by Kerry Gillespie (2003), Toronto homeless shelters, on average, each night sleep 4300 including another 800 in emergency homeless shelters. As well, each night there are 900 ex-psychiatric patients in rooming houses and around 1400 who sleep in the streets during the summer (200–300 in winter). What is less known is how many Canadians are one pay cheque away from being on the street. Increasingly, poverty, hunger, and homelessness are interconnected, since people using food banks can be seen as the "prehomeless," according to the executive director of the Canadian Association of Food Banks (Levy, 1999). Put bluntly, homelessness is not a simple problem with a single cause but a complex problem with multiple causes (Liddiard, 2001). Solutions must proceed accordingly.

To some, the homeless are largely victims of circumstances beyond their control, namely, a lack of low-end rental accommodation (Caragata, 2003). The deinstitutionalization of the mentally disabled as well as those in drug and alcohol recovery programs has swelled the homeless ranks (Turner, 2000). To others, homelessness is the price we pay for living in a freewheeling competitive society in which some win and others lose. Civic improvement projects that cater to the upwardly mobile may have the effect of eliminating inexpensive housing in city cores (Turner, 2000). For still others, homeless Canadians are seen as architects of their own misfortune. The poor can only blame themselves if they refuse to take medication or to comply with sometimes rigid house rules for overnight shelters. Such a blaming-the-victim mentality makes it difficult to generate empathy for the homeless or to commit resources for improving their welfare. Initiatives for improvement also cuts against the grain of many Canadians who believe that too much "mollycoddling" induces more dependency and laziness. This Victorian mentality of the "deserving poor" defuses the political will and financial investment to take action

The different needs of the homeless—from addiction treatment and job training to housing or mental health support—can also complicate the possibility of common solutions: Some homeless require access to simple and basic shelter, even if this accommodation comes with a set of rules. Others need to find jobs, while still others incapable of working require information about how to stay off the streets and collect the welfare or disability cheques they are entitled to (Bulla, 1999). Those with mental health problems require a caring community agency. In short, there is no simple solution to the com-

(continued on next page)

plex problem of homelessness. Only a blanket of initiatives along a broad front can possibly address the homeless problem, the complexity of which may well compromise Canada's commitment and reputation as a compassionate and caring people. That makes it more important than ever to replace short-term emergency reactions to homelessness with long-term approaches that prevent homelessness by re-engaging the homeless into the social and economic fabric of society (Lankin, 2003; Caragata, 2003).

Case Study Questions

1   Why is it so difficult to define the nature and extent of homelessness as a social problem?

2   What are some of the difficulties associated with trying to solve the homelessness problem?

Initiatives to reduce poverty are thwarted by popular misconceptions. The poor are poor, it is argued, because they are idle, lack a work or saving ethic, preferring hand-outs to labour. The poor are responsible for their own plight, according to this line of thinking, since individuals can control their destiny. This mentality of assigning primacy to personal responsibility plays into a conservative and market-oriented mindset. Government interventions such as pay equity or employment equity are decried for lowering standards while interfering with the free play of market forces. Welfare, in turn, is accused of undercutting Canada's international competitiveness while perpetuating the very conditions—including dependency and addiction—that caused the problem in the first place.

Others disagree with this assessment. In her *Dispatches from the Poverty Line*, Pat Capponi reminds us that poverty is a complex problem that cannot be reduced to simple slogans or quick-fix formula. Poverty, she observes, is hardly a lifestyle choice, but a by-product of generations of neglect, hunger, and domestic abuse. It may be inadvertently perpetuated by social service agencies that inflict humiliation on the poor by inducing patterns of dependency and powerlessness. Governments are responsible too, thanks in part to fiscal retrenchment policies. Poverty among Canadian women is systemic, that is, it goes beyond labour discrimination or entrenched gender attitudes but entails government cutbacks that affect women more than men (Nares, 2003). No less troubling is the obsession with deficit reduction in the name of global competitiveness, even at the expense of long-cherished social programs. At a time when keeping a lid on social spending remains a key priority, blaming the poor for their predicament cannot be justified (Hurtig, 1999). But not all blame can be attributed to government austerity or market forces. Individuals must take some responsibility for their choices, although options may be limited because of context. Not surprisingly, according to Bricker and Greenspon (2001), Canadians are both tender-hearted and hard-headed in preferring to provide the poor with a hand-up to get them back on their feet, rather than a handout and the expectation that we owe them a living.

This conclusion is disheartening, but inescapable. In a country with such bounty and beauty, Canada's reluctance to move on the poverty problem must come as a shock. The persistence of poverty is not an inevitability as suggested by the book of John where it is said the poor will always be with us. Nor is it the result of market forces beyond people's control. True, the utopian ideal of complete equality may never exist, but does this excuse justify unconscionable levels of poverty in Canada that have drawn fawning admiration for doing what is workable, necessary, and fair. Punishing rates of poverty are the result of decisions and choices that people make, especially by political authorities who withhold resources or lack the political will to challenge the causes of poverty. Structural changes related to downsizing and deregulation are no less suspect in throwing people out of work or into minimum-wage jobs. Policy changes in the past decade have further eroded Canada's safety net for the poor. In other words, poverty is not created by poor people but by the interplay of the economic system, political decisions, and social institutions that have been designed for those at the top. The root cause of poverty, Yunus (2003: 364) writes, is the "failure at the top rather than the lack of capability at the bottom." The conclusion seems inescapable: Now is the time to hold the affluent and powerful accountable for actions that render many Canadians powerless by keeping them mired in poverty.

EXPLAINING INEQUALITY

That inequality exists is an established fact of life. Inequities reflect patterns of social stratification by which society is divided into unequal "strata" along the lines of class, race and ethnicity, gender, age, sexual orientation, or disability. Less well established are the reasons behind its origins and persistence. What causes inequality? Should blame be pinned on individuals or on the institutional structures of the system at large? Should persons be held responsible for their predicament, or are they victims of forces beyond their control? Do we look to genes or developmental schedules as probable causes or shift to the social and the cultural? Numerous answers exist, given sociology's knack for connecting surface manifestations with root causes. Yet most responses can be sorted into four explanatory streams: biological, psychological, cultural, and structural. Responses will shape proposed solutions.

Biology

Some prefer to blame individual poverty on inherited genetic characteristics. Those who subscribe to the theory of biological determinism portray certain racial and ethnic minorities as genetically and intellectually inferior. Evolutionary principles argue that certain individuals are better suited for success than others in the competitive struggle for survival (Herrnstein and Murray, 1994). Individuals of "superior stock" will prevail and succeed in keeping with the Darwinian doctrine of "survival of the fittest." Conversely, those without the "right stuff" will be banished to the edges. In his most provocative work, *Race, Evolution, and Behavior: A Life History Perspective* (Rushton, 1994), Philippe Rushton of the University of Western Ontario posits a theory of evolution to account for racial differences across a broad spectrum of physical, social, mental, and moral domains. Rushton argues that separate races, namely "Oriental," "Caucasoid," and "Negroid" (Rushton's terminology), evolved distinctive packages of physical, social, and mental characteristics because of different reproductive strategies in diverse environments. A racial pecking order can be observed, according to Professor Rushton, because of this evolutionary adaptation. "Orientals" are superior to "Caucasoids" on a range of sociobiological factors, who in turn are superior to "Negroids" on the grounds of measurements involving skull size, intelligence, strength of sex drive and genital size, industriousness, sociability, and rule following. "Orientals" as a group have proven more intelligent, more family-focused, more law-abiding, but less sexually promiscuous than "Negroids." "Caucasoids" happily occupy the terrain in between these extremes. Although a theory of genetic inferiority appeals to some people because of simplicity and self-interest, there is little scientific evidence in support of such racist speculations.

Psychology

Others believe that the origin of inequality rests with the psychological attributes people acquire as they mature. For various reasons, some individuals do not develop normally but internalize a host of attitudes contrary to commonly accepted definitions of success. This line of thinking holds that victims of poverty and discrimination are responsible for their plight. Under a blaming-the-victim approach, the poor are blamed for their predicament because of weak "moral fibre," or personality flaws for which they alone are responsible. The proposed solution is consistent with this assessment: With hard work and application to the task at hand, anyone can succeed in a society organized around the virtues of merit, equal opportunity, and open competition. Alternatively, inequality arises because of prejudice towards "others," once again demonstrating the relevance of psychological attitudes in fostering inequality.

Culture

Another perspective focuses on the primacy of culture (and socialization to a lesser extent) as an explanatory variable. Inequalities continue to arise and are resistant to solutions because the cultural lifestyles of the poor and marginal are self-perpetuating. Oscar Lewis' (1964) work on the culture of poverty underpins this school of thought. For Lewis, living in poverty creates a cultural response to marginal conditions. This response is characterized by low levels of organization, resentment towards authority, hostility to mainstream institutions, and feelings of hopelessness and despair. Once immersed in this culture, a self-fulfilling prophecy is set in motion (a belief leads to behaviour that confirms the original belief), which further amplifies those very attributes that inhibit mobility and advancement. To be sure, the emphasis on kinship, sharing, and generosity that one finds in families of the poor may be commendable; nevertheless, critics argue, such lifestyles may be an anachronism, at odds with a competitive and consumerist present, and contrary to the blueprint for success in the future. The interplay of welfare dependency with female-headed households and lack of acquired resourcefulness reinforces the perpetuation of poverty from generation to generation.

Not everyone concedes the validity of a cultural interpretation. Recourse to culture as an explanation is perceived as yet another version of the "blame-the-victim" approach. Social problems are "individualized" by locating their causes within the culture of the victims. Ignored in this type of explanation is the external environment: Structural constraints such as social class and social barriers including racism and sexism may preclude full and equal access, thus reinforcing a lifestyle of poverty because of social exclusion. Even the very status of a culture of poverty is challenged. What passes for a "poverty culture" may be less a coherent lifestyle in the anthropological sense than a strategic response to destitute conditions. Nor is cultural deprivation per se the problem. Cultures themselves are not inferior or deprived in the absolute sense of the word. More accurately, certain cultures are defined as inferior or irrelevant by the powerful and are dismissed accordingly as unworthy of equitable treatment.

Structural

There is yet another set of explanations at our disposal. For many sociologists, inequality is not necessarily the fault of individuals or of cultural deprivation. People are deprived because of social circumstances rather than depraved because of their moral blemishes. Inequities of power, wealth, and status are created by and embedded within the structures of society itself (Agocs and Boyd, 1993). Social structures refer to those aspects of society that involve a patterned and recurrent set of rules, roles, and relations. These regularities are seen as structures in themselves or reflect manifestations of deeper structures that produce or regulate behaviour (Gillespie, 1996). Structures may include the following: institutional arrangements, economic opportunities, class entitlements, role expectations, racist/sexist ideologies, discriminatory practices, and imperatives of the prevailing economic system. Inequality and barriers to advancement are contingent on structural constraints, many of which are largely systemic and reflective of a society constructed around ruling class priorities. Structural explanations of inequality often include the broader contexts of domination, exploitation, and exclusion—including the idea that the root cause of all social problems revolves around the capitalist commitment to profits rather than people (Bolaria and Li, 1988).

Inequality, then, is framed within the context of structure or system, not individual differences or defective genes. It is not that social actors are irrelevant for understanding inequality as a social problem; on the contrary, individuals are ultimately responsible for their actions. But human behaviour does not materialize in a vacuum. It is embedded within specific social contexts that are limiting and constraining without being coercive or deterministic. Individuals are free to choose, yet must make selections within the context of structural constraints and culturally prescribed options. Institutional structures have powerful agendas that can open or close the doors of opportunity. For these reasons, most sociologists prefer to couch human behaviour in social terms by looking for causal explanations in social structures. Two theoretical approaches prevail: functionalist versus conflict theory.

The Functionalist Approach: Inequality As Solution

Functionalist theories portray society as the metaphorical equivalent of a biological organism. That is, both society and non-human organisms can be interpreted as integrated systems composed of interrelated and interdependent parts, each of which contributes to the "needs" of the organism, even if superficially they do not appear to do so. In the case of society, each of these components (such as institutions, values, and practices) is properly understood in terms of their contributions to survival and stability. By definition, then, if inequality exists in society, it must be functional and good—a solution to some societal problem.

For functionalists, then, inequality is integral to a complex and productive society. All societies must devise some method for motivating the best qualified to occupy the most important and difficult positions. A sophisticated division of labour in an urban, post-industrial society demands a high level of skill and training. A hierarchy of rewards entices skilled individuals to compete for positions in short supply, thus releasing pent-up creative energy. Differences in the rates of reward are thus rationalized as the solution to this problem. For skilled personnel to occupy key positions, adequate levels of motivation provide an incentive for recruitment. Failure to do so would dilute the pool of talent, with disastrous consequences for society as a whole. Reward structures under this model are supported by the "law" of supply and demand. Premier hockey players such as Mats Sundin or Markus Naslund are reimbursed more generously than unskilled labourers, not because hockey is more important to society than manual workers, but because crowd pleasing pucksters—unlike manual labourers—are in short supply compared with the demand. Their value is further enhanced because of a capacity to generate more income for team owners—either by putting more spectators in seats or by inflating revenue from advertising, merchandising, or endorsements. A similar line of reasoning applies to different occupations and incomes. Physicians are compensated more for their services than childcare workers because of a regulated shortage of such highly valued skills, even though, arguably, both are socially important for the smooth functioning of society.

A functionalist perspective interprets inequality as normal and necessary: necessary, because of the need to fill critical positions in society with skilled but scarce, personnel; normal, because a sorting-out process is inevitable in a complex division of labour. Inequality is condoned when the rules of the game are applied fairly and according to market principles. In an open and democratic society, people have a "right" to distribute themselves unequally, provided the competition isn't rigged but based on merit and open competition rather than arbitrary or irrelevant factors such as race or ethnicity. To be sure, a minimum degree of government intervention may be required to ensure everyone has a "fair go." "Imperfections" in the system, such as unfair trading practices or monopolies, may interfere with the proper functioning of the system, putting pressure on governments to curb these market impediments. But such intervention should be kept to a minimum lest it disturb free market expression. Excessive interference also runs the risk of fostering dullness and uniformity, while stifling the creativity and initiative necessary for progress and prosperity. That some individuals suffer more than others in an open competition is unfortunate, even regrettable but unavoidable in advancing a functioning society.

The Conflict Approach: Inequality As Structural

A (radical) conflict perspective opposes functionalist interpretations of inequality. As noted, functionalists see society as fundamentally sound while dismissing as dysfunctional ("a social problem") anything that tampers with its coherence and stability. By contrast, conflict theorists tend to view contemporary societies as fundamentally unsound because of their inherently exploitative nature. Conflict theorists approach society as a site of inequality in which opposing groups compete for scarce resources. Those groups with preferential access to scarce resources will do anything—including create conditions, fosters myths and misconceptions, devise policies, and erect barriers—to protect interests and priorities (Turner, 2000). Conversely, those who see themselves as relatively deprived will engage in actions that secure a more equitable distribution of scarce resources.

Inequality is also embedded within the capitalist framework of wealth creation—an observation popularized by Karl Marx in the 19th century and subsequently promulgated by legions of followers. In capitalist societies such as Canada, the ownership of property and control over economic processes are key defining criteria in sorting out who gets what. A capitalist system by its nature is riddled with social contradictions and class conflict. The owners of the means of production (the ruling class) are constantly on guard to reduce labour costs and protect private property. In turn, the working class is locked in a struggle to contest this inequity along a more equitable basis. The clash of these competing interests can only encourage intergroup conflicts over scarce resources. In this cut-throat game of winners and losers, individuals are sorted out in ways that foster social inequality.

Is inequality inevitable in complex societies? Are capitalist societies "naturally" inclined towards inequality? To what extent is inequality inherent in human nature, or does it reflect social imperatives relative to a mode of production? The inevitability of inequality—a basic tenet of capitalism and functionalism—is an anathema to Marxist conflict theory. Inequality is not inevitable for Marxists because capitalism is not inevitable, despite ongoing efforts by the ruling classes to naturalize free enterprise as normal. Rather marked inequities occur only in those societies that pit one class against another in the struggle for control over productive property. In contrast, according to Marx and Engels, primitive societies lived in a "natural" state of equality and cooperation. With few exceptions, formidable economic disparities rarely intruded into primitive cultures given the absence of material conditions to solidify patterns of stratification. Blatant forms of exploitation could hardly hope to flourish in contexts where everyone had relatively equal access to the basic necessities. For Marx and Engels, such an egalitarian state of affairs will be reinstituted with the end of capitalism and its replacement by a socialist Utopia.

Competing Perspectives

Man is born free, and he is everywhere in chains.

—Jean-Jacques Rousseau

In a prophetic way, this 18th century indictment of society strikes at the core of inequality debates. Despite its lack of gender inclusiveness, Rousseau's assessment captures the ambiguity inherent in society as a moral community. For Rousseau, society had betrayed "man's" natural liberty, equality, and "fraternity." The forces of domination and exploitation had subverted "his" innate goodness by transforming "him" into something "unnatural." The legacy of Rousseau continues to persist in Marxist interpretations of inequality as a departure from human "nature." Not everyone concurred with Rousseau's observations. The English philosopher, Thomas Hobbes, concluded that social restrictions were necessary for keeping our innately destructive impulses in check. Society represented a collective agreement (social contract) to protect individuals from the predations of others. Unfettered individualism had to be sacrificed for the safety and survival of the collective whole. This society-as-prior line of thinking eventually culminated in a functionalist perspective with its foundational belief that the whole must be greater than the sum of the parts.

The significance of this proto-sociological observation should be clear by now. If Rousseau was right, then inequality is an artifice perpetuated by vested interests for self-serving reasons. If Hobbes is correct, then inequality and stratification are natural and normal to society, requiring only ground rules to ensure fair play. Both functionalists and conflict perspectives agree on the universality of inequality; after all, even the simplest hunting and gathering societies are stratified by age or gender. Disagreement, however, arises over the nature of the chains that historically have shackled women and men. For Rousseau and conflict theorists, these social bonds enslaved the human species by crushing natural creativity and inherent freedom. Hobbes disagreed, arguing that restrictions are necessary and defensible in a world where life is "nasty, brutish, and short." For Hobbesian functionalists, as for Rousseauian conflict theorists, inequality per se is not a problem. Inequality becomes a problem when this inequity is relatively enduring and permanent; based on irrelevant criteria such as skin colour rather than on merit; rooted in the exploitation of others; entrenched in the institutional structures of society; and seemingly impervious to solutions. For conflict theorists, extremes in inequality are inescapable in those societies organized around the trifecta of private property, class relations, and profit-making. Conflict and instability are inevitable in a highly competitive system as each group struggles to preserve—or reclaim—its privilege, power, or wealth. Efforts to justify these gaps as natural and necessary are dismissed as ideological ploys to shore up societal inequities, in part, by cushioning the blows of exploitation.

In the final analysis, neither functionalism nor radical conflict theory is more correct. Each appears to be "trapped within the framework of its own truths," in the process drawing attention to different aspects of social inequality but not others. Neither perspective (with the possible exception of the Marxist variation of conflict theory) seems to acknowledge an uncomfortable truth: Inequality has proven a problem for some, not others; it has also proven a solution for some, but not others. And both perspectives seem to endorse different views on conceptualizing equality.

TOWARDS EQUALITY

That most Canadians aspire to social and economic equality is a widely accepted ideal. Many Canadians would also agree that equality is to be preferred over inequality. But the concept of equality is subject to diverse interpretations. Mutually opposed definitions may be endorsed by different groups or individuals, depending on their location on the social spectrum. The situation is further complicated by the possibility of concurrent versions at a given point in time in response to changing circumstances. This proliferation of definitions has culminated in confusion and misunderstanding over the politics of entitlement with respect to who gets what and why. This element of uncertainty has also complicated the process of solving problems. Without new solutions to the historical problem of inequality, the goal of equality will remain lofty but elusive.

Competing Equalities

The concept of equality is employed in three different ways. First, equality is used as equivalent to "sameness." All are treated the same regardless of their background or circumstances. No one is accorded special privileges in a system designed around equal opportunity and universal merit. This type of "formal" equality dwells on due process and legal equivalents. Second, equality is used in the sense of numerical or "proportional" equivalence. Under systems of preferential hiring and promotion, each group is allocated positions according to its numbers in society or the workforce. Third, the concept of equality is directed towards the principle of "different but equal." With its emphasis on equal outcomes or conditions rather than opportunities, this position takes into account the unique circumstances of a person or group as a basis for entitlement. People cannot be treated alike because some groups have special needs or unique experiences. Differential treatment is required to ensure the conditions for equal opportunity in the competition for scarce resources.

Consider for example the so-called "special" treatment that extends to individuals with disabilities. Wheelchair ramps, closed-caption TV, and designated parking spots are common enough. Yet these concessions can hardly be thought of as special or preferential but rather as removing barriers to ensure equality of opportunity. Likewise, historically disadvantaged minority women and men encounter barriers that are every bit as real as physical impediments and equally in need of removal for levelling the playing field. In other words, those with social disabilities require different treatment if only to ensure their right to compete with others on an equal basis.

Each of these perspectives on equality differs from the others in terms of objectives and scope. Formal equality is concerned with mathematical equivalence and a market-driven means for establishing who gets what. For purposes of allocating scarce resources, everyone is deemed to be the same—that is, as asexual, deracialized, classless, and lacking a history or context (McIntyre, 1994). Differences are not taken seriously on the liberal-universal grounds that what we have in common as rights-bearing individuals supersedes differences that divide because of membership in some group. Any measure that rewards individuals on criteria other than merit or competition is criticized as contrary to the natural sorting-out process. With its emphasis on formal equality, equality of opportunity and treatment, and sanctity of the individual, this perspective is at odds with more substantive versions of equality known as equity. For equity perspectives, identical treatment may entrench inequality by virtue of treating everyone the same without regard to histories of exclusion or restricted opportunities. Under equity, differences are taken into account in securing more equitable outcomes according to needs, rights, and aspirations of the vulnerable group. This makes it doubly important for social policies to consider inequities based on the demands of the real world rather than on formal abstractions that ignore the realities of race, gender, and class (McIntyre, 1994).

Such a debate raises a host of questions about which version of equality should prevail. Is one more important than the other, or is it a case of one serving as a necessary precondition for the other? The distinction between equal opportunity (competition) and equal outcomes (conditions) is critical. Equal opportunity focuses on the rights of individuals to be free from discrimination when competing for the good things in life. It operates on the principle that true equality can only come about when everyone is treated equally regardless of gender or race. By contrast, equal outcomes concentrate on the rights of historically disadvantaged groups to a fair and equitable share of scarce resources. True equality arises when differences and disadvantage are acknowledged as a basis for divvying up the goods. On the one hand, a commitment to equal opportunity openly advocates competition, inequality, and hierarchy as natural and inevitable. Consider the contrasts: On the other hand, an equal-outcomes perspective is concerned with controlled distribution and egalitarian conditions for members of a disadvantaged group. This perspective not only recognizes the need for collective over individual rights when the situation demands it, but it also endorses the principle of social intervention for true equality, since equal outcomes are unlikely to arise from competitive market forces.

By themselves, equal opportunity structures are insufficient to overcome the debilitating effects of systemic discrimination and institutional bias. The application of abstract standards to unequal situations may have the controlling effect of freezing the status quo. Context and consequences must be taken into account for righting wrongs and establishing equity. The taking of context into account means dealing with actual situations rather than abstract principles. The taking of consequences into consideration suggests the importance of what actually happens rather than just intent or awareness. Consider, for example, how the unintended consequences of seemingly neutral or beneficial practices may have the effect of unintentionally excluding the qualified regardless of motive or awareness. Of course, outcome-oriented equity is not opposed to equal opportunity as principle. But ultimately, a commitment to equality of opportunity cannot achieve a fair and just equality since fairness and justice acknowledge the importance of incorporating both differences and disadvantage for breaking the cycle of inequality.

DISCUSSION QUESTIONS

1   The concept of social inequality as a social problem is not nearly as obvious as many would think. Problematize the notion of social inequality as a social problem.

2   Indicate how social class continues to structure patterns of inequality in Canada.

3   Indicate why it is so difficult to define poverty. What are the major debates in defining poverty?

4   How would sociologists go about explaining the causes of inequality and poverty?

5   Indicate why the goal of equality is so elusive to attain.

 ## WEBLINKS

Inequality of wealth and income distribution. Global policy forms.   **www.igc.apc.org**

Inequality in Canada. News and analysis from a socialist perspective.   **www.wsws.org**

Canadian Council of Social Development.   **www.ccsd.ca**

chapter three

Prejucice, Discrimination, Racism

FRAMING THE PROBLEM

From afar, Canada looks like a paragon of racial tranquility. Racism may loom as the single most explosive and divisive force in many societies, including the United States, but surely not in Canada where racism is publicly scorned and officially repudiated. In contrast with the United States, where race is seen to exclude or deny, racism in Canada is thought to be relatively muted, confined to fringe circles, or relegated to the dustbins of history. Laws are in place that not only prohibit racism and discrimination but also punish those who flout Canada's multicultural ideals. Brazen racists such as White supremacists are routinely charged and convicted for disseminating hate propaganda. Race riots are virtually unheard of, while blatant forms of racial discrimination have been driven underground. To their credit, Canadians have learned to "walk their talk": Establishment of multiculturalism and employment equity initiatives have catapulted Canada to the forefront as a beacon of sanity for living together with differences. The demographic revolution that has transformed stodgy provincial cities such as Vancouver and Toronto into vibrant, racially tolerant cosmopolitan centres is yet another positive indicator. The fact that the UN has repeatedly ranked Canada as a premier place to live must surely say something about its peoples and their commitments.

Up close, the picture blurs. We could be smug about our enlightened status if racism were a mere blip on Canada's social and historical landscape. This, sadly, is far from the truth. Rather than a historical anomaly of minor consequences, racism in Canada was inextricably linked with Canada-building (Satzewich, 1998; Walker, 1998). Racism not only rationalized the removal and subjugation of Canada's original inhabitants (Wotherspoon, 2003). It also secured the ideological life-support for capitalism by creating a cheap and disposable labour force for the domestication of an "untamed" land (Bolaria and Li, 1988; Li, 2003). Minority women and men experienced varying degrees of intolerance and discrimination because of racial and national origins. Chinese immigrants in particular bore the brunt of mainstream xenophobia toward anything that remotely challenged White privilege (Baureiss, 1985; also Ip, 1997; Levin and McDevitt, 2002). Hate and fear compelled authorities to intern thousands of ethnic minorities, including Ukrainians and Germans during World War I—at great personal cost to themselves and their families. An even more spiteful internment was inflicted on Japanese–Canadians in British Columbia during World War II. Those on the west coast were rounded up for relocation, their property confiscated and civil rights suspended, before being placed in labour internment camps, which were viewed as a prelude to deportation (Samuels, 1997). An apology and modest reparations did not materialize until 1988.

The present may be equally racist, in consequence or by default if not always in intent. Critics charge that racism is alive and well in Canada; however, its worst effects are camouflaged by a Teflon veneer of politeness, denial, and good luck. Canadians are less likely to express hatred of others preferring, instead, to hide behind the gloss of politeness and coded expressions. Racism may be less blatant than in the United States, but people of colour continue to suffer indignities while confronting barriers that complicate access to full and equal participation. Consider only the persistence of hate crimes in Canada; the proliferation of racial hatred over the Internet; incidents of police racial profiling; patterns of systemic institutional bias; and anti-Muslim representations in mainstream media (Lauder, 2003). Visible minorities continue to experience discrimination at all levels of employment, from entry to access to middle and senior management (Jain, 2002). New immigrants are not doing as well economically as they once were, despite impressive educational credentials and a potent work ethic, suggesting that who you are and who you know is more important than how hard you work (Kunz, 2002). Mainstream institutions such as the police or the media are routinely condemned as discriminatory as are their oft-criticized counterparts in the United States (Cryderman, Fleras, and O'Toole, 1998; Fleras and Kunz, 2001). Canada's relations with aboriginal peoples since 1990 have been marred by racial violence, from the 78-day standoff at Oka in 1990, to the arson and destruction at Burnt Church in 1999/2000, with violent encounters at Gustafsen Lake and Ipperwash in between (Coates, 2000). Hate crimes continue to rise in major urban centres, with Blacks and Jews as the most frequent targets, followed by high levels of prejudice towards immigrants, "Arabs," and aboriginal peoples (Jedwab, 2003; Scrivener, 2003). Contrary to popular belief, racist violence usually involves the spontaneous outbursts of often inebriated young men rather than the plots of organized racist groups such as Neo Nazi skinheads (Pinderhughes, 1997; Cogan and Marcus-Newhall, 2002). Racism in sport persists as well, including the use of racial slurs to denigrate minority hockey players in Canada (Sanders, 2003; Sapurji and Mudhar, 2003).

Even Canada's much-lauded initiatives to accommodate diversity through equity-based and multicultural policies are increasingly denounced: Critics on the left dismiss these initiatives as thinly-veiled racism that inflicts more harm than good; critics on the right pounce on their inherent unfairness in a society that claims to be colour-blind (Abu-laban, 2003; Jonas, 2003). Nor can Canadians take much solace from Canada's relatively peaceful race relations record. Incidents of racial conflict may confirm the presence of racism; their absence, however, does not disprove the pervasiveness of dormant hostility toward outgroups (Brown and Brown, 1995). Expressions of racism may resemble an iceberg: You can see a bit at the top, but hidden from public awareness are those discriminatory structures underpinning the very fabric of society (Nakata, 2001). For example, Toronto's overall hate crimes may have declined from 338 incidents in 2001 to 219 in 2002, (according to the FBI, reported hate crimes also dropped in the United States from 9730 in 2001 to 7462 in 2002) but only a small percentage may be reported to authorities, with the result that what we don't know may be more important than what we do (Keung, 2003). That Canada has managed to escape the debilitating race riots that periodically engulf the United States is commendable in its own right. Yet such a fortuitous state of affairs may reflect exceptional good fortune and a powerful myth-making machine rather than enlightened policies.

Which picture is more accurate? On one side, there is talk of the "end of racism," because of official multiculturalism, elimination of overtly racial laws, progressive government policy and sanctions, and general improvement in the tenor of minority relations. On the other, there is growing evidence that racism is alive and well: A report by the UN Committee on the Elimination of Racial Discrimination in 2002 criticized Canada for discrimination against aboriginal peoples, Asians, Blacks, immigrants, and refugees. A special envoy of the UN Commission on Human Rights has also singled out racial profiling and discrimination in housing, the workplace, health, and education (Canadian Press, 3 October, 2003). So what is going on? Is Canada as racist as critics say, or is it essentially an open and tolerant society, with only isolated and random incidents of racism (also Seiler, 2003)? Who says so and why? Responses vary: For some, racism is something that happened in Canada's past, while others believe racism reflects new immigration flows and aboriginal politics. For some, racism reflects random and isolated incidents involving poorly socialized individuals, whereas others see racism as routine, systemic, and structured within mainstream institutions. Some see racism as real and growing, while others are concerned over its manipulation as a political slogan to: (a) silence individuals; (b) close off public debate over complex or controversial ideas; and (c) demonize those with different philosophical assumptions about the nature of society (Satzewich, 1998). Is Canada properly described as a society where individuals are rewarded on the basis of merit, where no group is singled out for negative treatment, and where racial attributes are irrelevant in determining a person's status? Or is there a different slant that mocks Canada's official multiculturalism (Fleras, 2001)? Answers to these questions largely depend on who is asking the question and the kind of responses they are looking for in seeking clarification (see the Case Study in Chapter 5) (Kim, 2002; Brown et al., 2003).

A sense of perspective is badly needed. Canada is a bit of everything: An awkward and conflicting blend of hard-core racists coexists with resolute anti-racists in Canada, with the vast majority of individuals wavering somewhere along this continuum. Such ambiguity makes it just as wrong to exaggerate a view of Canada as irrevocably racist, with countless hate groups resorting to violence to achieve supremacist goals, as it is to underestimate the tenacity of racism in conferring privilege on some, yet disadvantaging others. The contested notion of Canada as racist provides a framework for analyzing racism as a social problem. Both conditions of racism (including "causes, consequences, characteristics, and cures") and its constructions ("acting upon these conditions") through anti-racism are addressed, in hopes of improving our understanding of the so-called "race relations problem." The structural conditions that give rise to various forms of racism are explored as well; so too is the manner by which racism (a) defines who gets what in society; (b) pervades institutional practices and everyday encounters; and (c) resists eradication because of its chameleon-like quality to change with the times. Different dimensions of racism are analyzed and assessed in casting about for a definition, including racism as (a) race; (b) ideology; (c) culture; and (d) power. The magnitude and scope of racism will be assessed by dissecting its constituent elements, namely, prejudice (including ethnocentrism and stereotyping) and discrimination (including harassment). Particular attention is focused on the diverse types of racism, from the interpersonal (including hateful and polite) and the institutional (including the systematic and systemic) to the societal (including everyday and cultural). Insight into the many faces of racism provides a blueprint for challenging racism. Anti-racist strategies are classified as personal or institutional then examined with respect to differences in objectives, means, and outcomes. Finally, the chapter addresses why racism continues to persist, despite the fact that "we should know better" in these enlightened times. The chapter does not pretend to solve the problem of erasing racism in Canada. But it does raise useful questions about the complexities of racism as a social problem, including (Nakata, 2001):

- What are the causes of racism?
- In what forms does racism appear?
- What are the effects and impacts of racism?
- How can racism be stopped?
- How can we insure a future without racism?

THEORIZING RACISM

Awareness is mounting that (a) racism is an everyday reality for many Canadians, (b) racist practices affect individuals in very real ways, and (b) racism is not some relic from the past, but is dynamically active and socially intrusive (Satzewich, 1998). Rather than sitting still, racism more closely resembles a moving target that is difficult to pin down or control (Frederickson, 2002). Incidents of racism can span the spectrum from the openly defamatory to the quietly systemic, with the subtle and polite in between. Certain types of racist behaviour are unplanned and unpremeditated; they are expressed in isolated acts at irregular intervals because of individual impulse or insensitivity. Other expressions of racism are less spontaneous or sporadic; they are systemic and manifest instead through discriminatory patterns that may be unintentional but no less real. Expressions of racism can be wilful, intentional, or conscious; alternatively, they can be involuntary, inadvertent, or unconscious. Racism may be expressed by individuals or entrenched within institutional systems. Some see racism as something individuals do or don't do, while others define it as structural arrangements that inadvertently exclude and unconsciously deny. Racism may reflect an exaggeration of differences or, conversely, a denial of difference. For some, racism consists of any actions that single out a minority for positive or negative treatment. For others, racism is the refusal to recognize people's disadvantages and differences as a basis for recognition or reward. In other words, racism means whatever people want it to mean, and, while such breadth may be helpful, it can also confuse or provoke.

Part of the problem in securing a definition stems from reality itself. Racism is so expansive, with such an array of references from context to context, that most despair of a common meaning in the conventional sense of a single definition. Definitional difficulties are compounded by an indiscriminate use of the term itself. While references may imply a singular type of racism or a population that is divisible into racist and non-racist, in reality, racism represents an astonishingly fluid concept with a remarkable capacity to bend, elude, twist, conceal, and shape depending on context and consequences. Negative comments involving racially different persons are assumed to be racist; nevertheless, the remarks may more accurately reflect ignorance, bad manners, greed, fear, or laziness on the part of the speaker (Wieseltier, 1989). For example, resentment toward employment equity or immigration policy may have little to do with race but involve a complexity of motives, from concerns over core Canadian values to worries over levels of government intervention, in which racism is but one dimension (Satzewich, 1998). Conversely, seemingly neutral or complimentary comments may be interpreted by others as patronizing at best or racist at worst. Repeated references to racism as the precipitating cause of behaviour may gloss over the complexity of motives in shaping actions (Palmer, 1996). Blaming racism for everything when race is irrelevant may be racist in its own right. Doing so may draw attention to racial rather than social causes of minority problems, in effect contributing to the notion that when everything is defined as racist, then nothing is racism. Constant and repetitive use of the term also runs the risk of reducing racism to a harmless slogan thus trivializing its consequences for genuine victims. Finally, racism is vulnerable to manipulation by various interests along the political spectrum. Racism as a smokescreen may divert attention from the issues at hand; likewise, it may cow people into silence for fear of being branded a racist. Such labelling raises the question of what it is about racism that makes it so cringe-inducing within the general public.

Did You Know?

The nature, extent, and effect of racism may appear to be self-evident to some. Yet the reality of such an assessment is much different, largely because of the difficulties in conceptualizing racism. The following questions secure a framework for theorizing racism as a social problem:

1. Is racism increasing across Canada, or are Canadians becoming more aware of racism, with a growing willingness to report violations to proper authorities? Do Whites tend to "underestimate racism" to protect themselves from guilt or charges of racism, while minorities "overstate" it to comply with peer pressure (Holmes, 1999; Kim, 2002)?

2. Is racism a relatively recent departure from the norm in Canada by misguided individuals, or is it chronic and embedded within the history of Canada-building?

3. To what extent is racism about attitudes or structures? Is racism a case of cultural ignorance, intense dislike, or inherent fear? Or is racism embedded within the social fabric and institutional framework of Canada?

(continued on next page)

4. Is racism a "thing" out there, or an attribute that is applied after the fact by the victim in light of the context or consequence? Rather than a thing out there (a noun), is racism better conceptualized as a dynamic of interaction (a verb)?

5. Is it possible to be colour-blind, yet racist? Can colour-consciousness be regarded as progressive and non-racist? Is racism any kind of differential treatment based on race, regardless of intent or benefit, or does such a label depend on the intent or the context?

6. A generation ago it was racist to treat people differently; at present, it may be racist to treat everyone the same. Is it racist to treat everyone the same irrespective of difference or disadvantage, or is it racist to determine a person's worth by race or ethnicity?

7. Is racism about something that is done to someone, or something that is *not* done when it should be?

8. Can Canada be divided into two camps of racist and non-racists, or is the potential for racism within each of us?

9. How valid are all references to racism? Is any criticism of minorities an expression of racism by definition? Is there a danger of overuse by seeing racism in everything? Can constant repetition diminish or trivialize the impact of racism on those who routinely endure its presence?

10. What would a non-racist society look like? Is such a utopian state of affairs possible in a changing and diverse society of multiple publics?

Put bluntly, there is no timeless essence or absolute standard that applies exclusively to racism (Winant, 1998). Racism has been described as a "scavenger" ideology that is both persistent and changing in borrowing rationales from a variety of sources, losing its precision in the process, especially when used loosely and unreflectively to describe feelings of dislike toward others and actions that result from such negative attitudes (Frederickson, 2002). The possibility of consensus is further undermined by demographic changes, shifts in intellectual fashion, and global developments. Conceptualizing racism has varied over time and place, has undergone shifts in emphasis and scope, reflects variations in context and consequences, and upholds the cliché of the "eye of the beholder" (also Solomos and Back, 1996). To further complicate the matter, people's references to racism may depend on their location in society (Brown et al., 2003). Discrepancies in perception between different groups can be expected, given the widely divergent experiences and life chances in society. Whites may not deny the existence of racism; however, they tend to see it as an individual and irrational aberration from the norm (i.e., normal functioning of society) that can be isolated and eradicated. Racism is dismissed as a small bunch of "bad apples" in an essentially sound social "barrel." Minority women and men, by contrast, tend to view this barrel as fundamentally "rotten to the core," with the "bad apples" being simply the most obvious manifestation of the rot that has set in (see the case study in Chapter 5 on Crime). For minorities, racism is a central and recurrent aspect of a racialized society in which patterns of power and privilege are reproduced in overt and covert ways. The racism that is experienced by minorities is not necessarily blatant. It is conveyed discretely in ways that "other-izes" people of colour as inferior or irrelevant, and inappropriate (Gosine, 2003). In other words, White refusal to endorse power-sharing in pursuit of equality may be perceived as self-serving and racist, inasmuch as such a stance may have the effect of perpetuating a racialized status quo. This perceptual gap between Whites and people of colour makes it difficult to convey a one-size-fits-all definition of racism that meets with everyone's approval.

Definitions of Racism

Conceptual uncertainty over racism is a surprising admission. In light of racism's profile and pervasiveness, one would expect a critical mass of consensus. To the contrary, as many definitions exist as there are specialists in this area. Certain actions are unmistakably defined as racist; others are defined as such because of context or consequence. Generally speaking, reference to racism is multidimensional (Winant, 1998). The multidimensionality of racism appears to sort itself out into several categories of definitions: racism as biology, as ideology, as culture, and as power. Definitions of racism are expressed in terms of who people are (biology or race), what they believe (ideology), what they do (culture), and where they stand in the broader scheme of things (power). These distinctions are analytically useful for conceptual purposes; in reality, however, they are interrelated (Fleras, 2004).

Racism As Biology ("Racism As Race")   This definition of racism is derived from the root, "race," with its attendant notion that biology is destiny. Racism as biology (or race) can be used in three ways. First, it entails a belief that people's behaviour is determined by genes or biology. For example, many regard as racist those references to Blacks as naturally-born athletes, Japanese as naturally-gifted scientists, Arabs as fanatics, and Hispanics as hot-blooded. Second, racism may be defined as the use of race as a basis for entitlement or evaluation of others. To exclude others because of skin colour is racist; to include others on similar grounds is no less racist. For example, to include visible minorities as an employment-equity target is racist regardless of the intent or outcome, since it assigns privilege or preference on the basis of appearance rather than actions (Jonas, 2003). Third, racism as biology refers to the process of attaching an evaluative and moral quality to perceived biological differences. People who are racially different may be perceived as inferior or threatening not because of actual differences but because of perceived meanings attached to these differences and their significance for society (Pinderhughes, 1997).

Racism As Ideology   Racism as ideology transforms race-based differences into a hierarchy that justifies the dominance of one group over another (Jakubowicz et al., 1994). With racism, a relatively cohesive set of beliefs ("ideology") and practices is imposed that labels, classifies, evaluates, and ranks members of a group along a hierarchy by virtue of their inclusion in a predefined category. Racism as race begins with the ideological belief that people can be divided into "races" and assessed or treated accordingly. The human world is partitioned into a set of fixed and discrete categories of population. Each of these racial categories contains a distinctive and inherited assemblage of social and biological characteristics that can be arranged along ascending/descending orders of importance. Unequal treatment of others is then justified on the grounds of innate differences between races. Racial doctrines not only define certain types of behaviour (such as intelligence) as bio-genetically programmed. A moral value of inferiority or superiority is also assigned to human differences. Certain races are judged inherently unequal because of social or mental deficiencies and subsequently denied rights and opportunities for full participation because of these imputed differences. In some cases, hatred toward others is reflected in and reinforced by this rationale for justifying unequal treatment.

Racism As Culture ("Racism Without Race")   The biological focus of racism has shifted in recent years to take into account assumptions about cultural inferiority rather than a preoccupation with pigment-focused inferiority. Racism is no longer perceived as a universalist discourse about biological dominance, as was the case with colonialism. The objective then was to destroy the "other," to exploit them on the grounds of their biological inferiority, or to subordinate and assimilate them to the colonizer's concept of progress (Stolcke, 2001). The new racism is rooted in a dislike toward the "other," not only because of who they are ("biology") but also because of what they do ("culture"). Minorities are denied or excluded by racializing cultural differences as a basis for denial or dislike. Instead of assertions about the differing endowments of different races, what we have is a discourse about racism without reference to "race." A cultural framework is invoked for framing debates about inclusion and exclusion with respect to belonging and acceptance.

Under cultural racism, ethnic minorities are no longer dismissed as racially inferior. Dominant sectors are not defined as racially superior but as culturally normal. This cultural racism prevails when people of one culture assume their way of doing things is normal and necessary, together with the power to impose these beliefs and practices on others. This newer racism is rooted in a coded language that links social cohesion with national cultural identity (Jayasuriya, 1998). Such exclusion is no longer about biological dominance but about the necessity for cultural uniformity in the guise of citizenship, patriotism, and heritage (Fleras, 2004). Racism as culture is predicated on the principle that the cultural "other" poses a danger or threat to the mainstream. Culturally different migrants are defined as the source of a society's social problems, Wieviorka (1998) writes, with dominant groups drawing on racial definitions that combine biology with culture to demonize or scapegoat the "other" on the grounds that they are too aggressive, too uppity, too demanding, too successful, or not successful enough. Contemporary racist discourses are aimed at criticizing the cultural "other" when differences are seen as beyond the pale of integration. Cultural differences are racialized or vilified to marginalize a group as inferior or irrelevant. Conversely, these differences are subject to intense assimilationist pressure in hopes of preserving a preferred way of living (Madood and Berthoud, 1997). In more extreme cases, those who are defined as outside the cultural nation are expelled or eliminated.

Racism As Power (Racism As "Racialization")   Another set of definitions focuses on racism as power. Racism is approached as virtually any type of exploitation or process of exclusion by which the dominant group institutionalizes its privilege and power at the expense of others (Al-Krenawi and Graham, 2003). A specific strategy and process of political and social control is imposed that excludes certain groups from opportunities, rights, and benefits (Nakata, 2001). This broader dimension goes beyond racism as a set of ideas or individual actions; proposed instead is reference to racism as a network of power relations (Dei, 1996; Gosine, 2003). Power can be variably defined but normally is situated within social relationships and the institutional structures of society that unintentionally advantage some, disadvantage others (Barrett, 2002). Those with power can impose their definition of the situation to the exclusion of others, thereby influencing others to think and act accordingly.

Reference to racialization exposes the linkage of power and racism. Racialization begins with the notion that there is no such thing as race relations involving discrete biological races in relationship to one another (Holdaway, 1997). What prevails instead are relations that have been racialized, involving a process by which some groups have the power to attach social significance to, draw boundaries around, and take advantage of others because of perceived inferiority. For example, consider how urban crime in Canada is "racialized" around the image of Black criminality. With racialization, meanings associated with race are negatively assigned to particular practices or devalued groups (Al-Krenawi and Graham, 2003). Those routine, recurrent, and organized features of society become infused with racial undertones by virtue of racial distinctions that define, evaluate, and compare. Finally, racism as power also entails the capacity for some to establish agendas regarding what is normal, necessary, desirable, or acceptable, thus reinforcing the superiority of one group over another.

Racism, then, is about power, not pigmentation (Khayatt, 1994). It involves the power held by one group of individuals that has a controlling effect over another on the basis of appearance, intelligence, or moral worth. In contrast to perception of race as the prejudices of individuals, racism as power points to the primacy of structures, values, and institutions in allocating rewards according to race (Bonilla-Silva, 1996). The notion that racism is about power, not prejudice, is reinforced by bell hooks (1995: 154–155) when she writes:

> Why is it so difficult for many White folks to understand that racism is oppressive not because White folks have prejudicial feelings about Blacks … but because it is a system that promotes domination and subjugation? The prejudicial feelings some Blacks may express about Whites are in no way linked to a system of domination that affords us any power to coercively control the lives and well-being of White folks.

To be sure, power should never be reduced to the level of a static resource, with Whites holding all the power in some kind of zero-sum game. Power is increasingly perceived as a dimension in social relations involving competition, negotiation, and compromise (Holdaway, 1996). Minorities are not powerless; people of colour may tap into pockets of power to resist, remove, redefine, or renew. Still, only White power is institutionalized within the structures, values, and institutions of society. And it is these institutionalized power relations that empower some groups to impose frameworks that reflect, reproduce, and advance relationships of inequality (Guibernau, 1996).

A Working Definition   Acknowledging the different dimensions of racism is a blessing and a curse. Some want to define racism as the inclination to "biologize" the intellectual, moral, and social characteristics of a person or group. A racially based ideology of "who gets what" involves a so-called hierarchy of superior and inferior races that unjustly diminishes others and justifies this discrimination by reference to biological reductionism. Others are leaning toward cultural definitions of racism. Boundaries between groups are drawn by racializing culturally different groups and signifying them as different and threatening ("racism without race") (Malik, 1996). Still others prefer to define racism as any act of denial or exclusion against any identifiable group perceived as inferior. Racism has the intent or effect of reproducing a racially unequal social structure by naturalizing perceived differences as necessary and normal (Winant, 1998). For that reason, racism should be interpreted as a system of power relations in defence of the status quo, with a complex array of practices and discourses that are historically defined, embedded within institutional structures, woven into the ideological fabric of society, and acted out through daily actions.

A comprehensive definition of racism should incorporate as many dimensions as possible without losing any sense of integrity or cohesiveness in the process. For our purposes, then, racism is defined as those ideas and ideals ("ideology") that assert the normalcy or superiority of one social group over another, together with the institutionalized power to put these beliefs into practice in a way that has the intent or effect of demeaning those in a devalued category. Racism is ultimately based on patterns of power involving relations of dominance, control, and exploitation. Those in positions of power are able to invoke a doctrine of dominant superiority to enforce social control over those deemed inferior in the competitive struggle for scarce resources (Levin and McDevitt, 2002). In that racism is about power, and because those with power rarely want to share it with those perceived as social inferiors, the pervasiveness of racism is unlikely to diminish in the foreseeable future.

CONSTITUENTS OF RACISM: PREJUDICE AND DISCRIMINATION

Racism does not exist as a monolithic reality. Nor is it a "thing" out there that everyone can agree on. Racism ultimately touches on a variety of social processes, from the immediate and everyday to the remote and systemic. Each of the components that constitutes racism contributes to its totality as an ideology and practice. For purposes of analysis, the building blocks of racism consist of prejudice (including ethnocentrism and stereotypes) and discrimination (including harassment).

Prejudice

The concept of prejudice refers to negative, often unconscious, and preconceived notions about others. Prejudice arises because of our tendency to prejudge persons or situations as a way of imposing a definitional order on the world around us. Prejudicial thinking is normal and necessary. It is fundamental to the way that individuals process information with respect to ingroup–outgroup relations (Thomas, 1998; Abel, 2001). Prejudice also refers to a set of generalized attitudes and beliefs that encourages the perception of others at odds with objective facts (Holdaway, 1996). Ignorance is closely linked with prejudice. Unlike ignorance, however, prejudice is characterized by an inflexible refusal to modify beliefs when presented with contrary evidence.

Many regard prejudice as a psychological phenomenon involving a corresponding set of authoritarian personality traits (Adorno, 1950; Allport, 1954). Others link these prejudgments with a visceral and deep-seated fear of those whose appearance or practices challenge a cherished and comfortable status quo. Still others equate prejudice with (a) feelings of superiority; (b) a perception of subordinate groups as inferior; (c) a belief in the propriety of White privilege and power; and (d) reluctance to share scarce resources (Blumer, 1958). In that such perceptions may involve a projection of the "us" onto the "them," prejudice may say more about public anxieties than anything intrinsic about minority women and men.

For sociologists, however, prejudice is inseparable from the nature of group dynamics in society. Prejudices do not materialize out of nowhere; nor are they the by-product of unhealthy personal development. The nature and content of prejudice is situated within a broader context to seek to control minorities.

National surveys confirm what many probably suspect (Jedwab, 2003): Many Canadians are inclined to negatively prejudge others because of ignorance or visceral dislike. Tests, such as the Implicit Association Test, suggest that the vast majority of people have unconscious prejudices that are strikingly different from explicit or conscious values (Banaji 2003; Dow 2003). Prejudicial attitudes are perceived as particularly hard on certain visible minority communities such as Blacks and Chinese, according to the *Toronto Star's* "Beyond 2000: Home to the World" study project, with 68 percent of Blacks and 64 percent of Chinese acknowledging prejudice against their community (Carey, 1999). A parallel situation is found in the United States. According to Dr. Banaji, the discrepancy between implicit and explicit attitudes can be staggering, with upwards to 95 percent of respondents revealing an unconscious bias against African Americans. To be sure, the nature of prejudice may be changing: The strongly held sense of biological inferiority and hateful stereotypes has given way to rejection and denial on the basis of cultural differences that are deemed unacceptable or incompatible (Fleras, 2004). Nevertheless, the consequences of such cultural rejection may be racist and controlling in reinforcing a racialized pecking order.

Ethnocentrism

Every society socializes its members to accept the normalcy and naturalness of their way of life. People grow up believing that what they think and how they act are universally applicable and that others tend to think or act along these same lines. Ethnocentrism is the term to describe this prejudgment about ourselves and the world out there. It can be defined in two ways. First, it consists of a process whereby individuals tend to be "trapped within their truths" because of a universal tendency for people to interpret reality from their cultural point of view as normal and necessary, while assuming that others will do the same if given a chance. Other realities are dismissed as inferior or irrelevant. Second, ethnocentrism refers to a set of beliefs in the superiority of one's own culture compared to others. It represents an uncompromising loyalty to one's own ways as the unquestioned norm that prejudges others. Others are dismissed as inferior, an assessment that arises from ripping their cultural practices out of context for comparison, then judging these practices against the familiarity of their own standards.

There is nothing intrinsically wrong with embracing one's cultural lifestyle as self-evident and preferable. Difficulties arise when these standards are used as a reference point for negatively evaluating others as backward, immoral, or irrational. Status differences are the key: The dominant sector doesn't have to look outside itself for meaning, in effect remaining largely oblivious to its own assumptions regarding what is normal (Al-Krenawi and Graham, 2003). By contrast, minority identities are powerfully shaped by mainstream attitudes because of the imbalances of power in society. Problems also arise when these ethnocentric judgments are used to condone the mistreatment of others. In other words, ethnocentrism is a two-edged social phenomenon: Favouritism towards one's group may forge the bonds of cohesion and morale but can also foster intergroup tension and hostility.

Stereotyping Ethnocentrism often leads to a proliferation of stereotypes about outgroup members. Stereotypes are essentially generalizations about others, often reflecting first impressions that are thought to be unfounded on the basis of available evidence. The dangers of exaggeration may result in oversimplified distortions. To be sure, stereotyping may be inevitable in the processing of information. Stereotyping reflects a universal tendency to reduce a complex phenomenon to simple(istic) explanations that are generalized to a whole category without acknowledging individual differences (Isajiw, 1999). In an information-rich environment, stereotypes allow people to cope with an economy of effort. Others concede that stereotypes are generalizations, but in the sense of statistical approximations rather than a literal description that applies to everyone in a group (Seligman, 1999).

Like ethnocentrism, stereotypes have the potential to create problems. Stereotypes tend to dehumanize whole groups of people by isolating a tiny anomaly among some individuals, then amplifying outward to the entire group (Pickering, 2001). Problems further arise when these preconceived mental images give way to discriminatory practices. The dispossession of aboriginal peoples from their lands was facilitated by circulation of negative images of First Nations as savages, cannibals, or brutes (Ponting, 1998). A pervasive anti-Asianism in British Columbia fostered hatred against Asian populations, thereby simplifying the task of expelling 22 000 Japanese–Canadians from the West Coast in 1942. And hostility toward Arab/Muslim Canadians continues to fester in light of demeaning stereotypes that portray Arab Canadians as (a) an uncooperative visible minority; (b) colonized peoples without democratic traditions; and (c) pro-terrorist religious fanatics bent on liquidating the West (Siddiqui, 1998). Finally, stereotypes continue to drive a wedge between young people and the police, each of whom appear willing to believe the worst of the other (Neugebaur, 2000). According to one youth, in confirming that young people won't respect police because police don't respect them:

> [T]he police perceive me as being a bad person … they judge me by how I look. Just because I am Black, wear baggy jeans, have a gold tooth, and wear a cap or toque, they won't even talk to me properly (cited in Moss, 1998: D-1).

All negative stereotypes are hurtful. Failure of minority women and men to perform well in society may have less to do with ability than with the circulation of stereotypes that tend to deny, demean, or distort (Steele, 1999). Nor can the public appreciate the insult and hurt when people are stereotyped by race or ethnicity instead of being judged as individuals on grounds of achievements and personality. But not all stereotypes are equal in impact (Elmasry, 1999). Context and consequence are crucial, especially for vulnerable minorities. For example, members of a dominant group may diffuse negative stereotyping about themselves since they, as a group, have control over a wide range of representations that flatter or empower. Even a constant barrage of negative images can be absorbed without harm or damage if buffers are in place. Stereotypes might make White men uncomfortable; yet many possess the resources to resist or neutralize them because power and privilege provide a protective layer.

For minorities, however, stereotyping is a problem. Each unflattering representation reinforces their marginal status in society. The media are a major source of stereotyping; so too are ethnic jokes. Ethnic jokes often portray minorities in a demeaning way not out of malice but because such humour by definition is simplistic and prone to exaggeration. While unintended, the consequences are damaging: Minorities are portrayed in unidimensional terms such as "comics," "athletes," "victims," "vixens," or "violent." These images, in turn, can be employed to justify daily violence or structural oppression through the negative effects of a "chilly climate" (Holtzman, 2000). In short, stereotypes are not an error in perception, at least no more so than prejudice reflects psychological flaws. In terms of its social dimension, stereotyping is yet another instrument of social control in preserving the prevailing distribution of power and resources (Pickering, 2001).

Discrimination

Prejudice refers to attitudes and beliefs; by contrast, discrimination consists of the process by which these prejudgments are put into practice. The term "discrimination" can be employed in different ways. Non-evaluative meanings indicate a capacity to distinguish (for example, a colour-blind person may not distinguish between blue and green). Evaluative meanings of discrimination can be used positively ("a discriminating palate") or negatively ("a differential treatment") depending on whether the distinction is appropriate or legitimate. Section 15 of the Charter prohibits discrimination on the basis of race, ethnicity, or origin; yet it also concedes the necessity for "discriminatory" measures, such as employment equity, to assist historically disadvantaged minorities to compete on a level playing field. Discrimination may also involve taking evasive action because of perceived risks created by others' actions, even if these group generalizations are unfair and reflect badly on targeted group members. The noted Black leader, Jesse Jackson, spoke candidly to this effect in 1994:

> There is nothing more painful for me at this stage in my life than to walk down the street and to hear footsteps and to start to think about robbery and then to look around and see it's someone White and feel relieved.

Some forms of discrimination are defined as acceptable and reasonable to the functioning of society. For example, the Supreme Court of Canada upheld a discriminatory law that favoured Canadian citizens over non-citizens in public service competitions, and defended the ruling by arguing that such a violation of equality rights is reasonable and justifiable (MacCharles, 2002).

Discrimination involves treating people differently and negatively without a good reason (Canadian Human Rights Act). In the context of unequal relations, discrimination entails the differential treatment of minority groups not because of their ability or merit but because of irrelevant characteristics such as skin colour or lifestyle preference. Intrinsic to all types of discrimination are the realities of power. Neither institutions nor workplaces can be regarded as neutral sites that are devoid of intent or consequences. Rather, workplace institutions and practices are loaded with ideological assumptions that inadvertently favour some at the expense of others. The values, perspectives, and expectations of those in charge tend to define how "things are done around here" with respect to "who gets what." Those with access to institutional power possess the capacity to put prejudice into practice in a way that denies, excludes, or controls. This discrimination may be open and blatant; alternatively, it may be covert, thus prompting companies to determine whether their hiring or promotional procedures may unintentionally exclude otherwise qualified applicants. In some cases indirect discrimination happens because the outcomes of seemingly neutral rules or procedures that apply equally to everybody have an unintended discriminatory effect on vulnerable minorities. For example, criminal laws are not usually seen as discriminatory because they apply to everybody; in reality, laws are essentially designed to target personal and property offences that often involve individuals from lower classes and racial minorities (Nakata, 2001). Combining these dimensions produces a workable definition: Discrimination can be defined as any act, whether deliberate or not, that has the intent or the effect of adversely affecting ("denying" or "excluding") others on grounds other than merit or ability.

Harassment

Harassment is commonly categorized as a type of discrimination. Yet there is no consensus regarding what is encompassed by this concept (Saguy, 2003). Racial harassment consists of persistent and unwelcome actions of a racially oriented nature by those who ought reasonably to know that such attention is unwanted. In the words of Monique Shebbeare (McGill, 1994: 6), harassment involves:

> [t]he abusive, unfair, or demeaning treatment of a person or group of persons that has the effect or purpose of unreasonably interfering with a person's or group's status or performance or creating a hostile or intimidating working or educational environment....

As is the case with discrimination, harassment constitutes an abuse of power that need not be explicitly directed at a specific target. Seemingly minor and isolated incidents may amount to harassment when viewed over time or in context. The creation of a chilly climate, or "poisoned environment," because of harassment can also have an adverse effect on work, study, involvement, or well-being (Baker-Said, 2003). Others disagree. A distinction should be posited between harassment and causing offence. Harassment should be restricted to speech or behaviour that repeatedly targets a particular individual or group in a way that inhibits that person(s) from full and equal participation within the institution. Merely offending someone because of an isolated ethnic joke or thoughtless racist remarks should not be considered harassing (Stockholder, 1997). In any case, what passes for harassment is ultimately "receiver-dependent," that is, harassment is defined from the perspective of the victim in distinguishing between those actions that constitute an abuse of power and those that are simply annoying or awkward.

To sum up: Many have equated racism into the following formula: Prejudice + Discrimination = Racism. In theory, racism entails a complex interplay of ideas and actions, with its admixture of prejudice (stereotyping and ethnocentrism) and discrimination (harassment). Although discrimination is often paired as the behavioural counterpart of prejudice such a distinction or relationship is not always clear-cut. Discrimination can exist without prejudice; conversely, prejudice may flourish without its expression in discrimination. Racism also encompasses an ideology with a patterned set of responses that combine to explain, justify, rationalize, and legitimize the unequal treatment of minorities through political exclusion, economic exploitation, or social segregation. The key element in this equation is power. When combined with power, the interplay of prejudice and discrimination culminates in many different forms of racism.

THE FACES OF RACISM

Racism is not a uniform concept around a singular experience or common reality. On the contrary, different modes of racism can be discerned that embody variations in intent, levels of awareness, magnitude and scope, styles of expression, depth of intensity, and consequences. These variations have culminated in the recognition of diverse types of racism, including: (a) interpersonal (including hate and polite); (b) institutional (including systematic and systemic); and (c) ideological (including everyday and cultural). Comparing and contrasting these admittedly ideal types expose the complex and multidimensional nature of racism as principle and practice. Acknowledging the different types of racism should also assist in devising diverse solutions for purging racism from society (also Augoustinos and Reynolds, 2001; Pincus, 2003).

TABLE 3.1	Types of Racism		
Interpersonal		Institutional	Ideological
hate		systematic	everyday
polite		systemic	cultural

1. Interpersonal Racism   Interpersonal racism entails a pattern of interaction that occurs primarily between individuals. It reflects a degree of dislike that is directed at others because of who the person is or what the person stands for. Two types of interpersonal racism can be discerned: hate and polite.

a. Hate Racism   Hate racism is the kind of racism implied by most references to racism. It refers to the kind of old-fashioned racism that prevailed in the past and prevails into the present among a handful of reactionary, ignorant, or defiant individuals. With hate racism, violence is directed at all persons because of their membership in a devalued group in response to increased competition for scarce resources (Levin and McDevitt, 2002). Intrinsic to hate racism is its explicit and highly personalized character. Whether through physical or verbal abuse, hate racism consists of highly personal attacks on others perceived as culturally or biologically inferior. These personalized attacks often consist of derogatory slurs and minority name-calling. Hate racists are not intimidated by labels of racism. Unlike many Canadians, who cringe at the prospect of being labelled racist, hate racists take boastful pride in being defined as such, and acting accordingly.

Even a cursory glance at Canada's past exposes a legacy of hate racism (Walker, 1998; Backhouse, 2000; Lauder, 2002). This may come as a shock to many readers. Few are surprised by references to the United States as a hotbed of hate racism. With its historic claims to slavery, the Ku Klux Klan and segregation, and convulsive urban riots, the United States is easy to single out as a bastion of racism. But surely not Canada, with its espousal of multiculturalism and human rights! Certain myths are deeply entrenched in our collective memories, especially those that extol Canada's progressive outlooks. Foremost is the absence of American-style race riots, the lack of racist symbols, the omission of prolonged slavery, and the entrenchment of multicultural philosophies within Canadian society. How accurate are these perceptions? Are Canadians really superior to Americans when it comes to the treatment of racial minorities? Close scrutiny suggests not. Canadian society has long been stratified along a social ranking in which racialized groups were hierarchically arranged on grounds of their proximity to the norm of 'Whiteness' (Kobayashi, 2001).

Until the late 1950s, racism was central in shaping attitudes, state policies, and institutional arrangements—particularly in the fields of immigration and aboriginal peoples-state relations. Minority women and men were regularly exposed to: (a) economic exploitation as disposable labour; (b) social and physical segregation; (c) separate cultural development; (d) enforcement of a colour bar through public policy and private acts; and (e) legislation to exclude or deny equality (Walker, 1998). These initiatives created a vicious circle by moulding public perception of minorities as unacceptable, thus intensifying the demand for yet more restrictive legislation.

Expressions of hate racism in Canada persist into the present. Blatant acts of anti-Semitism—including harassment, hammer and acid attacks, and bomb threats—jumped to 459 incidents across Canada in 2002, a 60 percent increase over the previous year, possibly in response to growing mid East tensions (Scrivener, 2003). Racial violence in recent years has been perpetuated by White supremacist groups ranging from the White Aryan Nation and Western Guard movements to neo-Nazi skinheads in urban areas (Kinsella, 2001). Groups such as these are committed to an ideology of racial supremacy in which the White "race" is seen as superior and destined, thus requiring a strict separation of races to ensure purity and salvation. They are also prepared to transform society along White supremacist lines by seeking out converts to their ideology of hate (Li, 1995).

The popularity and potential of White supremacist groups are difficult to gauge. Only a small number of hardcore supremacists are thought to exist in Canada; nevertheless, these extremists have the potential to destabilize a society by stoking dormant prejudices (Lauder, 2002). Many supremacists may see themselves as White Christians, fusing race and religion in a single nationalist crusade against the forces of "evil" (Jaret, 1995). Hate groups sustain their credibility and legitimacy by capitalizing on a sputtering economy and social instability. Disaffected youth are an obvious target because of their perception that the government is indifferent to their plight in a changing and diverse world. Demographic imbalances resulting from immigration are likely to ignite supremacist ire, as is the perception that certain minorities are mollycoddled by excessive levels of political correctness. Hatred toward minorities is conveyed in different ways but primarily through telephone hotlines, the Internet, which allows dissemination without fear of reprisals or court challenges, and disinformation campaigns by hate-mongers recruited by the movement (Kinsella, 2001). The combination of music, pamphlets, and the Internet concocts a poisonous but appealing mishmash of neo-Nazi philosophies, KKK folklore, pseudo-Nordic mythology, and anti-government slogans (Wood, 1998). The courts in Canada have defined these diatribes as "hate propaganda" and a violation of Canada's criminal code. Technicalities have often overturned such verdicts.

b. Polite Racism

> In some ways I prefer to live in a society where they just say "You're Black, we don't like you. Here in Canada, people are hiding behind a mask (Kolawole Sofowora, *Toronto Star*, 2 May, 1999).

Few people at present will tolerate the expression of racism. Yet racism at one time was openly expressed, institutionalized in government policy and practice, and socially acceptable. There was no need for pretense—everything was up front and openly visible (Griffin, 1996). But the risk of social or legal consequences, not to mention the potential for physical retaliation, serves as a deterrent at present. The passage of constitutional guarantees, such as The Charter of Rights and Freedoms and the Human Rights Code, has banished hate racism from public discourse. But while blatant forms of racism have dissipated to some extent, more subtle references to bigotry and stereotyping remain in force. Instead of disappearing in the face of social reprisals and legal sanctions as might have been expected, racism is now couched in a way that allows people to talk around their aversion to others by using somewhat more muted (polite) tones.

Polite racism then can be seen as a contrived attempt to disguise a dislike of others through behaviour that outwardly is non-prejudicial in appearance. It often manifests itself in the use of coded or euphemistic language to mask inner feelings and attitudes. In contrast with the open bigotry of the past, racist attitudes are increasingly cloaked in codes that make it difficult to prove motive or awareness (Wetherell and Potter, 1993). This politeness is especially evident when people of colour are turned down for jobs, promotions, or accommodation (Henry and Ginzberg, 1985). For example, when approached by an undesirable applicant, an employer may claim a job is filled or requires Canadian experience rather than admit "no Blacks need apply." Polite racism may appear more sophisticated than its hate equivalent; nevertheless, the sting of this hidden racism erects invisible barriers when visible minorities apply for jobs or promotions.

Canadian racism is often depicted as polite and subdued. This racism is rarely perpetuated by raving lunatics who engage in beatings, lynchings, or graffiti. Rather, racism among Canadians is unobtrusive, often implicit, and couched in a political correctness that reveals as much as it conceals. Hostilities to minorities continue to be expressed, to be sure, but they are usually restricted to remarks in private or to friends. Polite racism is increasingly popular with an educated population. With higher education, individuals become more adept at compartmentalizing and concealing racist attitudes behind coded expressions, lest they blurt out statements at odds with career plans or public image (Fleras, 1996). This gap between the fairness that Canadians profess and the subtle discrimination they practice is often undetected—except by those who experience the sting of this subtlety. Such hypocrisy makes it difficult to confront—let alone eradicate—the expression of polite racism.

2. Institutional Racism   Much of the discussion to this point has dwelt on racism as an individual attribute. Other types of racism go beyond the interpersonal in terms of scope, style, and impact. Racism at the institutional level represents such a shift in expression. Institutional racism refers to the process by which organizational practices and procedures are used either deliberately or inadvertently to discriminate against others. With institutional racism, the issue is not of individual acts of racism within the confines of an institution or workplace. Rather, institutional racism refers to organizational rules, procedures, rewards, and practices that have the intent (systematic) or effect (systemic) of condoning discriminatory practices.

a. Systematic Racism   Systematic racism involves organizational rules and procedures that directly and deliberately prevent minorities from achieving full and equal institutional involvement. This institutionalized racism appears when discriminatory practices are legally sanctioned by the state and formalized within its institutional framework, thus reflecting the values and practices of the dominant sector. It consists of formal rules and official procedures that are embedded within the design (structure and function) of the organization to preclude minority entry or participation. These institutional norms and values may be based on ideologies that uphold the superiority of the mainstream. As well, informal principles and practices may also be accepted, either consciously or unconsciously, reinforcing the institutional adage of "that's how we do things around here" (Isajiw,1999).

Systematic institutional racism flourished in societies that endorsed racial segregation. The regime of apartheid in South Africa was a classic example, as was the pre-civil rights United States. Nor was Canada exempt from the tarnish of institutionally racist practices (Reitz and Breton, 1994). Institutional racism was once a chronic and inescapable component of Canadian society (Walker, 1998). Minorities were routinely barred from even partial participation in mainstream institutions. But evidence now suggests that minorities are unlikely to be directly victimized by blatant institutional racism. Institutions can no longer openly discriminate against minorities, lest they attract negative publicity, invoke a lawsuit, or incite consumer resistance. Nevertheless, institutional racism continues to exist. It can incorporate various discriminatory actions, from hate to polite, all of which combine to preserve the prevailing distribution of power. Systematic racism may refer to the way in which organizations deliberately manipulate rules or procedures to deny minority access or participation. It can take the form of harassment from supervisors or co-workers, often defended as unintentional or not meant to harm, but involving a process by which workers act on behalf of the corporation or these actions are condoned by the company. The revelation that both Denny's restaurant chain (United States) and Texaco went out of their way to discriminate against African-Americans provides proof that systematic racism is alive and well (also Watkins, 1997). More recent cases include charges that Wal-Mart conspired with contractors not only to hire illegal migrants but also to violate their civil rights and wage protections (American Press, 12 November, 2003).

b. Systemic Racism   There is another type of institutional racism that comes across as impersonal and unconscious. Its unobtrusive and implicit character makes it that much more difficult to detect, much less to isolate and subdue. Systemic racism is the name given to this subtle yet powerful form of discrimination that reflects the normal functioning of the institution. That is, institutional-based practices from recruitment to reward are themselves free of bias but, in their even-handed implementation, exert a negative effect on vulnerable minorities (Frederickson, 2002; Pincus, 2003). Even explicitly colour-blind policies and well-intentioned initiatives may be systemically racist if differences as a basis for recognition and reward are ignored. In other words, the normal operations of an institution may culminate in a systemic bias because of the unintended consequences of seemingly neutral rules and practices that adversely effect those who differ cultural or racially.

With systemic racism, it is not the intent or motive that counts: context and consequences do. Policies, rules, priorities, and programs may not be inherently racist or deliberately discriminatory; for example, institutions do not go out of their way to exclude or deprive minorities. But rules may have a discriminatory effect in that they exclude certain groups, however inadvertently, while conferring advantage on others. Systemic racism is thus defined by its consequences. It rests on the belief that institutional rules and procedures can be racist in practice, even if the actors themselves are free of prejudicial attitudes. Institutions are systemically racist when they ignore how organizational practices and structures reflect and reinforce White experiences as normal and necessary. Or institutional policies are formulated that may be well intentioned but rest on faulty assumptions that penalize those with radically different cultural assumptions and social needs (Shkilnyk, 1985). Put baldly, systemic racism is difficult to discern because it is (a) embedded within institutional rules and procedures; (b) beyond our everyday consciousness; (c) undetected and disguised by reference to universal standards; (d) taken for granted; and (e) duplicitous in reflecting an appearance of fairness and impartiality.

Even a few examples will demonstrate how the implicit bias of a system designed by the mainstream can create unintended yet negative effects on minority women and men. For years, a number of occupations such as the police, firefighters, or mass transit drivers retained minimum weight, height, and educational requirements for job applicants. In retrospect, we can interpret these criteria as systemically discriminatory because they favoured males over females, and White applicants over people of colour. Valid reasons may have existed to justify these restrictions; nevertheless, the imposition of these qualifications imposed a set of unfair entry restrictions, regardless of intent or rationale. No deliberate attempt was made to exclude anyone, since standards were uniformly applied. But these criteria had the net effect of excluding certain groups who lacked these requirements for entry or promotion. Other examples of systemic racism include an insistence on Canadian-only experience—a catch-22 conundrum that ensnares many immigrant professionals who must also confront the devaluation of minority experiences and credentials, unnecessarily high educational standards for entry into certain occupations, and other demanding qualifications that discourage membership into professional bodies. The situation is particularly acute with foreign trained medical doctors who have settled in physician-starved Ontario in hopes of qualifying as physicians yet confront quota barriers, which severely restrict the number of doctors that are allowed to sit medical exams or take retraining programs to become licensed (Keung, 1999). Well meaning people may have drawn up immigration policies, with Canada's national interests at heart, and the policies may have been administered as even-handedly as possible. Nevertheless, the logical consequences of these actions are systemically discriminatory because they inadvertently prevent minorities from full and equal participation.

3. Ideological Racism   As noted by many, racism is more than a structure or ideology (Essed, 1991). It also constitutes a process that is created, reflected, reinforced, and reformulated through everyday interaction and routine practices. Ideological racism constitutes that level of racism that occurs in the general functioning of society. It consists of interactional patterns, often without people being consciously aware of how their actions may inadvertently deny or exclude. This notion of racism as routine is not intended to trivialize racism. As with any expression of common-sense thinking, societal racism represents the natural and normal way in which people view and interpret the world, process information, engage with others, and deal with the practicalities of everyday life (Essed, 1991). A distinction between cultural racism and everyday racism is useful: Everyday racism refers to unconscious speech habits and behaviour that have the effect of denying or excluding. Cultural racism, in turn, reflects ambiguities in our value system in which underlying tensions have the effect of reinforcing a racialized social order.

a. Everyday Racism   Contemporary racism is no longer expressed in direct aggression but in more culturally acceptable ways that deny or exclude (Sirna, 1998). Certain ideas and ideals are widely circulated that explicitly or implicitly assert the superiority of some people at the expense of others. The internalization of these racist ideas and their expression in daily behaviour is called everyday racism. It entails racist practices that infiltrate everyday life and become part of what is accepted as normal by the dominant group (Essed, 1991). The mechanisms of everyday racism are well established. Individuals interact with one another in ways that implicitly condone a racialized reality. As a process and social practice, everyday racism is created and reconstructed through daily actions that are repetitive, systematic, familiar, and routine. The complex and cumulative interplay of attitudes (prejudice) and practices (discrimination) (a) is diverse in manifestation, but unified through constant repetition; (b) permeates daily life to the extent that it is viewed as normal or inevitable; and (c) falls outside people's awareness.

The role of language in perpetuating everyday racism is increasingly recognized. Many think of language as a kind of postal system; that is, a neutral system of conveyance between sender and receiver for the transmission of messages created independently through a process called thinking. In reality, language is inextricably linked with the social construction of reality. Language is intimately bound up with our experiences of the world and our efforts to convey these to others. Ideas and ideals are "trapped inside" language, with the result that patterns of thought and behaviour are influenced by how we speak. Or as the critic Kenneth Burke once concluded, language does our thinking for us. Language can be employed to control, conceal, evade issues, draw attention, or dictate agendas about what gets said. Words are not neutral; rather they have the capacity to hinder or harm when carelessly employed. Words also have a political dimension: They convey messages above and beyond what is intended. Inferences can (and are) drawn about who you are and where you stand in the competition for who gets what and why.

Language, in short, represents an ideal vehicle for expressing intolerance by highlighting differences, enlarging distance, and sanctioning inequality through invisible yet real boundaries (Sirna, 1998). Words are a powerful way of conveying negative images and associations. They may be used to degrade or ridicule minorities, as Robert Moore (1992) demonstrates in his oft-quoted article on racism in the English language, by way of obvious bigotry ("niggers"), colour symbolism (black = bad), loaded terms ("Indian massacres"), and seemingly neutral phrases that are infused with hidden anxieties ("waves of immigrants"). Negative meanings can become part of everyday speech as the following passage from Robert Moore (1992) demonstrates:

> Some may blackly (angrily) accuse me of trying to blacken (defame) the English language, to give it a black eye (mark of shame) by writing such black words (hostile) … by accusing me of being black-hearted (malevolent), of having a black outlook (pessimistic; dismal) on life, of being a blackguard (scoundrel) which would certainly be a black mark (detrimental fact) against me.

The association of "blackness" with negativity illustrates how certain values are embedded in our everyday speech. Daily speech patterns provide an example of racism as everyday and interactive. For this reason and others, some Canadians of African ancestry prefer to be called "African-Canadians" rather than "Blacks." To be sure, the racism implicit in words and metaphors may not be intended or deliberate. Nor will the occasional use of such loaded terms explode into runaway racism. Moreover, it is inaccurate to say that language determines our reality. More precisely, it provides a cultural frame of reference for defining what is desirable and important. In short, those who trivialize the impact of language in perpetuating racism through discourses of everyday life are in for a rude shock.

b. Cultural Racism   Cultural racism points to cultural values that privilege dominant interests at subordinate expense. Mainstream cultural values are defined as the unquestioned norm and neutral standard by which others are judged—regardless of their impact on others. These values may be specific in openly denying the right of minority women and men to equal treatment. Alternatively, they may indirectly endorse dominant value orientations by privileging them as necessary and normal, while dismissing others as irrelevant or defective, and a prime cause of minority failures. For example, consider the conflict of interest between the liberal-universalist values of treating everyone the same versus minority demands to be different and to have these differences taken into account (Fleras, 2004). Liberal-universalist principles are based on a belief that what we have in common as rights-bearing individuals is much more important than our differences as members of groups; that what we do and accomplish is more important than who we are; and the content of our character is more important than the colour of our skin. Differences are tolerated only to the extent that everyone is different in the same kind of way. Compare this universalism with the particularism of ethnicity with its focus on difference rather than similarity as a basis for sorting who gets what. This gap between the universal and the particular also generates misunderstanding, conflicts, and problems.

This ambivalence within a cultural values set is called subliminal racism (Fleras and Elliott, 2003)—or alternatively is referred to as "democratic racism" (Henry et al., 1999); "non-racist racism" (Elliott and Fleras, 1991); or "aversive racism" (Dovidio, 1986). In acknowledging the circulation of messages beneath the level of individual awareness, the subliminality of cultural racism appears to reflect an inescapable dichotomy in our core values (Myrdal, 1944). This dichotomy not only enables individuals to internalize two apparently conflicting values, one rooted in universalistic notion that everyone is equal before the law and be treated the same regardless of who they are; the other is the egalitarian notion that differences have to be taken into account for justice and fairness. Subliminal cultural racism is located within that category of persons who are aware of injustices and openly abhor discriminatory treatment of minorities, yet appear unwilling or incapable of doing something about it (Taylor, 2003). Individuals may profess a commitment to the principle of equality but at the same time oppose measures for remedying the situation because of costs or inconvenience (Henry et al., 1999; Augoustinos and Reynolds, 2001). Even those who profess egalitarian attitudes may be incapable of seeing how their criticism—or compliment—of minorities may unintentionally reinforce a "racialized" status quo. For example, consider what transpires when a White person says she does not think of you as a minority. Does this seemingly complimentary remark reflect deep-seated negative attitudes toward the minority in question, with you as the exception, while subconsciously reinforcing White supremacy as the norm and standard that you have successfully internalized (Smith, 2003)?

How does subliminal racism work? Evidence suggests that Canadians as a whole are receptive to the principles of multiculturalism and racial equality (Fleras, 2002; Jedwab, 2003). Many Canadians express sympathy for the plight of those less fortunate than themselves. For example, immigrants are frequently portrayed as industrious contributors to Canadian well-being. Yet negative and prejudicial attitudes continue to distort our assessment and treatment of the foreign-born. Immigrants are acceptable as long as they know their place in society. Immigrant demands that fall outside conventional channels or mainstream approval are criticized as a threat to national identity or social harmony. People of colour are chided for making too many demands at odds with the character of Canadian society, yet are criticized when not taking the initiative to make a difference. Diversity is encouraged, but minority espousal of genuine cultural differences is criticized when these differences are seen as violating individuals' rights, the laws of the land, and core Canadian values or institutions. A Catch-22 combines with double standards to marginalize minorities who are damned if they do, and damned if they don't. Finally, government initiatives to protect and promote diversity may be acceptable—as long as they don't cost money or impose burdens in terms of sharing power or cultural space. For example, employment equity programs for improving the status of historically disadvantaged minorities may be valid in principle but in practice disparaged as unfair to the majority, inconsistent with core values, and contrary to the spirit of sound business practices.

How then do we explain this ambiguity in cultural values toward minorities in Canada? Cynics would argue that Canadians are hypocrites whose deep-seated racism is camouflaged by platitudinous pieties. Opposition to multiculturalism or immigration by way of polite put downs is more acceptable than open expressions of intolerance (Palmer, 1996). Yet subliminal racism differs from polite racism. Whereas polite racists disguise their dislike of others behind coded terms, subliminal racism reflects an unconscious aversion to assertive minority demands. In hiding behind a smokescreen of higher principles, subliminal racism is not about disliking minority women and men per se but disliking minorities who "don't know their place" or "don't play by mainstream rules." Criticism of minority assertiveness is rationalized on principled grounds, namely, mainstream values, national interests, or values of fair play, equality, and justice. A general principle may be invoked to deny the legitimacy of a specific instance, as when refugees are perceived as acting unfairly by "jumping the queue" for entry into Canada. Clearly, then, a degree of cultural ambiguity is apparent. Mainstream individuals may endorse progressive attitudes as a matter of principle, yet disapprove of minority means to bring about substantial change (Essed, 1991). Values that endorse racial equality are publicly reaffirmed in the name of multiculturalism. Nevertheless, there is deep-seated resentment at the prospect of moving over and making space for minority women and men. These aversive feelings are not about outright hostility or hate, but rather entail discomfort or unease, often leading to patterns of avoidance rather than intentionally destructive behaviour. Such an indictment suggests racism is more pervasive in Canada than many assume, perhaps even implying that Canada is a racist society.

CASE 3-1	**Is Canada a Racist Society?**

Are Canadians racist? Is Canada a racist society? Is racism a major problem in Canada? Responses to these questions are much more complex and problematic than many admit. What exactly constitutes a racist society? What is meant when Canadians are accused of being racist? On what grounds are judgments made? The charge that Canada is racist is not sim-

ply an intellectual parlour game, even though raising the question may seem unusual at a time when a commitment to diversity has never been stronger (Levitt, 1997). Accusations of such magnitude run the risk of eroding Canada's international reputation. Fears also are intensified of a looming race relations problem which, if left unchecked, may prove the undoing of

(continued on next page)

Canada as a society. How accurate are these accusations and appraisals?

Problematizing the Charges

Canada is widely regarded as a socially progressive society in which initiatives for engaging with diversity are second to none. Yet there is gnawing concern that things are not what they seem to be, and that racism continues to flourish in Canada, albeit in ways that are unlikely to conform to conventional forms of racist thought and practices. Even positive initiatives are given a negative spin. Consider how the inception of multiculturalism or employment equity may be predicated on the premise that Canada is fundamentally racist, and that Canadians are racists in need of government intervention to reverse the trend. Recent developments would appear to uphold this unflattering assessment of Canada as a "racist society" (*National Post*, 24 April, 1999). The gravity of such a charge makes it doubly important to deconstruct the notion of a "racist society." After all, it is one thing to make this charge; it may be quite another to prove it by way of argument and empirical evidence.

First, what exactly is meant by the concept of racism? Racism is not a static entity but is evolving and situational more of a process rather than a thing, and increasingly defined in terms of consequences and context, rather than intention or essence. The equating of racism with swastikas or burning crosses is also losing ground. Pressure is on moving away from classic conceptions that equate racism with: (a) formally prescribed boundaries between groups; (b) opportunity structures defined by inherited racial attributes; (c) codification of prejudice and discrimination into laws that openly dis-

criminate against identifiable minorities; and (d) conscious exclusion of others from full and equal participation in spheres that enhance social and material rewards (Holdaway, 1996). South Africa's apartheid regime may have been racist according to these criteria, but surely not Canada, at least not since the 1950s, when new Canadians were routinely racialized as different and ranked accordingly. Rather, racism has become increasingly subtle in terms of its process and effects, in the process becoming less visible as Canada becomes more demographically visible. Racism is the glass ceiling that deters visible minorities from advancing in the workplace; racism entails those daily indignities that confront people of colour; racism is expressed in the differences that inadvertently yet adversely affect outcomes within the criminal justice system (James, 1998); racism is criticism of immigrants behind the camouflage of national interests; and racism consists of those tacit assumptions that bolster dominant ways of thinking or doing, while cavalierly dismissing minority ways as irrelevant or inferior. In short, racism in Canadian society has become overwhelmingly covert, beyond explicit slurs and put-downs, and is increasingly embedded in the normal operations of institutions, reflecting the context and consequences of actions rather than attitudes or intent. Such invisibility not only complicates the challenge of detection and eradication; it also detracts from any consensus over the magnitude and scope of racism in Canada.

Second, what exactly is meant by a racist society? To answer this question, we need to unpack the notion of a racist society. What criteria must be invoked in defining a society as racist, and on

(continued on next page)

what grounds? Is a racist society defined by what it is or is not; by what people do or don't do to others; and by what is said or not said? How can racism be measured—by way of incidents that come to the attention of authorities or through victim self-assessments? To what extent are statistics or national surveys a valid measurement of racism in society? Is a racist society based on a minimum number of racial incidents per year (if so, how many?), or should we look more closely at systemic biases that unobtrusively but systemically perpetuate a racialized and unequal social order? Statistical measures are known to be riddled with inherent drawbacks. Pollsters are cautious about drawing sweeping conclusions from a few survey questions on race or ethnicity, according to Donald Taylor of McGill University. Not only are polls a crude measure of public attitudes because of their superficiality in addressing complex problems. Intolerance is difficult to measure because of responder's reluctance to answer truthfully for fear of blowing their cover. Indirect questions must be designed to reveal people's true attitudes, Jacquie Miller (1998), writes, even if such questions are confusing, subject to interpretation, or may be easily taken out of context. Statistics cannot reveal the number of unreported acts. An increase in reported acts may reflect: (a) increased anti-racism awareness in school curricula; (b) greater public awareness and police willingness to press charges; (c) expanding media interest and reportage; and (d) more open access to grievance articulation, such as a hate-crime hotline with a 1–800 number.

What constitutes a non-racist society? Broadly speaking, a racist society is one that officially and routinely condones a hatred toward others. A racist society is one in which racism is: (a) institutionalized as a normal functioning of society; (b) supported by cultural values and expressed through widely accepted norms; (c) tacitly approved by the state or government; (d) intrusive in many interpersonal relations; and (e) largely impervious to reform or eradication (Aguirre and Turner, 1995). A society is racist when it systematically oppresses others through denial, exclusion, or exploitation on the basis of race or ethnicity. Discrimination toward others is formally institutionalized as a basis for defining who gets what. Formal mechanisms do not exist to prevent or to deal with the outbreak of racist incidents at individual or institutional levels. Mindful of these criteria, it may be necessary to reassess the charge that Canada is racist. Canada officially prohibits racism and racial discrimination at policy and statutory levels. Canada as a society tolerates differences as a motivating core and legally protected goal, encourages freedom of expression and dissent, respects minorities, has an independent judiciary, and holds the government accountable for upholding multicultural principles (Abella, 2003). Canada also possesses human rights legislation, criminal codes against racial hatred, and sentencing procedures that severely punish hate crimes. On these grounds, Canada can no longer be regarded as a racist society—as was once the case in our not too distant past. Nevertheless, racism does exist in Canadian society.

Third, are Canadians racists? Some would say that all mainstream Canadians are racist by virtue of living in a pale-male world where disproportional benefits are derived from exposure to institutions, values, and structures that

(continued on next page)

exclude some, and privilege others. Others would say that pockets of bigotry persist in Canada. Still others would label many Canadians as "closet racists," given the degree of their thinly veiled hostility toward immigration, employment equity, or multiculturalism. While professing a commitment to equality and inclusiveness, these fair-weather racists criticize any initiative to improve minority life chances as too costly, too quick, too accommodative, too pushy, too "un-Canadian," or contrary to national interests. Yet there is no proof that a dislike of government policies or minority initiatives is automatically indicative of racism, even if the unintended consequence of such criticism may reinforce a racialized social order. In fact, critics may argue that it is supporters of special programs who are racist, by treating others differently because of race, and that to be criticized for criticizing such programs is racist in its own right, since such "political correctness" suggests that minorities are immune to criticism. Moreover, the very idea of a non-racist population or society may be an anomaly in its own right, given the range of publics that exist in society. Racism and intolerance are unavoidable, since Canadians are humans with pockets of resistance or resentment inevitable during periods of change and diversity. A certain level of ethnic friction in liberal-democratic societies is inevitable, in other words, and its existence may reflect the cost of living together with differences in a society that encourages freedom, equality, individualism, and rule of law.

Racist Society Or Racism in Society? From Either/Or to Both/And

What can we conclude? There is little doubt that racism exists in Canada both personally and institutionally as well as openly and covertly. But however accurate such an appraisal, this observation is not the same as accusing Canada of being racist. The combination of racist incidents with racist individuals is not synonymous with or reducible to such labelling. Just as we must never underestimate the pervasiveness of racism in sectors of society, and exercise constant vigilance to that effect, so too is a degree of caution required in exaggerating the notion of a racist Canada. A sense of perspective is critical: Most racist incidents are instigated by a relatively small number of protagonists. The actions of a few are hardly representative of society at large and should not be manipulated as a measure by which to judge the inactions of many. Compare racism in Canada with the situation in Europe, where a European Union survey of 16 000 Europeans in 15 countries yielded staggering results: 55 percent of Belgians identified themselves as very or quite racist; 48 percent of the French, and 35 percent of the British (Bates, 1997). Comparable figures for hard-core bigotry in Canada are not available, given the notoriously unreliable responses to survey questions in this area, but evidence suggests a figure of about 15 percent (Henry and Tator, 1985; Reitz and Breton, 1994). Neither the proportion of racists in Canada nor the number of racist incidents can define Canada as racist. What counts in defining a racist Canada is how Canadians deal with racists and racist incidents—from prevention to punishment.

A sense of perspective helps. It has been said that the smallest indiscretion in a society of saints would be sufficient to elicit outrage (Levitt, 1997). In societies where hatred toward others is the norm, even the most egregious

(continued on next page)

form of racial intolerance will go unnoticed or unpunished. In a society such as Canada where racism and racial intolerance are widely repudiated and illegal, the slightest provocation becomes cause for public remorse, national breast-beating, or social rebuke. And it is precisely these high standards that encourage, yet complicate, the process of debating Canada as a racist society. There is yet another dimension: Canadians may not be racists in the conventional sense of close-minded bigots that deny or exclude. Racism in Canada is more likely to embody seemingly neutral acts of behaviour that have the unwitting effect of perpetuating an unequal status quo. The unanticipated consequences of universally applied institutional rules and practices—largely created by Whites (and males) to normalize the preservation of power and privilege— may have the cumulative, if inadvertent, effect of privileging some and disadvantaging others. White experiences continue to be defined as the norm by which others are measured and evaluated. When combined with the power to put these normative expectations into practice, an arrangement prevails that empowers some, while disempowering others.

In other words, Canada is racist in endorsing discourses in defence of dominant ideology—that is to say, tacit assumptions that privilege mainstream values and institutions as natural, superior, and inevitable. Racism is manifest in the articulation of policies and ideologies that promote so-called "national interests," reflected in the collective belief system of the dominant culture, and woven into the language, laws, rules, and norms of Canadian society (Henry et al., 1999). Inasmuch as the mainstream values and institutions may inadvertently advantage some, disadvantage others, Canada may be regarded as racist. It is also racist in that foundational principles that underpin Canada's constitutional order remain anchored in a Eurocentric colonialism that does not take kindly to deep differences. A racism that is systemically embedded within a constitutional framework may make it difficult to detect but no less real and powerful in denying and excluding. In short, perhaps, answers to the question of whether Canada is racist must escape the trap of "either/or" (yes or no). A position that concedes "both/and" (yes and no), depending on circumstances and criteria, may provide a better insight into the paradoxes of living together with our differences.

Case Study Questions

1   What is the distinction between a "racist society" and "racism in society"?

2   According to the evidence presented above, would you agree or disagree with the claim that Canada is a racist society? Justify your response.

EXPLAINING RACISM

People, why can't we just get along?

—Rodney King, 1992

Well, why can't we? Racism as a social problem exacts an unacceptable toll. It represents a blot upon Canadian society, with the capacity to squander our potential as an ordered and tolerant country. Racism costs all Canadians in the following ways: (1) it perpetuates inequality by infringing on fundamental human rights; (2) it reduces the number of people who can contribute to Canada; (3) it expends useless energy that otherwise could be funnelled into more productive channels; (4) it inflicts damage on minorities through loss of self-esteem and cultural identity; and (5) it diminishes Canada's competitive edge both domestically and internationally. The costs of racism are absorbed unevenly across society, with some capitalizing on racism to preserve privilege or power, while others suffer. Racism also adds an additional burden to minority lives (Ford, 1994). Minorities live in perpetual fear of physical retaliation; the loss of personal security intensifies isolation or self-defensive behaviours; a restricted set of economic and social opportunities constrains options and opportunities; and many are dismayed by negative media messages that demean and dismiss because of who they are (Thomas, 1998). Moreover, racism is known to intersect with and be constitutive of other forms of exploitation related to class, gender, ethnicity, or sexual preference (Stasiulis, 2000). To add insult to injury, exposure to racism may contribute to poor health, both physical and psychological (Maioni, 2003). A few may even lash out in violence from frustration.

That racism in one form or another exists in Canada is widely accepted. With the benefit of some prodding and sharp reminders, Canadians are increasingly facing up to their checkered past, with its bewildering mixture of tolerance and repression (Satzewich, 1998). Racism may be equated with a particular psychological complex of emotions, feelings, and thoughts; it also entails the symbolic, cultural, and institutional expressions of society that are systematically and systemically organized around the suppression of some, and the privileging of others (Wetherell and Potter, 1993). Some forms of racism are now widely condemned and detested, even by those who are indifferent to the principle or promotion of diversity. Other varieties of racism continue to be endemic to Canada, with few signs of relinquishing their tenacious grip. No less worrying is the persistence of racism: Removal of openly discriminatory barriers appears to have had the effect of driving racism underground or morphing into new forms. The fact that racism continues to persist despite its costs and rejection is cause for concern, and raises the question of what if anything can be done to eliminate racism.

How do we account for this anomaly? Is it because of societal inertia or public disinterest, with the result that racism drifts along, irrespective of its dysfunctional effects on society? In the same way that people appreciate the need for ecological sustainability, yet do not always act on that awareness, so too has public knowledge of racial harmony not necessarily resulted in behaviour modification. Some attribute the pervasiveness of racism to our genetic wiring from an evolutionary past when outsiders posed a threat to survival in an uncertain environment. Such a visceral reaction to the fear of the unknown continues to operate in the present, it is argued, with the result that it is only natural to recoil from what is different. Some like to think of racism as the by-product of ignorance or fear of the unknown because of improper socialization. Racism will vanish with improvements in people's stock of knowledge about differences and minorities. Others believe that racism persists because of its self-serving properties. As many have noted, racism does not just penalize victims but also benefits the perpetrators by affording them privileges; after all, for every person of colour who is turned down for a promotion because of her colour, another majority person is awarded the position because of his or her colour (Frederickson, 2002). Or consider how racism has a way of making the mainstream feel good about itself by bolstering individual and collective self-esteem, whether people are aware of it or not.

Hence, racism is not an aberration associated with a lunatic fringe but a normative means of asserting racial identity relative to the victimized other by reinforcing the 'natural scheme of things' (Cogan and Marcus-Newhall, 2002). This notion of racism as "functional" for Whites is captured in these words by Julian Bond, head of the NAACP, when referring to the tenacity of White supremacist racism (White, 1998: 25):

> It's still White supremacy. It stills means so much to those who practise it. It defines who they are. It makes them feel that they are better than others. It ensures them positions in employment and college admissions they otherwise might not have. It still puts a lid on the dreams of Black people....

Still others look to social institutions as the primary culprit responsible for racism. Mainstream institutions are racialized: institutional structures are designed by and for dominant groups, and either deliberately or inadvertently reflect dominant values, priorities, agendas, and practices, and normalize these as superior, necessary, and inevitable. Racism also has the effect of enhancing majority privilege by reducing uncertainty and imposing control over those likely to challenge the status quo (Levin and McDevitt, 2002).

Each of these explanations of racism is accurate. But reference to racism as a function of biology or psychology is secondary to most sociological analyses. Racism does not reside solely in the minds of demented individuals; nor is it an error of perception or belief. The roots of racism go beyond the conduct of aberrant individuals, even though individuals are the carriers and targets of this outgroup hatred. Racism persists because of its usefulness to a capitalist economy (Bolaria and Li, 1988; Satzewich, 1991). The economic well-being, standard of living, and cultural history of Canada are constructed around a contrived hatred towards others, both in the formal and informal sense (McKenna, 1994). Through its ideological underpinnings, racism has played and continues to play a formidable role in establishing and maintaining patterns of inequality and control. Racist ideologies are employed as rationalizations to foster acquisition of a disposable labour supply; to destabilize minority movements by undermining any potential show of unity or strength; and to justify intrusive devices for regulating the activities of troublesome minorities. The interests of capitalism are also served by fomenting a degree of inner turmoil within the ranks of the working class. Rather than a departure from the norm, in other words, racism exists because it is supportive of a system designed to augment "pale-male" power and privilege. Those in positions of power take refuge in racism to preserve privilege in the competition for scarce resources. Sowing the seeds of racism provides this advantage without drawing unnecessary attention to the contradictions and dysfunctions within the system.

In short, racism is linked to patterns of social control in contexts of inequality. Racism in Canada is neither a transient phenomenon nor an anomalous and unpredictable feature. The origins of racism have deep roots in Canadian society: That is, racism is intrinsic to Canada's historical and economic development; embedded within the institutional structures of society; endemic to core cultural values; and integral to Canadian society-building. Racism continues to flourish because of its positive functions in support of White, ruling-class interests. Not surprisingly, responses to the question of why racism persists continually miss the mark. The reason why there is no correct answer is because the question is wrongly worded. Rather than asking "Why does racism exist?" the focus should be on "Why isn't there *more* racism, given the combination of pressures to preserve an unequal status quo, the systemic bias inherent within mainstream institutions, and the Eurocentrism inherent within the social fabric of society?" Why, indeed, should racism *not* exist, in light of the benefits it confers on those in positions of power and privilege? Put bluntly, racism is not a departure from society and its ideals, but is constitutive of the existing social order, whether by intent or in consequence. To the extent that Canada is irrevocably tainted by racism, both covert and overt, personal as well as institutional, the prospect of eliminating racism is, indeed, formidable.

SOLVING THE PROBLEM: ERASING RACISM

Most Canadians are no longer racists in the classic sense of openly vilifying different races. Yet racism continues to exist in unobtrusive ways, deliberately or unconsciously, by way of action or inaction. Racism exists in tolerating practices and arrangements that have the intent or effect of discriminating against others. Doing nothing to confront such racial discrimination is racist in consequence because fence-sitting (through inactivity or silence) is not impartiality, but tacit acceptance of the status quo (Abella, 2003). By contrast, anti-racism can be defined as the process that isolates and challenges racism through direct action at personal and institutional levels (also Dei, 1996). Minorities in Canada have relied on different strategies to erase racism (Allahar, 1998). Anti-racism is egalitarian in outlook insofar as it seeks equality, not in the liberal sense of everyone being equal in the same way, but through structural changes that foster power-sharing (Dei, 1996: 25). An integrative anti-racism constitutes an educational and political action-oriented strategy for institutional and systemic change that addresses racism as part of an interlocking system of social oppression involving sexism, heterosexism, ethnocentrism, and classism (Dua and Robertson, 1999). Anti-racist measures may include: confronting racist hate groups; direct action through protest or civil disobedience; boycotts; litigation; or legislation (Jaret, 1995).

Solving the problem of racism can take different forms: Much depends on how racism is defined (as race, ideology, culture, or power) and the level of racism under consideration (interpersonal, institutional, or ideological). The emphasis is not on minorities to erase racism but for mainstream members to become informed about "eracism," then taking appropriate action to rid society of racism and racialization. Two styles of anti-racist strategy can be discerned. One is concerned with modifying individual behaviour through education, legal sanctions, or interaction; the other with removal of discriminatory structural barriers by eliminating their systemic roots, either democratically through political channels, through institutional reform, or by revolution through protest and forcible seizure of power (Bonilla-Silva, 1996).

Individual "Eracism": Change from Within

Racism is normally envisaged as a personal problem of hatred or ignorance. There is an element of truth to this assertion. Racism is generally expressed through the thoughts and actions of prejudiced individuals. Thus, strategies for containment or control are endorsed that focus on behaviour modification through attitude change. Three of the more common personal anti-racist strategies for improvement are interaction, education, and law.

Interaction   Learning through interaction represents one of the many anti-racist techniques available for individual change. Interaction with others will remove barriers that stem from ignorance or fear. Lack of knowledge is replaced with mutually reinforcing understanding. Yet contact in its own right is not necessarily beneficial (Tilbury, 2000). It is doubtful if the thousands of Canadian tourists who pour into the Caribbean each winter have done much to ameliorate race relations, given that such hospitality patterns have a tendency to reproduce the colonialism that created the problem in the first place. Under such potentially exploitative encounters, the degree of resentment and contempt escalates as the indigenous populations are compelled to serve, defer, and grovel.

Reduction of racism through interaction depends on the nature of the interactional setting. For any positive effect, interaction must be conducted between individuals who are relatively equal in status; who collaborate on a common endeavour in a spirit of trust and respect; whose interaction receives some degree of institutional and societal support; and who derive mutual benefit from cooperation (Jaret, 1995). Interaction between unequals simply upholds the status quo by perpetuating stereotypes in a negatively-charged environment.

Education   It is widely assumed that education can reduce racism (Nakata, 2001). Racism is viewed as a case of individuals subscribing to an irrational belief; thus the cure lies in educating people to realize that racism is wrong. Once aware of what they are doing and why, appropriate adjustments will fall into place. This notion of enlightenment through learning has put schools in the vanguard of institutions dealing with diversity. Education has long been seen as the most popular policy prescription for curing us of racism (Bonilla-Silva, 1996).

Two styles prevail in accommodating diversity within schools: multicultural and/or anti-racist (see Chapter 9). Multicultural education refers to a philosophy of "celebrating differences." It consists of activities or curricula that promote an awareness of diversity in terms of its intrinsic value to minorities and/or society at large. The aim of multicultural education is largely attitudinal; that is, to enhance sensitivity by improving awareness about cultural differences. Emphasis is on becoming more aware of ourselves as cultural carriers; of the customs that underpin non-Western cultures; and of the role of ethnocentrism and cultural relativism in supporting or denying diversity. Strategies for this kind of sensitivity awareness are varied, spanning the spectrum from museum displays to multi-faith Christmas pageants, with cross-cultural enrichment in between.

Multiculturally-based training sessions have proliferated outside of school settings. Training sessions may involve workshops for new and established employees, with content ranging from cultural awareness modules to cross-cultural communication sessions, to pointers about prejudice and ethnocentrism. Police forces in the larger metropolitan areas are increasingly involved in multicultural-relations training programs for cadets, patrol officers, and management (Fleras and Desroches, 1989). Program sessions are generally geared toward the elimination of discrimination in policing; promotion of cultural diversity within the police force; development of sensitivity to culturally diverse constituencies; improvement of cross-cultural communication; and implementation of community-based policing principles. Yet diversity training programs can be counterproductive in the hands of poorly trained and inadequately motivated instructors. Blame-and-shame programs can backfire because they are openly confrontational or preachy, tend to make people defensive, and often foster resentment among participants because of perceived political correctness (Jaret, 1995). Even in the hands of skilled practitioners, there is no guarantee of positive change in attitude or behaviour because of the difficulty of isolating, let alone unlearning, something that was internalized unconsciously and is perceived as positive rather than irrational or inappropriate. Such an indictment suggests the futility of multicultural initiatives in favour of anti-racist programs.

Anti-racist education seeks to overcome the limitations of multicultural education, arguing in effect that cultural solutions cannot adequately address structural problems (Fleras and Elliott, 2003). Anti-racist education takes a critical view of power relations in society by directing its attention to how the dominant sector exercises power over subordinate groups within and beyond the school system (Cheyne et al., 1997; Dei, 1998). Anti-racist education links racism to politics and economics against a backdrop of policies, practices, and social structures. The historic relations of domination within institutional structures are analyzed and assessed, thus exposing both minorities and the mainstream to the structural sources of oppression in society. Anti-racist education is also focused on encouraging individuals to look inside themselves and their culture as sources of racism. Whites are encouraged to examine their own racism and privileged positions, on the assumption that White awareness is critical to understanding personal privilege and taking responsibility for disempowerment of others (McIntosh, 1988). In short, anti-racist education differs from multicultural equivalents in several ways; namely, it: (a) privileges power at the centre of any reconstruction; (b) acknowledges institutionalized power to establish ideological dominance; (c) provides a discursive framework for analyzing how different oppressions intersect and overlap; (d) problematizes the notion of "culture" in multicultural education as a basis for transformative change; and (e) challenges the notion of what is valid and legitimate knowledge, and how other forms of knowledge can be incorporated in contexts that historically denied their value (Dei, 1998). It remains to be seen if an anti-racist initiative can galvanize society into activity in defence of its self-defined democratic ideals of freedom, equality, and social justice.

Law and Legal Sanctions   Recourse to law is sometimes upheld as an effective personal deterrent. Laws exist in Canada that prohibit the expression of racial discrimination against vulnerable minorities. The scope of these laws is broad. Some legal measures consist of protection for identifiable minorities through restrictions on majority behaviour. For example, the Supreme Court of Canada has ruled repeatedly that prohibiting racist propaganda is a justifiable and reasonable limitation on the freedom of speech in a Canada that aspires to multicultural principles. Other measures are aimed at removing discriminatory barriers that deter minority participation in society. The objective is to make it illegal to discriminate by making people aware of the consequences of breaking the law.

Passage of these and related laws is not intended to alter people's attitudes, at least not in the short run. A democratic society such as Canada entitles citizens to their own private thoughts, however repugnant or anti-social. But this right disappears when private thoughts become discriminatory behaviour: Legal sanctions apply at this point. To be sure, laws are limited in their effectiveness for modifying individual thought or behaviour. The legislative advances of the United States Civil Rights Act in 1964 neither resolved African-American inequities nor eliminated prejudice and discrimination. Racism simply assumed different guises or went underground. Similarly in Canada, Section 319 of Canada's Criminal Code prohibits the promotion of hatred against identifiable minorities; yet this hate law may well have the outcome of: (a) driving racism underground; (b) reinforcing the ingroup's belief in the rightness of its actions; and (c) fostering a sense of hero worship or martyrdom in defence of the cause (Kinsella, 1995). Nor can laws eliminate disadvantages by dispersing the concentration of wealth or distribution of power. Passage of laws may be designed to minimize majority inconvenience, rather than to assist minorities. But laws can modify people's behaviour through the imposition of sanctions. On the assumption that most individuals are law-abiding because of the threat of punishment or social ostracism, passage of anti-racist laws ensures compliance with the letter of the law, at least outwardly, if not by personal conviction. In time, however, people's thought may converge with behaviour in an effort to reduce the dissonance between thought and action.

Institutional Eracism: Moving Over and Sharing Power

There is room for cautious optimism when dissecting the effectiveness of individually tailored anti-racist programs. But are these initiatives of sufficient scope to expunge racism at its roots? Are the structures of society amenable to reform through personal transformation? Social explanations are key: If racism were simply a reflection of prejudice or ignorance, the problem would have long disappeared because of a growing liberalization of attitudes since the 1960s. Such a perception ignores the depth of institutionalized racism, with its most significant expression reflected in denying minorities jobs, equality in the criminal justice system, and discrimination in housing (Taylor, 2003). Racism is inextricably linked with the process of social control for preserving the status quo in complex societies. This assertion is consistent with fundamental sociological premises: that the social is real; that it transcends individual personalities; that behaviour is contextual and constructed; and is amenable to analysis and reform by modifying the social environment. Racism may be expressed in and through people (who may be regarded as precipitating causes), but individuals are merely the conduits of racial antipathy. When the personal is the social, it is the social context that counts.

Racism can only be resolved by excising it at its source; namely, the institutional structures that support a capitalist society. Racism is not just about good individuals who do bad things because of misguided ideas or dormant prejudices that can be eliminated through sensitivity training (Gosine, 2003). Rather racism is rooted in institutional structures and systems of power that are deeply entrenched and resistant to change. Personal solutions such as multicultural education are comparable to applying a bandage to a cancerous growth—compassionate and humane to be sure but ultimately self-defeating in light of the magnitude of the disease. The symptoms are addressed, not the cause or source. The problem of racism cannot be eliminated except by confronting it within the wider confines of political domination and economic control.

Institutional anti-racism strategies consist of measures and mechanisms for dismantling the structural basis of organizational racism. The removal of discriminatory barriers is central: Selection and recruitment procedures as well as rules for promotion and reward are scrutinized for hidden bias, in the interests of promoting accessibility. Values and practices are monitored that historically have propelled the organization, but are irrelevant in a changing and diverse context. Anti-racist strategies must focus on dominant beliefs and values within the institution, the organizational system related to rules and practices, and the experiences and behaviours of organizational actors. Any institutional enterprise will foster racism, intentionally or unintentionally, when it perpetuates mission statements that are exclusionary; refuses to share power or decision-making; promulgates a monocultural set of values and beliefs as normal and necessary; maintains an inflexible or unresponsive set of structures and operations; and endorses unequal distribution of resources (Fleras, 1995).

These systemic biases imply the need for anti-racist initiatives at the level of mission statement, culture and subculture, power and decision-making, structures (including rules, roles, and relationships), and the distribution of physical, financial, and human resources. In theory, these multi-pronged, anti-racist initiatives sound plausible; their implementation may be another story. In the final analysis, then, the objective of anti-racism is not simply to erase racism from our midst but to create a new society based on living together with our differences in ways that enhance diversity without sacrificing equality.

Toward a Comprehensive Solution: Think Socially; Act Personally

Dealing with racism in Canada demands that we recognize our colonial past, that we come to terms with the historic and violent oppression of aboriginal peoples, and that we talk about the race-based inequalities that pervade nearly every sphere of society. Racism is a messy matter, and if we are really interested in challenging it, we can't afford to just keep trying to tidy things up.

—Andil Gosine (*Toronto Star*, 21 March, 1999)

Racism is clearly a major social problem for both Canada and Canadians. That makes it doubly important to find improved ways to combat racism, encourage effective methods of control and reform, and improve legislation to protect those victimized by racism and discrimination (Layton-Henry and Wilpert, 2003). Who to blame and what to change? It is relatively easy to dismiss racism as little more than a personal problem. It is equally tempting to situate racism within a system of vast and impersonal forces that are largely beyond individual responsibility and outside the bounds of human agency. Racism is deeply embedded in Canadian society, as well as in the tradition of liberal-pluralism upon which Canada is secured. Dismantling racism is also complicated by the interlocking nature of social oppressions such as gender, race, ethnicity, and class.

Do we need to change people or to change structures? Is it possible to change people without changing structures, or vice versa? Perhaps the dichotomy is a false one (Nakata, 2001). Neither of these positions—racism as individual or as institutional—is entirely correct if either is excluded. Individuals may not be the root cause of racism, but racism is located within and is carried by the person. Systems may generate root causes, but institutions do not exist apart from individuals who interact to create, support, maintain, or transform patterns of racism. Racism is implicit in our daily encounters through the perpetuation of countless actions, gestures, and speech patterns. Each of us must be held accountable for our actions, no matter how powerful the social context and social forces. Unless there is an awareness of people's contribution to the problem, it becomes difficult to be part of the solution. Put differently, when applied to the realm of racism and proposed solutions, the personal is indeed the political. The political in turn defines the personal. That is, changing the system invariably changes people's attitudes; changing people's attitudes may result in transforming people's behaviour, with corresponding revisions to society. Only a comprehensive approach can deliver the goods with any hope of success. It remains to be seen whether any system driven by materialism as the measure of all things can banish racism from its midst. After all, a system devoted to greed, competition, and profit-making—and built upon a bedrock of racism—may contradict those anti-racist values related to diversity, inclusion, and equality.

DISCUSSION QUESTIONS

1 Racism is sometimes referred to as prejudice + discrimination + power. Explain.

2 Briefly compare the different types of racism: individual, institutional, and ideological.

3 How would you respond to the assertion that Canada is a racist society?

4 Racism involves a variety of different dimensions: biology, ideology, culture, and power. Comment on the differences.

5 The anti-racist struggle involves both personal and institutional approaches. Compare.

 ## WEBLINKS

Canadian Race Relations Foundation. **www.crrf.ca**

Canadian Human Rights Commission. **www.chrc-cchp.ca**

Reports on systemic racism and discrimination. **www.web.net/~ccr/arpolicy.htm**

chapter four

Gender Inequality

FRAMING THE PROBLEM

In 1963, Betty Friedan published *The Feminine Mystique*, a scathing critique of gender relations that proved as revolutionary in raising consciousness as had Rachel Carson's *The Silent Spring* in launching the environmental movement. The Feminist Mystique was not the first to draw attention to this "problem with no name." Two years earlier, another ground-breaking book by Simone de Beauvoir, *The Second Sex*, reinforced the perception of women as second class citizens whose worth and work suffered because of a male dominated world. Earlier still, Helen Mayer Hacker published an article in 1951 that framed women as a "minority" whose caste-like status reflected discriminatory practices at educational, economic, political, and social levels. Yet it was Friedan who captured the pulse of an era by comparing the unhappiness and boredom of middle-class women within "comfortable concentration camps." According to Friedan, a profound sense of emptiness and discontentment tormented those women who sought fulfillment and identity by being "sexually passive," accepting male domination as natural and normal, obsessing over children and husbands, and fixating on their housework to the exclusion of their inner needs. Gender options were tightly scripted. Boys were taught to do and accomplish; girls, in turn, were conditioned to defer or demur while toiling at keeping unwanted dirt at bay. So pervasive and internalized was this presumption of women as "natural-born nurturers" that few dared to step outside the gender blue-print for fear of rebuke or rejection.

Women indeed have "come a long way" since those heady consciousness-raising days. In a relatively short period of time, gender relations have evolved beyond the days when (a) women and children were regarded as male property; (b) rape within marriage was dismissed as a contradiction in terms; (c) a woman's place was in the kitchen or between the sheets; (d) a working woman was pitied as irresponsible or an embarrassment to her husband; (e) unwed mothers were stigmatized and shunned; and (f) universities were institutes for snaring husbands rather than securing credentials. Emergence of feminism as a powerful social movement has challenged conventional views over the status of women in society; the rules, roles, and expectations associated with womanhood; and their relationships to men. Women are increasingly occupying the corridors of power at both economic and political levels. A growing number of women are now in paid work, including making inroads into occupations traditionally perceived as male. The income gap between women and men is closing as well, albeit slowly. In fact, certain categories of women, namely, single, university-educated women, are doing as well as their male counterparts. Girls are performing so well at school that their success is drawing attention to a pending crisis in male performance, if contemporary trends persist. Finally, women are exerting control over many aspects of their lives, including: (a) deciding if and when to have children; (b) raising children on their own or with novel combinations of partners; (c) suing employees for harassment and discrimination; and (d) exerting pressure on hidebound institutions to embrace female realities or risk bottom-line credibility. This "gender quake" of change has banished the most egregious expressions of sexism, with the result that many young women are questioning the relevance of feminism in a post-feminist world (Dicker and Piepmeier, 2003).

How do we account for this transformation in gender relations? Perhaps the reason why women have come such a long way is because there was such a long way to go. Sexist assumptions had the effect of marginalizing women, undervaluing their achievements and contributions, relegating them to lesser-paying jobs, ghettoizing them into less prestigious corporate domains such as staffing functions (human resources), and excluding them from positions of power. Paradoxically, the past is still with us. Substantial gains in opportunities and choice, notwithstanding, women as a group still have a long way to go before attaining economic parity, social equality, agenda-setting powers, and political power-sharing. Progress yes, equality no, argues Diane Francis (2003), in part because of women's ambivalence toward the business world of "blood sport" that grinds women down by ruthless attrition in the Darwinian struggle for survival, and survival of the fittest (also Greer, 1999). Improvements have proven more symbolic than real, with the result that inequities in the workplace are showing surprising resistance to changing realities (MacIvor, 2003). Women are more likely than men to earn less, to be on benefits, to suffer from abuse and violence at the hands of men, and to be excluded from the highest echelons of corporate or political decision-making. They continue to be taken less seriously, judged on the basis of what they look like rather than what they do, and assumed to excel as caregivers rather than money makers. Politics remains a no (wo)man's land because of an "old boys network" that refuses to discard a creaky political culture (Trimble and Arscott, 2003). Stereotypes persist: Women continue to be perceived as passive, emotionally "soft," and obsessed with appearances, in contrast to men who are defined as assertive, ambitious, competitive, and goal-oriented. The term "women's work" resonates with a coded subtext, either as a way of describing unpaid maternal-domestic work around the home, or the relegation of women to largely low-paying "girl ghettos" such as service, sales, or clerical jobs. Opportunities for women are short-circuited by the persistence of the "second shift," with the nerve-wracking demands of balancing paid employment with unpaid household work—culminating in a punishing cycle of wired days and wasted nights. Double standards are alive and well as well: Women are criticized for undermining family values when gainfully employed, yet chastised as irresponsible layabouts by working at home. Women are seen as having a rightful place in the workforce, with an obligation to augment household income, yet they must also endure the wrath of those who believe children suffer with two working parents. The end result? Yet more mixed messages that unnecessarily complicate women's lives.

Any verdict on the status of women is wildly inconsistent. Compared to the past, woman at present have it good (Francis, 2003). In contrast to the status of women in many developing world countries, where brutal suppression may be the norm, the status of women in Canada is enviable (Wax, 2003). Yet this era has its share of problems as well that reflect the complexities and contradictions of profound social change (Lemieux and Mohle, 2003). For example, women may be living longer than ever, with a life expectancy of 82.2 years for a women born in 2002, compared to 77.1 years for a male born in 2002—the gap reflecting bad habits and riskier behaviour (McCabe, 2003). Yet living longer is small consolation if the quality of life for elderly women is compromised or undervalued. The onset of the new millennium is proving a confusing mixture of progressive and regressive as traditional gender scripts prevail in practice, if not always in principle. Gender lines are blurring even as gender identities continue to be politicized for purposes of recognition and reward, in effect reinforcing the contradictions of coping within a predominantly patriarchal framework (MacQueen, 2003). Women may have more freedom and choice than ever before, but these choices and options are routinely second-guessed as wrong or unfeminine, resulting in a restless lack of fulfillment that drives women to over-do (eating binges) or under-do (anorexia) rather than getting in touch with their desires and wants (Knapp, 2003).

However lamentable the mixed messages, women aren't the only ones experiencing a gender crisis. Men, too, are being buffeted by the gender quake that is challenging gender relations. Men, in general, have experienced as much perplexity as women in redefining who they are, what they can do, and what they can get away with. Consider the onslaught against masculinity in recent years. The certainties once associated with masculinity have dissolved under a wave of technological, economic, and cultural changes—prompting critics to ask if men today are the downtrodden gender. Social forces have combined to topple men from their lofty perch by eroding their sense of importance and identity, according to Susan Faludi in her book, *Stiffed*. Others, including Angela Phillips, in *The Trouble with Boys*, believe that men have been effectively neutered by a feminist-dominated status quo—in effect reminding us of Gloria Steinhem's fractured howler that women need men like fish need bicycles. In *Blood Rites: Origins and History of the Passion of War*, Barbara Ehrenreich contends that, because men are no longer central as hunters and providers in the lives of women and children, the legitimacy of malehood has suffered accordingly. Similarly, in his book, *The Decline of Men*, Lional Tiger argues that discriminatory public policy initiatives have disconnected men from significant involvement in family life. Masculinity is increasingly under assault as irrelevant—a point reinforced by a Body Shop ad featuring a woman holding a small mammal, with an accompanying text "Why test on poor defenceless little animals when they could use my husband?" (Valpy, 2003). In short, men have been challenged to change, yet have not had a chance to reinvent themselves like women have, as noted by a contributor in Marion Botsford Fraser's *Solitaire:*

> I don't think men have had a chance to catch up. Women have spent the last 30 years reinventing their role in society, lobbying for change to laws and social culture, to accommodate their growing role. And all men have had a chance to do is react ... I don't think men have had the chance to reinvent themselves in relationship to the new woman, the evolved woman.

To add insult to injury, the situation looks particularly grim on the genetic side. The male species is doomed, writes Bryan Sykes, professor of human genetics at Oxford University. Not only are men genetically modified women, but the male Y chromosome is decaying at such a rapid rate because of molecular damage that men run the risk of extinction (*Sunday Star-Times*, 28 September, 2003).

Yet appearances are deceiving if implying a massive role reversal between women and men. For all the talk of a gender quake, with ominous predictions of men as second-class citizens, rhetoric may not match reality. Canada continues to be governed by men, men call the shots at corporate Canada, men monopolize the legal profession at the level of private practice and equity partners, and the media remain wholly male controlled despite a dumbing down of men for programming ratings (Kingston, 2003). More importantly, Canada remains arguably a (White) man's world in terms of foundational structures, core values, institutional frameworks, and constitutional principles. The structure and organization of Canadian society are hardly culturally neutral. Society continues to be organized around a gender-specific agenda that privileges male interests and priorities, with the result that women must work within a framework that reflects, reinforces, and advances male interests. Such an arrangement is not without consequences in disempowering women. Governor General Adrienne Clarkson put it into perspective when chiding the legal profession "as built by men for men," thus forcing women to play by male rules, at the expense of female careers (Tyler, 2003). True, more than half of the graduating students from Ontario law schools may be women, argues Clarkson, but many recoil from the prospect of lifelong employment in a female-unfriendly workplace of pecking orders, billing pressures, networking, and long hours. Relatively high dropout levels are the result.

Of course, the most egregious expressions of sexism and patriarchy have been dismantled. Men no longer have the right to "have it all," as was once routinely the case. Rather, male power and privilege are being whittled away by a combination of demographic shifts, changes in intellectual fashion, government initiatives, and female assertiveness. Nevertheless, societal values and agendas continue to bolster male experiences and aspirations, either by intent or by default. In monopolizing most of the powerful positions of authority, men as a group remain firmly in control of those decisions that shape political, economic, social, and cultural outcomes, with just enough exceptions to prove the rule. Such a scenario may prove paradoxical for women: They must buy into the system if they hope for mainstream success; yet incorporation along these lines may be difficult or costly in personal terms. Even those women who manage to crash the glass ceiling by scaling the corporate ladder find success elusive. Acceptance is contingent on playing the male game by men's rules, without compromising claims to femininity. Yes, women are challenging those ready-made scripts that historically secured the foundation of patriarchal society. Yet moving into uncharted territory is fraught with uncertainty and confusion. Women find themselves in a combat zone where a pit-bull mentality may be critical for success, but inconsistent with female-friendly sensibilities (Galt, 2002).

The question is clearly before us: How to analyze and assess a situation in which women have made remarkable progress in closing the gender gap, yet continue to be hobbled because of patriarchal biases? Conversely, how to assess the fact that men appear to have lost their unquestioned right to power and privilege, yet they remain firmly in control? The juxtaposition of these intersecting yet contradictory trends generates a host of complex social problems that have proven difficult to solve. In such uncharted territory, social conventions are up for grabs, and it is precisely this contestation that is proving both rewarding yet costly (Heilbrun, 1999). Insofar as gender constitutes a constructed and contested site of progress and regress, of empowerment and disempowerment, this chapter explores the evolving and enigmatic relationship between men and women from a social problem perspective. Gender as a social problem is approached from a conditionalist (with its focus on causes, consequences, characteristics, and cures) and a constructionist perspective (with its focus on those claims-making activities known as feminist social movements). In defining gender as social construction, the following questions are inevitable: How different are women from men? Are differences of degree or kind, of culture versus biology? What does it mean to be a man or a woman in contemporary Canada?

Of particular importance to this chapter are the politics of inequality. The chapter is predicated on the assumption that gender relations are ultimately unequal relations with respect to power, privilege, and property. In that gender inequity is social in origin, definition, and treatment, the chapter focuses on how these relationships of inequality are constructed, expressed, maintained, as well as challenged, and transformed by way of politics and protest. The structural basis of gendered inequalities is examined by looking at the problems women confront as they walk up the down-escalator of corporate success. Also addressed is the notion that men are a gender too, one whose precipitous decline in privilege and corresponding crisis in identity is proving both real yet illusory. Finally, efforts to re-prime gender relations on a more equitable basis are linked to feminist social movements. To the extent that the gender problem is differently defined by diverse feminisms, with varying proposed solutions, the domain of gender will continue to excite—and incite—in the foreseeable future.

A sense of perspective is useful. Gender per se is not a problem. The social constructedness of gender and gender relations generates social problems because these largely arbitrary creations confer more power, privilege, and wealth to some at the expense of others. Three scenarios are problematic: First, gender is a social problem when inequities between women and men continue to persist in a society that espouses gender equity. Perceived differences between women and men are manipulated as grounds for sex discrimination to preclude entry of women into certain activities or unequal treatment if admitted (Hacker, 1951). Second, gender is problematic because the growing estrangement between men and women is not without consequences. Competition over scarce resources tends to create unhealthy friction at great interpersonal costs and risk to social stability. Third, gender is rendered problematic when the scripting of masculinity and femininity into rigid roles and stereotypical rules restrict personal choice, foster sexism, and create unequal outcomes. Paradoxically, a loosening up of the gender script may prove equally disruptive as both men and women fumble about for gender blueprints that are workable, necessary, and fair.

(DE)CONSTRUCTING GENDER

We are told that the social gap between the sexes is narrowing, but I can only report that having, in the second half of the twentieth century, experienced life in both roles [male and female], there seems to be no aspect of existence, no moment of the day, no contact, no arrangement, no response, which is not different for men and women. The very tone of the voice in which I was addressed, the very posture of the person next in [line], the very feel of the air when I entered a room or sat at a restaurant table, constantly emphasized my change....

—Transsexual British journalist, Jan Morris,
after her surgical change from male to female

Interest in the politics that define male–female relations has escalated in recent years, thanks in part to the feminist movement and in part to workplace changes. The growing prominence of women in previously male-dominated domains has riveted public attention as have few other contemporary issues. For personal and professional reasons, individuals express a consuming interest in the cultural meaning of womanhood ("femininity") or manhood ("masculinity"), especially as they vary over time and place. Sociologists take as axiomatic the notion that neither manhood nor womanhood qualifies as the purely biological attributes of individuals. Biology may determine our sex as male or female (or one of several other sexes including intersexed (between sex) or trans-sexed (wrong body) (O'Keefe and Fox, 2003). But culture shapes the content and conduct of what is perceived as male and female. Similarly with sexuality, according to O'Keefe and Fox, which many believe is more fluid and context-dependent than either heterosexual or homosexual, with most people lying on a continuum between entirely gay or entirely straight.

Those socially constructed and culturally specific attributes about manhood and womanhood that are acquired by individuals through socialization are known as gender. Masculinity consists of that package of attributes associated with an ideal typical male; femininity exemplifies the cultural characteristics that define the blueprint for female. As social and cultural constructs, concepts of femininity and masculinity are known to vary spatially (from culture to culture), laterally (within culture), historically (from one period to another), and longitudinally (across a person's lifespan) (Kimmel, 1992; 2000). The fact that gender is cultural and constructed rather than biological and innate confirms the centrality of the social in understanding male-female relations. It also reminds us that gender consists of identities that have been assigned by a largely patriarchal imagination: A view of humanity is promoted that suppresses how inventive, adaptive, adventuresome and resourceful people can be in defining sex and gender diversity (O'Keefe and Fox, 2003).

A Gendered Society

Contrary to popular belief, gender is not a natural consequence of biological differences. Rather, gender constitutes a culturally-defined prescription about what is or should be (Nelson and Robinson, 1996). But gender is more than a label assigned to men and women that varies from one culture to another (Harding, 1986). The concept of gender has proven critical in shaping how we think about ourselves and our relationship to the world. Gender constitutes a central element in our personal lives by providing a primary point of contact with the world out there thus reinforcing how our gender location in society profoundly influences our experiences and opportunities. (Renzutti and Curran, 1999). As conveyed by the contributors to *Politics, Policy, Pedagogy: Education in Aotearoa / New Zealand* (Marshall et al., 2000), children and adults are constantly conditioned to absorb the dominant ideals of masculinity and femininity, either through sanctions or media images, with the result that ideas about how to act as a man or woman are deeply embedded in the realities that constitute our everyday lives. Boys learn about attitudes and behaviour consistent with manhood, which in most cultures involves strength, competitiveness, domination, and control (Cleaver, 2002). Girls, in turn, internalize those complementary roles that rarely evoke admiration.

Reality is itself gendered. Every society divides the world into male and female, imposes different meanings upon women and men, reinforces the domination of men over women, and evaluates and rewards each gender on the basis of these perceptions (Kimmel, 2000). Society is gendered because foundational principles that govern the constitutional order are designed to reflect and reinforce male power, privilege, and priorities. A gendered society is organized so that male ways of thinking, perceiving, and behaving are regarded as natural and normal, while others are dismissed as irrelevant or inferior. Gender also constitutes a primary axis around which social life is organized in terms of defining who gets what in society. Its centrality in determining patterns of entitlement and engagement further reinforces how gender, like social class or race, is subject to similar patterns of inequality, hierarchical distinctions, and (dis)advantages. Such a dynamic invariably leads to questions about how gender relations as unequal relations are constructed and secured, in addition to being challenged and subjected to change.

Thirty years of social upheaval have dramatically altered public perceptions about gender. Women are no longer dismissed as inferior or submissive in status; roles are not nearly as rigidly scripted as before; rules defining masculinity and femininity are increasingly contested; differences among women are accepted as empowering; and the principles of partnership provide the blueprint for getting along. Feminism has helped to redefine this shift in the balance of power by expanding options and choices for women in contemporary society. But social practices have not always kept pace with cultural beliefs, with the result that Canadians are increasingly unsure of how to embrace changes in gender roles, rules, status, and relationships. Traditional rules about gender relationships no longer seem applicable. But new norms have yet to be formulated to everyone's satisfaction or without eliciting a backlash (Smith, 1998). Nowhere is this more evident than in television or film. Both media are filled with confident, assertive, intelligent, and independent women whose professional moxie and "butt kicking" skills match those of men. Nonetheless, women continue to be portrayed as vacuous, vulnerable, sex objects, and marriage material (Pozner, 2003; Mintz, 2003; Byers, 2003; Leong, 2003).

Of course, women are not the only ones undergoing change and adjustment. Men too have had to renegotiate their relationship with women on the basis of equality (Benwell, 2003). Double standards prevail: No sooner do men show a "softer" side than they are precluded from female-dominated professions, discouraged from working with children, and criticized for acting "wimpy" around the guys. Many of the attributes once negatively associated with femininity are now perceived as strengths; conversely, male virtues of independence and control are defined increasingly as vices. For example, many believe male leaders prefer a command and control style, in which they view job performances as a series of transactions with subordinates, with power defined as an end in itself. By contrast, female leaders embrace power as a means to an end, appear more willing to share information and encourage participation, prefer to motivate by negotiation, diplomacy, and compromise, and are more comfortable with ambiguity. In theory, neither style is superior, but the female style is no longer dismissed as weak and vacillating, but is increasingly valued as a preferred style in the teamwork oriented workplace environment of a freewheeling global economy. Not surprisingly, men are experiencing an identity crisis in trying to figure out who they are and what is expected of them in this topsy-turvy world.

Men Are from Mars/Women Are from Venus?

How many times have we heard this one? Bad men may have created a mean world, but good women will grab power and everyone will live happily ever after (Vanstone, 2002). The caring, cooperative, and more empathetic world of women would replace male-dominated hierarchies based on power, violence, and aggression. Such gender fundamentalism has essentialized women and men around innate differences, according to Phyllis Chesler in her *Woman's Inhumanity to Women*, in the process ignoring how woman can be as domineering and aggressive as men (also Sismondo, 2002). This notion of woman as fully, fallibly human reinforces the concept of gender and gender roles as socially constructed. It also raises two related issues, each of which has had a powerful impact in defining gender-related "rules," "roles," and "relationships." First, how different are women from men? Are differences based on degree ("minor and superficial") or kind ("major or fundamental")? Are women more cooperative and consensual compared to male aggression; or are these differences superficial and reflective of situational adjustments irrespective of gender?

Some would argue that women and men are basically alike: Similar outcomes will result if women and men are equipped with the same opportunities and expectations, situated in a comparable context, and exposed to similar pressures and competition (Kanter, 1977; Kimmel, 2000). Others propose a radical difference between women and men. For some, the differences are rooted in biogenetic wiring; for others, differences reflect the radically different social and cultural experiences that each encounters in society. Belief in the existence of radical differences raises several questions. To what extent should similar treatment apply if people are fundamentally different? Should women chase success by embracing traditional male virtues of aggressiveness, toughness, and competitiveness (Fukuyama, 1999)? Or should women try to shift the political and economic agenda away from the male obsession with hierarchy, competition, and domination? The fact that responses to these questions remain as contested as ever is itself indicative of the complexities involved.

Second, what is the nature of female-male differences? Are behavioural differences the result of biology or culture? Innate or situational? Essential or culturally specific? Is there any biological basis to the allocation of roles and rewards along gender lines, either in the past or at present? Is it possible to resocialize men to be more like women or women to be more like men? Or are manhood and womanhood largely unalterable by modifications to culture, socialization, or situational circumstances (Fukuyama, 1999)? Many continue to believe that gender relations reflect innate and inherited qualities. Virtually all evolutionary biologists believe differences between women and men are profound and genetic, reflecting differential reproductive strategies. These differences extend to the mind as well as to the body and behaviour. Consider how the brains of women and men are thought to process information differently; for example, women's brains are perceived to be more adept at solving problems involving spatial relations. Reference to innateness makes it extremely difficult to alter deeply ingrained patterns of behaviour like male violence.

Most sociologists reject the idea of genetic hard-wiring as grounds for explaining gender differences and similarities. Of course, biological claims are not categorically dismissed as irrelevant in influencing gender behaviour. Furthermore, references to the genetic are not to be confused with the fixed or predictable but may be subject to modification or override, in effect reinforcing the primacy of the social and cultural. The preference of the social over the biological is sociologically consistent: That is, similarities and differences in gender are the result of social forces, such as cultural values, socialization processes, structural constraints, group dynamics, and situational cues. The concept of what it means to be a woman or a man ("femininity" and "masculinity") is socially constructed, relative to a particular time and place, culturally defined, internally differentiated, politically contested, and responsive to broader societal changes. Gender represents a convention created at a particular point in time and place by those in positions of power to enforce these scripted notions of right or wrong. And historically, men have manipulated the levers of power to promote their interests, priorities, and ambitions.

Did You Know?

Men and Women Are from Earth

What do cross-national studies say about gender and gender roles? Anthropology has performed a yeoman-like service in expanding our horizons on the social and cultural basis of gender relations. Anthropological evidence is overwhelming in the direction of gender differences as socially constructed and culturally relative (Peoples and Bailey, 1997). All societies construct distinctions between women and men; assign certain rules, roles, and responsibilities to the categories of women and men; and allocate a different value to men's work versus women's work. The seeming inequality of gender relations is no less subject to debate. Men are defined (or have defined themselves) as superior to women in terms of authority, prestige, and access to power. By contrast, women's activities are normally devalued compared to male endeavours—no matter how critical to the local economy. A complex set of ideologies and symbols are also employed to denigrate women as irrelevant, dangerous, polluting, or untrustworthy—a view not necessarily shared by women who work around these restrictions even as they pay lip service to male domination (Harris, 1993; Abwunza, 1997; Chagnon, 1999).

Three key issues appear to animate much of the controversy surrounding gender relations from a cross-cultural perspective. First, the so-called "universality" of male dominance and female subordination despite the centrality of women to production and reproduction. Second, a worldwide sexual division of labour in which men hunt and women forage. Third, the pervasiveness of gender-linked attributes pertaining to men as aggressors and women as nurturers. Societies are stratified by gender: men and their activities are associated with prestige, not because of the activity per se but because their gender is linked with that particular activity (hence, women are cooks, men are chefs (Henslin, 2000). But things are not what they seem to be. There is growing awareness that appearances are deceiving in assessing the status of gender relations around the world. Gender differences and inequities are not an either-or phenomenon but often reveal how those women with even nominal amounts of power can work the system to their advantage. In other words, rather than assuming that men are from Mars and women from Venus, let's remember that both women and men are constructions from Earth.

THE MASCULINE MYSTIQUE

Turn to the gender chapter in any sociology textbook. Virtually all focus on the social problems that confront women, with particular emphasis on women and inequality, the devaluation of women's experiences, violence against women, changes in women's status and identity, and sexist discriminatory barriers at odds with full and equal participation in society. A section on feminism and different types of feminist movements is routinely included. This focus on a female dimension is to be expected, given that women initially problematized the notion of gender (Cleaver, 2002). Yet this one-sided look glosses over the male component of gender and gender relations. Such an exclusion is unfortunate: Not only are male contributions to the gender equation excluded; after all, "men are gender" too, and, besides, it does take "two to gender." Also ignored is how men themselves are undergoing a profound transformation in terms of status, roles, expectations, and responsibilities—in ways both empowering and disempowering.

What does it mean to be a man in today's rapidly changing environment? Masculinity may be defined as a combination of biology, evolutionary psychology, shifting social relations, media images, and capitalist consumerism. Nonetheless, separating biology from culture and society is elusive (Valpy, 2003). Both women and men have experienced confusion about male roles in light of changing definitions of masculinity and femininity. The days of the Marlboro Man (a rugged individualist) are rapidly disappearing; so too has the Sturdy Oak model personified by the "Duke" (John Wayne). Even the quintessential 1980s man, Alan Alda (Hawkeye Pierce) of the television series "M*A*S*H," appears to have fallen into disrepute. Nothing seems to have taken the place of these earlier models except for vague and contradictory appeals for men to be sensitive yet manly, family-friendly yet corporate phenoms, warmly intelligent yet well-chiselled, and good-natured yet calculatingly decisive. There is less agreement than ever on defining manhood, with the result that men are experiencing a crisis of confidence with respect to identity. Men are floundering in a masculinity quicksand in trying to figure out who they are writes Michael Valpy (2003). Many want to reject machismo stereotypes they dislike or can't cope with, yet are repeatedly massaged by media messages about buying into metrosexuality—the new dandified version of a straight urban male who is eager to embrace his gay/feminine side by buying into designer suits, manicures, moisturizers, and facials. Young men carry around a lot of stereotypically masculine baggage such as being cool, never cracking under pressure, never crying, never allowing people to see how they really feel, while honing a knack for accumulating money, power, and relationships (Valpy, 2003). This ambiguity is conveyed by Leah McLaren in her article entitled "The Perfect Guy: Smart, Manly, and Just Gay Enough" (*The Globe and Mail,* 10 November, 2001). No wonder contemporary males are in a quandary over what to do or who they ought to be. Traditional rules no longer apply, while new rules are floating around in a kind of limbo. Moreover, the support systems for any significant shift in behaviour are not in place, with the result that working outside the script can derail career plans or invite ridicule. Uncertainty and pressure will continue to mount even further as men begin to want it all—a fast-paced career; a nurturing role as father; sensitive, reflective, self-aware and communicative relationships; insatiable sexuality; fabulous pecs and washboards abs; and loads of cash.

Put bluntly, men are experiencing an identity crisis. The crisis of confidence over the norms and values that traditionally informed masculinity is not without consequence, according to Carol Gilligan in her book *The Birth of Pleasure.* Confusion of such magnitude can erupt into hostility and violence as men grope around for the meaning of masculinity in an unyielding and unforgiving world. This fractured and complicated picture may prove an opportunity in disguise for some, or a recipe for chaos for others, given the difficulties of "operationalizing" the concept of "new age guy." Context appears critical. A take-charge kind of guy is appropriate at times, especially in boardrooms and bedrooms, but so too is the sensitive and thoughtful type who can relate equally well to politics and playdough without sacrificing masculinity in the process. Women too are casting about for a blueprint in defining the new woman. Yet their experiences and tribulations have received greater exposure from contemporary critics and authors. And, as women have gained more control over their lives and life chances, men have had to rethink the once unimaginable: The world does not revolve around them.

From Ruling the Roost to Roasting a Chicken

The great male identity crisis shows no sign of abating, with pressure mounting to dislodge men from their lofty pedestal at the universal centre. Historically, men were not troubled by questions about who they were. Their status as social superiors furnished them with ready-made answers as the norm and standard by which others were judged and assessed accordingly. A "real" man embodied core cultural values, including that of a rugged heterosexual individual with a penchant for action, accomplishment, and competition, without abandoning unquestioned loyalty to country, corporation, and family. The John Wayne model for men—tall, tough, and silent—secured generations of male wannabees. To be sure, entry into a "man's" world did not come easily or automatically. To become a man entailed a struggle involving formidable hurdles. By contrast, women were thought to have it easier: They were naturally inclined toward motherhood through normal biological maturation. Not surprisingly, women were unthinkable outside of their relationship to men as doting mothers, loving wives, hero-worshipping daughters, "girlfriends," "castrating bitches," and trophies of male competition and conquest.

Revolutionary changes have challenged the place and privilege of men. Males entered the 20th century in firm control of themselves and the world around them, including obedient wives, dutiful children, jobs for life, and prerogatives of citizenship to define, build, and make a difference (Faludi, 1999). But they are entering the new century in a more precarious position because of disempowerment at home and the workplace as (a) women have seized more power; (b) children are asserting rights; (c) computers are taking their jobs; (d) their value to society is eroded by technological advances; and (e) their command and control skills are becoming obsolete in a global economy that emphasizes female skills (*Economist,* 2001). Even an ideal body image for men has undergone substantial change toward a sleeker body shape, including square-shouldered, V-shaped torso, narrowed waist, pumped-up pecs, and washboard abs. For young men approaching adulthood, the very definition of manhood is being transformed before their eyes. The transition from an alpha male ("competitive") to a beta male ("compassionate") is littered with cultural landmines and mixed messages about relating to women, to other men, and to children. To be sure, among younger, more educated men, they are willing to accept the principle of gender equity, especially in once female-dominated spheres such as child-rearing and housekeeping. But, generally, men appear unhappy about having to share power and privilege with those once defined as inferior or irrelevant, preferring instead to secure as much of the status quo as possible, without looking like a knuckle-dragging Neanderthal in the process (Johnson, 1997). Insofar as the gains by women are perceived to be at the expense of men, the mounting resentment breeds an unhealthy hostility.

The dislocation is proving disruptive. Men as a group have had it good for such a long time that most cannot conceive of having to move over and share power. For most men, their status and stature are being diminished and demeaned. Instead of respect and deference, men are increasingly criticized as deadbeats or dolts who cannot be trusted or admired. Not surprisingly, men find themselves beleaguered on all sides. Those males with education and emotional resiliency will prosper from the transformation; others for whom the slope of life is slippery have reacted to this emasculation by lashing out vindictively in a last-ditch effort to snatch a shred of respect. Still others respond to this loss of power and privilege by withdrawing deeper into themselves. The implications are disturbing; The very social fabric that sustains our existence may well rupture under the strain of genders in disarray.

The forces of change and diversity have been relentless and disruptive. The fanning of male anxieties is inevitable with the erosion of once reassuring images. Confusion is so pervasive because of perceived unfairness and perceptions of double standards that it borders on resentment. Consider the conundrums that puzzle or infuriate many men: Why is it that the violence of women in domestic relations is treated less harshly by the legal system than male violence, asks a report released by support groups for battered husbands (Remington, 2002)? Answer: Men and women are not equal in a violent relationship since the physical and economic consequences are potentially more serious for women than men. Or how do we justify women-only clubs—from health spas to golf clubhouses—yet the Augusta National Golf Club is severely criticized for not allowing female members (Ferguson, 2002)? Answer: in the context of a patriarchal society, women-only and men-only are not the same thing, feminists have argued, since men are trying to monopolize power while women are trying to acquire power while creating safe space in a society that disdains female culture. In other words, equity demands that equal standards cannot be applied to unequal situations. Or why does conventional wisdom continue to emphasize how powerful men are, yet male powerlessness is increasingly the norm for most men? Answer: Men as a group retain the levers of economic and political power while the foundational principles of society are unmistakably gendered in reflecting, reinforcing, and advancing male privilege.

Men's movements and male-rights groups have attempted to enter into dialogue with the new realities. Some of these movements seek to advance feminism through support and empathy. But while awareness of inequities provides a useful start, insight and sympathy are not the same as challenging the system. Other male movements are more interested in preserving any further erosion of male privilege, rather than advancing the concerns of women. And still others are willing, in theory, to address issues pertaining to power-sharing. For most men, however, privilege and power are hard to relinquish to those once perceived as inferior or irrelevant. Moreover, for many men the path of least resistance is to do nothing, especially since the status quo is organized around preserving male privilege and power (Johnson, 1997).

In sum, the masculine mystique has been unzipped and exposed for what it is: a social construction in defence of power and privilege. For too long men have been the primary beneficiaries of a world unmistakably male in norm and standard. But male ways of doing things are no longer automatically assumed the best. Gender scripts are being fiercely contested. The rules of the game have undergone change because the personal is political while individual troubles are seen as public issues and social problems. And yet there is no clear direction as to what the new gender relations rules should look like, much less how they should be put into practice. Such a massive gender quake has splintered the relationship as both genders fumble about in securing the scripts for living together with their differences. Estrangement between women and men in Canada is growing at times, in some cases bordering on "gender wars," because of male bewilderment over the pace of change.

GENDER INEQUALITY

A commitment to gender equality is highly valued in many parts of the world. According to the World Values Survey 1995–2001, this commitment is true even of the Middle East, although attitudes toward abortion and homosexuality differ markedly indicating a real schism between East and West (Inglehart and Norris, 2003). But the persistence and pervasiveness of gender inequality persists even in societies that aspire to equity between women and men. As the UN likes to remind us, no country treats its women as well as its men, with wildly varying degrees of gender inequality. Women and men are differently situated economically and politically because of unequal access to cultural and material resources that define who gets what (Cleaver, 2002). These inequities in power, privilege, and wealth are neither random nor isolated but patterned, persistent, and resistant to change. Nor do they necessarily reflect individual shortcomings: The combination of power relations, opportunity structures, discriminatory barriers, and workplace practices points to structural causes (Agocs and Boyd, 1993).

The relationship between women and men in all human societies is characterized by disparities of various sorts, although the intensity and scope of this gender gap is subject to cross-national variation. Throughout the world, politics remains a "no (wo)men's land," where women are routinely excluded from most involvement in government, state, or political life. Similarly, women languish near the bottom of the socio-economic ladder, despite making a disproportionate contribution to most economies. Women are increasingly subject to violence, with recourse to mass rape as a weapon of war—either to punish husbands suspected as collaborators or, in the case of the Congo, to infect women with the HIV virus, thus ensuring catastrophe for rape victims and their country (O'Reilly, 2003). Gang rape is so systematic in Eastern Congo where thousands of women are suffering from vaginal fistula (a condition which does not allow women to control their bodily functions, leading to social ostracism and health-related problems unless the vagina is surgically reconstructed) that the mutilation of the vagina is considered a war injury and recorded by doctors as a crime of combat (Wax, 2003). Admittedly, women around the world have taken strides in uprooting ideals and practices surrounding their status in society. But patterns of inequality remain deeply entrenched. That is, women represent about half the world's population and perform nearly two-thirds of the work, but earn about one-tenth of the income, while owning less than one one-hundredth of the property.

Canada is no exception despite encouraging signals. In a United Nations Development Programme survey of selected countries ranked according to the Gender Empowerment Measure, 2001, Canada came in fifth—behind Norway, Iceland, Sweden, and Finland. Canada's score of 0.783 meant that Canadian women were about four-fifths of the way to equality with men based on women's share of Parliamentary seats, proportion of administrative, professional and managerial jobs, and the amount of women's earning power. Evidence of disadvantages is clearly evident. Many Canadian women live in a climate of fear of violence and poverty; are marginalized into occupational ghettos; have fewer job options and earn less income; are discouraged from excelling in traditional male pursuits; are subjected to harassment; and routinely confront discriminatory barriers and double standards. Their contribution to society is undervalued in some circles, except in their roles as mother, wife, sister, or daughter (Hacker, 1951). The disproportional amount of unpaid domestic work performed by women remains largely invisible, writes Peggy Kome, in her book *Somebody Has to Do It: Whose Work Is Housework?*" Yet the value of housework is equivalent to nearly 40 percent of Canada's GDP, according to Statistics Canada, thus conceding the collapse of Canada's market economy without the invisible labour of women's unpaid work (Morgenson, 2002). Despite their centrality to society and the economy, women's self-confidence is under perpetual siege by vested interests, including those who would like nothing better than to endorse "family values" while keeping women "kept." The net effect of linking workplace success with perpetual makeovers has led to unrealistic expectations about what is attainable, an obsession with appearance at the expense of health, and a preoccupation with weight loss and body image that borders on the pathological.

A sense of perspective is required in balancing the bad with the good. By comparison with other parts of the world, Canadian women receive more equitable treatment. In relationship to Canadian men, women have also made astonishing strides in a remarkably short period of time. Yet the reality of the situation is much more complex, with advances in some areas matched by stagnation or regression in others, depending on the context (MacIvor, 2003). Paradoxically, gender is not always the most important dimension of inequality for women. Gender may be superimposed on class, race, and ethnicity to create intersecting and interlocking patterns of inequality that have the intent or effect of denying or excluding women of colour, immigrant and minority women, and aboriginal women (Stasiulis, 2000; Cole and Guy-Sheffall, 2003). In short, disparities persist and this gender discrimination is manifest in the employment picture, income earnings, education, politics, and victims of violence.

Employment Status

Women are prominent in the labour force. Nearly 46.7 percent of Canada's labour force is comprised of women, according to the 2001 Census Data, compared to 45 percent of the workforce in 1991. Nearly 58 percent of all adult women were in paid employment, compared to only 24 percent in 1950. The number of women in info-technology jobs nearly doubled to 110 000 from 61 000, while the number of female managers grew from 408 000 in 1991 to 574 000 in 2001 (compared to nearly 1 million men), including 50 900 who identified as senior management, up from 23 800 in 1991. As well, according to Catalyst Canada, women in 2001 occupied 9.8 percent of board seats on the FP-listed companies, up from 6.2 percent in 1998 (MacNamara, 2002). Women in Canada created 34 percent of all businesses (Smythe, 2003).

On the downside, a gendered division of labour restricts women from higher paid "male" jobs while slotting women into lower status, lower paid jobs—a trend unlikely to change judging by the enrolment of female students in female typical studies (MacIvor, 2003). Women continue to be concentrated in four occupations—elementary teaching, nursing/health related jobs, secretaries and office clerks, or retail sales/service, including cashiers (Statistics Canada, 2001 Census). Further progress in desegregating occupations has stalled because of the challenges that women confront, including the double shift, part-time work, wage gaps, and shortage of high quality daycare (MacIvor, 2003). And while women continue to make major advances in their careers, they spend more time than their male partners in looking after children and doing housework. In 2001, nearly 15 percent of women did 30 or more hours of unpaid family related work; only 6 percent of the men achieved this level. Not unexpectedly, a major reason for marital break-up is failure to create an equitable division of household labour, second only to abusive domestic relations (Morgenson, 2002).

Income Earnings

The message is most mixed when income differences are analyzed. Overall, women earn about 61 percent of what men earn. Women in full-time full-year employment earn around 70¢ for every dollar a man earns, according to 2001 census data—an improvement from the 58¢ in 1967, but down from the 73¢ in the mid 1990s. Single women earned 95.5 percent of what single men earned, whereas married women earned only 67.5 percent of what married men earned. Women between 15 and 24 earned 90.9 percent of what men earned. Women between 45 and 54 earned only 67.2 percent. However, women between 45 and 54 who were single and university-educated earned the same as their male counterparts. Lastly, young female university graduates earned more than young male university graduates in only one occupation—social work—but overall the most common occupations held by women are lower paying ($37 185) than the most common occupations held by men ($41 509) (Carey, 2003).

Differences based on annual earnings may be misleading. Gaps may reflect the fact that annual earned wages increase with experience, with men working longer hours and without interruption to careers because of less family responsibility (Canadian Press, 12 March, 2003). Men are also more likely to ask for a raise or promotion while women often don't get what they deserve because they don't ask for it, reinforcing female under-representation in top jobs and lesser earnings (Babcock et al., 2003). A slightly different picture appears with hourly wages. The gap between women and men is 80 percent based on an hourly rate, with women on average earning $17.14 and men on average earning $21.54. Part of the gap can be explained by looking at workplace differences. Women tend to work in less progressive companies that are less likely to offer incentives, merit pay, and profit sharing. They are more likely to work in more part-time oriented firms that slot men into management and technical jobs while women do sales and administration. And they are more likely to be employed in Canadian corporations that tend to pay less than foreign-owned companies (Carey, 2002). Women also are prone to jobs which they believe can help individuals or society or, as secondary wage earners, choose lower paying jobs consistent with family obligations (Canadian Press, 12 March, 2003).

Education

Women and girls are now surfing the wave of education success. Girls are outperforming boys across the board in math, writing, and reading in Ontario primary schools (Galt, 1999)—in effect prompting debates about the need for all-boys classes to provide extra assistance for underachievers (Owens, 2002). Young women make up 58 percent of university graduates, up from 52 percent a decade ago. And women are gradually moving into disciplines once reserved for "the guys." This gender shift may reflect a tilt in school culture: Young women are excelling at schooling, in part because schools are teaching girls what they can do; conversely, young men are taught a different message by reminding them of what they can't be, namely, too aggressive or too wild (Valpy, 2003).

So where is the problem? A gap still persists between women's lived experience and the university's official commitment to equality. As Keahy and Schnitzer (2003: 12) write in castigating the elitist and self-serving nature of the academy:

> It is a system that ranks my productivity by measures I cannot endorse; that promotes research that is often deliberately inaccessible and is valued because its focus is compatible with a university-bred publishing industry that is closed and egocentric; that asks me to teach and knows that by and large I have no training and less incentive to improve my practice for it for, in fact, it is my research that will determine whether or not I will perish; that puts me on a variety of task forces whose work is usually undone or forgotten from one year to the next.

The distribution of women in universities remains skewed as well. Only about 25 percent of university faculty are women, most of whom are relegated to the lower echelons. Women have been awarded only 15 percent of federal research chairs since the program was first created in 2002 (Sokoloff, 2002). Faculties such as computer science or engineering still remain overwhelmingly male, while women tend to graduate from the "softer" disciplines in arts and social sciences. A gender divide persists in the use of computers, according to a study by sociologists Dianne Looker and Victor Thiessen, with girls showing a lower level of computer skills competence that could hamper future computer-literate jobs (Akin, 2003). And theories continue to circulate that girl's brains are hard-wired very differently than boys, with the result that only a small percentage can ever hope to become engineers, no matter how hard they try (Swainson, 2002).

Political Status

The gender gap is especially striking at the political front (Trimble and Arscott, 2003). With 63 seats in Parliament, women represent 20.6 of the total—a figure that has stalled after climbing for 30 years. Canada ranks 31st in the Inter-Parliamentary Union's ranking of 179 countries by the number of female legislators, well behind Sweden with 45.3 percent of Parliamentary seats but ahead of the United States at 14.3 percent (Laghi, 2003). The situation could become bleaker with the retirement of top ranking party leaders such as Alexa McDonough (Speirs, 2002). For the first time in 14 years, none of the federal political party leaders are female, all the provincial premiers are men, and only two female party leaders in British Columbia and New Brunswick are waiting in the wings (Goar, 2003). The few women who make it into Parliament find themselves on "soft" legislative committees pertaining to culture or welfare, while those in Cabinet tend to occupy pink-collar portfolios such as health or human resources (MacIvor, 2003).

Domestic Violence

Domestic violence remains a major problem in Canada. Between 1995 and 2001, according to Statistics Canada, rates of spousal violence reported by the police rose from 302 per every 100 000 of women to 344 per 100 000, possibly reflecting a growing willingness of victims to report incidents to the police rather than absolute increases (Carey, 2003). Male victims remained relatively steady at about 50 per 100 000. While the murder rate has dropped from 16.5 women per 1 000 000 couples in 1974 to 8.3 in 2001, criminal harassment by a spouse increased substantially by 53 percent between 1995–2001, with women 90 percent of the victims. To be sure, both men and women display aggressiveness in the pressure cooker of domestic relations (Foss, 2002). Yet the study by Statistics Canada on family violence makes it abundantly clear: Women are much more likely to suffer serious injuries from domestic battles including a much higher risk of requiring medical attention because of beatings. Moreover, ignoring context, meaning, and motive in such violent encounters is misleading, notes Desmond Ellis, a York University sociology professor, with men using violence to control their partners, while women resort to violence in settling a conflict (Foss, 2002).

Explaining Gendered Inequality

Few sociologists would deny the asymmetric quality of gender relations in Canada. For some, gender differences cause inequality; for others, the structure of inequalities tends to accentuate differences between women and men (Kimmel, 2000). In either case, gender relations are anything but abstractions between categories. What we have instead are patterns of interaction between unequals involving power and control in contexts of patriarchy. Women continue to be "put down" because of institutional and systemic bias, or "put in their place" by way of outright harassment or subtle forms of intimidation. Many are denied equality in the workplace or deprived of spousal support to compete equitably within the corporate boardroom. By the same token, many men believe that women have achieved equality. Women are seen as gaining ground at male expense, with the result that any further concessions are seen as unfair and unnecessary. The tension reflects a conflict in interest between the "half-fulls" (those who focus on how far women have come) versus the "half-empties" (those who focus on how far women still need to go).

Men's perceptions and women's experiences differ in how each sees gender inequality (Saguy, 2003). Take sexual harassment: Sexual harassment involves attention toward individuals, both deliberate or inadvertent, that is unwanted, unwarranted, and persistent in terms of actions or words. Also included under sexual harassment is the creation of a female-unfriendly environment by words or actions that threaten women or make them feel irrelevant or inferior. While a sexual component may prevail in some cases, most harassment is about power and control over the workplace, either though quid pro quo (sex for favours) or creation of a "poisoned climate." The structure of the workplace reinforces the potential for the abuse of power since the inferior status occupied by women invites male hostility and harassment. As Catherine MacKinnon (1976) concluded, sexual harassment can no longer be dismissed as a personal problem involving an unwanted advance by a male because of a woman's appearance or behaviour. When linked with the power that men have possessed over women in the workplace and their determination to keep it that way, sexual harassment must be viewed within a patriarchal context because of its embeddedness within the structures of the male-dominated workplace (Henslin, 2000). But men tend to see it differently. Harassment as structure and power is widely misunderstood by men because, as a rule, (a) they fail to connect specific instances of sexual harassment with broader patterns of sexual inequality and power relations; (b) they ignore how both abuse and harassment constitute strategies of dominance and exclusion that have had the effect of keeping women in place and out of the way; and (c) they have a corresponding reluctance to challenge workplace structures and underlying cultural values that would make women less vulnerable (Rhode, 1997).

How do we account for gendered disparities? Are they the result of innate differences or market forces? Should the blame be laid on capitalism or patriarchy (and its correlates, androcentrism, sexism, and misogyny)? Biological theories are generally discounted by sociologists; psychological theories of maturational development are best left to psychologists. Sociological theories emphasize social factors as key explanatory variables. These social factors are not necessarily intentional. Rather, they reflect the logical consequence of a system designed for preserving male privilege. The structure of capitalism has long been acknowledged as a key source of gender inequities. Under capitalism, women are subject to inequality because of the need to maintain a cheap and disposable workforce, to ensure divisions within the existing workforce, and to secure the domestic life for nurturing male labour. For Marxism, then, capitalism exploits everybody; women are simply more exploited than men.

In conjunction with capitalist structures is the prominence of patriarchy. Prominent feminists from Carol Gilligan to Marilyn French agree that patriarchy remains the prevailing form of social and political organization in society. Patriarchy refers to a society that is designed by and organized around male interests. It can be defined as a system in which: (a) the social, political, economic, and cultural are controlled by men; (b) masculinity is more highly valued than feminine values; and (c) males have preferential access to the good things in life because of their gender (Renzutti and Curran, 1999). Patriarchy itself consists of several interrelated constituents. Misogyny refers to hatred of women. Sexism covers that constellation of beliefs and practices that openly assert the superiority of one gender over the other because of preconceived notions of what is normal, acceptable, and superior. Androcentrism, by contrast, reflects an inclination by men to automatically and routinely interpret reality from their point of view; to posit this interpretation as natural and normal, while assuming that others will think so too, if given half a chance; to judge others on the basis of this masculinist standard; and to dismiss alternate interpretations as irrelevant or inferior. With androcentrism, men are defined as natural-born leaders—ranging from household heads to heads of state; women, in turn, are defined as natural-born nurturers. The dynamics of patriarchy with capitalism are sharply etched in the corporate setting, as this case study demonstrates.

CASE 4-1	**Walking Up a Down-Escalator: Women in the Corporate Workplace**

One of the more extraordinary developments in recent years reflects the changing composition of the corporate workplace. Women, people of colour, and individuals with disabilities have challenged the once-exclusive male domain of status and rewards. Corporations have had to rethink the rules, structures, and priorities that once underpinned the expression, "That's the way we do things around here." The concept of institutional change may sound good in theory and have the best intentions at heart, but reform efforts face a host of barriers that historically resist even minor adjustments. Every concession is met with an

(continued on next page)

equally powerful reaction. Relations between women and men have become more political and antagonistic, as previous male strongholds must move over and share space with those once relegated to the margins as social inferiors. But, rather than arguing that males are deliberately colluding to control women, the case study suggests that gender inequalities stem from systemic biases associated with organizational structure. Women and men display different patterns of organizational behaviour not because of gender, either innate or acquired but because of different cultural expectations and opportunity structures (also Kimmel, 2000). The interplay of variable access to opportunity structures with the prevalence of ingrained cultural values invariably result in a process by which some prosper, while others falter. The case study serves as a primer for thinking sociologically about social problems by reinforcing a key assumption: Our location in society with respect to gender or race will profoundly influence our experiences and opportunities in shaping how we act toward others and others toward us.

In 1977, Rosabeth Moss Kanter published what has become a classic in sociology. *Men and Women of the Corporation* received countless accolades, including the coveted C. Wright Mills Prize for its contribution to a critically informed sociology. The significance of Kanter's book went beyond exploring gender-based organizational behaviour within corporate America. The book provided a sociological look at how social forces impacted on human behaviour since, as Kanter observed, organizational actors tended to respond predictably when confronted by similar structural circumstances. Capitalizing on a sociological dimension symbolized a major departure from conventional studies of organizational behaviour, with their emphasis on psychological attributes and attitudinal predispositions.

Kanter focused on the structural determinants of organizational behaviour by concentrating on the dynamics of a particular corporation. For Kanter, organizational behaviour stems from unconscious responses of actors to their status (or "placement") within corporate structures. Kanter concluded that, as a group, men prevailed in corporate settings, not necessarily because of male personality features or predispositions but because of advantageous placement with respect to preferential opportunity structures, access to power, and numerical superiority. Women, by contrast, were often excluded or put down for precisely the same reasons that groomed men for success. Behaviour differences also arose from confining women to the velvet ghetto of public relations, advertising, staff support, and personnel, in part, because of a patriarchal perception that women excelled in people-handling and emotional fine tuning, but men took care of business. The few exceptions merely confirmed the rule: the prominence of structure was critical in understanding organizational behaviour. Organizational structures embodied something more than a passive backdrop for corporate games. These structures were logically prior and external to the individual; they also reflected the values, interests, experiences, and aspirations of those who created and controlled the corporation.

Opportunity Structures: "Nothing Succeeds Like Success"

The behaviour of corporate actors reflected their placement within the opportunity structures of the organiza-

(continued on next page)

tion. Those who were labelled as having potential by virtue of being streamed into the fast track behaved differently from those defined as having limited opportunities. High achievers acted in a manner that reflected and reinforced a commitment to the corporation, with sights firmly locked on entry into the upper echelons. Those on the fast track of opportunity acted in a competitive, dedicated, and instrumental manner. Their confidence and assertiveness reinforced the expectations of others in a kind of self-fulfilling prophecy, subsequently opening even more doors for corporate scaling. In contrast, those without high expectations of them acted accordingly, by displaying behavioural patterns consistent with marginality. Those on the slow track behaved predictably: they were inclined to be peer-oriented, to exhibit signs of complacency and resignation, and appeared bereft of ambition, in the process reinforcing their peripheral status, both real and perceived. In a classic re-enactment of a self-fulfilling prophecy, the "no-hopers" related to the corporation by way of hostility to management, displayed an unwillingness to put out for the company, a refusal to take risks to enhance upward mobility, and conducted themselves with an air of resignation and defeat.

The significance of structures for corporate gender behaviour is critical. Corporate structures have the potential to reduce or enhance organizational commitment; they can also dampen or accelerate enthusiasm and aspiration. Men do not monopolize these fast opportunity tracks simply because of superior work habits or heightened ambition. Nor are women shunted aside because of their skills or lack thereof. Rather, men find themselves in posi-tions where they are encouraged and rewarded to move upwards, whereas women are located in structures that inhibit career enhancement. As proof, those men derailed from the fast-tracking express tended to exhibit many of the same symptoms—from passivity to resistance—as those on the female track to nowhere. In sum, individuals are successful not necessarily because they have the "right stuff" (although that is obviously important). The fact that they have been centred out for success has a tendency to elicit the right corporate stuff. The person, in other words, does not make the job; more to the point, the job makes the person.

The Structure of Power: "Powerlessness Corrupts"

Those who possessed power tended to act in a powerful fashion. They could take advantage of power to get things done, define situations, propose solutions, establish agendas, draw on resources when necessary, enhance performance, and improve productivity. These objectives were often achieved through discretionary decisions that went beyond the "rulebook." Powerful individuals also knew how to delegate responsibility without having to check with superiors. They were in a position to enforce decisions, yet were rarely victimized by second guessing, in effect, reinforcing the idea that power is most powerful when quietly exercised.

Conversely, those without power displayed behaviour patterns consistent with their powerlessness. Those unsure of their power because of limited opportunity structures tended to act in a manner that underscored their peripheral status. Through displays of rigid, coercive, and vindictive behaviour, powerless people concentrated on what

(continued on next page)

little residual power they had over subordinates by "throwing their weight around." Even when occupying positions of formal authority within the corporate chain of command, the powerless resorted to excessive authoritarianism or displaced aggression, reinforcing yet again the observation that the most powerful are those least inclined to flaunt it. Throwing this "weight" around may have achieved the goal of compliance and ritual subordination, but ultimately sabotaged productivity while eroding cooperative manager-labour relations. Without power, a person's credibility was in doubt and openly contested, making it doubly difficult to receive deference, ensure compliance, and impress superiors. In short, Kanter asserts that it is not so much that power corrupts; rather, that powerlessness is corrupting.

The Structure of Relative Numbers: "Token Effects"

Relative numbers refer to the proportional distribution of certain categories of persons within the corporate setting. The behaviour of those who constituted the majority differed from members cast as minorities (measured statistically). The majority did not have to worry about being excluded, since they set the norm and established the standard by which others were judged. Majority members were exempt from double standards that plagued minorities. Conversely, minorities and women of the organization behaved differently because of their minority status. Differences in behaviour did not necessarily reflect variations in the human capital that people brought to the company (although these may have been important). Rather, behavioural differences stemmed from different expecta-

tions and diverse pressures imposed on those along the margins. Minorities such as women are likely to be treated as tokens, a situation that culminated in the circulation of both double standards and stereotypes regardless of what they did or did not do, including:

1. Minority tokens are viewed as representatives of their race or gender when they fail but exceptions when they succeed.

2. Tokens are constantly reminded of their differences but must conduct themselves as if these differences were immaterial—even as forces conspire to exaggerate their uniqueness, yet depersonalize their individuality.

3. Tokens tend to be thoroughly scrutinized and evaluated for any weaknesses, yet strengths and contributions may be ignored.

4. Tokens are extremely visible and the most dramatized of corporate performers, yet they are rendered invisible by exclusion from centre stage where props are set, scripts are rehearsed, and casts are assembled.

5. Tokens find the organizational settings stressful and constraining, even more so during times of relaxation or socializing (such as office parties), largely because of intensified levels of scrutiny.

6. Tokens are undervalued as potentially disruptive to the firm. Yet this perceived disruptiveness is primarily a function of their historic exclusion from meaningful participation within the organization.

The repercussions of this token effect should be obvious. Constant exposure to scrutiny and monitoring

(continued on next page)

inevitably takes it toll on those hand-picked as standard-bearers for their "kind." Their imposed status as ambassadors and role models practically guarantees that any missteps will confirm the worst in reinforcing stereotypes. Worse still, they carry around the weight ("guilt") that the future success of others depends on them. The combined impact of this token effect, Kanter explains, is anything but token in its impact and implications.

Glass Ceilings, Brick Walls, and Slippery Surfaces

What can we conclude from Kanter's work? First, organizational structures are important in shaping differences in behaviour between men and women. Maleness or femaleness is not the issue for corporate success. Personality characteristics or attitudinal predispositions are not nearly as important as many believe. What appears to be critical is the structural location of individuals that shape people's expectations, interactions, and responses. Women and minorities occupy the lower echelons of a corporate hierarchy not because of personal deficiencies that make them a liability to the organization. Rather, any passivity and non-commitment orientation is largely a behavioural response to structural inequities involving denied opportunity, an inadequate power base, and numerically induced tokenism. To be sure, cultural factors are also important. For example, in pigeonholing women and minorities into preconceived slots, mainstream cultural values may influence who is eligible for access to organizational opportunity or rewards. Organizational behaviour is also derived from situational circumstances, including personality differences among the social actors. But

structural limitations restrict the range of behavioural options, primarily because the system "… set limits on behavioural possibilities and defined the context for peer interaction" (Kanter, 1977: 239). These structures were systematic and deliberate in some cases; otherwise, they were systemic and unintended but nevertheless had a controlling effect on behaviour and outcomes.

Second, Kanter drew attention to the unmistakably androcentric logic at the core of organizational cultures. Corporations are very much a "pale-male" world, with masculine values and male priorities embedded into organizational styles and agendas. This gendered corporate reality extends from managerial styles on outward to include standards for appointments, entitlements, and conduct. Core organizational values are typically male-linked, including a commitment to aggressiveness, competitiveness, achievement orientation, individualism, analysis and an emphasis on rationality and logic, toughness, and lack of emotional display. Values pertaining to connectedness and other-directedness are shuffled aside in the rush for success at all costs. Even organizational conduct is unmistakably androcentric. Survival techniques focus on the need to be unemotional (avoid feelings); to depersonalize issues (never point the finger at anyone); to be subordinate (never challenge authority); to be cautious (better the devil you know); to be focused (mind your own business); and to stay competitive (keep your guard up). Routinely dismissed as career-limiting (at least until recently) are female styles of discourse, with their adherence to accommodation, relationships and communication, supportiveness, deference, and approval seeking. Who, then, can be surprised

(continued on next page)

when women and minorities find corporations user-unfriendly, and have experienced difficulties in navigating their way through the cultural mine fields of male-dominated institutions?

Third, Kanter's work was directed at dissecting behaviour patterns within organizations. Much of her analysis is equally applicable to understanding the behaviour of women and minorities in society at large. For example, just as corporate dynamics are unmistakably male in structure and ethos, (men are the prime beneficiaries of continuous employment and minimal domestic responsibilities (Sydie, 1987), so too is society an essentially masculine construction. Those whose interests and styles fall outside the "pale-male" mould are subject to criticism or second guessing. Pressures for conformity lead to frustration and despair, as well as disinterest because of the androcentric demands of contemporary institutions. A seeming lack of ambition and commitment among minorities is not necessarily a sign of inferiority or indifference. Unproductive responses reflect minority perceptions of themselves as undervalued and irrelevant to society. In such a situation, behavioural responses, from deviant acts to passive resignation, appear to be consistent with the structural location of the devalued.

Fourth, what can be done about transforming organizations in a manner consistent with minority needs and female aspirations? Programs and policies that focus on attitudinal changes or personality modifications are insufficient because they avoid the root cause. Organizational structures themselves need to be overhauled if any substantial change is anticipated. Productivity and satisfaction are contingent on structural arrangements that either facilitate or inhibit the best in each worker. A proposed replacement of males by minorities or women without any corresponding structural changes is unlikely to alter the status quo. Only the players would change, while the corporate game merrily rolls along.

Postscript: "Business As Usual"

Ten years after the publication of her book, Rosabeth Kanter provided an update on the intervening years in the journal *Management Review* (1987). On the one hand, modest organizational reforms had materialized, some of which came about because of her book, Kanter added. Women and minorities began to chip away at the glass ceiling that had inhibited upward mobility. Yet it was pretty much "business as usual." Male stereotypes continued to extol deeply held values about a woman's "rightful place" that pigeonholed women into communications, human resources, and corporate cheerleader jobs, thus denying them the line experience that they needed (Smith, 1998). As far as Kanter is concerned, the combination of constraints of power, lack of opportunity structure, and relative numbers remain as formidable as ever. The traditional image of a company as castle-like does not seem farfetched (Hacker, 1951)—a small number of highly paid White males in charge of an army of poorly paid clerical workers (mostly women), remains the reality in many cases, despite modest initiatives for improving the employment and promotion of targeted minorities.

Admittedly, a loosening of the corporate structures had encouraged upward mobility among women and minorities. Beyond a certain point, however, movement upward had ground to a halt, leaving women to ponder whether to persist

(continued on next page)

or resign in the face of subtle and not-so-subtle pressures. Over and over again, women spoke of upward mobility patterns that hit a "brick wall" because of male refusal to take them seriously. Women cited an inability to fit into a competitive corporate mould as an obstruction. As well, there was burn out from the conflicting and impossible demands of the double shift. Not surprisingly, many have pointed a finger at uncooperative spouses, not bosses, as a major impediment. To the surprise of no one, women and minorities are fleeing corporate cut-throat competition for the friendlier confines of small business and individual entrepreneurship.

Case Study Questions

1 What organizational structures help to account for differences in male/female behaviour?

2 According to Kanter, what must be done to transform the organization into a workplace that is more consistent with minority needs and women's aspirations?

"Dancing Backwards and Doing It in High Heels"

Ginger Rogers and Fred Astaire appeared in numerous movies as a gifted and graceful dancing team. Inevitably, comparisons raised the question of who was better. Ginger was known to have once quipped that she was every bit as good as Fred; however, she had to *dance backwards and do it in high heels*. That astute observation may apply to gender relations in general, corporate contexts in particular. Structures and values continue to pervade reality in a way that secures male advantage even if no intent or sexism is involved. Many of the barriers are unintentional but continue to have the effect of favouring men over women in the corporate rat race. This undervaluation of women is unfortunate and counterproductive. Corporations are losing qualified women because of sexist values, androcentric mindsets, and patriarchal structures. Stereotypes about what makes a good manager continue to hobble women, despite growing evidence that a female management style addresses 21st century realities (Carey, 2003). This bleeding takes place at precisely the time when companies can least afford to ignore the competitive potential of a wider talent pool.

Corporate Canada continues to be structured around a military model of hierarchy and power-seeking. For women the challenge is two-fold: They must cope in a cultural environment created by and for men while trying to juggle a career, children, and personal life. This creates a no-win dilemma for women in those gendered institutions already established to sustain masculinity: To the extent that corporate women must become more "manly" to succeed, femininity is sacrificed and punished. Those that refuse to sacrifice their feminine side are trivialized as irrelevant or superficial, and discriminated against accordingly (Kimmel, 2000). Or as Kimmel (2000: 17) puts it: "Either way—corporate frump or sexy babe—women lose, because the workplace is, itself, gendered and standards of success, including dressing for success, are tailored for the other sex." Career progress is rendered doubly difficult by increasingly intense pressures that subject women to additional restriction, including a workplace culture that makes it easier for men to succeed, the old boys' network, male discomfort in dealing with women at a professional level, and the challenge of balancing career with personal and domestic life (Galt, 2002). Despite these structural barriers, few appear ready to abandon hard-fought economic gains in exchange for the reassuring but increasingly unrealistic confines of hearth and home. In their quest for female-friendly workplaces, women are stepping off the corporate ladder and creating businesses at twice the rate of their male counterparts, with the result that female entrepreneurs now own or lead about 34 percent of all businesses in Canada (Crowley, 2003). Or alternatively, they are moving into high-tech jobs (Galt, 2002) where there are fewer barriers because the old boys' network has not been established, where they can work from anywhere, including their home, and where people tend to be judged by the quality of their work rather than the quantity of testosterone they bring to the workplace.

RE-GENDERING SOCIETY

To borrow Dickens's oft-quoted phrase, it is both the best of times and worst of times for women. Social, political, and economic advances are matched by inactivity in other areas that reinforces the status of women as "couched in compromise." Yes, the worst forms of discrimination have been eliminated. Left untouched, however, are the systemic biases that inadvertently hinder and hurt. In other words, the battle for equality is far from finished despite the fact that young women tend to reject feminism as a label while accepting feminism as a principle and politics. As Denise Campbell, president of National Action Committee on the Status of Women puts it, media demonizing of feminists as man-hating lesbians has not deterred young women from choosing to explore feminism in a different way (Trichur, 2001). This last section will explore the extent to which the different feminisms have addressed the problem of gender inequality together with corresponding solutions in creating a more inclusive Canada both diverse yet equitable.

Social Movements As Solutions

The concept of social movements has long been a staple of social problem study (Carroll, 1997). Its popularity has expanded even further because of contemporary dynamics in reshaping the contours of Canadian society. Canada has emerged as a site of many social movements, ranging in scope from the 1960s civil rights and feminist movements, to the AIDs and breast cancer advocacy groups of the 1980s, with the recent rise of neo-Nazism, gay rights, and quality of life movements as markers for the 1990s. Included as well are newer movements that focus on the environment; denounce fur and leather as clothing apparel; decry the use of alcohol and tobacco in public; engage men in the search for the male within; and are defining diversity as the "new" tobacco. Social movements vary in terms of scope, organization, and style (Aberle, 1966). Some are concerned with partial change (reform), others with a total revamping (revolution), still others with reversing current trends by reasserting conventional values or traditional structures (reaction). "Old" social movements often entailed labour issues; by contrast, "new" social movements may be concerned with the politics of identity or community renewal in light of rampant urbanism, creeping globalization, innovations in telecommunications and technology, and the tide of modernization (Adam, 1993). Tactics and strategies may also vary. Certain social movements advocate peaceful change (conventional channels and behind-the-scenes); others involve civil disobedience or flamboyant, media-catching actions; and still others endorse violence as the only course of action for achieving visionary goals.

Such diversity is a healthy sign. Yet it can hamper the creation of a coherent body of thought for theorizing the nature of social movements. When the range of phenomena spans everything from well-financed international organizations such as Greenpeace to spontaneous street activists such as Queer Nation, the prospect of a pattern may appear daunting. Social movements can be defined as conscious, collective efforts by a group of aggrieved individuals who initiate (or resist) social change through actions that fall outside institutional frameworks (Wilson, 1973). Such movements arise when individuals become disenchanted with disreputable aspects of society, with a willingness to do something constructive about their disenchantment. Involvement comes about not only because people know something is wrong. They must also be mobilized into action groups under recognizable leadership in pursuit of shared goals. A focus on claims-making activities aligns the concept of social movements with a constructionist perspective on social problems.

Feminism As Claims-Making

I myself have never been able to find out precisely what feminism is. I only know that people call me a feminist whenever I express sentiments that differentiate me from a doormat or prostitute.

—Rebecca West, English author and critic, 1913 (Gibbs, 1992: 39)

Women in Canada and the United States have long struggled to address issues about gender inequality. Marching to the slogan that the "personal is political" enabled various women's groups during the 1970s to politicize "the problem with no name," as Betty Friedan aptly called it. Feminism took off when women escaped dependence on men for their livelihood while claiming (birth) control over their fertility (Weldon, 1997). Emboldened by civil rights and anti-war activism, feminism drew inspiration from seeking social solutions to hitherto ignored or seemingly unimportant personal problems. Women united around the one thing that they shared in common, writes Dorothy Smith (2003)—the patriarchal exclusion of women from the sphere of public discourse (from the political to the cultural) and their subordination across a broad spectrum of family and work. Once this predicament was shared with other women, it quickly became a matter of social significance. Moreover, once women began to compare notes, says Fay Weldon, it became impossible for men to pick them off one by one. Nor was it permissible to bully, insult, and assault women behind closed doors. Imbalances over power would now be openly challenged in the public realm because of their rootedness in the structures of society, not simply in individual acts (Tweedlie, 1995). In brief, a social problem had emerged and feminism evolved into the vehicle for solving this problem once the personal was transformed into the social and politicized.

The impact of this collective protest has proven transformative. Feminism as a social movement has altered people's perceptions of gender relations as anything but natural or normal. It has also reshaped the status and role of women in society, while striking at the very foundational knowledge of a constitutional order that is anything but gender blind. To be sure, some have vilified feminism as a source of all social problems including family breakdowns. Others have praised it for its emancipatory qualities in releasing both women and men from rigidly scripted expectations; still others question the wisdom of portraying women as innately good, exploited by "phallocentric" structures, and perpetually destined to victim status, in effect denying the truth about the multi-dimensionality of women. The emergence of feminism has also been instrumental in changing cultural values by reshaping structural arrangements that historically have defined and distorted "who gets what."

Feminism, in general, consists of ideas and ideals pertaining to the goal of gender equality, even though the nature and characteristics of this equality is open to debate. It is predicated on the once rejected proposition that women are human beings whose normalcy and moral worth are equivalent to those of men (Gray, 1995). With feminism, women are treated as a central point of reference by bringing their experiences and realities into the foreground (Burt and Code, 1995). A gender-based analysis is now included in an information kit provided by the Status of Women in Canada (2003), one that dismisses gender neutrality (or gender blindness) on grounds that policies and programs do not have a neutral impact on recipients and that the genders are differently affected. Central to most feminisms is a proposed vision of society in which women and men can learn to equitably live together with their differences. Also integral is the rejection of a rigidly scripted and gendered division of labour that privileged men while disempowering women. True, challenging gender rules may make people uneasy since such a challenge privileges the counterintuitive notions of gender as constructions of culture rather than laws of nature (Heyding, 2003).

Yet feminism is not a single voice, much less a singular voice of experience. As a multi-vocal movement of criticism and activism, feminisms differ in terms of how they define the problem of gender inequality, as well as how best to solve this problem. Two dimensions prevail in sorting out the different types of feminism. First, can the problem of

TABLE 4.1	Comparing Feminisms	
	MEN/WOMEN = ALIKE	MEN/WOMEN = DIFFERENT
FEMINISMS THAT WORK WITHIN THE SYSTEM	**Liberal Pluralism** *Main Problem:* Unequal opportunities	**Conservative Feminism** *Main Problem:* Role changes
	Root Cause: Sex discrimination	*Root Cause:* Radical feminism
	Proposed Solution: Remove discrimination	*Proposed Solution:* Traditional division of labour
	Anticipated Outcome: Level playing field	*Anticipated Outcome:* Knowing one's place
FEMINISMS THAT REJECT THE SYSTEM	**Marxist/Socialist Feminism** *Main Problem:* Inequality as working class	**Radical Cultural Feminism** *Main Problem:* Devalued female culture
	Root Cause: Capitalist structures	*Root Cause:* Patriarchy
	Proposed Solutions: Transform society/capitalism	*Proposed Solutions:* Ideological transformation/ Abolish patriarchy
	Anticipated Outcome: An egalitarian Communism	*Anticipated Outcome:* Celebrate women's voices

gender inequality be solved by working within the system or by dismantling it? Second, in seeking solutions, are women and men basically alike or fundamentally different? The intersection of these two lines of thought creates four possibilities in securing a blueprint for feminist social movements, namely, liberal (working within the system + women and men are alike); Marxist/Socialist (working outside the system + women and men are alike); Radical Cultural (working outside the system + women and men are different); and conservative (working within the system + women and men are different). The table on the previous page provides a brief comparison based on the definition of the problem, root causes, proposed solutions, and anticipated outcomes.

Liberal Feminism: Levelling the Playing Field

Liberal feminism arises from classical liberal principles that extol individual freedoms and rights. With liberalism, what we have in common as rights-bearing, equally seeking, and autonomous individuals is more important in allocating outcomes or rewards than group-based differences. Yet women as a group rarely enjoy equal rights or equality of opportunity, much less equality of outcomes. Women in Canada are devalued because of their unequal participation in institutions outside the family or pink-collar ghetto jobs. For liberal feminists, this inequality arises from imperfections within an essentially sound system in which some degree of inequality is inevitable and necessary for individual and societal prosperity. Liberal feminists do not propose to dismantle the system or rearrange the basic institutions of society. Rather, their aim is to equalize the distribution of individuals (women and men) within the existing institutional arrangements by affirming women's rights to economic, political, and social equality. Liberal feminists endorse the basic integrity of the system. Equality can be achieved if women are allowed the opportunity to compete on level terms with men through the removal of sexist discriminatory barriers. Liberal feminism also rejects the possibility of essential differences between women and men, at least none that could justify the differentiation of employment or opportunities. Excessive emphasis on gender differences may have the effect, if not necessarily the intent, of reinforcing inequities through sex-role stereotyping. Not surprising, liberal feminists are criticized for their willingness to work within those male-constructed structures and existing power relations that created the problem in the first place (Gray-Rosendale and Harootunia, 2003).

Marxist/Socialist Feminism: "Workers (Women + Men) of the World Unite"

This variant of feminism is largely consistent with a radical conflict view of society as largely exploitative. Also endorsed is the idea of men and women as fundamentally alike in terms of their common interests and experiences as exploited. A Marxist feminism corresponds to a conflict perspective in situating inequality within the framework of capitalism, with its correlates of profit, private property, and class relations. Under capitalism, contend Marxist feminists, women are oppressed in the same way as men because both must sell their labour power to ensure physical survival. However, women, as a group, constitute the more exploited segment within the working class, and this division is exacerbated by the forces of patriarchy and the contradictions of the nuclear family arrangement. Because the problem is chronic and structural, a system devoted to the principles of private property and rational pursuit of profit is viewed as hopelessly flawed and inimical to female interests. In contrast to liberal feminism, Marxist feminism insists on a complete restructuring of society before true gender equality can kick in. The aim is to minimize private property, maximize the importance of human needs over profits, and abolish or reduce gender and class-based division of labour (Gray-Rosendale and Harootunia, 2003).

Radical Cultural Feminism: Dismantling Patriarchy

Radical cultural feminism rejects the legitimacy of the existing system, while arguing that women and men are fundamentally different (Greer, 1999). The celebration and politicization of women as different and valuable is central to radical cultural feminism. Gender differences are neither superficial nor the result of social conditioning. Rather, they reflect fundamentally different experiences. Women and men possess different interests and strengths, together with different aspirations, in part because of biology, in part because of different experiences pertaining to inequality, the threat of violence, and demeaning media images. Women speak in a different voice and are defined by their relationships to others, their ability to nurture and cooperate, and to engage in contextual thought. Men, by contrast, are thought to be locked into abstract analysis, driven by materialism and competition, and possessed by commitment to individual achievement. Women and men approach leadership differently: A women's voice is potentially transformative because of its commitment to connection, community, and communication; men's voices dwell on combativeness, hierarchy, and self-interest. In that the problem resides in the suppression of the distinctiveness of female experiences and values, the solution resides in privileging female difference by re-validating undervalued women's voices. By championing a matricentric society in which female interests and principles are central to the public sphere, a radical cultural feminism hopes to remodel society by transforming ideology along the lines of pacifism, cooperation, and nonviolent settlement of difference (Gray-Rosendale and Harootunian, 2003).

For radical cultural feminism, the basic source of oppression for women is not the capitalist system but the subjugation of women by men under patriarchy. Patriarchy is ultimately rooted in patterns of male superiority as it pertains to female subjugation and servitude. Just as the subordination of the proletariat is made natural under capitalism, so too is the subordination of women "naturalized" by patriarchal assumptions (Code, 1995). While capitalism and patriarchy are linked, even though analytically separate, the starting point for radical feminism focuses on how male hegemony is constructed and construed through everyday actions. The focus is on deconstructing the patriarchy in order to reassert the centrality and validity of female experiences. Patriarchal institutions that historically have enslaved women as women are criticized, particularly the nuclear family, which is seen as little more than domestic servitude in disguise. Finally, working within the system is counterproductive: According to Germaine Greer, women are robbed of their identities and opportunities when they desperately pursue equality with men within the existing structures instead of focusing on the liberation of women from their enslavement in a patriarchal system (Greer, 1999).

Did You Know?

Broadly consistent with radical cultural feminism is the emergence of rainbow feminism. White feminists are perceived to have a specific agenda, one rooted in issues pertaining to sexism or to classism, with men portrayed as the "enemy." Women of colour confront an additional set of pressures related to racism and ethnicity that are superimposed on and intersect with gender and class in creating overlapping and intersecting patterns of subordination that simultaneously amplify yet contradict (Stasiulis, 2000). Consider the contrasts: White women focus on issues ranging from glass ceilings, the cost of daycare facilities, job and pay equity, and workplace harassment. By contrast, women of colour worry about basic survival skills related to employment, rather than employment equity; about getting and holding a job, rather than harassment on the job or barriers to promotion; and about access to any childcare facilities, rather than shattering the glass ceiling. In the case of aboriginal women, they experience both physical violence but must also contend with the psychological violence of colonialism (Monture-Angus, 2003). In short, references to "woman" can no longer be defined as a static category encompassing a single shared ideal, but rather as a series of fluid identities relative to shifting political and economic contexts that impact differently on women because of radically different experiences, realities, and expectations (Gray-Rosendale and Harootunian, 2003). A rainbow feminism hopes to capitalize on this internal diversity by incorporating differences as a strength rather than a weakness (Roth, 2004).

Conservative Feminism: "The Good Old Days"

The last feminism is perhaps the most contentious, and many would prefer to exclude it altogether because of its seemingly regressive and reactionary stance. While most feminisms are challenging society to expand choices and chances for women, conservative feminism endorses a restriction of options anchored around a conventional division of labour. Conservative feminism is predicated on the idea that the system is fine, that women and men are fundamentally different, and inequalities will persist unless women and men do what comes naturally. Conservative feminism, as exemplified by the initiatives of groups such as "R.E.A.L. Women," espouses a view of equality that acknowledges women in traditional, maternal, domestic roles within the framework of a conventional social order. For conservative feminism the real problem involves too much change, rather than not enough, with predictable costs to family and traditional values. The solution rests with bringing back a traditional society in which "men were men" and "women knew their place." In short, the world would be a much better place if women reverted to their natural role in society ("barefoot and pregnant") through acceptance of women's scripted maternal–domestic role and scripturally ordained status.

A Post-Feminist Era or Third-Wave Feminism

We live in what is commonly defined as a post-feminist era. Post-feminist thinking is based on the notion that feminism as a social movement is irrelevant, in part because the battle for equality has been won, in part because the feminisms of the past focused too much on women as victims, while expounding agendas that seemed excessively rigid, confrontational, standardized (White), and humourless (Dicker and Piepmeier, 2003). In the belief that the battle against inequality and sexism has been won, a creeping complacency has set in that dismisses feminism as passé as the Cold War (MacIvor, 2003). Such a perception is not entirely correct, especially since the gains from the past cannot be taken for granted against the forces of resistance, backlash, and apathy. Gender equality in terms of political power, economic success, and institutional decision-making falls beyond the reach of women as a group. Both sexism and gender barriers remain persistent and pervasive in a patriarchal society, albeit in ways less blatant than before.

In short, reference to post-feminism is problematic. To one side, ours is hardly a post-feminist era that can claim victory in the struggle for gender equality. To the other side, the feminisms of the past no longer seem relevant. Feminists find themselves in a historical moment of unrest in which "… feminism of the 1970s is problematized, splintered, and considered suspect, one in which it is no longer easy, fun, empowering, or even possible to take a feminist position (Mascia-Lees and Sharpe, 2000). Multiple feminist positions co-exist with the result that we must speak of feminisms rather than feminism (Gray-Rosendale and Harootunian, 2003). New forms of feminism are engaging with feminisms in the past to create what is widely known as "third-wave feminism" (Dicker and Piepmeier, 2003). Third-wave feminism is as critical as ever, write Dicker and Piepmeier, one that is personally aware yet politically engaged and grounded on (a) the material realities and cultural productions of the 21st century (from globalization to the information revolution); (b) acknowledges a diversity of women's experiences, from White women to women of colour; and (c) concedes that identity is multifaceted, fluid, and intersectional so that gender intersects with other identity markers such as class or race to create both opportunities and costs that do not fall along a single axis. Of particular relevance to third-wave feminism is the high level of paradox. Political engagement and collective action may be critical, not by rejecting appeals to beauty, sex, and power, but by utilizing these attributes strategically to advance women's interests, while criticizing traditional approaches that fixate exclusively on appearances to demean and deny (Heywood and Drake, 1997). The dynamics of these contradictions promise to make for lively, if somewhat messy, politics.

DISCUSSION QUESTIONS

1   Compare and contrast the different types of feminisms in terms of their underlying logic.

2   What is meant by the expression that gender and gender relations are socially constructed and culturally constitutive?

3   Gender inequality remains a pervasive problem in Canadian society. Demonstrate how this is the case.

4   How can sociologists account for gender inequities? Use the case study in this chapter to illustrate your answer.

5   How and why has the concept of masculinity changed?

 WEBLINKS

Status of Women, Canada.   **www.swc-cfc.gc.ca**

Canadian Aboriginal women.   **www.canadianaboriginal.com/womenissues**

The National Organization of Immigrant and Visible Minority Women. **www.diversewomen.com**

part three

Institutions in Crisis

Canada in the new millennium is fundamentally different from the Canada that evolved during the 20th century. The demographics have shifted dramatically: From a predominantly French and English society, Canada has evolved into one of the world's most cosmopolitan societies with a level of institutional inclusiveness that is the envy of most. The politicization of this heterogeneity has challenged those colonialist constitutionalisms that once defined who got what, and why. Formerly marginalized groups, including women, First Nations, and people of colour have also taken advantage of this demographic shift to redefine the allocation of power, privilege, and wealth. A new horizontal society has emerged instead. As Lawrence Friedman writes in his book *The Horizontal Society*, a virtual reality in which traditional authority, conventional wisdom, existing institutions, and inherited hierarchies are no longer relevant or deferred to, much less able to provide the organizational basis for identity, meaning, or attachment (also Neil Nevitte's *The Decline of Deference,* 1998). Personal identities, once organized around the core institutions of religion, family, and political allegiance, are increasingly contested and subject to a host of conflicting definitions and provisional attachments. People increasingly endorse the idea that they possess both the right and the powers to define a life, a meaning, and an identity for themselves as unique individuals (Curtis, 1999). The idea that only centralized institutional structures can contribute to the building of society is being challenged by a belief that people will have to become self-organizing by way of internalized rules and provisional norms for behaviour (Fukuyama, 1999). In other words, it seems that we are living in an era where the prevailing rule is to break the rules.

The transformation of society from a reliance on vertical structures to increasingly horizontal processes is not without a host of social problems. Top-down authority cannot be casually discarded, given that any functioning social system depends on a moral centre with a corresponding set of rules. Challenges and transformations, notwithstanding, all societies must make arrangements for carrying out the basic functions related to the survival of its members. Of those imperatives at the forefront of human adaptation, few are as important as the following: production and distribution of food and material goods; maintenance of social order; protection of external boundaries; channels for effective decision-making; linkages to the supranatural world through religious practices; and arrangements for the socialization of children. Tribal ("premodern") societies tended to carry out these functions informally and without the benefit of specialists. By contrast, complex, modern societies often rely on formal agencies and trained professionals to discharge these social obligations.

Every society may be interpreted as a system of institutions for securing existence. Such an interpretation is particularly important to sociologists who rely on institutions as primary units for the analysis of society. An institutional approach begins with the assumption that human social life is organized around a set of responses for facilitating adaptation and survival. Formal agencies are established in which their mandate is to carry out activities of significance to society and the privileged classes. Institutions are examined from the vantage point of functions (what is supposed to happen or intended goals) for society, structure (how it looks including social roles and the prescribed rules for engagement or entitlement), and process (what really happens, both deliberately and inadvertently). Each institution possesses common features, namely, a set of underlying rules, role networks, and patterned relationships, all of which contribute to a relatively smooth operation. Certain questions come to mind in sorting through the thicket of institutions: Why do institutions exist in the first place; how effective are they in doing what they are supposed to do; are alternative social arrangements preferred during times of social change; and what are their impact and implications for society at large? Do institutions advance the interests of all individuals, vested interests, or interests of the institution? Do social problems arise when institutions don't do what they are supposed to do, thus posing a risk to individual well-being and societal survival? Not everyone agrees with this institutional approach to the study of social problems. The classification of reality into such self-contained units of reality is often repudiated as artificial or ethnocentric (Lee and Newby, 1983; Hale, 1989). Proposed instead are more process-oriented frameworks that focus on the claims-making experiences of those who collaborate to construct social reality.

Institutions have long proven a mainstay of human societies across time and space. Yet these same institutions have come under criticism with the onset of the present millennium. Outdated structures and monocultural mandates appear incapable of coping with the dizzying demands of a globalizing world and postmodern outlooks. The authority and deference that institutions routinely elicited are increasingly contested by those who defy the rigid and conformist scripts of the past. The need for informed and critical thought about what is happening, and why, is futher sharpened by the "crisis" of legitimacy that most institutions are experiencing, with an attendant loss of public confidence in their identity and rationale for existence. Still, for all the talk about crisis or collapse, modern institutions are not about to disappear from the social screen. Institutions appear to be taking their cue from the principle of "continuity within change"—that is, they are bending, but not breaking, in response to social transformations. Time will tell if the "crisis" that afflicts many contemporary institutions is temporary and transitional or the convulsive gasps of a collapsing arrangement.

In this section, the concept of institutions in crisis provides a conceptual peg for exploring select institutions from a social-problem perspective. The institutions chosen for analysis vary in terms of how they are structured, the role they play in people's lives, and the impact they exert on society. Nevertheless, each of these institutions has several attributes in common, not the least of which is growing public perception that they are in trouble. The interplay of diverse and demanding publics, together with social, political, economic, and cultural changes has undermined any consensus regarding the role and status of these institutions and their relationship to society. This identity crisis in confidence may be attributable to often contradictory sources: Institutions are criticized for undergoing too much change, or not enough change; for accommodating too much diversity, or having insufficient commitment to engagement with differences; for being too scripted to bend with changing and uncertain times, or too loosely organized to anchor guidelines for behaviour; and for catering to too narrow a target, or being too expansive in trying to be everything to everyone.

The institutions chosen for analysis in this section include the family, the criminal justice system, the mainstream media, health and health care, education, and the workplace. Each of these institutions is framed as a social problem in its own right by virtue of institutional design or dynamics. Each is also seen as creating social problems for those whose lives are implicated by these institutions, either as participants or recipients. Proposed solutions to the problems of institutions in crisis are addressed as well. To the extent that most solutions tend to generate more problems, thus intensifying the crisis at hand, the contradictions are not necessarily indicative of poor planning, design, or implementation. Rather, the elusiveness of solutions to complex and contradictory social problems is a function of a world that is diverse, changing, interconnected, and increasingly uncertain. Inasmuch as these institutional crises may also herald new opportunities for creative growth—that these institutions are in *transition* rather than in *trouble*—this section imparts a decidedly positive spin to the future of criminal justice, family, media, health care, education, and the workplace.

chapter five

Crime and Control

FRAMING THE PROBLEM

Most sociology aims at improving our understanding of human behaviour. Sociologists focus on why we behave the way we do by looking at social factors as explanatory cues. No less sociologically interesting is the study of human misbehaviour, that is, why do we engage in antisocial actions that many regard as deviant or break the law? Yet the study of deviant behaviour poses an interesting challenge, sociologically speaking. On the one hand, many Canadians routinely obey traffic signs, pay their bills on time, do as they are told, and would never think of breaking the law even if their life depended on it. On the other hand, there are those Canadians who would rather cut corners than conform, take pride in not giving a damn about breaking rules, routinely ignore traffic signals, engage in provocations that activate law enforcement, and think nothing of ripping off the establishment at every opportunity. In between these admittedly extreme types— the law-abiding on one side and the criminally-oriented on the other—are those who will tempt fate by cutting corners if the opportunity arises. They will conform under normal circumstances but are not averse to bending the law if the risks are low and the rewards worthwhile.

Is there an explanatory framework that can span such a continuum of behaviour? Sociologists have long acknowledged the pervasiveness of conformity in human behaviour. The vast majority of people observe the roles expected of them while playing by the rules in coping with everyday challenges. Both a stable and coherent social order depends on such compliance and control. Yet deviance and crime are no less integral a strand of the social fabric, albeit in a perverse way. Just as people are conditioned by a culture of conformity and restraint, so too do they internalize rules that encourage them to tempt fate, skip corners, bend rules, play brinkmanship, or take advantage of others—all the better if they think they can get away with it. In other words, deviance and crime are remarkably mundane and routine activities. The idea that "everybody's doing it" reinforces the ubiquity of deviance and crime: that is, the same pressures that encourage conformity and consensus may also stimulate deviance and criminality if the timing is right.

Not that criminality is restricted to a certain class of individuals. Even the most hardened criminals behave normatively when necessary (think of the TV series "The Sopranos"); conversely, so-called "normal" people can act out of character by resorting to misdeeds that transgress social norms or laws of the land. This makes it difficult to divide the world into "good guys" and "bad guys," given the situational nature of rule-following or rule-breaking. Still, another paradox complicates a distinction between "social" (normative) and "anti-social" behaviour (deviant). Under some circumstances, rule-following may be interpreted as deviant, for example, driving the speed limit on multi-lane highways; in other contexts, certain deviant actions may be deemed "normative." For example, jaywalking or speeding are but two deviant activities in which violations may be the rule rather than the exception.

This continuum of commitment to the social order perplexes sociologists. Why do some obey and conform? Why do others commit crime and act uncivilized in a civil society? And why do still others engage in both regardless of the consequences? Sociologists have long debated the responses to these questions, with little unanimity to show for it. Nevertheless, most look to the centrality of social context in explaining people's behaviour, both normative and deviant. Solutions to the problem of crime must be customized accordingly. But the prospect of controlling crime is no less of a paradox insofar as the so-called solution to the problem of crime (the criminal justice system) generates an additional set of problems. Many Canadians believe the criminal justice system has lost the fight against crime: The police can't keep our streets safe; courts no longer dispense justice; and prisons represent a bottomless pit of tax money. For some, crime is increasing because the system is too "soft" on offenders; for others, the system is too rigid and exclusive, thus inciting more crime than necessary; and for still others, the enormous expenditures do not justify the outcome (Jackson, 2002). Massive outlays in expense and energy notwithstanding, public fears of victimization are escalating, although concerns are often misplaced or baseless, in large part because what is known about crime depends on who is caught and what is reported. Consider the following debates:

- Do minorities or youth commit more crimes, or are they just more likely to be apprehended because of greater visibility and selective police surveillance?
- Do police apply the law uniformly, or are they abusing their discretionary powers by victimizing some while turning a blind eye to others?
- Are there race and ethnic differences in rates of violent crime? What are the causes of these disparities, assuming they exist (Hawkins, 2003)?
- Why do some get caught and pay the price for law-breaking while others get off lightly despite the enormity of the crime?

- How is it that specific types of deviant activities (for example, street crime of the dispossessed) are vigorously enforced, while white-collar crime is relatively immune to the discretionary arm of the law?
- Who are the main beneficiaries of law and law enforcement: Society? Individuals? Vested interests?
- How do individuals become deviants; how do they sustain their involvement in deviant subcultures; how do they come to be labelled as criminals by the dominant culture; and how do they respond to institutional efforts at control?
- Is the criminal justice doing its job or does it provide a fertile breeding ground for more criminality

The list could go on; let it suffice, however, to conclude with a warning to the wise. While many Canadians regard crime and control as a pressing social problem, there is little consensus about what is going on, and why. Even more elusive is any convergence over how to solve the seemingly insolvable problem of controlling the seemingly uncontrollable.

Sociologists aren't the only ones fascinated with the topics of crime and control. The trifecta of "cops," "courts," and "corrections" remains a staple of the entertainment industry. The combination of "cops 'n robbers," together with "nuts, sluts, and perverts," has proven a sure-fire money maker for Hollywood. The sensationalization of crime on TV is megabusiness despite mounting concern over the impact of distorted coverage on audience perceptions and institutional policies (Doyle, 2003). News is no less hooked on crime and the criminal justice system because of the competition for audience ratings and advertising revenues. Such massive and relentless exposure is not without consequences since most individuals acquire their understanding of crime and control from the mainstream media. Not surprisingly, the public is increasingly worried that a crime-storm is brewing to the detriment of society (Sher and Marsden, 2003). The social stabilizers of society are thought to be collapsing under the relentless onslaught of gun-toting punks and cowering authorities, in effect, prompting yet more calls for punitive measures in stamping out crime.

The problem of how to deal with crime in a modern society is one that plagues most countries (Consedine, 2003). Canadians are genuinely worried about their safety, are quick to endorse measures that appear to do something about the crime problem, and readily pounce on perceived shortcomings in the criminal justice system. Crime rates may be falling and positive alternatives are available; nevertheless, the criminal justice system remains stuck in a 19th century time warp. State-centred responses to law and order are failing badly judging by people's growing concern over safety and control (McLaughlin et al., 2003). Prisons are dinosaurs of the modern age that fail to rehabilitate or are expensive—an expensive way of making "bad" people worse by taking large numbers of hopeless people and turning them into bitter hopeless people (Consedine, 2003). In other words, the retributive model of criminal justice, with its focus on punishment and imprisonment, appears to have morphed into a "monster" that many define as criminally unjust. Yet, paradoxically, the public seems to want more of the very policies and programs that are failing them and which they criticize. Such warped thinking seems to strike at the very root of crime and control as a social problem.

This chapter explores the dynamics of crime and control as a major social problem in Canada. The chapter is organized around a sociological perspective on crime and control, with an emphasis on the broader context of causes, characteristics, consequences, and cures. The concept of crime as a social problem pivots around key questions: (a) "how much" (b) "what kind," (c) "who commits crime," and (d) "why." The reasons behind crime vary with the sociological perspective that is employed, namely, functionalism, conflict, and social interactionism. Each perspective is shown to differ in assumptions, subject matter, and conclusions, while expanding on those aspects of crime that others tend to underplay. This chapter also addresses the perils and promises of crime control in Canada. The criminal justice system is analyzed as a "solution" to the crime problem, with particular emphasis on the challenges confronting "cops," "courts," and "corrections." Evidence suggests that structural flaws and operational loopholes in Canada's criminal justice system have proven as much of a problem as a solution. The chapter concludes by exploring several initiatives to reform the system along the lines of restorative/aboriginal justice.

The social dimensions of crime and control—that is, the relationship of crime to society—is a central theme of this chapter. Crime is interpreted not only in the legal sense, but as a social problem resulting from an unequal distribution of power, privilege, and resources. As a social problem, crime (a) originates in a social context (from need to greed); (b) is defined as a problem by laws that may reflect vested interests; (c) exerts a disruptive impact on victims and society; and (d) is amenable to solution by way of treatment—at least in theory, if not always in practice. Three themes prevail: First, to inform readers about crime and control in Canada by debunking widely accepted myths that feed into people's fear of crime. Second, to better understand Canada by examining Canadian society through the prism of crime and control. Third, to sharpen our knowledge of social problems by filtering the issues through a crime and control lens, without trivializing either social costs or consequences to victims. The conclusion is inescapable: Crime is a problem that costs all Canadians, thus making it a responsibility of every Canadian to help solve a problem that is more social than legal.

WHAT IS CRIME?

Even casual observation confirms the obvious: The vast majority of people play by the rules in coping with daily demands and everyday challenges. Most observe the roles expected of them, defer to norms that underpin a variety of circumstances, and accept punishment as the cost of breaking widely accepted rules. Those who routinely follow the rules tend to congratulate themselves as integrated, well-adjusted, and law-abiding. Conversely, those who stray from the straight and narrow find they are labelled as misfits or degenerates (or venerated by some as "cool"). The fact that law breakers conform most of the time, while conformists will break laws when opportunity knocks confirms the complexity in defining the problem.

Two lines of thought approach crime in Canada. For some, Canada should be congratulated as a relatively safe place to live. Rates of crime, especially those involving weapons and violence, are deemed as low by international standards. To be sure, there is a growing perception of crime surges in major cities as youth turns to guns and gangs for revenge or profit. Others are concerned with immigrants who allegedly import criminal practices into Canada. To its credit, Canada is seen as an oasis of tranquility when compared with the anarchy in other parts of the world. But comparisons across time and place pose problems. Each country may use different categories for definition or assessment. Nor is it clear if crime rates are based on arrests, charges, or convictions. Nevertheless, there is a perception that crime is under control in Canada, especially by comparison with pockets of lawlessness in the United States.

There is yet another perception of crime in Canada at odds with this glowing assessment. Public fear of crime continues to escalate despite official reports that the situation is improving. A crisis of confidence in the criminal justice system is escalating as well: Police are not catching enough crooks; sentencing and enforcement are too lenient; recidivism continues to baffle the best minds; and laws are not tough enough, especially on the young. Moreover, police themselves may be the problem: Youth at risk in high risk zones such as Jane–Finch in Toronto rank police and police harassment as their second greatest worry just behind drug activity (Smith, 2003). People are also perturbed by inefficiencies in the criminal justice system. Take, for example, the so-called crime funnel: Most crimes do not result in arrests, most arrests do not result in convictions, and most convictions do not result in imprisonment.

Not surprisingly, Canadians appear poorly informed about the magnitude of crime in Canada. They are even less well-informed about the often-beleaguered efforts at crime control and social order. Who can blame them? Most people's knowledge of crime and control is not first hand but derived primarily from mass media. The news media tend to focus on the sensational with the result that newscasting exaggerates what rarely happens while glossing over the routine and mundane (Fleras, 2003). Film media depictions of random violent acts by strangers tend to be disproportionate to their real-world occurrence. TV programming is no less guilty of glorifying crime. As a staple of many prime-time shows, crime is often depicted as a way of solving problems that conveys an air of finality. But TV depictions of crime and control are so one-sided, that what audiences see on television may contradict what really happens (Surrette, 1998). This ignorance or confusion not only makes it more difficult to solve a major social problem; public anxieties about the scope of criminal activity may also contribute to poor policy making. Such a glaring omission makes it doubly important to understand the relationship of crime to deviance.

Crime As Deviance/Deviance As Crime

Crime falls under the broader category of deviance. Deviance can be defined as public disapproval of those actions that violate a "widely accepted" norm. Norms themselves consist of rules or ideas about how people should act in a particular situation. Deviance entails a breach of a norm, followed by some kind of reaction or punishment. This recognized violation of norm is remarkably routine; after all, the proliferation of rules in society makes it nearly impossible to observe all social norms or legal statutes. Such universality also makes it futile to divide the world into deviants or non-deviants, conformists or criminals. Even the most saintly or sanctimonious engage in some deviant acts, often inadvertently, and do so for the same reasons as "hardcore" deviants: namely, to achieve culturally defined goals without excessive cost or commitments. Moreover, not all references to deviance imply negativity. As the authors of *The Deviant's Advantage* point out, deviation as a marked departure from the norm provides a source of innovation, font of new ideas, and catalyst behind new products and markets.

Disapproval is central to the notion of deviance. Without disapproval, there is no deviance. The centrality of reaction reminds us that deviance is not something inherent within the individual or intrinsic to reality, with a readily fixed label that proclaims "deviant." Deviance is a label assigned to certain individuals or groups of activities because they threaten authorities, undermine tradition, challenge privilege, or upset the status quo. Reactions to deviance can run the gamut from gentle rebuke to outright ridicule and rejection, depending on the magnitude of the misdeed, namely: (a) how harmful or dangerous the violation is; (b) the intent of the deviant; (c) the repetitiveness of violations; (d) the competence of the person committing the act; and (e) the degree of group consensus regarding the seriousness of the violated norm. Disapproval is mild at best for acts that are annoying rather than dangerous; others, such as drinking and driving, are condemned as serious infractions worthy of formal attention. Not surprisingly, what constitutes deviance and crime varies across place; what is normal in one society may be deviant in another place or time. Chewing gum is socially acceptable in many circles, but regarded as mildly deviant in formal settings, is discouraged in public venues such as movie theatres, and is punishable by law in some Malaysian countries. Definitions of crime and deviance also vary over time. For example, consider changing public reactions to smoking in public venues. What once was accepted as the norm was gradually redefined as deviant and eventually formalized as unlawful behaviour when second-hand smoke was framed as a public health risk.

Defining Crime

In general, crime is about breaking the law. More specifically, crime can be defined as a complex process involving an offender, a victim and law intersecting at a particular point in time and space (Andresen et al., 2003). Viewed in this light, crime is a subset of the broader category of deviance, while law itself is subsumed under the category of norm. Crime itself may be classified in different ways. For example, the legal system in Canada distinguishes between crimes punishable by two years less a day (provincial jail) or more than two years (federal penitentiary). Sociologists often utilize a different typology based on what happens. Some

Key Definitions

What is the relationship between norms and deviance? Norms and laws? Deviance and crime? Laws consist of those norms that have been formalized into legal statutes of right or wrong. Public disapproval of certain actions deemed as deviant may exert pressure on central authorities to codify this growing intolerance into law. Those who break a law commit a deviance known as a crime. In that criminal acts pose a threat to society or vested interests, they are subject to control by formal state agencies better known as the criminal justice system.

Norm
A widely accepted and expected rule of behaviour in a particular context

Law
A formalized (legalized) norm

Deviance
Recognized violation of a widely accepted norm

Crime
Violation of a norm that has been formalized into law

Social Control
Both formal and informal practices to ensure conformity with norms or laws, prevent antisocial behaviour, or deal with incidents of deviance or crime

Criminal Justice System
A formal (or institutional) response to violations of law by way of the police, courts, and prisons

divide crime along the lines of violent, property, white-collar, and victimless. Others, such as Kendall et al. (2004), divide crime into street crimes (violent, property, and morals), corporate crime (crime committed during the course of employment), organized crime (business that supplies illegal goods and services), and political crimes (involving an abuse of power).

CRIME IN CANADA: HOW MUCH?

How much crime is there in Canada? Such a question would strike many as pivotal in the fight against crime. Yet there is no consensus with regard to responses. What we know about crime reflects what is reported to the police or by victims. Such reporting is not entirely reliable in its own right. Data are not like tangible objects for the picking. Rather data are a social construction since they have to be collected, coded, and interpreted in a particular context, for a particular reason, and for particular interests. Furthermore, crime rates cannot include what is NOT reported to police or by victims. But like the tip of the proverbial iceberg, what is exposed may be less formidable than what is hidden. For example, sexual offences comprise about 1 percent of official crime statistics. Yet more than 90 percent of sex crimes are never reported—an underreporting rate that may be higher than for any other criminal category. Furthermore, despite increased enforcement, prosecution and imprisonment, including a 400 percent increase in the last decade, only one sex offender in 100 is apprehended and sent to jail (Aboriginal Healing Foundation, 2002). Finally, certain types of white-collar crimes tend to be underrepresented. Many are difficult to detect or prosecute, and are treated more leniently by the courts—despite the enormity of the costs such as human injury or environmental destruction.

Despite these caveats, what is known about crime in Canada? With several exceptions, reported crime in Canada has declined over the past decade. Since peaking in 1991, according to Statistics Canada, the national crime rate has dipped by 27 percent, with police reporting a total of 2.4 million Criminal Code violations in 2002, excluding minor charges such as traffic offences. Criminal Code offences (excluding traffic offences) stood at 7589 per 100 000 population in 2002—a drop from 8136 per 100 000 population in 1998 (Statistics Canada, 2004). Robberies and sexual assaults continue to decline, with property crime at its lowest level in 30 years. Still, it is a little early to uncork the champagne: The current figure is still about triple the rate of about 3000 per 100 000 population in 1962. Moreover, bucking the downward trend are violent youth offences and certain types of organized crime (including drug dealing, prostitution, and fraud) (Canadian Press, 25 July, 2003). True, the number of youth murders has remained static; of growing concern, however, is the increasingly random pattern of vicious assaults by those youths in gangs who appear unfazed or lack any remorse (Canadian Press, 8 December, 2003). Finally, local patterns can buck national trends. For example, the overall crime rate in the Waterloo Region increased by 2 percent in 2001 and 2002, partly because of car thefts, fraud, and break-ins (*KW Record*, 15 May, 2003). Yet the region's violent crime (murder, abduction, assault, robbery) declined by 9 percent over the same time period.

Homicide rates are considered an indicator—a social barometer—in exposing the magnitude of crime and violence in Canada (Andresen, 2003). Unlike property crimes, which may not be reported to the police, homicides are unlikely to go unnoticed, thus reflecting a reasonably accurate snapshot of what is "going down." In 2001, there were 554 homicides in Canada, compared to 582 in 2002—an increase largely attributable to the 15 bodies found at Robert Pickton's Port Coquitlam pig farm. At 1.78 per 100 000 of population,

Canada's homicide rate puts it around the middle of the pack for industrial countries. A 30-year decline is noticeable: the 701 murders in 1975 represented a ratio of 3.09 per 100 000 of population. However, a degree of caution is necessary. Statistical techniques that focus on an age-adjusted homicide rate suggest a somewhat different picture (Andresen et al., 2003). Furthermore, the decline in homicide rates may reflect life-prolonging improvements in medical technology and ambulance response times.

Who does it? Friends, spouses, and acquaintances commit most of the homicides, with 53 percent of the victims killed in their home. Strangers commit comparatively few random acts of murder, despite massive media coverage to the contrary (Doyle, 2003). Of the 429 solved homicides in 2001 (125 remain unsolved), 13 percent were committed by strangers, 20 percent by spouses or partners, 23 percent by other family members, and 44 percent by acquaintances. Children under the age of two were the most likely homicide victims according to a 1997 Statistics Canada report. At 33 per 1 000 000, the rate for children was seven times higher than for those between two and 17, five times higher than for those 18 to 64, and eight times higher than for those over 65. Homicides related to gang activity are up sharply as well, from 21 in 1995 to 71 in 2000. Rates of homicide also vary by city. Winnipeg (2.77 per 100 000) and Edmonton (2.61 per 100 000) led the pack in 2001, while Ottawa (0.36 per 100 000) and Quebec (0.72 per 100 000) ranked lowest. Toronto was in the middle at 1.6 per 100 000. Guns continue to be the weapon of choice, according to the 1997 annual homicide survey by Statistics Canada, with 33.2 percent of the deaths gun-related, followed by stabbing (28.9), beating (19.8), and strangling (9.0).

Did You Know?

A similar pattern of crime decline can be discerned in the United States. With the exception of murder, which showed a slight increase, violent crimes fell by 9 percent in 2001 (Associated Press, 2002). Data collected from the National Crime Victimization Survey, FBI, and Bureau of Justice confirmed violent offending at its lowest level since the inception of surveys in 1973. Violent crime has dropped by nearly 50 percent since 1993, partly because of a more robust economy, smarter policing, an ageing population, and tougher sentencing laws. But homicide by guns continues to be a major problem. The rate for gun deaths in the United States is 14.24 per 100 000 people in 1998, compared to Japan at 0.05 deaths per 100 000. Handguns may have contributed to 99 deaths in Canada, whereas the handgun total in the United States was 9976. In Toronto, 26 of the 58 homicide victims in 2003 (inclusive to the end of November) involved gun play. These figures should come as no surprise according to Fred Matthews, director of research and development at Central Toronto Youth Services. Guns are the great equalizer for marginal youth seeking acceptance or deference. Guns not only follow an illegal drug trade, but they also draw attention to youth, create power among peers, establish identities, and defy the adult world.

To sum up: Evidence points to a gradual decrease in reported crime in Canada. Yet this statement needs to be qualified. First, changes in rates of criminal offending may say more about changes in police cataloguing procedures than in public behaviour. For example, a decline in youth crime rates is anticipated because of new federal law that diverts youthful offenders away from the criminal justice system into alternatives or rehabilitation (Blackwell, 2003). Second, a sense of perspective is valuable: Of the 5399 serious injuries in Canada between 1999 and 2000, according to the Canadian Institute for Health Information, 48 percent were caused by motor vehicle collisions, 27 percent by falls, and 17 percent by other. Criminal acts contributed to only 8 percent of all serious injuries. Third, people's perception and fear of crime continues to escalate despite evidence to suggest otherwise. Such a divide suggests that public attitudes are driven by media coverage and political electioneering. Media preference for the negative and sensational creates an overrepresentation of random violent acts. Nor is there any evidence to suggest that smarter policing is having an appreciable effect on reducing rates of criminal offending, although the impact of community-based policing initiatives should not be dismissed. The drop in criminal offending may simply reflect a declining proportion of younger people than in the past.

CRIME IN CANADA: WHAT KIND?

The face of crime has shifted. Thirty years ago, gambling was illegal, robberies were uncommon, as were auto thefts, and sexual assaults were reported to the police only as a last resort. Today, gambling has become socially acceptable, robberies are commonplace, auto thefts doubled to 177 286 between 1986 and 1996, and both domestic and sexual assault are routinely processed by authorities (Barrick, 1998). In 2002, about 2.4 million Criminal Code offences (excluding traffic offences) were reported, a drop from about 2.5 million in 1998 and 27 percent below the peak rate in 1991 (Statistics Canada, 2004). Of these, about 53 percent were property crimes, 13 percent were crimes of violence, and about 34 percent were other Criminal Code offences. A more detailed breakdown revealed that the most common property crimes were theft under $5000, followed by break and enter, motor vehicle theft, and fraud. Police reported about 300 000 violent crimes in 2002 with decreases in most major categories including attempted murder, assault, robbery, and abduction. Assaults from level 1 to 3 including sexual assaults were the most common violent crimes, with nearly two-thirds of these deemed to be minor assaults. Of growing concern is the explosion of organized criminal gangs who operate with relative impunity in corrupting, extorting, smuggling, and swindling their way through life (Humphreys and Bell, 2003). According to a confidential report by the RCMP (Blackwell, 2004), massive police raids to dismantle the Hell's Angels and other motorcycle gangs have yielded little appreciable effect on their criminal activities.

In assessing how much and what kind of crime, white-collar crimes are often overlooked. How do we account for the underenforcement of white-collar crime—most frequently associated with the likes of the Enron Corporation, Martha Stewart, or Hollinger Inc.? Law enforcement revolves around those street crimes that are more easily detected and punished. The police are more likely to patrol densely populated areas, in effect resulting in higher charge and arrest rates. Attention is directed away from crimes that stray outside this context, including those that pose problems for policing (including white-collar crime dealing with forgery, embezzlement, and work safety violations). White-collar crime is difficult to detect, still harder to prevent or punish once uncovered (Powell, 2003). Most white-collar crimes are committed by individuals with higher status in the community, making it difficult to bring criminals to justice when business ranks close. Finally, white-collar criminals possess the resources with which to fight the charges, making it even more difficult to prosecute them.

CRIME IN CANADA: WHO DID IT?

Sociologists are interested in studying who commits crimes. Crime in general is common across the entire population; nevertheless, criminal activity varies unevenly across sectors of society. Individuals who commit crime tend to fall into five major categories based on age, gender, ethnicity, class, and region.

Age

Those between the ages of 18 and 34 are most likely to be charged with breaking the law. According to Statistics Canada, less than 5 percent of people aged 12–17 were charged with a Criminal Code offence, a figure that has remained relatively stable for over a decade. Most Canadians believe that youth crime is on the rise. But the rate of youths charged for all criminal code offences (excluding traffic offences) continues to drop to 3955 per 100 000 population in 2002, compared to 4386 per 100 000 population in 1998 (Statistics Canada, 2003). Youth crime is generally more property oriented than violent crime, accounting for 44 percent of youth crime in 2002, while violent crimes represented 24 percent and other criminal offences at 32 percent (Statistics Canada, 2004). Property crimes by youth declined from 2206 per 100 000 to 1732 per 100 000, with theft under $5000 the most common offence (991 per 100 000), followed by breaking and entering (653 per 100 000) and motor vehicle theft (254 per 100 000). Crimes of violence increased slightly to 933 per 100 000 in 2002 from 906 per 100 000 in 1998 and 832 per 100 000 in 1991. A total of 42 youths were charged with homocide in 2002, up from a low of 30 in 2001 but down from a high of 68 in 1995. Nearly 70 percent of violent crimes committed by youths were assaults, although this figure represented only 17 percent of all youths charged. All levels of assault increased to 680 per 100 000 including sexual assault (64 per 100 000), while robberies decreased to 133 per 100 000 as did homocides 1.7 per 100 000 and attempted murders (2.6 per 100 000). Other Criminal Code offences such as public mischief remained relatively stable at 1290 per 100 000 population.

Young people are often depicted by the media as more offending and law-breaking than was once the case. Evidence would suggest otherwise: According to Statistics Canada data, there has been little change in the level of youth crime since the late 1980s (Carrington, 1999). Even here caution is necessary. Allegations of increased youth offending may reflect growing public awareness and willingness to report certain incidents. Zero tolerance toward certain forms of deviance had led to automatic charges and arrests. For example, what may have been a schoolyard scuffle followed by an after-class detention may now result in a police visit. Even parents are increasingly willing to transfer responsibility of their unruly children over to the proper authorities.

Gender

For the most part, both violent and property crime that come to the attention of authorities are concentrated among young, unmarried males. Males tend to dominate in virtually all crime statistics categories. Most crimes are committed by male adults against other males, according to Lydia Miljan, director of the Fraser Institute's national media archive, and they usually involve drugs or alcohol and often occur late at night. Men constitute 85 percent of the accused, with the median age of the accused rising from 26 in 1974 to 32 in 1997. Half of those accused, and a third of the victims, had consumed alcohol or drugs. But while men commit most of the crime, the rates for women are increasing. Young women between the ages of 12 and 17 accounted for 22 percent of those charged in 1997, up sharply from 16 percent in 1987. The rate of violent crime by female youths (5652 charged in 1998) has increased twice as fast as for male youths (16 493 charged in 1998). Men continue to be the primary victims, constituting nearly two-thirds of the total.

Why do men do it? The reasons are many and open to dispute but often point to relatively unstructured lifestyles that encourage aggression, risk-taking, and the acting out of violence for public display. Cultural reasons may reflect a desire for adventure and non-conformity, a craving for the respect of others, a defence of status or turf, or an expression of virility. Fascination with guns and gangs has long underpinned male youth culture. Precipitating causes are apt to include drink or drugs, while root causes extend to broken families, child abuse, and exposure to violence in the media. Additional root causes may extend to defective socialization, breakdowns in informal pressure, and inefficient formal agencies. Young men may experience a disconnection from society. Many are caught in the crossfire of conflicting demands involving the new economy, changing definitions of masculinity, and the erosion of traditional privileges.

In short, crime is gendered. Men, especially those between 18 and 34, commit nearly all the violent crimes in society, prompting a European report on crime to conclude that if men behaved like women, the courts would be idle and the prisons empty. To be sure, women and girls are hardly innocent, particularly as young women turn to crime for fun and profit but not nearly to the same extent as males. Even the rationale for crimes may be different (Silverman and Kennedy, 1998). Women may aggress in reaction to domestic violence or to protect themselves and their children from further male violence. Women may not be able to walk away from an abusive relationship because they (and their children) are economically dependent or risk the possibility of being murdered if they dare to leave. By contrast, males' violence toward others is aimed at controlling or subjugation—either by intimidating or terrorizing victims.

Region

Crime (both volume and types) varies by region in Canada. Canada averaged 8102 incidents per 100 000 population in 1998. This figure conceals variation by province and cities.

- Provincially, Newfoundland had the lowest rate at 5803 per 100 000, while British Columbia, with 12 141 per 100 000, and Saskatchewan with 12 403 per 100 000, had the highest. Ontario's rate stood at 7020 per 100 000, a drop of 5.8 percent since 1997. The Northwest Territories had the highest rate of crime at 23 266 per 100 000 population.

- Cities are no less variable: According to Statistics Canada, property crimes over a three-year average between 1999 and 2001 varied from a low of 2403 per 100 000 of population in Mississauga and 2720 per 100 000 in St John's to 10 337 per 100 000 in Vancouver and 7543 per 100 000 in Halifax. Toronto ranks near the bottom with 3500 per 100 000. Or consider vehicle thefts: Regina with 1996 per 100 000 of population and Winnipeg with 1581 per 100 000 of population ranked highest in 2001, while Victoria at 354 per 100 000 and Toronto with 370 per 100 000 ranked at the bottom (*Toronto Star,* 9 January, 2003).

- Violent crime in cities also varies. According to 2002 Statistics Canada data, Regina had the highest violent crime rate, followed by Saskatoon, Thunder Bay, Winnipeg, and Halifax. Sherbrooke had the lowest violent crime rate, followed by Saguenay, Quebec City, Trois Rivieres, and the Waterloo Region. Homicides vary by cities as well.

Class

Crime rates are not immune to distribution by class. Some have assumed that the poor and working classes were more criminally inclined because of denied opportunities and harsh social circumstances. Others disagree: The poor do not necessarily commit more crime than the affluent; they are simply more likely to be caught, charged, and convicted. Poverty is not necessarily a cause of crime; nevertheless, the root causes of criminal offending reflect the reality of being poor, unemployed, undereducated, and victimized by substance addiction and a history of abuse (Consedine, 1999). Neither poverty nor inequality per se are causes of crime; rather an inequality and poverty that is perceived by victims as unfair or inescapable may prove a factor.

Others have proposed a correlation between social class and certain types of crime: Serious crimes involving drugs and guns are more common in the lower classes, while "less serious" crimes are more evenly distributed through all sectors. For still others, such as conflict theorists, even the nature of the criminal activity reflects a class bias. A class bias can be detected in what is defined as crime, who is singled out as criminal, and how individuals are processed through the criminal justice system. Laws that define crime tend to reflect the interests of the rich and powerful, with the result that street crime, rather than corporate crime, is more likely to be detected. A class bias is also reflected in differential conviction and sentencing for working class and ruling class offences (Samuelson, 1998). In other words, official statistics may distort the relationship between class and crime since "white-collar" crimes rarely come to police attention or lead to prosecution (Jack, 2003).

Ethnicity

Does race or ethnicity have anything to do with criminality (Hawkins, 2003)? Do certain ethnicities endorse values and norms that prompt law-breaking? Do minorities commit more crime, or are they just more likely to be caught and charged because of their appearance, the visibility of street crimes, police prejudices and profiling, and greater likelihood of successful prosecution? Police bias may stem from unconscious racial stereotyping that makes it easier for police to bust some poor Black kids smoking crack on the street corner rather than to grab some rich White kids snorting coke in the bedroom of their gated community (Taslitz, 2003). Rates of minority offending may be distorted by the selectivity inherent in processing minority women and men through the criminal justice system. This bias also has the effect of racializing crime along racial and ethnic lines, thus further amplifying the risk of detection and apprehension.

Information about ethnicity and crime is spotty and unreliable. Studies suggest that, while immigrants commit less crime than the Canadian-born, with some exceptions, some immigrant groups tend to be jailed at higher rates than their proportion in the population. For example, according to Wortley (2003), the federal incarceration for Black Canadians was 146 per 100 000, or almost five times the rate for White Canadians at 31 per 100 000. Ethnicity may be a variable that correlates with certain types of crime, according to the Canadian Centre for Justice Statistics (Galloway, 1999; also Humphreys and Bell, 2003). Canada's five major organized crime groups are thought to be divided along ethnic lines, with each perceived to have its own area of criminal expertise. Eastern Europeans are perceived to specialize in counterfeiting; Asian groups prefer extortion; aboriginal groups are focused on firearms trafficking and contraband smuggling of cigarettes and alcohol; White motorcycle gangs tend to smuggle both guns and explosives; and Italians are linked with money-laundering through the use of legitimate businesses.

How do we account for these connections? There is no reason to assume an innate biological disposition for minorities to commit crime. Social factors provide answers: First, high rates of criminality (assuming they exist) reflect conditions of control and oppression that minorities have historically encountered (Hawkins, 2003). Under conditions of profound and prolonged subordination, minority groups may turn hostility and violence inwards against members of their own group (Fanon, 1968). Young men gravitate toward gangs as one way of preying on their "own kind," while asserting some degree of social status and deference from the community at large. Second, many minorities and aboriginal peoples are economically disadvantaged groups, with few resources to escape charges or avoid prison. Prejudices and stereotypes increase the risk of police attention. Minorities' visibility and cultural lifestyles may also foster negative encounters with the police. The interplay of street life and petty crime with police contact become increasingly interlinked, feeding into each other and making it difficult for street youth to break this cycle. Arrests add further links to this chain of adversity, with the result that minority youth are further embedded within a criminal justice system that cannot possibly address the cumulative disadvantages they confront (McCarthy and Hagan, 2003: 137). Third, the presence of both open and systemic discrimination intensifies the divide. The law appears to be protective of the White middle class, yet remains a source of worry for people of colour. For minorities, the criminal justice system is perceived as racist by virtue of the power differences; by contrast, most Whites reject this blanket charge as needlessly provocative without necessarily denying the existence of some racists within the system. In other words, there is no reason to conclude that minorities are committing more crime than the general population. Even if minorities do commit more of a certain crime, these offences are not the result of their race or ethnicity, at least not any more than white-collar crime can be attributed to "Whiteness" (Siddiqui, 1999). The crisis in police racial profiling exposes some of these contradictions, as the next case study reveals.

CASE 5-1	Racial Rashomon: Police Racial Profiling—A Few Bad Apples Or Rotten Institutional Tree?

The Theory

People see the world differently depending on who they are or what they do. In his film, "Rashomon," the revered Japanese film producer, Akira Kurosawa, explored this multi-perspectival theme. This brilliantly conceived film revolved around the competing perceptions of those who "witnessed" a brutal incident involving a woman, her husband, a bandit, and a peasant onlooker. Each of the witnesses not only interpreted the rape in a different way but did so in a way that reflected favourably on themselves. The process by which divergent and self-serving interpretations define the same incident has come to be known as the "Rashomon effect."

The radical relativism implicit in the Rashomon effect can help untangle

(continued on next page)

a paradox in race relations. That is, why do some believe that racism in Canada is under control while others think it is out of control? According to the Rashomon principle, Whites and non-Whites tend to have different outlooks on the nature and causes of racism. Put bluntly, Whites usually underestimate the scope and impact of racism, preferring to see it as a random and individualized incident that can easily be controlled through attitude modification. Rather than fists or epithets, racism is perceived by Whites as a quieter failure to treat others as equals while assuming that "our" way is the right way—multiculturalism be dammed—and that minorities best conform if they want equality or acceptance. Opposed to this sanguine view are victimized minorities who tend to emphasize the magnitude and effects. Racism is deemed to be systematic or systemic, embedded within the institutional structures of society, and the removal of institutional barriers and power sharing is easier said than done. In other words, the divide is largely perceptual: Minority discourses suggest Canada is a fundamentally racist society; for the mainstream, Canada is perceived as basically sound with a few misguided racists. Such a perceptual gap is not without repercussion. A lack of agreement in assessing the problem of racism compromises a capacity for solutions consistent with the definition.

The Rashomon effect has come into play with the politics of police racial profiling. Consider the following questions: Do police stop *what* they see or *who* they see? Is an expensive car stopped because it is speeding and swerving or because the driver is a young Black male? Do police have articulatable grounds (a reasonable and clearly expressed cause) for the stop, or, are minorities profiled on improper grounds such as race? Responses will vary with the definition: According to the Ontario Human Rights Commission (2003), racial profiling can be defined as actions undertaken for reasons of safety or security that rely on stereotypes of race to target members of a group for negative treatment. By contrast, criminal profiling relies on actual behaviour or information that meets the description of suspects. Racial profiling may be a kind of criminal profiling but, rather than reflect objective evidence, it involves a mindset based on stereotypical assumptions related to race and preconceived ideas about a person's character. With racial profiling, a process is activated by which authorities single out minorities for negative treatment (from stops to searches to detainment, in hopes of uncovering a crime) because of perceived criminal propensity applied to an entire racial group (Wise, 2002). Criminality is attributed to an individual on the basis of his or her racial appearance, resulting in the targeting of all members of the group regardless of whether they fit the profile (Canadian Press, 20 April, 2003).

The Practice

On the weekend of October 19, 2002, the *Toronto Star* published a series of articles that exposed the nasty reality of policing and diversity in Toronto. Data collected from police reports over a five-year period (1996–2001) accused the Toronto police of practising a form of polite racism known as racial profiling. The *Star* analyzed police data and concluded that those Blacks charged with simple drug possession were treated more harshly than Whites with the same

(continued on next page)

charge. The *Star* investigation also concluded that a disproportionate number of Blacks were ticketed with offences that would only come to light after a traffic stop (for example driving under suspension or without insurance)—a pattern of behaviour that the paper deemed to be consistent with racial profiling.

The controversy took a disturbing twist the following week when the *Toronto Star* reported that Blacks who comprised 8 percent of Toronto's population were charged with 27 percent of the violent offences in the city, including homicide, sexual assault, and gun-related incidents. The study also indicated that violent criminal activity was disproportionately attributed to Caribbean born Canadians (Blatchford, 2002). Tragically, four young Black men were gunned down and killed over a two-hour span in late October, prompting some to justify racial profiling as regrettable but necessary. People may complain that police are targeting Blacks because of "racist presumptions of heightened criminality," writes Mark Kingwell (2002), but a certain amount of targetting is "reasonable." Others, however, saw it differently. The killings underscored the disadvantages and prejudices that confront young men who are racialized by a police service that profiles them yet fails to provide protection (Cheney, 2002). According to this line of thinking, racial profiling creates such a climate of distrust toward police that minority communities become unpolicable, thus creating a climate conducive to Black-on-Black crime.

Admittedly, no one is saying that race ("genes") is a determining factor in accounting for patterns of crime. Individuals commit crime, not races, in large part because of social factors, such as powerlessness, poverty, discrimina-

tion, dysfunctional families, derelict housing, availability of guns and drugs, irregular immigration patterns that separate children from parents, inadequate social programs, cultural values, and lifestyle habits (James, 2002). Yes, people are responsible for their actions, but choices occur in a constraining context. Options for many border on the illusory: Either make $1500 a day selling crack or $250 a week flipping burgers at McDonalds? The net result? Black youths buy cars, carry guns, become involved in gangs and drugs, and "hang" in nightclubs where every dispute boils down to saving face (Cheney, 2002).

The Reactions

Reaction to these charges of racial profiling proved predictable. Police authorities at both local and provincial levels vehemently denied the existence of racial profiling within their services—either as principle or practice (Perkel, 2002). Yes, a few rogue officers might be out there spoiling it for everyone, but these bad apples can be dealt with accordingly. Not surprisingly, both news media and political correctness were accused of exaggerating the so-called problem, which police authorities argued reflected criminal behaviour rather than police racism. Besides, if Blacks are overrepresented in crime statistics, it is because they commit more crime. The findings of the *Toronto Star* were also discarded as little more than "junk science"—an accusation that assumed some credibility when another sociologist (hired by the police) debunked the study's methods and conclusions.

Opposed to this denial was the reaction of the Black community, legal bodies, and concerned academics (Henry and Tator, 2002). Each supported the

(continued on next page)

Toronto Star findings as consistent with what Black male youth have long experienced: Police tend to stop who they see rather than what they see (Hurst, 2003). Allegations of racial bias have long dominated the criminal justice system (Wortley, 2003). For example, the Ontario Court of Appeal ruled that police racial profiling is likely since some officers do target racial minorities in the belief they are more likely to commit crime (Canadian Press, 20 April, 2003). According to members of the Black community, Blacks tend to be overpoliced in contexts that don't count, but are underpoliced in contexts that, if unchecked, can lead to Black-on-Black conflict. Rather than good police work involving apprehension of suspicious behaviour, racial profiling is neither ethically acceptable nor logical as a law enforcement strategy but widely perceived as a device for socially controlling troublesome constituents (Harris, 2002; Wise, 2002). Profiling promotes the social control of those less powerful by reinforcing public fears of minorities as dangerous and in need of additional scrutiny (Wise, 2002). Worse still, profiling begins a progressive spiralling that is hard to halt. A disproportionate number of arrests and jailings leads to criminal records, limited job opportunities, poverty, alienation, and ultimately more crime. (Rankin et al., 2002b).

Analysis

Reaction to charges of racial profiling was varied: Some said no, never; others said yes, always; and still others said maybe, occasionally. Who is right and who is wrong? Perhaps the question is misleading: Neither police denials nor Black community accusations can be framed as a distortion of reality since there is no mind-independent reality (truth) to distort. Perception is everything when it comes to gauging racism (including profiling) because "what you see depends on where you stand." Hence the racism paradox: For Whites who have rarely experienced colour-coded discrimination, racism is dismissed or underestimated because of protected lived experiences. Racial profiling is seen as little more than an inconvenience that is essentially harmless or a practice that is justified in improving police work and the safety of everyone (also Wortley, 2002). To the extent that racism exists, it is restricted to a few bad apples who can be isolated and reformed through sensitivity training.

For Blacks, however, racism is a lot worse than many Whites believe. Racism is a pervasive reality that impacts on the daily life of minorities (Henry and Tator, 2002). "Racism is everywhere," claimed Lincoln Alexander, former lieutenant-governor of Ontario and chair of the police-minority summit meeting: "There's racism all over the bloody place" (Duncanson, 2003: A16). True, the most blatant forms of racism have been purged from public circles and polite company. Nevertheless, more subtle and nuanced expressions continue to deny, insult, or exclude at both institutional and individual levels. Police racism is not restricted to a few bad apples. According to this line of argument, it is the whole institutional tree that is rotten to the core because of deeply embedded racist structures that generate arrests from random stops, strips, and searches. This racism is deemed to be systemic since police use their authority to "overpolice" street and traffic crime where visibility becomes a factor.

(continued on next page)

Reference to Rashomon may explain the disparity in police and Black responses to the crisis. For Whites such as senior police officials, the magnitude and scope of racism is underestimated because of who they are and where they stand in society. Their power and affluence ensure that they will not be victimized by a discrimination that denies or excludes. By contrast, Blacks and minorities may dwell on the frequency and intensity of police profiling because of their visibility, powerlessness, and poverty. Minority street youth see themselves as disproportionately targeted for negative police attention, and respond with hostility or defiance (McCarthy and Hagan, 2003). Not surprisingly, both groups often miscommunicate by talking past each other. Each not only sees racism differently, but different types of racisms are seen as well, with Whites acknowledging the possibility of a "few bad apples" in the police service, while minorities define the institution of policing as "rotten to the core."

The crisis also draws attention disparities within the police service. A discrepancy can be discerned between what upper management says and what the rank and file actually does. My involvement with police services in Canada and New Zealand confirm the perceptual gap between management and labour. Management is often accused of making policies that curry political favour rather than improve the lot of front-line officers. Management policies are also criticized because even well-intentioned initiatives may be deemed as largely out of touch with the "real" world of everyday policing. Thus, the police chiefs were technically correct in discounting a racial profiling mandate as something not tolerated within the police services. But what constitutes official policy is not necessarily what happens in reality, particularly since individual officers must make split-second decisions. In other words, profiling may persist at ground level and outside of individual consciousness, regardless of mission statements, strategic plans, and corporate commitments.

Implications

What can we conclude? Regardless of whether profiling can be proven in every case, its widespread perception among racialized minorities is cause for concern; after all, justice must be seen to be done (Wortley, 2003). Community perceptions cannot be ignored and, if police hope to restore public trust, improve community relations, and become more effective in fighting crime, they must respond to the reality of the perceptions by going beyond denial or patronization (Ontario Human Rights Commission, 2003). Police leadership must acknowledge perceived injustices when confronting conflicting perceptions—"You think we profile; we think we don't"—not as indictment but as an opportunity for dialogue (Hurst, 2003). Such an assertion does not imply that police are racist. Nor does reference to Rashoman exonerate police services of blame. Racism exists, only its extent is contested. As the Ontario Court of Appeal concluded, the attitude underlying police profiling may be largely unconscious, that is, police officers are not necessarily openly racist since their conduct may reflect a subliminal stereotyping (Canadian Press, 20 April, 2003). Moreover, profiling is not an across-the-board enforcement. Police profiling is more likely with discretionary street offences. By contrast, mandatory

(continued on next page)

responses to 911 or emergency calls for violent crimes leave very little latitude for discretion (Rankin et al., 2002b; James, 2002).

The analysis is the easy part. Doing something about it is a lot tougher since solutions are contingent on how the problem is defined. If the problem of racial profiling is to be solved, it is important to define the problem in ways consistent with proposed solutions. If the problem of profiling is a personal one, then the focus must be on attitude change through a mindset shift. If the problem is structural, then institutional changes are necessary that focus on rules, priorities, and agendas. If the problem is a function of the job, it may be time to rethink the very concept of policing in a multicultural society. In either case, something has to give for healing to happen. Racial profiling exerts a punishing cost—emotionally, psychologically, mentally, and sometimes physically—for those "usual suspects" who need protection from those who are obligated to protect them. Little can be gained by the cynicism toward the criminal justice system engendered by racial profiling, as well

as social costs related to alienation and diminished sense of citizenship (Ontario Human Rights Commission, 2003).

The last word belongs to Royson James, a columnist with the *Toronto Star* who put racial profiling into a perspective that many Canadians can relate to. When he watches his son drive away in the family car, the parent in him worries that his son might get into trouble for no other reason than driving while Black (DWB). If stopped, the police may prove more of a trigger than a tonic by making a bad situation even worse. By comparison, as a White parent, I too worry when our sons drive off. But my gut reaction is that the police will bail them out should they get into trouble. The Rashomon effect could not be more forcefully profiled.

Case Study Questions

1 Explain how the concept of racial Rashomon may account for the diverse reactions to the concept of police racial profiling.

2 Indicate why the solution to the problem of police racial profiling depends on how the problem is defined.

CAUSES OF CRIME: NEED, GREED, OR GENES

Deviance and crime exist in all human societies, despite pressures and sanctions for conformity. How then do we explain the universality of crime and criminality in general and its existence in Canada in particular? Several explanatory models exist, often based on need, greed, or genes, each of which differs in defining who or what is to blame. Key factors include: poverty, bad influences, warped values, defective genes, personality defects, or structural constraints.

Biological theories of deviance have varied over the years but generally rely on the concept of "natural born killers." Criminals are not made, but born, and often carry physical stigmas as "proof" of their depravity such as bumps on their skulls or an extra "Y" chromosome. Psychological theories tend to approach crime as a pathological disorder that results from arrested personality development, childhood disturbances, frustration-aggression impulses, and maligned superegos ("conscience"). Deviance is seen as common among those with poor self-esteem. It is also common among those with an obsessive desire to repress rage or hostile urges under the guise of self-control (over-superego). Conversely, those with poorly developed superegos because of arrested childhood development are equally prone to deviate and stray (under-superego). Finally, rational, thinking-based arguments have proven helpful in accounting for crime. A rationalistic approach operates on the premise that individuals engage in rational behaviour to achieve certain goals, within a restricted range of choices, in environments not of their making. According to this economic model, most criminals are rational beings who choose to commit crimes by weighing expected costs against benefits. When the benefits of deviance outweigh the costs, a criminal act is more likely.

For the most part, sociologists tend to avoid biological explanations (ranging from chromosomal disorders to biochemical/neurological impairment). Not because biology is wrong or irrelevant but because such explanations fall outside the expertise of most sociologists. Sociologists are equally dismissive of psychological reductionism (from psychopaths to alcohol damage), although impulsive acts of crime and deviance may be better explained by psychology. Economic models are useful but may not go far enough in explaining the contextual basis of rational choices. Proposed instead are references to social and cultural factors. Sociologists tend to focus on social dimensions of crime by looking at the relationship of crime to society, and vice versa. Generally speaking, the sociological perspective reflects a view of deviance and crime within the framework of structures, values, and institutions. The focus is on the root causes by examining the social and cultural context in which deviance is constructed, defined, and controlled. In brief, sociologists prefer to look at the bigger picture with respect to what constitutes crime, which criminal acts attract formal authorities, and what causes crime. To be sure, there is a psychological dimension to all human activities, including crime; nevertheless, all human thoughts and actions occur in a social context. For convenience, these explanatory perspectives include functionalism, social interactionism, or conflict.

Functionalism

Functionalists define society as an integrated whole of parts that gravitate toward stability, order, and cohesiveness. Crime is seen as a disruption to the moral consensus that binds a society. Three major functionalist explanations include: anomie, subculture, and strain:

- Anomic explanations of crime revolve around breakdowns in culture, society, or socialization. In times of rapid and disorienting social change, individuals fail to internalize normal patterns associated with conventional values, beliefs, and practices. The lack of clear cut rules creates an absence of conformity which, in turn, "draws" individuals into crime for attainment of culturally defined goals.
- Crime may arise from exposure to subcultural values at odds with mainstream standards. Involvement in gangs may reflect participation in subcultural groups that provide a sense of meaning and security while securing benefits that challenge core cultural values.
- According to strain theory, crime is caused by relative deprivation: Everybody may embrace the same goals and values (wealth, power, and prestige), but not everyone has the legitimate means to achieve these goals. When expectations outstrip the reality of achievement, individuals fall back on alternative (unconventional) means to acquire those valued resources they feel entitled to.

Conflict Theory

The second major perspective is known as conflict theory. Conflict theorists differ from functionalists in how they assess the status and role of crime in society. For conflict theorists, society itself is a structured system of inequality and domination. Competition between social classes becomes inevitable as each attempts to advance, defend, or consolidate its position. The centrality of class conflict points to class-based explanations of crime and control. The ruling classes will do everything to secure their status, including creating a control system that favours them rather than the working classes. Dominant groups possess both the power and the resources to define patterns of behaviour as criminal; they also monopolize the power to punish those who break the law. Conversely, working-class people may commit crime not only out of need but as a protest against existing class inequities.

Clearly, then, crime and control are neither self-evident nor uncontested (Hawkins, 2003). Nor are they fixed concepts that are divorced from the power differentials that exist in class societies. Class interests determine which acts are defined as criminal and subject to punishment. Criminal acts are defined as those that impede the operation of capitalism, including theft of property, refusal to work, defiance of authority, and challenge to social order (Macionis and Plummer, 2002). Laws are implemented to criminalize behaviour that threatens the power and privilege. In addition, class inequities create economic imbalances that induce property crimes by the poor and peripheral (Samuelson, 1998). Corporate practices involving capital accumulation, from fraud to unsafe working practices, are rarely treated as a problem, let alone defined as illegal and prosecuted accordingly. By contrast, punished more vigorously are crimes by the working classes, few of which rarely match the costs of corporate crime.

Social Interactionism

Social interactionism takes a different approach to crime and control. As a major perspective in sociology, social interaction rejects a view of society as a straitjacket of social forces for conformity or conflict. Society is neither good nor bad; it just is. Social action theorists argue that society is a dynamic process in which reality is constructed and reconstructed through a process of meaningful interaction. Rather than some durable force out there, the social reality of society is an ongoing and evolving human accomplishment, constructed through individuals engaged in meaningful and jointly linked interaction. Social actors define situations in a certain way, and then interact with others on the basis of these definitions within contexts that are shifting and situational. Criminal activity is acquired in the same way as conformity: that is, through meaningful interaction with others in group settings. Exposure to a deviant subculture reinforces rules and values that are likely to bring someone into trouble with the law.

Labelling represents one of the more popular social interaction theories of crime and control. Labelling theory begins with the premise that social actions in their own right are neither deviant nor normal but acquire this label through a collective definition process known as labelling. Through labelling, society "creates" crime by making rules about behaviour whose infractions are defined as deviant or criminal. Formal mechanisms of control are thus established to reduce deviance. Paradoxically, however, labels that are affixed to persons by the criminal justice system may amplify criminality, since those labelled as such may act in conformity with these public expectations. Once labelled and stigmatized as criminal, individuals are inclined to act in a self-reinforcing manner because of restricted occupational opportunities, limited interpersonal relations, and reduced self-concept. In other words, any response to crime is criminogenic since it amplifies the very behaviour that it seeks to control (Jackson, 2002). Police encounters do not discourage offending; to the contrary, arrests add to already historical disadvantages, thereby contributing to a street context that further elevates the risk of criminal involvement (McCarthy and Hagan, 2003). Briefly then, crime is not a quality intrinsic to an act, person, or situation. It consists, instead, of an attribute conferred on an action or person by those with the power to make their labelling stick, often resulting in a reinforcement by way of self-fulfilling prophecies. Laws may be established to curtail crime; yet crime flourishes—not because people are bad but because of laws that label people as "bad."

Matching Solutions with Perspectives

Is it possible to construct an explanatory framework that accounts for all levels of crime and criminal behaviour? Such an explanation will have to embrace criminal actions from the trivial to the heinous, from violent crimes to misdemeanours, from premeditated and intentional to crimes of passion, from crimes of property to so-called "victimless" crimes. Such explanatory frameworks have their work cut out for them: Variables such as age, gender, class, ethnicity, and location must be addressed. Explanations must also account for the causes of crime—need or greed, without excluding a range of motivations in between.

Explanations will vary according to the sociological perspectives that link crime to society. For functionalists, who see society as fundamentally sound and deserving of protection, deviance and crime are social problems because of dysfunctional effects. Conflict theorists, by contrast, interpret society as essentially unjust because of structural inequalities. As a result, crime is not only inevitable under such circumstances, but potentially subversive in challenging the foundations of an unjust system. Finally, social interactionism is not interested in the functionality or dysfunctionality of crime. Crime is approached as a socially constructed exercise involving a host of definitions and jointly linked lines of interaction that eventually coalesce into a human accomplishment called "society." For functionalists, in other words, society is basically good; therefore, crime is bad; for conflict theorists, society is fundamentally bad; hence, crime simply reflects inequities in society. Finally, for interactionists, society just *is*, and crime needs to be analyzed as a socially constructed process involving meaningful interaction. Notwithstanding differences in emphasis and scope, however, each theory shares a common sociological commitment. That is, crime must be analyzed in sociological terms, either by reference to culture and structure, situational circumstances, or group context.

The importance of perspectives goes beyond mere problem definition. How a problem is defined will shape particular types of solutions. If deviance and crime are the result of defective socialization, then solutions must focus on improving value internalization. If the problem is rooted in the structure of society, a restructuring of cultural norms and societal arrangements is in order. But the focus on structures leads to a paradox of sorts. When a crime is committed, who is at fault? Do we pin the blame on the individual since everyone must take personal responsibility for his or her actions? Or does the fault lie with the system, in effect negating individual blame or responsibility? What precisely is the nature of the relationship between personal responsibility (agency) and societal context (structure)? To what extent are individuals shaped by their social environment? Or should individuals be seen as essentially autonomous persons who can transcend social and cultural constraints? The question of who is responsible is suspended in the tension between blaming the victim (agency) or blaming society (structure). Locating the balance between agency and structure has long challenged sociologists, and will continue to do so in the foreseeable future.

CONTROLLING CRIME: THE CRIMINAL JUSTICE SYSTEM

Broadly speaking, social control consists of collective efforts to enforce conformity to norms. Control can be achieved either formally or informally. Socialization is a key informal factor, including the deliberate (family, education) or the unintentional such as the mass media. Informal pressures for ensuring compliance often entail approval or disapproval by family, friends, or peer groups. Ridicule, gossip, shaming, or social ostracism are commonly used to informally ensure compliance, especially in pre-industrial societies or in rural areas where face-to-face encounters are the norm rather than the exception. As a result, social control functions are inherent in all institutions since some degree of socialization or re-socialization is involved. Formal (institutional) methods of control come into play when informal pressures are ineffective, especially in more impersonal environments with more serious crimes. Urban-industrial societies increasingly rely on "courts, corrections, and cops" as well as mental hospitals and the military as formal sources of social control.

The topic of social control raises a number of perplexing questions. Foremost among these is the question: Why are some deviant actions defined as problems of control, both formal and informal? How is it that certain categories of drug-taking are regarded as an offence (although this was not always the case as recently as the early 1900s in North America); conversely, other drugs, such as tobacco and alcohol, are legally permissible, albeit subject to certain constraints? Why are the affluent in the corporate world less likely to be charged (and even less likely to be convicted) despite the enormity of the crimes? To be sure, white-collar corporate crime may lack the flair or flamboyance of everyday criminal behaviour. But who can underestimate its capacity to pollute the environment, violate consumer health, and risk worker safety? Yet the criminal justice system tends to punish more readily detected crimes rather than the more destructive forms of criminal activities in boardrooms and computer networks. These questions are not easily answered; nevertheless, their very elusiveness reinforces the notion of social control as a socially constructed artifice, often in defence of vested interests but at the cost of impartiality and legal equality.

The Criminal Justice System: Cops, Courts, and Corrections

Canada has much in common, procedurally speaking, with the system of criminal justice in the United States (Cunningham, 1998). Both systems, in turn, evolved from the 18th century system of England. Differences exist, of course, not the least of which is the universality of Canada's criminal code across the country, rather than the state-to-state variability of criminal law in the United States. Nevertheless, Allison Hatch Cunningham (1998) observes, Canada too has a constitutionally defined division of power and responsibilities between federal and provincial jurisdictions that ensures provincial control over administering justice.

There is an additional commonality. Critics in both countries have criticized the criminal justice system for losing the fight against crime. None other than Julian Fantino, Toronto's Chief of Police, has blamed the criminal justice system for failing to deter brazen young criminals claiming that "... the system has broken down ... I think it needs fixing and I think we have the victims to prove it" (Borcea, 2003: A-17). For some, the system is too lenient, particularly with respect to sentencing; for others, the system is too strict and insensitive to differences. For many, however, the criminal justice system comes across as too costly for the returns, prompting the questions: Is it working; is it effective; is it fair; and can it be improved? Not surprisingly, Canadian policy-makers have sought ways to reduce reliance on a cops-courts-corrections approach to crime by fostering alternatives to custody or imprisonment for low-risk offenders.

Policing   One of the primary sources of formal control is the police. A wide range of roles and duties are encompassed under its protect-and-serve mandate, most of which revolve around the goals of protection (of life and property) and service through law enforcement and public order maintenance. With an annual cost of $6 billion, or $195 per capita, police costs take the biggest bite out of the criminal justice budget each year. Nearly 55 000 police officers work at federal (RCMP), provincial (OPP), and municipal (Waterloo Regional) levels. This works out to about 181 officers per 100 000 population, or, alternatively, one police officer for every 554 Canadians, a decrease of 11 percent since 1991 (Cunningham, 1998). Police departments vary in size from 5000 uniformed officers in the Toronto Police Service to one-member detachments of RCMP officers in remote communities. Nearly 40 percent of all police officers belong to the RCMP, making it one of the largest police services in the entire world.

Thanks to the media, what we know about the police portrays them chasing dangerous criminals in hot pursuit, routinely making drug busts, and collaring callous murderers (Knutilla, 2002). Yet police functions tend to be much more mundane, with goals related to preventing crime, apprehending criminal offenders, maintaining local order, regulating traffic, responding to emergencies from crowd control to missing persons, and providing information of relevance to the community. As the "thin blue line" that separates civilization from disorder, police are empowered with the right to apply force in discharging their obligations but only to the extent that its use is reasonable and demonstrably justified in light of Canada's democratic and legal traditions. This monopoly of force on behalf of the state makes police work "political" in the sense that policing is perceived as supportive of some sectors but detrimental to others (McDougal, 1988; also Neugebauer, 2000).

This expansion of functions is not without difficulties in shaping police-public relations. Questions abound: What is the relationship of the police to the public? Are they servants of the people who must submit to civilian control or are they accountable only to the uniform? What can police really accomplish in society? Many of the demands made on the police reflect social problems of such magnitude that they are virtually resistant to solutions. Moreover, the police are hardly in a position to address the underlying causes of conflicts that come to their attention (Verdun Jones, 1994) With their limited resources, the best they can do is address the symptoms of crime rather than the root causes of societal or personal problems. Or, as put by Verdun Jones (1994: 71), the police cannot prevent crime, they can only respond to it.

In recent years, a community-oriented relationship has infused community-police relations. Community policing is about establishing a closer and meaningful partnership with the local community as part of a coherent strategy to prevent crime in the first place. The community is defined as an active participant in crime prevention rather than a passive bystander. The police, in turn, are expected to shed their "crime-buster" image in exchange for proactive styles that embody a willingness to cooperate with increasingly diverse communities through establishment of liaison and communication (Shusta et al., 1995). Five principles undergird the concept of community-based multicultural policing; namely, community partnership, prevention, problem-solving, power-sharing, and pluralism (Fleras, 1998).

The concept of community policing continues to be widely endorsed. Virtually every police mission statement has institutionalized a commitment to community policing, while senior police officials routinely trot out this commitment as a new way of doing policing in a changing and diverse Canada. Its acceptance at lower ranks is somewhat more problematic. More often than not, community policing is not taken seriously as a policing alternative or dismissed as a career-stalling move. Moreover, as police services become increasingly strapped for resources, even management is shifting its priorities (including budget and human resources) from community policing into more conventional policing. Such a shift should serve to reinforce a major theme in this text: Even promising solutions to major problems may be difficult to implement because of complexities beyond people's control.

Courts The court system in Canada is similar to that in the United States. Both are adversarial in principle and practice; each also utilizes the same key doctrines, including presumption of innocence, the right to trial within a reasonable period of time, and reasonable doubt as the burden of proof. Differences exist, including no statute of limitations for most crimes in Canada. Court sentences differ too: State–federal distinctions in the United States reflect the type of offence (Cunningham, 1998), while Canadians are sentenced to provincial or federal prisons on the basis of sentence length, with federal penitentiaries reserved for sentences two years and over.

Additional similarities reflect the processing of young people through the courts. Few jurisdictions have attracted as much attention or notoriety as the enactment of the national Young Offenders Act in 1994, now replaced by the Youth Criminal Justice Act. Canada, like the United States, adopted a separate court for juvenile offenders at the turn of the 20th century. Initially based on a paternalistic model of early intervention ("as the twig is bent, the tree will grow"), the YOA bestows all rights of due process afforded to adults as well as some additional protections for youths between 12 and 17 years of age, including: limits on the length of custody (two years maximum for most crimes); a ban on publication of the names of offenders and the purging of all incriminating records; sentencing based on the characteristics of the offender rather than solely on the severity of offence; and absence of jury trials except for charges of murder (Cunningham, 1998).

Yet not all is dovey in detention. The violence and brutality that is increasingly commonplace in juvenile institutions is directly related to overcrowding created, in part, by putting all juvenile offenders, regardless of their crime, in the same correctional facility. Prisons become finishing schools for gang members and career criminals, resulting in high rates of reoffending (McClelland, 2003). Not surprising, the new Youth Act is premised on the notion that juvenile behaviour can be modified without incarceration. The objective of the new Act is twofold: To keep all but the most serious youth crimes (such as murder) out of the criminal justice system by mandating police to consider a range of alternatives (from warnings to community service) to laying charges for first time offenders (Tyler, 2003). Second, the focus is on rehabilitation by bringing the victim back into the healing and renewal process. How? The challenge lies in addressing underlying causes by getting the cooperation of family and community members to prevent future crime through sanctions that have "meaningful consequences" (Goodfellow, 2003; Doob and Cesaroni, 2003).

Courts have also come under pressure to take differences into account when sentencing—culture- (or colour-) blind or colour- (or culture-) conscious? Cultural differences are seen as a factor in shaping behaviour yet minority norms and values may be at odds with acceptable practices in Canada. Taken into consideration is the broader context in which historically disadvantaged minorities find themselves. Courts have also instructed judges to look at root causes of criminal behaviour, for example, persistence of systemic racism, to determine why a Black or aboriginal person is before the court (Rudin, 2003). Controversial questions come to mind: Should imprisonment for nonviolent offences be the first line of defence in the fight against crime or a last resort? Should judges exercise leeway when meting out punishment especially in seeking creative alternatives to costly imprisonment, including remedial sentences in the community or rehabilitative programs? Consider this case: Two women were caught smuggling cocaine into Canada from Jamaica. Typically, drug offences of this nature carry a prison term of two to three years. However, the judge sentenced both women to less than two years of house arrest. According to the judge, there were mitigating factors: both women were Black, first-time offenders, single parents of three children each, and both had pleaded guilty. The sentence reflected a host of relevant factors, from the overrepresentation of Black women in Canada's jails to taking into consideration the children's best interests (Parsons and Chen, 2003). The judge also ruled that the women may have been victims of systemic discrimination, thereby precluding conventional channels of making it in Canada.

Criminal Justice: Is it culture-blind or culture-conscious? Reaction varies: For some, the problem rests in dwelling on differences in a system that abides by the principle that everyone is equal before the law. For others, a one-size-fits-all justice that doesn't take differences seriously is the problem rather than the solution. For some, special treatment because of skin colour is wrong since it removes personal responsibility for actions, insults the law-abiding members of the Black community, and constitutes a type of reverse discrimination that violates the basic principle of "justice is blind" (Editorial, *Toronto Star*, 4 April, 2003). For others, a colour-conscious approach is necessary as the basis for "reversing discrimination" in contexts where treating everyone the same according to similar standards is itself unjust. The inequities and systemic racism that pervade Canada's criminal justice system put pressure on judges for alternatives that may rehabilitate rather then perpetuate the revolving door of street to jail and back again (Rudin, 2003). Judges have also been encouraged to adopt a contextual approach to justice, rather than one based on abstract principles of right or wrong, by taking into account the circumstances in which people find themselves and for which they are not entirely responsible.

Finally, there is a perception that the courts are much too lenient with white-collar and corporate crime, especially in light of the Enron and WorldCom debacles. Nova Scotia's Westray coal mine exploded in 1992 with a loss of 26 miners because of flagrant violation of rudimentary safety rules by management, yet the case was thrown out in 1998 (Jobb, 2003). Investors continue to be bilked of millions by white-collar con artists, yet punishment for "suite" crime is a slap on the wrist. For example, a former stockbroker received a four-year sentence when he pleaded guilty to defrauding about two dozen investors of $7.5 million, including retirement funds of the elderly (Powell, 2003b). Studies confirm significant disparities in the conviction rates and sentencing between "suite" crime and street crime. It is much easier to nail a petty criminal than to process someone whose crimes are complex, take time and expertise to solve, and involve economic resources to bring charges. White-collar criminals often can afford better legal advice or have a better ability to negotiate a plea that ensures leniency or a fast-track parole (Powell, 2002; 2003a).

Corrections (Prisons)

The corrections system in general is equally prone to criticism. Of Canada's 30 million population, about 35 000 can be found in prison at any given time, reflecting an adult population rate of 135 per 100 000 of population (1999–2000). This puts Canada near the midpoint of all countries based on the highest prison population per 100 000 of the national population as of July 1, 2002. The United States is highest with 690 per 100 000, according to the International Centre for Prison Studies, followed closely by Russia at 670 per 100 000. The United Kingdom (England and Wales) ranks 90th with 133 per 100 000. Still, figures in Canada are disturbing: According to the book, Justice Behind the Walls, the federal prison population in 2000 was approximately 22 000, with 13 000 offenders incarcerated and 9000 on conditional release in the community. The correctional service has a budget of $1.3 billion, with 14 000 staff and 47 federal penitentiaries for men and 17 correctional centres for offenders on day parole. There are five regional centres for federally sentenced women. Prisons are expensive. The average annual cost for inmates in a federal penitentiary reached $51 202 in 1998 (but $70 326 for maximum security, and $91 753 for female prisoners). It cost $43 734 for each inmate in the provincial/territorial jail system.

Prisons vary with respect to levels of confinement, with maximum, medium, and minimum security. Conditions vary as well, with some jails defined as barbaric and in violation of fundamental human rights (Jackson, 2002). These holding pens are so degrading and dehumanizing that inmates become even more bitter and hardened when they leave. This indictment of the Don Jail in Toronto (mainly a custody jail for those awaiting trial) captures the brutality of doing time in the Don:

> The prisoners are crammed into tiny cells—two on the bunk bed and another sleeping on a stinking mattress on the floor. They can be locked up for days, weeks even, deprived of recreation and visits. Water leaks out of the cells and the overpowering smell of urine, feces, and unwashed bodies hangs in the air (Editorial, *Toronto Star,* 8 May, 2003)

The situation is so harrowing—"a medieval brutal place" and an "embarrassment to the Canadian criminal justice system" —that judges routinely reduce the sentences of prisoners who have done Don time while awaiting trial. Even improvements in squalid cells, antagonistic guards, or ritual humiliations cannot change the potential for abuse inherent in the relationship between the keepers and the kept (Jackson, 2002).

Other prisons are perceived as luxury pads that make a mockery of justice for the victims. Consider these country club conditions in BC's Ferndale minimum security prison:

> [A prisoner] can have his own room in a duplex style home, with access to telephones and cable TV. It comes with laundry facilities, private showers, patio, and gas barbecue. Nearby is a duck pond. Not too far away there is a tennis court, and once there was a stable for horses. There is also a retreat for conjugal visits, six greenhouses, a sweat lodge for aboriginal inmates, a children's playground, pool tables, and a picnic area. Prisoners can even order in pizza and catch a film on the Movie Channel (Arnold, 2003).

What is the verdict? Should imprisonment for nonviolent offences be the first line of defence in the struggle against crime or, alternatively, the last resort when other means have been exhausted? Are Canadian prisons an innovative approach to rehabilitation by which prisoners learn to cope with daily life or are they the "soft underbelly" of Canada's criminal justice system? Contradictions abound: To one side is a growing commitment to find alternatives to prisons, given the high costs and dubious outcomes of imprisonment. To the other side is evidence that more inmates are serving full sentences rather than released after two thirds of their sentence (Tyler, 2003). No less contradictory are prison functions. Prisons are expected to carry out a variety of often conflicting functions, including:

- punishment: retribution for those who break the law
- protection: isolation of the offender from society
- rehabilitation: reformation of the offender and prevention of future offending through education
- deterrence: serving as a warning to the rest of society

Efforts to balance each of these functions have proven largely uneven. Punitive measures tend to prevail, and this retributive mentality has drawn criticism (Law Commission, 1999). Moves to reform the prison system are currently in place, with emphasis on replacing the somewhat depersonalized procedures of the state with a more personal and interactive dimension (Lozoff, 1998). The focus on retribution or punishment is shifting toward alternative measures in sentencing that stresses responsibility, restitution, and healing. According to most diversion programs, those offenders who do not pose a risk to the public can be released under conditions that include house arrest, restitution, treatment, or community work. Nevertheless, confusion and skepticism are mounting regarding the effectiveness of alternative sentencing (Makin, 1999).

Did You Know?

Corrections in Canada leave something to be desired. Yet the prison system in the United States strikes many as a classic example of a solution gone amok. Prisons are now the fastest growing segment of the U.S. economy. Despite falling crime rates, a whole prison-industrial complex has evolved to challenge the military-industrial complex of the Cold War (Lozoff, 1999; Consedine, 2003). The prison industrial complex is built around the lure of big profits and guaranteed jobs that encourage spending on imprisonment regardless of actual need, relevance, or benefits. As a world leader in incarcerations, some 2 million Americans are locked up in state and federal prisons, another 3.4 million are on probation, and 7 million are on parole. Inmates include the warehousing of the poor, homeless, mentally ill, drug addicts, alcoholics, socially dysfunctional peoples, and young Black males. National incarceration costs total $60 billion per year, in contrast to a national welfare budget of $25 billion. As prisons flourish, spending on rehabilitation inside the prison and prevention outside (for example, job training and early childhood education) has declined, with the result that states such as California spend more on prisons than on higher education. The irony is inescapable: While the United States lectures other countries on human rights abuses, the American prison system has been widely condemned for tolerating repressive control methods, physical and sexual abuses in direct violation of international human rights codes, and the making of profit out of human misery. Paradoxically, while major and violent crimes have dropped to their lowest levels since 1973, prison construction is soaring to record levels, particularly private prisons that have become a profitable "cash-cow" for cash-strapped communities.

RETHINKING CRIMINAL JUSTICE

The criminal justice system is under pressure to reduce its workload. It is also under pressure to make the system more inclusive of Canada's diversity. Such demands are understandable. Minorities tend to be disproportionately represented in the criminal justice system (Ontario Human Rights Commission, 2003). The 1995 Report on Systemic Racism in Ontario's Criminal Justice System indicated that Blacks and aboriginal peoples are much more likely to end up in prison. Prison admissions per 100 000 members of the total population stood at 827. By comparison, the rate for Blacks was 3686; for First Nations, 1993; for Whites, 706; for Asians, 353. In 1986, Blacks constituted 7.1 percent of Ontario's prison population; by 1992–93, 15.3 percent, an increase of 203.6 percent (compared to only a 23 percent increase for Whites), while comprising only about 3 percent of the population.

Of particular worry is the skyrocketing number of aboriginal males and females in prison. Despite decade-long declines in crime and incarceration, aboriginal peoples continue to be incarcerated in disproportional numbers, in part because of culture clashes, legacy of colonialism, structural factors and bias, and lack of access to scarce resources (Aboriginal Healing Foundation, 2002; Proulx, 2003). Aboriginal adults comprised 17 percent of federal jail admissions—up from 11 percent in 1991—despite constituting only 3 percent of Canada's adult population. Consider the prairie provinces: Aboriginal peoples occupy 50 percent of the federal and provincial prison space but less than 10 percent of the general population. Saskatchewan population is 11 percent aboriginal, yet 74 percent of the provincial jail population is aboriginal while 61 percent of the federal inmates are aboriginal. Not surprisingly, nearly three-quarters of aboriginal males will have been incarcerated in a correctional centre at some point by the age of 25 (Aboriginal Healing Foundation, 2002). The situation is equally grim for women. Although aboriginal women constituted only 3 percent of the female population in Canada in 1991, Carole LaPrairie (1996) writes, they formed 50 percent of the female inmates in provincial and territorial correctional institutions. In Manitoba, aboriginal peoples comprise 12 percent of the population, with males accounting for 63 percent of the male inmates in provincial prisons and females 73 percent of the female inmates. Not unexpectedly, a female Treaty Indian is 131 times more likely to be admitted to a provincial jail than a non-aboriginal person, while a male Treaty Indian is 25 times more likely, according to Professor Tony Hall of Aboriginal Studies at the Lethbridge Community College.

To say that Canada's criminal justice system has experienced a profoundly troubled relationship with aboriginal peoples would classify as a classic understatement (Royal Commission, 1996; Green, 1998; Proulx, 2003). Admittedly, some degree of caution must be exercised: Statistics may be misleading, since offenders may be convicted for relatively minor offences and end up serving time for offences that require only a fine, if they had the resources. As well, only a small number of individuals may get in trouble with the law, but they do so on a repeated basis (Buckley, 1992). Once arrests are made, aboriginal clients rarely receive proper legal representation, yet must appear before non-aboriginal judges whose hands historically were tied by precedent and the principle of uniformity in sentencing (Proulx, 2003). The revolving door of incarceration and recidivism has stripped many aboriginal peoples of any positive self-concept, in effect leading to self-fulfilling cycles of despair and decay. For some, prisons are an ominous and terrifying experience; for others, their level of indifference to White justice stymies the deterrent or stigma value of prisons (Waldram, 1997). Moreover, jails are neither the solution nor can they be considered a safe place which encourages disclosure, openness, and healing. As one Yukon elder explained (Green, 1998: 18):

> Jail doesn't help anyone. A lot of our people could have been healed a long time ago if it weren't for jail. Jail hurts them more and then they come out really bitter. In jail all they learn is "hurt and bitter."

Such bitterness undermines the very purpose of contemporary sentencing. Traditional penal sanctions have rarely had a preventative effect on most aboriginal offenders, thus failing to address the needs and concerns of both aboriginal victims and the community (Aboriginal Healing Foundation, 2002). State-centred criminal justice systems stand accused of investing more public funds in cumbersome bureaucracies that seem to have little impact on rehabilitation or recidivism, in part because offenders do not have to attend to the consequences of their actions or to the needs of the crime victims (McLaughlin et al., 2003). Not surprisingly, attention is focused on revising procedures and sentencing for aboriginal peoples. In response to the lopsided number of aboriginal persons in correctional institutes, the courts have acknowledged the need for greater aboriginal control over responses to community crime. Measures include separate justice structures such as band policing with jurisdiction over the reserve, to upholding culturally-sensitive programming within the prison system (Cunningham, 1998). Enhanced community participation in the sentencing and supervision of aboriginal offenders is encouraged by way of alternative measures both inside and outside of the criminal justice system (Green, 1998). Exploring sentencing alternatives for aboriginal offenders may reduce incarceration rates by diverting offenders from the court to community-based mediation committees such as sentencing circles.

Both government and aboriginal groups have made a commitment to address the problem of the criminal injustice system especially for urban aboriginal youth by relying on culturally appropriate diversion programs (Proulx, 2003). The most promising initiatives are those undertaken by aboriginal communities who design and implement solutions consistent with the principle of aboriginal self-determining autonomy (Aboriginal Healing Foundation, 2002; Douglas, 2003). Of particular note is the use of restorative justice principles in which the community cooperates with the courts to find non-incarceration alternatives as sanctions. Restorative justice tackles the underlying causes of criminality, builds safer communities, and cultivates pro-social values and responsibilities. Rather than punishing the offender for actions that are regarded as potentially harmful and disruptive to society, aboriginal justice is concerned with reconciling the individual with the family that has been wronged in order to restore community equilibrium. The processing of crime on the basis of abstract principles of justice is secondary to a holistic approach that integrates the spiritual with the social, cultural, and economic (Green, 1998).

The restorative principles of aboriginal justice rest on three assumptions: first, crime hurts individuals, not the state; second, restitution must be aimed at the victim; and third, victim input is important not only to repair the emotional distress but also to restore a degree of equilibrium within the community (Gaines, 2002). The punitive and adversarial focus of Canada's prison-centred criminal justice system stands in sharp contrast to a more conciliatory approach that emphasizes restoration, renewal, and rehabilitation. The differences are nicely captured in this observation: Canada's criminal justice system is based on determining (1) what law was broken; (2) who broke it; and (3) how much penalty must be applied. By contrast, the restorative system is grounded on an entirely different set of principles: (1) who was harmed; (2) how much harm was caused; and (3) whose responsibility is it to restore community equilibrium?

Time will tell whether restorative justice principles are effective in solving the crime problem (McLaughlin et al., 2003). After all, problems can be solved only by getting at the root cause. However, the root cause may be so deeply embedded as to escape detection, isolation, or reform. Even efforts to bring about reform face formidable obstacles. However much an improvement over the existing system, the more holistic approach to restorative justice would appear to be in conflict with the abstract and adversarial approach implicit in mainstream courts. Many questions remain contested: Should there be one set of rules for all Canadians, or should justice be customized to reflect the diverse realities of the disadvantaged or different? Should individuals take full responsibility for their actions, or must historical and social circumstances be incorporated into any assessment of wrongdoing? Should all crime be punished equally, or should differences be taken into account when decisions are made? Is it racist and paternalistic in sentencing to take into account race or ethnic background? Or does such an enlightened concession acknowledge the importance of taking differences seriously?

There is no certainty that a restructuring of the criminal justice system will pay off for aboriginal peoples. Key issues need to be addressed, including (1) how has the criminal justice system failed aboriginal peoples; (2) can the current system be modified to correct shortcomings; (3) should alternative systems be established; and (4) how would an indigenous justice system relate to the existing system in terms of jurisdictions and appeals (Douglas, 2003)? Two certainties prevail: First, a "do for" approach will not work (Aboriginal Healing Foundation, 2002). Solutions imposed on aboriginal communities tend to point to ineffective results and recipient resentment. Effective strategies must take into account history and culture, while conceding an aboriginal right to determine solutions to their problems. Second, no one should underestimate the challenges of incorporating a perspective at odds with Western principles. Resistance must be expected given that neither law nor the criminal justice system can be regarded as a neutral set of principles innocent of meaning or intent.

DISCUSSION QUESTIONS

1 Explain the relationship between crime and deviance.

2 What is the criminal justice system? Indicate the kind of rethinking that is transforming Canada's criminal justice system.

3 One must be extremely cautious in using crime rates as an indicator of crime. Indicate how this might be the case.

4 Indicate how the concept of "racial Rashomon" may prove useful in understanding minority offending in Canada.

5 Sociologists point to the social as probable causes of crime. Demonstrate this by outlining the functionalist, conflict, and interactionist approaches to crime.

 WEBLINKS

Canadian Criminal Justice Association.   **www.ccja-acjp.ca**

Centre for Restorative Justice and Peacemaking.   **www.ssw.che.umn.edu**

The World Factbook on Criminal Justice Systems.   **www.ojp.usdoj.gov**

chapter six

Family and Marriage

FRAMING THE PROBLEM

Families are generally regarded as one of the oldest and most durable of all human institutions (Egelman, 2004). Their centrality to human social existence is widely acknowledged. Most of us are born into a family; our preliminary point of contact with the world is filtered through family experiences; identities are defined by different stages within the family cycle; many are involved in establishing and nurturing new families, and younger family members may assume responsibility for elderly or infirmed parents. Like many other institutions, the family constitutes an interrelated system of rules, roles, and relationships for meeting the universal human needs of security, subsistence, and survival. Two levels of analysis are involved. For society, the importance of the family includes: producing new members; socializing and controlling children; serving the economy by consuming goods; conveying cultural values and beliefs; and regulating sexual relations. For individuals in search of intimacy, a family setting promises an oasis of tranquility in a competitive and calculating world. Families also serve as a primary social environment for learning about the facts of social life, including: gender relations; diversity and minorities; community involvement; the care and treatment of the elderly; and patterns of intimacy. Of particular relevance is the primacy of the family in the process of identity formation. Notions about who we are or would like to be are first nurtured within the reassuring confines of family support (McAdoo, 1999).

To no one's astonishment, the domestic context is often regarded as one of the most satisfying and fulfilling aspects of human existence (Browning and Rodriguez, 2002). For many, being part of a family is a defining feature in their daily lives for which few, if any, alternatives can be as emotionally gratifying (Conway, 2001). To be sure, the reality of family life is far more complex than the sugar-coated fantasy conveyed by mainstream media. Much heartache has resulted from politicians who bandy about nostalgic if unrealistic images of the family as a repository of moral values and refuge of safety. Nevertheless, perceptions of the family as a haven in a heartless world cannot be dismissed. Nor should we ignore the positive things that families do, in part by dismantling the barriers that prevent them from doing what they do best (Alvi et al., 2000).

Yet another picture is apparent, and the flip side of family—as hell rather than haven— cannot be casually brushed aside. Consider the challenges: the modern, urban family is being eroded by a lack of long-term commitment; shattered by divorced parents; destroyed by domestic bickering; hounded by mouthy kids; undermined by family-unfriendly work bosses; conflicted by spouses who barely know each other because of punishing work schedules; and ridiculed by those who mock anything that smacks of conventionality. Heartless government cutbacks and deficit-fighting philosophies have pulled the rug out from under the most vulnerable families. By the same token, some of the historic functions associated with the family have been co-opted by state agencies, including education, with a corresponding diminishment in status and role. Designer families by way of genetic engineering may convey a perception of improvement, but perils await a too casual acceptance of such controlling technology—from test tube babies to surrogate mothers to selling babies on the Internet (McKibben, 2002). To add insult to injury, there is mounting concern over the relevance of parents and parenting. The paradoxes are staggering: To one side, studies suggest that even positive parenting is of marginal influence in shaping children's behaviour outside the home context—at least in comparison to the role of peers or the media (Harris, 1998). To the other side, evidence is equally compelling that poor parenting is the prime cause of problem children (Fellegi, 2003).

Many Canadians believe the institutions of marriage and family are experiencing a "national crisis" (Conway, 2001). The pace of change has contributed to this crisis mentality: As recently as 1969, divorce was difficult to obtain without adultery as grounds; birth control pills were illegal except for medical reasons; and the mere mention of same-sex unions could land you in trouble because homosexuality was illegal. At present, critics are more worried about runaway reproductive technologies, no-fault divorce, permissive sex, and sex-same marital unions (Conway, 2001). The volume of changes has proven equally punishing. Canadian parents are adrift, depressed, and stressed out; many are mired in a confusing patchwork of family policies and conflicting expectations; most are desperately seeking a balance between home and work; and many are unsure whether parents (including themselves) are fit for the job of raising children (Shellenbarger, 1999). Contemporary families remain structured around an untrained and isolated pairing of relative strangers, both of whom may be poorly equipped even to look after goldfish, let alone to carry a heavy functional load of family responsibilities under trying circumstances. Domestic arrangements are also proving hazardous to people's health. Violence and spousal abuse are as common as domestic bliss, while inequities of power within domestic arrangements are deeply entrenched and resistant to reform. Family relations, like all social relationships—even the most intimate and egalitarian—are pervaded by inequities of power, both deliberate and manipulative as well as subtle and inadvertent. And yet many continue to uphold the cliché, the "stranger is danger, the familiar is safe" (Miller, 2000), while reject-ing the counter-intuitive notion of family as a danger zone.

There is still yet another picture. For all the turmoil and dismay, the family remains a central institution in the lives of most Canadians, with an overwhelming majority declaring its importance to their lives (Kendall et al., 2004). The institution of family is so pivotal to human social existence that many cannot imagine life without it. For most Canadian adults, marriage and family may be the most political institution they will enter, a commitment involving a more highly calibrated complexity than the gushy "diamonds are forever ads" would have us believe (Kingston, 1999). Survey after survey keeps telling us the same thing: Family provides the greatest source of happiness for many Canadians, including young people who rank an emotionally satisfying family life as one of the most important goals in life—surpassing even career, thinness, or popularity. According to a study entitled, "Canadian Attitudes on the Family" (Nickson, 2002), 80 percent consider a stable marriage as their top priority, 76 percent consider being a good parent the second most important priority, 88 percent say that having children was the best thing that happened to them, 78 percent believe the family is undervalued, and 83 percent think the government should do more to strengthen families. A Maclean's poll indicated that 96 percent of the 800 parents polled described their children as healthy and well-balanced, while 93 percent considered themselves good or excellent parents and 92 percent said raising kids was a satisfying experience (Wilson-Smith, 2002), prompting some to conclude that today's parents may be in denial. Or consider this: When young adults were asked in a *Time* magazine survey what they would want most if stranded on a desert island, 24 percent said music, 21 percent their computers, 15 percent their books, 10 percent their television, *but 29 percent opted for their parents* (*New Zealand Herald*, "Fill in the Blanks Generation," 10 August, 1997).

A sense of perspective is helpful. Families are neither a heavenly interlude, as implied by sitcoms or the moral right. Nor are they a punishment from hell, as implied by critics and statistics. Perhaps the answer lies somewhere in between the poles of bliss and brutal-ity, with banality thrown in for good measure. From its endorsement as the cornerstone of a healthy society to its vilification as evil personified, the family as institution continues to reassure and be revered by some, while provoking and dismaying others, with confusion and uncertainty sandwiched in between because of social changes and public demands. To many, the traditional family is an ideal to be protected and encouraged; for others, "family values" are little more than a patriarchal ploy whose thinly veiled codes—namely, the white picket fence, traditional family structure with pop on top, sticking it out for the kids, family commitment more important than career—neither reflect reality nor provide emo-tional solace (Browning and Rodriguez, 2002). A number of questions come to mind in determining the magnitude of marriage and family as a social problem, including:

- Is the family in crisis? Who says so, why, and on what grounds?
- Does anyone care? Will the family continue to matter in light of contemporary develop-ments and demands? Have media and peer groups overtaken family as the primary agents of socialization?
- How should we interpret changes to the rules, roles, rights, and relationships within the family—as demise; transition; reincarnation; or opportunity?
- Is the so-called family crisis a portend of more problems yet to come or simply a transi-tional phase, given the inevitability of tension and conflict in any transformational process?

- Is diversity within and among family arrangements a sign of an adaptive and resilient institution or a worrying sign of an institution in trouble?
- In what ways has the traditional nuclear family evolved into a contested site, involving a terrain of political struggles and resistance because of diverse expectations and oppositional ideologies (McDaniel, 1998)?
- How does the structure of a modern nuclear family contribute to domestic abuse and spousal violence?
- Why do many regard alternative family arrangements as deficient or deviant, while blatant weaknesses within nuclear families are ignored or excused (Miller, 2000)?
- Are escalating divorce rates a sign of a decaying institution or a confirmation of the centrality of marriage and family as a revered institution?

Responses to these questions are highly varied, lack consensus, require nuance, and are subject to constant second guessing. Nevertheless, responses do provide a basis for deconstructing an institution that is being buffeted by the winds of change; they also cast light on the reconstruction of new domestic arrangements in an era of choice, individuality, and freedom. Furthermore, the very act of posing these questions provides a blueprint for analyzing the family and domesticity from a social problem perspective.

This chapter begins with the premise that neither marriage nor the family is dying or irrelevant. Rather, contemporary families embody institutional arrangements that are experiencing (a) a crisis of confidence because of what they are; (b) a crisis of legitimacy in what they are doing; and (c) an identity crisis in what they are supposed to do. The crisis can be broken down into four themes:

What is the family for? For God, for country, for the kids, for personal fulfillment?

Who is a family? Straights, gays, brother–sister ties, multiple partners?

Why is the family? Is it genetically-rooted; socially constructed; an emotional release?

How should a family look? One standardized model for all or customized to reflect varied needs and experiences?

A shift from the scripted formats of the past to the increasingly customized arrangements at present has made it abundantly clear: The monolithic bias of conventional families is under challenge. The transformation of marriage and family from practical arrangements involving duty and obligation, to increasingly egalitarian partnerships in search of personal fulfilment, has proven a problem for some, a solution for others. In that families in Canada are evolving into a variety of viable options in their own right, contemporary families are sites of social problems, with potentially negative impacts for individuals and society.

Crisis or opportunity? This chapter puts a positive spin on the family in crisis; after all, what humans have socially constructed may be reconstructed when these frameworks prove inappropriate. Our collective genius lies in this ability to reconstruct institutional arrangements around the emergent realities of a diverse, changing, and postmodern world. What can we conclude about this evolution of diverse experiences with emergent types? Family can no longer be seen as a noun (thing) but rather as a verb (process). Family is not a kind of programmed script that people accept out of duty or resignation. Rather, we increasingly "do" family by working at creating new forms for living together domestically with the resources at hand.

Family — social problem

Reference to the family as a social problem is conveyed in five ways: First, the modern nuclear family is defined as a site of social problems, ranging in scope from domestic abuse to work–home imbalances, especially since individuals are conditioned to conform to roles that no longer resonate with relevance in the 21st century. Married couples are expected to transcend traditional scripts for living together, yet are punished for defying those conventions that clash with (post-)modern realities (Alvear, 2003). Second, the family may be regarded as a problem because of people's inflated expectations about domestic life, together with the inevitable disappointment that results from falling into this delusional trap of trying to live happily ever after. Worse still, people are being set up for failure by privileging the nuclear family ideal as natural and inevitable, while "problematizing" alternatives as inferior, unstable, or irrelevant (Baker, 1996; McDaniel, 1998). Third, despite diversity and change within families, cultural norms are failing to keep pace with social changes. Such a reality gap invariably generates confusion and conflict as dual-income families grope about for ways to balance home with career. Fourth, the family itself constitutes a structure of inequality, given the disparities in power and privilege between partners and parents and children. Insofar as family contexts reflect relationships of inequality within contexts of power, these unequal relations can be explored in terms of how they are created, expressed, and maintained, in addition to being challenged, and transformed. And fifth, families are normally regarded as the building blocks of society—for better or for worse. Their demise may have a catastrophic impact on society as individuals are cast adrift without a firm moral compass to guide, secure, or cushion.

Two assumptions prevail: If families are the site of social problems, the causes of these social problems must reside in the institutional structures of society rather than in individuals. Each of us is expected to fit into a standardized institutional framework at odds with our needs, experiences, and expectations, then are labelled as a failure for failing to conform or be successful. Each of us is set up for failure through the creation of institutional structures that may be impossible to attain, yet the tendency is to blame the victims rather than point the finger at the system. Second, the normalcy of family structures is problematic in its own right. Domestic problems are not an aberration or departure from some ideal norm but a "normal" component of an antiquated, male-dominated power structure (Miller, 2000). The conclusion is unequivocal: Any solution to the social problems of family and marriage depends on challenging social structures and inequities that created the problems in the first place (McDaniel, 1998). This position does not absolve individuals of responsibility when things go wrong. Rather, it acknowledges the contextuality of people's choices in a world where options and opportunities are more restricted than many would like to believe.

DEFINING FAMILY: EXPANDING INCLUSIVENESS

Sociologists are very good at analyzing the structure and dynamics of contemporary modern societies. They are less adept at proving the cross-cultural validity of their conceptualizations. They are even less keen on assessing the universality of human thought or behaviour in light of postmodern realities. This dearth of a comparative mindset characterizes the study of family and marriage. Questions are left unanswered: To what extent do marriage and family constitute universal categories of human institutional experience? In what ways does the logic of family and marriage differ from that of the West? Are current descriptions of non-Western families an imposition of ethnocentric discourses upon unsuspecting realities? To what extent do family types involve a series of socially constructed conventions rather than something natural or normal about the world (Egelman, 2004)?

Ponder for a moment the "bizarre" logic behind a monogamous nuclear family arrangement. Two strangers are thrown together into a context that compresses a small number of individuals into a highly dependent relationship without much kinship support, expert guidance, and ongoing training for carrying out a high functional load across a broad range of domestic fronts. How natural or normal is it for two relative strangers to establish a permanently monogamous household to discharge a host of functions pertaining to life and love when perhaps humans are predisposed to loosely informal arrangements (including what we call infidelity or adultery)? The institutionalization of such arrangements into marriage and family may well go "against the grain" of what it means to be human (Fisher, 1997). The implications are disturbing: Individuals are conditioned to conform to impossibly difficult standards, in effect setting families up for a fall, according to Stephanie Coontz in her book, *The Way We Never Were: American Families and the Nostalgia Trap* (Basicbooks, 1991).

Admittedly, the processes associated with establishing a household may be universally applicable. All societies must find ways of regulating sexual behaviour, procreating, socializing children, dividing labour, and transmitting property and inheritance. These relationships are sometimes formalized into institutions and practices called marriage and family. Yet the rationale underlying non-Western families differs from the logic that informs urban industrial societies. Few formal institutions exist in traditional tribal societies that resemble their Western counterparts. Furthermore, family arrangements are rarely static. The ideas and practices associated with marriage and family have evolved over time and across space, with the result that diverse forms and functions respond to the shifting demands of a changing society (Murray, 2003). Even the popularity and emergence of a monogamous nuclear family as the norm in Canadian society may be of relatively recent vintage, bolstered by a unique set of circumstances after World War II (Stacey, 1990; 1997). Moreover, as a *Life* magazine special on the family concludes, no particular family form guarantees success, and no particular form is doomed to failure, reinforcing the fact that how a family functions on the inside is more important than external appearances. Such an orientation also confirms the socially constructed nature of family—not as something natural or normal—but as a convention created by human accomplishment across time and place.

The Politics of Definition

Even the most obvious of social phenomena can pose definitional dilemmas. The concept of family is an especially instructive example, particularly since the meaning of the word has changed appreciably in response to the question, "What is family for?" (Browning and Rodriguez, 2002; Kingston, 2002). Complicating the definitional process is the application of family to an astonishing array of interactions and arrangements—from Ozzie and Harriet to Ozzy and Sharon. Consider the cross section of family households taken from the U.S. Bureau of the Census (1980). They include households with a father as sole wage-earner, a mother as full-time homemaker, and at least one child; a household in which both husband and wife are wage-earners, with more than one child at home; households of married couples with no children at home or who are childless; households headed by a single parent (mother or father) with one or more children at home; households of unrelated persons living together; single-person households; and households that include relatives other than children. If we add same-sex couples and ethnic families to this already teeming category, few should be surprised by the challenge of collapsing such variation into a single definition. Canada is no slouch in this area either, with Statistics Canada listing 36 kinds of family arrangements.

Defining a family is not merely an academic exercise. Revenue Canada relies on a definition for various tax purposes, while Immigration Canada must determine who qualifies as an immigrant under the family category (Owens, 1999). Those who are excluded from a definition may experience problems in terms of institutional participation, identity validation, and social equality. To ensure inclusiveness by incorporating as many arrangements as possible, the Vanier Institute defines a family as "any combination of two or more persons who are bound together over time by ties of mutual consent, birth, and/or adoption/placement, and who assume responsibilities for variant combinations of some of the following: physical maintenance and care of group members; addition of new members through procreation or adoption; socialization of children; social control of members; production, consumption, and distribution of goods and services; and affective nurturing love" (Owens, 1999: A-7). Others prefer to define the family around the core themes of commitment, obligation, and responsibility, in effect leading to definitions that focus on "… coming together of two adults, usually but not always a man and a woman, usually but not always legally married, to express their mutual love and commitment. If the relationship lasts, children are often produced, and then the family is made of mother, father, and children living under one roof, developing a long-term economic, social, and emotional unit" (Conway, 2001:1).

Common sense would be inclined to define "family" as an enduring social entity composed of a male and female, together with their statistical 1.7 children. For many, the creation and care of children cuts to the core of "what family is for" (Conway, 2001). Yet common sense is easily misled by surface appearances that camouflage deeper dynamics such as commitment and love as a defining feature. To avoid the taint of ethnocentrism, this text defines a family as a relatively durable relationship between individuals who are conjoined in some kind of domestic arrangement for practical and/or personal reasons. This domestic arrangement involves those persons who are related by blood, marriage, or adoption; share a common residence apart from other domestic units; consume shared meals; work to a division of labour; and possess a set of mutual obligations and responsibilities (between spouses, and between spouses and offspring). This definition is broad enough to encompass a diverse range of practices and images, yet sufficiently specific to retain a focused subject matter, thus averting the paradox of defining everything as family, with the result that nothing is family. Deconstructing this social construction yields a host of interesting variations in family arrangements and types, each of which reflects a distinct logic and situational adjustments.

THE NUCLEAR FAMILY: RECIPE FOR LOVE OR HOTHOUSE OF HATE?

When people think of family, most refer to nuclear families. Nuclear families can be defined as a social and residential unit consisting of a married couple (traditionally a stay-at-home mother and working father) and their unmarried children who reside in a single dwelling apart from their immediate relatives, with a corresponding division of labour around a reciprocal exchange of rights and obligations (Gee, 1990). This observation is consistent with the Statistics Canada definition of a nuclear family as a relatively self-contained domestic arrangement involving parents and dependent children. Childless couples, single-parent arrangements, and common-law unions are included as well by Statistics Canada, in the sense that these alternatives are catalogued as temporary "departures" from the standard. The nuclear family is a popular type of arrangement in urban-industrial societies where: (a) the family ceases to serve as the unit of production; (b) the state assumes a number of key functions related to socialization and elderly care; (c) kin are less important because of comprehensive social security systems; and (d) geographical mobility is central in pursuit of subsistence and wealth. It should be noted that two-parent nuclear families are declining, according to Statistics Canada, down from 64 percent of families in 1971 to 41 percent in 2001. By contrast, common-law relations account for 13.8 percent of households (3 percent of common-law couples are in same-sex relationships), up from 6 percent in 1996 (Arnold, 2002).

[handwritten margin note: nuclear family]

Did You Know?

The much-touted traditional nuclear family of a working dad, homemaking mum, two kids, with a house in the suburbs of "Pleasantville" is more an ideal than a reality (Stacey, 1990; 1997). The primacy of the nuclear family in Western societies is neither timeless nor inevitable, but historical and constructed. Its entrenchment as the Western ideal can be traced to the Industrial Age. Pre-industrial families tended to be larger, rooted in economic needs and social necessity, and based on pragmatism rather than on frivolous reasons related to romance, love, sexual attraction, or companionship. They constituted a large and diverse household of kin, lodgers, and servants, in which the community often played a key role (Miller, 2000). With industrialization, as Marx and Engels noted, the face of the family shifted. Men became increasingly estranged from the domestic realm; conversely, women tended to withdraw from the public domain. Both became intensely dependent only on each other, unlike the past when husbands and wives constituted a cooperative unit of production within the context of the community. Even attitudes toward children have shifted. Children rarely received much attention in the past since few parents could afford to invest emotionally in their children; they had neither the time nor the means. But in contrast to a time when children were meant to be seen, not heard, the modern family is increasingly child-centred. Childhood is a distinct social category, with parents now assigned the primary responsibility of making it work out, thus reconstituting the concept of homemaking as the central mission of modern womanhood (Miller, 2000).

The inevitability or desirability of nuclear families is widely assumed. The nuclear family continues to be widely celebrated as an ideal living arrangement that brings out the best in humanity. Benefits include provision of support and mutual assistance, nurturance, emotional satisfaction, protection, and positive socialization. Others are not so sure, and critics have depicted the nuclear family as conflict-driven and oppressive. Nuclear families are reproached as largely unstable arrangements at odds with individual needs in a changing society. The instability of nuclear families is inherent in the structure. Intense emotional attachments can provoke conflict and violence when individuals are forced to rely on a small support group for a host of functional needs in contexts of relative isolation (Peoples and Bailey, 1997). Not surprisingly, the same context that may generate passion and intimacy can unravel into fits of hate and abuse. The reassuring confines of marriage and family are just as likely to induce control and exploitation as they are to foster emotional gratification. In short, the combination of economic isolation with social dependency on few individuals can generate a "hothouse" quality that intensifies extremes of behaviour, from passion on the one hand, to raging hostility on the other, with unremitting boredom or indifference in the middle.

Tension and conflict are inherent components of any relationship, even more so in contexts that isolate individuals and make them highly dependent on each other across a broad range of needs and concerns. But there is a much darker side of the family that puts women and children at grave risk. Images of comfort and coziness are just that: fantasies. In reality, the family is now considered one of the most dangerous environments for dependents. Violence and abuse within families is of epidemic proportions, according to numerous surveys, reinforcing an alignment of domestic relations along a continuum of unsafety (Alvi et al., 2000). Violence can range from physical force that breaks bones to emotional abuse that may scar for life. It can include the typical victims of family violence, namely, women and children, but also extend to elder abuse and the rarely discussed aggression between siblings. No one can say for certain if family violence is increasing. But it is getting the attention it deserves as a horrific violation of human trust and human rights.

Violence within the context of intimacy is the cruelest of social problems. With domestic violence, those to whom we place our trust for safety and security betray that bond. Nor can anyone derive much satisfaction by pointing to increased awareness as an improvement over the past when domestic violence was neither openly discussed nor defined as a social problem. Domestic violence has long existed, of course, but until recently was swept aside as a regrettable but necessary component of domestic life. The premier journal for the sociological study of marriage and family did not have a single article with the word "violence" in its title or even a single article on domestic violence between 1939 and 1969 (Nuefeld, 1993). Authorities, from police to physicians, refused to intervene out of deference to a man's prerogative as king of the castle and master of his house. It was assumed that men had certain passions in need of release; women and children were offered as appropriate targets for male virility. Assaults against women were trivialized, deemed inconsequential, or the butt of jokes. Violence against women was accepted as normal, even necessary, and reflected a view of children and women as property that could be punished or pushed around. The private nature of violence and abuse has complicated efforts in gauging its historical extent. Such is also the case at present despite more awareness of domestic abuse, less acceptance of its presence, and greater willingness to report violations to authorities. There are few assurances that statistics and national surveys are telling the whole story rather than merely exposing the surface of the problem. The fact that many are reluctant to acknowledge the reality or magnitude of the problem, much less do something about it, may itself be seen as a form of violence.

The brittleness of the nuclear family goes beyond internal flaws. Its relationship to the world at large is also problematic, especially with growing distortions in the family–work balance. Work is so central to the lives of dual-income parents that many find it increasingly difficult to separate work and home into distinct spheres. People do not leave their problems at home when they go to work. Quite the opposite: The domestic intrudes into the public, and vice versa, with the result that contradictory messages are inevitable, as Alvi et al. (2000: 213) astutely points out:

> The children may have to get ready for school themselves. A debate starts over who will cook dinner tonight. If any banking or grocery shopping must be done today, someone will have to make time during the lunch hour. Worse still, if a child falls ill one parent must stay at home, which means that someone will miss work. If a parent must work overtime, special arrangements must be made by the entire family to deal with that individual's absence. To accommodate the demands of the new workplace, one or both spouses may have to bring work home, which means taking time from family activities such as homework or leisure. At work, both spouses may encounter resentment from co-workers if they "sneak out early" or arrive at work late to deal with family responsibilities. Bosses may tell either partner that "family problems should be left at home where they belong" so as not to interfere with work.

This excerpt makes it clear why family life can be so stressful at times that working spouses may seek refuge and relaxation in the orderly and disciplined world of work (Hochschild, 1997). And while some family-friendly policies are in place, most employees continue to see family responsibilities as a liability. Structural constraints are no less punishing since raising a family may be incompatible with the hierarchical organization of work, with the uninterrupted pace of upward career mobility, and with the emphasis on "face time" as an indicator of dedication and commitment to the job (Alvi et al., 2000).

FAMILY DIVERSITY: CHALLENGES AND ALTERNATIVES

The nuclear family may be widely endorsed as natural, normal, and necessary. In practice, it has proven to be structurally flawed, culminating in major social problems around intimacy and commitment. The traditional family can no longer deliver what it promises, namely, emotional gratification for men and women and minimum emotional and physical security for children as a precondition for adulthood (Conway, 2001). Additional domestic arrangements are emerging in reaction to the crisis of the family, but the transition invariably entails uncertainty and confusion. For some, the proliferation of these new family types represents a solution to the monolithic bias of nuclear family arrangements. For others, the new arrangements are proving more of a problem than a solution by discarding what many regard as the cornerstone of Canadian society.

The Postmodern Family

The institutions of marriage and family reflect different shapes and sizes. The term "postmodern family" seems to capture this sense of diversity. In 1981, for example, married couples with children constituted 55.9 percent of all families in Canada; married couples without children, 28.1 percent; common-law couples with children, 1.9 percent; and common-law couples without children, 3.7 percent. Single-parent families constituted 11.3 percent. By 2001, the percentage of married couples with children had dropped to 41.5 percent of all families, while common-law couples had increased to 13.8 percent (6.3 percent with children at home; 7.5 percent without. Young adults are driving the increase in common-law relations, with 53.3 percent of women between 20 and 29 years of age preferring common law as their first union, compared to 30.7 percent choosing marriage (Schmidt, 2002). Lone-parent families had increased to 15.7 percent. Nearly 41 percent of twentysomethings live with parents, while 33 percent of men aged 30 to 34 and 22 percent of women live with parents. Interestingly, each Canadian household is composed of 2.6 individuals, in contrast to 2.9 in a typical home in 1981. People are marrying at a later age: the average age of first-time brides in 2000 is 28 years old; first-time grooms, 30 years. Just as Canadians are postponing marriage, so too are people postponing families, with the average age of motherhood in 1999 at 26.7 years compared to 24.9 years in 1983 (Vallis, 2001). Similarly in the United States: The traditional nuclear family (working dad, stay-at-home mom with children) constituted 26 percent of all households, down from 45 percent in 1972.

In rejecting the normalization of modern nuclear families as the ideal or standard by which to judge others, the postmodern family does not posit a single alternative (Stacey, 1990). A multiplicity of family arrangements is recognized instead that are undergoing constant change in response to changing circumstances. Postmodern families include arrangements such as adult children returning to live at home; blended or reconstituted families; and same-sex families. An open mindset is critical: These customized arrangements that depart from the cult of domesticity are neither a problem nor a deviation, with no claim to legitimacy as real families (Miller, 2000). Such arrangements are just as capable as conventional families in assisting individuals to fulfill their full potential as humans. Insofar as they represent departures from the tightly scripted notions of family a generation ago, postmodern families may be riding the wave of the future.

The Single-Parent Family

Single-parent families are an emergent phenomenon in those contexts with sufficient infrastructure (state support) for supporting a parent–child relationship. The proliferation of single-parent families reflects a fundamental shift in attitudes in North American society. It also heralds a growing array of options for women because of increased economic independence and a more supportive social climate. Nearly half of all children in Canada and the United States may spend all or part of their childhood in a single-parent arrangement. Yet the jury is still out regarding the impact of such arrangements. For some, living with a single parent may have a negative effect on children, mentally and emotionally (Lash-Quinn, 2002). According to a long-term study by Statistics Canada involving 23 000 children, guardians, and teachers, single-parent family children tend to be in poorer health, have more behavioural problems, do less well in school, and have poorer interactional skills with their peers or adults. Other studies disagree, arguing that anything is an improvement over an abusive domestic context (Milstone, 1999).

In principle, there is nothing inherently wrong with such arrangements for raising children and making ends meet (Murray and Herrnstein, 1995). Nevertheless, single-parents families tend to be especially vulnerable to poverty. They also are subject to manipulation and control by state agencies. But female-headed households are not the cause of poverty, crime, or homelessness, since marital stability is not the same as family stability, and female-headed households may be stable over time (Sudarkasa, 1999). Once again, it is important to discard the notion that only nuclear families can provide stability and support to ensure survival. The cooperation and reciprocity that allow single- or female-headed households to thrive within the broader context of kin and friends may prove equal to the task.

Blended Families

Blended families are increasingly common because most divorced people end up remarrying or cohabiting. New domestic arrangements are reconstituted that creatively combine the past with the present in ways both innovative yet awkward. The combinations are headspinning, from the relatively simple, in which only one partner has children from a previous relationship, to more complex arrangements in which there are children from both marriages who live in both their new home with their step-siblings and in the homes of their biological parents. There are arrangements in which men in a second marriage are paying child support to their first wives, while the children they actually live with are being supported by their partner's former husband.

Such arrangements are both an opportunity and a danger: an opportunity, for exploring novel scripts; a danger, in creating unscripted relations that may confuse or provoke. Blended families are prone to considerable tension, including conflict between step-siblings; mixed emotions toward the new arrangement; hostilities toward the stepmother who must replace a child's most revered figure, her natural mother (Sachs, 1999); separation anxieties; general ambivalence about the divorce; and financial problems related to child support payments. Not surprisingly, second marriages run a higher risk of divorce, in effect creating the conditions for even more innovative blends to mix and match.

Gay and Lesbian Families

Gay and lesbian ("homosexual" or same-sex) families are increasingly part of the Canadian social landscape. The presence of gay and lesbian families may rankle or provoke, including denunciations from politicians and the pulpit. Nevertheless, these families are here to stay, judging by their popularity and recent court actions. Court decisions have recognized the legitimacy of same-sex unions by granting spousal entitlements comparable to those of opposite-sex, common-law relations. These rulings are having the effect of eroding arbitrary and pointless distinctions that have existed for no other reason than the tyranny of custom and historical prejudices (Coyne, 1999). Partners registered under domestic partnership arrangements enjoy many of the benefits of married couples (Knopff, 1999). In Ontario, for example, provincial employees in same-sex relations receive the comparable pension benefits or spousal support rights of an opposite-sex, common-law relationship. On June 17th 2003, the yardsticks of acceptance shifted even further. One week after Ontario's Court of Appeal ruled that same-sex marriages were constitutionally legal, the federal government announced the drafting of a bill that would make Canada the third country in the world (besides the Netherlands and Belgium) to give legal status to same-sex unions (*Economist,* 21 June, 2003)

Reaction to gay and lesbian unions is mixed. To one side are those who cite principles of tolerance and equality as the basis for same-sex unions; to the other side are those who oppose such arrangements in defending the sanctity of faith, family, and the fabric of society (Editorial, "Middle Ground for Marriage," *KW Record,* 9 August, 2003). Many disagree with the logic or morality of recent court rulings over same-sex marriage, arguing that marriage by definition is heterosexual (Coren, 2003). For example, lawyers for the province and Ottawa contend that same-sex marriages are unnatural and illogical as well as a violation of common law (practices according to tradition or practice). Marriage must be restricted to heterosexual relationships since that arrangement alone contributes to the survival of society (Knopff, 1999). Interest groups, such as the Canada Family Action

Coalition, also maintain that only heterosexual marriage provides the core relationship to pursue "family values"; reflects the Biblical injunction to go forth and multiply; is the only natural union with the capacity to secure a strong society; and fosters the best environment for the socialization of children.

But others have argued that denying marriage to gays and lesbians constitutes a further violation of the Charter's equality provisions and human rights commitments. Why should same-sex couples not have the same entitlements as heterosexual couples when (a) procreation is no longer the sole purpose of marriage; (b) personal love and commitment is the defining feature of long-term relations; (c) marriage provides a validation of social status; (d) equality between and among genders is assumed; (e) interracial marriages are no longer illegal; (f) and intimate relationships are not about hierarchy or biology (Graf, 1999)? Besides, most people are social by nature, and those who seek stable relations tend to live longer, healthier, more productive, and happier lives than those dependent for their care on an impersonal state (Knopff, 1999). It remains to be seen if a middle ground can be broached.

Ethnic Families

Canada is a society of extreme diversity, particularly in the larger urban centres of Toronto, Montreal, and Vancouver. Nearly 40 percent of the population in Toronto are visible minorities, while the percentage of foreign-born is rapidly approaching 60 percent. With diversity, the potential for problems increases—not because differences are a problem per se, but because of pressures to conform to the status quo. This racial and ethnic diversity is reflected in and reinforced by the proliferation of diverse family arrangements that may prove at odds with mainstream practices. Consider how the logic of non-Western ethnic families appears to be at odds with Western nuclear family practices. Family and marriage in our society is predicated on the principle of relationship between individuals, voluntarily entered into on the basis of free choice and romantic love. By contrast, ethnic marriages such as some Indo-Pakistani families are more likely to involve parental input, kinship obligations, economic calculation and exchange, or political expediency. This is not to say that personal choice is nonexistent or unimportant. Relatives may be less concerned with relatively unimportant proposals for marriage, while the introduction of a wage economy has loosened the grip of elders in determining who can marry whom. Still, few would deny the existence of a logic at variance with the Western ideal of family and domesticity (Handa, 2003).

Ethnically diverse immigrants may hold socially conservative views with respect to domesticity. In the area of parenting and child-rearing, ethnic families may subscribe to permissive or authoritarian styles, or both depending on circumstances, and reflect variation in practices such as punishment, reasoning, setting of limits, and reinforcement (Martinez, 1999). Tensions within ethnic families reflect a conflict of interests, including balancing conventional families values pertaining to children, the elderly, the role of punishment, and family honour with mainstream emphasis on individual independence and success (Lin and Lin, 1999). Gender relations may be problematic: Ethnic families may be uncomfortable with the concept of loosely scripted gender relations (from reservations about dating and premarital sex to equality in husband–wife relations). In traditional ethnic families, a woman as wife and mother must know her place if domestic peace and social harmony are to be maintained. Violence may be tolerated in some ethnic families: Men are expected to be aggressive in discharging their duties, and this aggressiveness is tacitly assumed as divinely ordained or naturally normal, thus reinforcing the notion of domestic abuse as a mechanism of social control rather than personal pathology (Cribb and Barnett, 1999).

Did You Know?

The most popular types of families are unlikely to be found in large numbers in Canada. Extended families are by far the most common type of family from a cross-national perspective. They tend to proliferate in contexts with a relatively secure source of subsistence, low levels of geographical mobility, and the presence of immovable property as a primary determinant of wealth creation and inheritance. They also are common in agriculturally-oriented societies where cooperative hands are critical to productivity and success. The extended family can be defined as a complex household of smaller family units of at least three generations, consisting of parents, one or more of their married children, their spouses, and their unmarried offspring. This combination of conjugal (marriage) and consanguineal (blood) bonds occupy a single dwelling while cooperating to achieve subsistence goals. The benefits of an extended family should be clear. The larger the size of the family, the more equitable is the workload. Expanded size also broadens the range of role models to emulate; enhances the circle of intimacy and support, especially in times of emergency; reduces the strain of sustained interaction with a small number of intimates; and encourages the pooling of resources for survival or wealth creation. Compared to the small but more intense circle of relations within nuclear family arrangements, extended families offer flexibility and a "diffuseness" that may work to the advantage of family members.

Plural marriage (polygamous) families are widely admired as the preferred family type in many parts of the world. A productive unit is created by plural marriage families in which the different members pool their resources to enhance adaptation or success. Yet polygamous unions involving multiple partners are not necessarily the most common because of the realities of demography and costs of supporting such an arrangement (Peoples and Bailey, 1997). Two types predominate: polyandry and polygyny. In polyandrous families, a woman is allowed two or more husbands simultaneously (or perhaps it is a case of a man sharing his wife with another male such as his brother), while in polygynous families, it is the man who can have two or more wives. Contrary to Western mindsets and the perception of fractious jealousy in polygynous unions, relationships between the husband and his wives, as well as among the wives, may be relatively tranquil. Co-wives may cooperate across a range of activities, often encouraging husbands to take additional wives not only to alleviate their workload, but also to bolster the status and prestige of the household. In other cases, where rivalry or jealousy prevails, adjustments may be required to compensate older wives for displacement by younger wives. In both types of family settings, a broader circle of intimacy may create a more supportive environment for raising and socializing children. Polygamy is currently outlawed in Canada and the United States despite its prevalence in specific locales such as Utah. But with the extension of marriage rights to same-sex unions, it may be a matter of time before polygamy becomes contested as a valid alternative.

FAMILY IN CRISIS: OPPORTUNITY OR DECAY?

Many myths inform the domain of marriage and family. The myth-making machine may exist to paper over cracks which, when exposed, may trigger deeper anxieties. Of the many myths, few are as pervasive or debilitating than popular beliefs about the normalcy and inevitability of conventional nuclear families. No less myth-making are concerns over the crisis in familyhood. Consensus is growing that conventional families don't work any more. Heightened anxieties over the family may reflect challenges to its status as the cornerstone of society, coupled with a belief that further relapse will undermine the quality of human social life. Critics and concerned citizens point to those indicators that portray the family to be in trouble. Among these trends are rising divorce rates; dysfunctional domestic arrangements; a proliferation of family types, especially single and same-sex unions; and punishing levels of domestic violence. New reproductive technologies may have an even more revolutionary impact on the nature of the family, what it means to be a parent, and the rights and obligations of family members (McKibbon, 2002). To be sure, stresses and strains are inevitable in an arrangement that conjoin two inexperienced strangers into a lifetime of diverse and demanding functions under pressure-cooker conditions. The cost in tempting fate is captured by this television quip:

> At the core of the 1990s TV sitcom "Home Improvement" is an underlying creed: Men and women were not meant to live together and, therefore, married life is a series of consequences couples face for having defied fate (*The New York Times,* Sept. 18, 1994).

Not surprisingly, efforts have focused on propping up the structure of the nuclear family through threats or incentives. Reference to family values conjures up reassuring images of a refuge of last resort in a chaotic and calculating world. Yet family dynamics have become contested and confused, with corresponding impact on individual lives and institutional foundations of society. Reactions to this turmoil and transformation are equally divided. Many regard these trends as evidence of an institution in trouble or decline. According to this line of thinking, neither society nor many of its victims can expect relief from dysfunctional families, domestic violence, sexual abuse, philandering spouses, and juvenile delinquency. Others are pleased that conventional forms of marriage and family are ceding ground to more humane alternatives. The logic behind modern families is contemptuously dismissed as little more than institutionalized "slavery" in defence of male power and privilege. That this patriarchal arrangement routinely encourages abuse and/or indifference is further justification to hasten its demise.

Still others believe that talk of crisis and decay is misplaced or premature. The institutions of marriage, family, and domesticity are not experiencing a crisis in the negative sense of the term. There is no evidence of some decline from some mythical past when everyone knew her place and performed accordingly. Families such as the depression-era "Waltons" or pioneer families portrayed by the "Little House on the Prairie" series rarely existed except in the minds of TV programmers, fundamentalist Christian sects, or advertising jingles. Yet such idealistic images had the effect of fostering failure since people were conditioned to defend, emulate, or aspire to institutional ideals beyond the scope of reality. For some, then, there is a crisis in the family that portends the end of the family as we know it; for others, the crisis reflects an increased awareness of the gaps between egalitarian ideals and unequal realities, between the unrealistic portrayals of made-for-TV families and the banalities of everyday reality. Needless to say, no institutional arrangement will please everyone. The institutional framework undergirding human social life is constraining and restrictive by definition, and those who insist on seeking the perfect arrangement are asking for trouble. The crisis also reinforces a growing belief that a 20th century ideal may not be equipped to meet 21st century challenges.

Simply put, women and men are dazed and confused by the conflicting demands imposed on them by marriage and family (LeMasters, 1977). Changes in the norms and expectations have had disruptive consequences for established patterns of interaction. Consider the following dilemmas when individuals are thrust into playing the roles of marriage and family: Parental and spousal roles are poorly defined (what is a perfect parent or perfect spouse?); there is little margin for error, especially when you hedge your bets on one partner and 1.7 children; parental and spousal roles cannot be abandoned without payment of penalty; parents have responsibility but increasingly are losing authority to schools, children's aid societies, and peer groups; parents are judged by professionals who never raised children; parents often feel they must follow fashions and fads that experts endorse, then discard; parents and spouses are often victimized by poor advice regarding communication and interaction; parents must raise children who are better off than they were as youths; parents do not receive training for parenting but must learn as they go along; and parents and spouses are expected to pursue career goals without straying from the collective needs of the family.

Of particular concern is parental lack of basic knowledge about child rearing and child development. The dearth of awareness is especially acute in the formative years when parenting is thought to exert a powerful influence on children's development. Yet parents rarely possess the expertise to deal with developmental or emotional problems. Not surprisingly, there have been calls for mandatory parenting classes to help parents cope with the complexity of child rearing in modern Canada, especially if involving a single child within the context of a dysfunctional home (Hiller, 2002). The more extreme position argues that parents should not be allowed to have children until they have finished high school, completed a parenting course, and obtained a licence (Andrews, 1999). Others disagree, arguing that parenting comes naturally for most adults, that parents know better than experts what their children need, that incompetent parenting can never be proven to cause antisocial behaviour, and that people have been parenting successfully for centuries without government interference.

Talk of the family in the throes of demise may be greatly exaggerated. Conventional families will not disappear in the future; both formal and informal messages continue to privilege the moral authority of nuclear families, thus making them resilient and difficult to dislodge (Miller, 2000). Perhaps the so-called "crisis" is not really a problem but a solution with yet untold opportunities. The family as an institution is not necessarily in decay or decline but undergoing a transition to a postmodernist reality of single-parent families, blended families, common-law arrangements, same-sex unions, and ethnic families. The traditional one-size-fits-all family is giving way to more democratic forms that not only encourage different styles but also foster more egalitarian and loving relations. Are marriage and family obsolete? Is the family disappearing? Yes, if we think of the family as a noun or a thing, with a scripted set of rules and roles in defence of the status quo. No, if we approach the family as a social construction in contexts of diversity and change. No, too, if families are regarded as a verb or process, involving socially constructed ways of making them work. In other words, the concept and importance of families is not declining. What is disappearing is a particular type of mid-20th century family ideal whose claim as the exclusive norm and standard may not stand the test of time.

SOCIOLOGICAL PERSPECTIVES:
THE BINDS THAT TIE OR THE TIES THAT BIND?

Marriage and family as social institutions have come under increased scrutiny and criticism. The critique is mild in some cases, with barbs aimed at drawing attention to inconsistencies between ideals and reality. In other cases, the critique has been withering and severe. Family and domesticity are depicted as a "chamber of horrors" because of structural weaknesses, systemic inequities, and high costs. Nothing is left unscathed in castigating the ideal of a monogamous, nuclear family as little more than a "comfortable concentration camp" (Frieden, 1963). The conventional family is deemed a training ground for conformity and control, with an oppressive set of rules and roles that lock both women and men into rigidly scripted relationships (Alvear, 2003). Women are robbed of individuality and a sense of self-worth because of dependency and demeaning patterns associated with maternal–domestic spheres. Similarly, men are locked into behavioural patterns that preclude "softer" definitions of masculinity. Contradictions abound because of this inequality. For example, men have the final say in critical matters but prefer to remain aloof from involvement in domestic affairs except to "help out." By contrast, women continue to shoulder the bulk of domestic drudgery without much reward or recognition, while adjusting their careers around maternal responsibilities and spousal priorities. Admittedly, patterns of dominance are less obvious than in the past, thanks to human rights awareness and progressive legislation. Yet evidence suggests that power and privilege do not have to be blatant to be coercive or controlling.

Sociologists have responded to growing awareness of "the dark side of the family." As is the case elsewhere, perspective matters. Those of a functionalist persuasion see domestic conflict as an aberration (a deviance from the norm) in a system that craves consensus and cooperation for social stability. For functionalists, a functioning society is an orderly one, and the dynamics and design of society are geared towards creating, maintaining, and restoring equilibrium. Of particular importance in maintaining a cohesive and stable society is a healthy and functioning family (Yoest, 1994). Strong, stable family ties can reduce the incidence of violence, poverty, substance abuse, educational failure, and social drop outs. Societal stability and regulation are achieved by carrying out the basic functions associated with the family, including reproduction, socialization, sexual control, economic production and consumption, and emotional satisfaction. Fulfillment of these functions enhances the integration of individuals into society as long as everybody knows their place and complies with the script.

Conflict theorists agree that marriage and family are functional, but "functional for whom" and "for what purposes"? According to conflict theorists, inequality is a central feature of society, and institutional arrangements are designed to secure class-based inequality. As Frederick Engels (a lifelong collaborator of Karl Marx) remarked over a century ago, nuclear families exist to serve capitalist class interests, in part by creating a division of labour that separates the private world of women from the public domain monopolized by men. The consequences of this gender-based segregation proved disruptive to women's lives and life chances. The status of women deteriorated because of the marginalization under a patriarchal arrangement that reduced their status to little more than kept property. Abusive relations and domestic violence are inevitable in situations involving such an exploitative context.

Variations on this line of argument contend that the conventional family arose for political rather than strictly economic reasons (Hite, 1994). With urban-industrialism, the new political order was confronted with the problem of ensuring the flow of inheritance through males. The modern patriarchal family was created to establish male control over a woman who would produce children for "him." Restrictions were placed on women's lives and sexuality to ensure that "his" children were the sole beneficiaries of family inheritances. Male control over children completed the confinement of women within the patriarchal framework of a nuclear family. It also reinforced perception of marriage and family as institutions for controlling men from wandering while securing a relatively safe environment for women and children (Alvear, 2003).

Divorce: Problem Or Solution?

How does each sociological perspective connect the institutional crisis in the family with divorce? Sociological responses are clearly divided in judging divorce as cutting edge or a downward spiral. For some, divorce is defined as a problem, for others a solution. Escalating rates of divorce in Canada are criticized by some as the cause of major social problems, by others as a symptom of broader moral decay and social disintegration, and by still others as a sign of growing maturity in customizing institutions to fit people's needs, not vice versa. For functionalists, divorce poses a danger to the system; for conflict theorists, the crisis represents an opportunity for healthier alternatives. For some, galloping divorce rates are a sign of society in distress. For others, high rates of divorce confirm that the institutions of marriage and family are as resilient as ever.

Divorce is denounced by those who uphold the fundamental soundness of the existing institutional framework. Most divorces, it is argued, are accompanied by emotional stress and financial strain, with children often experiencing disruption and distress, while the burden of single parenting becomes even more onerous because of responsibility overload, task overload, and emotional overload (Kornblum and Julian, 1995). Worse still, divorce has become so common and casual that many now trivialize it as little more than a temporary inconvenience, with little impact on either parents or children—despite some evidence to the contrary, given the delayed effects of such a life-transforming experience (Lash-Quinn, 2002; Wallerstein et al., 2002). A cavalier attitude to divorce is also thought to contribute to sexual permissiveness, juvenile delinquency, deterioration of "family values," and trivialization of key human relations. Others disagree: They applaud escalating rates as a progressive sign in heralding the demise of rigid and patriarchal family structures, followed by their replacement with more humane alternatives. Even the harm to children may be overstated. In a study that appeared in the *American Psychologist*, Louise Silverstein and Carl Auerbach of New York's Yeshiva University argue that most children do not suffer significant long-term effects from divorce, especially when escaping abusive domestic contexts. Those who suffer from divorce tend to land in poverty, lose contact with extended family, and are uprooted from familiar neighbourhoods (Milstone, 1999). Children rarely need both parents to flourish; usually one responsible adult with a positive emotional connection and a consistent relationship is sufficient. Still others see escalating divorce rates as inevitable for an institution in transition. Rather than a rejection of family and marriage as institutions, divorce can be interpreted as an affirmation of core values and key institutions. They also criticize how divorce rates can be manipulated by vested interests. I leave it to the reader to decide—on sociological grounds—whether contemporary families are experiencing a "positive" or "negative" crisis, and if divorce should be interpreted as "good" or "bad" or "in between."

Let's put divorce into a statistical perspective. In the year 2000, there were 157 395 marriages in Canada, representing a small increase of 1.1 percent over 1999. A total of 71 144 couples finalized their divorces in 2000, an increase of 3 percent since 1998. Nevertheless, divorce rates are beginning to fall, from 137.6 divorces per 100 000 of population in 1971, up to 307.8 per 100 000 of population in 1989, down to 262.2 per 100 000 of population in 1995, and continuing downwards to just over 231.2 per 100 000 of population in 2000 (Statistics Canada, *Canada Social Trends*, Summer 2003). Still, Canada's divorce rate, which is thought to be a main index of social stability and health, is one of the highest in the world, according to the OECD data, behind those of Sweden but well above Turkey and Mexico. Nor can we ignore the costs: A total of 1.8 million Canadian children (or one in five) are growing up in single-parent households. According to a 1998 Human Resources Development Centre report, more than half of the single-parent families earned less than $20 000 per year, compared to only about 5 percent of two-parent families. Eighty percent of these single parents were women, and 60 percent lived below the low-income cut-off line. Lone father families do better than single mother families, but they still earn only about 54 percent of two-parent family incomes.

What can we say about divorce as a social problem or solution? First, divorces are not nearly as common as people think. For example, it is commonly believed that between one-third and one-half of all marriages will end up in divorce. Those figures are extremely misleading: They are derived from tallying the number of divorces in any given year, then dividing that figure into the total number of marriages for the same year. For example, in the year 2000 a total of 157 395 Canadian couples married, while 71 144 divorces were granted (Statistics Canada, 1998). But comparing the number of marriages with the number of divorces in each given year to arrive at a divorce rate is misleading, since the couples who divorce in each year are unlikely to come from the group that married that year (Kendall et al., 2004). What becomes ignored in these tabulations is the overall number of marriages that stay intact from year to year. By tracking marriages from start to finish, nearly 85 percent of first-time marriages will survive until death does them part. The revolving door rate of divorce and remarriage in the remaining 15 percent may inflate the divorce totals.

Second, divorces reflect a gradual deinstitutionalization across society. Changes in people's perceptions of what they expect from marriage reflect broader social changes. Primary emphasis in the past lay with the discharging of role obligations and moral necessity. People did what was expected of them out of duty or from fear of social disgrace and ostracism. In a life filled with drudgery and economic uncertainty, the pursuit of marital happiness as an explicit goal was rarely a priority. With lowered expectations, a happy marriage and family life may have been defined as reflecting an absence of mutual antagonism. A shortened life span may have eased the burden of unhappiness without having to resort to divorce. But attitudes toward marriage are shifting because of the increased value placed on personal contentment and emotional satisfaction, a marked relaxation in patterns of authority and convention, and the growing assertiveness of women at political, economic, and ideological levels. Higher divorce rates can be attributed to a variety of factors. These might include: higher expectations of the marriage partners; easier access because of relaxed grounds for divorce; longer lives, thus eliminating early death as a means of dissolving an unhappy marriage; a commitment to personal growth and self-actualization as the ultimate value; a growing willingness to terminate an abusive relationship if emotional needs are unsatisfied; discontent with an existing partner because of shifting expectations; increased economic independence of women; access to birth control and sexual freedom without the "obligations"; and increased acceptance of divorce as inevitable and necessary. Moreover, divorce rarely elicits the moral indignation or social stigma that it once did except within certain religious circles. Rather than being defined as a personal failure or problem, divorce is increasingly tolerated as an unfortunate but inevitable dynamic of a "me-first" society that is becoming more tolerant and accommodating, yet also more self-centred and indulgent.

Third, there is no proof that higher divorce rates signify an institution in decline. The fact many remarry suggests that most accept the concept of marriage in principle. People are not looking for something outside marriage; rather they are seeking greater emotional fulfillment within the framework of a less-scripted format. This suggests that the pursuit of happiness rather than fulfilment of legal obligations is a primary motive for marrying. Marriage and family are no longer about imperatives or obligations, but about options (Mooney et al., 2001). There is a much higher commitment to the relationship than to the institution than once was the case. In contrast to the past, people now define "happy" marriages and family life in terms of positive predictors pertaining to support, personal satisfaction, and individual growth. There are less compelling bonds for supporting an emotionally bankrupt relation. This emphasis on relationships and emotions creates a more unstable and unrealistic condition, amenable to rupture and dissolution. It also creates the basis for a more satisfying and egalitarian partnership by relieving the pressure to stick it out, for better or for worse.

In short, high divorce rates may not necessarily reflect greater unhappiness or institutional rejection. Relatively high rates may reflect evolving notions of domesticity in shifting from "scripted" duty (where everything is in its place) to customized satisfaction (where everything is up for grabs). Divorce does not symbolize a rejection of marriage or family as institutions, but an acknowledgement that individuals make unfortunate choices within the institutional framework of society. To be sure, suggesting that divorces are a "healthy" sign is not the same as endorsing them; nor should we casually dismiss their impact at large, especially on the lives of children or grandparents. Nevertheless, the lack of institutional stability in contemporary families is not necessarily reflective of a "lost" society. This crisis and confusion may be attributable to the persistence of antiquated structure and institutional norms in coping with the demands of the 21st century.

A sense of perspective is useful. What could be less "natural" than two strangers making a lifelong commitment only to each other along a broad range of fronts and responsibilities. Similarly, there is nothing unnatural about two people not conforming to such highly demanding expectations, especially in a culture based on "looking out for number one" (Lash-Quinn, 2002). Like it or not, approve or disapprove, divorce has emerged as a response to those who want to terminate destructive relationships, achieve personal growth and identity, and to alleviate stress because of fear, violence, and boredom. The social anchors that once made marriage an evitable step in a young person's life—a rite of passage into adulthood—are no longer there (Hutsul, 2002). The traditional rationales for kin and community have been replaced by personal commitment, with the result that young people no longer look to the church or state to approve what they believe is a private decision.

The deinstitutionalization of marriage cannot be separated from divorce rates. Perhaps divorces are one way of reminding us that social conventions may be necessary for social order, but contrary to human needs or emergent realities. That many marriages *do* survive until death rents asunder what women and men have put together is a testimony to the powers of socialization and social control.

Into the 21st Century: From Traditional Script to Contested Site

The modern family cannot be interpreted as neutral or devoid of interest. Inasmuch as the family is a social institution that shapes and is shaped by other public institutions, the conventional family in Canada is highly idealized. Yet modern families originated and continue to exist to reflect national interests, advance the demands of capitalism, bolster male experiences and ideologies, and embrace masculinist definitions of the world (McDaniel, 1998). Rules that establish a relationship between the roles of husband and wife have evolved over time in the context of capitalist patriarchy. From the Industrial era onward, the traditional relationship was based on the male as breadwinner, the female as homemaker (Skolnick, 1973; Eichler, 1983; and Mandell, 1987). Gender roles were fixed for the most part along traditional patterns associated with the ideals of masculinity and femininity. These scripted roles contributed to and shaped the nature of family interaction, including patterns of domination, control, and dependency.

It is apparent that the institutions of family and marriage are undergoing change. Uncertainty prevails under such disruptive conditions. Many believe the family is worse off than ever, in part because people compare the complex and diverse families of the new millennium with 1950s families, a unique era when every long-term trend of the 20th century converged around a national consensus on family values and norms, albeit in a climate of coercion, censorship, deprivation, and discrimination (Stacey, 1997). Concerns about the family reflect how much better we want to be, rather than how much better we used to be when problems from spousal rape to housewife depression were routinely swept under the rug. Admittedly, there is still no clear-cut answer with regards to what women and men want from each other in a spousal relationship. Do women look at marriage and family as an opportunity to be taken seriously as a productive partner in an equitable relationship? Do men look for old-fashioned virtues, coupled with modern skills but with none of the hang-ups? National surveys clearly indicate that the vast majority of Canadians marry, raise families, and remarry when the opportunity arises. What is being abandoned are specific and scripted styles of domesticity that sculpted individuals into a one-size-fits-all family format.

No less transformative is the institution of marriage. In less than a generation, the concept of marriage has morphed from a straight path down the aisle to a zigzag gauntlet of unions, breakups, and blends. Consider the following: the growing popularity of cohabitation ("living together"), the percentage of children born outside the family or with a single parent, the rising age of first marriages and rising rates of divorce, and the belief that happy and stable unions are the stuff of Hollywood, not reality (Amato et al., 2003). Public reaction is contradicted: Judging by national census data, marriage may be losing some of its lustre among Canadians (Kueng, 2003), yet others suggest a growing popularity as the new "it" accessory in times of emotional high alert (Kingston, 2003). Young people are rejecting some of the formal trappings associated with institutionalized marriage, but nearly every survey says that having a happy marriage-like relation remains the number one goal—over career, popularity, or good health (Hutsul, 2002). Judging by the number and popularity of TV reality shows that revolve around 'tying the knot' such as Trista and Ryan's Wedding, the fantasy is alive and well. The fact that gays are demanding official marriage status for same-sex unions while straights appear to be increasingly indifferent about such formality also speaks volumes about the state of institutional disarray.

CASE 6-1	Rethinking Spanking: Children Are People Too

The roles, rules, and relationships that accompany familydom are confusing and contradictory. What exactly does it mean to be a husband or wife—or partners—in these changing and confusing times? Spousal roles are not the only ones to undergo redefinition. The role of parents with respect to rules that govern their relationship to children are no less subject to change and confusion. How should parents relate to children—as friends, as guidance councillors, as disciplinarians? Consider the case of physical punishment as indicative of the reversal in rethinking parent–child relations. Until recently it was routinely accepted that sparing the rod would spoil the child; parents who did not apply such discipline were seen as derelict of duty. But the tide is shifting, together with the underlying assumptions that justify physical punishment. Children are increasingly defined as having fundamental rights that are protected under the charter, including equal protection under the law. No wonder then that spanking children in public is likely to be greeted with social disapproval or a charge of assault, in contrast to the past when a "cuff" was seen as a corrective.

The issue came to a boil in 2001 when the Family and Children Services of St. Thomas and Elgin County in Southern Ontario removed seven children from their home after learning the children had been disciplined with objects from fly swatters to electric cords by their parents, former Mennonites who now belonged to the Aylmer Church of God (Harries, 2003). The removal sparked heated reactions. Some argued that all parents and guardians possess the right to physically discipline children as long as this force is applied judiciously, for corrective purposes, without malice, and with care and compassion. Others questioned the so-called right of parents to punish children physically. Such discipline is seen as ineffective, publicly degrading to a child or to the parent, and conveying mixed messages about violence as a problem-solving alternative. Children need to be disciplined or forewarned of pending danger, to be sure, but resorting to physical blows is by definition abusive. Besides, how can we justify using force against the most vulnerable members of society when assault toward others is unacceptable in this era of zero tolerance?

What does the law say? According to section 43 of the Criminal Code, "reasonable" force may be used to correct a child. First introduced in 1892, the Code allowed the use of corrective force against women, employees, and prisoners as well as children, although the UN

(continued on next page)

has criticized Canada's reliance on corporal punishment to discipline children (Edwards, 2003; Vallis, 2003). Over a century later, children remain the only class of Canadians whose behaviour can be modified through reasonable force by parents, teachers, guardians, and babysitters. But even defining "reasonable" has proven elusive, despite repeated efforts by the Supreme Court of Canada to clarify the criteria for reasonableness (including the nature of the child's offence, the age and character of the child, the likely effect of the punishment on the child, the type of punishment resulting in injury, and whether the punishment was motivated by anger or arbitrariness (Silver, 1999). Such indecision is not without consequences. Ambiguities around the concept of "reasonableness" may equip parents with an escape clause should children be injured under the guise of correcting them (Robertshaw, 1999). Yet many are afraid of the implications if the law is pushed to its logical conclusion. Fears are expressed that repealing section 43 may undermine parental authority by denying protection to parents and teachers who are behaving reasonably but find themselves charged with assault for applying force without consent (Goddard, 2003). The dilemma is all too palpable: How to protect children without criminalizing parents by turning mild punishment into a criminal offence?

This case raises a number of issues related to parent–child relations in the new millennium. First and foremost are the topsy-turvy shifts in the rules that guide appropriate behaviour. Solutions of the past can become problems in the present: Consider how what once was seen as conventional wisdom, even virtuous, ("spare the rod and spoil the child") is now dismissed as dangerous or deviant. Second, there are questions about what it means to be a good parent in a world where the rules, roles, and responsibilities of parenting are increasingly contested. Is physical punishment a useful way of raising children, or is it a way of making parents feel better in releasing anger and frustration? With parents already experiencing guilt over their decreased involvement with children, the lack of answers only intensifies the confusion. Third, to what extent is parenting a private rather than public affair? Historically many viewed the relationship between parents and children as private, in the same way that husband–wife relations were regarded as nobody's business. But the politicization of family violence has changed all that. The moral panic over widespread child abuse has implicated state authorities and the general public. Finally, children are no longer viewed as property under parental control and discretion. Children do have human rights, with the same protection as adults from physical harm and assault (Covell and Howe, 2001). With the primacy of human rights as the basis for rewards and recognition, the interests of children are challenging parental rights and autonomy (Harries, 2003), further reinforcing how both religion and political leadership are losing moral authority as arbiters of right and wrong.

Repercussions from this shift is staggering. A revolution is emerging not only in the nature of parent–child relations but also in shifting the focus of family from parents to children. Key issues must be addressed as a result of this shift, including the role of parents in correcting children. Should parents be more permissive and run the risk of inflating children's self-esteem to the point where spoiled kids call the shots,

(continued on next page)

lack real-world coping skills, have little concern for others, and lack any moral compass for distinguishing right from wrong (Underwood, 1999)? Removal of the right to physically punish in other countries such as Sweden appears to have reduced rates of child abuse. Such a challenge should also remind the general public that parenting within a conventional family is an extremely underrated yet complex job for which few are properly equipped. The challenge of new disciplinary techniques makes it more enticing than ever to introduce mandatory training for new parents in coping with the perils and promises of parenting in the new millennium.

Case Study Questions

1 How has the issue of parents spanking their children reflected and reinforced evolving trends in parenting and how the family is conceptualized?

2 How can spanking be regarded as a social problem if the law allows the use of "reasonable force" to correct children's behaviour?

Postscript: The Supreme Court ruled in January 2004 that parents and teachers may use force to correct a child's behaviour as long as this force is minimal ("reasonable"), but not with children under two or with teens, and not administered out of rage.

How can changes to the family be assessed? One might argue that the institution is cresting the wave of social changes at large. The transition from an elitist (authoritarian) society to a more egalitarian society is reflected in the contesting of rules, roles, and relationships that constitute a modern family. Conversely, one might suggest that neither the traditional authoritarian family nor its modern-day counterpart represents an accurate reading of what is really happening. Most families fall somewhere in between these ideal forms, with the result that many family types incorporate confusing mixtures of the authoritarian and egalitarian. For example, most Canadians would endorse the principle of an egalitarian partnership with respect to duties and responsibilities. Whereas 42 percent of Canadians in 1983 agreed that the father of the family must be the master of his own house, that figure dropped to 17 percent in 1998— although ironically support for the notion of the man as king of the castle remains consistently high in the United States (*Maclean's,* 25 January, 1999; Adams, 2000).

The reality is much different in practice: Most relationships continue to reflect fundamental inequalities, even in situations in which women work outside the home. As Jan Mannette (1966: 11) observed a generation ago: "Nobody objects to a woman being a good writer or sculptor as long as she manages to be a good wife, mother, good looking, good tempered, well dressed and well groomed." In effect, the labour-force status of women does not necessarily mean equality at home. It is more likely instead to double the workload, with corresponding frustration and resentment because of role conflicts. Yes, men are more likely to "assist" with domestic activities, especially in the care of children, but this is perceived as "helping out," rather than any fundamental restructuring of the division of labour. Society may be responsible for this double standard: Women and men appear to be caught in an unforgiving vice between traditional role models and a changing world. Once they decide to have children, there is a corresponding tendency to backslide into traditional arrangements that intensify women's dependency on maternal–domestic roles but reduce economic power (Carter and Peters, 1996). Refusal to take domesticity seriously may suit male interests and resistance but is a major source of tension in contemporary families.

But new relations are emerging that embrace more egalitarian ideals. Family roles are much more flexible, determined in part by experience and choice, and in part by dual-income careers and a freedom associated with financial security. Relations between partners are not nearly as rigid or authoritarian as in the past. Decisions to stay together are voluntary and personal, and based on balancing duty with companionship and personal empowerment. Advances in levels of education, employment, and income of women have improved their status within a family. These advances have also enhanced women's decision-making powers while securing the potential for less abusive and more egalitarian relationships (Amato et al., 2003). This shift is not complete by any stretch of the imagination: More accurately, families can be interpreted as sites of contestation in varying stages of transition. Many of the rules that governed patterns of interaction within the family are under scrutiny, with the result that conventional norms are less applicable than once was the case. Family dynamics are undergoing change in response to the gradual decoupling of women and men from tightly scripted rules, roles, and relationships. The family is no longer a nested hierarchy in which everyone knows their place and what to do. What we have instead of a conventional "script" is a contested "site" that is subject to negotiation and compromise (Alvear, 2003). Patterns of interaction within domestic arrangements are increasingly varied as people look for ways to balance their roles as career persons with obligations as family members, without necessarily discarding personal aspirations and goals. Even relationships between parents and children have shifted to embrace a more enlightened set of "rules" for living together as family.

DISCUSSION QUESTIONS

1   Respond to the statement: "The modern family is in crisis." Be sure to include in your answer reference to who says so, why, and on what grounds.

2   Indicate some of the ways in which the rules, roles, rights, and relationships have evolved within the family, in the process creating families as "contested sites."

3   Indicate how the concept of divorce in relationship to family and society is approached differently by functionalist versus conflict theorists.

4   How does the structure of nuclear families contribute to domestic abuse and spousal violence?

5   Define family and defend your choice.

6   Demonstrate how public and legal attitudes toward the spanking of children reflect changes in parent–child relations within the context of the family.

 WEBLINKS

Focus on Family, Canada.   **www.family.org**

Divorce Magazine.   **www.divorcemag.com**

Same-sex marriage in Canada.   **www.religoustolerance.org**

chapter seven

Mainstream Media

FRAMING THE PROBLEM

A generation ago, references to mass media conveyed images of household furniture: In one corner, a rectangular TV cabinet with "bunny ears" to improve reception; in another corner, an equally boxy stereo console with an automatic record changer; and in yet another corner, an upright radio with glowing dials that promised programming from exotic overseas locales. Most of us believed that media could be regulated by turning over a page, or clicking the off button, or simply looking the other way. How times have changed: Today media are everything and everywhere. Our lives are awash in the media —from television to films, from radio to the Internet and video games. Their pervasiveness is such that media infiltrate into our lives without much awareness or resistance from us. Boundaries are blurred, orthodox wisdom is being eroded, and conventions of order from hierarchy to loyalty are undermined (Tarlow and Tarlow, 2002). The link between the "in-here" and the "out-there" is increasingly "media-ted." Reality is not lived except through images that, in turn, shape the reality of lived experiences. Personal identities and interpersonal relations are so inextricably linked with the media that human existence is unthinkable without their input. To their credit, many Canadians generally seem vaguely cognizant of the media as a powerful social force, with the capacity to distort, conceal, or distract. Few, however, possess the critical skills necessary to unpack the techniques behind mass persuasion. Even fewer are equipped to put these deconstructions into practice in a way that challenges and resists.

Few would dispute the role of media in shaping how people look at the world, how they understand it, and the manner in which they relate to it (Lorimer and Gasher, 2001; Attallah and Shade, 2002). Put bluntly, our lives are informed by, take refuge in, and revolve around media images. In a media-saturated world such as ours, the challenge is not more information but in deciding which opinions and insights have the most credibility (Williams, 2003). Young people increasingly rely on media for models to emulate or reassure; after all, nothing in their lives is of sufficient import to neutralize the impact of television, movies, the Internet, or video games as substitute parental authorities. Incidents that matter become media events; media events matter, by definition. The implications are unnerving: In an image-based world of media where life imitates art rather than vice versa, the ability to distinguish reality from fantasy can no longer be taken for granted since media messages reformulate the very reality under observation. Such formidable power reinforces the absurdity of reducing the media to simply a mechanical transmission of information on a massive scale. The media are this, yet more, with consequences as dismaying as they are disruptive.

Consider the agenda-setting functions of mass media. The power of mainstream media—either to challenge or control—is based on defining which issues are on the agenda, how these issues are to be discussed, and whose voices will be included or excluded from the debate (Polzer, 2003). A media-dominated society tends to elevate electronic and print media to a privileged status in articulating what is right or wrong, acceptable or unacceptable. Those in control of the media define the beliefs, values, and myths by which we live and organize our lives. They impose a cultural context for framing our experiences of social reality, in the process sending out a clear message about who is normal and what is desirable (Abel, 1997; Seale, 2002). In their ability to redefine normal conduct and reshape behavioural standards, popular media discharge a double duty as "weapons of mass persuasion": They not only change people's notions of what is accepted; popular ideas of what is expected are altered as well (Altheide, 2002; Doyle, 2003). Our dependence on the media for reality construction assumes even greater relevance in the absence of direct experience. Without necessarily impugning the integrity of the news media, how do we know what really happened, except as interpreted by the press? Whose interpretation made it onto the screen or into print? The taint of propaganda is unmistakable, in other words, and may reflect an institutional bias that is inherent rather than inserted.

References to media as a social problem remain a lively source of debate. The controversy over the use of embedded journalism in the Iraqi conflict attests to this, as does the popularity of reality programming on television, a growing reliance on product placement within films, and an increased commercialization of the Internet in displacing its democratic potential (Fleras, 2003). Reaction to media's ubiquitous presence has been mixed. For some, media are endorsed as a positive force in advancing human progress. Mainstream media are touted as indispensable in the construction of a democratic and cosmopolitan society (Gans, 2003). Others are less sanguine about media effects. Media are deplored as (a) an insult to the human spirit; (b) an instrument for promoting mediocrity or stifling creativity while encouraging antisocial behaviour; (c) a system of social control that reinforces racism and sexism; (d) a tool of propaganda at odds with social goals; and (e) a discourse in defence of privilege (Wilson II et al., 2003). In Canada's multicultural society where diversity is endorsed as inseparable from society-building, mainstream media have come under additional criticism for compromising the goals of a diverse society (Fleras and Kunz, 2001). To be sure, the media cannot be blamed for all the social problems in society; nor can they be expected to provide all solutions. Yet media-bashing has become a favourite pastime among those looking for a quick fix to society's problems. Scapegoating the media may have the virtue of simplifying the problem for blame. Unfortunately, such simplicity does little to advance our insight or offer a solution.

Clearly, then, we must go beyond the knee-jerk reaction that automatically conflates mainstream mass media with a social problem. The challenge lies in accepting the media as a normal and important component of contemporary life without excluding its potential to harm, deny, or exclude. Four themes prevail in pinpointing the media as a social problem: First, the media are interpreted as a problem in their own right. Media content is riddled with hidden values and agendas that benefit some and handicap others. The media establish standards of performance, then fail to live up to these expectations, in effect creating a warp between anticipation (what they say they do) and reality (and what they really do). Promises to enlighten, educate, and inform often are forgotten in the rush to entertain, titillate, and distort, if necessary. Second, the media are known to generate social problems by virtue of their impact and effects. Media create problems by circulating images and narratives that twist personal attitudes, distort people's perceptions, foster antisocial behaviour, shape public discourses that encourage poor choices and imperil individual safety, and help formulate public policies at odds with national interests. Their status as big business, as discourses in defence of dominant ideology, and as thought control in a democratic society make it doubly important to explore how media bolster patterns of privilege, social control, and domination. Third, problems arise because of debates over the nature of media relations with society. Media are defined as a social problem for their failure to advance a particular vision of Canada. Should media help to foster a pluralistic and socially responsive Canada as a community of communities? Or should media reinforce a market-driven society that exults in profit, competition, and unfettered individualism? This lack of consensus regarding media–society relations creates a context for problem proliferation. Fourth, defining media as a social problem reflects different public expectations. Those who look to the media as a source of entertainment, fantasy, and distraction will not be disappointed by the current fare. Those who believe the media have a responsibility for critically informed citizenship and progressive change continue to be dismayed.

How, then, are media a social problem? Who says so, and why, on what grounds, and by what criteria can such an assessment be made? If the media are a problem, what is the solution? This chapter approaches mainstream media within the context of the "good," the "bad," and the "in between." Emphasis is on the social dimensions of media–society relations by focusing on how this often contested relationship is constructed, expressed, maintained, challenged, and transformed. The concept of media as a social problem is examined at several levels, including: (a) the media's impact on Canada as a democracy; (b) the role of advertising, newscasting, and the Internet in shaping public attitudes; (c) negative effects of televised violence; (d) harm inflicted on minority women and men; and (e) the media's tendency to generate public discourses that weaken Canada's social fabric. This chapter begins by asking the question "What are media?" Deconstructing the media by challenging its assumed autonomy as a privileged mode of communication clearly reveals a hidden agenda of class, power, and control (Mickey, 2003). Advertising is discussed as capitalist propaganda insofar as values and beliefs are conveyed that reflect commercial interests rather than community well-being. The concept of media impacts is examined next by problematizing the concept of newscasting. The biases that drive the social construction of news are shown to create public discourses at odds with a critically informed democratic citizenship (Nadeau and Giasson, 2003; Gans, 2003). Media (mis)representation of minorities at the level of image, symbol, and narrative provides further insight into media impacts, while references to the Internet clearly reveal its ambiguous impact, with the positive intermingling with the negative to yield a fundamental ambiguity. The final section of this chapter explores the problem of media effects. A look at the relationship between television violence and violent behaviour exposes some of the complexities in sorting out media effects. Exposed, as well, is the fallacy of media determinism in shaping behaviour. The chapter concludes by trying to assess whether censorship is a solution to a problem or creates more problems than its worth.

WHAT ARE MEDIA?

Defining media is not as simple as it looks. The term "media" (plural) may look singular, but this simply disguises a diverse range of products and processes, including: books, movies, magazines, advertising, radio, TV, newscasting, and the Internet. Each medium (singular) embraces yet more internal diversity. Newscasting can consist of news on television, radio, the Internet, and newspapers (including broadsheets, tabloids, dailies, weeklies, mainstream, ethnic, and so on) (Loseke, 2003). Moreover, media are increasingly contradicted by paradoxical trends. Ownership of media is more concentrated than ever as fewer owners own more media, but audiences are fragmenting into many niches as populations diversify (Weston, 2003). Technology may be taking the "mass" out of mass media, but the same technology is making it easier to target a broader mass of people. Exposure to media may improve understanding, but the level of understanding may be so superficial that confusion and conflict are intensified. The list could continue, but the point should be clear: How we define the media depends on many factors that are not necessarily consistent with each other.

Historically, media could be defined as a rapid, mechanical, and one-way transmission of standardized information to a mass audience. With the advent of new technologies, media are better defined as interactional systems of communication in which customized information is exchanged from many to one rather than one to many. While such definitions are accurate enough, they fall short of our purposes. Framing the media as a social problem is not necessarily self-evident. Attention must be drawn to what the media really do, why and how, by probing both beneath and behind. A peek into the "hidden agenda" exposes mass mainstream media for what they really are: Systems of thought control within contexts of power and politics (Fleras, 2003). Media contribute to thought control in democratic societies along three dimensions: (a) commercial logic; (b) discourse in defense of dominant ideology; and (c) institutional propaganda.

Commercial Imperatives

Of those dynamics that animate media content or process, few are as pervasive as the commercial imperative and the perpetuation of values consistent with conspicuous consumerism (Giroux, 2003). The media do not exist to inform or to entertain. As a rule they are not interested in solving social problems or fostering progressive social change unless profit margins are directly involved, even if critics think they have a social responsibility to do so. They are a business whose raison d'être is simple: to make money by connecting audiences to advertisers (Lester and Ross, 2003). Veteran TV producer Aaron Spelling put it succinctly when asked to account for media miscasting of minorities: "Our industry is not about Black or White. It's about money ... the only colour that matters in TV is green" (*National Post*, 26 July, 1999: B-7).

Contemporary news media (both print and broadcast) are driven by big business dynamics (Winter, 2002). The struggle to absorb companies and consolidate power by multimedia companies such as AOL-Time Warner embody this corporate feeding frenzy to be top dog in the convergence game (Pitts, 2002). This is certainly the case in Canada, where independent news sources are a vanishing breed. In lieu of independents are chains such as CanWest or Osprey, in addition to Rogers, Shaw Communications, BCE, and Quebecor. These corporations approach the news sector as a money-making business venture. Even publicly owned networks such as the CBC appear to be increasingly market-driven (Taras, 2001). A commercial imperative compromises the integrity of the news media. It sharpens the potential for a conflict of interest between corporate needs and consumer concerns. Distance is created because of corporate ownership in which the chief concern is a return on investment, with audiences as little more than a marketplace for cheaply produced information (Miller, 2003). A preoccupation with profit can lead to erratic (or non-existent) coverage of issues of relevance to an informed society (Gans, 2003). This "bottom line" mentality ensures a version of the news that may sacrifice impartiality or detachment. The cumulative effect of this implicit collusion between news and big business (and the government) is not necessarily conspiratorial in intent as much as a convergence of mutual interests.

Discourses in Defence of Ideology

Many perceive mass media as little more than a content delivery system. Like a postal system, mass media are thought to involve processes that mechanically but disinterestedly deliver prepackaged bits of information from sender to receiver. Nothing could be more wrong: Media are not simply passive or neutral channels for delivery of content; more accurately, media convey information because they embody ideological values that reflect and reinforce the status quo. Rather than neutral conveyors of disinterested information, media are themselves actively involved in shaping the content of information by privileging some perspectives, denying others (Sharmarke, 2003).

Reference to media as discourses in defence of ideology reflects this notion of a politicized media. According to this line of thinking, the media are loaded with ideological assumptions that not only reflect the ideas and ideals of a dominant discourse, but also preclude the values and views of those that might contest an unequal order (Abel, 1997). As discourses in defence of ideology, the media are effective in drawing attention to certain aspects of reality as natural, normal, and superior. Other aspects are dismissed as irrelevant or inferior. Media messages combine to "normalize" contemporary social arrangements as "natural" and "non-political" rather than as self-serving social constructs. Inasmuch as they secure consent and domination through consensus and control rather than coercion, mainstream media are hegemonic. This hegemony is achieved in several ways, including: (a) to represent dominant interests as universal and progressive rather than particular and parochial; (b) to deny contradictions such as those related to capitalist production and distribution; and (c) to privilege the present as "common sense." (Engstrom, 2003).

Thought Control As Institutionalized Propaganda

There is little question that the media are powerful agencies with the capacity to dominate and control. Media define issues, impose frames on them, and decide whose voices will prevail in the discussion. In some cases, the exercise of power is blatant; in others, media power is sustained by an aura of impartiality, objectivity, and balance. A capacity to set agendas by framing issues around the status quo reinforces the notion of media as thought control in democratic societies (Hermann and Chomsky, 1988). This agenda-setting property also reinforces a view of the media in advancing national interests at global levels (Chomsky, 2003).

Propaganda can be defined as a process of persuasion by which the few influence the many (Pratkanis, 2002). Symbols are manipulated in an organized and one-sided fashion to modify attitudes or behaviour (Qualter, 1991). By contrast, an institutionalized propaganda dismisses the element of intent or consciousness as part of the persuasion process. Proposed instead is the idea of consequence or effect: That is, the way in which information is defined, organized, and distributed may have a controlling effect by promoting one point of view to the exclusion of others. In taking this perspective, institutional propaganda is neither equated with blatant brainwashing nor synonymous with crude displays of totalitarian censorship. Nor is it a kind of lying that is deliberately inserted into the media. Rather, institutional propaganda is inherent within media rules and intrinsic to daily operations, in the same way that systemic discrimination reflects the negative but unintended consequences of even-handed rules or well-intentioned procedures that, when equally and evenly applied, have a discriminatory effect (Fleras and Elliott, 2003). The net result is the same in both cases: a one-sided interpretation of reality that normalizes even while it marginalizes.

Media objectives are directed towards the goals of "manufacturing consent" and "generating compliance." The shaping of public discourses can be accomplished in several ways, as Herman and Chomsky (1988) remind us: First, powerful interests can fix the parameters of debate by circumscribing the outer limits of acceptability for discussion; second, government and the corporate elite have monopolized access to what eventually is defined as news; third, major advertisers can dictate the terms of media content; and fourth media owners can influence what will or will not appear by suppressing information at odds with powerful interests. Admittedly, the media do not act in collusion when presenting a monolithic front. Even less plausible is the idea of media driven by a cabal of conspirators. Media authorities are known to disagree with one another, criticize powerful interests for betraying national interests, and expose government corruption and corporate greed. Even the relationship between media and military within the context of conflict is highly unstable and complicated by divergent interests and expectations, corporate agendas, political interests, military strategies, and ongoing shifts in culture and technology (Menon, 2003). But such debates are more apparent than real, suggest Herman and Chomsky (1988), reflecting disagreement over means rather than tacitly accepted ends or goals. Left largely untouched are the underlying principles of capitalism, liberalism, democracy, and Western supremacy. Spirited discussion and lively dissension may be encouraged but only within the framework of assumptions that constitute an elite consensus, with the result that debates are limited to squabbles over details, not substance. For these reasons, the media can be interpreted as systems of institutionalized thought control ("propaganda") in democratic societies, especially when applied to advertising.

Did You Know?

Media coverage of the war in Iraq provides an excellent study of propaganda in action (Fleras, 2003). The propaganda factor has proven as important to the war effort as the movement of troops, offensive sorties, and deployment of resources. In a world where there is no mind-independent reality, only representations of reality by way of images (both verbal and non-verbal), those in charge of media can control what people think about. Not surprisingly, concerns are mounting that both the US and British governments have duped the public, thanks to the complicity of the free press (Edwards and Cromwell, 2003). On the coalition side, coverage of the war reflects propaganda that sanitizes the war by making it more palatable—little more than a video game—for those Americans without the stomach for a protracted conflict. The idea behind this sterile coverage is to legitimize the coalition forces by stupefying Americans into a false sense of security.

The inception of embedded journalism within the coalition forces is complicit in this endeavour. Journalists may have been excluded from the fighting during the First Gulf War in 1991, according to John R. McArthur in his *Second Front: Censorship and Propaganda in the Gulf War* (1992), thus keeping Americans in the dark about events and politics. But the use of US media alongside the US troops provides first-hand coverage with a pro-military slant. With footage that glorifies coalition courage and invincibility, embedded journalism is clearly a made-for-TV strategy in defence of Pentagon ideology. Coverage is so lacking in objectivity (given the necessity of living and working alongside the very military that is protecting you while restricting coverage to rules approved by combat unit commanders) that many refer to this "war porn" as jingoism, not journalism. No one should be surprised that war journalism hides behind a fog of patriotism. During times of war or crisis, the news media routinely surrender their normal functions to criticize, expose the mighty, and afflict the comfortable while comforting the afflicted (Kishan and Freedman, 2003). What we have instead is news that is censored, distorted, and even falsified—as little more than a weapon of mass persuasion (Schlesinger, 2003). To do otherwise is seen as treason and a betrayal to the memory of fallen comrades.

Advertising As Capitalist Propaganda

Many of us express a love-hate relationship with the world of advertising. We enjoy being massaged by the message of more, yet bristle at the banality and superficiality that this implies. Much of our unease stems from exposure to the sheer volume of advertising: Most of us will see millions of ads that cumulatively squander months of our life. Reaction to advertising is mixed as one might expect. A problem for some is seen as a solution for others, and shrugged off as indifferent by yet others still (Kenway and Ballen, 2001). Many endorse advertising as part of the cost of doing big business in a capitalist society. Media such as television are heavily dependent on advertising revenues: That alone may explain why ABC can charge US$2.2 million for a 30-second ad during the Superbowl match

(Canadian networks charge "only" CDN$100 000 per 30 seconds of the Superbowl (and Academy Awards)). By contrast, a 30-second spot during CBC's coverage of the Grey Cup is a relative bargain at CDN$57 000 (Westhead, 2003). Others are less benign in their assessment of advertising as capitalist propaganda. Advertising is accused of everything from the decline of the West to intellectual dwarfism, with social pollution in between. Of particular concern is its role in fostering discontent and creating insecurity by exploiting our fears, hopes, and anxieties. By harnessing these emotions to the purchase of a product, advertising not only exploits an obsession with our self-image but also encourages weakness and dependency by defining relief as a purchase away (Knapp, 2003). Youth, in particular, are bombarded with and defined by brand names because of marketers who target their minds, wallets, and identities in hopes of "branding" them for life (Klein, 1999; Quart, 2001; George, 2003). Finally, advertising encourages waste, contributes to the disfigurement of the environment, and creates an imbalance in human values. Even so-called "green advertising" is no solution, since the underlying message is the same; that is, use more, not less. An environmentally friendly car, is still a gas-guzzling, steel-bending commodity at odds with the principle of public transit and the commitment to pure, clean air.

Generating Discontent/Glamorizing Consumption

Advertising encompasses a number of functions. Foremost is the need to generate profits by selling products, generating brand-name recognition, and bolstering corporate legitimacy (Williamson, 1978). Central to all advertising is a simple message: For every so-called problem need, there is a product solution (Andersen, 1996). Widely regarded strategies are employed for emotionally connecting consumer with product, including targeting a market, capturing attention, arousing interest, fostering images, neutralizing doubts, and creating conviction (Fleras, 2003).

A distinction between manifest (articulated) and latent (unintended) functions is reflective of advertising logic. The manifest function of advertising is to sell a product by symbolically linking consumers with a commodity or service. A social value component is added to the product by glamorizing it through images and messages that strike a responsive chord. The selling of fantasies represents a latent function. As recently as the mid-20th century, ads sold a product by touting its virtues and practical applications. But contemporary advertising sells fantasies by employing images that promise more of everything without specifying why or how. Buying into fantasies of popularity, sex appeal, attractiveness, or success not only transports people into an image-world of glamour and popularity. Advertising is also associated with selling a lifestyle anchored in the pursuit of conspicuous consumption. The underlying logic? Consumer advertising exploits audiences by preying on gaps in their self-esteem through seductive images in reminding us that we are never good enough.

In short, advertising is much more than a process of moving goods off a shelf. It goes beyond a fact sheet about the product in question. Advertising upholds a philosophy of life commensurate with ruling class interests. This association makes it difficult to separate advertising from discourses embedded in a dominant ideology (McAllister, 1995). Advertising is ideological in that it represents ideas and ideals that secure the existing social order while excluding values at odds with a consumerist philosophy (Andersen, 1996). Equating advertising with dominant ideology reinforces its links as institutionalized propaganda on behalf of capitalism, while reaffirming the hegemonic properties of advertising. To the extent that every ad says it is better to buy than not to buy, advertising is propaganda; in that every ad reinforces the social ideals of consumerism as desirable, advertising is propaganda; insofar as advertising teaches us that external appearances are more important than what's inside, it is propaganda; and by equating consumerism as a matter of individual choice rather than a socially structured process, advertising is propaganda (also Jhally, 1989).

The cumulative effect of advertising as propaganda is overwhelming. At the heart of this propaganda is the irrefutable message: "Buy and you will be saved." On its own and taken out of context, each ad may not make much difference. Collectively, however, their impact cannot be discounted. For, in the final analysis, advertising instils the essential cultural nightmare in our society: namely, the fear of failure and envy of success.

Advertising As a Social Problem

The 20th century may well go down as the age of advertising (Marchand, 2003). Advertising evolved as a tool for creating and amplifying demand by transforming consumerism into a culture and lifestyle. Such a transformation is unlikely without attendant problems, and many of the social problems associated with advertising reflect ethical issues within the industry (Singer, 1986). These ethical issues are deemed a problem because of a potentially negative effect on society or certain members.

- First, there are debates about what should be allowed in advertising. Should the industry tolerate the advertising of products that are legal but lethal? Both the tobacco and alcohol industries depend on advertising, in part, because sales are directly related to transforming dubious products into desirable social commodities. But many regard it as irresponsible to advertise products that are anything but healthy when used precisely as prescribed. A similar line of reasoning is applied to advertising of cars that promote excessive speeds, especially among the testosterone-driven segment of the market.

- Second, questions have been raised about access to advertising. Corporate sponsorship has been singled out as a major culprit in abusing this responsibility. In the case of tobacco or alcohol companies, event-marketing ads represent one of the few outlets currently available in Canada. Underwriting symphonies, sports tournaments, and rock tours is a favourite way of reaching out to audiences, while bolstering an image as a good corporate citizen. Corporate sponsorship of "high-brow" events may secure access to a sophisticated market that otherwise would shun conventional advertising. Yet such corporate links are widely criticized as unethical in taking advantage of captive audiences. Even political advertising is frowned upon, since techniques perfected to sell consumer goods are applied to political candidates, in effect transforming elections into market exercises and voting into consumer options (Rose, 2001; Brennan, 2003). Still, politicians have little choice except to play along in an era where sizzle counts for more than substance.

- Third, there are moves to regulate specific techniques and target groups. Product placements and promotional tie-ins are directed at children and families by subliminally manipulating the subconscious (Madger, 1997). For example, many critics are concerned about the use of children's shows—from G.I. Joe and Mighty Morphin Power Rangers to Sailor Moon and Pokémon—as a carefully orchestrated market strategy involving an imaginary world of consumer goods (Kline, 1995). Interestingly, marketers now focus directly on children to take advantage of guilt-ridden, purchase-happy parents. Of special concern has been the use of prepubescent girls to sell perfumes or sun blocks. In a society in which child abuse is of worrying proportions, the inclusion of youthful seductresses in ads sends out a mixed message about who is sexually desirable.

• Fourth, the depiction of women in advertising has come under criticism for its tasteless-ness in perpetuating sexist stereotypes (Martin, 1997; Graydon, 2001; Ganahl et al., 2003). This accusation reinforces the notion of media as gendered, that is, women and men are known to use the media differently; media, in turn, tend to have a different relationship with men and with women (Fleras, 2003). Images of women in advertising revolve around messages that define and measure a women's worth around material possessions or physical appearances (Kilbourne, 1999). Women are portrayed in ways that have nothing to do with the product except to confirm the principle that sex sells. They appear as obsessed with their appearance (thin, youthful, beautiful, fit, and White) or preoccupied with domestic-maternal activities (cleaner, brighter, and whiter). To be sure, women in ads are appearing in a broader range of roles. The lessons of feminism are so densely woven into the cultural fabric of society that media images implicitly buy into gender equality (Kuczynksi, 1999). This concession conceals more than it reveals. Put simply, advertisers have taken advantage of the double shift by expanding the number of products for pitching at working women who continue to work at home. In addition to domestic consumer goods, women now require additional products for coping with the demands of paid employment. The challenge of "having it all" demands a look that exudes femininity without compromising career advancement. Women also require more labour-saving devices for unpaid domestic work. In other words, media portrayals of women remain couched in compromise: advances in some areas are matched by setbacks in others without disrupting the commercial status quo (Mintz, 2003; Polzer, 2003).

MEDIA IMPACTS

Responses to the question of "what are media" yield the unexpected. Mainstream media constitute a socially constructed system of technologically driven communication that are anything but neutral or passive in delivery. Realities are defined around "frames" of inter-pretation that "normalize" media priorities around vested interests rather than consumer needs. Bias and ethnocentrism may not be openly articulated by the media but intrinsic to and implicit in media processes. The constructed character of the media is rarely conveyed to audiences, many of whom are often unaware of the production process behind the appar-ent "naturalness" of media products (Abercrombie, 1995). Or, as Brian Maracle (1996) puts it, mainstream media are so steeped in Eurocentric values (including liberal pluralism and universalism) that the perception of bias is elusive, especially when directed at those who are different. The existence of media bias is not the problem. Problems arise from media refusal to admit the inevitability and pervasiveness of this bias while claiming to be neutral, fair, and objective.

There is little question that media exert an impact on society. At one time it was assumed that media impact was powerful and direct, thus compelling authorities to intro-duce controls for the sake of national interests. For that reason alone, the 822-page report, "Our Cultural Sovereignty: The Second Century of Broadcasting" (2003) recom-mends less cross- and foreign-ownership to ensure a variety of Canadian voices. But ref-erence to media impacts has shifted. Media impacts are increasingly defined as indirect and inconsistent—indirect, in that media generate messages which create public discourses about what is normal or acceptable; inconsistent, because media messages involve public discourses that audiences may or may not tap into. The agenda-setting properties of the media do not tell us what or how to think but rather what to think about. As a result, the outcomes of media messages cannot be defined as good or bad, but both good and bad, depending on the context, criteria, and consequences.

The double-edged nature of media impacts is nicely captured by debates over the Internet (Schofield and Davison, 2002). The Internet is rapidly establishing itself as the medium of choice: Among Canadians with a connection, one-third say the Internet is more important than TV, including 56 percent of the 15 to 19 years old (Macklem, 2003). Among its many virtues, two are uppermost: interactivity and immediacy (Bricker and Greenspon, 2001). Supporters of the Internet tout its virtues in enhancing democracy and freedom through delivery of information to people without pre-screening by central authorities. This "anarchic" dissemination of information has the potential to strip large organizations of their monopolistic access to information, thereby eroding the hierarchies that inform institutional life (Tarlow and Tarlow, 2002). The potential for broader participation in political and policy-making decisions is also enhanced through two-way flows of information. Computer-mediated communication may produce a life that is profoundly democratic and emancipating in levelling the playing field between big and small, rich or poor. As an instrument of democracy in our profoundly disengaged society, the Internet not only provides a political platform for generating votes. A culture of civic engagement among connected participants is created as well. In short, the Internet is more than a vehicle for disseminating content; more importantly, it embraces a networking tool for civic action and engagement, thus enhancing the social capital at the heart of a truly democratic society (Davis et al., 2002; Neff, 2003).

Yet detractors remain skeptical. It is one thing to advance the free flow of information; it is quite another to concede that much of this information is manipulated by elites with hidden agendas who prefer fostering the illusion rather than the reality of power-sharing (Dines and Humez, 2003). The end result is more and more information but less and less knowledge. Equally worrisome are the commercial implications. The democratizing of information may become secondary to establishing a powerful medium for advertising. In addition, there are problems of access, interaction, privacy, regulation, and copyright. Damage that hackers can do to websites (from corporate secrets to national security systems) is widely known and feared (Thompson, 2002). The unfettered flow of digital information also complicates the preservation of cultural borders, to the detriment of national decision-making and sovereignty. No less disturbing is the proliferation of hate sites with their espousal of multicultural-bashing White supremacist dogmas (Kinsella, 2001). Relatively easy access to porn sites is also deemed a major problem, especially when conveying distorted messages about sex education and gender relations to impressionable minds. Finally, in a world where everything is recorded and nothing is forgotten, computer-mediated communications can also lead to loss of freedom, individual surveillance, invasion of privacy, and centralization and control of power (Hunter, 2002).

In between are those who acknowledge Internet impact without necessarily passing judgment. Computer-mediated communications are more than a quick-fix solution in search of a problem. They are not simply a machine for doing what print does, only more quickly and less expensively. The Internet is much more than an efficient instrument for data retrieval or distribution, notwithstanding public perception of digital technology as just another labour-saving device for simplifying repetitive tasks. What we have instead is a fundamental shift in how we relate to the world "out there," as radically different in laying the foundations of a new society as the urban-industrial system was from the feudal-agricultural order. With the institutionalization and popularity of the Internet, we live in a "wired world" (or wireless world of laptops and Blackberrys), one in which human social existence is inseparable from the instantaneous exchange of information across vast distances (Pendakur and Harris, 2002). By redefining patterns of interpersonal communication, the emergence of digital information may further obliterate traditional notions of time and space, while transforming the dynamics of an increasingly networked society. The possibilities are so vast and subversive that reducing the discourse about computer-mediated communication to the level of good or bad, progressive or regressive, is both simplistic and trivializing.

In brief, the Internet possesses contradictory impulses: The same digital forces that compress data may coerce people; they may control, yet create resistance; and they may empower, yet disable. Consider varied reaction to computer hackers: the establishment denounces hackers as criminals who must be punished; those who do not see media content as private property tend to embrace hackers as heroes or frontier outlaws who advance the boundaries of cyberspace while interrupting (subverting) the status quo (Thompson, 2002; Macklem, 2003). The lesson is clear: Little is gained by pigeonholing the impact of the Internet into slots of good or evil. Internet processes and their outcomes appear to be sufficiently complex and contradictory that they often blur any distinction between positive and negative. As a complex social construction of contradictory roles, ambiguous messages, multifaceted functions, and diverse impacts, the Internet is neither good nor bad, but simultaneously both. Such ambiguity may even help explain its popularity.

Shaping Public Discourses: The Impact of Newscasting

We live in a world inundated by news. Newspapers continue to hold their own despite the growing popularity of television news. TV news can be found in regular time slots or in 24/7 news channels such as CNN or CTV's Newsnet. The proliferation of news may create greater awareness about the world out there; too much of it may also distract from the real issues at hand. Did the capture of Saddam Hussein by American troops merit blanket television coverage or the entire news hole (19 pages) of the first section in the *National Post* (15 December, 2003)? Such exposure can complicate the notion of what constitutes news. News can be viewed as a system of communication that facilitates dialogue and interaction. News can also be viewed as a body of knowledge for expanding our understanding of the world as it unfolds in time and space. In some cases, this knowledge is not necessarily consistent with official doctrines and dominant ideologies; in many cases, it is.

News as a professionally defined set of values and practices elicits varying responses. Mainstream news media are criticized, alternatively, as too conservative, too radical, too liberal, or too in-between by not taking a stand on controversial issues. Too much media may lull us into a false sense of security or, alternatively, a 24-hour TV-newsworld may accelerate and intensify our fears, resulting in media-induced panic (James, 2003). For example, wall-to-wall coverage of SARS as an out-of-control and random epidemic may have done more to fuel fears than calm concerns (Doyle, 2003). Criticism of news as panic cannot be lightly dismissed since news media are key institutions of the public sphere involving exchanges of information that shape public discourses and debates (Hackett and Zhao, 1998). News that fails to connect performance with standards and expectations is no less problematic, and this privileging of profit over public service provides a starting point for defining news as a social problem (also Solomon, 2002). News becomes a social problem when it (a) detracts from fostering a democratic society of critically-informed citizens (Nadeau and Giasson, 2003); (b) obsesses over market shares rather than quality control (Miller, 2003); (c) serves as a commodity to be manipulated and sold as cheaply as possible; (d) provides a largely one-sided point of view rather than balanced coverage; (e) is driven exclusively by commercial interests and corporate agendas rather than public interests; (f) is framed exclusively as entertainment rather than a source of information and knowledge; (g) relies exclusively on conflict and violence as a catalyst for storytelling and narrative structure; and (h) fails to acknowledge diversity in its personnel, process, and output (Henry and Tator, 2002).

Consider media coverage of political news. Many would agree that a lively news media are central in advancing a critically informed citizenship, improved decision-making, and more accountable democracies (Gans, 2003). Yet fears are mounting that media coverage of politics has contributed to a declining level of trust in politicians, loss of confidence in political institutions, voter apathy, and increased cynicism toward the entire political process (Nadeau and Giasson, 2003). Political journalists are criticized for many reasons: exaggerating the negative and superficial aspects of policies; usurping the role of elected officials by drawing unnecessary attention to the story or storyteller, redirecting voters' attention to secondary issues, exercising undue influence in the process of defining the political agendas, and cheapening the image of politics by focusing on partisan conflict between political actors rather than investigative journalism (also Entman, 1998). Emergent trends account for this malaise, according to Nadeau and Giasson. Political journalism is practised under a different set of conditions than in the past, especially with the importance of tele-visuals in driving the coverage (also Taras, 1991). A "gotcha" mentality creates a journalism that is more interested in uncovering scandals than covering political debates. Journalists increasingly rely on stereotyped, superficial, and sensationalist coverage because of increased workloads within a cost-slashing environment. And increased media concentration has intensified pressures on profitability with a corresponding weakening of the public service news tradition. In his piece in Vanity Fair, entitled "Round up the Cattle," James Wolocott indicts the American press for failure to do its job in a post 9/11 era. He writes:

> The press in this country has never identified less with the underdog and pandered more to the top pedigrees. The arrogance of the Bush administration is mirrored in the arrogance of the elite media, which preens even as it prostrates itself. TV punditry, with its exclusive skybox view, has genetically modified all political coverage. Bulbous-ego'd cable-news hosts, celebrity reporters and political operatives posing as experts are far more interested in prying information loose than in popping off with their own stale insights and psychic hot line predictions.

Who can be surprised, then, by news coverage that rarely advances public interest. The common good suffers when commercial media want to maximize profit, political actors crave more visibility, and journalists must work under punishing conditions in processing information for the masses (Nadeau and Giasson, 2003).

Defining News: The Only Good News Is Bad News

What passes for news is normally associated with a property called newsworthiness (Abel, 1997). Generally speaking, news in North America is regarded as an "event" with one or more of the following characteristics: It must be immediate; be proximate (events further away are less likely to be reported); feature prominent individuals or flamboyant personalities; employ direct quotes and authoritative (although often unnamed) sources; involve magnitude in terms of cost or loss of life; embrace the odd or the deviant; be obsessed with conflict, anguish, and tragedy; and be easily labelled and condensed for quick reference and recall (Fuller, 1996). Unexpected events that constitute a break from norms and the routine also qualify as news values (Madger, 1997). Not surprisingly, in a profession consumed by negativity and the "un-normative," coups and earthquakes get top billing, as do crimes, clashes, and crises (McGregor, 1996). The editor of *The Globe and Mail* did not mince words when he wrote to this effect:

> Let's not be coy here. Journalists thrive on the misery of others. It's not, as some have supposed, that the media dwell on the negative. It is that we dwell on the unusual and extraordinary … If it happens everyday, it ain't news. Which creates a natural bias toward the negative since most of life actually unfolds as expected (Greenspon, 2003).

Situational factors may account for why one news item takes priority over another. Time and budgetary constraints may intrude (Abel, 1997). An item of local interest may take precedence over a global issue in a regional paper; conversely, a large urban daily may ignore regional interests. On balance, however, conflicts involving Hollywood celebrities are more newsworthy than mass killings in Africa. The media seem more mesmerized by the Annika Sorenstams and Janet Jacksons of this world. They appear less interested in telling readers why such admittedly fish-out-of-water stories should consume so much space. Items for inclusion also depend on their "presentability," and this is determined by the media's access to visuals, easily identifiable protagonists, the availability of quotable reactions, and the novelty of the sound bites. Adversity and adversarial situations are preferred over the cooperative; so too are angles involving the unusual or the perverse. A preference for "bang-bang" journalism creates a tendency to blow things out of proportion to the risk they pose, with the result that media hype may fan public panic and unnecessary fears. The dangers of applying a conflict framework to most news items is nicely captured by Gwynne Dyer (1998) who believes the world is not nearly as "stupid" or "nasty" as the news would have us believe, despite the heavy predominance of bad news but a far more "rational, less violent, and even kinder place than it used to be." In that newsworthiness prefers the negative and confrontational over the positive and cooperative, the impact of newscasting in skewing public discourses is indeed a problem.

News As Social Construction

What passes for news is not simply a formulaic process; it consists of a series of judgment calls within the framework of organizational values and commercial commitments. The pervasiveness of these biases subjects newscasting to charges of bias (Hackett et al., 2000). In purporting to present only the facts, mainstream media have long endorsed the goals of objectivity in terms of fairness, accuracy, balance, and impartiality (Hackett and Zhao, 1998). However admirable such objectives may be, barriers are ignored that interfere with their attainment. News is not something out there waiting to be plucked for placement as newsworthy. Rather, news is a constructed reality that is susceptible to various demands and pressures, both intentional and inadvertent (Weston, 2003). Rather than detachedly covering the news, the news media are themselves part of the news story; after all, the very act of observing people alters their behaviour (Doyle, 2003; Sharmarke, 2003). Collectively, these constraints blunt the media's capacity for balanced and accurate coverage. Many of the difficulties arise from the bias and selectivity inherent in the newscasting process. Each of these factors—coverage, collection, and packaging—undermines the potential for an informed citizenry.

Coverage   There is a lot going on in the world at any particular point in time. How do the news media decide what is worthy of coverage? What is included, what is excluded, and on what grounds? Why are events and personalities framed in a certain way? Whose voices are heard or not heard, and why? The news industry is nominally committed to the principle of selecting only what is newsworthy (Miljan and Cooper, 1999). In reality, the industry is equally bound to making a profit by "selling" as much copy or airtime as possible through advertising or subscription rates. This dual commitment puts a premium on bolstering audience size and network ratings by appealing to the broadest possible audience. Corporate ownership of the news media frames issues in ways that reinforced this commercial imperative (Winter, 2002). The news collection process is driven by a focus on the dramatic and spectacular, with particular emphasis on conflict, calamity, and confrontation. Newsworthiness is enhanced by the presence of flamboyant, preferably corrupt personalities with a knack for the outrageous or the titillating. The noncontroversial and cooperative are often ignored because they lack intrinsic appeal for audiences with a short attention span and an "action" mentality.

The "jolts" and "jiggles" mentality inherent in the news process has been widely criticized. Tabloid-style journalism is taken to task for fixating on the trite. Mundane but important topics are pushed aside for eye-popping spectacles, in the process marginalizing the realities that inform everyday life (Solomon, 2002). Religion may be important to many Canadians and Americans, but few would glean that impression from the paucity of articles that grace the broadsheets. The lack of context is especially disturbing since it not only imparts a sheen of superficiality to news but also robs events and developments of any meaningful rationale, while conveying the impression that individuals make choices for which they alone are responsible. Minorities in Canada and abroad have complained about news portrayal of them as belligerent, ruthless, or indifferent towards human life. No less unflattering is their depiction as victims, vulnerable to social decay and societal disorder, enmeshed in graft and corruption, and without much capacity for cooperative enterprise. Stereotypes, prejudice, and discrimination become easily entrenched under these circumstances (Henry and Tator, 2002). Finally, a preoccupation with conflict is no less a problem. A relentless barrage of the confrontational and catastrophic may have the effect of diminishing people's capacity for genuine outrage, compassion, or commitment, while pandering to the lowest common commercial denominator through sensationalized choreographies of conflict or calamity (Moeller, 1998; Rieff, 1999; 2002).

Collection   Another source of bias is in the news collection process itself. The investigative journalist with a nose for news may also be an unwitting agent in relaying bias.

Professional assumptions create particular frames of reference that rarely reflect a neutral view of reality (Abel, 1997). Even a fierce commitment to objectivity and neutrality does not preclude the possibility of bias in news collection. Words may be manipulated (unconsciously in many cases) when drawing attention to certain aspects of reality but away from others that are deemed less significant. The camera lens or camcorder may not "lie" in the conventional sense of the term; nevertheless, each instrument only records a minute portion of what occurs around us. The ubiquity and pervasiveness of this bias undermines any pretext of objectivity and value-neutrality. For that reason alone, audiences must cautiously approach what they see, hear, or read— especially if they lack first-hand knowledge of the situation in question.

Bias also arises from official sources of news. Reporters are heavily dependent for their livelihood on official sources in the government, bureaucracies, police forces, and corporate sectors (Fishman, 1980). Collectively these sources are difficult to access and prone to secrecy. Yet they are highly sought after because they lend credibility to stories or offer the promise of a "scoop." Not surprisingly, many organizations employ professional public relations and media consultants whose job description rarely includes truthfulness. They appear more interested in impression-management than in providing the facts (Peart and Macnamara, 1996). What emerge from these news "scrums" are highly selective bits of information that make the organizations look good at the expense of balance and accuracy.

Even unofficial sources of information can be suspect. On-site reporting conveys the impression of painstaking and meticulous objectivity. Reality is reported as it unfolds before our eyes without the filter of interpretation. In fact, however, what passes for reality may be as contrived and manufactured as official reports. Demonstrations and protest marches may be staged and managed for the benefit of the evening news slot. The rhetoric produced by these telegenic displays is focused on manipulating sympathy or extorting public funds for political purposes. And while many would argue that media continue to under-, over-, or misrepresent minorities (Mahtani, 2002), there are those who believe that media political correctness and cultural cringe ("fears of being labelled a racist") exclude coverage of anything that could be construed as negative or critical about minority women and men— to the detriment of so-called objective collection (McGowan, 2001).

Packaging and Presentation   Bias in newscasting is compounded by problems in presentation. Distortions can be attributed to a variety of factors. Journalists live in a world of "bang-bang" journalism according to Jeffrey Simpson, a columnist with *The Globe and Mail*, a world of hard facts, brevity, punishing deadlines, reduced resources, little time for reflection, with pressure to make sense of the world by transforming random events into riveting stories that people can understand (Weston, 2003). An adversarial format is frequently superimposed to give some "bite" to the presentation, thus privileging those with loud voices, extreme views, and strange appearances. Coverage of both violent and nonviolent events are portrayed through a conflict paradigm, in which one side is deified as good, the other demonized as bad. Isolated and intermittent events may be spliced together to create the illusion of a story, thereby accentuating the magnitude of crisis or urgency where none actually existed. Problems arise from the very act of packaging such a complex and fluid reality into the straitjacket of visual images and sound bites, with a beginning and end, separated by a climax. Such a dynamic demonstrates the importance of understanding the grounds for editorial decisions: What is kept and what is discarded? Who decides and why?

Television is no less selective than newspapers collection, coverage or presentation. Reality is beamed into our homes, not in the sense of an exact replica but as a form of realism purged of any sordid elements lest it rattle queasy audiences or nervous advertisers. In effect, then, TV news is packaged to meet audience demands and advertising priorities. In an age of zappers and satellite transmission, what passes for (or is passed off as) news are visual bites for fun and profit. Without visuals, a story is unlikely to get on the air. Complicated ongoing issues with unclear protagonists are likely to be shunned as well (Madger, 1997). There is nothing wrong with having news packaged in an entertaining fashion. But separating fact from fantasy is tricky when all subject matter is reduced to entertainment, as Neil Postman (1985) writes in his biting commentary on television. This ambivalence has turned the news into an electronic equivalent of Orwellian doublespeak, a process whereby two opposing thoughts (entertainment and information) are accepted simultaneously without experiencing the dismay of contradiction.

To sum up: It should be clear, then, that the news is not an objective exercise in information processing and transmission (Hackett et al., 2000). What eventually is defined as news is not something intrinsic to reality, with clearly marked labels. Neither an impartial slice of reality reported by trained professionals nor a random reaction to disparate events, news as "invented" reality is shaped by organizational values and commercial concerns (Parenti, 1992). The concept of news as socially constructed is important: Rather than representing anything natural or normal about the world out there, despite efforts by vested interests to make it seem so, news is a socially constructed product, created by individuals who make choices in specific contexts. Both journalists and newscasters play a "selection" game—what's on, what's not, who's quoted, what sources, and which spin (Weston, 2003). To define news as socially constructed is not the same as saying that news is a fiction, fantasy, or fabrication. Nor is it intended to slur journalists. The words of Graham Fraser (2003) seem appropriate:

> Journalists are storytellers. That is what drew us into this craft—the hunger for narrative, the unquenchable desire to fill the silence, to tell what happened next, to contribute to the national conversation.... For those of us who take this work seriously—and that is most of the reporters I know—there is a sense of mission. There are few words in this paper today that were not stared at, reconsidered, and worried over. Is this worth knowing? Is it interesting? Fair?

The intent is to draw attention to news, not as a thing (noun) but as a process (verb). An attribute called "news" is applied to the "world out there" by those with the power to make such a label stick. Put candidly, the news process is subject to numerous biases and hidden agendas. Newscasting is formatted to attract audiences and secure advertisers, and then filtered through selective mechanisms that tend to enlarge the reality gap. News media become increasingly incapable of transmitting complete, objective, and relevant news on most issues to citizens because of its visually-driven, negative-mired, and profit-oriented domain of the short, superficial, episodic, and dramatic (Nadeau and Giasson, 2003). This selectivity is not intentional, but institutional; it is not conspiracy but consequences; it is not personal but cultural. And when information becomes inseparable from entertainment values, a public discourse about fear is fostered that not only cripples people's outlooks and opinions but messages of fear can also be manipulated by authorities for social control purposes (Atheide, 2002)—as demonstrated in the Case Study on page 208.

CASE 7-1	Portraying Minorities: News Media Propaganda

It is said that in times of change or crisis, people often rely on media for information or reassurance. People also enlist the media for insights into racial, ethnic, and religious diversity. An inclusive media can bring people together; by contrast, myopic and stereotyped coverage can divide and antagonize (Miller, 2003). The very practice and conventions of newscasting—the way news is defined, collected, and presented—may perpetuate popular yet incorrect images that injure minority women and men (Weston, 1996; Lester and Ross, 2003). What is at stake here is the vexing issue of cultural representation: How to depict a diverse, complex, and evolving minority in a broadly informative yet nuanced way without getting tangled up in preconceptions and prejudgments (Weston, 2003)?

Historically, media portrayal of minority women and men has left much to be desired (Holtzman, 2000; Cottle, 2000). Mainstream media have tended to underrepresent minorities in areas that count, to overrepresent minorities in areas that don't, and to misrepresent minorities in countless ways (Fleras and Kunz, 2001). For purposes of analysis, media (mis)treatment of minority women and men can be categorized under four headings: minorities as invisible, stereotyped, problem people, and adornments.

(1) Minorities As Invisible

Numerous studies have extolled what many regard as obvious. Çanada's multicultural diversity is poorly reflected in those aspects of media pertaining to programming and newscasting sectors (Murray, 2002). Visible minorities are reduced to an invisible status through "underrepresentation" in programming, staffing, and decision-making. With several exceptions, they are underrepresented in TV programming in any meaningful way. Even proportional presentation in the media may be misleading if minority women and men are slotted into a relatively small number of programs such as sitcoms, reduced to victim/assailant in cop-based reality programming, or so whitewashed that their distinctiveness is bleached in favour of a middle-class norm of acceptability.

Newscasting is particularly guilty of making minorities invisible. Not deliberately, mind you, but because of constraints that prevent news media from matching ideals with practices or products, including workplace pressures and institutional values that influence who is covered, how, and where (Weston, 1996). Nevertheless, it would be inaccurate to say that the news media ignore minorities. Rather, a "shallows-and-rapids" treatment is a more accurate appraisal. That is, under normal circumstances, minorities are ignored by the mainstream press ("shallows"). But coverage snaps into action ("rapids") in response to crisis or calamity, involving natural catastrophes, civil wars, and colourful insurgents. When the crisis subsides, media interest is suspended until the next big thing. Of course, minority commuities are afflicted by conflicts and calamities; Nevertheless, the dearth of balanced coverage results in distorted perceptions of needs, concerns, or aspirations. This distortion may not be deliberately engineered. Rather, the misrepresentation reflects a media focus on audience ratings and advertising revenues.

(continued on next page)

(2) Minorities As Stereotypes

Minorities have long complained of stereotyping by the mainstream media (Mahtani, 2001; 2002). Historically, people of colour were portrayed in a manner that did not offend prevailing prejudices. Liberties taken with minority depictions in consumer advertising were especially flagrant. In an industry geared toward image and appeal, the rule of homogeneity and conservatism prevailed. Advertisers wanted their products sanitized and bleached of colour for fear of lost revenue. People of colour were rarely depicted in the advertising of beauty care and personal hygiene products, so entrenched was the image of "Whiteness" as the preferred standard of beauty (Bledsloe, 1989). Elsewhere, images of racial minorities were steeped in unfounded generalizations that emphasized the comical or grotesque. This stereotyping fell into a pattern. People from the Middle East continue to be portrayed as sleazy fanatics or tyrannical patriarchs who link terrorism with religion; Asians have been type-cast either as sly and cunning or as mathematical whizzes. Blacks in prime-time shows remain stuck as superheroes/athletes, or sex-obsessed buffoons against a backdrop of secondary characters such as hipsters or outlaws. Newscasts continue to portray Blacks as athletes, entertainers, or criminals (Henry and Tator, 2002).

Consider how media have historically portrayed Canada's aboriginal peoples as the "other," a people removed in time and remote in space (Alia, 1999; also Weston, 1996; Churchill, 2003). Perception of aboriginal peoples as the "other" has been filtered through a Eurocentric lens, with images ranging from their portrayal as "noble savage" and "primitive romantic," to their de-basement as "villain" or "victim" or "comical simpleton," with the stigma of "problem people" or "menacing subversives" sandwiched in between (also Blythe, 1994; Fleras and Spoonley, 1999). Images of tribalism continue to resonate with a spicy mixture of meanings, from backwardness to spiritual mysticism to ecological custodians (Jakubowicz et al., 1994). Most portrayals embraced a mythical image of an imaginary warrior who occupied the plains between 1825 and 1880 (Frances, 1992). A so-called "Indian Identity Kit" (Berton, 1975) consisted of the following items, few of which even were indigenous to aboriginal peoples prior to European settlement: wig with hair parted in the middle into hanging plaits; feathered war bonnet; headband (a White invention to keep the actor's wig from slipping off) buckskin leggings; moccasins; painted skin teepee; and armed with tomahawk and bows and arrows. This "one-size-fits-all" image applied to all First Peoples, regardless of whether they were Cree or Salish or Ojibwa or Blackfoot. These images could be further divided into a series of recurrent stereotypes, in effect reinforcing a "seen one Indian, seen 'em all" mentality.

Collectively, these images reinforce a perception of aboriginal peoples as a people remote in time and place. Their histories are thought to begin with European colonization, their reality only makes sense in terms of interaction with Whites, and their salvation rests in becoming more like the mainstream (Churchill, 2001). To be sure, media have begun to invert conventional stereotypes of Whites and First Peoples, with much greater emphasis on the courage or durability of the indigenous people of the land versus

(continued on next page)

the rapacious greed of White settler colonization (think of Dances With Wolves). Nevertheless, there is a long way to go, according to Maurice Switzer, a member of the Elders' Council of the Mississaugas of Rice Lake First Nations at Alderville, Ontario (1997: 21–22):

> The country's large newspapers, TV and radio news shows often contain misinformation, sweeping generalizations and galling stereotypes about natives and native affairs. Their stories are usually presented by journalists with little background knowledge or understanding of aboriginals and their communities ... As well, very few so-called mainstream media consider aboriginal affairs to be a subject worthy of regular attention.

(3) Minorities As Problem People

Minority women and men are frequently singled out by the media as a "social problem"; that is, as "having problems" or "creating problems" in need of political attention or scarce national resources. As problem people, they are taken to task by the media for making demands that may imperil Canada's unity or national prosperity. Consider the case of Canada's aboriginal peoples when depicted as: (a) a threat to Canada's territorial integrity (demands for nationhood and self-determining autonomy), or to national interests (resistance to proposed changes to the Indian act by way of First Nations Governance Act); (b) a risk to Canada's social order (the violence from Oka to Burnt Church, New Brunswick); (c) an economic liability (the costs associated with massive land claims settlement or restitution for residential school abuses); (d) a thorn in the side of the criminal justice system (ranging from the Donald Marshall case to police shootings of aboriginal people, including the killing of Dudley George at Ipperwash, Ontario),

or an unfair player (cigarette-smuggling or rum-running across borders). Aboriginal activism is demeaned as a departure from established norms; protestors, in turn, are dismissed as dangerous or irrational, reflecting a conflict of interest between destabilizing forces on one side and the forces of order, reason, and stability on the other (Lambertus, 2004). The subsequent criminalization marginalizes the legitimacy of dissent, trivializes aboriginal issues, and distracts from the issues at hand. Compounding this negativity are reports of an excessive reliance on welfare, a predilection for alcohol and substance abuse, a pervasive laziness and lack of ambition, and an inclination to mismanage what little they have. The combined impact of this negative reporting paints a villainous picture of Canada's First Peoples as people with a "plight" unable to cope with the complexities of contemporary society (Weston, 2003).

Minority men and women are also problematized by the media. People of colour, both foreign- and native-born, are targets of negative reporting that dwells on costs, threats, and inconveniences. Media reporting of refugees usually fixates on illegal entries and the associated costs of processing and integration into Canada. Immigrants are routinely cast as "troublesome constituents" who steal jobs from Canadians; cheat on the welfare system; take advantage of educational opportunities without making a corresponding commitment to Canada; engage in illegal activities such as drugs or smuggling; and imperil Canada's unity and identity by refusing to discard their culture. Newsmedia are accused of Muslim-bashing in the wake of September 11th (Raza, 2003), in part intentionally, in part, because of the different expectations that Muslims have

(continued on next page)

of the media versus the cultural values that drive newscasting (Saloojee, 2003; Taheri, 2003). Race and crime are often linked together by the media, according to John Miller (2003) and others (Henry and Tator, 2002). Double standards persist: White criminal behaviour is treated as an aberrant individual act; with minorities such as Blacks, it is seen as a "group crime" for which the entire community is held responsible. The cumulative effect of this hypocrisy has had the controlling effect of criminalizing race, while racializing crime.

(4) Minorities As Adornment

The media tend to trivialize minority women and men as mere adornments to society at large. This decorative aspect is achieved by casting minorities in token roles that are meant only to amuse or embellish. Or coverage is of a superficial nature, focusing on festivals, individual success stories, and the cultural esoterica of ethnic minority communities (Cottle, 2000). Minorities are associated with the exotic and sensual, portrayed as congenial hosts for faraway destinations, enlisted as superstar boosters for athletics and sporting goods, or ghettoized in certain marketing segments related to "rap" or "hip hop." Most minority roles on television consisted of bit parts, usually restricted to sitcoms or dramas, which mercilessly stereotyped minority women and men. Blacks on television remain locked into roles as entertainers, criminals, or athletes. Rarely is there any emphasis on intellectual or professional prowess, much less recourse to positive role models to which Black youth can aspire outside of athletics or entertainment. Such a restriction may prove inherently satisfying to mainstream audiences who historically have enjoyed laughing at Blacks when cast as comics or buffoons. The depoliticizing of Blacks as "emasculated" cartoons ("playing 'm for laughs") has the effect of reassuring nervous White audiences that little has changed.

Media relations with minority women are no less demeaning (Kunz and Fleras, 1999; Graydon, 2001). Both women and men of colour are vulnerable to misrepresentation as peripheral, stereotypes, problem peoples, and the "other." Women also are subject to additional media mistreatment because of gender. The intersection of gender with ethnicity and race relegates aboriginal women, women of colour, and immigrant women to the status of decorative props. Minority women are generally reduced to commodities; this objectification equates women with objects for control or consumption. They are sexualized in a way that equates "the good life" with "snaring" and supporting a man to the exclusion of anything else. This sexualization is thought to infantilize women by casting them as silly or superfluous, obsessed with appearances, and devoid of intelligence. They also are racialized in a manner that draws inordinate attention to their status as "other," together with the demeaning implications associated with being "otherized." Their bodies are gratuitously paraded to sell everything from esoteric fashions and sensuous perfumes to a host of exotic vacation destinations. Minority women are cast in roles of domestication, a process that tends to diminish their status and contributions to society. Finally, women of colour are portrayed as dangerous or evil, with the potential to destroy everything good about society or civilization (Jiwani, 1992). Such demonizing tends to trivialize the realities and contributions of minority women to the level of adornments in contexts where style prevails over substance (Dines and Humez, 2001).

(continued on next page)

To be sure, the media's treatment of minority women and men has shifted in recent years (Fleras and Kunz, 2001). Both the quantity and quality of minority representations have improved if only to take advantage of a growing ethnic market. Not all media have complied, however: Certain media processes such as advertising are increasingly embracing diversity; others such as newscasting have shown less improvement in coverage; and still others such as television reflect a confusing mixture of progress and regress. The continued (mis)representation of minority women and men is neither intentional nor deliberate but systemic in consequences. Visible minorities are rendered invisible through underrepresentation in programming, staffing, and decision-making. Conversely, people of colour are visibly overrepresented in areas that count for less, including tourism, sports, international relief, or entertainment. Media portrayals tend to depict minorities as the "other." The need to frame all stories around the theme of conflict puts an onus on dividing the world into "good guys" and "bad guys." While Whites are portrayed as the norm and standard by which others are judged and found wanting, minority women and men are given short shrift as humans removed in time and outside the pale of civilization. Minorities complain of being scapegoated as "foreigners" or "outsiders," whose lives seem to revolve around their "defining" status of race or religion, to the virtual exclusion of other attributes. Images of "them" as "those people" are filtered through the prism of "Whiteness," in the process projecting mainstream fears or yearnings onto the "other."

What is conveyed by these racist depictions? Overtly negative representations combine with the absence of complex characterization to create a racist impact—by consequence, if not always in intent. Negative public discourses about minorities can lead to a skewing of public perceptions (Weston, 2003). Minority audiences are no less affected by negative coverage. Through images and codes, children are taught that cultural differences outside the imprint of White, middle-class culture are inferior, deviant, irrelevant, or threatening. Children of colour also learn to dislike who they are because of these depictions. Both the collective and individual self-esteem of minorities plummets as a result of this "otherizing," process (hooks, 2003). A spokesperson for an American Islamic association said this about the film Alladin (Giroux, 1995: 40):

> All of the bad guys have beards and large, bulbous noses, sinister eyes and heavy accents, and they're wielding swords constantly. Alladin doesn't have a big nose; he has a small nose. He doesn't have a beard or a turban. He doesn't have an accent. What makes him nice is they've given him this American character. I have a daughter who says she's ashamed to call herself an Arab, and it's because of things like this.

The paradox is unmistakable: Negative portrayals say more about the mainstream media than minorities—a projection of fears or fantasies by those making decisions about who or what to include or exclude. Not surprisingly, the solution must come from those who create the problem (Weston, 2003).

Case Study Question

1   How are minorities underrepresented, overrepresented, and misrepresented in the mainstream media?

MEDIA EFFECTS

Most debates about media as a social problem revolve about its role in shaping behaviour. Do the media directly or indirectly influence what people think or do? Are the effects positive or negative, or do they depend on the person, context, and media? How do we make sense of studies that say too much TV impairs reading skills of young children (Galloway, 2003), while another study touts the virtues of the Internet for improving literacy among low-income kids (Carey, 2003)? Not too long ago, such mixed messages were rarely taken seriously. Media were depicted as all powerful, with formidable powers of persuasion, while audiences were dismissed as passive and absorbent sponges (McQuail, 2000). Contemporary analysis has shifted. The deterministic framework that existed in the past has been replaced by a mindset that is much more skeptical of direct media effects (Perse, 2001). Instead of being treated as cultural dopes that can be easily duped, audiences are thought to actively engage with media by selecting patterns of interpretation that fall outside the preferred reading (Strasburger and Wilson, 2002). Media effects are increasingly seen as indirect rather than direct, negotiated rather than imposed, variable rather than uniform, and conditional rather than causal (Fleras, 2003).

Such an interpretation may be applied to television. Television is arguably the most powerful yet enigmatic of contemporary social forces. Such ambiguity may explain the varied reactions to television. For some, it is a "revolution in a box" with a capacity to enlighten and reform; for others, it is a "tyranny of the trivial" with few redeeming qualities. Television tends to portray a nasty and dangerous world that audiences may readily accept in the absence of first-hand experience. No less worrying for many is television's role as a nemesis of democracy. Instead of substance and stance, the art of politics now revolves around telegenic candidates, stage-managed platforms, and eight-second visual bites. For still others, especially on the moral right, TV is a "moral sewer" because of its "filth," "vulgarity," "coarseness," "sex," and "violence," and only the return of "family-safe TV" can possibly save America. For yet others still, television is harmless fun with no long-term or detrimental consequences (Menon, 2003). Finally, there are those who see television as a device to distract and amuse the population, thus dissipating any threat to the status quo. Its impact as an opiate of the masses is even more pronounced for those without access to alternate sources of information. This loss of connectedness with the real world invariably is thought to breed indifference and insensitivity.

The commercial dimension of television is widely acknowledged. Once a device for celebrating consumerism as an acceptable lifestyle after World War II, television continues to promulgate the virtues of consumerism through programs and advertising. Television is bound up with capitalism both as a set of economic activities as well as a cultural force that is constituted by and constitutive of the conditions of capitalist modernity. Not surprisingly, the content of TV programming is driven by commercial imperatives rather than audience concerns. Programming is created to please and appease advertisers who prefer programs that foster the right atmosphere for product amplification. The product that is bought and sold is not the program but the audiences: The networks sell audiences to advertisers while advertising buys "eyeballs" from the networks (Starowitz, 2003). To the extent that audiences are important to programmers, they are seen as products (or commodities) for sale to advertisers. The bigger the audience, the merrier the profits (Tehranian, 1996). If this line of argument is true, and evidence supports these assertions, the relationship between advertising and programming may need to be inverted (Ellul, 1965). Programming is not the normal function of television, with advertising as an interruption to the norm. Rather, programming may be interpreted as an interruption to television's normal function of advertising—a kind of filler between commercials. Even the distinction between programming and advertising has blurred ("commercialtainment") because of the proliferation of placement ads, programming environments (certain products will advertise only on certain types of programs), MTV (music videos are ads), and tie-ins (especially on children's shows). In short, television is one long commercial with programming breaks for connecting advertisers with the right kind of audience. Such an inversion provides fresh insights into "what's on" by asking, "What's behind?"

Violence on TV and Violent Behaviour?

Violence may be a universal phenomenon insofar as no human group is absent of aggression. Yet it remains one of the least understood aspects of human existence: its universality has not made it easier to explain or control (Aijmer and Abbink, 2000). Unlike aggression, which may be defined as unprovoked action, violence has a reason, and is instrumental in attaining goals or solving problems (Muro-Ruiz, 2002). Defining violence is tough enough; even tougher is assessing its cause, scope, and impact (Lee and Stanko, 2003). Nowhere is this more evident than in debates over the relationship of media violence to violence in society (Menon, 2003). Interest in negative effects of mass media spiked in the aftermath of highly publicized events involving violence in high schools and colleges. From the Ecole Polytechnique de Montreal to Columbine in Littleton Colorado to the Georges Vanier Secondary School in Toronto, words could barely capture the pain and bewilderment—much less convey the indignation and outrage—of knowing that innocent people were killed only because they happened to be in the wrong place at the wrong time. Finger-pointing was inevitable under such duress, if only to extract a measure of meaning from the meaningless, while asserting control over the uncontrollable. Bad parenting came under blame; so too was ready access to guns; youth subcultures that glorified nihilism and alienation as "cool," rebellious, or self-expressive; an amoral capitalism that has commodified violence as a lifestyle option; and the class structures that transformed high schools into cultural time bombs.

Of those culpable, however, only the media drew universal condemnation for their complicity in causing violence to run amok among youth. From Natural Born Killers to Pulp Fiction, films were singled out as the "usual suspects"; the Internet was criticized for its accessibility to seductive antisocial sites; popular music from gangsta rap to Eminem endured the usual slings for corrupting youth; also vilified were point-and-shoot splatter video games, including "Quake" and "Doom," the latter involving people on a room-to-room killing spree. But violence on television programs appears to have borne the brunt of criticism for misleading the nation's youth. The ensuing debate between television violence and violent behaviour has proven useful in drawing attention to a major social problem. The proliferation of violent imagery tends to make violence seem normal and acceptable rather than unusual and destructive, in effect condoning its use while contributing to exaggerated fears of victimization by the most vulnerable (Carter and Weaver, 2003). Insofar as this debate tended to be emotional and impressionistic, the relationship of television to behaviour requires clarification.

Concerns continue to be raised about how violence is portrayed. Graphic portrayals of violence as pathological are one thing; depictions of random and explicit violence as a joke in itself (for instance, Kill Bill) or as an aesthetic (The Matrix and its sequels) is another. Violent excitement is the key, and no amount of moralizing about pain, harm, or evil seems to diminish the glamour or appeal. The degree to which this violence is "sugar-coated" is also disconcerting. Violent encounters are glorified as humorous, exciting, and glamorous, in part, to suit the entertainment demands of prime-time audiences. Thus, what would by all accounts be a sordid and grisly event is transformed into something relatively painless or of little consequence, even ennobling, thus promoting its usefulness for solving interpersonal problems. Negotiation and compromise tend to be time-consuming and inconclusive as problem-solving devices; by contrast, violent solutions are clear-cut and unambiguous. Not surprisingly, violence for the sake of violence no longer has shock value but simply encourages people to see more but experience less (Giroux, 1996).

In recent years, attention has focused on the role of video games in fostering violence. The passive experience of watching television is one thing; the act of acting interactively with violent video games is deemed quite another. Escalating levels of gratuitous violence in video games are difficult to assess: Harmless fun? Release valve for dark fantasies? Or deadly conditioning for a violent outburst? Even more disturbing is the perception that military conditioning and video games rely on similar conditioning strategies. Soldiers are conditioned (desensitized) to be at ease with weapons and killings by repeatedly firing at human targets as a reflex response. The dangers in encouraging a violent mindset are all too evident, with the result that the shocking realities of mass murder are simply fictionalized in impressionable minds (Cribb, 1999). With adolescents, moreover, even the most repulsive act of aggression may be interpreted as an act of rebellion or self-expression. Dr. Liss Jeffrey of Toronto's McLuhan Program in Media Studies refers to this aggression as a "sicko star syndrome: that is, a sociopathic lack of compassion that gives a person the right to wreak revenge by turning the immediate environment into an immersive lethal video game" (Flynn, 1999). And this combination has proven a recipe for disaster in contexts where violence is considered cool because, as the media constantly remind us, control over others brings deference and respect (Cribb, 1999).

Rethinking the Connection: Relation Or Correlation? The statistics confirm what many suspect. The average Canadian watches a lot of television—about 23 hours of television a week—which translates into about 20 percent of our waking hours. The amount of television that people watch varies by region (those in Atlantic Canada watch the most), by gender (women watch more than men), and by age (older people watch more than younger people). The importance of television in people's lives is reflected in somewhat perverse relations. People "die" to be on television and some will kill as a ticket to 15 seconds of TV fame. No less worrying for many is the unacceptable high levels of violence on television. Programs designed for adults are violent enough, but the violence in children's programs is even more prevalent, with estimates ranging to ten times the amount of violence as in adult shows. And rather than subsiding in response to growing concern or outrage, prime-time television in the United States is getting more violent, particularly among pay cable networks, according to a $3.5 million study conducted between October 1994 and October 1997, and commissioned by the National Cable Television Association (Associated Press, 1998).

How do we interpret the relationship of violent behaviour with the proliferation of violent images on television? Is there a causal relationship? Will increased exposure to violence on TV activate aggressive behaviour in the viewer, as many are prone to believe? If so, what precisely is the nature of this cause-effect relationship? Does TV provide the cues, establish the models, serve as reinforcement, or stimulate the learning of violence patterns? Or does the causality work in reverse? That is, is it possible that more aggressive individuals are drawn to violent fare on television? Is the effect of TV violence primarily to reinforce a pre-existing disposition? Even more intriguing is the denial of any direct relationship between TV and violence. TV violence does not exist in a social vacuum. In a society saturated with violent images and symbols, it is difficult to isolate one component as the causal factor. In fact, the media-violence relationship may be correlational simply because of the difficulties in isolating causes (TV violence) from effects (violent behaviour) in a society where competition and aggression are the norm rather than the exception (Freedman, 2002). Finally, the entertainment industry has defended its depiction of violent excess by: (a) denying conclusive proof of any relationship; (b) claiming only to be reflecting society; (c) giving the public what it wants; and (d) reminding people of alternatives such as switching channels if their sensibilities are offended (Medved, 1996).

Sociologists are confronted by a host of questions when problematizing the link between television and violence. Foremost is the question of whether prolonged exposure contributes to antisocial behaviour in society. Most published results in this area—more than 3 000 since 1940—support a direct link between media violence and violent behaviour (Freedman, 2002). Prolonged exposure to TV violence is thought to generate several negative side-effects, including: (a) learning about aggressive behaviour; (b) a calloused indifference to the suffering of others, together with a lack of outrage to challenge even the most depraved atrocities; and (c) exaggerated fear of becoming a victim of violence in a world that is increasingly perceived as mean and dangerous. The harmful impact of screen violence is intensified when people lack first-hand experience to offset media messages.

Common sense would have us believe that such conclusions are reasonable. Not all sociologists would agree, however, and the basis for this disagreement may well reside in the different research strategies of different disciplines. Most laboratory experiments conclude that those who consume screen violence tend to behave in antisocial ways, but this relationship should not be taken at face value. Many of the studies in this area have lacked what researchers call external validity. That is, the studies were conducted in artificial contexts involving preschool children in which social significance and sanctions did not apply. As a result, these studies looked good on paper but bore little application to reality. To overcome this lack of external validity, natural environments are sought that allow observation in an undisturbed setting. Naturalistic studies to date confirm the general pattern of evidence from the laboratory (McBeth, 2001).

Prolonged exposure to explicit violence is thought to induce aggressive behaviour, especially among young males. Yet a causal relationship is not nearly as certain as many people would believe. A number of variables must be taken into account; after all, the influence of TV varies from person to person. Any effect may be indirect in that viewers tend to interpret TV images in ways that reflect personal needs and aspirations while reflecting their social status in society. Even more important is the reason for watching TV. Older people may watch it for entertainment and presumably are less affected by it. Younger people may turn to television as a source of information about how they should act or what to believe—thus reinforcing its effect on more impressionable audiences.

Put differently, people may only see what they want to see; they may absorb only what they are predisposed to accept. Too mechanical an interpretation of cause-and-effect relations is equally problematic. Perhaps the media only create a social climate, with a corresponding cultural frame of reference that defines some things as acceptable, others as unacceptable. Whether a person chooses to accept one option rather than another depends on a complex array of factors. Finally, protracted exposure to media violence may influence people's attitudes or beliefs. Exposure to televised violence tends to desensitize people by diminishing their empathy toward others while solidifying their apathy, indifference, and callousness to others. Yet negative attitudes do not lead to antisocial behaviour; after all, most people are adept at compartmentalizing attitudes and divorcing them from actions. This disconnection between beliefs and behaviour complicates any definitive conclusion.

In short, research conclusions on the causal relationship between TV violence and violent behaviour are tenuous and inconclusive. A relationship may well exist, but a causal connection may be difficult to prove or disprove, suggesting a need to think in terms of probabilities. Despite advances in statistical analysis and qualitative research, there are difficulties in "isolating" media effects within the context of a complex environment. Many factors are at play, and a misleading picture is created by efforts to isolate the media at the expense of other forces. This suggests a rephrasing of the original question. Instead of asking if TV violence creates violent behaviour, it might be more advantageous to inquire how it occurs (Perse, 2001). A useful hypothosis might read: "Under what circumstances and for what group of people is prolonged TV exposure a contributing factor to violent behaviour?" But if exposure to televised audiences is the problem, is censorship the solution?

CENSORSHIP—A SOLUTION IN SEARCH OF A PROBLEM?

In times of convulsive social change, people frequently turn to quick-fix solutions to complex problems. For every problem, many believe, there is an automatic solution. But superficial responses are not the answer, given a tendency to ignore the context of the problem or the consequences to society at large. A similar line of reasoning (but on a grander scale) pertains to issues of censorship and televised violence. Censoring the bad and the ugly on television has a certain appeal: It is reasonably simple to introduce through rating systems or technological devices, monitoring is relatively easy, and public acceptance can be counted on. Yet censorship in a free and democratic society is as much a problem as a solution. The right to "freedom of opinion and expression" as enshrined in Article 19 of the United Nations' Declaration of Human Rights is widely regarded as a cornerstone of democracy. For others, censorship is a minor but necessary irritant. Its restrictions are seen as reasonable limitations that are demonstrably justifiable, and a small price to pay in protecting society from the offensive.

Everyone is against censorship, Philip Marchand wrote in the *Toronto Star* (21 October, 1999), yet everyone wants to censor something (if only to censor people who want to censor!). Those on the left want to purge anything that is seen as insensitive to gender or diversity; the right wants to expunge material that is anti-family and pro-change (Humphreys, 2003). For our purposes, censorship can be defined as an interruption—either deliberate or unconscious—in controlling the flow of information from a sender to a receiver. This definition is admittedly broad, but it reinforces the notion of censorship as a process applicable to a wide range of human activities. Censorship is endorsed by people with a desire to muzzle those whose visions do not coincide with their own vision of reality. An important, if improbable, behavioural principle stands at the core of censorship: Change what people see or hear, and their behaviour will change accordingly. For example, eliminating violence from television programming will prompt people to act nonviolently. This assertion implies a direct relationship between thought and behaviour, an assumption that is increasingly dubious in light of recent evidence. Several conclusions follow from this definition and characteristics.

- First, censorship is going on all the time. To be human and live in society implies entanglement in a web of restrictions. Interruptions in the flow of information, such as self-censorship in talking or writing, are a routine and constitutive feature of any system of social relations (Petersen and Hutchinson, 1999). Thus, the issue is not one of censorship per se, which is unavoidable, but of where to draw the line in defining acceptability in a society that seriously upholds the freedom of expression.

- Second, there is no such thing as absolute freedom of speech. Nobody anywhere has ever had the right to do and say exactly as he or she pleased. Rather, the right to free expression is relative to time and place. What is permissible in one era is not in another, especially in times of uncertainty, change, and diversity. Context is also important. Yelling "theatre" in a crowded firehall is not an arrestable offence, although your circle of friends could shrink drastically. Shouting "fire" in a crowded theatre is an entirely different matter. Context is important in another way. Almost everyone agrees on banning child pornography, but there is less agreement on censoring material involving consenting adults. However repulsive blatant sexual exploitation may be, not everyone concurs that scuttling free expression is the solution. Admittedly, some degree of censorship may be necessary in protecting the innocent, securing safety, and ensuring order, but the question of drawing the line is still open to debate.

- Third, there is no agreement on how effective censorship is in curbing the flow of unacceptable information. Is censorship a solution to problems or simply a knee-jerk reaction that dodges key issues and costly commitments? Does censorship accomplish what it sets out to do, given growing doubts about media effects as direct and conclusive? What proof do we have of this, either for or against?

- Fourth, are restrictions on media violence an effective way of improving attitudes, modifying behaviour, empowering women and minorities, and changing social structures? Or is the move to marginalize rather than muzzle by way of more speech, not less, the best line of attack against offensive material? Will restrictions make people crave what has been censored more, on the assumption that people want what they can't get? Will censorship convince people to avoid, or will it have the effect of creating the right kind of noise and provide a million dollars' worth of free publicity? For example, program advertising that carries a warning of violence is likely to attract rather than repel young audiences; they are also more likely to express positive attitudes towards the products being advertised during that program (Strauss, 1997). In short, if censorship is the solution, what problem is it trying to solve?

DISCUSSION QUESTIONS

1   Provide arguments both for and against censorship of the media.

2   Collect a body of data to determine whether media continue to mistreat minorities in how they are portrayed.

3   What is meant by the notion that media are a kind of propaganda?

4   Demonstrate the idea that news is a socially constructed process.

5   Problematize the notion that media violence leads to violent behaviour.

 ## WEBLINKS

Mass Media in Canada.   **www.massmedia.nelson.com**

Diversity in Media.   **www.ryerson.ca**

Media Watch.   **www.mediawatch.org**

chapter eight

Health and Health Care

FRAMING THE PROBLEM

Healthwise, we are living in strange times. First, the good news. Rarely have Canadians as a group enjoyed such high health standards. We are living longer; many are living better because of health technology advances such as screening tests for genetically-related diseases. Other indicators of wellness are equally promising: health-related risks such as smoking are widely challenged, fatty foods may become the new tobacco, many infectious diseases are under control, and awareness is growing of environmentally-related diseases such as multiple chemical sensitivities (Ausubel, 2001). The system of health care in Canada is universally admired as a model to be emulated for its balancing of compassion with universality and efficiency. The system may not be as fast or as comprehensive as some would like, but it is fair, judging by studies that confirm both rich and poor wait equally long for elective surgery (Canadian Press, 2003). Not surprisingly, Canada's health-care system is embraced by many Canadians because of its enormous symbolic value in defining our national identity—who we are—even if many think the system is starting to fray at the edges (Armstrong and Armstrong, 2001; Burke and Silver, 2003; Carey, 2003).

Now, the bad news. Canadians are not as healthy as they like to believe. The odds of dying from cancer haven't changed much since the 1960s, including virtually no progress against the deadliest tumour of all, lung cancer, despite new drugs, better radiation techniques, improved surgery, and vast expenditures on cancer research involving thousands of scientists (Papp, 2003). To add insult to injury, those diagnosed with cancer must endure long waiting times for treatment, provincial variation in the quality of service, and inadequate support services (Carey, 2003). Yes, the triumph over infectious diseases may be one of the success stories of the 20th century. Yet this modern day scourge remains the leading cause of death in the world at present (Doyle, 2003). Malaria claims 2 million lives annually while sleeping sickness transmitted by tsetse flies is spinning rapidly out of control, with 250 000 deaths in the Congo alone (DiManno, 2003). Paradoxically, Canadians are becoming victims of medical success as new infectious diseases keep out-witting our capacities or complacencies (Gorrie, 2003). Advances in medical technology, notwithstanding, there are growing fears of new deadly diseases —from West Nile virus to Severe Acute Respiratory Syndrome (SARS) —because of their mysterious origins, resist-ance to conventional drugs, an ability to go global by overwhelming the immune system, and deep-seated anxieties over out-of-control plagues with a Black Death capacity to kill millions (Gorrie, 2003). New "epidemics" pose additional problems (Reany, 2003). A widening obesity problem among youth threatens to strip our health-care resources as they mature into overweight adults, prompting Toronto's medical health officer to lambaste sloth, not SARS, as the true epidemic (Freeze, 2003; also *New Statesman,* 18 August, 2003; *The Economist,* 13 December, 2003). And the Walkerton tainted water scandal that took eight lives has made it abundantly clear: The fragility of health should never be taken for granted as well, especially when carelessness and arrogance replace caution.

Even our widely ballyhooed health-care system has proven porous. Few take note when the public health system is doing its job, but complacency and political inattention, cou-pled with a lack of cash and resources, have stretched the system to the limit, making it almost impossible to keep up (Editorial, *Toronto Star,* 28 June, 2003). The SARS outbreak in 2003 clearly demonstrated weaknesses in Ontario's public health system. Think about it: It took only a single Chinese doctor who contracted the virus in Guangdong province and then passed it on to 13 people in a Hong Kong hotel, one of whom flew into Toronto (Houpt, 2003), to cripple a city of 2.5 million by virtue of 44 SARS-related deaths, hun-dreds of illnesses, thousands of quarantines, and abundant negative international publicity. More than bad luck was involved. Years of underfunding by the Ontario government had left health care so thinly stretched that the entire health system in Canada's richest province was one crisis away from a complete meltdown. Without a surge capacity to handle the SARS crisis, resources had to be diverted, including closure of operating rooms, with a corresponding backlog of heart and cancer surgeries, MRI diagnostic imaging, and organ transplants. Responses to SARS not only exposed deficiencies in cash, resources, and political attention. Relief was also hampered by lack of staff, outdated equipment, and con-fusion of responsibilities between different authorities (Editorial, 28 June, 2003).

SARS exposed yet another flaw in hospitalized health care. Hospitals are no longer seen as places to get better; they are rather germ-infested emporiums that make people sicker because of chronic emergency room crowding or shoddy infection control. Or as Andrew Nikiforuk (2003: A21) writes: "SARS is a reminder that if you're not deathly sick, a hospi-tal visit just might change your prognosis." Exposure to toxic materials such as dioxins—a confirmed carcinogen—is yet another hospital hazard. Chemicals in our environment are killing us as well, judging by worry over genetically modified and industrial produced food (Laidlaw, 2003). Our dependence on synthetic chemicals and refusal to acknowledge how profoundly they disrupt the environment is captured in this dispiriting metaphor of what has gone wrong: The discovery that human mother's milk is among the most toxic of human foods because of dioxin (Ausubel, 2001). Predictably, then, people are becoming increasingly aware of alternative medicine in complementing conventional medicines with their narrow focus on symptoms, negative side effects, and many failures (Grigg, 1997).

Other health-care indicators related to access are no less disturbing. Canada may have a universal health-care system but the reality is that one in seven Canadians (4.3 million) cannot find a family doctor—even in major centres such as Toronto or Vancouver (Wong, 2003). The number of physicians in Canada has declined by 5 percent since 1993, despite a 13 percent increase in population, with the result that Canada's ratio of doctors to population (2.1 per 1000 residents) is one of the lowest in the industrialized world (Editorial, *National Post,* 25 October, 2003). A government study in 2001 concluded that Ontario's nursing homes provide one of the lowest levels of daily personal care in North America or Europe (Welsh, 2003). Vulnerable residents don't get the care they need because of neglect while workers are burning out from excessive demands. Equal health care access is a myth for many minorities: Cultural taboos, language barriers, embarrassment, and fear of racism are preventing some minority women and men from seeking the medical assistance they require (Jimenez, 2003). Aboriginal peoples are experiencing a major crisis in health problems, yet often lack access to health care for various reasons. As many as one in seven disabled persons report they cannot access health care or afford the drugs they need, according to a study by the Canadian Council on Social Developments based on statistics Canada data (*National Post,* 20 May, 2003). And the fourth annual report by the Canadian Institute for Health Information pointed to widespread disparities in the calibre of health care and health outcomes across the different regions in Canada (Vallis, 2003).

In short, not all Canadians benefit from a commitment to create a common sense care for everyone, regardless of income. Inequalities in health and health care because of age, gender, race, or social class tend to contradict the ideals that Canadians value. In particular, social inequality is harmful to people's health because of the "health and longevity gap" between the wealthy and the poor (Wermuth, 2003: 1). As many have noted, income has the largest impact on health; as a result, a person's wealth dictates his or her level of health rather than lifestyle factors such as exercise or not smoking (MacIntyre, 2003). To the extent that the rhetoric of universal health care does not match the reality of expectations, these inequities are deemed a social problem. The World Health Organization in its World Health Report 2000 clearly articulated the challenge:

> The health system ... has the responsibility to try to reduce inequalities by preferentially improving the health of the worse off.... The objective of good health is really twofold: the best attainable average level—goodness—and the smallest feasible differences among individuals and groups—fairness.

Finally, international bodies (including the WHO) have ruled that health and care are basic human rights; after all, without health, what is the point of other individual and human rights?

Welcome to the 21st century. To one side, Canadians are justifiably proud of their level of health and health care. Public health insurance remains a cornerstone of Canada's identity and uniqueness in distinguishing us from the United States (Maioni, 2003). Canadians are telling Canada's new prime minister, Paul Martin, that more spending on health care is the number one national priority, followed by improved federal–provincial cooperation and increased funding for education and training (CRIC, 2003). To the other side, neither health levels nor health care are matching strides with our expectations and lifestyles (Holford, 2003). Healthy or unhealthy? Crisis or hype? Legitimate criticism or carping? Under control or out of control? Responses to these questions are of such fundamental interest to Canadians that this chapter explores the topic of health and health care as an institution in crisis (also Gauld, 2003). This chapter argues that health and health care in Canada can be framed as a social problem for three reasons: First, inequities in access and outcomes reflect social factors; second, health inequities impact differently on those most vulnerable; and third, solutions to health problems are solvable through human action. The chapter begins by analyzing health as a social problem. What is considered health and illness is shown to be socially constructed, culturally specific, and evolving over time and place (Henslin, 2000). The following questions reflect a concern with the social determinants of health and health care:

- What are the social influences on health and disease?
- Why do members of some groups, but not others, become ill and die prematurely?
- What effect does social cohesion have on individual and a population's health?
- How do social inequities bring about differences in health outcomes?
- Can social policies protect individuals from disease or prevent faster health improvements (Wermuth, 2003)?

To emphasize the social dimensions of health and health care, a sociological approach is compared with a medical model. For in the final analysis, health is as much social as it is medical. That is, health and illness are the result of broader social and environmental factors; accordingly, solutions to the health problem must be social and ecological (Ausubel, 2001). Data on the health of Canadians are discussed next, with particular emphasis on how poverty underpins many health problems—especially in aboriginal communities. This is followed by an overview of health-care arrangements in Canada, with a focus on what is distinctive about Canada's national health-care system as compared to the United States. Also discussed are the how and why behind the crisis in Canada's national health-care system with respect to both demographic changes and Canada's ageing population. Two key questions provide a conceptual framework: Is the health-care system fundamentally flawed, thus requiring an entire overhaul in the financing, allocation, and delivery of health services? Or is the system basically sound with only moderate reforms required to restore its health?

This chapter does not flinch from asking some tough questions about what many regard as the most vital ingredient in the quality of life. For example, references to Canada's health-care system as "broken" or "a failure" (Robson, 2003) cannot be taken at face value. What precisely is meant by "broken" or "a failure," and who says so, why, and on what grounds? To what extent is a market-based health delivery system relevant or inevitable? Consider, for example, how the continued deterioration in the quality and quantity of America's health care has not deflected Canadians from debating the merits of a private for-profit service to complement a private but publicly funded, "not-for-profit" health-care delivery (Devereaux, 2003; Redmond, 2003). Nor does this chapter recoil from answers that puncture the gloss behind Canada's much vaunted health-care system. The chapter debunks many myths that have infiltrated health and health-care fields, especially by those with a vested interest in inflating the so-called crisis in health care. Or as nicely put by Barer, Morgan, and Evans (2002: A-16):

Health care debates are "blessed" with more than their fair share of zombies—unsupported claims that just won't die. No matter how much damning evidence is rolled out, or how well-reasoned the counter-argument, or even if temporarily buried, the claims always rise again at opportune times, to confuse or deliberately mislead those struggling to understand the truth about their health-care system.

Finally, this chapter acknowledges an emergent paradox in the field of health care (Bricker and Greenspon, 2001). During the 1990s, the numbers of doctors and nurses declined in the face of cutbacks to admissions and emigration to the United States; hospital beds were sharply reduced; and investment to new medical technologies was radically curtailed. Yet during the same era a new health consumer emerged, both demanding of answers and updated treatments, as well as less deferential to medical authorities, advice, and answers than in the past (Bricker and Greenspon, 2001). This mismatch between growing assertiveness and declining access may yet prove a key flash point in the politics of health care.

HEALTH AND ILLNESS: MEDICAL MODEL OR SOCIAL PROBLEM?

Most people think of medicines, doctors, and hospitals when thinking about health and health care. You are not alone: A medical model has long dominated discourses on disease in Western societies. According to this medical model, illness is the result of biological breakdowns within the individual; sicknesses have specific causes like viruses that can be isolated; the focus of attention is on the physical body of the individual rather than on general well-being or the broader social context, and responses to treatment rest within a medical environment that happily dispenses pharmaceuticals or hospital care (Macionis and Plummer, 2002). With its emphasis on cause, care, and cure rather than prevention, this model embraces a trifecta of assumptions. First, there is the belief that risk factors are responsible for the disease. Risk factors will disappear by changing people's behaviour and their environment, according to this line of argument. Second, disease is unnatural and its elimination is necessary and normal. Third, all things are possible since humans have the power to control destiny, despite the unanticipated consequences of many of our actions (Grob, 2002).

It is widely assumed that people get sick because of poor health or natural causes such as chronic heart disease. That's true in a technical sense. Public health messages routinely warn us about the side effects of negative behaviour such as smoking, while encouraging healthy alternatives like exercising. High-tech medicine further improves our chances for survival. But these medical/individualized models have shortcomings, especially since spending more on medicine and health care does not necessarily improve overall health (Health Canada, 1994). Many diseases are a natural and inevitable component of human existence—especially as life expectancy increases (Grob, 2002). By contrast, approaching health as a social condition and illness as a social problem shifts the focus of study away from the medical model. Rather than thinking about health in individualistic terms, emphasis is on social factors that affect health with respect to causes, consequences, characteristics, and cures. The relationship of health to social context cannot be denied, ranging in scope from workplace safety and job stress, to family dynamics that can induce fear and loathing (Alvi et al., 2000). For example, the SARS epidemic clearly revealed the social dimensions of health and health care because of government cutbacks. Just 16 months before SARS hit Toronto, the Ontario government mothballed its research labs as part of a cost-cutting measure that left a stripped-down, public-health system poorly prepared for any crisis (Abraham and Priest, 2003). To combat SARS, Toronto had to divert funds from critical programs such as West Nile virus (Diebel, 2003). Health-care operations had to be put on hold. And those entrusted with our health care paid the ultimate price; two nurses died in the line of duty.

Gaps in health and health care are exerting pressure to rethink "wellness." Proposed are models that emphasize the importance of thinking socially and responding accordingly (Wermuth, 2003). Health is more than just feeling good or being fit. It goes beyond an absence of disease or infirmity. Health at an individual level is related to a sense of physical and mental well-being, an indicator of our quality of life, and a marker of identity in terms of how we feel about ourselves (Jones, 2001). Society at large is no less interested in health. Investment in health is endorsed as an expenditure that not only maintains a healthy population, thus reducing costs in the long run, while reducing workplace absences because of illness (Kelleher, 2001). Health care also creates wealth by generating nearly 10 percent of Canada's GDP through the sales and delivery of services, equipment, and salaries (Fiesen, 2003). The overall prosperity, social stability, and well-being of Canadians are enhanced as well (Health Canada, 1994).

The conclusion seems inescapable: Public and personal health must be situated in the broader context of society. Living and working conditions may have a greater impact on people's health than the quantity or quality of health care. The likelihood of becoming ill or dying prematurely may reflect a variety of factors related to the social and physical environment (Wermuth, 2003). Social factors that influence the determinants of good health or illness, include the following: income and social status, social support networks, education, employment and working conditions, safe and clean physical environment, personal health practices and coping skills, and access to adequate health-care services (Health Canada, 1994). A more concise breakdown reveals the broader context that accounts for wellness or illness.

1 **Environmental Factors.** The environment created by humans can pose serious health risks (Barlow and May, 2000). There is growing awareness that our health depends on a healthy planet (Ausubel, 2001). The interplay of social and biological forces have interacted with war, famine, and ecological damage (from climate change to destruction of natural habitats) to create human disruptions that lead to reviving old diseases, creating new ones, and intensifying existing plagues.

2 **Lifestyle Factors.** Smoking, excessive use of alcohol and drugs, poor diet, lack of exercise, and social isolation are contributing factors to illness and premature death. Specific living conditions such as work or housing may contribute to varied outcomes. Important, as well, is the presence or absence of social support and community networks.

3 **Health Care and Public Health Factors.** People's health depends on public and private means to improve health by preventing and treating disease. The public health system is composed of government-run programs to guarantee access to clean drinking water, sewage and sanitation facilities, and inoculation against infectious diseases. Health care involves facilities such as hospitals for ensuring health and treating illness.

4 **Socioeconomic Status.** Many studies confirm that the most powerful indicator of population health is the prosperity of society in which people live, especially in how wealth is distributed (Health Canada, 1994; Wermuth, 2003). Social class, income inequality, and deprivation are linked with indicators of national health, that is, those who are less

well off are less well (Olsen, 2002). Those with low incomes or living in poverty are more likely to die at a younger age or endure poorer health related to physical and psychological illnesses. Poverty is a proven killer: For example, according to the WHO, nearly 1 billion people suffer from serious ailments linked to poverty, including not enough to eat, an unbalanced diet, and lack of clean drinking water. Similarly, poverty creates imbalances in health care in Canada for the poor for the following reasons:

- Unequal access to health resources
- Lack of access to information
- Higher stress levels with fewer skills for coping with severe stress
- Greater exposure to environmental and workplace risks
- Lifestyle patterns that harm

In short, the health-care paradigm is shifting. There is greater acceptance of health and illness that goes beyond the individual/biological/medical/technological model of the past. Awareness is growing that good health recognizes the interconnectedness of many factors and the interplay of numerous social and personal forces that intersect to make people healthy (Ausubel, 2001). Of course, nobody really knows how much of a group's health is explained by social variables. According to studies by Tarlov and St Peter (2000), 56 percent of the variations in health can be attributed to social and ecological factors, 21 percent to health behaviours, followed closely by medical care and the public health system at 19 percent. Genes and biology at 4 percent account for the smallest proportion of variation in the disease burden.

The conclusion seems inescapable: Social factors overlap with behavioural and ecological factors to exert a major impact in shaping individual and population health (Wermuth, 2003). As noted by the Canadian Health Network, these determinants of health and well-being do not exist in isolation from one another but intersect in complex ways to complicate outcomes. Context is critical too, since people's circumstances such as housing, income, social support, work stress, and education profoundly affect life expectancy and quality of life.

THE HEALTH OF CANADIANS

Canadians, for the most part, are a relatively healthy lot. Many of us are living longer and living better than we did in the past. Medical triumphs have contributed to the quality and quantity of life. For example, life expectancy in 1831 was 40 years for men, 42 years for women (Lavoie and Oderkirk, 2000). By contrast a boy born in 2002 can expect to live to 76.7, while a girl's life expectancy is 82—a gender gap that is slowly closing (Gray, 2003). Paradoxically, Canada's health-care system may be a victim of its own success in that diseases that need time to develop are becoming more common. Increased life expectancy provides an opportunity for degenerative diseases such as cancer or heart problems to flourish in ways not possible a century ago. Solving health problems can lead to additional health-related problems that will require new and sometimes more expensive solutions. For example, the overuse of antibiotics has spawned resistant microbes that magnify the threat of tuberculosis and other infectious diseases to haunt us yet again.

Canadians tend to take health and health care for granted. They also have a tendency to poorly assess and distort risk factors because of media panic attacks (Durbin, 2003). Excessive fear over some relatively modest health risks tend to hog the spotlight while deadly killers are dismissed as part of "life" (Gatehouse, 2003). Consider that by the end of May 2003, one Canadian had died from Creutzfeldt-Jakob (human form of mad cow) disease, 18 had died from West Nile virus, and 44 had died from SARS. By contrast, in the year 2000, 76 426 had died from circulatory diseases, 62 672 from cancer, 17 745 from respiratory diseases, including 4399 from pneumonia, 3605 from suicides, 1405 from motor vehicles, 511 from AIDs. As well, 404 pedestrians were killed, and 546 Canadians were murdered. On a worldwide basis, 808 died from SARS, while about 2 million die each year from diarrhea-related illness. Which of these is regarded as a social problem? Which gets the funding and publicity? Why are fears disproportionate to the actual risk? According to Allan R. Gregg (2003), fear has little to do with reason but reflects deeply embedded anxieties, especially in contexts where random victimization intensifies the terror of being next.

Mortality rates reveal an interesting pattern. In 1901, the leading cause of death was tuberculosis with 12 percent of all deaths or 180.8 deaths per 100 000 population; followed by bronchitis and pneumonia at 10 percent of all deaths or 150.9 deaths per 100 000 population; and affections of the intestines (diarrhea and enteritis) at 9.1 percent of all deaths or 136.9 per 100 000 population. In 1997, cancer was the leading cause of death accounting for 27.2 percent of all deaths or 181.2 per 100 000 population (cancer was the tenth leading cause of death in 1901 with only 2.8 percent of all deaths). Death by cancer is followed by heart disease with 26.6 percent of all deaths or 173 per 100 000 (heart disease was the sixth-highest cause of death in 1901 with 5.6 percent of all deaths) and strokes with 7.4 percent of all deaths or 47.8 per 100 000 population. The figures for 2000 are largely unchanged from 1997 except for cancer, which now claims 29 percent of deaths (Gray, 2003). Sadly, this figure is expected to creep upwards since cancer rates increase with increases in longevity. Not unexpectedly, the perception is growing that the fabric of Canada's health-care system will unravel because of the costs of caring for an ageing population.

Most Canadians are relatively healthy in comparison with the developing world where a host of poverty-related diseases continue to debilitate or destroy. According to a report by the United Nations Population Fund, millions of young people are doomed to blighted lives because of poverty, lack of education, threat of HIV/AIDS, violence, gender discrimination, and human rights violations in war-torn countries (Ward, 2003). The contradictions are stunning: while half of the world must cope with hunger and starvation on a regular basis, part of the other half is more worried about putting on the pounds by dining to excess. No wonder the World Health Organization has declared obesity an epidemic that ranks among the world's most serious public health issues (*The Economist*, 13 December, 2003). To be sure, health in general has improved in many parts of the world: Infant mortalities have plummeted as childhood illnesses caused by infections are under greater control (Mooney et al. 2001). People live longer because of medicines and lifestyles, but improving life spans exert increased pressure on already scarce resources, thus creating the conditions for more disease and epidemics. Comparing health indicators in Canada with those in other parts of the world acknowledges gaps in health and care.

- Infant Mortality: The world average is 57 deaths per 1000 live births, with Afghanistan at 150 per 1000 live births at the top of the infant mortality list (Schaefer and Smith, 2004). Japan and Canada have one of the lowest rates at about 4 per 1000 live births. Among Canada's aboriginal peoples, the rate is 8 infant deaths per 1000 live births, a drop from 27.6 a generation ago.

- Life Expectancy: Medical scientists tell us the maximum average human lifespan under ideal conditions is 87 years (the record is held by a French women who died at the age of 122 in 1997) (Olshansky, Carnes, and Cassel, 1990). Japan comes closest to the ideal with a life expectancy of 81 years in 2000. In Canada, life expectancy is 79, in India it is 61 years, but it is only 41 years in the poor African country of Niger. According to World Health Organization figures (1998), 50 million people live in countries where life expectancies are less than 45 years, while 300 million people live in 16 countries where life expectancies declined between 1975 and 1995.

- AIDS is the leading cause of death in the poor regions of Africa south of the Sahara. More than 29.4 million sub-Saharans were living with HIV/AIDS, roughly 70 percent of the world total, compared to 0.58 percent of North Americans and 0.23 percent of Europeans. The cumulative number of deaths from AIDS on January 1, 2000 was about 14.5 million, with 80 percent of this total in sub-Saharan Africa. In 2002, according to the World Health Organization and UNAIDS, about 1.3 million people worldwide had died of AIDS. Tragically, the global AIDS situation is worsening, despite international efforts to control the spread of HIV/AIDS, with more deaths and infections in 2003 than ever before and nearly 46 million people living with the virus (Kleiss, 2003). The situation in Canada is less grim but no less deadly: 50 000 Canadians have been infected with HIV/AIDS, with an estimated 4200 new infections each year, including 511 deaths in 2000. Aboriginal peoples and African-Canadians are experiencing the country's fastest rising rates of AIDS infection, a trend attributable to poverty, despair, and social dislocation (Bueckert, 2003), including a sevenfold increase in the aboriginal community since 1990 (Picard, 2003). Spending on research and access to treatment remain overwhelmingly concentrated in Europe and North America.

- While an outbreak of disease can put a crippling burden on health-care systems, Canada's experience with the SARS epidemic pales by comparison to what confronts developing world countries. In 2002, AIDS, TB, and malaria killed up to 6 million, creating both social and economic devastation in parts of sub-Saharan Africa because of lost productivity (St Denis, 2003).

Aboriginal Health: Prognosis? Not Good

Not all Canadians are equally healthy. Nor do we have to go outside Canada to find developing world conditions in a land of astonishing wealth. Different groups in Canada suffer disproportionately from disease and illness, especially Canada's aboriginal peoples. Modest improvements, notwithstanding, aboriginal peoples as a group are the most disadvantaged with respect to health status (Health Canada, 1994). Something as basic as access to clean water provides a deadly indictment of what is wrong. In 2000, Health Canada estimated that at least 79 of 863 reserves had drinking water systems that were deemed potential health hazards (Hanrahan, 2003). Of Ontario's 134 reserves, 20 have endured boil-water advisories for at least 18 months, according to the Chiefs of Ontario who tabled a report at the Walkerton tainted water inquiry (Avery, 2003). The conclusion is inescapable: As bluntly put by John Richards (2000: 39), "Aboriginal poverty, family distress, and the general alienation of Aboriginal people from the mainstream of Canadian society is by far the most serious single social problem facing the country."

Health gaps persist along a broad range of fronts. Illnesses resulting from poverty, overcrowding, polluted water, and poor housing have contributed to a national death rate for aboriginal peoples, which is more than double the rate for the Canadian general population (Frideres, 1998: 180). Aboriginal intravenous drug users in communities such as Vancouver have an infection rate for HIV/AIDS twice that of non-aboriginals and comparable to the hardest hit communities in parts of Africa (Picard, 2003). Tuberculosis rates for registered Indians are about eight times that of the general population. Compare the aboriginal rate of 81.3 cases per 100 000 versus 7.4 for Canadians at large, and 80 for Africa (Frideres, 1998). According to Statistics Canada, 45 percent of all aboriginal adults report having one or more chronic conditions, with arthritis and rheumatism at the top of the list (Durst, 2003). Diabetes, which was unknown prior to the 1940s, is now bordering on the epidemic, with rates double the national average (Moore, 2003). Other negative indicators include: infectious and parasitic diseases; endocrine, nutritional, and metabolic diseases and immunity disorders; diseases of the respiratory and digestive systems; complications from pregnancy and childbirth; and injury and poisonings (Health Canada, 1994). Social, nutritional, and ecological factors continue to contribute to their decreasing quality of life, with the result that life expectancies are well below (upwards to 20 years) that of Canadians living in the south (Frideres, 1998).

No less dismaying is the degree to which aboriginal individuals are internalizing this powerlessness and impotence into an expression of self-hatred. The internalization of white racism and/or indifference is reflected in violent death rates, which are nearly four times the national average. Infant mortality rates are about 60 percent higher than the national average. With a suicide rate that is six times the national average for certain age-specific groups, including rates that are 36 times the national average in some aboriginal communities, aboriginal peoples represent one of the most self-destructive groups in the world at present (Samson, 2000). Alcohol and substance abuse are widely regarded as the foremost problems on most reserves, with alcohol-related deaths accounting for up to 80 percent of the fatalities on some reserves (Buckley, 1992). Domestic abuse is so endemic within aboriginal communities, according to some observers (Drost et al., 1995), that few aboriginal children grow into adulthood without first-hand experience of interpersonal violence. Finally, over one-third of all aboriginal deaths are due to accidents and violence, including car accidents, drowning, and fires, a rate that is nearly four times the national Canadian average (Frideres, 1998: 181).

HEALTH, DEMOGRAPHY, AND AGEING

Canada's health picture is more than a spreadsheet of health facts and disease indicators. The determinants of health and health care cannot be found in some kind of social vacuum, replete with statistics about who is healthy and who is not. Health is about people, how groups of people define themselves in terms of health and well-being, and the reactions of others to these definitions. This human dimension makes it doubly important to determine who are Canadians, demographically speaking. No less important is determining how the health-care system is coping with those Canadians who now constitute Canada's fastest growing population segment: the ageing.

Demography: Highlights from the 2001 Census of Population

1   The 2001 Census counted 30 007 094 people in Canada on May 15th 2001. Ontario is the most populous province with 11 874 436 people, followed by Quebec (7 410 504), British Columbia (4 095 934), and Alberta (3 064 429). The population of the major census metropolitan areas include Toronto at 4 751 408 people, followed by Montreal at 3 480 342 and Vancouver at 2 048 823.

2   Between 1996 and 2001, the population increased by 1 160 333, a gain of 4 percent, which is one of Canada's smallest census-to-census growth rates. Compare that with the 14.8 percent increase between 1951 and 1956. The five-year growth rates for the world at large are 7 percent, including 5.9 percent for Australia and 5.4 percent for the United States.

3   Of the provinces, Alberta's population increased by 10.3 percent, Ontario gained 6.1 percent, British Columbia, 4.9 percent, and Nunavut, 8.1 percent. The population for Newfoundland and Labrador decreased by 7 percent while the Yukon and Northwest Territories declined by 5 percent.

4   Immigration was the main source of population growth between 1996 and 2001, off-setting a decline of about one-third in the natural increase compared to the previous five-year period.

5   In 2001, 79.4 percent of Canadians lived in an urban area with a population of 10 000 or more.

6   Urban areas continue to grow, with the largest growth rates in Calgary, Oshawa, Toronto, Edmonton, Vancouver, and Kitchener. Both Greater Sudbury and Thunder Bay continue to lose population.

7   Canada's population continues to be concentrated in four major urban regions, claiming 51 percent of the population: The extended Golden Horseshoe in Southern Ontario; Montreal and its adjacent regions; lower mainland of British Columbia and southern Vancouver Island; and the Edmonton–Calgary corridor. The population of these four areas grew by 7.6 percent compared to virtually no growth in the rest of Canada.

8   Population by age group as of July 1, 2000 includes the following breakdown:

0–14 years	5 870 888
15–24	4 152 800
25–44	9 699 740
45–64	7 176 762
65+	3 848 897

Based on data cited in Canada at a Glance 2003 **www.statcan.ca**

The Ageing of Canada

Canada is greying. In 1981, 10 percent of Canada's population was 65 years and over; by 1995, the figure had increased to 12 percent, three years later to 12.3 percent. By the year 2016, possibly 21.5 percent of Canadians will be older than 65; another 5 percent will be over 80 years. The implications for health care cannot be sloughed off, given the perception that the elderly impose a greater cost on the health system. Health costs per person quadruple from middle age to retirement age: Per capita costs (adjusted for inflation) for males 45–54 totalled $514 in 2001 but $2409 for a 65–74 year male and $8689 for males over 85 (Won, 2003). Can Canada afford the added pensions and health-care costs associated with the retirement of the baby-boom generation and the heavy financial burden imposed on those of working age because of reductions in the workforce (Cheal, 2002)? Or is the crisis vastly exaggerated because of erroneous assumptions about ageing and the elderly (McDaniel, 2002; Hicks, 2003)? Will the government need to make significant changes to its retirement and pension programs—especially in light of Canada's relatively low birth rate of 1.5 (2.1 births per woman are required to keep the population stable) (Thorpe, 2003). Regardless of the responses, a mindset shift will be necessary: An ageing population is not necessarily a problem in the making but may prove an opportunity in disguise if channelled correctly (Hicks, 2003).

Growing old may conjure up images of the "Golden Years." Ageing as a social and physical process over time has a powerful impact on our social identity, that is, how we see ourselves and how others relate to us (Hockey and James, 2003). Yet the reality of ageing and retirement may be very different from the myth. In our rapidly changing and highly technological society, with its premium on youth, vitality, and participation in the workforce, the elderly tend to be treated as culturally irrelevant, no more so than in media depictions of the old as grouchy or infantile. Such disparagement was not always the case. The elderly were once accorded respect and deference because of their accumulated wisdom, experience, and courage. They continue to be venerated in many communities. But the contribution of the elderly is sharply devalued in a world of rapid social and technological change, where today's knowledge is tomorrow's kitty litter. Where once revered for their endurance and knowledge, the elderly are increasingly associated with degeneracy, death, senility, incontinence, frailty, and losing touch with reality. They are stereotyped as childlike, sclerotic, forgetful, asexual, unaware, and demented. Moreover, these stereotypes are internalized by older people, resulting in a reinforcement of negative self-images, low morale, lack of confidence, and higher morbidity. This internalization can also lead older people to avoid other older persons for fear of being stigmatized by association with a senile and incontinent group.

Immigrant elderly are known to experience disruptive patterns of adjustment in coping with the demands of Canadian society (Isajiw, 1999). Initial exposure to a radically different climate, culture, and social practices may trigger culture shock. Culture shock arises from disruptions to conventional values and norms that once defined the normal, correct, and useful. The subsequent settlement period may also induce a delayed culture shock, especially when immigrants become increasingly aware of their diminished status in Canada. For example, take the case of elderly immigrants who arrive from cultures where they are venerated, respected for their wisdom, and recipients of deferential treatment. Upon arrival, the immigrant elderly may find themselves in circumstances that tend to demean the aged as a burden or a bore, without much to offer to the household except often thankless tasks such as babysitting. Not surprisingly, first generation elderly immigrants may hold on tightly to their ethno-cultural roots rather than embracing the new (Elliot, 1999).

Much of the immigrant culture shock occurs within the context of intergenerational relations (Anisef and Kilbride, 2003). This should come as no surprise. The elderly of today are living much longer than in previous generations, with a corresponding increase in multigenerational families and intergenerational tensions. The tradition of maintaining filial piety and family obligations to parents becomes increasingly untenable from an economic perspective. True, the elderly may not have to rely on their children for social or economic support because of Canada's comprehensive social security system. But continued reliance on children for information and communication may breed an unhealthy dependence—culminating at times in awkward role reversals or, worse, elder abuse. Intergenerational conflicts are further intensified by parental efforts to compensate for lost status and authority in Canada by imposing yet more control over children (Desai and Subramanian, 2003).

Of particularly concern for the elderly is ageism—a belief in age as a determinant of behaviour. Ageism can be defined as those prejudgements and discrimination toward people (usually the elderly) primarily on the basis of their age (Mullaly, 2002). Often unwarranted assumptions are invoked about a person's physical, social, and mental skills—in effect reinforcing popular perceptions of old age as disease or affliction (Glover and Branine, 2001). Ageism reflects and reinforces a belief that the elderly are a burden on the economy, a drain on the resources of society, and irrelevant in having outlived their usefulness. Their exclusion from the labour market implies they are no longer making a contribution to a society in which one's worth is measured by their degree of involvement in the economy. Paradoxically, new research indicates that ageism at work—once the curse of the over-60s— is now affecting the thirtysomethings, resulting in depression, frustration, and antisocial behaviour (Doward, 2003). Finally, as Mullaly points out, ageism tends to smear the elderly in homogenous terms, rather than acknowledging differences along the lines of gender, race, or class, in addition to different levels of wellness, independence, and involvement.

Yet times are changing. Research warns against exaggerated concerns about population ageing as a social problem or an ageing society as problematic as many assume (Cheal, 2002). A multidimensional approach is proposed as a way of studying ageing, thus reappraising the place of older people within a broader political, economic, temporal, and familial context; recognizing the internal diversity of older people as a population category; acknowledging the complexity of factors that affect the lives of older Canadians; and rethinking the multiple linkages between sectors of society such as family, work, and the public (McDaniel, 2002; Cheal, 2002). The very idea of ageing as a personal opportunity rather than societal crisis will take on an added resonance as greying boomers move into this age bracket. Even the concept of old age is no longer as self-evident as many believe, given the arbitrariness of age 65 as a boundary between involvement and retirement. Time will tell if a new normative framework can be adjusted to reflect, reinforce, and advance the notion of ageing as part of a natural life course that has much to offer to all age groups.

CANADA'S HEALTH-CARE SYSTEM

Canada's response to the health-care challenge has resulted in a universal (national) and publicly funded health-care system that balances the public with the private in ways that evoke the envy of many countries. Canada's national health-care system is much more than a simple program that secures free doctor visits or hospital care. Reference to health care resonates with national pride and provides a source of national identity, which may help to explain public vehemence to any proposed changes. To be sure, the introduction of a national health-care system was not without incident or resistance, especially on the part of doctors and provinces (Maioni, 2003: 308–310). A publicly funded national system that covered medical and hospital expenses did not materialize until the early 1970s despite its earlier introduction in the provinces such as Saskatchewan—and in other parts of the world like Britain and Israel in 1948 and New Zealand in 1935 (CRIC, 2003). Still, Tommy Douglas's vision of a common sense health-care system for everyone regardless of income is now firmly anchored in the hearts and minds of Canadians.

But Canada's much touted health-care system appears to be crippled because of under-funding and over utilization. Criticism persists, despite evidence that the health-care system is doing what it originally set out to do: namely, to eliminate inequality among Canadians in relation to basic health care (Brym et al., 2003). Concern is mounting that a major crisis is looming: Canada may not be able to afford government programs for the elderly in the future, due to the expected retirement of baby boomers. With fewer Canadians contributing, either services cutbacks are inevitable or an increased burden will be placed on younger workers. In response, the 2003 federal budget injected $34.7 billion into health care over the next five years, including $1.25 billion for aboriginal health (Lahgi, 2003). This infusion is helpful, but throwing money at a problem is rarely a long-term solution. Any improvement must take into account related policies involving education, employment, and housing (Jones, 2001).

The Principles of Universal Health Care

Any health-care system is composed of three main dimensions: financing (who pays—public or private or both), allocation (how is service purchased from the deliverer—market choice or government control?); and delivery (who provides the service—for profit or not for profit) (Sullivan and Baranek, 2002). A national health-care system usually includes the following levels of government involvement: (1) regulates the financing and organization of health services; (2) provides direct payment for providers such as physicians; (3) guarantees equal access to health care; (4) tolerates some private health care for those who are willing to pay or where government coverage is inadequate; (5) is regarded as a need-related right rather than a commodity for sale along market lines.

National health care (including both health-care services and income security benefits to cover loss of earnings during illness) can be categorized according to the nature of state involvement in the funding and delivery of health care (Olsen, 2002). European countries such as Sweden have a national health service model in which the financing and provision of health services are publicly owned and administered with tax payers' monies, while providers such as doctors and nurses are salaried public employees. The United States is characterized by an entrepreneurial system that positions the private market as dominant in the provision and funding of health services. Without some type of national, public, and universal health-care system in the United States, government spending is much less extensive than in Europe although overall costs are high. Most Americans must take individual responsibility for health insurance, primarily through employment-based insurance programs. About 20 percent are covered by Medicare and Medicaid, in addition to some coverage by military and veteran programs. Nearly 20 percent have no or little coverage.

Canada's approach to health care is a hybrid of American and European models: funding is largely European (public) but delivery is more American (private) with physicians in self-employed fee practice and hospitals akin to corporations with an independent Board of Trustees (Evans, 2000; Marchildon, 2003). Like Europe, health care is defined as a collective responsibility for shared vulnerabilities. Comprehensive health-care coverage is provided for all citizens by government funding but, unlike Europe, care is not delivered by the state but by private doctors and hospitals. But while Canada does not allow the purchase of private insurance for services that are insured by the public health system, European countries like Sweden permit citizens to pay for private services if they are unhappy with the public system (Editorial, *National Post*, 26 May, 2003. Like the United States, both the public and health-care providers have choice and autonomy since public hospitals are defacto corporations, while doctors are not public servants but employees whose conditions of employment are governed by contractual agreement. Most health-care services in Canada are purchased by the government from private physicians in private practice (a fee-for-service arrangement), while hospital services are paid for by a national health insurance program. To defray the cost of hospital and doctors' services, 70 percent of financing comes from general taxation. Compare this figure with health-care costs borne by the government in Britain at 97 percent, 44 percent in the United States, and 13 percent in India (WHO, 2000). In its role as a single payer of health, the Canadian government can deliver a cheaper service than in the United States by reducing the administrative costs associated with universal health care (Olsen, 2002).

Putting Principles into Practice

How does Canada's system work? Canada's system is geared toward ensuring that all citizens will have access to the necessary medical care within a reasonable time without incurring catastrophic financial obligations in the process. Medically necessary services are obtained from a physician who is a private sector player delivering a publicly funded service. The fees are uniform across the province and paid directly by the public plan without patient involvement. Hospitals are funded through a global operating budget negotiated annually with the provincial governments. Private insurance is accepted for services that are not covered by public plans. Nevertheless, private services are increasingly tolerated, such as contracting out hospital services to private for-profit clinics, as a way of easing spiralling health costs (Wente, 2003).

Health Care by Numbers

Total health-care costs in Canada amounted to $121.3 billion in 2003, up from $78.5 billion in 1997, with government spending at $84.8 billion (that is, 70 percent of the total or $2681 per Canadian). An additional $36.6 billion (that is, 30 percent of the total or $1157 per Canadian) was spent in private costs, either out of pocket or by employers (Kennedy, 2002). With health care consuming 10 percent of the GDP, Canada now has the fourth highest level of health spending in the world, trailing only the United States (13.9 percent), Germany (10.7 percent), and Switzerland (11.1 percent) (Picard, 2003). Hospitals remain the largest cost component at $36.4 billion, followed by drugs ($19.6 billion), physician services ($15.6 billion), other health professionals such as dentists ($14.5 billion), health institutions such as nursing homes ($11.6 billion), and public health ($7.9 billion).

Canada's health-care system is not well understood by many Canadians. For example, medicare does not promise payment of all medical bills. All Canadian residents are fully covered for all medically necessary hospital and physician services through a program administered and financed by the province in which they live (Evans, 2000). For the most part, pharmaceutical drugs are not covered by the public health-care plans. Private coverage is generally required for dental plans or long-term care outside the hospital. Compounding the misunderstanding is the system itself: The organizational dimensions of a universal and publicly funded system are complex and increasingly contested by the politics of funding, access, and jurisdiction (Begin, 2002). Several core elements characterize the program:

Subsidy and Transfer   Both health-care and social programs in Canada are based on the principle of shared and reciprocal responsibility (Sullivan and Baranek, 2002). To pay for this collective service, health care is funded along two lines: First, a progressive taxation in which those who earn more pay more in taxes; second, the transfer in subsidies from the rich provinces to the poorer provinces to ensure a comparable degree of health care in those have-not provinces with a smaller tax base. Under the equalization provisions of the Canadian constitution, the federal government transfers tax money from the have provinces (Ontario, Alberta, and British Columbia) to the have-not provinces to provide a reasonably uniform service across the country regardless of regional disparities.

Risk Pooling   Canada's national publicly funded health system is predicated on several principles. First, everyone, regardless of who they are, should get the same (and the best) health-care treatment available. The objective is to ensure that those most in need, yet least likely to afford health care, are provided access to reasonable services. Second, the system must be universal: There should *not* be one health-care system for the rich and one for the rest. Third, priority should be given to those who are most in need of urgent health care rather than those who can buy their way to the front of the line (Sullivan and Baranek, 2002). The burden of the cost for these services should not be borne by the poor and unhealthy but rather progressively distributed according to income (Sullivan and Baranek, 2002). Hence, in a publicly financed health-care system, service is provided on the basis of need rather than ability to pay, although costs are distributed according to the ability to pay. The public pooling of health spending—one in which citizenship trumps consumerism— has served Canadians well and appears consistent with Canada's constitutional values.

Simplicity and Cost   A single public payment mechanism keeps administrative and overhead costs to a reasonable minimum. Costs are further controlled because of the bargaining power of a single payer (Olsen, 2002; Sullivan and Baranek, 2002). The Canadian Health Act of 1984 provides the legislative foundation that administers Canadian health care. According to the Act, federal funding is contingent on five prerequisites, namely, *public administration* (a not-for-profit implementation of health insurance); *comprehensiveness* (provinces must insure/ensure all medically necessary health services related to hospitalization and physician services but not necessarily extended health services such as home care or pharmaceuticals); *universality* (all residents of a province are entitled and must be covered on a uniform basis); *portability* (health coverage must be maintained when people move from province to province or outside Canada; and *accessibility* (reasonable access to necessary medical care must be available to all Canadians) (Health Canada, 2001 in Shaefer and Smith, 2004).

Standardization   Of particular importance is a commitment to national standards of public coverage for most medically necessary services involving hospitals and physicians. However, health care is considered a provincial responsibility, with each province imposing its own set of rules about coverage, eligibility, and payment to doctors and hospitals (Maioni, 2003). Provinces have the sole constitutional authority to organize, regulate, and deliver health services, except in cases of aboriginal health and public health (Sullivan and Baranek, 2002). Yet the federal government can control how provinces administer their health-care services through its spending power. Funding is transferred to the provinces in exchange for provincial promises to accept certain conditions for a national health-care standard. The federal government not only plays an active role in ensuring national standards by virtue of its spending power, but it also can ensure compliance to these conditions and standards by threatening to withhold funds for a breach of promise.

The overlap in health care created by federal and provincial overlap is creating dysfunctionalities, while the lack of accountability and transparency in spending creates a jurisdictional straitjacket (Robson, 2003). Not surprisingly, a conflict of interest between provincial jurisdiction and federal spending power is inevitable: To one side are the "have" provinces that resent the financial impositions; to the other side are the "have-not" provinces that are doubly dependent: first, on the federal government and, second, on their more affluent counterparts (Sullivan and Baranek, 2002).

Crisis? What Crisis?

Canadians take health care seriously. An end-of-year poll of 1000 adult Canadians for *Maclean's* magazine and Global TV found that health care topped the list of concerns, with unemployment and the economy a very distant second (Kennedy, 2002). Americans, too, regard health care as the most important problem for the government to solve, ahead of drugs, crime, education, or economy (Henslin, 2000). Nevertheless, the domain is replete with preconceived myths and dogmas that refuse to disappear in the face of evidence to the contrary, reinforcing the notion that emotional issues are swayed not by facts or evidence but by interests. Yet, despite the centrality of health care to our quality of life and national identity, most Canadians appear confused about the health-care crisis, except for a vague sense of waiting times, overcrowding, and rationing. Evidence-based assessments suggest improved performance—from consulting a specialist to receiving diagnostic tests or non-emergency surgery—implying that things are not as bad as they seem, despite public perception to the contrary.

Polls expose this confusion and ambiguity. An Angus Reid survey in 2000 indicated that only 25 percent of Canadians rated the health-care system as excellent or very good, compared with 61 percent in 1991 (Sullivan and Baranek, 2002; also Evans, 2000). According to Statistics Canada based on health indicators released by Canada and the provinces in September 2001, 84.4 percent of Canadians between 2000 and 2001 rated the quality of health-care services they received as either excellent or very good (*National Post*, "Quality of Life, Quality of Service," 23 January, 2003). Elsewhere, however, principles and practices clash: More and more Canadians are dissatisfied with the health-care system in principle, in other words, although not necessarily with the quality of health care they receive in practice (Maioni, 2003).

Perceptions of a crisis in public health care cannot be lightly discounted. Canadians are increasingly accustomed to the idea of a perpetual health-care "crisis." After all, health-care systems are prone to emotional debates because they involve money and health

(CRIC, 2003). Provinces are blaming Ottawa for underfunding; Ottawa is blaming the provinces for mismanagement; hospitals blame both Ottawa and the provinces; and the public and health practioners are blaming everybody (Harter and Ball, 2003). Worries are mounting over a national icon that is showing signs of ageing, particularly among those who live outside major urban areas, immigrants, low-income Canadians, aboriginal peoples, and people with disabilities (Schaefer and Smith, 2004). Concern is also growing over the provision of health care, out-of-control spending and funding, and increased pressure to privatize by imposing a market logic to alleviate a financially-strapped health-care system. Concerns continue to focus on waiting lists for surgeries, access to specialists in remote areas, growth of private fee-for-service clinics, long waits in emergency wards, lengthy delays in accessing specialized tests such as MRIs, closing of rural hospitals, reduction of beds in urban hospitals, and a shortage of nurses (Canadian Institute for Health Information, 2001). With international trade agreements such as NAFTA, Canadians fear a commercialization of health services by transnational corporations while accountability shifts from government to boardrooms. Health providers and professionals such as doctors and nurses are also experiencing additional pressures because of fiscal cutbacks, increased workload, punishing demands on expertise and expectations and, in the case of the SARS outbreak, extreme personal risk. The end result is staff shortages and burnout that must surely impact on the quality of services delivered to the public (Sullivan and Baranek, 2002).

Costs are soaring as well: Health-care costs in Canada have risen from $23 billion in 1980 to $121 billion in 2003, with an estimated rise to $145 billion in 2004. But bigger budgets have not staunched the closings of hospitals or emergency care; shortage of skilled personnel from technicians to surgeons; lack of costly diagnostic equipment; growing waiting lists for surgeries especially elective surgeries; and geographic differences in access to health care especially in rural areas. Part of the problem reflects a curious paradox in the funding formula. Put simply, hospitals get a lump sum of money to stay open, regardless of how many operations they perform. Not surprisingly, the incentive for hospitals is to avoid operations but to close hospital beds—in contrast to private for-profit clinics who are motivated to do as many as they can as quickly as possible (Wente, 2003). Not surprisingly, hospitals such as those in British Columbia are contracting out day surgery to private for-profit clinics who can do the procedure cheaper and faster.

Health-care costs are increasing at twice the rate of inflation and tax revenues (Francis, 2003). Increased costs reflect growing cases of catastrophic illnesses or confinement in nursing homes; reliance on specialists; treatment of cancer or Alzheimers and other chronic illnesses that require custodial care; and expensive drugs and technology such as CAT scanner or MRI machines (Schaefer and Smith, 2004). Provincial health-care systems are under pressure to reduce costs as well, and have done so by controlling the supply of health care through changes in treatment protocols, closure of hospitals or beds, and imposing limits on doctor billing and salary caps (Maioni, 2003). Moreover, given current funding levels, there are growing doubts whether the health-care system can be sustained because of escalating health costs and demographic pressures of an ageing population (medical costs increase four-fold once people reach 65 years (Cheal, 2002).

Costs are a factor in other ways as well. According to the 1984 Canada Health Act, the federal government is only obligated to provide insurance for physician care and hospital visits, thus protecting Canadians from the debilitating wipe out of uninsured services. Yet the most significant challenge confronting Canada's health-care system reflects an increased transfer of services away from hospital-based health care to placement in the community, including home care. Health care has been moving out of institutions into communities and homes with the result that home care is emerging as the new frontier for health-care coverage (Sullivan and Baranek, 2002). Clients are allowed to stay in their own homes, while having access to hospital-based services and long-term care facilities at a fraction of the cost. But the federal government appears reluctant to get financially involved in extended health care under terms of the existing agreement (Sullivan and Baranek, 2002).

Clearly, then, public confidence in Canada's health-care system is eroding. Canadians perceive a deterioration in access to health-care services, are highly critical of the government's performance in delivery of health care, and wonder whether an injection of private health care might do some good for the public. Calls for reforms range from radical surgery to incremental reforms. Central to many debates is increased pressure to impose market logic on health-care services, including the alleged merits of the American-based system of managed care as a possible alternative.

| CASE 8-1 | Managed Health Care in the United States: Solutions Or Problem? |

The confidence that Canadians have in their health-care system has been badly shaken (Evans, 2000). Public spending is unsustainable, according to those in favour of a privatized health-care system such as pharmaceutical manufacturers, partly because costs are out of control and can no longer be sustained under the present (Barer, Morgan, and Evans, 2002). Critics argue that a mixed funding system based on a public and entrepreneurial model could solve the problem of too much demand and not enough supply. Under a two-tier system, those who could afford to purchase health care outside the public system would free up space and improve general accessibility. A more competitive insurance market would make it more efficient while privately purchased health care would provide more choice. A win-win situation?

Canada embraces a largely universally based, publicly funded system that already incorporates aspects of the private sector. The United States, by contrast, has a largely market-oriented system with a few government supports

thrown in for good measure. Privatization of health care involves a process that restricts the role of the public sector by redefining health as a commodity, health care as a private responsibility, and treatments driven by market lines (Armstrong and Armstrong, 2001). More specifically, it involves transferring the burden of payment to individuals, expanding opportunities for private for-profit health-care providers, offloading the onus of care from public institutions and paid employment to home-based responsibility and unpaid caregivers, and allowing the market to rule how health-care treatment is to be defined, delivered, measured, and assessed.

To be sure, Canada and the United States do share some similarities in addressing health-care inequities. For example, health insurance in the United States is tied to employment and, while much of Canada's single-payer national health scheme is publicly funded through taxation, employers contribute to health care costs either through payroll tax or by providing employees with health

(continued on next page)

benefits such as dental care (Alvi et al., 2000). As well, governments in Canada have agreed to deregulate and privatize the funding and delivery of services, including the contracting out of services such as home care in Ontario or day surgery clinics in British Columbia. There are three privately funded, for-profit hospitals in Ontario, in addition to private diagnostic MRI (magnetic resonance imaging) and CT (computer tomography) clinics, implying a two-tier health-care system that provides preferential access for the wealthy (Laghi, 2003; Boyle, 2003). Nevertheless, ideological differences persist. For Americans, health care is regarded as commodity-driven by an employee-based, private, for-profit system; for Canadians, it is deemed an essential service and basic human right (Redmond, 2003).

The system of managed care in the United States promises more than it can deliver. A three-tier system operates in the United States reflecting a complex maze of programs, including HMOs (health maintenance organizations), HCOs (health-care corporations), PPOs (preferred provider organizations), and IPAs (independent physician associations) (Olsen, 2002). There is no publicly funded system of national health insurance that covers the entire population. Some Americans pay for private coverage, but most are covered by private insurance programs run by employers and unions who buy their health coverage from profit-seeking health maintenance organizations. These HMOs are quite restrictive: The average American has little choice except to accept the service provider of a particular HMO. Doctors and other service providers have less autonomy because of bureaucratic monitoring and control (Sullivan and Baranek, 2002).

Government involvement is limited to federal and state programs under Medicare and Medicaid. The elderly and the disabled who qualify for social service are covered by Medicare; the extreme poor are means-tested for programs under Medicaid (Maioni, 2003). In between are about 80 million Americans who have no coverage or are inadequately covered. The net result? Health care is a costly luxury for those who can least afford it, including the chronically or recently unemployed, low-wage workers, and African Americans (Redmond, 2003).

Curiously, the United States spends more on health care than any other country (Brym et al., 2003), with 14 percent of its GDP spent on health expenditures compared to 10 percent for Canada and 7.2 percent for Japan. Recent studies suggest that the United States spends about US$5427 per capita on health care in 2002 with the government contributing nearly 60 percent or US$3245 of the costs (Redmond, 2003). Not only does the United States spend twice as much per capita on health care than other leading industrial countries, including Canada, it also spends nearly $300 billion (or US$1059 per capita) on administration and paperwork—compared to approximately US$307 in Canada (Editorial, *Toronto Star,* 24 August, 2003). Yet the United States has less bang to show for its spending buck than other countries. For example, the U.S. model does less to improve children's health while having a higher infant mortality rate (seven per 1000 live births) compared to Canada and Japan (four per 1000 live births). Moreover, outcomes do not improve for patients with more lavish access to medical services (from visits to doctors to expensive procedures). More does not result in better, especially when

(continued on next page)

measured in terms of people living longer or functioning better, or being any happier with the quality of their health care compared to those equally sick patients who do not receive such costly services (Branswell, 2003). Not surprisingly, many Americans believe the current system has major problems and requires fundamental change (Parmelee, 2003). The system may be ailing and in need of strong medicine, but those in position to make changes are incapable of doing so (politicians because of ineptness) or are unwilling (health industries because of greed and the lobbying power of insurance companies and doctors' associations.)

How do we account for this anomaly? Why do Americans spend far more on health care than others yet, on average, have a population that is less healthy than those of other rich countries? The American system is burdened by a complex and expensive administrative bureaucracy that does not necessarily improve outcomes (Olsen, 2002). Yes, Americans in theory can choose from a wider variety of options for depth or range of coverage—but only as long as they can afford it. Those who can pay worry they won't be able to afford either services or insurance if health-care costs continue to escalate (Parmelee, 2003). For those who can't pay, their choices are more restricted than ever, perhaps even restricted to less than zero (Evans, 2000). No wonder Marcia Angell, editor of *The New England Journal of Medicine*, says, "The American health-care system is at once the most expensive and the most inadequate system in the whole world" (Evans, 2000:22). Even proposed reforms to Medicare including prescription drug plans, private for-profit hospitals, and a proposed shift of seniors to private managed-care

plans for controlling costs do not appear to be making much headway in light of vested interests (Gleckman, 2003; Weintraub, 2003; Barro, 2003). Entrenched ideologies are further marginalizing a growing interest in the possibility of Canadian-style universal health care delivery and proposals for a single-payer publicly funded health system (Marchildon, 2003).

It has been said that you have nothing, if you don't have health. Many of life's major concerns pale by comparison in the face of even relatively minor health ailments and are overwhelmed entirely by chronic illness, intense pain, or the shock of a grim prognosis. Failure to afford or to have access to appropriate health-care exacerbates the pain, prompting Lisa Ferraro Parmelee, editor of *Public Perspective*, to hope that no one ever gets caught "between the rock of financial insufficiency and the hard place of human suffering." That indictment alone should be sufficient to caution Canadians against uncritically hopping aboard the American health-care wagon.

Case Study Questions

1 Should health care be treated as any other good or service (commodity) that can be purchased on the market? Or should it be seen as a public good based on the principle of need and rights of citizenship?

2 Should Canada adopt the system of managed care from the United States?

3 Americans tend to see health care as an industry for profit, with Canadians perceiving it as a service based on needs. Discuss the differences between the philosophy and practice of a universal and publicly funded health-care system versus a private system.

THE CANADIAN WAY

Canada's national and publicly funded health-care paradigm is based on a bedrock of collective principles: government intervention in the funding and provision of health delivery; a recognition of shared risk and responsibility; and acknowledgement of health as a fundamental citizenship right (Armstrong and Armstrong, 2001). The public–private hybrid system has served Canadians reasonably well, judging by people's insistence on health care as the number-one priority. Most Canadians are satisfied with the status quo, according to the Romanow Report on Health, wanting only to tweak the system to improve outcomes by making the existing single-payer system better, broader, and more efficient. To the extent that a private for-profit system is incorporated, it must remain secondary to a national and publicly funded heath care.

Admittedly, a publicly funded system has its flaws. For one thing, the existing system is more privatized than many realize, including private for-profit acute care hospitals in Ontario, extra billing charges, blood labs and fee-for-service clinics such as MRI (magnetic resonance imaging) and CT (computer tomography) scanners (Canadian Press, 2003; Arnold, 2003). Second, the potential for reckless spending is constant in a system without user fees or tax consequences, resulting in overdemand without consequences and with corresponding pressure on limited services (Francis, 2003). Take hospitals: Hospitals may be excellent places for the sick in need of cardiac care or cancer surgery, but not for minor cases that are better left at private, for-profit clinics with lower overhead, high volume specialists, incentive profit plans, and non-unionized support staff (Wente, 2003). Or consider how Ontario's fee-for-service system tends to undervalue health promotion since doctors are anxious to maximize the number of patients, treat individual illnesses, and deal with symptoms rather than causes. By contrast, health promotion simply increases expenditures without increasing income (Benecki, 2003).

Is the market the solution to Canada's health-care crisis? To one side, there is growing support for an American-style business model of health as a marketable commodity, patients as consumers, and with a value on private, for-profit health-care strategies to improve effectiveness and efficiency through choice and accountability. To the other side are the critics. The for-profit system in the United States is expensive (prescription drug costs are much higher creating a situation where Americans are ordering Canadian drugs through the Internet), reflects a conflict of interest between consumers and health-care providers and insurers, and is tied to gainful employment with the result that people who get sick may lose their jobs and health coverage—just when they need it most! Why then are there calls for a more privatized health-care paradigm? Put simply: *Profits*. Those who view the provision of health-care services as a pot of gold to be plundered for corporate interests, especially pharmaceutical drug firms, are glomming on to the fact that health care in a regulated system is a largely untapped source of revenue (Douglas, 2003). Transforming health care along commercial lines yields distributional advantages for vested interests, ranging from for-profit providers and insurers, to the affluent who see an opportunity for more health choice while sharing a smaller proportion of the overall costs.

Yet evidence for privatizing health care is underwhelming: A greater reliance on markets to process health care leads to inferior outcomes in efficiency, high costs, public dissatisfaction—and deaths (Devereaux, 2003). Markets left on their own do not lead to equity. A for-profit insurance system is based on the principle that profit-making is enhanced if fewer and less sick people are insured (i.e., shift the risk so that those most in need are uninsurable). The goal can be achieved by eliminating coverage of high-risk individuals, providing less coverage of fewer services to low-risk individuals, and placing limitations on the access and amount of service (Sullivan and Baranek, 2002). This is consistent with the philosophy that those with lower incomes neither deserve nor should they expect to have the same level of care as those who can afford it (Evans, 2000). Such a Darwinian outlook is so incongruous with the "Canadian way" that its adoption would fundamentally alter the very notion of what "Canada is for."

If It Ain't Broke, Fix It

In late 2002, Ottawa released a royal commission report by former Saskatchewan premier, Roy Romanow, entitled *Building on Values. The Future of Health Care in Canada.* The Report focused on what values should drive the debate in directing the future of Canada's badly listing health-care system. Should health care be based on the ability to pay or make a profit? Or should it reflect the principle of need for medically necessary health services? The Report clearly endorsed the values of equity and collective responsibility—that is, health care as a public good to which all citizens have a right rather than an economic commodity for sale on the market (Douglas, 2003). The Report also listed 47 recommendations that would assist the government in modernizing health care to reflect contemporary realities. Among these were issues related to (a) funding—the need for stable, generous, and predictable transfers of federal monies to the provinces to ensure long-term planning and transformative change; (b) extending the mandate of the 1984 Canada Health Act to include three of the fastest growing and costliest programs—prescription drug coverage, extended home care coverage, and medically necessary diagnostic services coverage; (c) establishment of a national Health Council to ensure more accountability and community input into the spending of health dollars; (d) possible private sector involvement as long as for-profit services are compatible with the Health Act, provide a better or cheaper alternative, not result in queue jumping, and do not diminish Canada's ability to protect medicare in international trade agreements; and (e) going beyond illness management by focusing on prevention and health promotion. To date the government has done little to implement the recommendations outside of an additional $30 billion over five years for medicare (Walkom, 2003).

To conclude: Canadians are justifiably proud of their universal, publicly funded health-care system (Begin, 2002). A commitment to a national system of health care has contributed to Canada's lofty ranking as one of the world's best countries to live in (according to a UN Human Development Index). Only 30 years old, the national health-care system is the most popular and successful of Canada's social programs, evoking a visceral appeal and passionate defence, in part, because its very existence says a lot about our values as Canadians. The program is so deeply entrenched in the national identity that Canadians are sometimes defined as unarmed Americans with a national health plan. Kidding aside, Canada's health-care system is more than an administrative mechanism for paying medical bills. National health care is an important symbol of community, a tangible expression of mutual concern, and a fundamental commitment to the equality of all Canadians (Evans, 2000). The way we choose to treat the sick defines who we are as Canadians, the Romanow Report reminds us. The good news is that this image of Canada is sustainable—if we want it to be.

DISCUSSION QUESTIONS

1   What is meant by the expression: "Canada's health-care system is a hybrid of European and American models"?

2   How would you describe the health of Canada's health-care system? Is it in crisis? Why or why not? What are its strengths and its weaknesses?

3   What do we mean when sociologists say they prefer to study the social dimensions of health and health care?

4   Ageism is a major social problem. Indicate how this is true with respect to the elderly in Canada.

5   Describe the health problems of aboriginal Canadians. What can or should be done to improve the health and health care of aboriginal women, children, and men?

WEBLINKS

Health Canada.   **www.hc-sc.gc.ca**

Canadian Health Information.   **www.cihi.ca**

Canada's universal health care system under attack.   **www.socialistalternative.com**

chapter nine

Schooling and
Post-Secondary Education

FRAMING THE PROBLEM

All societies must socialize their children for participation in adult life. The means for achieving this goal are diverse and evolving, both formal and informal in process, with outcomes that vary over time and place. Pre-contact societies survived without formal arrangements for education and schooling, relying instead on informal socialization procedures such as observation, practice, and community instruction. These informal routines have been increasingly displaced by formal structures in urban-industrial societies. Formal institutions for schooling are characterized by a host of defining characteristics, including: a constellation of formal rules, values, and practices; a team of specialists both in the class and out; a specific location for systematic induction; and appropriate equipment and apparatus (Robertson, 1987). The universality of formal schooling is currently the rule rather than the exception; after all, a literate population is seen as a precondition for progressive development. To be sure, both schooling and education are confronting crises because of social changes. A digitally-driven information age is challenging a print-based knowledge system, with corresponding disruptions to educational aims, conventional divisions of knowledge and disciplines, methods of teaching and learning, the role of teacher and nature of the student (Spender, 1997). Nevertheless, the main functions of schooling and education continue to prevail, namely, to impart knowledge, culture, and skills; to prepare individuals for citizenship and the workplace; to secure social and political integration; to impose social control; and to foster individual self-growth (Brown and Schubert, 2002).

Canada is no slouch when it comes to expenditure in formal education. The cost of educating Canada's 4.9 million primary and secondary students during the mid to late 1990s was about $35 billion or $7200 per student, with about 67 percent of the costs devoted to instruction. Such a commitment provides Canada with the brain power to address the demands of an information-based and rapidly changing global market economy. Where Canada sparkles is in its post-secondary commitments (Guppy and Davies, 1998). Canada invests more in post-secondary education than almost any other country, according to Statistics Canada Report, *Education Indicators in Canada* (Beauchesne, 2000). Canadians remain one of the most educated populations in the world, ranking fourth in university participation behind the United States, Norway, and the Netherlands, and second overall in college education behind Ireland (Corak, 2003). The number of Canadians with university education grew by 39 percent between 1991 and 2001, with the result that 53.4 percent of Canadians between 25 and 64 had some post-secondary schooling in 2001, up from 43.8 percent in 1991, and 1.9 percent in 1951. As well, 41 percent of Canadians aged 25–64 had a post-secondary degree, either university or college, ahead of the United States with 37 percent. Future prospects remain bright as well, despite tuition fee hikes and punishing debt loads.

Yet these largely positive indicators are misleading. The ideals of equality and inclusion that Canadians expect of schooling and education are not necessarily reflected in reality (Dei et al., 2000). In terms of literacy or numeracy, Canada may rank first among English-speaking countries, yet up to 40 percent of Canadians lack basic literacy skills to function effectively at work, including some 20 percent of recent high school graduates (Bolan, 1997; ABC Canada Literacy Foundation, 2003). Education is often touted as the path to personal growth and social progress; unfortunately, the opposite appears equally true. Canada may be one of the most educated countries in the world, yet four workers in ten earn less than $20 000 per year, a figure that hasn't budged since 1981 (Carey, 2003). For many, education or schooling is neither creative nor progressive, but more a qualification earning process that is "… ritualistic, tedious, suffused with anxieties, destructive of curiosities, and imagination; in short, anti-educational." (Robertson, 1987: 383). What passes for schooling and education continues to be driven by the dictates of a print-based industrial era, in effect creating reality gaps within the system itself while short-changing students for the realities of the 21st century. The interplay of boredom with outdated teaching methods may be contributing to student alienation—at least judging by rates of truancy that are among the highest in the world, according to Douglas Willms, Director of Canadian Research Institute for Social Policy (Canadian Press, 16 October, 2003).

Much of Canada's education and schooling seems stuck in the past: For some, however, a reversion to the past is precisely the key for solving the problems of the present. Or as the late Neil Postman (1995) put it, schools are no longer inclined to create a coherent, stable, and unified culture out of diverse students preferring, instead, to focus on economic utility and career prospects, consumerism rather than criticism, reliance on technology rather than informed judgment, and the primacy of information over knowledge and wisdom. Not surprisingly, schooling and education are experiencing an identity crisis. Unsure of their roles and responsibilities in contemporary society, yet resigned to plod along as best they can without resources and outdated mandates, all schooling levels are under pressure to do more with less.

Primary Schooling

No level of education is exempt from scrutiny (Keith, 1997). At the primary level, there is growing parental concern over the combination of declining educational standards, demoralized teachers and principals, deteriorating pupil performance levels, laxity in discipline, and learning without the "basics." (Leithwood et al., 2002). Public schools in remote and isolated parts of Canada continue to underperform because of depleted resources, a dwindling population and tax base, and a funding formula that tends to favour the urban and affluent boards (Friscolanti, 2003; Sokoloff, 2003). Students, parents, and teachers are expected to abide by ministry decisions despite the remoteness of educational bureaucracies from local concerns and needs (Orpwood and Lewington, 1995). Parental involvement is encouraged in theory but discouraged in practice for fear of disrupting the smooth implementation of board policy. Lip service to the creative and the critical is betrayed by the harsh realities of authority, dogma, routine, conformity, cost-cutting, and credentials at all costs. Even well-intentioned initiatives are known to backfire because of unanticipated consequences: Consider how efforts to fix the gender gap that once penalized girls may be inadvertently affecting boys' performance. A school culture has emerged that is so feminized that boys are set up for failure—in part, by pathologizing normal so-called masculine behaviours such as running and shouting while privileging so-called feminine attributes such as sitting quietly (Summer, 2001; Owens, 2003).

Educational philosophies continue to flip-flop between the "progressives" and "traditionalists." To one side, an outcome-oriented, curriculum-driven schooling ("back to basics") focuses on competition for high grades through standardized testing and measurable performance indicators. To the other is a process-oriented, "child-centred" system which aims to bolster individual self-esteem through customized learning reflecting a child's interests rather than a structured curriculum (Owens, 2003). Not surprisingly, parents are worried that students are unschooled in basic literacy skills but swamped with pedagogical mumbo-jumbo about self-esteem and personal creativity. Stroking the ego is fine to a point, it is argued by Osborne (1999), but how does ego-massaging prepare children to cope with the demands of a knowledge-based, global economy? The end result is an inadequate focus on academics, followed by a hollowing out of academic standards ("dumbing down"), in part because schools are assuming social functions traditionally performed by family or church (Rochester, 2002). Front line workers such as teachers must increasingly cope with the results of poor parenting, a tendency to dump all social problems on the school system, and intense competition with instant forms of electronic gratification (Crispo, 1997). No less disruptive are ministerial directives that confuse, anger, or alienate both teachers and parents, in effect creating bottlenecks in debates over what to teach and how.

Secondary Schooling

The secondary level is equally subject to finger-pointing and second-guessing. High schools are demonized as ticking time bombs because of alcohol and substance abuse, teenage pregnancy, sexual activity and disease dissemination, racism and right wing recruitment, and overt sexism. Violence appears to be a major problem, and its ugliness is seared into our consciousness by media reports of guns, drugs, and bullying. Young women remain the target of male chauvinism, but while girls are overcoming the gender gap in science and math, boys continue to struggle with reading and writing—with dire long-term consequences

(Canadian Press, 2 June, 2003). The calibre of students appears to be declining, critics say. Students are thought to suffer from a terminal overdose of media exposure, resulting in (a) diminishing attention spans; (b) a discomfort with the written word; (c) acceptance of discontinuity and fragmentation as normal conditions of existence; and (d) a disrespect for the past as a source of inspiration or wisdom (Keith, 1997). Also worrying is the erosion of respect for convention and growing defiance of authority. Most young adults are so attuned to peer-group pressure and so seemingly indifferent to adults that many resent parental involvement in youth issues (Eckhler, 1999). The pressures and demands that students confront are both bewildering and stressful. At the same time that young people are expected to excel academically, they must also adjust to bodily changes, separate themselves psychologically from parents, develop a working network of friends and allies, think hard about education or vocational goals, and establish their sexual orientation.

Administration comes in for its share of blame. Students continue to be sorted into categories for placement from advanced to basic (often behind the smokescreen of French immersion as the new tracking); teachers are increasingly specialized and excessively accredited; curricula reflect philosophies of senior administration or popular pedagogies; administrative convenience supersedes student needs; credentials prevail over learning and have little relation to intelligence or parental concerns; and procedures are standardized to ensure order and predictability. The fact that educational authorities are aware of these flaws, yet appear unwilling to or incapable of addressing the problem in any substantial fashion—notwithstanding constant mantras about empowerment or partnership—attests to the power of inertia in defence of the status quo.

Tertiary Schooling/Post-Secondary Schooling

Post-secondary institutions have come in for their share of criticism. The deteriorating health of the post-secondary system is lamented in light of chronic underfunding, dwindling resources, increased commercialization, mounting workloads, inadequately prepared students, and impossible teaching conditions. Universities are depicted as imperious ivory towers, not only out of touch with business realities and globalizing forces but impervious to the demands of diversity and change. The university enterprise is being buffeted by relentless pressures to be everything to everyone but with less resources than before. Pedagogical styles have not kept up with student skills or outlooks (Giroux, 1996). Antiquated teaching techniques that worked well when the professor owned the only book in the land are hard to justify in a multimedia society (McSherry, 1993). Consider the gaps between how students like to learn (practical applications and active learning) and how faculty prefer to teach (abstract and theoretical material with passive pedagogy). As a result, students are bombarded with yet more information at a time when they already absorb more raw data than they can possibly process. This mismatch between faculty and student perceptions regarding skills for coping with the outside world converges with perceptions of universities as assembly-line factories in which faculty manage while student-drones defer in pursuit of credentials and careers. But like any oversized corporation, McUniversities too are too bureaucratized, insular, and over-administered to do much more than deliver bits of "packaged education" (Berezin, 2003; also Pocklington and Tupper, 2002). Rationalization and routinization have had the effect of Wal-Marting the academy into something safe, sanitized, and predictable (Ritzer, 1998; Olive, 2003).

External pressures are no less disruptive to the academy. The core of higher learning—the cultivation of the intellect and moral character through liberal arts education—is threatened by the corporate pressures of the marketplace, with its clarion call for global competitiveness and plea for knowledge workers (Axelrod, 2002). Fears are mounting that corporate interests are increasingly calling the shots, in part, by limiting academic freedom around research results consistent with their narrow commercial interests as clearly demonstrated in the Nancy Olivieri case at the University of Toronto, thus upsetting the balance that historically anchored the relationship between the practical and the contemplative (Donnelly, 2003; Giroux, 2003). Yes, some degree of relevance to the economy is necessary, if only to retain legitimacy and students, but many balk at the notion of university as corporations for delivering products and services to the market rather than developing critical and creative skills of benefit to society at large (Flynn, 1997).

Talk of a fiscal crisis and corporate links camouflages a deeper malaise, namely, a crisis of identity as elitist assumptions jostle with shifting government priorities, student expectations, ideological changes, and economic imperatives (Price, 1993; Reading, 1996; Brown and Schubert, 2002). Admittedly, the crisis goes beyond dollars and cents as universities try to steer a middle course between the discipline of the marketplace and the self-regulating confines of the ivory tower. Nevertheless, both politicians and the public are demanding yet more accountability and transparency from the academy. True, there is no shortage of ideas for reforming the academy to alleviate the crisis, including reducing class size, raising teachers' pay, and considering new pedagogical theories about what works in the classroom. Yet research on the effectiveness of reforms is weak, inconclusive, or difficult to implement in a context where educators have yet to agree on what university is for (Miller, 1999).

Let's be candid: Schools are designed for conformity rather than change, for consensus rather than disagreement, for social reproduction of the status quo rather than the reconstruction of social reality, and for preparing people to cope with the demands of the industrial age (traditional workplace, 9–5 jobs) rather than those of an information-driven global economy. Many of these paradoxes are neither superficial nor transitory, but chronic and embedded, yet resistant to facile solutions. Moreover, in those cases where problems are deeply entrenched within education, proposed solutions that only skim the surface may complicate the situation by creating new imbalances. Rightly or wrongly, only one thing is certain: criticism will persist because of the gap between reality and the impossibly high standards expected of education by a demanding and diverse public. A sense of perspective is critical. There is nothing wrong with the public education system in Canada if we were addressing the problems of the *19th century*, according to Michael Fullan, dean of OISE. But a radical revamping is necessary for education to play a leading role in the 21st century.

This chapter explores the idea of schooling and education as social problems in their own right. In a world convulsed by the dizzying pace and deafening scope of social change, schools are faltering under the pressure to be all things to all people—parent, guardian, moral guidance, social worker, and babysitter (Webber, 1994). The external world is changing faster than internal mechanisms can cope with in light of rising expectations, conflicting messages, and shrinking budgets (Orpwood and Lewington, 1995). Not unexpectedly, education and schooling are experiencing an identity crisis in figuring out what they should do in relationship to society at large. In this context of turmoil and second guessing, the social dimensions of education and schooling—particularly post-secondary schooling and education—are analyzed as a social problem with respect to origins, definition, impact, and treatment.

Three problems are uppermost: first, the problem of inequality. Education has long been endorsed as an instrument for the attainment of social equality. Yet the educational system has proven a site of inequality as competing interests struggle for control of the agenda. The system may also perpetuate patterns of inequality because of differences in class, family (1) expectations, cultural background, language competence, teacher attitudes, and peer group influences (Bowles and Gintis, 1976; Giroux, 1996). Gender inequities continue to persist, except now it is girls who have overcome the gender gap in science and math at school, having long outdistanced boys in literacy tests by a wide margin. The struggle that boys have with reading and writing raises concerns over lifelong deficits unless schools customize instruction to capitalize on the different ways that boys and girls learn in an era of mass testing and standardized curricula (Landsberg, 2003). Second, the challenge of diversity is proving problematic. Schools are demographically diverse because of robust levels of immigration. A commitment to constructively engage diversity has elicited a variety of responses normally associated with multicultural education (Fleras, 1995; Dei et al., 2000; (2) Fleras and Elliott, 2003). But multicultural initiatives have proven superficial, to date, while moves to take differences seriously under an anti-racism education tend to go against the grain of education and schooling as instruments of assimilation and control— as brutally evidenced with the forced "domestication" of aboriginal peoples under the residential school system (Schissel and Wotherspoon, 2003). Third, problems arise from the mismatch between ideals and reality. Much is promised, but for many non-mainstream students the promises are (3) empty in a one-size-fits-all system that rewards conformity rather than unconventionality. Schools espouse democratic values, yet routinely revoke the principle of democracy in everyday practice. Promoting equality of access, participation, and outcomes may be high on the priority list, yet the opposite is likely. Diversity is embraced, then discarded when priorities shift or costs escalate. Simply put, schooling and education don't always deliver.

Of course, the labelling of education and schooling as a problem or failure can be challenged. Widespread criticism of schooling and education indicates a need to rethink the label of "failure." Who says schools are failing, why are they saying this, and on what grounds are these accusations being made (Barlow and Robertson, 1993)? The "let's-solve-it-through-schools" mentality tends to inflate the importance of education as an agent of socialization, while underinflating the significance of the media and peer groups as forces for change or conformity. Such a mindset also allows primary caregivers to wriggle out of responsibilities by scapegoating schools for shortcomings that rightfully belong to parents. To add insult to injury, education is being blamed for the miscalculations of Canadian business when it fumbles opportunities to compete globally. Such a multi-dimensionality of perspectives reinforces the notion of education as a "contested site," with progressive and reactionary forces aligned opposite each other (Brown and Schubert, 2002). Ambiguity and paradox are inherent in a system that is neither homogeneous nor monolithic but contradictory, ambiguous, and subject to internal dissonance (Stone, 1993).

MASSIFYING SCHOOLING/DEMOCRATIZING EDUCATION

People tend to take the social world for granted. Common sense dictates a view of society or social institutions as durable and enduring—timeless realities that have existed without change since time "immemorial." However reassuring, this perception is wrong. Human realities are socially constructed conventions rather than anything natural, normal, or inevitable, created by social actors who interact with others to make choices in contexts that are not necessarily of their making. The idea of reality as constructed and contested is not without consequence. The values and customs that shape people's lives are neither impervious to change nor divorced from a broader context.

Institutions, too, are in a constant state of turmoil and flux in response to social changes, cultural challenges, and political demands. Institutional forms emerge because of criticism, reform, or need; they persist and undergo modification because of internal and external pressures; and they decline because of ineptness or disinterest. This interpretation would appear true of all institutions, with schooling and education no exception to this rule. An overview of formal education in Canada from the 19th century onwards provides a look at an institution in the throes of change and transformation. The democratization of schooling has proven of benefit in advancing a more inclusive society. Yet this achievement has not been without costs; accordingly, many of the social problems attributed to schooling and education may reflect this commitment to be all things for all people.

Early Education: Elitist and Exclusionary

Compulsory mass education under the state's auspices is a relatively recent phenomenon. This is true of the primary level, and even more so at the secondary and post-secondary levels. Prior to the mid-1800s, education for the most part was a privilege restricted to children of the ruling class. Education and schooling had little practical value for the masses; its existence was justified for the express purpose of cultivating the minds of those with money for "idle" pursuits (Robertson, 1987). Religious instruction was paramount, with reading and writing directed at the Bible rather than preparation for work. Estimates suggest that perhaps only half of all children in Upper Canada (Ontario) attended school in the 1830s, and even then for a total of only 12 months (Johnson, 1968). Ordinary Canadians were excluded from schooling for various reasons, including a reliance on labour-intensive agriculture as a basis of making a living, direct involvement in food production as a means of wealth creation, concentration of the population in rural areas, a highly stratified system that emphasized a hierarchical gulf between gentry and the masses, and prominence of the church and family as agents of socialization. A pervasive elitism may also have inhibited any inclination for compulsory, mass education except for the privileged classes. As a result, education for the masses consisted of direct parental observation or entry into an apprenticeship for some trade (Nock and Nelson, 1993).

Educating the Masses: From Class to Mass

The principle of mass schooling evolved with the onset of an urban, industrial Canada. By Confederation, both Protestant and Catholic schools systems had been established; the principle (if not the practice) of universal education was accepted; teacher training was in force; and text and curricula under board control (Johnson, 1968). The Constitution Act of 1867 outlined a national system of local school boards to be governed by municipalities (Flynn, 1999). Traditional forms of socialization (churches or extended families) were no longer as relevant in urban environments, in effect, creating a demand for the state to assume responsibility through a regulated school system. Ontario first introduced compulsory schooling in 1871 in hopes of instilling the values of good citizenship (Sears, 2003). In 1883, Toronto became only the second jurisdiction in North America to incorporate kindergarten into the school enterprise. By 1920 compulsory education was instituted to the end of elementary school (or about 16 years of age). Schools were designed to reflect the dominant mode of economic organization, namely, the factory, with its assembly-line outlook and one-size-fits-all mentality. Schools were places where rules mattered: In a society based on rigid expectations of class and gender, drill and obedience shaped the school day. Learning by rote was commonplace; emphasis was on the awe and majesty of the British Empire; and a military character predominated that involved high levels of regimentation, standardization, and discipline (Flynn, 1999). The rationale for taking education to the masses reflected additional social concerns. Curriculum remained basic and geared toward employment, including math, reading, writing, spelling, and history. Compulsory education was also endorsed as a means of distracting the attention of crime-oriented, unemployed children. Many of these custodial functions persist into the present where the potentially disruptive costs of unemployed youth are all too real. Mass primary education not only prevented the outbreak of class conflict or ethnic strife; it also legitimized the values and norms of a competitive, hierarchical society. Then as now, a concern with the "moral character of pupils" was paramount. In seeking to socialize or civilize, a one-size-fits-all model of education prevailed in hopes of fostering obedient, God-fearing children.

Yet the massifying process proved uneven. First, the commitment to mass education extended only to primary level. By the 1950s only about a half of all 14- to 17-year olds were enrolled in secondary schools (Nock and Nelson, 1993). Even by the mid-1960s, nearly a third of adult Canadians went no further than grade eight (Bricker and Greenspon, 2001). Resistance to mass post-secondary education stemmed from resentment over increased costs, the loss of cheap labour, and fear of spoiling it for the elites. Second, the introduction of mass education altered peoples' perception of children and childhood. As long as farming provided a primary employment for the masses, children were viewed as a productive addition to the household. Even early industrialization did not really question the morality of young children in mines and factories. Children who outgrew infancy were expected to assume "adult" status and responsibilities. With the massification of schooling, however, the notion of childhood was reinforced, ultimately leading the way toward post-war acceptance of adolescence as a specific age group with its own lifestyle outlooks. Third, for some Canadians schooling proved nothing short of a collective nightmare rather than a learning process. From the late 19th century onwards, numerous aboriginal children were removed from family, communities, and culture and placed in residential schools where many were abused, humiliated, and deprived of dignity, culture, and skills (Miller, 1999; Schissel and Wotherspoon, 2003). In 1998, the federal government apologized for its part in the residential school system and allocated some resources to atone for the neglect (see the case study in this chapter).

It is generally assumed that the technological changes associated with industrialization put a premium on skilled workers. Yet there is some question whether the expansion of 19th century manufacturing prompted the "massifying" of education. The scientific management philosophies of the early 20th century tended to treat workers as mindless extensions of an assembly-line machine. In some cases, vocational skills demanded a rudimentary level of literacy and numeracy; in other cases, it did not. Many jobs required only basic entry-level skills; further skills were built into the job. The credentials associated with education may have evolved instead to preclude the entry of unwanted masses into certain occupations. An emphasis on accreditation allowed professionals such as doctors or engineers to consolidate their privilege against indiscriminate entry. In short, schooling and education became universalized for reasons only partially related to job placement. Compulsory education may have sought to keep youth off the streets, reduce unemployment and crime rates among the young, instil optimism for the masses in an oppressive society, inculcate obedience and sub-missiveness to authority, and reproduce the social order through patriotism and citizenship. The regulatory functions overrode other considerations; hence, the democratization of edu-cation may reflect a perennial concern with controlling the masses.

Towards an Inclusive Schooling

The universality of primary and secondary schooling was firmly in place by the early 1960s. Elementary school enrolments increased by about 50 percent between 1951 and the early 1990s, while preschool numbers increased sixfold and secondary schools by a factor of four. The notion of mass education for post-secondary levels came into play as well, although entry restrictions remained in countries such as Japan and Britain. Historically, higher education was restricted to the ruling class elites (Price, 1993). Universities served as "finishing schools" for the well-heeled and upwardly mobile. Post-secondary education was aimed at creating a trained professional class: This cadre of pampered elites was expected to staff the private and public bureaucracies of an expanding Dominion, as well as preserve the cultural assumptions of Christian civilization through knowledge and research.

University enrolments accelerated dramatically in response to a growing democratization of society, with its commitment to equal opportunity for everybody, not just the elites. The numbers speak for themselves: In 1939, only 3 percent of 18- to 25-year-olds were in univer-sity; by 1963 the figure had risen to 7 percent; by 1994, the figure had increased to 30 percent. In 1951, 1.9 percent of the population aged 15 and over had a university degree; by 2001, the figure leapt to 15.4 percent, according to Statistics Canada, including 36.5 percent with some post-secondary schooling. In 1948, Canada had one MBA school; in 2002, the figure stood at 35 with skyrocketing enrolments even in the face of a worker glut. Post-secondary education is now the norm rather than the exception in Canada, with no country having as high a pro-portion of 18- to 21-year-olds enrolled in college and university or as large a percentage of 25- to 64-year-olds with college diplomas or university degrees, according to the Organization of Economic Cooperation and Development (Bricker and Greenspon, 2001). The forces behind this shift were complex but invariably included: a burgeoning baby-boom population; changes in the Canadian economy; continued rural–urban movement; complicated technolog-ical advances; consolidation of the welfare state coupled with a government willingness to underwrite educational costs; and a growing belief in education as a key to Canada's economic success. This commitment was further bolstered by competition with Communist Russia for Cold War supremacy and Space Age advantage (particularly following the launching of the Soviet Sputnik satellite into orbit in 1957). Cost appeared irrelevant as governments funnelled endless resources into the construction and expansion of universities. Rarely subjected to pub-lic scrutiny or widespread criticism, post-secondary institutions were recipients of seemingly limitless funding by governments who revered them as catalysts for economic growth, social equality, cultural sophistication, and political democracy. Intellectuals flocked to them as sites of enlightenment and research. Taxpayers didn't mind the extra burden since universal access to post-secondary education opened avenues of social mobility for their baby-boom offspring.

The Paradox of Democratization

This democratization process has had a profound effect on higher education. Universities have become more inclusive by accommodating the historically disadvantaged, including members of the working class, women, and people of colour. Yet success has unleashed many of the problems associated with underfunding and overcrowding (Keith, 1997). The democratization of post-secondary education has challenged elitist assumptions at the heart of the academy, in effect leaving the university enterprise perplexed and rudderless (Price, 1993). Democratization is accused of sabotaging deference to authority, esteem for hard-earned accomplishments, reverence for heritage and knowledge of the past, a commitment to rationality and science, and a willingness to assert the superiority of one idea or standard over another (Henry III, 1994). In the place of small intimate environments are sprawling bureaucratic organizations where routine and regulation prevail in pursuit of efficiency and standardization. Whereas public colleges in the United States receive 30 percent more funding support per student than they did 20 years ago, governments in Canada are providing 20 percent less, according to the Association of Universities and Colleges in Canada, with the result that student to faculty ratios in Ontario are at about 30 to 1 compared to 4.5 to 1 for undergraduate programs at MIT (Schmidt, 2003). Overcrowded classes and overworked professors have eroded a commitment to foster excellence. In its place is a tedious ritual entailing memorized input and scheduled regurgitation, an exercise not dissimilar in consequences to intellectual bulimia.

The democratization of education has trickled down to primary schools. The rigidity and regimentation of the past has evolved into an inclusive system that is more diverse, receptive to freedom of choice, and amenable to reform. There is growing debate over what schools should teach, and how and why; how to assess and monitor student progress; and how to prepare students for the future. On the one hand are conservative forces, consisting largely of those concerned parents with an eye on the three Rs. For example, in Ontario, teachers are expected to implement a tougher fact-filled curriculum that provides detailed lists of specific and mandatory expectations (not vague outcomes) that are tested on standardized exams in hopes of raising standards to international levels and encouraging greater accountability (Small, 1997). On the other hand are progressive forces that endorse a "life-skills" philosophy. Proponents of "process" are critical of "outcomes," arguing that any return to basics may prove inconsistent with the demands of a changing and diverse reality. Students, they contend, already receive too many facts but need more understanding to ensure (a) they can apply what they know to explain other events and (b) they have a framework for thinking historically and comprehending important relations (Chamberlain, 1999). The conservatives reply by pointing to process education as irresponsible and soft. Those streamed in process are accused of being improperly equipped to meet current challenges; they are also portrayed as rebellious and defiant of authority, with no respect for custom or convention.

Put bluntly, radically different perspectives coexist, both of which would appear immune to comparison or evaluation because of opposing assumptions about human nature and its relation to schooling and society. Neither is right or wrong since each defines differently the roles and responsibilities of formal education. This controversy is interesting in its own right: It also symbolizes a broader struggle in Canada: To one side are the proponents of free-market principles, with their commitment to institutional adaptation in the direction of global competition; to the other side are those who must live with the consequences of systems increasingly directed toward the rational pursuit of profit and privilege (Barlow and Robertson, 1994). The paradox is fuelled by educational reforms in Canada (especially Ontario) involving a broad-ranging strategy that recasts the focus on schooling for citizenship to schooling as preparation for the market. According to Alan Sears (2003), this agenda shift is characterized by three dimensions: the growing commercialization and corporatization of schooling; an emphasis on sorting out students through standardized testing; and the privileging of programs and disciplines of relevance to the market. This shift in focus from citizenship (the state) to consumer (the market) reflects broader changes in capitalist restructuring and establishment of a meaner and leaner state (Sears, 2003).

MULTICULTURAL AND ANTI-RACIST EDUCATION

The educational system has for the most part embraced a fundamental commitment to mono-culturalism. Historically, schooling and education were inseparable from the absorption of diversity into the mainstream. This conformist ideology sought to absorb immigrant children directly into Canadian society by stripping them of language and culture. All aspects of schooling, from teachers and textbooks to policy and curriculum, were aligned with the principles of Anglo-conformity. Anything that veered outside this Anglocentric framework was deemed to be irrelevant or dangerous, and punished accordingly. Special curricula or references to other languages or cultures were rejected as inconsistent with the long-term interests of Canadian society-building. The end result? Schooling had evolved into a site for the reproduction of social inequality in that it denied equal opportunity and fostered outcomes at odds with the concerns and aspirations of minority students (Dei, 1996).

The explicit assimilationist model that once prevailed within educational circles is no longer officially endorsed—even if assimilation remains an unspoken yet powerful ethos that animates the logic behind schooling. These opposing dynamics have transformed schooling and education into a contested space: To one side of the struggle are those who endorse the status quo; to the other side are those who have been historically excluded and want changes (Giroux, 1994). In theory, the impetus for multicultural education constitutes a departure from conventional ways of doing things. Multicultural education initiatives wrap themselves around the rhetoric of "cross-cultural communication," "racial awareness and sensitivity," and "healthy identity formation." Its introduction has challenged how schools should relate to diversity, while raising questions about the form, function, and processes of formal education in a changing and diverse society (Dei et al., 2000). By fostering a learning environment that acknowledges the culture of its students (Henry et al., 1999), multicultural education provides a framework for a more responsive schooling culture (Turner, 1994). The more demanding forms of inclusiveness revolve around a commitment to anti-racism education. Challenging those relationships of power that racialize the school social order is central to anti-racism education, with an emphasis on dismantling the structural roots of educational inequality (Giroux, 1994).

Post-secondary schooling has also achieved a level of internal diversity. Students of colour are common enough on some campuses to create a critical mass in terms of influencing administration decisions. The academy has also managed to eradicate the most blatant forms of racism on campus, although systemic biases continue to prevail in upholding Eurocentric standards, procedures, outcomes, and rewards as they pertain to curriculum, classroom, and the pathway to convocation (Fleras, 1995). But it still has some distance to go before it fosters an environment that promotes diversity as a strength and an asset where people can come together and challenge each other, learn from each other's differences, be enriched by coping with diverse perspectives, and learn that differences are assets that broaden the academy and define its excellence (Brown, 2002). To the extent that multicultural education seeks to institutionally engage diversity, it is eminently worthwhile. In light of the fact that multicultural education may not accomplish what it sets out to do because of entrenched interests, any move to constructively engage diversity will prove a challenge.

Monocultural Education: Schooling As Social Control

Education and schooling are secondary agents of socialization in which social functions are often at odds with formal mandates. The following functions of education prevail in society: (a) socialization, or transmission of culture; (b) self-actualization and individual self-development; (c) preparation for workplace, consumerism, and citizenship; (d) improvement in Canada's competitive edge; and (e) reproduction of the social order. Education plays both a conservative and progressive role in society, depending upon the level of schooling under examination. For example, elementary school education discharges a conservative function in promulgating mainstream values and social patterns. Post-secondary education, by contrast, endorses a more creative and informed agenda in advancing progressive change—at least in theory, if not practice. Yet a tacit commitment to assimilation remains a central objective. Alok Mukherjee (1992: 73) writes:

> Traditionally, the school has been a conservative institution. Its function, on the one hand, is to legitimize the dominant social, political, economic, and cultural ideas of society and, on the other, to perpetuate existing relations. The ownership, organization, and activities of the school reflect this dual role.

From daily routines to decision-making at the top, education is organized to facilitate cultural indoctrination and social control of minority students. These reproductive functions can be accomplished in a direct manner by the selection of textbooks that reflect mainstream experiences or values. The streaming of minority students into lower level programs restricts access to higher education and useful employment. Indirect and largely unobtrusive measures are also employed, including the use of French immersion programs to separate students into "winners" and "losers." The school system screens out certain information by projecting certain views of the world as necessary and normal, others as inappropriate. Diminished teacher expectation may be a problem for some. The widely accepted practice of grading students may have the effect of reinforcing competitive individualism at the expense of consensus or cooperation. Through schooling, in other words, the reproduction of the ideological and social order is realized without much public awareness or open debate. By linking power with culture without acknowledging the connection, schools tend to perpetuate prevailing distributions of power and resources (Smith, 1998). This "hidden curriculum" is aptly described by Apple and Franklin (1979):

> Schools … help control meaning. They preserve and distribute what is perceived to be "legitimate knowledge"—the knowledge that "we all must have." Thus schools confer cultural legitimacy on the knowledge of specific groups (Mukherjee, 1992: 76).

The assimilationist dynamic ostensibly interferes with a multicultural agenda. A commitment to diversity and change may be fundamentally compromised in a context where monoculturalism prevails. Rarely do schools seriously contemplate the magnitude of commitment to foster substantive changes around curriculum, language, and culture programs for children, placement and assessment, employment and promotion, teacher training, and relations with community (McAndrew, 1992). *Ad hoc* adjustments are more common than principled reform. Nor does there appear to be any wholesale move to reject the assimilationist ethos of the school system (Cummins and Danesi, 1990). Discriminatory structures are not easily dismantled in the light of entrenched interests and ideologies, many of which are unlikely to tolerate significant changes without considerable resistance. Reforms tend toward the cosmetic, with minimal impact on the key domains of decision-making, agenda-setting, and power-sharing. These impediments should warn against any excessive expectations regarding the potential of multicultural education. The next case study provides a disturbing example of education as assimilation.

CASE 9-1	"TO KILL THE INDIAN IN THE CHILD" Education As Assimilation

The Canadian government recently apologized to the First Nations for decades of systematic assimilation, theft of their lands, suppression of cultures, and the physical and sexual abuse of aboriginal children. "To those who suffered the tragedy of residential schools," the Minister of Indian Affairs Jane Stewart announced, "we are deeply sorry." For many, federal response was overdue. For over a century, thousands of aboriginal children passed through the residential school system where many were exposed to ruthless absorption in an atmosphere of neglect, disease, and abuse (Aboriginal Healing Foundation, 2002). The government acknowledged its role in enforcing policies that forcibly removed children from their families and placed them in residential schools. As a token of atonement, the government pledged $350 million to fund counselling programs and establish treatment centres for residential school victims of emotional, sexual, and physical abuse. To be sure, not everyone agreed with the tone or scope of this assessment (Hunter, 2001). To demonize all residential schools as symbols of cultural genocide, critics argued, reinforced the negative at the expense of the positive, dismissed the testimony of those who benefited from the experience, relied heavily on anec-

dotal testimony, stigmatized the schools as scapegoats for aboriginal failures, and fed into white liberal guilt by cultivating a grievance industry (Donnelly, 1998; O'Hara, 2000). Moreover, the tone of the criticism implied a deliberate attempt by the school system to hurt aboriginal children. However, the negative impacts of a residential system may stem instead from the logical ("systemic") consequences of well-intentioned programs based on faulty assumptions ("progress through development," or inaccurate reading of the situation ("they want to be like us whether they know it or not"), or cultural misunderstanding ("judging others on the basis of mainstream standards"). Still, the number of testimonies by victims appeared to outweigh the success stories, with the result that the government may have had little choice but to apologize as a kind of plea bargain to limit damages from further revelations (Coyne, 1998).

Context

Founded and operated by Protestant and Roman Catholic missionaries but funded primarily by the federal government, the system was designed to educate a colonized people against their will while eliminating the Indian problem by "killing the Indian in the child"

(continued on next page)

(Aboriginal Healing Foundation, 2002). Residential schools (or "industrial schools" as they were called initially because of the emphasis on manual skills acquisition) for aboriginal children were built in every province and territory except Prince Edward Island, Nova Scotia, and Newfoundland, with the vast majority concentrated in the prairie provinces. According to figures from John Siebert (2001), a researcher with the United Church, only a small number of aboriginal children attended residential schools (average of 7100 native children per year from 1890 to 1965), compared to those in federal or provincial day schools (average of 11 400 per year over the same period).

Officially, the Indian Residential school began in 1892 with an Order in Council to aggressively civilize Indians in preparation for citizenship through exposure to industry and the arts of civilization (Aboriginal Healing Foundation, 2002). From two residential schools at the time of Confederation, the number of schools expanded until nearly 80 residential schools existed by 1931. They were shared among the Roman Catholic (44 schools), Anglican (21), United Church (13), and Presbyterian (2) (Matas, 1997). Some aboriginal parents opted to send children to residential schools in hopes of preparing their children for the new realities. Others refused if there were day schools nearby. And still others' children were forcibly removed to residential schools, especially after 1945 when residential schools served a child-protection function for children from dysfunctional homes (Siebert, 2001). Between 100 000 and 125 000 aboriginal children (about one in six) entered the system before it was closed down in the

mid-1980s, although four residential schools continued to operate under aboriginal jurisdiction (Miller, 1996). The last school in Yellowknife did not close until 1996.

To be sure, Canada was not the only jurisdiction to remove children from their parents and resocialize them in schools or foster families. From the 1910s to the 1970s, about 100 000 Australian part-aboriginal children were placed in government or church care in the belief that Aborigines would die out—a practice that was tantamount to cultural genocide, according to a Report by the Australian Human Rights Commission, aptly entitled "The Stolen Generations." A similar practice prevailed in the United States and, to a lesser extent, in New Zealand. In short, the system in each jurisdiction elicited two unflattering interpretations: At best, residential schools could be described as ethnocentric and paternalistic attempts to assimilate indigenous children by stripping them of their language, culture, and identity. At worst, they embodied a type of institutionalized assimilation that bordered on the genocidal (Schissel and Wotherspoon, 2003; Neu and Therrien, 2003).

Rationale

From the mid-19th century onwards, the Crown engaged in a variety of measures to assert control over the indigenous peoples of Canada (Rotman, 1996). The Indian Act of 1876 proved such an instrument of control—a codification of laws and regulations that embraced the notions of European mental and moral superiority to justify the subjugation of aboriginal peoples. The Indian Act provided a rationale for misguided, paternalistic, and cruelly implemented initiatives to assimilate

(continued on next page)

aboriginal peoples into White culture. The mandatory placement of aboriginal children in off-reserve residential schools fed into these racist assumptions of White superiority and aboriginal inferiority. With the assistance of the RCMP when necessary, the government insisted on removing aboriginal children from their parents by putting them in institutions under the control of religious orders. The rationale for the residential school system was captured in an 1889 annual report by the department of Indian Affairs:

> The boarding-school dissociates the Indian child from the deleterious home influence to which he would otherwise be subjected. It reclaims him from the uncivilized state in which he has been brought up. It brings him into contact from day to day with all that tends to effect a change in his views and habits (Roberts, 1996: A7).

Its guiding philosophy embraced the adage "that how a twig is bent, the tree will grow." Federal officials believed in the necessity to transform the entire child by segregating children at school until a thorough course of instruction was acquired. However, the residential school system had a more basic motive than simple education: The removal of children from home and parents was aimed at their forced assimilation into non-aboriginal society through creation of a distinct underclass of labourers, farmers, and farmers' wives (Rotman, 1996; Robertson, 1998). This program not only entailed the destruction of aboriginal language and culture but also invoked the supplanting of aboriginal spirituality with Christianity in hopes of "killing the Indian in the child" (Royal Commission on Aboriginal Peoples, 1996).

Reality

This experiment in forced assimilation through indoctrination proved destructive (Hodgson, 2002). Many of the schools were poorly built and maintained, living conditions were deplorable, nutrition barely met subsistence levels, and the crowding and sanitary conditions proved incubators of diseases (Aboriginal Healing Foundation, 2002). Many children succumbed to tuberculosis or other contagious illnesses (Fournier and Crey, 1997). A report in 1907 of 15 schools found that 24 percent of the 1537 children in the survey had died while in the care of the school, prompting the magazine *Saturday Night* to claim "Even war seldom shows as large a percentage of fatalities as does the education system we have imposed upon our Indian wards" (Matas, 1997). Other reports indicate that disciplinary terror by way of physical or sexual abuse was the norm in some schools according to the Royal Commission on Aboriginal Peoples (1996). As one former residential student told the Manitoba Aboriginal Justice Inquiry:

> My father, who attended Alberni Indian Residential School for four years in the twenties, was physically tortured by his teachers for speaking Tseshalt: they pushed sewing needles through his tongue, a routine punishment for language offenders ... The needle tortures suffered by my father affected all my family. My Dad's attitude became "why teach my children Indian if they are going to be punished for speaking it?"... I never learned how to speak my own language. I am now, therefore, truly a "dumb Indian" (Rotman, 1996: 57).

Punishment also included beatings and whippings with rods and fists, chaining and shackling children, and

(continued on next page)

locking them in closets or basements. Many suffered long-term effects: Children grew up hostile or confused, caught between two worlds but accepted in neither. Young impressionable children returned as older Western-educated people but without the skills to communicate with older members of the community or to identify with community life (Rotman, 1996). Adults often turned to prostitution, sexual and incestuous violence, or alcohol to cope with the emotional scarring from the residential school system.

Implications

The single-mindedness of residential schools makes disturbing reading when judged by contemporary standards of human rights, government accountability, multicultural education, and aboriginal self-determination. Admittedly, it is easy to judge and condemn historical actions by the standards of today. Not only did most Whites subscribe to the principle of White supremacist superiority. Many also believed that they were acting as good Christians by improving the lot of the First Nations and congratulated government initiatives as enlightened or necessary (Editorial, *The Globe and Mail*, 8 January, 1998). Nor should the role of aboriginal parents be ignored: According to Miller (1996), aboriginal leaders insisted on a European style education for their children while federal authorities acknowledged a fiduciary obligation to oversee such education. Finally, while incidents of abuse and violence can never be condoned, the concept of corporal punishment was routinely accepted as necessary and normal. After all, sparing the rod was tantamount to spoiling the child.

Still, the Royal Commission concluded that the residential school system was an "act of profound cruelty" rooted in racism and indifference, and pointed the blame at Canadian society, Christian evangelism, and policies of the churches and government. Aboriginal parents may have endorsed the principle of a residential school system, but surely not those practices that physically maimed their children or psychologically scarred them. The apology and proposed reparations may prove a useful starting point in acknowledge past injustices that rejected aboriginal people as full and complete citizens and human beings (Editorial, *The Globe and Mail*, 8 January, 1998). Ottawa has paid more than $37 million in compensation for about 600 out-of-court settlements since 1996, with additional proposals to fast track cases to ease the litigation trauma—and wait—for more than 12 000 plaintiffs (Bailey, 2002). It remains to be seen whether psychologically scarred natives, broken families, and dysfunctional aboriginal communities will respond to the balm of counselling centres and the establishment of healing programs. However, given that aboriginal peoples have managed to survive the religious indoctrination of the mission schools, the brutality of residential schools, and integration of provincial day schools (Tremblay, 2000), the prognosis looks good (Schissel and Wotherspoon, 2003).

Case Study Questions

1 Demonstrate why the residential school system has been accused of "profound cruelty rooted in racism and indifference."

2 Indicate the rationale for the establishment of the residential school system.

MULTICULTURAL EDUCATION: ENRICHMENT, ENLIGHTENMENT, AND EMPOWERMENT

The fact that diversity initiatives have materialized at numerous schools points to the arrival of multicultural education as an idea whose time has come. Yet multicultural education can mean different things—ranging from lessons on how to be nice to cultural others, to sessions that challenge the prevailing distribution of power, privilege, and wealth in society. It can also encompass the study of many cultures or an understanding of the world from diverse perspectives; alternatively, it may convey how power and politics are inextricably connected with unequal group relations. Different styles of multicultural education can be observed, including *enrichment, enlightenment, and empowerment.* An *anti-racism approach* constitutes a fundamentally different style.

An enrichment multicultural education is aimed at all students. Students are exposed to a variety of different cultures to enhance a knowledge of and appreciation for cultural diversity. The curriculum is enriched with various multicultural add-ons. Special days are set aside for multicultural awareness; projects are assigned that reflect multicultural themes; and specific cultures are singled out for intensive classroom study. Additional perspectives include a focus on healthy identity formation, cultural preservation, intercultural sensitivity, stereotyping awareness, and cross-cultural communication. A desirable side effect of the enrichment process is greater tolerance, enhanced responsiveness, and more cooperative intercultural relations. A less beneficial consequence is a failure to initiate sweeping institutional changes because of reluctance to challenge the racism within and outside the school (Dei et al., 2000).

The enrichment model is widely acceptable because it is non-threatening. Yet this very innocuousness has brought it into disrepute with critics. Enrichment styles have been criticized as too static and restrictive in scope. They tend to focus on the exotic components of a culture that everyone can relate to, rather than the more substantive issues such as values or power. Diverse cultures are studied at the level of material culture, stripped of their historical context and discussed from an outsider's point of view (Mukherjee, 1992). There is also a danger of overromanticizing minorities by focusing on a timeless past or, worse still, crippling them as social problems within the context of the present. Stereotyping is always a problem: Even sensitive presentations must grapple with dilemmas as varied as (a) how to discuss elements of other cultures that are fundamentally opposed to Canada's democratic principles; (b) how to emphasize the positive features of minorities to the exclusion of problems that many confront; (c) how to present cultural differences without reinforcing stereotypes or an "us" versus "them" mentality; and (d) how to convey the idea that everyone is basically different in the same kind of way or, alternatively, everyone is fundamentally the same in radically different ways (MacAndrew, 1992). That these questions have yet to be answered to everyone's satisfaction reflects the muddles in this model.

A second approach entails an enlightenment model of multicultural education. This approach is similar to the enrichment model insofar as both seek to modify people's attitudes by changing how they think about diversity. Enlightenment models are less concerned with celebrating differences as a basis for attitudinal change. The focus is on informing students about race relations in society and their impact on education and schooling. They go beyond description of specific cultures. Advocated instead is a broader, analytical approach toward diversity not as a thing but as a process or relationship within contexts of power and inequality. Attention is directed at how minority-majority relations are created and maintained as well as challenged and transformed. Enlightenment models focus on analyzing those arrangements that have the intent or the effect of compromising minority school success (a) school policies and politics; (b) the school culture and "hidden" curriculum; (c) languages—official, heritage, and other; (d) community participation; (e) assessment, testing procedures, and program tracking; (f) instructional materials; (g) the formal curriculum; (h) the ethnic composition of the teaching staff; (i) and teacher attitudes, values, and competency. Stronger versions of enlightenment approaches may expose students to Anglo-European complicity in crimes of racism, dispossession, and imperialism, and the corresponding concentrations of power in colonial hands. Specific group victimization may be included, for example, genocide against First Peoples.

Both the enrichment and enlightenment style of multicultural education concentrate on the needs of non-minority pupils. In contrast is a third model, called empowerment multiculticultural education, which is directed essentially at the needs of the minority student. A minority-centred or minority-focused school provides an alternative learning environment that caters to students for whom mainstream (Eurocentric-focused) schools are inappropriate and alienating, even with incorporation of "other-centred knowledge to achieve a multicentric, inclusive school" (Dei, 1996: 106). For example, an Africentric or African-focused school arrangement seeks to improve academic and social achievement by emphasizing the centrality of Black experiences in social history and cultural development. The minority-focus empowerment model is predicated on the belief that monocultural school systems are failing minority pupils. Minority students do not see themselves in a Westocentric curriculum that rarely acknowledges minority achievements and contribution to society except as "victims or vultures." What minority students require is a school context that capitalizes on their strengths and learning styles as a basis for achievement. Empowerment models have proven controversial since not everyone necessarily shares in the assumption that separate but equal is the appropriate multicultural path to take (Smith, 1998).

Aboriginal people's struggle for control of aboriginal education typifies empowerment education. Education has proven something of a paradox for aboriginal peoples. To one side, aboriginal peoples have embraced education as an emancipating way to improve their social and economic conditions without denying their indigenousness. To the other side, exposure to mainstream education has had the effect of marginalizing, alienating, or oppressing. Aboriginal peoples may have looked to education to assist in fostering the personal identity and social success of aboriginal students. Yet aboriginal aspirations for improving prospects have been derailed by the very structures that they were intended to assist. Whereas residential schools may have deliberately set out to "kill the Indian in the child," a contemporary system designed for the mainstream is no less hegemonic in disempowering most aboriginal children. Not surprisingly, control over education has long proven a focal point of aboriginal politics for self-determining autonomy—not in the assimilationist ways envisaged by central authorities but in advancing the interests and aspirations of aboriginal peoples (Schissel and Wotherspoon, 2003; Maaka and Fleras, 2004). Towards that end, aboriginal peoples have sought to implement a variety of reforms around the need to (a) decentralize the educational structure; (b) transfer funding control to local authorities; (c) devolve power from the centre to the community; and (d) empower parents to assume increased responsibility for their children's education. The aims of aboriginal-controlled education are twofold. First, it seeks to impart those skills that aboriginal children will need to succeed in the outside world. Second, it hopes to immerse children in an environment that is unmistakably aboriginal in content, style, and outcome. The logic is unassailable: Overall outcomes for aboriginal youth are unlikely to change if they are expected to operate within a framework designed by the needs and priorities of the dominant sector. The challenge lies in producing children who possess a strong sense of who they are and where they came from, without forsaking the skills to compete in the dominant sector.

To put each of these models into perspective, Table 9.1 provides a succinct comparison of enrichment, enlightenment, and empowerment models of multicultural education.

TABLE 9.1	Models of Multicultural Education		
	Enrichment	Enlightenment	Empowerment
Focus	Celebrate	Analyze	Empower
Objectives	Remove prejudice	Study discrimination	Achieve success
Goals	Diversity	Equality	Achievement
Outcome	Lifestyle ("heritage")	Life chances	Biculturalism
Focus	Cultures	Race relations	Cultural renewal
Style	Experience	Understand	Immersion
Target	Student	Student	Minority students
Scope	Individual	Interpersonal	Collective

Anti-Racism Education

Multicultural education revolves around a philosophy for celebrating differences. It consists of activities or curricula that promote an awareness of diversity in terms of its intrinsic value to minorities and/or society at large. The aim of multicultural education is largely attitudinal and analytical; that is, to enhance sensitivity by improving knowledge about cultural differences (enrichment) or race relations (enlightenment). Yet there is no proof that enriched or enlightened attitudes will lead to behavioural changes. By contrast, anti-racism education is concerned with the identification and removal of discriminatory barriers through direct action. Anti-racism education begins with the assumption that minority underachievement is not necessarily caused by cultural differences. Thus, cross-cultural understanding will not result in any fundamental change to the structural roots of inequality (Kivel, 1996). Improving minority status depends on removing the behavioural and structural components of racial inequality through direct and open challenges, along with the power and privileges that sustain racialized inequalities. Sweeping changes in the content, structure, and process of education and schooling are called for—not simply a tinkering with multicultural concessions at curriculum levels.

Anti-racism education can be defined as a pro-active and process-oriented approach that balances a focus on difference with a sharing of power (Dei, 1996). The pedagogy becomes political, as Giroux (1994) points out, when it challenges the production of knowledge, social identities, and social relations that inform schooling and education. This approach acknowledges that schooling and education are racially, culturally, and politically mediated through asymmetrical power relations between and within groups (Dei et al.,

2000). Only a redistribution of power can bring about transformative change. Five dimensions are implied (a) critical insight into the interlocking inequities of race, class, and gender that are brought into the classroom; (b) a critical discourse that focuses on race and racism as issues of power and inequality rather than matters of cultural difference; (c) a deconstruction of White power and privilege, and its accompanying rationale for domination; (d) challenging existing school practices to uncover the structural roots of monoculturalisms and inequality; and (e) changing the status quo through political and social activism (Dei, 1996). Under an anti-racism education, both students and teachers can see how culture is organized; who is authorized to speak about different forms of culture; which cultures are worthy of valorization; and which are not. They also come to understand how power operates in the interests of dominant social relations, and how such relations can be resisted, challenged, and transformed (Giroux, 1994). Put candidly, the goal of anti-racist education is transformative: that is, to deconstruct, to delegitimize, and to dissolve the colonialism at the core of contemporary society by critically interrogating the system of power relations that bestows privilege to Whiteness.

Anti-racism education differs sharply from multicultural education. One is about insight and analysis; the other is aimed at critically informed action. Anti-racist education goes beyond acknowledging differences (enrichment) or analyzing race relations (enlightenment) by focusing instead on transforming the structural roots of racism and racial discrimination. Whereas multicultural education is about attitude change, anti-racist education is about behaviour modification. While multicultural education is merely intolerant of racism in its practice, anti-racism seeks to actively eradicate racism through resistance, challenge, and confrontation (Kivel, 1996). Anti-racism education shifts attention away from minority cultures; emphasis instead is on institutional reform by analyzing how mainstream racism is historically created, symbolically expressed, and institutionally embedded at various levels in society (Giroux, 1994). Finally, different styles of anti-racism education can be discerned. Anti-racism at individual levels concentrates on modifying people's behaviour through education and training (Stern, 1992). Institutional anti-racism strategies are aimed at dismantling the structural basis of school racism through removal of systemic discriminatory barriers. These systemic biases are most apt to occur at the level of mission statement, culture and subculture, power and decision-making, structures (including rules, roles, and relationships), and distribution of financial and human assets. The next table provides a summary of multicultural versus anti-racism education in terms of focus, objectives, concerns, scope, and outcomes.

TABLE 9.2	Comparing Multicultural and Anti-Racism Education	
	Multicultural Education	Anti-Racism Education
Focus	Culture	Structure
Objectives	Sensitivity	Removal of discriminatory barriers
Concerns	Ethnocentrism	Systemic racism
Scope	Student	Institutions
Styles	Accommodative	Challenge/uproot
Outcomes	Understanding	Transformation

CRISIS IN POST-SECONDARY EDUCATION

Most of us regard a post-secondary education as a normal and fundamental right. This was not always the case, and the notion of post-secondary schooling for the masses came into play only during the 1960s. Historically, higher education was just that: education for the higher ups. Universities were once the most pampered and privileged of all institutions (*Economist*, 1993/1994). They represented communities distinct in both mission and values that fed into mainstream society by shaping law, diplomacy, policy, politics, and civil bureaucracy. In serving as finishing schools for the well-heeled and upwardly mobile, higher education represented a socializing, civilizing, and even moralizing agent (Logan, 1997). But the demise of both exclusivity and the belief in education as a privilege rather than a right has impacted powerfully on post-secondary education. The democratization process has profoundly transformed the post-secondary workplace through solutions that create more problems. Universities have become more inclusive by accommodating the historically disadvantaged, including members of the working class, women, and racialized minorities. Yet success has spawned many of the problems associated with underfunding and overcrowding because universities are expected to accomplish what they were never designed to do: to cater to the masses. The levelling trends associated with this massification are contrary to the elitist principle at the core of post-secondary education (Keith, 1997). The universality of post-secondary education has also challenged many of its operating assumptions, in effect leaving the university enterprise perplexed, stretched to the limit, and rudderless (Price, 1993).

The post-secondary bubble has burst, with the result that the ivory towers are under siege to rethink, redo, and reform. Universities increasingly are distrusted by governments as an expensive luxury in a no-frills economy, lampooned by politicians for perceived excesses in political correctness and minority pandering, ignored by decision-makers as irrelevant to intellectual life in a world of think tanks and information technologies, criticized by the private sector for inappropriate workplace material, and accused of trying to be everything for everybody. They no longer possess the moral and intellectual high ground to be either the critic or the conscience of society, but appear to be driven by their own self-serving impulse for power and money (Logan, 1997). Martin Loney (1999) takes the universities to task because of their ivy-wall elitism: "Funded by taxpayers and student fees, they are run in the manner of a medieval guild for the benefit of tenured academic staff whose jobs-for-life guarantee requires no commensurate commitment." It is impossible, he writes, to think of another occupation that offers such maximum rewards for such minimal output. Yet moves to improve quality are compromised by economic realities. New faculty are not being hired; sessionals and contract workers are replacing full-time faculty; and students are shouldering an increased burden of operating costs by way of spiralling tuition fees (Rajagopal, 2002). The ratio of full-time faculty to university students has subsequently declined, according to Statistics Canada, from 17.7 per professor in 1992/93 to 19.7 per professor in 1999/2000 (and 21.1 in Ontario)—a trend that is worrying, given the possibility of a 30 percent increase in demand over current totals of 645 000 students (Sokoloff, 2002).

Funding Crisis and Tuition Increases

The crisis in funding is the most obvious of the problems confronting post-secondary schooling. Post-secondary education is no longer seen as an investment for Canada's future but as a highly subsidized service to students who should pay more up front. Not surprisingly, while per capita spending on university students in the United States has increased by 30 percent in the last 20 years, the figure in Canada has decreased by 20 percent. Canada's funding of post-secondary institutions by way of federal cash transfers continues its freefall, according to data from CAUT, from a high of 0.56 percent of the GDP in 1978 to 0.24 percent in 2002, a figure relatively unchanged since 1998. The proportion of revenues from all levels of government declined substantially during the 1990s to 55 percent in 2000/01 compared to 69 percent in 1990/91 (Greenway, 2002). Universities in Ontario and Nova Scotia had the lowest proportion of their revenues provided by the government—48 percent and 43 percent respectively—with the result that tuition fees accounted for 25 percent of revenues in Ontario and 27 percent in Nova Scotia. The financial situation at the University of Waterloo may be typical of Ontario universities. Waterloo generated $379 million in income for the year ended April 30, 2002. Government operating grants accounted for 30 percent; research grants and contracts, 20 percent; sales services and other income, 20 percent; donations, 2 percent; investment income, 2 percent; and student fees, 26 percent. Compare this with Quebec, which received the largest proportion of revenue from government at 66 percent while the proportion from tuition fees (which are the lowest in the country) stood at 11 percent. A comparison with the United States is also instructive: Between 1995 and 2000, total post-secondary spending in Canada increased by 2 percent, according to the Council of Ontario's Universities, while state expenditures in the United States increased by an average of 37 percent, including 76 percent in California. By contrast, Ontario's spending dropped by 3 percent, in the process reducing Ontario to last among 60 state/provinces in spending per capita on post-secondary education.

Did You Know?

Universities increasingly rely on tuition fees because of greater pressure to find alternative sources of funding. Canada's undergraduate universities paid an average of $3733 in tuition fees in the 2002–03 year or 135.4 percent more than they paid in the 1990–91 academic year. Graduate students paid 11 percent more with an average of $4948 while foreign students saw an increase of 6.1 percent to $10 476 for undergrads and $10 181 for grads. Only two provinces did not increase fees (Manitoba and Newfoundland, while fees increased by 25.2 percent in British Columbia. In Ontario, undergraduate fees have increased to $4923, second highest in the country behind Nova Scotia. For the sixth year in a row, tuition fees were frozen in Quebec for residents of the province at $1675, easily the lowest in the country (out-of-province students pay tuition fees comparable to the provinces in which they live). Tuition hikes in non-regulated programs took a sharp hike, jumping 11 percent to $6125 in applied sciences and engineering. Law increased to more than $14 000, medicine $15 435, and MBA program fees to $23 500 (Mascoll, 2002). With annual costs of about $11 000 for fees, books, rent, and transport, the average debt burden of each graduating student is between $17 000 and $25 000 compared to about $8000 in 1990, according to the Association of University and College Teachers (Duff, 2003; EKOS Research Associates, 2003). And the situation will get worse. According to the Toronto Dominion Bank analysis, the cost of sending today's newborns to university for four years could leap to nearly $125 000 per child (Beauchesne, 2002).

Tuition fees have escalated to offset this loss of revenue. Three key questions come to mind in the debate over rising tuition fees. First, are high tuition fees justified? To a large extent, the answer depends on who is defined as the prime beneficiary of a post-secondary degree. For some, a university degree is seen as a private gain rather than a public good, thus, users should pay at prices determined by supply and demand (Klassen, 1999). Others, especially students and parents disagree, arguing that an educated workforce is a public good, not just a private gain. Second, do higher tuition fees exclude the working classes from entry despite Canada's commitment to universal access for every qualified student? Post-secondary education continues to be less accessible because of rising costs, according to the authors of the *Missing Pieces Report* (Delorme and Shaker, 2003). Young Canadians from the wealthiest quarter of the population were 2.5 times more likely than the poorest quarter to attend university in 1998, according to a 2001 report from Statistics Canada entitled *Family Income and Participation in Post-secondary Education*. But while individuals from higher-income families are more likely to attend, the participation gap between the poorest and richest continued to narrow during the 1990s, partly because of increased participation from students in lower-income families and declining rates among students from higher-income families. Particularly disadvantaged are those less affluent students who did not live within commuting distance of a university. Also under pressure are those middle-income families whose income precludes access to student loans (Bruser, 2003). Third, are high tuition fees worth it? It appears so: Consider the annual income breakdowns for the year 2000:

- Average income in Canada, both full-time and part-time was $31 757
- Average full-time earnings in Canada, regardless of education, was $43 231
- Canadians with a high-school diploma earned $36 278
- Canadians with a college degree earned $41 825
- Canadians with a university degree earned $61 823
- Men with a university degree in full-time employment earned $72 000

Job opportunities differ as well. According to Bruce Little (1998), from 1990 to 1997, the number of jobs for those with a post-secondary certificate increased by 1.83 million, while total employment for those who didn't finish high school dropped by 962 000. In 1997, 73.3 percent of all Canadians with a post-secondary degree or diploma had a job, whereas the employment-to-population ratio for those with less than a high-school diploma was only 35.1 percent. The unemployment picture is consistent with employment levels: The unemployment rate in Ontario in 1999 for those with a high-school diploma or less stood at 8.6 percent; the figures were 3.9 percent for those with a BA and 3.4 percent for those with a graduate degree. Interestingly, even the much-maligned arts degree appears to be holding its own in a world of highly skilled workers as employers look for candidates who are flexible, adaptive, capable of lifelong retraining, and possessing communication and group skills. The communicative, social, and analytical skills that arts students are thought to acquire may culminate in more financially lucrative careers over the long run than the specialized but potentially dated skills of highly trained professionals (Lewington, 1998; Cook, 1999).

Free Speech in the Academy

A growing commitment to institutional inclusiveness has paid dividends to the post-secondary enterprise. Yet this commitment to inclusivness has played havoc with cherished principles such as free speech. Academics continue to see themselves as autonomous figures engaged in the unencumbered search for truth. But academic freedom is attacked on all sides by bureaucracy and political correctness, while intellectual fashions are contesting the concept of academic freedom in a postmodern world of contested truths (Tierney, 2001). Universities and colleges are now confronted by the paradox of preserving academic freedom without trampling on gender or minority rights for inclusion within a bias-free environment (Drakich, 1994). Post-secondary institutions are under pressure to foster environments in which all individuals can enjoy the freedom to study, teach, and conduct research. Yet such inclusiveness may compromise the historic role of higher education. Critics have argued that universities are losing their status as bastions of freedom by curbing free expression, abdicating an attendant "right to offend" if necessary, or caving in to unproven allegations of racism and sexism without due process (Fekete, 1994; Furedy, 1995). Others contend that a commitment to an inclusive environment implies restrictions to ensure that no one is excluded because of fear, intimidation, or threats. Efforts to reconcile these mutually exclusive yet seemingly valid perspectives—the right to free expression versus the right of minorities to be free of hateful statements that may endanger—may prove elusive.

This debate continues to be hotly contested in Canada. Should universities allow all speech on campus, regardless of how offensive and inaccurate, in the name of free expression and commitment to cover both sides of an issue? Or should universities openly bar the right to certain forms of speech that eschew their responsibilities to both the academy and to society? Consider the case of Holocaust deniers and revisionists: To one side are those who would deny a platform for Holocaust deniers (those who refute the fact that Germany killed 6 million undesirables such as Jews) or Holocaust revisionists (those who maintain that something evil happened but deny the magnitude of the extermination process). To the other side are those who would deny a university platform for those Jewish speakers who defend the right to Israel's existence even at the expense of Palestinian disempowerment. How should the academy align itself in these politics?

These issues cannot be taken lightly. For many, the centrality of academic freedom as a fundamental principle cannot be compromised (Berger, 1993). Other values pale by comparison, as confirmed by the CAUT when it adopted its Policy Statement on Academic Freedom in 1977:

> The common good of society depends upon the search for knowledge and its free exposition. Academic freedom in universities is essential to both these purposes in the teaching function of the university as well as in its scholarship and research.... Academic members of the community are entitled, regardless of prescribed doctrine, to freedom in carrying out research and in publishing the results thereof, freedom of teaching and of discussion ... in a manner consistent with the scholarly obligation to base research and teaching on an honest search for knowledge (*McGill*, 1994: 12–13).

In short, the academy is predicated on the premises and principles of academic freedom. A capacity to pursue impartial truth and value-free knowledge without fear of reprisals is seriously compromised without guarantees of non-interference by bureaucrats or political correctness. Support for free expression presupposes that your adversaries have something

Free Speech and the University: Politics, Power, and the Pursuit of Truth

When it comes to free speech at university, not everyone aligns along the extremes of yes or no. Some prefer a more moderate position that balances rights with responsibilities. In an interesting paper by Deborah Tannen (2003), she argues that the academy in any democracy must be a bastion of free speech, knowledge, and reason. But she also points out that the academy must take the responsibility to ensure it stands for factual history and accurate knowledge. Otherwise, it can no longer claim to be a centre of learning, but rather an "echo chamber for the spread of disinformation in the name of free speech" (p. 9). According to Tannen, the problem lies in how the issue of free speech is framed. The strengths of any democracy rest on a commitment to free speech and the belief that truth is possible through open debate in which both sides are heard. Yet there are dangers in such an approach, confirming again that strengths can also prove liabilities, depending on the context. The problem arises around the concept of "two sides to every issue." This tendency to frame all issues as debates between two sides may distort the issue or even obscure "truth" because of the need to provide a platform to those whose claims may incite hate, are patently false, trigger antisocial behaviour, and undermine a commitment to social justice, cultural diversity, and national unity. Moreover, most issues don't have just two sides but many complex, nuanced, and overlapping sides that are obscured when an issue is polarized around two sides. The most extreme views come to define the debate, with the result that intermediate positions are ignored and people often despair of any solution.

In short, Tannen argues, universities have an obligation to encourage open debate over a wide range of issues. But they also have a responsibility to withhold a platform for the dissemination of false information or to lend credibility to those who spread it. Yes, individuals should have a right to say what they want. There are places in a free society for that kind of unfettered speech, including speakers' corners from London's Hyde Park to Kitchener's King and Benton commons. But universities do not have an obligation to amplify the message of those who spread disinformation; nor must they confer credibility implied by the invitation and platform to speak. For that reason, Tannen concludes, Holocaust deniers and revisionists, have no place in the academy because such deliberate misinformation goes against the grain of universityhood. In that the right to free speech is never an absolute right, but relative to time and place, contested, and subject to change, the politics of free speech (and censorship) are closely linked with the politics of power.

useful to say, with every right to articulate it, provided a similar right is extended to others (Dickson, 1993). The principle of "agreeing to disagree" is not simply a luxury or post-secondary perk; it is critical to the process of sorting out competing truth claims as a precondition for intellectual discoveries. Impartiality and objectivity are seriously compromised without guarantees of non-interference by political or outside interests. Moves to "muzzle" open inquiry through outside interference are criticized and openly resisted as fundamental infringements to academic freedom and institutional autonomy (de Toro, 1994). Without academic freedom, in other words, what is the point of the academy?

Commercialization and Corporatization

The rules, roles, relationships, and structure of the university are changing in response to internal and external pressures (Reading, 1996). Many believe the central functions of the academy are to prepare students for citizenship in a democratic society, to provide the skills to contribute to the economy, and to advance the frontiers of knowledge through creation and transmission of information. Yet these functions are increasingly contested by a climate of multiple perspectives, an absence of an embracing consensus, and rejection of any claims to absolute truth or good (Brown, 2002; Brown and Schubert, 2002). Without a firm centre to hold their focus in place, universities are losing the sense of historical mission that defined and legitimated their status in society. Historically, the university was linked to the destiny of the nation-state that it served by promoting the idea of a national culture. But nation-states are declining as the prime creator of wealth or sources of identity. Not surprisingly, the protection and promotion of national culture is less urgent than in the past, given the increasingly tenuous relationship between higher learning and nation-state status in a globalizing era. As a result, universities are turning into bureaucratic corporations with a focus on a market-driven excellence rather than cultural transmission.

The cozy links between business and education are controversial (Pocklington and Tupper, 2002). In an era of dwindling resources and increased competition, universities are increasingly corporatizing around the new three Rs—restructuring, refocusing, and retrenchment (Lewington, 1997). Hard-pressed universities have little choice but to balance the intellectual mission with the demand for corporate dollars to defray operational costs as governments trim funding. For cash-strapped universities, a pipeline between the boardroom and the classroom provides a much-required dose of relief from relentless government underfunding. To stave off insolvency, universities are closing down departments and programs on the grounds that they can't do everything with current funding and human resource levels. Businesses, in turn, look to universities for connections, personnel transfers, and contract work arrangements. Commercialization continues to infiltrate universities, ranging from ads in washrooms to corporate donations to foreign buyouts of campus bookstores (Klein, 1997). The dilemma is palpable: if universities are too closely identified with established powers and measurable outcomes, they risk sacrificing their independence and creative scholarship. If they are too divorced from the outside world, they risk losing a lucrative source of funding. To be sure, a university disconnected from the real world is hardly an option that Canadians can afford. Although some degree of relevance to the economy is necessary, if only to secure legitimacy, many balk at the prospect of universities as corporations for delivering products and services to the market rather than for developing critical and creative skills of benefit to society at large (Flynn, 1997).

To the extent that universities now resemble money machines, they have embarked on a path altogether different from the immediate past. The convergence of academic interests with those of business and government is widely criticized (Brown and Schubert, 2002). Instead of preserving its defining mission of reflective inquiry, independent thought, and free dissemination, the university is becoming subservient to the master goal of research and market sites for private interests. Universities have adopted a corporate motto based on achieving new efficiencies and serving the new knowledge economy. This view of universities as little more than credential factories is expressed in the following trends: the specialization of the academic labour force, assembly-line work processes in teaching and research, conveyor-belt outputs for students as consumers, increased professionalization of university administration, and the hierarchy of administrative/academic entrepreneurs devoted to fund-raising, marketing, and project management (Pocklington and Tupper, 2002; Melchers, 2002; McMurtry, 2003) Furthermore, the "bean counters" of the world have managed to convince decision-makers that everything worthwhile, including universities, is quantifiable, and that failure to measure something is tantamount to being unaccountable. Such a shift may explain the popularity of *Maclean's* annual "measurement of excellence" ranking of Canadian universities to help prospective customers make a more informed choice. However interesting and entertaining, *Maclean's* can only base rankings on measurable indicators that imply educational quality, such as library holdings, entrance standards, and alumni support (Cameron, 1997). Educational "outputs" related to the creation and dissemination of knowledge are not included because they are notoriously difficult to quantify. Yet as Mark Giberson observes, education and schooling are not a commodity for consumption or comparison shopping; rather, post-secondary institutions embody unique personalities that shape people's lives, challenge their minds and imaginations, nurture a sense of self-worth, and transform them into good citizens.

Gendered Academia

A gender bias has long prevailed in post-secondary schooling. Up until the 1970s, for the most part, women did not attend universities or, if they did, the purpose of snaring a spouse was uppermost. Women who attended university were rarely taken seriously or were subject to harassment, in part because of personal bias by indifferent teachers and bullying males, in part because of structural factors related to curriculum and testing procedures. But times have changed: Women now excel in terms of university enrolment; they accounted for over three-quarters of all university enrolment growth in the past 20 years. And these trends are likely to continue, given that young women between the ages of 13 and 16 have achieved near parity with young men in math and science, while pulling even further ahead in reading and writing, according to a study by Statistics Canada and the Council of Ministers of Education (Seeman, 2000). In 1978, 10 percent of all women between 18 and 21 attended university; by 1997, the figure had increased to 20.5 percent. Men, by comparison, saw their participation rate increase only slightly, from 12 percent to 14.2 percent. Women are graduating in much higher numbers: In 1997, 99 616 women received a degree compared to 72 120 men. Men earn more PhDs than women, 2519 versus 1395, but women earned slightly more MAs and substantially more BAs, 86 264 compared to 58 261. These figures are consistent with the performance of young women in primary and secondary schooling.

However impressive on the surface, there remain conflicting messages and patterns. Women may have overtaken men in many disciplines: Women outnumber men in biology and pharmacy as well as medicine, dentistry, law, and biochemistry. Women now earn 50.2 percent of MD degrees, including 60.4 percent of Quebec's medical school graduates. But other disciplines remain female-unfriendly, including computer science and engineering. Consider how the most popular fields of study for university graduates in 2001 remain gendered, with women predominantly in teaching (20.1 percent) and nursing (6.5 percent), compared with men in engineering at 15.4 percent and business and commerce at 10 percent. Engineering remains a problem for women: women were granted 35.6 percent of all doctoral degrees in 1997/98 but only 9.5 percent in engineering and applied science. Ottawa's decision to create 2000 Canadian Research Chairs (endowments to universities and hospitals to attract research stars) appears to discriminate against women. Only 16 percent of the chairs have been awarded to women, in part because the majority of chairs go to science, engineering, and medicine, with women making up only a small percentage of the applicant pools. Only 20 percent of the chairs are set aside for the Humanities and Social Sciences where women comprise 50 percent of the researchers (Sokoloff, 2003). Other trends are no less conflicted: Full-time faculty by gender and rank in Canadian universities in 1997 are mainly tenured males at 20 580 positions compared to 6616 tenured females, with the vast majority of full professors (both contract and tenured) being male (10 507 versus 1574) (*SWC Supplement*, 1999).

Gendered inequities reflect the experience of many female faculty, thus reinforcing the perception that appearances are deceiving and universities are not what they seem to be. To one side, universities routinely endorse a commitment to excellence in teaching, research, and service. To the other side is a darker picture at odds with mission statements and public relation spins. Universities tend to be remarkably exploitative, despite their ivory tower gloss, with a decided reluctance to put into practice what they preach. Put simply, universities have become increasingly dependent on contract faculty. The relentless drive to manage enrolments, balance budgets, and trim teaching costs has created a bifurcated labour force split hierarchically into tenure versus contract (part-time) faculty. Part-timers have evolved into a permanent and inexpensive source of labour. Last hired, first fired, they produce a surplus value that helps universities overcome government-underfunded fiscal shortages. According to Indhu Rajogopal (2002), part-timers—most of whom are women—comprise approximately one-third of all faculty members in Canadian universities. They contribute significantly to overall academic output, despite consuming only a marginal share of the universities' economic resources. Yet as a whole they remain largely alienated, underappreciated, and marginalized by administration and tenure faculty. Not only are they rendered invisible, but, advancement is also precluded by seemingly insurmountable barriers including: university policies and economics; discriminatory treatment in the workplace; conventional academic practices; and myths about their temporariness that conceal differing career motivations. This devaluation of teaching puts part-timers in a Catch-22 bind: They are hired to do the very thing that the university devalues, but time in the classroom displaces time from research. A vicious circle prevails: that is, part-timers need the resources associated with full-time employment to escape this marginality, but the very nature of teaching part-time makes it impossible to cultivate those research skills that enhance employability and tenure.

CRISIS OF CONFIDENCE/IDENTITY CRISIS

The relationship of higher education to society at large remains ambiguous. On the one hand, the ivory towers prefer to remain detached and aloof from the grubby reality beyond the ivy walls. On the other, they are implicated in social ferment that invariably challenges the rationale behind post-secondary education. Universities are in crisis not only because of budgets or high enrolments; rather, they are experiencing a crisis of identity because they are no longer sure of what is expected of them in balancing the elite with the democratic, the intellectual with the pragmatic. Growing uncertainty over roles, rules, relationships, and responsibilities in a rapidly changing and increasingly diverse world raises the question: What are universities for? Must education improve the human condition by advocating a critically-informed citizenry? Should it foster intellectual excellence and encourage curiosity-driven research? Should schools emphasize the transmission of skills to ensure productivity? Should universities abandon elitist claims to higher learning in exchange for more pragmatic vocational training? For institutions that historically have enjoyed the equivalent of diplomatic immunity from public scrutiny, the call for accountability and transparency is as disruptive as it is dismaying. And in trying to be responsive to everything, there is a danger of being relevant to nobody, with a corresponding loss of legitimacy. This ambiguity is encapsulated in debates over the primary goal of post-secondary schooling as (a) enlightened sites of higher learning; (b) catalysts for social action; and (c) credential factories for career success. These goals are mutually related yet analytically distinct, having evolved over the past generation to occupy an uneasy coexistence.

Higher Learning

Universities have historically prevailed as institutions for the acquisition and transmission of knowledge. They have evolved over time into a distinctively modern way of exploring the world out there that not only transcends the specifics of different academic disciplines, but also imparts a coherent unity to the whole scholarly enterprise (Berger, 1993). Central to the higher learning enterprise is the unremitting search for dispassionate truth, as reflected in the ideals of objectivity and according to the canons of cognitive rationality (Martin, 1993). A single definitive reality is thought to exist; this reality is subject to discovery and analysis by properly trained individuals with a capacity to transcend social and cultural barriers in the quest for excellence. Such a positivist outlook embraces the logic and methods of the natural sciences, with its embrace of quantifiable objective facts and neutral observation (Darder, 1990).

For others, we live in a world of truths, not truth. A postmodernist turn in recent years has challenged the notion of truth or objective knowledge. According to postmodernism, there is no such thing as absolute truth or objective reality (or at least no humanly possible way of discovering it): We can only have discourses about truth and reality in a mind-dependent and culturally-specific world. Truth or knowledge is relative to an interpretive framework, each of which is socially constructed as culturally specific embodiments across time and place. Nor, is there any way of stepping inside a mind-dependent framework to determine which construct is superior or correct. Truth, in other words, has little to do with knowledge or objectivity but more with "muscle" in terms of whose truths prevail. As Paulo Friere reminded us many years ago, learning and education are never neutral but inherently political, with the result that politics and pedagogy are inseparably linked process (Marshall et al., 2000). Conducting research in these postmodernist times is no less political; and those who fail to grasp this fundamental notion will require a "thick skin" if they hope to flourish in academia.

Social Activism

Not everyone is pleased with an an ivory tower view of the universities. Universities are criticized as remote and removed from the realities of life, as producers of knowledge that do not improve the quality of life, and as discursive (discursive = from discourse) frameworks in defence of dominant ideology. Critics have taken the universities to task as excessively cognitive instruments where the preference for abstraction empowers some while disempowering others because of the potential for elitism, racism, sexism, and colonialism. Institutes of higher learning are criticized as handmaidens of the status quo, more concerned with careerism and empire-building than with progressive social change. Put bluntly, critics believe the university must do more than think; it must focus on doing by encouraging social activism. For in the final analysis, doing nothing to challenge social injustices is not neutrality but rather makes people complicit in the status quo, thus implicating each of us in the struggle for social transformation (Dei et al., 2000).

A commitment to social activism clashes with the pursuit of objective knowledge and truth-seeking as guiding principles. Learning for learning's sake is less important than the pursuit of equality and justice according to social activists. The validity of an idea should no longer be based on its degree of truthfulness, (i.e., on whether it upholds minimum standards of evidence and argument) but on its potential to address minority interests in the struggle for liberation and empowerment. The objective is not memorization or recall: The goals are to deconstruct assumptions underlying the organization and transmission of this knowledge, and to use this as a basis for renewal and reform (Smith, 1998). Of particular note is the role of university as social critic. As Bernard Shapiro, principal of McGill University, says:

> We must be able to hold up a mirror of society to itself in such a way as to make clear not only the gap that continues to exist between society's rhetoric of its soaring objectives and the less impressive reality of its achievements, but also the inadequacy of the objectives themselves compared to the alternatives that may be considered (Galt, 1997: A-6). We don't want financial people who don't understand the human implications and social implications of what they do.

To be sure, post-secondary education has always been implicitly political in terms of who gets what, and why. But advocates of the social activist position argue that the mission of higher education should be overtly political, with objectives directed at nothing less than comprehensive social change. Yet imposing a transformative agenda by discrediting the legitimacy of higher learning has confounded the very foundation of the university as a cornerstone of Western society. After all, once the pursuit of objective knowledge is abandoned as legitimate or worthwhile, those supports underlying higher education—objectivity, reason, and science—are likely to collapse.

Credential Factory

There is a saying that, students once attended university to learn, but now they come to earn. There is no way of proving or disproving this cliché; nevertheless, many believe that students flocked to universities to engage in a process of self-discovery through learning. Life was seen as an adventure to be savoured and experienced, while thoughts of a career were rarely contemplated or treated with startled disdain. Students, of course, could afford such lofty ambitions since jobs were readily available to anyone who decided to re-enter the establishment. A secure economic future enabled people to become reflectively engaged, Edward Renner (Carey, 1995) reminds us, while learning for learning's sake proved an affordable luxury in an era of plentiful jobs.

At present many students attend university to enhance career success. Learning is fine, but they know only too well that a degree is a prerequisite for a well-paying job. Parents, too, are increasing pressure by telling sons and daughters to pursue a career-focused education (Morgenson, 2003). A conflict of interest is inevitable: While students want more training for jobs, many faculty continue to uphold the primacy and principles of higher learning. And the universities have fallen into the trap. They have evolved into mass-produced assembly lines that dispense credentials in a manner not altogether different from

Taylorist principles of scientific management. Consider the parallels in linking university education with a conveyor belt within a factory system: Managers (teachers) think, workers (students) do; course work is divided into minimal units for assessment; students are thought to be motivated entirely by extrinsic rewards (markets); and the entire system operates on and is modelled after private enterprise. Both students and professors may strive to reclaim higher learning or social activism, but the system conspires against both.

Is there a solution? More than ever, a liberal arts education is critical. Without the humanities and social sciences, universities run the risk of becoming sites for vocational training (Napran, 2003). True, universities are part of the real world, and can no more return to the elitist exclusion of the past than they can abandon claims to higher learning without compromising the very reason for their existence. Nevertheless, some degree of distance is critical. This raises a key question of balance: Should universities see themselves as vocational training schools with a few liberal arts morsels thrown in for good measure? Or should they focus on educating creative minds, creating knowledge for the sake of knowledge, and performing a broader social role than preparing students for business? The balancing of the contemplative with the practical may sound good in theory; putting it into practice may be something altogether different. Time will tell whether the university can be transformed to play a leading role in forging social cohesion while producing critically informed knowledge workers for an information driven global market economy. It also remains to be seen if a largely premodern (even medieval) institution can cope with the market-driven realities of the modern era while attending to the fractured discourses of the postmodern turn.

DISCUSSION QUESTIONS

1 Indicate how and why schooling and education—especially post-secondary education—is experiencing a crisis of confidence, that is, an identity crisis regarding what it should be doing, why, and how.

2 Demonstrate how the democratization and massification of schooling and education has contributed to the social problems that confront schooling and education at present.

3 In what way can the debate over academic freedom of expression be defined as a social problem? What is the solution?

4 Compare the different types of multicultural education in terms of objectives and means.

5 Compare multicultural and anti-racist education in terms of how each defines the problem that needs to be addressed and the kind of solution that is consistent with the definition of the problem.

 WEBLINKS

Education in Canada. **www.ca.dir.yahoo.com/Education**

Canadian Association of University Teachers. **www.caut.ca**

National Association for Multicultural Education. **www.nameorg.org**

chapter ten

Work, Working,
and the Workplace

FRAMING THE PROBLEM

The cliché "nothing is constant except change" resonates with meaning when applied to the world of work, working, and workplaces. The very concept of work has undergone a change of such startling proportions that a paradigm shift is looming in response to the demands of: (a) an intensely competitive and freewheeling global market economy; (b) massive restructuring because of job-stripping automation and "labour"-saving technologies; and (c) a reconsideration of wealth creation in a networking and information-highway age. Institutional rules and workplace wisdom have taken such a "pounding" that what once were virtues are now regarded as vices, and vice versa. New technologies have transformed how people work, the skills they need, the demands imposed on them, the knowledge they can contribute to the workplace, and the kind of careers that can be planned in a just-in-time work environment. Workplaces, too, find themselves subjected to a constant barrage of demands and regulations, each of which has the potential to complicate or confuse (Higgins and Duxbury, 2002). Radical shifts in the business environment due to globalization have also disconnected the moorings that once secured the "way things are done around here." Businesses today are expected to embrace risk-taking as a matter of course, although the dot-com crash in 2001 has put a damper on daring as companies retrench and recoup. Even the concept of work is evolving. Work is no longer wage-by-age activity from nine to five, five days a week, but a zigzag of patterns and routines that individuals customize by way of choices, contracts, and credentials. Thanks to the telecommunications revolution, millions of office workers are already working from home, while others are exploring the concept of co-workplace—a new kind of neighbourhood-based workspace that offers the benefits of boundaries between home and work while combining the framework of a good corporate office with the convenience of a home location (Johnson, 2003).

Put bluntly, the very concepts of work, working, and workplaces are under pressure to adapt and evolve or become irrelevant. Pressures for transforming this domain are often internally driven, spanning the spectrum from increasingly alienated workers in search of empowerment, to harried CEOs under the gun to maximize profit, with an increasingly diverse workforce equally adamant in demanding "space" through the removal of discriminatory barriers. Further pressure is imposed by disgruntled clients who bristle at the prospect of tolerating shoddy goods or indifferent services. An upheaval of such magnitude will undoubtedly generate a host of social problems for some, yet opportunity for others. Even the problems that plagued workplaces in the 1990s may not apply in the new millennium. Previous editions of *Social Problems* focused on the impact and implications of a stagnant economy to work and workplaces. But Canada's economy at present is booming: strong job creation, surging consumer confidence, low inflation, rock-bottom interest rates, receptive export markets, and predictions of healthy growth in the future. Unemployment rates by the end of 2003 had declined to about 7.5 percent nationwide; a total of over 16 million Canadians are employed; the economy churned out 560 000 jobs in 2002, with most in the higher wage sector (Little, 2004); exports to the United States are piggybacking because of a robust American economy and an undervalued Canadian dollar; and the manufacturing sector continues to rebound, despite gloomy predictions to the contrary. Those who predicted the end of work because of automation and globalization (Rifkin, 1995) may have trouble accounting for the creation of nearly 2 million jobs since 1992, a labour force participation rate of 66 percent, and growth in self-employment to 17.6 of the total (Finlayson, 1999).

Yet there is a downside. Not everyone is hopping aboard the "gravy train," judging by key economic indicators. Almost 1.1 million Canadians are looking for work, while upwards of 500 000 have given up the search (Canadian Press, 2000). Subdued growth in real wages and weekly earnings suggests anything but prosperity for workers at lower and middle levels. Canadians may take pride in their highly educated population, yet 6.6 million earn less than $20 000 per year compared to 447 000 who earn more than $100 000 per year. Problems arise when people's expectations clash with workplace realities. The expanding gap between the working haves and working have-nots does not bode well in strengthening the social fabric.

Several themes provide a conceptual framework for problematizing the concept of work, working, and workplaces:

1 Workplaces and organizations are social problems in their own right because of design and definition. Workplaces are particularly problematic sites for those who are exposed to dangerous, dehumanizing, or demeaning jobs. In cases where automation is eliminating jobs, people's right to work and to sustain themselves is being jeopardized. Shift work may be critical to the economy, but it exacts a physical and emotional toll on those 30 percent of employed Canadians who work non-standard hours (Shields, 2003). Technology has made it easier than ever for employers to monitor and investi-

gate workplace behaviour. Such close scrutiny has disrupted productivity or morale—in effect, making it important to rethink the balance of the legitimate privacy rights of employees with the equally valid privacy interests of employers in a security-conscious era (Lane III, 2003). Of particular concern is violence in the workplace as disgruntled employees displace their frustrations on bosses or co-workers. Conflict-producing workplaces may culminate in random acts of work rage because of wearying workloads combined with a brooding sense of powerlessness and injustice in a mean and lean environment (Cole, 1999).

2   Workplaces are thought to be responsible for creating social problems because of work-related stresses (Lowe, 2003). Job stress is now at epidemic proportions: According to Statistics Canada, a survey of about 25 000 adults acknowledged long work hours and heavy workloads as primary sources of workplace stress (Galt, 2003; Theobald, 2003). One in three workers is stressed out due to excessive work demands, with stress-related absences costing businesses an estimated $3.5 billion annually (Lowe, 2003). Workplace stress may be especially acute among those who must balance career plans with personal and family life (Laver, 1999). Many spend more time performing supplemental work at home and unpaid overtime than time in paid overtime (Higgins and Duxbury, 2002). As noted by Linda Duxbury and Chris Higgins in their survey of 32 000 working Canadians in the 2001 *National Work–Life Conflict Study*, many Canadians are experiencing "role overload" because of jobs and overtime that are literally making them mentally and physically sick, resulting in less commitment to jobs and more absenteeism from work, to take care of elderly parents (*KW Record*, 18 October, 2003). Health-enhancing work environments that pay attention to the underlying determinants of health, including trust and cooperative relations, are critical in creating healthy employees (Lowe, 2003). Yet employers avoid addressing the cause of workplace stress, preferring instead to deal with the symptoms by offering employee-assistance programs such as glide time hours that alleviate the strain of long working hours but do little to lighten the workload for their overworked, cynical, and disengaged workers (Galt, 2003; Williams, 2003).

3   Workplaces themselves are structured as social problems because of inherent inequalities. Workplace relations are unequal relations, and these inequities may induce resentment and conflict, and erode the social fabric if allowed to spiral out of control, particularly if certain minoritized groups are denied full and equal participation. A diverse workforce is widely endorsed as a bottom-line investment, yet can prove disruptive and costly if not "managed" properly (Wang, 2003).

4   Workplaces are known to resist problem-solving changes. By the same token, proposed solutions to the problems of work and organizations often generate conditions that create more problems. Workplace solutions such as downsizing may be great for the bottom line; they also have the effect of shedding workers by the thousands, who then have little chance of re-entering the labour market regardless of retraining.

5   Workplaces are problematic because of their relationship to the economy. What is the economy for? For some, the point of the economy is to make a profit; for others the economy exists to create meaningful and stable jobs (Laxer, 1999). Not surprisingly, critics respond differently to the prospect of even profitable corporations eliminating workers in the name of efficiency and profit (Bartram, 1999).

This chapter explores the trifecta of work, working, and workplaces as social problems in a rapidly changing, increasingly diverse, and uncertain world. Workplace organizations are interpreted not as smoothly functioning "things," but as highly contested sites where competition and confusion are the rule rather than exception in coping with internal pressures and external demands. By approaching workplaces as an ideological battleground involving different competitive groups in a constant struggle for control of the agenda, workplace realities are shown to fall somewhere in between the poles of chaos and regulation, structure and agency, continuity and change, and resistance and control. Such an interpretation may not yield elegant models of organizations and neat workplace flowcharts. Nevertheless, it does capture the dynamics of workplace politics as sources of inequality yet simultaneously as sites for social transformation (Dei et al., 2000). The first part of this chapter surveys the evolving and contested nature of work, working, and workplaces against the backdrop of a new work world. Work is not disappearing per se; but work as conventionally defined is now superseded by new forms that reflect a shift in how we work, workplace design, and the dynamics of working. The inception of a human resources approach is widely approved as humanizing the workplace. Nevertheless, many workers continue to be treated as little more than glorified robots, as demonstrated by the case study on conveyor-belt burgers. Finally, the politics of inclusiveness are discussed in light of Canada's growing diversity. The barriers that preclude workplaces from becoming more inclusive are explored at the level of community policing across Canada.

WORKING IN THE 21ST CENTURY: FROM CRISIS TO CHALLENGE

Work has been around since the beginning of time. It remains the most essential of human activities in providing the basis for both personal identity and self-esteem (Krahn and Lowe, 1994). Studs Terkel captured its centrality to the human condition accordingly:

> Work is about daily meaning as well as daily bread. For recognition as well as cash; for astonishment rather than torpor; in short, for a sort of life rather than a Monday through Friday sort of dying ... (*Utne Reader*, May/June, 1995).

Work comes in all shapes and sizes, and its pervasiveness in people's lives is rarely disputed. Students engage in work when going to school; upon graduation many will begin to work at jobs or pursue careers. Some will continue to work at home by looking after children but without formal payment. Others will work out of their homes by exchanging goods and services for payment. Still others will be paid for working outside the house, often in large corporate settings but at the risk of losing their creativity, control, and individuality. A few see work as the crowning feature of a meaningful existence and source of identity; others prefer to shirk their jobs as a source of aggravation or humiliation. In short, working is so central to many people's lives and to society at large that a world without work is unthinkable, and it is precisely this tension between work as an opportunity and a problem that provides the impetus for this chapter.

Work is commonly defined as earning a living through paid (sometimes unpaid) employment in the production and distribution of goods and services (Livingston and Sawchuk, 2003). Until the 19th century people did work rather than had jobs per se (Keegan, 1996). As pointed out by William Bridge (1995), author of *Job Shift*, work historically was an activity for doing at a certain time and place, according to personal and seasonal rhythms rather than something that a factory provided in exchange for pay. The institutionalization of work (having a job in a factory) evolved with the Industrial Revolution and the mechanization of the productive process. Even so, barely 50 percent of the workers in the industrialized world were employed by a company a century ago. Workplaces were small, family-owned, and rudimentary in organization (Campbell, 1996). It was not until the early 1970s that labour-intensive industrialization raised the job figure to 90 percent of the workforce.

But the concept of work has continued to evolve. No sooner did the culture of work begin to take hold—including the notion of a full-time job for life, well-defined career paths, and corporate loyalty in exchange for job security—than countervailing forces combined to dismantle the very nature of work, the process of working, and the structure of the workplace (Keegan, 1996). Both the private and public sector embarked on a labour-shedding process that eliminated jobs involving repetitive aspects of production. Even white collar jobs are being "out-sourced" and "off-shored" to developing world countries (Gwyn, 2004). A corporate downsizing further bifurcated the workforce: To one side, a core of permanent employees (stressed out and demoralized by pressures to produce or else); to the other, a wobbly perimeter of part-time or contract workers with little opportunity for security or success. The "work-rich" have secure jobs with continuous, high-value employment as a function of their skills; by contrast, the "work-poor" are relegated to semi-employment status with generally lower wages and few benefits (Gwyn, 1996). Adding insult to injury are untapped pools of workers on the margins of society without even a hope of finding a decent paying job.

Five dimensions reflect, reinforce, and advance this perception of workplaces as breeding grounds for social problems: namely, (1) transforming workplaces; (2) diversifying the workforce; (3) workplace inequities; (4) rethinking working; and (5) a world without work. The fact that each of these dimensions can be construed as both an opportunity and problem adds yet another wrinkle in conceptualizing the problem-solution link.

Transforming Workplaces

The winds of change pose a menacing and disruptive challenge to institutional life. In the midst of a free-market revolution, modern workplaces are under pressure to change and adapt. Rules and priorities that once governed work and workplaces are increasingly contested, exposed to uncertainty, and prone to confusion in response to intense global competition over capital and investment. Global forces exert a powerful impact both internally and externally: internally, at the level of group dynamics; externally, through institutional links and customer relations. Workplaces are evolving as new philosophies influence management style and strategies, worker-management relations, and the design and the organization of work. A restructuring of the workplace has flattened the organizational pyramid. Layers of management have been peeled away, thus creating more horizontal forms of decision-making and power-sharing. The combination of worker demands and consumer dissatisfaction has compelled companies to restructure from within or lose the flexibility for coping with external changes. With younger workers valuing balance and flexibility in addition to security and responsibility, it becomes more important than ever to foster workplaces in which people feel as though they make a difference, have a sense of purpose and fulfillment, and are valued for their contribution (Laver, 1999).

Innovative thinking about workplace organizations is proving to be cutting edge. Revisions are apparent in how we think and talk about the workplace with respect to structure (what it looks like), functions (what it is supposed to do), and process (what it really does). Workplaces were once dominated by a set of simple physical tasks around a mechanistic mindset for maximizing productivity (Chorn, 1991). A managerial mentality prevailed, with its commitment to rationality, the pursuit of goals, and cost-benefit ratios. Management–labour relations were organized around the principle that managers managed and workers worked. But workplaces in the new millennium are no longer bound by such tightly defined scripts with respect to organizational design and workplace practices. The corporate air is filled with slogans extolling the virtues of the "new economy," "the information highway," "total quality," "empowerment," "total quality management," "quality circles," "downsizing," "restructuring," and "delayering." Traditional bromides such as "seniority," "job security," "company loyalty," "benefits," and "pensions" are rapidly fading from memory. But rhetoric is one thing, reality another.

The effect has been twofold: The logic of decentralization has replaced centrality as the key organizational principle in the modern workplace. The era of paternalistic management-subservient worker relations is drawing to an end. So too is the notion of lifelong employment and corporate loyalty, thanks to the troika of downsizing, restructuring, and delayering. A one-size-fits-all managerial mentality may have once prevailed, according to Peter Drucker in his *Management Challenges for the 21st Century* (*Harper Business*, 1999). Contemporary management styles now need to be flexible, reflect the specific task to be accomplished, and to capitalize (rather than manage) on change as an opportunity rather than as a problem. Reliable suppliers and stable markets are virtually a thing of the past. Patterned and predictable environments have given way to fluid and dynamic contexts that promise to reward creativity and risk-taking. For other workplaces, however, the situation is depressingly similar to the work environments of the last century (Ritzer, 1998). The principles and practices of a conveyor-belt mentality continue to dominate the workplace, no more so than in the fast-food industry where "McDonaldization" as process, principle, and organization (including an obsession with efficiency, predictability, calculability, and control) has confirmed the prescience of Henry Ford's quip: "You can have a Model T in any color you want, as long as its in black."

Diversifying the Workforce

In addition to the challenges of intrusive and disruptive social change, the workplace must engage with the demands of diversity, both internally and externally. Almost every workplace must now hire people from different generations, genders, and races—in part from "need," "greed," or "good deed." Workplace inclusion of people with disabilities and aboriginal peoples has further diversified the organizational mosaic, with corresponding pressure to formulate innovative ways of working together with differences. The movement of women into the labour force, as well as into the corridors of power, is but one dimension of this surging diversity (Little, 2000). Another sign of the times is the expanding presence of visible minorities. People of colour now constitute nearly 14 percent of Canada's population, with the majority concentrated in the largest urban areas. Racialized minorities are no longer content to linger by the institutional sidelines. Recognition and participation are the norm instead, within the framework of inclusiveness, even if demanding equality means getting "uppity."

The focus on diversity goes beyond a simple "celebration" of workplace differences. With diversity in place, rules for entitlement (who gets what, and why) are being revised in response to minority demands for a bigger slice of the corporate pie. Business and bureaucracies have had little choice except to rethink the delivery of goods and services to an increasingly diverse and discerning public. Attention is aimed at providing services that are culturally safe, ethnically sensitive, and community-based. Equally important is the commitment to the principles and practices of institutional inclusiveness. Central to this notion of inclusiveness is the removal of discriminatory barriers at odds with equality of recruitment, retention, promotion, and reward. Of course, talk of more inclusive workplaces is one thing, action quite another, especially as resentment mounts over measures to improve minority access, representation, and treatment (Loney, 1998).

As well-intentioned as these initiatives might be, moves to engage diversity pose a challenge to existing structures and vested interests. Women and minorities want to be defined as productive and vital members of the workforce. They are anxious to be taken seriously for what they *do*, rather than for what they are or how they look. Yet the process of transforming workplace structures along minority and gender lines is fraught with ambiguity, tension, and hostility. A diversified workforce sounds good in theory; after all, the creative energies (synergies) and connections of workers with varied backgrounds should never be underestimated (Wang, 2003). But differences are just as likely to divide and frustrate as they are to empower and enrich, resulting in conflict, loss of commitment, absenteeism, and higher employee turnover. Entrenched interests have not taken kindly to proposals for institutional reform. The end result is barely concealed anger in the workplace. The escalating spate of violence in the workplace may be attributable to "worker rage" over changes they cannot control (Girardet, 1999). To no one's surprise, there are no easy solutions in sight. Many companies balk at implementing the concept of "inclusiveness" except when they are backed into a corner, preferring to do just enough to stay one step ahead of the law. Still, the demand for engaging with diversity is no longer a luxury or an option. In a diversifying Canada and the global marketplace, a commitment to diversity may prove a necessity whose time has come.

Workplace Inequalities

Inequities continue to pervade the workplace. Rhetoric about worker empowerment notwithstanding, the lines of command and control remain firmly entrenched, except, perhaps, for those dot-com companies that are bucking the corporate way. Record revenues and profits have not diminished an enthusiasm for downsizing: Canada's major banks may be earning profits by the billions, but employees continue to be slashed from the payroll to sustain corporate profitability. "Tier-ism" is rampant: In the current lean and mean business climate, companies will do anything to retain valued staff; by contrast, those with undervalued skills will be bounced around with relative impunity. Income levels suffer: Annual average earnings for Canadians may be $31 757 (full time + part time) in the year 2000. But while 447 000 earn $100 000 per year, up 70 percent since 1991, with the annual income for the top 1 percent averaging $469 656 in 2000, 6.6 million earn less than $20 000, a figure largely unchanged since 1981. While the annual income for the top 10 percent of working Canadians stood at $185 070, up 14.6 percent since 1990, the annual income for the bottom 10 percent was $10 341, up 0.8 percent since 1990. Can these disparities be justified or condoned, or are Canadians settling into a consumerist "soma" where a person's worth and the meaning of life is judged by his or her wealth (Willis and

MacDonald, 2003)? The mantra of economic rationalism—"greed is good," "market rules," and "competition cures everything"—provides an all-embracing ideology that justifies any bottom-line mentality, however disruptive or destructive. Paradoxically, companies that downsize rarely perform more productively. Just the opposite: Indiscriminate downsizing may induce absenteeism, cynicism, creative blockage, demoralization, passive resistance, open sabotage, and risk aversion (Robertson, 1997).

Gendered inequities in the workplace remain a problem. Yes, women are making strides in climbing the corporate ladder. They hold 14 percent of corporate positions in 2002, up from 12 percent in 1999, according to an exhaustive study by FP500 Corporate Ratings, but the numbers still remain small compared to men who hold most of the top jobs with the highest pay (Perry, 2003; Kuitenbrouwer, 2003). Working women as a rule tend to earn less than men, regardless of the type of employment, although differences largely disappear for female workers who are single, university-educated, and childless. For women of colour, the situation is even more grim (Dwyer, 2000). Rather than bumping into a concrete ceiling when scaling the corporate ladder, many remain mired in the "sticky floor" of the workplace, often dealing with sweatshop conditions, low-paying jobs, unpaid overtime, and sexual harassment (Malneaux, 1999). To be sure, corporate executives are proclaiming changes in the rules that govern the workplace behaviour of women and men, according to Shere Hite in her book *Sex and Business*, but such announcements may pay politically correct lip service rather than reflect a genuine commitment to inclusiveness (Flynn, 2000). A ten-year study of women's advancement in business by the *Harvard Business Review* (*The Globe and Mail*, 12 February, 2000) concluded accordingly: "Most workplaces are created by men and for men, and are based on male experiences, with the result that workplace structures and cultures rarely accommodate women's value systems, styles of interacting, or complexities in their lives."

Rethinking Working

The centrality of work to the human condition cannot be denied. Historically, people's lives and identities revolved around work and their relationship to workplaces. However, human labour is gradually being redefined or discarded because of computer-mediated automation and corporate reorganization (Rifkin, 1995). As Michael Dunkerley writes in his book, *The Jobless Economy*, "People are now the most expensive optional component of the production process.... People are now targeted for replacement as soon as the relevant technology is developed to replace them." (Gwyn, 1996, F3). Much of the uncertainty can be attributed to rule changes that formerly governed "how work was done around here." Work is rapidly disappearing in certain quarters, as automation kicks in and corporations kick out. Robots are appearing on more assembly lines, elbowing out old-fashioned workers in an attempt to reduce costs and stay competitive in global markets (Stinson, 2000). Changes are also evident in the nature of work. Lean production is based on three principles: elimination of waste associated with older mass production techniques; introduction of new forms of workplace organization and labour discipline such as outsourcing of work to cheaper sites; and the casualization of workers deemed less necessary to production (Sears, 2003). The prospect of job permanence is vanishing because of restructuring, managerial delayering, and workforce downsizing. The days of lifetime job security are numbered. Both legally and psychologically, the employment contract that linked job security with employee performance is going the way of the dodo bird.

Individuals and corporations alike are continually shopping around for the best deal, resulting in turnstile operations where team composition varies from year to year (Capon, 1999). The ideals of loyalty and commitment are showing their age: Once cherished as a mark of virtue, corporate loyalty is now likely to be caricatured as a sign of weakness, lack of ambition, or a stalled career.

For those with skills and connections, work is not necessarily a penalty for pay as much as an opportunity for empowerment (Chiose, 1997). Highly skilled workers are increasingly looking for three preconditions in securing a relationship with their employers: education (opportunities for growth and skill enhancement); rewards (work that is interesting and challenging); and freedom (to excel, participate in success, and exercise a high degree of self-reliance) (Bricker and Greenspon, 2001). For others, however, work will remain a dreary cycle of dead-end jobs, from fast-food marts to white-collar factories (for example, telephone operators who handle customer calls), with few rewards and fewer opportunities (Clement, 1997). Access to adequately waged jobs is further jeopardized by a combination of people-displacing technologies and a globalizing economy with its outsourcing to lower-paid offshore workers (Lerner, 1997). The net result is a bifurcated workforce: Some have so much work that their personal and family lives suffer because of overtime; others have so little work that they experience a kind of "Monday to Friday dying." Even the public sector, once the employer of last resort, is increasingly adopting a downsizing mentality. Instead of a well-paid job for life as was once the case, public servants are exposed to slash-and-burn management whose bottom-line mantra is efficiency and zero deficits. Career patterns may entail a combination of contract work for a variety of companies, interspersed with periods of unemployment or underemployment. Such a mean and lean mentality is wreaking havoc with career plans.

A World Without Work?

The logical result of rethinking working is to envision a world without work. Jobs may become an endangered species with the onset of a new, information economy. Computers may be creating more jobs than they absorbed, but this technology is undermining the security of unskilled workers in repetitive jobs (Little, 1997). The forces of automation and digital technology have also expanded the volume of work done by robots and machines— neither of which require costly dental plans or inflict labour disputes. Admittedly, not all jobs will disappear because of the new economy. A knowledge-based economy will produce jobs for scientists, engineers, software analysts, and biotechnology researchers (Rifkin, 1995). Those in the caring sector (from teachers to caregivers for the elderly) should prosper. But there is little hope for those on the margins. For them, part-time and temporary jobs will be the rule, despite a culture that dismisses casual or part-time labourers as dilettantes and failures (Rajagopal, 2002). No amount of retooling or upgrading will help the millions who are discarded because of planned obsolescence, especially if there is no meaningful work out there. Blue-collar workers may become obsolete in a workerless world, with massive unemployment as computer-guided machines displace most workers from the production process. The gradual decline of smokestack industries is no less a problem as profit-hungry companies seek offshore locations to reduce production costs.

The consequences of a world without work are both fascinating yet dismaying. Those employees clever enough to seize the opportunity will prosper at the expense of the less fortunate, in the process rupturing the sense of community at the core of a sustainable society (Stewart, 1997). A large reservoir of underemployed (or never-employed) will intensify the gap between rich (skilled) and poor (unskilled). Young Canadians have been hit especially hard by this rupture, with unemployment rates for Canadians under age 25 at twice the national rate, even without taking into account dropouts (those who have stopped looking and are no longer counted), part-timers, and school-returners. A recipe for social disaster looms as well: The disenfranchised may see few options except crime and violence, for no other reason than having nothing to lose when nothing is at stake (Keegan, 1996). Yet there is little consensus in dealing with the thousands of workers who have been cut adrift from the rhythms of the world, unsure of how to make their contribution in a society that defines personal value by work.

Are we at the end of work, or of particular types of jobs? The rules of the new economy have altered the nature of work, how work is organized, and how wealth is generated by workers. A globally-based, knowledge-driven economy cannot possibly provide work for everyone. By the same token, the resiliency of a free-enterprise system should never be underestimated. The ongoing creation of new jobs at record levels attests to that. In other words, the demise of work is greatly exaggerated. Each new technological advance has the potential to create new products, redefine workplace routines, invent new needs, and alter existing employment patterns. The introduction of a computer-driven, knowledge-based technology is not the end of work so much as the end of work as we know it. And for many, this transformation cannot come too soon.

HUMANIZING THE WORKPLACE

A globalizing free market revolution has exerted bewildering pressure on workplaces. The combination of intense global competition with automation and technological innovations are proving both dismaying and disruptive. Manufacturing jobs are disappearing as one way of squeezing labour costs. Disappearing too are white-collar jobs, often being replaced by highly skilled professionals employing state-of-the-art computer technology and just-in-time support personnel. A rethinking of management–labour relations is taking place in the knowledge economy. A restructuring of the workplace has flattened down the organizational pyramid, with layers of management pared away to encourage more horizontal forms of decision-making and power-sharing. The era of paternalistic management–worker relations is waning. Even the distinction between management and labour is increasingly fuzzy as more humane workplace models challenge conveyor-belt philosophies. Not surprisingly, the prospect of a more inclusive and democratic workplace is showing signs of modest improvement under equity directives. Yet appearances may be deceiving because of the "greed" and "grubbiness" that informs the workplace, sometimes discreetly, other times openly.

The Old (Fordist) Workplace

For most of the 20th century, mass production was the dominant organizational framework, influencing both corporate strategy and the design of jobs. Central to the principle of mass production was a commitment to maintaining stocks of inventory as security against possible disruptions to production (Perry et al., 1995). A mode of production named after the practices that Henry Ford introduced to car manufacturing, Fordism focused on mobilizing masses of labour into huge factories to produce large batches of standardized goods for mass consumption (Holly, 1996). Fordist means of production dovetailed with Taylorist principles of scientific management, namely, mass production, standardized products, large inventories, strict division of labour, labour deskilling, vertical integration, and global firms. Taylorism (named after Frederick Taylor) sought to make complex organizations more efficient and productive by applying the principles of rationality for controlling the workforce. The drive for efficiency by controlling costs transformed the workplace into a glorified machine with mechanistic precision and control. The following procedures were deemed critical in maximizing workplace production:

1   A simple division of labour, best summarized in the aphorism, "Managers think and command; workers do and obey."

2   The use of carefully calibrated methods to determine the most efficient work routine. Through precise measurement and reliance on time-and-motion studies, an optimum level of performance could be devised.

3   The division of the production process into its smallest constituent units for assignment to trained workers. Train the best person for each particular job and no other.

4   Encourage productivity by increasing monetary rewards as the central incentive for hard work.

5   The elimination of the human element by establishing work routines (i.e., uncertainty, risk, or choice) in the production while improving control over the entire process.

The old (Taylorist/Fordist) workplace environment sought to regulate and control both the internal and external environment by eliminating uncertainties from all facets of production or distribution. Fordist models were driven by the principle of an integrated assembly line, rationalization of production and labour, product standardization, economies of scale, and principles of scientific management (Perry et al., 1995). The workplace was rigidly stratified and regimented, with king-bee managers on top and worker-drones compartmentalized into cubicles or conveyor belts who produced something in exchange for rewards and promotion. The workplace could also be described as autocratic, with routines organized around the bureaucratic principles of everything in its place and in a proper sequence. Work skills relied heavily on the physical strength or manual dexterity normally associated with smokestack industries. The mind, for all intents and purposes, could be parked at the factory gate. Workers were seen as cogs in the machine of industry because of a specialized division of labour. It was assumed that workers were motivated primarily by extrinsic rewards (money) rather than job satisfaction. Work itself was seen as a full-time, lifetime activity. Company loyalty and commitment to corporate goals over the long haul (seniority) secured the secret to career success.

In short, the traditional workplace was authoritarian by nature. Most workers exerted little control over the production process; the work itself was often alienating or exploitative, if not openly dangerous; stress factors contributed to high rates of staff turnover and absenteeism; and mind-numbing routines could induce thoughtless complacency or open sabotage. Managerial interests took top priority at the expense of workers who were relegated to the bottom or the background. Not surprisingly, the traditional workplace has come in for its share of criticism. Labour unions and worker advocates reprimanded the workplaces as places fit for machines rather than humans. Academics have pounced on organizational workplaces as inhumane and counterproductive by exposing the logic behind the process of exploitation and control. But rather than fading away as might be expected in enlightened times, the principles of an authoritarian workplace—with its notions of imperious managers, worker-drones, and robotic routines—continue to define fast-food industries.

CASE 10-1 | Conveyor-Belt Burgers

Any trained monkey could do the job.
—Reiter, 1992: 167

Talk of workplace revolution, notwithstanding, the fast-food industry continues to rely on a conveyor-belt mentality in dealing with customers and employees (Ritzer, 1993). This portrayal of work experiences at a Toronto-based Burger King restaurant demonstrates how the preoccupation with standardization applies not only to food preparation but to customer relations and workplace dynamics. The fact that everyone is reduced to a cog in the fast-food machine confirms the tenacity of Taylorism as a principle of organization and process.

The principles of scientific management inform the fast-food industry in Canada and the United States. Central to this philosophy is a commitment to regulate the workplace by dehumanizing both process and output. Rigid operational procedures and standardization are adopted, not to improve food quality but to eliminate the uncertainty—the human element—from the production process. Or, as one of the original McDonald brothers once said about his golden arches: "If we gave people a choice, there would be chaos" (Love, 1995: 15). Success is defined by the principles of quality (the ideal of standardization and predictability in the preparation of food), service (speed in the delivery of food to each customer), and cleanliness (associated with "order" and consumer "appeal" rather than healthfulness). Each outlet combines unskilled machine operators and auxiliary staff with sophisticated technology to produce a highly polished product through painstaking attention to design

and planning (Reiter, 1992: 75). To the extent that these goals are achieved, each fast-food outlet conforms with the ideals of scientific management. Many of the examples below are taken from Ester Reiter's (1992/1996) book on a Burger King franchise in Toronto, *Making Fast Food: From the Frying Pan into the Fryer*.

The operations of a Burger King franchise are regulated down to the most minute detail. Pots and pans, as well as chefs and dishwashers, have been replaced by automated routine and a crew of undifferentiated machine-tenders. With the aid of computer technology, Burger King can slot almost any crew person into any food processing function at the outlet by simply cross-training workers to conduct a number of simplified tasks. Both movements and emotions are controlled by the franchise. Those who work at counters and take customer orders are expected to display a ready smile, a cheerful yet energetic disposition, and clichéd lines in promoting the sale of meals. Kitchen workers are no less programmed in terms of appearance and lines of interaction. Jobs are divided and arranged in a way that is easy to master and measure for the sake of efficiency. Workers are treated as little better than commodities along a conveyor belt. A worker at Burger King is expected to place her or his responsibility to the franchise above family or friends. Each worker is asked to work as hard as possible, to come to work on short notice, and to put in irregular hours. The patterns of authority over workers contrasts sharply with the image of self-indulgence offered to customers.

(continued on next page)

Consider the preparation of food. All food enters the store in its final cooking stages: Hamburgers arrive as frozen precooked patties, while buns are precooked and caramelized to ensure an appealing image. French fries, chicken, and fish are precooked to ensure a standardized product. Condiments such as onions or pickles (with the exception of tomatoes) are presliced or preshredded. The instore preparation of these foods is essentially that of machine-tending—the incorporation of assembly-line technology in the food service industry. For example, hamburgers are placed on a conveyor belt that transports the frozen meat patties through a gas broiler in a space of 94 seconds. A worker at the other end of the broiler picks up the cooked patty with tongs and transfers it to the bottom half of the bun. The ungarnished hamburger is then placed in a steamer where it can remain for up to 10 minutes before being discarded. Workers at the burger board "assemble" the burger by adding the condiments (cheese slices, pickles, onions, mayonnaise, lettuce, tomatoes, ketchup, and mustard). Pickle slices are spread evenly over the meat or cheese (no overlapping is allowed). Ketchup is applied by spreading it in a spiral circular motion over the pickles. Mayonnaise is applied to the top of the bun in a single stroke, while three-quarters of an ounce of shredded lettuce is sprinkled over the mayonnaise. Two slices of tomato (three is permissible, but only with management's permission) are then put on top of the lettuce. The assembly process itself should take no longer than 23 seconds for a Whopper. The finished burger is placed in a box or wrapper, reheated in a microwave for 14 seconds, and then placed in a chute.

The fast-food industry employs work processes and labour-management relations that reduce labour and work to its simplest components. The principle of formal rationality strikes at the core of this process and relationship (Ritzer, 1993). Rationality is characterized by a commitment to efficiency, predictability, and calculability, the substitution of non-human technology for human labour, and control over uncertainty. Applied to fast food, there is little question that the operation is predictable (consistent when it comes to taste, appearance, and speed of delivery) and calculable, since quantity is emphasized over quality (the bottom line is not in the taste of the food but in the number of customers processed, the speed with which they are processed, and the profits produced); that workers are expected to act in robot-like fashion (people are trained to work in an automatic, unthinking way whether preparing food or serving customers); and that control over the product is secured by enslaving the workforce. Customers are thus shielded from the exploitative work situation that confronts Burger King workers. To the extent that customers only see the benign image of service and smiles, this gap between illusion and reality may prove to be the biggest whopper of them all.

Case Study Questions

1   How does work and working in a burger outlet reflect and reinforce the principles of scientific management endorsed by Fordist/Taylorist workplaces?

2   What do we mean by the principle of rationality? How does it apply to fast food outlets?

The New (Post-Fordist) Workplace: People As Resources

The certitudes of the old work environment no longer dominate in a world of chance and uncertainty. Post-Fordist models of production have shifted to production processes that incorporate more flexible means of wealth creation as applied to product types. Reforms include delivery of parts as needed; availability of disposable labour; reliance on outsourcing (contracting out); small batch production to meet demand; and elimination of any operations (such as storage) that do not directly contribute to corporate value (Holly, 1996). Reliable suppliers and predictable markets are largely a thing of the past. Instead of pattern and predictions, fluid and competitive environments prevail that seldom lend themselves to regulation or control but entail risk-taking. New ways of organizing work are characteristic of the post-Fordist workplace, including reduced tiers of management, greater worker discretion, just-in-time production, and new approaches to industrial relations (Perry et al., 1995). Workplaces are no longer characterized by a rigid pecking order, with the lowly worker at the bottom and a maze of management on top. Appearing instead is a flattened hierarchy that invites decentralized and participatory decision-making. Innovative work practices and flexible job design are seen as bolstering productivity while fostering greater employee loyalty, although a study by Statistics Canada suggests mixed results because of these changes (Canadian Press, 2003).

The creation of wealth is now grounded on post-industrial employment patterns rooted in knowledge and services rather than in manufacturing (Castells, 1993). While the old work is organized around mass labour, the new work is advanced by knowledge elites, resulting in a two-tier system of labour: On the one hand are the knowledge workers, with high-paying, relatively secure jobs who are expected to serve as catalysts in generating wealth; on the other hand, are the poorly paid and underemployed, whose jobs have been de-skilled by automation. Equally noticeable is the disappearance of a large, permanent workforce. Companies are looking for ways to prune costs by shedding those layers of "fat" that do not actively contribute to the bottom line. CEOs prefer a workforce that can meet fluctuations in the business cycle: Just-in-time labourers can be hired quickly during business upturns and dismissed promptly when profits shrink (Lerner, 1997). The concept of working is also undergoing radical change. Job enrichment and enlargement replace the notion of simplification and excessive specialization. Workplaces are seen as constellations of competencies rather than a hierarchy around layers of management (Schellhardt, 1997). Teamwork and reliance on outside expertise are increasingly commonplace and widely touted. The shift from lifetime employment and career aspirations to just-in-time employment (part-time) puts the onus on personal "reskilling" and lifetime learning. Even the concept of a work site is losing its sense of physical locale. Corporate offices are being replaced by virtual offices/virtual corporations that exist only in name and modem address, in effect releasing contemporary work sites from the constraints of time or space (Arnault, 1995).

A human resources perspective challenges the Fordist/Taylorist assumptions about workers. Metaphorically, the employment contract has shifted from that of a conveyor belt to a quality circle involving a holistic and democratic environment of active and concerned participants. Instead of defining workers as purely economic animals to be pushed or prodded at the convenience of management, they are seen as whole persons who crave psychological satisfaction and creative outlets. Under human resources approaches, human intellect replaces warehouse inventory as a source of wealth, with workers expected to assume responsibility and control over the production process, rather than park their brains at home. In the past, workers may have been singled out for praise if they followed guidelines, avoided risks, minimized mistakes, justified action (or inaction) according to the book, and slavishly carried out what was expected of them. But the shift from command and control to employee empowerment has rendered these virtues increasingly obsolete and secondary. Instead of clockwork obedience, Marti Symes (1994) warns, employers now want workers who are not threatened by change or diversity, but thrive on risk-taking and multi-tasking.

To be sure, a distinction between Fordist and post-Fordist models invoke an opposition between ideal types. Or as Holly (1996) reminds us, a dualistic framework between Fordism and post-Fordism always distorts by oversimplifying; nevertheless, such a distinction provides a basis for analyzing differences and similarities. How then does the new (postmodern) workplace compare with the old (modern) workplace? Reality suggests that modern work is riddled with ambiguity, since it combines aspects of Fordism and post-Fordism. The new work is superimposed on the old without dislodging the latter. Since neither model is powerful enough to displace the other, the workplace may reflect an oppositional site involving competitive struggles between the new and the old. Contradictions also pervade the workplace: It is ostensibly more democratic and inclusive yet remains as autocratic as in the past because of its competitive pressures. Emphasis is directed at being more inclusive, flexible (less rigid, more participatory and discretionary), and worker-friendly (less harassment), yet the primacy of profit and productivity remain uncontested. Employees are touted as a company's greatest asset, but bottom-line calculations routinely compromise this commitment. Loyalty is disposable, since bottom line considerations are not averse to slashing these valued "assets" to cut costs and bolster profits. The introduction of modern technology is no less ambivalent. Labour-saving devices may reduce much of the drudgery associated with traditional tasks. Finally, appeals to the virtues of empowerment, partnership, participatory management, and quality circles may be interpreted as window-dressing. Illusions of meaningful involvement are fostered without actually relinquishing any of the levers of power. Substantial decisions regarding relocation or hiring remain firmly in the grasp of management. The irony is inescapable: That thousands of workers are losing their jobs in the midst of a human resources revolution makes references to worker empowerment an especially cruel hoax.

THE POLITICS OF WORKPLACE CHANGE: TOWARDS INCLUSIVENESS

Workplaces are under pressure to change. Younger workers are demanding that workplaces allow a balancing of careers with family and personal lives—and expect these demands to be met (Valpy and Anderssen, 2003). Yet facilitating reforms and achieving goals may prove difficult to achieve, given the magnitude of the challenges in transforming workplace dynamics and institutional design. There is growing awareness that things don't work like they used to. Environments are seldom controlled, individuals cannot be pre-progammed in a predictable way, and ground rules cannot be formulated in a way that will please all parties concerned. Theories of workplace change are known to operate on the 30–50–20 principle (Laab, 1996): 30 percent of workers will willingly accept imposed changes, 50 percent will resist initially but can be converted to the cause with persuasion or penalties, and 20 percent will resolutely oppose any change, and nothing can dissuade them. Resistance to change is both personal and structural. The most common of these obstacles are mistaken notions about workplaces themselves; namely, the pervasiveness of bureaucracy; the role of organizational culture and subcultural systems; questionable insights into human "nature"; and naiveté about the process of planned change. But pressures to change are relentless, and corporations that refuse to bend will find that they may break under the pressure.

Towards an Inclusive Workplace

It is one thing to contemplate the concept of workplace change. It is another thing to put these principles into practice in a way that makes an appreciable difference. Perils and pitfalls await those who underestimate the complexity and uncertainties associated with planned change. Nowhere is this more true than in creating a workforce that is reflective of Canada; a workplace that treats all employees equitably; and a service that is responsive to the needs and concerns of the local community. Historically, the workplace tended to marginalize disadvantaged groups such as women, visible minorities, aboriginal peoples, and people with disabilities. But the historically disadvantaged are demanding full and equal participation through removal of discriminatory barriers and creation of more inclusive workplaces.

Schooling for the Inclusive Workplace

What is an inclusive workplace? According to the authors of a critically informed yet hopeful book entitled, *Removing the Margins* by Dei et al. (2000), an inclusive workplace such as education revolves around creative ways to meet the unique needs of minority teachers, students, and families. The authors argue that an inclusive schooling is informed by programs and practices that allow each student to identify and connect with the school's social, cultural, and organizational environment. This puts the onus firstly on removing those barriers that contribute to educational inequality and exclusion, secondly on the introduction of alternative solutions that improve access (equality of opportunity) and equity (equality of outcomes), and thirdly, on instilling appropriate skills for living together with differences in a diverse, changing, and global world. The challenge lies in transforming schools from sites of control to sites of social transformation, in part by producing knowledge for social action, in part by ensuring minority contributions are not devalued or ignored, and in part by eliminating artificial boundaries between schools and community.

The concept of an inclusive workplace entails a process by which diversity is incorporated at the level of structure, function, and process but without undermining either profitability or cohesiveness in the process. Five components are critical in specifying the parameters of an inclusive workplace: (1) representation; (2) institutional rules and operations; (3) workplace climate; (4) service delivery; and (5) community relations. First, the workforce should be representative; that is, the composition and distribution of its workers should be relatively proportional to that of the regional labour force, taking into account both social and cultural factors as extenuating circumstances. Such numerical representation applies not only to entry-level jobs, but to all levels of management, access to training, and entitlement to rewards. Second, institutional rules and operations cannot deny or exclude anyone from the process of job recruitment, selection, training, and promotion. This commitment to root out discriminatory barriers, both systemic and personal, demands careful scrutiny of company policy and procedures. Third, the institution must foster a working climate conducive to the health and productivity of all workers. At minimum, such a climate cannot tolerate harassment of any form; at best, differences are accepted as normal and desirable to effective functioning and creative growth. Fourth, an inclusive institution ensures that delivery of its services is community-based and culturally sensitive. Such a commitment requires both a varied workforce and a sense of partnership with the community at large. Fifth and finally, workplaces do not operate in a social or political vacuum. They are part of a community and cannot hope to remain outside of it in terms of accountability and responsibility if success is anticipated. Institutions must establish meaningful relations with all community members to ensure productive lines of communication and some degree of community involvement in the decision-making process.

Barriers to Inclusiveness

An array of personal and social barriers precludes the process of workplace change. Debate in this field is polarized by those who advocate change without much thought to the costs and difficulties, versus those who are resolutely opposed and resist change at all costs. Such divergences are to be expected: implementing institutional change is not like installing a new computer system. Institutions are complex, often baffling landscapes of domination and control as well as of resistance and rebellion. Conservatives and progressives are locked in a struggle for power and privilege. Conventional views remain firmly entrenched as vested interests balk at discarding the tried and true. Newer visions are compelling, yet many lack the singularity of purpose or resources to scuttle traditional paradigms. The interplay of these juxtapositions can be disruptive or disorienting, as workplaces become reconstituted into a "contested site" involving competing world views and opposing agendas.

Numerous barriers exist that interfere with the process of directed institutional change. Stumbling blocks include people, hierarchy, bureaucracy, corporate culture, and occupational subcultures. People themselves are a prime obstruction. Workers are likely to resist any appeal to move over and make space without an understanding of what is going on, why, and how changes will affect them. This should come as no surprise, as few individuals are inclined to relinquish power or privilege without a struggle. Consider the resentment to diversifying the workforce by means of employment equity initiatives (Editorial, *National Post*, 29 May, 2003). The dimension of hierarchy will also inhibit inclusive adjustments. Those in higher echelons may be highly supportive of institutional change for a variety of reasons, ranging from genuine concern to economic expediency, with an eye towards public relations in between. Yet publicly articulated positions in defence of internal reform may be long-winded on platitudes but short-minded on practice or implementation. Middle and lower management may be less enthusiastic about changes, preferring to cling to traditional authority patterns for fear of rocking the boat through institutional adjustments. Corporate cultures may not be conducive to change because of a commitment to "the way we do things around here." To be sure, many talk of changing the corporate culture toward greater inclusiveness, but talk is one thing, reality quite another, since corporate cultures tend to resist all but the most superficial of changes. Even more disruptive to an inclusive workplace are occupational subcultures. The subcultural values of front-line workers may differ from those of the higher echelons because of differences in experiences or expectations. This slippage may prove fatal to the transformation process, especially if resistance turns to outright sabotage.

Of the many impediments to institutional inclusiveness, few are as daunting as the presence of bureaucracy. The concept of bureaucracy is often associated with certain structures and formal rules within large-scale, complex organizations. Bureaucracy can also be defined as a principle of control. Organizationally, bureaucracies are imbued with an explicit commitment to command, coordinate, and control through creation of a strict division of task, a supervisory hierarchy, and attachment to rules and regulations (Morgan, 1986; Hummel, 1987). Two themes prevail: First, bureaucracies resemble machine-like instruments designed for rational goal achievement or crisp efficiency in service delivery. Bureaucratic work can be partitioned into a coordinated set of specific tasks; each task is then assigned to trained specialists who are responsible for dealing with particular cases or issues. In this sense, bureaucracies are the epitome of scientific management principles. The second feature entails a commitment to the routine, the standardized, and the predictable as the preferred way of doing things in the organization. Bureaucracies are in the business of stamping out the informal, creative, or improvisational at odds with the principles of efficiency or control. In their place are appeals to universality and professionalism, coupled with the application of uniform standards and formal procedures. Rationality and standardization are implicit in bureaucratic efforts to rearrange the environment for maximizing control and predictability (Scott, 1998). This universality simplifies the administration of a large number of individuals (both workers and customers) without getting bogged down in paralyzing detail. Such a commitment not only has a controlling effect on behaviour; it also raises the question of whether a bureaucracy can respond to the challenges of an inclusive workplace.

Community Policing: Putting Inclusiveness into Practice?

In the 1990s, Canada's police services moved toward greater inclusiveness by adopting the concept of community policing. Interest in community policing has expanded to the point where it no longer symbolizes only a promising experiment in redesigning police–community relations (Fleras, 1998; Pruegger, 2003). The principles of community policing have catapulted it to the forefront of contemporary Canadian policing, even if the rhetoric may outstrip reality. This commitment to community policing has focused on transforming the police from a technically-driven, bureaucratic, and professional crime-fighting force to a customer-inspired service that is community-responsive, culturally sensitive, problem-oriented, and "user-friendly." Such lofty ideals raise the question, what exactly is meant by community policing; is it attainable; and what barriers prevent its implementation?

Professional Crime-Busters   Canada's police at federal, provincial, and municipal levels have relied for the most part on a "professional crime-fighting" model as a blueprint for appointed duties (Walker, 1987). Acceptance of this model drew its inspiration from developments in the United States. American police reformers adopted a professional ethic as one way of circumventing widespread corruption, questionable service, and political interference within local precincts. A commitment to professionalism defined the police as a highly trained force with a shared identity and code of ethics for crime control and law enforcement. Police effectiveness was measured by way of: (a) random patrol as a deterrent to criminal activities; (b) rapid response to calls for all services; (c) arrest, conviction, and clearance rates; and (d) citizen satisfaction surveys. An "incident-driven," "complaint-reactive" approach was bolstered by administrators who sought to bureaucratize policing by linking organizational procedures with technique and the latest technology. Structurally, the police were organized into a paramilitaristic model of bureaucracy involving a top-down chain of command and control, law enforcement by the book, a compulsion with internal rules and regulations, and an explicit system of checks and balances to deter corruption, enhance control, monitor activities, and maintain surveillance. Rewards and promotions were allocated to some extent on the basis of the "big catch," in addition to loyal and long-standing service to "the force."

Certain assumptions about the community underscored a professional crime-fighting model. The police envisaged themselves as a "thin blue line" between the community and chaos; their job was to keep disorder at bay. Community involvement was kept to a minimum; citizens were expected to report crime to the police by way of the 911 system, to provide information on possible criminal activities, and to cooperate in the apprehension and conviction of lawbreakers (Tomovich and Loree, 1989). Beyond that, however, police interaction with the community was brief and to the point, idealized by the immortal words of Sergeant Friday of the TV series "Dragnet": "Nothing but the facts, ma'am." Officers are not expected to look beyond an incident to attempt to define and resolve a particular problem. Once dispatched to handle calls, the patrol officers are encouraged to return to service as quickly as possible to resume random, preventive patrol. Little attention was directed toward the needs of citizens that had become victims of crimes.

In short, community participation was dismissed as irrelevant to the social-control process. Crime control was viewed as the prerogative of a professional and distanced bureaucracy. Confronted by this indifference, the police and community drifted apart. Such a rift did not imply that all police departments embraced the perspective of "two solitudes." Not all police officers subscribed to a detached and impersonal style of policing (consider, for example, those with roots in small-town environments). Rather, conventional policing may be interpreted as a specific style that flourished at a particular time and place in the evolution of modern urban policing. This professional crime-fighting model has prevailed to the present as a cornerstone of policing. For better or worse, its values and visions continue to frame police experiences on a daily basis.

Towards Community Policing   The introduction and popularity of community policing reflects an increased disillusionment with conventional police styles, many of which are perceived as inefficient, ineffective, inappropriate, and inequitable (Rosenbaum, 1994). Critics have raised questions about the value of a "cops, courts, and corrections" approach to curbing crime, fear of crime, urban disorder, incivilities, and social decay. Police in Canada have come under pressure from different quarters to change. They are accused of losing the fight against crime because of outdated workplace styles. Complaint-reactive, incident-driven styles of policing are largely incapable of dealing with the precipitating causes of crime, of preventing crime at the source, or of fostering cooperative relations with minority communities. The remoteness of bureaucratic policing is also thought to breed passive and unresponsive communities that further depress police effectiveness. Allegations of harassment, brutality, double standards, intimidation, abuse, corruption, and racism have fuelled the fires of criticism of the police. Additional questions arise over police effectiveness and efficiency in a society that is increasingly diverse, everchanging, and more uncertain. The concept of community policing is widely endorsed as one way of warding off this potential crisis in police legitimacy and restoring public confidence.

Community policing can be broadly defined as a rethinking of the nature of police work, the relationship of police to communities they serve, and the place of police in society. As principle and practice, community policing consists of a strategy (including a set of principles, policies, and programs) by which police are engaged with community members in the joint pursuit of local crime prevention. Objectives include a framework for assisting police to help communities to help themselves by way of citizen-defined community problems (Seagrave, 1997). It envisions demilitarization (debureaucratization) of police departments—a down-shifting of authority through management rank—to enhance discretionary powers for police on the street in hopes they will go beyond arrests and will focus on analyzing problems through community cooperation. Five recurrent themes distinguish community policing from conventional policing: (1) partnership perspectives; (2) proactive/preventative policing; (3) problem-solving orientation; (4) power-sharing; and (5) pluralism (also Bayley, 1994). Community policing is about establishing a closer and meaningful partnership with the local community as part of a coherent strategy to prevent crime through proactive efforts in prob-lem solving. The community emerges as an active participant in crime prevention rather than as a passive bystander, with the potential to deal with problems before they criminalize. The police in turn are expected to shed their "crime-buster" image in exchange for proactive styles that embody a willingness to work more closely with increasingly diverse communities through establishment of liaison and communication (Shusta et al., 1995). Policing from top to bottom must become better acquainted with the multicultural community in terms of its varied needs, entitlements, demands, and expectations. A commitment to diversity also com-pels the police to view cultural differences as a resource of potential value in preventing crime.

In many ways, community policy reflects and reinforces a human resources model of work, working, and the workplace. As a principle committed to greater inclusiveness, it embraces a wholesale transformation of workplaces that goes beyond the superficial or cosmetic. The organizational structure and culture are redesigned to ensure the primacy and needs of the clients or consumers; to maximize employee satisfaction and rewards through partnership and meaningful consultation; and to secure the involvement of both the community and management in spearheading a service culture that is locally-based and culturally sensitive (Perry et al., 1995). In contrast to impersonal and bureaucratic struc-tures that routinely impose decisions without client involvement—alienating many who recoil from a process they cannot hope to influence—the human resources model seeks meaningful consultation with clients and workers that goes beyond mere rubber-stamping but engages the public in the general problem-solving process. There is a commitment to delayer unnecessary levels of management by delegating decision-making powers to work-ers, thus empowering the workforce with control of productivity over schedules, outputs, service delivery, working conditions, and shop-floor waste. Under the human resources model, operational style must change from inward-looking (law unto themselves) to an outward focus (client needs), from bureaucratic rigidity to organizational flexibility (Rawson, 1991). Citizen's demands for involvement in the design and delivery of commu-nity-based social services are addressed, while public servants become more accountable for actions by making decision-making more transparent.

Bending Granite People who occupy a similar occupation may develop distinctive ways of perceiving and responding to their social environment (Chan, 1996). They also are likely to endorse a common system of norms and values related to work. The police are no exception. They belong to a type of occupational subculture defined by the demands of the job and the constraints of public expectations (Desroches, 1998). A distinctive set of norms, values, and beliefs has evolved and become entrenched through shared experi-ences, similar training, common interests, and continual interaction.

The grounds for this police occupational subculture are not difficult to uncover. Despite equity initiatives to improve diversity, most police officers in Canada continue to be male, White, able-bodied, French- or English-speaking, and of working-class origins. This homogeneity in sex, social class, and ethnicity is reinforced by similar socialization pressures related to common training and peer group influence. The resulting solidarity is reinforced by a sense of isolation from the community ("us versus them"), by police perception of the public as ignorant and unsupportive of law enforcement activities, and by the nature of police work, which encourages a degree of caution or defensiveness. Suspicion towards those outside the profession compounds the pressures of isolation, mutual distrust, and alienation. Adding to the divisiveness is the need to appear efficient and in control at all times as part of doing police work (James and Warren, 1995). Not surprisingly, police deeply resent those segments of the community that defy police authority or violate concepts of order and stability. Police solidarity and estrangement from the community are further reinforced by the requirements of the job, including shift work and mutual support in times of crisis and danger.

The values and priorities underlying the police occupational subculture are inconsistent with those of community policing (Seagrave, 1997). These differences can be summarized by way of contrasting outlooks (Seitzinger and Sabino, 1988: 45–46):

1 Officers define police work as "man's work," in that they condone aggressiveness and a take-charge mentality as a means of conflict resolution and a path to career success (Worden, 1993).

2 Officers feel comfortable reacting to crimes, but many are uncomfortable dealing with community organizations. Crime control continues to be defined as "real" police work, and everything else as a "soft option" or "luxury" for public relations reasons (Robinson et al., 1989).

3 Officers have been trained to believe in rapid response and random patrol as key crime-fighting tools. Walking the beat, by contrast, is often perceived as a punishment, the preserve of those who can't hack real policing, those about to retire, or a sign of a "stalled" career.

4 Community police officers tend to be isolated from their peers, in some cases actively disparaged as "traitors" or "phonies" who jeopardize the lives of fellow officers by not pulling their weight (Chan, 1996).

5 The lack of an opportunity structure for community policing undermines its potential as a stepping stone for career advancement.

The lack of enthusiasm for a community policing option is openly palpable. The police openly resist those aspects of community service at odds with the traditional policing subculture. Evidence indicates that many police officers do not want to be seen as "facilitators," "resource personnel," or "peacekeepers." They see themselves as law enforcement agents who define success by their number of arrests and citations. Many resent a "social welfare" tag, preferring a "take-charge" identity that reinforces their self-perception as professional crime-busters. Not surprisingly, the focus on community, communication, and service under community policing do not coincide with popular perceptions of police as professional crime-fighters. The community is viewed not as a problem under community policing, but as a "resource" with unlimited potential for dealing with local issues. Opposing this is the occupational subculture of the police, which tends to perceive the community as irrelevant to the point of being an impediment to effective policing, except in the most passive way by providing information (Gillmor, 1996). This clash of visions makes it difficult to imagine a situation more conducive to misunderstanding and distrust.

No less inhibiting of organizational change is the pervasiveness of police bureaucracy. The police as an institution are organized around bureaucratic principles. As a bureaucratic organization with paramilitary overtones, the police are governed by a central command and control structure, with a ranked hierarchy, complex division of labour, impersonal enforcement of formal rules, carefully stipulated procedures, and the provision of a rationally based service. Police bureaucracies exist to control a large number of persons (both internally and externally) without prejudice or explicit favouritism. This control function is attained through rational control procedures, standardization, conformity through rule-following, and accountability to the organizational chain of command. Despite remarkable degrees of discretion at their disposal, police officers tend to act as functionaries by dispensing their obligations "by the book."

The principles of bureaucracy and community policing appear mutually opposed. The partnership ethos and the reciprocity inherent in community policing are strikingly at odds with an entrenched bureaucracy. Community policing emphasizes collaboration, creativity, joint problem solving, accountability to clients, and co-responsibility for crime control and order maintenance (Normandeau and Leighton, 1990). Bureaucracies, by contrast, are destined to be remote, isolated, and case-oriented. They are also bound by rules, organizational procedures, and hierarchy. One model is programmed for control and routinization, the other for cooperation and consultation. These contradictions raise a key question: How can creative problem-solving techniques flourish under workplace conditions that expect obedience and compliance while discouraging questioning, self-motivation, and innovation (Tomovich and Loree, 1989)? Can innovative, even risk-taking solutions be reconciled with a mindset based on "not rocking the boat" or "shut up, and do as you're told"? Who can be surprised that the concept of community policing may be sound in theory but has proven a tough sell to the police services (Pruegger, 2003)?

DISCUSSION QUESTIONS

1   The concepts of work, working, and workplace can be defined as a social problem. Indicate how and why.

2   A Fordist workplace is seen as dehumanizing. A post-Fordist commitment is seen as humanizing the workplace. Explain.

3   Indicate what community policing is, and why it has been so difficult to implement a more inclusive type of policing service.

4   Explain what is meant by institutional inclusiveness. What are the components of and barriers to creating an inclusive institution?

5   How do the principles of scientific management apply to the fast-food industry?

WEBLINKS

Workopolis.   **www.workopolis.com**

Canadian Centre for Occupational Health and Safety.   **www.ccohs.ca**

Inclusiveness–Canadian Centre for Social Development.   **www.ccsd.ca**

part four

The Challenge of Diversity

C anada is widely regarded as a societal enigma. The sprawling land mass in the northern half of North America has no business being in existence as a nation, at least judging by the conventional standards of history or peoplehood that are normally invoked as grounds for statehood. Yet this apparent weakness has proven a blessing in disguise. Despite overwhelming odds because of geography, demography, and history, Canadians have managed to forge a unique and cohesive society by making virtue a necessity. This enigmatic character was nicely captured by a Mexican ambassador who grandly described Canada as "a solution in search of a problem." The sincerity of such flattery notwithstanding, this quip exposes what many regard as self-evident: Canada is indeed a progressive and prosperous society, with little to complain about when compared to the suffering and scarcity found in other parts of the world.

Accolades abound: Some marvel at Canada's ability to solve the problem of living next to the world's foremost economic and cultural colossus without abdicating its sovereignty or sense of identity. Others compliment Canada for its social programs, from health care to education, the envy of most of the world, despite cutbacks that have left many Canadians fuming. Still others, congratulate Canada on coping with the potentially divisive demands of aboriginal peoples, the Quebecois, and multicultural minorities. A willingness to proactively engage with diversity is widely praised as a beacon of enlightenment in a world that too often is consumed by xenophobia, ethnic cleansing, and genocide. Canada's diversity agenda is encrypted in a series of firsts: Canada was the first country to introduce a non-discriminatory Citizenship Act in 1947; the first to constitutionally entrench both aboriginal rights and multiculturalism in 1982; the first country ever to receive a UN medal in 1986 for its humanitarian work with international refugees; and the first and only country to formally endorse official multiculturalism with passage of the 1988 Multiculturalism Act. Not surprisingly, a UN Developmental agency declared Canada the best country in the world to live in each year between 1994 and 2001.

Accolades notwithstanding, however, Canadians are reeling from a period of convulsive social change. Everything is changing so quickly that nothing is certain or predictable except a pervasive sense of unpredictability or uncertainty. Rules and values of established and hierarchical orders are openly challenged, if not actively resisted and transformed. Moves to engage diversity by expanding Canada's human rights package must contend with balancing the competing demands of a universal humanity and national interests with the uniqueness of cultures and individual autonomy (Kallen, 2003). Not surprisingly, what once were endorsed as universal truths and self-evident virtues are no longer accepted as morally valid. Weaknesses are reconstituted as strengths; strengths, in turn, morph into weaknesses. Many of the initiatives that seemed so promising in the 1970s and 1980s— including multiculturalism—have been overtaken by a pessimism that nothing appears to work and nobody seems to care (also Kitaro, 1997).

A sense of perspective is helpful. Compared to societies that are plagued by catastrophic ethnic conflicts and "cleansings," Canada's relentless introspection of itself borders on the almost self-indulgent. While the politics of differences may elicit violence elsewhere, including nearly 4 million slashed or starved in the Congo during the past six years, Canada's national-unity crisis is largely confined to political corridors. While mid-East tensions spin out of control because of bullets and suicide bombs, the Canadian way is touted as a peaceful alternative to the challenges of living together differently (Kymlicka, 2001). Even the challenges that confront Canadian society-building and national unity often pale in comparison with other jurisdictions. Consider, for example, the enormity of the task that awaits India with its 16 official languages and five major religions in a country where religion still counts. Or consider Indonesia with its 200 million people across 17 000 islands and the home of 300 ethnic groups and 500 languages/dialects (Gee, 1998).

Canada may be internationally acclaimed as a trailblazer in forging unity from the strands of diversity. Nevertheless, its exalted status is neither automatic nor immediately transparent. Canada itself is a social construction: There is nothing natural or normal about Canada as a sovereign society, despite myth-making machines to the contrary. Canada as a whole has never been a nation-state in the orthodox sense of a people with a shared sense of history, language, culture, and identity. Canadian society represents an artificial construct carved out of North America by decisions within European salons. Society in Canada comprises a complex and divided personality of French settlers, United Empire Loyalists, British colonists to the east and west, and aboriginal peoples in various stages of interaction with the Crown. That said, Canada is properly interpreted as a contested site, that is, a kind of battleground involving a struggle between opposing groups in constant competition over power, status, and resources. The odds of fortifying this "excuse for a country" have proven daunting in the face of formidable obstacles related to geography, demography, regionalism, history, diversity, globalization, and inequality.

Society-building (or nation-building) in this "adventure called Canada," as Governor General Vincent Massey once deftly put it, is both complex and contradictory. Canada as a society cannot be taken for granted but must be continually "willed" into existence, as this excerpt clearly demonstrates:

> … Canada is a construct of the will. It is not a creation of free market forces, not a colony of any
> dominant civilization. It exists because every day, whether we were born here or came here as

immigrants, we must believe that Canada is worth creating and reinventing and act upon that belief. And how does a modern country exist? In the minds and hearts of its people ... (Robert Lantos, acceptance speech at Ryerson Polytechnic University, *The Globe and Mail*, 30 November, 1998).

In other words, Canada has had to define itself as distinctive and distinguishable from other nation-states, often in the face of formidable odds that continue to perplex and provoke. In doing so, Canada assumes the status of a socially-constructed and contested site, that is, a diverse and complex creation undergoing constant change and adjustment in response to internal pressures and external forces.

This section explores some of the challenges associated with Canada-building in terms of national unity, identity, and integrity. Both aboriginal peoples and the Quebecois claim to be a people or nations whose politicized interests as self-determining autonomies do not necessarily conform to the society-building aspirations of Canadians at large. Multicultural minorities, both Canadian-born and foreign-born, are also proving a factor in forging unity from diversity, despite implementation of an official multiculturalism as policy and program. The challenge is twofold: from a national-interest perspective, the objective lies in making Canada safe for diversity, safe from diversity; from a minority perspective, the goal revolves around making diversity safe from Canada, safe for Canada. This section makes it clear: The challenges for living together differently are defined differently by Canada's major ethnicities, and solutions differ accordingly. Time will tell if the "Canadian Way" for engaging diversity in a deeply divided Canada will save Canada from imploding.

chapter eleven

"Indian" Problems/
Aboriginal Solutions

FRAMING THE PROBLEM

Canada may rank as one of the world's best places to live judging by UN quality-of-life measurements. Canada's resources and resourcefulness are astonishing by world standards, prompting some to playfully mock Canada as a "solution in search of a problem." The problems that confront Canadians are relatively modest compared to the deprivations and depravities experienced by others elsewhere. Ethnic conflict is not unknown in Canada, to be sure, but there is grudging admiration for Canada's moxy in exploring models for cooperative coexistence that balance our universal humanity with a commitment to personal autonomy and cultural uniqueness (Kallen, 2003). Canada's exalted status as a "lucky country" is captured by the words of Professor Xavier Arbos, a Catalan and president of the International Council for Canadian Studies: "Canadians have reasons to be proud of a country that is balanced, democratic, a country that cares, where there is less violence...." Canada may not be perfect, he concludes, but it sure looks a lot better than most.

Yes, Canada may be the least imperfect society in the world. Yet for all its abundance, Canada is in danger of splintering along ethnic fault lines. Canada is not alone in experiencing a crisis of such proportions. The forces of ethnicity (as well as language, region, or religion) pose a greater threat to national unity than the threat of invasion by outsiders.

Traditional cross-border wars, in the conventional sense of force to capture coveted territory, have been replaced by threats "from within" because of disgruntled minorities. Of the 119 conflicts around the world between 1990 and 1999, according to a Berlin-based monitoring group, 103 of them involved interethnic confrontations of a civil war nature. The "ethnicization" of conflict should come as no surprise: The search for collective touchstones of ethnic identity may be the definitive challenge to an impersonal yet increasingly fragmented world. Yet existing states seem incapable of addressing these ethnically charged nationalisms because of cultural blindspots or constitutional limitations.

National unity crises are no stranger to Canada. These crises reflect a lack of fit between existing structural arrangements and the political ambitions of Canada's "deep diversities" (Taylor, 1994). Consider the following conflicts of interest: Canadian federalism is based on a division of jurisdictions between Ottawa and the provinces; by contrast, national minorities are claiming nationhood status beyond the territorial restraints of a federal-provincial framework (Kymlicka, 2001). Official multiculturalism may be highly commended as a blueprint for those minorities who want to "fit in." This model may not apply to national minorities who are looking to "get out" of the existing political arrangement. Canada's commitment to the shared commonalities of a liberal universalism is widely admired; however, a commitment to a "pretend pluralism" may clash with those "deep diversities" that want their differences to be taken seriously and taken into account in divvying up the goods. Admittedly, there is much to defend in promulgating individual equality, and equality before the law, with no special treatment for anyone. Yet such an abstracted and formal equality may prove counterproductive when collective rights are pivotal for group survival.

The list could go on. But the point should be clear: The existing social contract with its roots in the foundational principles of a liberal democratic constitutional order may have worked in the past. Such a blueprint may no longer apply when powerful national minorities demand post-colonial models for living together differently. Canada's national unity crisis is animated by the nationalist ambitions of aboriginal peoples and the Quebecois. For aboriginal peoples, the challenge lies in establishing a new relationship based on the principle of partnership and power-sharing. Aboriginal peoples are demanding recognition as relatively autonomous political communities that are sovereign in their own right, yet sharing sovereignty over Canada, with corresponding rights to indigenous models of self-determining autonomy over land, identity, and political voice (Fleras and Maaka, 2004). For the Quebecois, the goals are comparable, with an emphasis on restructuring their relationship with Canada along the lines of sovereignty-association. Like aboriginal peoples, the Quebecois want to transform the existing political framework that historically has framed them as a province rather than as unique peoples or nations. And like aboriginal peoples, the Quebecers do not see themselves as subjects of the Crown but as sovereign self-determining peoples—a situation unacceptable to the Canadian government, which can neither accept a power that is above the constitution nor relinquish its sovereignty over territory in deference to a doctrine rejected by the UN (Johnson, 2003).

In short, both aboriginal peoples and the Quebecois define themselves as nations or peoples with inherent and collective rights to self-determining autonomy as "nations within" (Fleras and Elliott, 1991). Each is seeking a new social contract by challenging the foundational principles that govern Canada's still colonial constitutional order. Both employ the language of nationhood to advance their nationalistic claims. In neither case is the objective to destroy or bankrupt Canada but rather to remodel it along radically different lines. A new social contract is proposed that is sufficiently decentralized to accommodate deep diversities with just the right amount of coherence to prevent Canada from collapsing into warring factions. New patterns of partnership are proposed that incorporate loyalty to the "nation" without rejecting a commitment to the "state." It remains to be seen if Canada can absorb such a provocation to its integrity without capitulating into chaos. Much depends on how adroitly aboriginal solutions to the so-called "Indian problem" can stave off the crisis for living together differently.

This chapter focuses on the question of "What is meant by the 'Indian problem'? Who says what, and why?" Particular attention is directed at aboriginal responses in constructing a new relationship (social contract) with Canada as the basis for solving the Indian problem. The chapter begins by exploring the socioeconomic dimension of the Indian problem, with particular attention to the social problems that confront aboriginal communities, especially when they impact on women, youth, and urban aboriginals. Billions of dollars may have been spent to counteract the legacy of disadvantage, dispossession, and disempowerment but often to demoralizing effect—in effect, prompting questions about "why" (Neill, 2003). The challenge is further complicated by a tendency to misread the so-called "Indian Problem." To one side are those who say the Indian problem is caused by too much assimilationist pressure at the expense of aboriginal difference. To the other side are those who believe the problem stems from aboriginal refusal to assimilate, with a corresponding drift towards isolation, dependency, and underdevelopment. Solutions follow logically: On the one hand, aboriginal solutions to the Indian problem pose a challenge to the existing system in hopes of realigning the relationship; on the other hand, government problem-solving solutions continue to be couched within the framework of the existing status quo (Day and Sadik, 2002). In that more of the same poses a greater threat to national unity than the risk of taking bold initiatives, there is much to commend in thinking outside convention (Land, 2002).To the extent that Canada's Indian problem may also be interpreted as the Indians' Canada problem because of history, power, and politics, any proposed solutions can be likened to the challenge of walking up a down-escalator.

A word of caution. Excessive emphasis on the Indian problem to the exclusion of positive dimensions has the effect of "framing" aboriginal peoples as a problem people. This focus on aboriginal peoples who "are" problems, who "have" problems, or who "create" problems tends to diminish the contributions of aboriginal academics, artists, and entrepreneurs. For in the final analysis, aboriginal peoples are not a problem but peoples whose lives are complicated by forces beyond their control. More disturbing still is a tendency to foist responsibility for the Indian problem on aboriginal peoples ("blaming the victim"), while overlooking the broader colonial context—from Crown treaty violations to mismanagement of aboriginal rights—that created the Indian problem in the first place. To be sure, there is no excuse for glossing over the dire circumstances that disrupt the lives and life chances of aboriginal peoples and communities. Yet aboriginal peoples have not stood by as passive and pliant victims of colonization preferring, instead, to mobilize in solving the problems that confront their communities, both on and off the reserve. Moreover, not all aboriginal peoples have suffered or failed. Nor should definitions of success or failure be construed on narrow material grounds. As a group, however, far too many aboriginal women and men, young and old, live under deplorable conditions that evoke images of grinding developing-world poverty. Violent confrontations at Oka or Burnt Church are signs of the dysfunctionalties in the relationship between aboriginal peoples and the rest of Canada. So too is the high level of self-violence inflicted by the demoralized and dispossessed, which may represent a form of self-medication to numb the boredom and pain of badly damaged realities (MacDonald, 2002).

CANADA'S HIDDEN SHAME: THE "INDIAN PROBLEM"

Nearly four hundred years of sustained contact have left Canada's relationship with aboriginal peoples in a state of denial, disarray, and despair. The imposition of a colonialistic framework has excrted a profoundly negative effect on aboriginal peoples (Adams, 1999). As noted by the 1996 Report of the Royal Commission on Aboriginal Peoples, aboriginal peoples were ruthlessly stripped of land, culture, livelihood, and leadership with devastating impacts in terms of poverty, powerlessness, and marginality. In some cases, government policies deliberately undermined the viability of aboriginal communities in the never-ending quest to divest them of land, culture, and tribal authority. In other cases, the demise of aboriginal peoples came about through unobtrusive, yet equally powerful measures such as education and missionization. In still other cases, the often unintended effects of possibly well intentioned but ultimately misguided programs—for example, relocation has collectively traumatized aboriginal peoples (Shkilnyk, 1985). In that solving any problem depends on how it is framed, two sets of paired questions loom large: Do we have an Indian problem or a Canada problem? Are aboriginal peoples poor and powerless because of a reluctance to assimilate into the mainstream? Or does aboriginal poverty and powerlessness stem from excessive pressure to identify with a system at odds with aboriginal realities and aspirations? Responses to these questions not only underpin the dynamics and content of Canada's aboriginal policy in the past and at present, but they also explain the lack of consensus in defining the problem and proposing solutions for restructuring aboriginal peoples–Canada relations.

Canada's mistreatment of aboriginal peoples has been called a national tragedy and a shameful disgrace (UN Report, 2002). No matter how evaluated or assessed, aboriginal peoples as a group remain at the bottom of the socio-economic heap (Wotherspoon, 2003; Canadian Labour Congress, 2003). For example, only 42 percent of aboriginal persons 15 years and older were employed, with an average annual income of $15 994, according to the 2001 Census data, compared to 66 percent of non-aboriginals who were employed with an annual average income of $26 914 (*The Globe and Mail*, 17 June, 2003). With rates nearly three times the national average, unemployment is a major cause of aboriginal distress that leads directly to poor housing, illness, a sense of powerlessness, and cycles of poverty (Drost et al., 1995). The overtones of government indifference and bureaucratic expediency represent nothing less than Canada's great moral failure (Gwyn, 1998). Only aboriginal peoples have been forcibly incorporated into an alien system that systematically and systemically reduced them to the status of the dispossessed, the demoralized, and the dysfunctional. International dignitaries as diverse as Nelson Mandela and Pope John Paul II have also taken Canada to task for its neglect (Owens, 2002).

Access to land and resources remains a key problem. Like indigenous peoples around the world, Canada's aboriginal peoples have endured repeated attempts at appropriating their resources through dodgy land deals and legal hocus-pocus (Alfred, 2000; Barnsley, 2001; Russell, 2004). Predictably, then, aboriginal protest and politics generally revolve

Did You Know?

The demographic time bomb that is ticking away in many aboriginal communities continues to cause concern. The aboriginal population has been rapidly increasing since the 1960s because of the interplay of high fertility and a declining infant mortality and longer life expectancy. Life expectancies for aboriginal males is 68.9 years, up from 59.2 in 1975; for aboriginal females, the life expectancy rate is 76.3—about five years less than for Canadian women in general. On average, according to the 2001 Census, each aboriginal woman bears 2.5 children—a fertility rate that is 1.5 times that of Canadian women on the whole. The youthfulness of many aboriginal communities is no less worrying. With a median age of 24.7 years compared with 37.7 in the non-aboriginal population, nearly a third of aboriginal children are under 15 years of age compared to 19 percent in the overall population (Philp, 2003). The implications of this demographic reality are staggering in terms of exerting additional pressures on already depleted resources.

around the ownership and control of land and resources (Kulchyski, 2003). The reasons are obvious enough: Without territory, aboriginal peoples find themselves in a no-man's-land. Their right to identity and culture is compromised, as is the right to speak the language of nationhood or to claim a self-governance by way of self-determining autonomy (Maaka and Fleras 2004). Any hope of socioeconomic improvement is also derailed: Former Assembly of First Nations Chief, Matthew Coon Come (1999: 1) puts it into perspective when underscoring the material basis of aboriginal impoverishment:

> But without adequate access to lands, resources, and without the jurisdiction required to benefit meaningfully and sustainably from them, we are given no choices. No number of apologies, policies, token programs, or symbolic healing funds is going to remedy this fundamental socio-economic fact.

A powerlessness associated with landlessness is pivotal in generating aboriginal social problems. So too was policy mistreatment of aboriginal peoples as human beings whose rights are expendable and expedient. As noted by David Courchene, a former president of the Manitoba Indian Brotherhood in emphasizing the psychological effects of alienation and a sense of irrelevance:

> One hundred years of submission and servitude, of protectionism and paternalism have created psychological barriers for Indian people that are far more difficult to break down and conquer than the problems of economic and social poverty (Buckley, 1992: 24).

No less dismaying is the degree to which aboriginal individuals have internalized this powerlessness and impotence into an expression of self-hatred. The internalization of White racism and/or indifference is reflected in violent death rates, which are nearly four times the national average. Infant mortality rates are about 60 percent higher than the national average. Aboriginal peoples represent one of the most self-destructive groups in the world at present, with a suicide rate that is six times the national average for certain age-specific groups, including rates that are 36 times the national average in some aboriginal communities (Samson, 2000). Alcohol and substance abuse are widely regarded as the foremost problems on most reserves, with alcohol-related deaths accounting for up to 80 percent of the fatalities on some reserves (Buckley, 1992). Domestic abuse is so endemic within aboriginal communities, according to some observers (Drost et al., 1995), that few aboriginal children grow into adulthood without first-hand experience of interpersonal violence.

The erosion of aboriginal cultural values has compounded the difficulties of poverty. Numerous aboriginal languages are currently under threat because of the pressure of English (and French) in the schools and mainstream media. Of the 60 aboriginal languages from a century ago, eight have vanished altogether, and only four (Cree, Inuktitut, Ojibway, and Dakota) have reasonably secure survival prospects. The rest are perilously close to extinction, including six languages with fewer than ten known speakers (Philp, 2000). According to the 2001 Census, only 25 percent of aboriginal peoples could carry on a conversation in their native language, down from 29 percent in 1996. Yet language is widely regarded as a definitive and defining symbol that sustains a distinct culture and self-determining society. As well, aboriginal peoples are experiencing a massive deculturalization process. Traditional beliefs, values, and practices are losing grounds to a culture of dependency and underdevelopment (Frideres, 1998). Thus, aboriginal peoples continue to be distinctive but not necessarily Indian, in part because this distinctiveness is reflective of communities lacking power to debate and control their future (Scott, 2001: 16; Boldt, 1993).

Of course, not all of Canada's aboriginal peoples are destined to fail even when measured by mainstream standards of material wealth. Individuals exist who possess secure and satisfying prospects and exceptionally enriched lives without rejecting either culture; they are successful at straddling both cultures. Aboriginal communities are gaining access to substantial sums of money and resources because of lucrative returns from successful land claims settlements. Corporate Canada is taking notice, and many companies have understandably established joint ventures with aboriginal communities, while expanding employment and business opportunities for aboriginal people (Frideres, 1998). In addition, there are currently 20 000 aboriginal businesses, 50 financial institutions, a native trust company and a native bank, thus confirming the relationship between wealth and power (Howes, 2001). Not unexpectedly, economic development will remain at the heart of federal government initiatives to build strong First Nations communities (Robert Nault, former Minister for Indian Affairs, *Toronto Star*, 1 June, 2002). But critics argue that an economic focus masks a hidden agenda (Alfred, 2001). Not only does economic development with its promise of "saving" aboriginal peoples entail greater political and social incorporation. Further integration into Canadian society may sacrifice the spirit of aboriginality on the altar of capitalism.

Off-Reserve Aboriginals: "Urban Indians"

The relationship between on-reserve and off-reserve remains complex and confusing. Reserves were once regarded as tools of colonialism and subjugation. They served as "holding pens" that made Canada safer for settlement while procuring the conditions for the assimilation and control of aboriginal peoples. Reserves have also evolved into locales of chronic poverty and structural powerlessness. Housing is inadequate or overcrowded on many reserves, failing to meet basic standards of amenities and structure (Editorial, *National Post*, 1 November, 2003). Fewer than 50 percent of aboriginal homes have sewer or water connections, while many houses are essentially flimsy firetraps (Frideres, 1998). On certain reserves, up to 95 percent of the population subsists on welfare or unemployment benefits. Some of the luckier ones prosper, especially those in control of band councils, but the emergence of a class system on the reserves has also exacerbated the chasm between the connected and the disconnected.

There is yet another spin: Reserves are widely endorsed as sites for the promotion of aboriginal identity, self-determination, and self-government. Cities, in turn, are deemed to be disempowering ("empowerment" equals a sense of control over one's life and life chances) in both the physical and social-cultural sense. Reference to reserves as places of empowerment points to a striking ambiguity: The very isolation of these reserves fosters the "essence" of aboriginality, both physical and psychological. The fact that reserves serve as a refuge from and buffer against a hostile outside world also improves their attractiveness. Reserve communities furnish spiritual assistance and social security for aboriginal persons—despite unacceptably high levels of unemployment and substandard living conditions. Yet, paradoxically, nearly one-half of the aboriginal population prefers to live off the reserve, including 44 percent of status Indians. About one-fifth of urban aboriginals are distributed across seven major cities: Regina, Winnipeg, Calgary, Edmonton, Saskatoon, Vancouver, and Toronto (Peters, 2002). Winnipeg has the largest number of residents who identify as aboriginal; at 46 000 it might well be called Canada's largest reserve, although estimates for Toronto can range up to 60 000.

Reaction to reserve life remains mixed. For some, reserves remain the one place where aboriginal difference can be taken seriously, where traditional social and cultural patterns can find an acceptable outlet, and where demands for self-governance are rooted in a territorial base. For others, the dysfunctionalities and inequities of a largely undemocratic reserve system without checks and balances confirm the obvious: that is, the implausibility of autonomy without accountability as the solution to the social problems that beset aboriginal peoples (Flanagan, 1999). Decades of government spending on reserves has generated an "Indian industry" that benefits a few at the expense of the rank and file, according to the Centre for Aboriginal Policy Change, in large part because the 1876 Indian Act relieves band chiefs of accountability for reserve expenditures (Friscolanti, 2003). Those closest to the ruling clique receive benefits, while those who fall outside that inner circle are denied access to scarce resources such as housing and jobs (Fontaine, 2003). For still others, life off-reserve is positive and amply rewarded. There are aboriginal lawyers, teachers, nurses, and successful entrepreneurs, many of whom earn high incomes and are actively involved in city life. Many are not so fortunate, and, coping with the demands of a city are fraught with peril (Moore, 1995). Life off the reserve is beset with missed economic opportunities, abysmal living conditions and homelessness, exposure to substance abuse, discrimination and lack of cultural awareness, and repeated brushes with the law (Maidman, 1981).

Imbalances between city-living and reserve-life have prompted some aboriginal migrants to accept dual residence (Dosman, 1972). Home in winter may be the city where welfare and heated accommodation make life bearable. Summer sees an exodus back to the reserve for the company of relatives in the great outdoors. Such mobility complicates access to reserve entitlements. As far as many aboriginal people are concerned tribal membership and benefits should continue even with migration to the city. Bertha Wilson (1998) writes to this effect:

> Most aboriginal peoples living in cities strongly resist the idea that they have, by relocating, abandoned their traditional land and people. Indeed, they stress that their connection to their land

has never been more important. It is fundamental to their culture and their identity and they have to work very hard to preserve it in the alien and often inhospitable setting of the city.

The federal government, for its part, disagrees with the portability of aboriginal rights. It offers little in the way of services to off-reserve aboriginals, citing jurisdictional conflicts of interest with the provinces as a stumbling block. Services that exist may prove inadequate. Government institutions are ill-equipped (both in terms of resources or needs assessments) to provide adequate culturally-sensitive services to aboriginal clients (Maidman, 1981). A patchwork of urban services and institutions has evolved instead, in part, because of government (in)actions and, in part, because of a quest for self-sufficiency (Graham, 1999). Establishment of aboriginal-run voluntary agencies may address issues of health care, traditional healing, shelter, and criminal justice. Nevertheless, the gap between supply and demand continues to escalate. Finally, treaty settlements continue to ignore off-reserve aboriginal peoples, thus compromising their transition from reserve to urban life (Richards, 2000).

Aboriginal Women: Marginalizing the Marginal

The complexity of issues that confront aboriginal women is gaining prominence (Hammersmith, 2002; Monture-Angus, 2003). Awareness is growing that gender and race impact on the experiences and realities of aboriginal women as individuals, as mothers, and as community members in ways that reinforce their distance from both non-aboriginal women and aboriginal men (INAC, 2002). Both formal studies and personal testimonies indicate that aboriginal women rank among the most severely disadvantaged people in Canada (DIAND, 1979; Silman, 1987; also Allen, 1986 and Witt, 1984). Economically, they are worse off than non-aboriginal women and aboriginal men in terms of income levels and employment options; not surprisingly, the feminization of poverty bites deeply especially for lone aboriginal women in cities (Williams, 1997). Social hardships are numerous; they include: abusive male family members, sexual assaults and rapes, inadequate housing, squalid living conditions, unhealthy child-raising environments, and alcohol and drug abuse. Levels of violence directed against aboriginal women and children are extremely high: As explained by the Native Women's Association of Canada in a 1991 brief (Razack, 1994: 910):

> We have a disproportionately high rate of child sexual abuse and incest. We have wife battering, gang rapes, drug and alcohol abuse, and every kind of perversion imaginable has been imported into our lives.

Depression and self-hatred among aboriginal women is reflected in high levels of suicide, alcohol dependency, or neglect of children. To that volatile mixture add the pressure of derogatory stereotypes that reinforce the marginality and despondency that many aboriginal women endure (Witt, 1984; also LaRocque, 1975; 1990).

Negative images make it doubly difficult to recognize the positive contributions of aboriginal women to community life and social change. Historical and social factors work against adequate recognition. Those stripped of status because of marriage to non-aboriginal males have suffered from loss of Indian Act rights, ostracism from involvement in band life, and exclusion from housing and jobs. Not even the repeal of the offending passage (Section 12(1)(b) of the Indian Act in 1985) has eased the barriers for some women. Their status and that of their children may be reinstated in theory; in reality, resource-strapped bands have refused membership and residence for political and economic reasons. Moreover, Bill C-31 women do not have the right to pass full status to their children unless they marry a status Indian, with the result that status eventually atrophies.

Nor is there much relief in sight for the foreseeable future. Aboriginal women claim their rights are being trampled upon by male-dominated band councils that are neither responsible nor accountable, with the result that what you get depends on who you know (Fournier, 1999). Efforts by aboriginal women for fundamental change or removal of blatant sexism have met with resistance on the grounds that tampering with the status quo could jeopardize existing protections and entitlements. And while the Charter of Rights provides a step in the right direction, its focus on equality does not address the experiences and realities of women in aboriginal communities (Hammersmith, 2002). Even moves toward aboriginal self-governance are met with fear, apprehension, and confusion (Fontaine, 2002). The pursuit of self government may promise a renewal, but it also runs the risk of reinforcing colonially imposed structures of governance.

Aboriginal Youth: Youth in Crisis

The images are still searingly clear: Sheshatshiu, an Inuit community of 1200 in central Labrador attracted national attention when Innu leaders removed 50 Innu children for their own safety. Canadians were stunned by video images of Innu youth who openly inhaled toxic gas fumes from plastic bags while their parents were nowhere in sight. Many complained of boredom; others sought escape from abusive or absent parents; still others didn't know why they did it, or care. The magnitude of the problem is reflected in the countless numbers of young people who are locked into patterns of substance and solvent abuse, prostitution and petty crime, and incarceration in correctional facilities. To the dismay of aboriginal peoples, Canada's governments have reacted slowly to this waste of human lives, appearing to be more concerned about preserving its international reputation rather than solving the problem.

Did You Know?

Aboriginal youth in Canada are opting for suicide at rates that are unprecedented at any time or place in recorded history (*Windspeaker,* Special Issue, January, 2001). In Davis Inlet, Labrador, the rate of suicide among Innu is the equivalent of 178 per 100 000 population—based on the figure of eight suicides since 1990 in a community of 600 individuals—as compared to the overall Canadian rate of 14 per 100 000. This situation has prompted a British group, Survival, to label the situation as "Canada's Tibet" (Barnsley, 2001). Eight young women killed themselves in the small northern Ontario community of Pikangikum during the year 2000, giving this small community a rate of 470 deaths per 100 000. Other remote communities are also plagued by obscenely high rates of suicides that speak volumes about the power of poverty and powerlessness. Even communities not burdened by remoteness are suffering: for example, the Siksika First Nations near Calgary experienced eight deaths and 247 attempted suicides in 2000.

The causes of aboriginal youth suicide are widely debated. Sociologists from Emile Durkheim onward point to changing social conditions as root causes. Individuals in societies who experience anomie (a state in which normal values are confused, unclear, or absent because of sudden and disruptive change) become dysfunctional and prone to suicide (Barnsley, 2001)). Social context is important. Young people, in general, are inclined toward suicide because many lack a positive identity, role models, or a clear direction to assist them in meeting the challenges of adult life. The lack of opportunity on aboriginal reserves, in addition to the despair and boredom that many confront, are also conducive to suicide. At the heart of this social problem, however, is the pervasive and persistent sense of powerlessness and loss of identity (Barnsley, 2001). Aboriginal youth are suffering from a profound sense of not knowing who they are or what they want to be. Many are trapped between two cultures, rejected by one but not fully accepted in the other, yet having to cope with both while in a state of suspended animation. Sadly, then, this self-inflicted carnage will continue until the issues of powerlessness and poverty are resolved in a way that connects aboriginal youth with the wisdom of their elders and the spirituality of the past.

FROM PROBLEMS TO PEOPLES

Canada as a multicultural society is a bit of a paradox. On the one hand, Canada is widely touted as a beacon of enlightenment for engaging aboriginality. Canada remains the first and only country in the world to have constitutionally entrenched a commitment to aboriginal and treaty rights, with passage of the Constitution Act in 1982, even if the specifics of that enshrinement have yet to be articulated or implemented. On the other hand, Canada is criticized for failing to match ideals with reality. This paradox rests on a widening disjuncture between Canada's lofty international reputation for engaging aboriginality versus its widely publicized mistreatment of aboriginal peoples. Or as critics are prone to ask:

> People are beginning to ask aloud how it is that this remarkable country called Canada could, year in and year out, be chosen the No. 1 nation in the world for its quality of life. And yet this same country could hold a massive, scattered aboriginal population that live in Third World conditions (Roy MacGregor, *National Post*, 8 February, 2001).

Another paradox is captured by public reaction to the government's aboriginal agenda. To one side of the critical divide is unstinting praise for the "Canadian way": in advancing aboriginal rights. From a people pushed to the brink of cultural and legal extinction because of colonial greed and arrogance, aboriginal peoples now constitute increasingly powerful social actors at the cutting edge of political change. They are no longer automatically dismissed as inferior or irrelevant to the Canadian society-building project. To the contrary, aboriginal peoples are seen as having a well-established collective and inherent claim to rights over land, identity, and political voice—albeit within the framework of Canada. Positive indicators abound: Escalating rates of aboriginal students at post-secondary institutions (up to 22 000 from 200 in the 1960s) are a promising sign for the future. Aboriginal entrepreneurs across Canada are creating businesses at rates faster than the national average, with more than 20 000 aboriginal-owned companies ranging from joint ventures in forestry to band-operated oil and gas companies (Howes, 2001; Canadian Labour Congress, 2003). Political changes are no less evident, The Nisga'a Final Settlement in British Columbia (see the case study in this chapter) provides a taste of what's in store in repriming the social contract for living together differently.

To the other side of the perceptual ledger are the critics. Canada is accused of pursuing policies of repression and violence that have had the intent or effect of denying aboriginal peoples their rights and resources (Alfred, 1999; Adams, 1999). Consider the words of Matthew Coon Come (2001) when accusing the government of racist policies that seek to extinguish aboriginal peoples by assimilation through entrapment in impoverished lifestyles:

> I have come to the conclusion … it has been a federal policy to not provide for adequate sanitation, drinking water, housing, health care, infrastructure and services to our people. What is happening is the continuing implementation of policies of assimilation and extinguishment through infliction of conditions of social despair. Canada's social policies are killing and stunting large numbers of our people … these conditions are tolerated because of racism.

A selective application of the law attests to this negativity, as does the capricious use of hypocrisy in revoking promises or obligations. Worse still is the continuing propensity of central authorities to change the terms of the debate for self-serving purposes (Deloria Jr., 1999). Several disturbing outcomes can be attributed to this duplicity and double-dealing, namely: (a) a disproportionate number of aboriginal peoples in prisons; (b) continued dispossession of aboriginal land and resources; (c) erosion of the aboriginal right to self-determining autonomy; (d) destruction of the environment; and (e) desecration of sacred and burial sites. Advances in some areas such as the Residential School compensation or Royal Commission on Aboriginal Peoples are offset by stagnation in other domains such as the Lubicon (Ominayak and Bianchi, 2002) or Innu (Ashini, 2002; Samson, 2003), thus reinforcing a perception that "nothing has changed" (Bird et al., 2002: xvi). The end result does not auger well: The prospect of constitutionally entrenching a nation-to-nation relationship with aboriginal peoples seems as remote as ever. Or as Taiaiake Alfred (2000) writes in castigating even enlightened overtures:

> Let us understand that it is Canada's goal, advanced through policy and the co-optation of our people, to undermine the strength and very existence of our nations by taking away … everything that makes us unique and powerful…. Historically and into the present day, it's clear the Canadian government believes that by forcing or enticing us into the legal, political, and cultural mainstream, every bit of distinction between us and them will disappear. Then in the future, with all the differences erased, there will no longer be any moral and political justification for laws that support special rights and separate lands for Indian people. Indian problem solved!

Denying the expression of aboriginal and treaty rights not only insults Canada's First Nations; such exclusion appears to be in violation of Canadian law as well, in addition to recent Supreme Court rulings and United Nations protocols to which Canada is a signatory.

Canadians appear to be of two minds in taking substantial steps. There is a consistent level of sympathy for the plight of aboriginal peoples and a desire to right historical wrongs. Yet Canadians are also anxious about how far these concessions should go; who will pay for them; whether core Canadian values will be protected in assisting aboriginal peoples; whether the integrity of Canada will be maintained; and whether a common ground can be found for living together. Indeed, not all Canadians are convinced that such a deplorable state of affairs actually exists, preferring, instead, to think that aboriginal peoples are better off than most Canadians (Nadeau et al., 1997). Aboriginal people are perceived as a pampered lot who get a free ride, don't pay taxes but receive $7.5 billion annually in reserve programs, and are treated with kid gloves by cowardly politicians.

In short, a paradox is falling into place. The combination of promises, commitments, and concessions is poised to transform Canada's First Nations from a "problem" to a "peoples" (Royal Commission, 1996; Fleras and Spoonley, 1999; Frideres, 2000). But rhetoric does not always match reality, with the result that the social problems engulfing aboriginal communities may well constitute the most serious challenge to Canada's national unity (Richards, 2000). Aboriginal peoples in Canada confront numerous social problems, all of which have proven extremely resistant to solution. Part of the problem stems from failure to adequately define the nature, scope, and source of the so-called "Indian problems." Part of the problem also stems from failure to define blame, with some believing that aboriginal peoples have only themselves to blame, while others believe aboriginal peoples are victims of social and political circumstances beyond their control. Is it the system (structures) that continue to victimize aboriginal peoples, or, should blame be apportioned to those who make choices but refrain from assuming responsibility? To the extent that the interplay of agency with structure may be responsible, in that people make choices—but within controlling contexts not of their own making—solutions to the "Indian problem" will prove vexing.

Duelling Discourses: More of the Same, Or Doing It Differently

Proposals to solve the so-called Indian problem revolve around two competing frameworks. One of these argues—as did the White Paper in 1969—that aboriginal people should become more like "us" if they want to be successful. As a *National Post* editorial (29 April, 2000) puts it in endorsing the principle of equality before the law, the choice is simple: either an aboriginal population that is richer, healthier, and Whiter, or, one that remains poor, sick, and Red because of special status, native rights, reserve isolation, and preferential treatment. Not surprisingly, some believe the government is moving in the wrong direction by encouraging aboriginal difference rather than encouraging assimilation into the mainstream (Flanagan, 1999). Others, however, argue that aboriginal people need to become further removed from the mainstream in the hopes of securing their distinctiveness and prosperity as a people. Unless aboriginal differences are incorporated into a framework for living together differently, aboriginal peoples will continue to chafe under a system that created the Indian problem in the first place.

Sociological analysis can be helpful. To one side are the functionalist theorists who look to assimilation as a solution. The Indian problem is caused by aboriginal people's refusal to modernize by discarding their backward cultures in exchange for the liberating principles of the free market, private property, and liberal-democracy. Refusal to assimilate is the root cause of aboriginal problems, and solutions must be focused on closing the cultural gaps between "Neolithic cultures" and the modern world (Widdowson and Howard, 2002). A commitment to formal equality under a liberal universalism insists that everyone is fundamentally alike. What we have in common is more important than the superficial differences that set us apart. Personal responsibility and individual rights must take precedent over collective rights, race-based entitlements, and preferential treatment. The entire edifice of laws, arrangements, and programs that distinguish aboriginal Canadians from non-aboriginal Canadians is thought to be discriminatory, fosters dependency and under-development, and should be dismantled in favour of equality of all before the law. The solution is inescapable: If only "they" could become more like "us," their problems would disappear. Towards that end, aboriginal policy objectives must focus on eliminating all invidious distinctions that not only distinguish aboriginal people from the mainstream but also preclude them from full and equal participation.

To the other side are the conflict theorists who believe the protection of aboriginal difference (exceptionalism) is critical for advancing a post-colonial Canada (Alfred, 1999; Macklem, 2001). Implicit within a conflict perspective is a radical assessment of society as foundationally flawed and in need of a structural overhaul if there is any hope of living together differently. According to a conflict paradigm, a modernization model proposed by functionalism is the cause of the Indian problem. Involvement with capitalist societies accounts for aboriginal poverty and powerlessness, as well as dependency and underdevelopment. Both a liberal democratic commitment and a market mentality are deemed to create more problems than solutions. Liberal universalism homogenizes that which must remain distinct, while the market commodifies those very things that should not respond to profit motives. Even an official multiculturalism is of little help in advancing autonomy principles. A multicultural commitment to a "pretend pluralism" not only flattens aboriginal difference, but it also slots aboriginal peoples into a one-size-fits-all ethnic landscape while denying the specificity of aboriginal difference (Ignace and Ignace, 1998; Fleras, 2002; Day and Sadik, 2002). By contrast, an aboriginal agenda acknowledges the primacy of aboriginal rights. Under an aboriginal rights agenda, aboriginal peoples are defined as fundamentally autonomous political communities who are sovereign in their own right ("self rule"), yet sharing in Canada's sovereignty by way of multiple yet interlocking jurisdictions that clearly stipulate what is mine, what is yours, and what is ours ("shared rule") (Alfred, 1999).

What will it be: Is the Indian problem best solved by making "them" more like "us" or by taking aboriginality seriously as the basis for engagement and entitlement? For aboriginal peoples, the solution to the Indian problem lies in taking aboriginality seriously, that is, in becoming less like the mainstream (Alfred, 1999). That makes it doubly important to take aboriginal differences into account when formulating policies, implementing programs, or defining agendas (Fontaine, 2003). The challenge may well lie in avoiding the extremes of absorption or separation by ensuring aboriginal peoples have the same rights as all Canadians as well as additional rights as indigenous peoples.

Did You Know?

An intermediate position is proposed by Alan Cairns in his book *Citizens Plus: Aboriginal Peoples and the Canadian State* (2000, UBC Press). According to Cairns, a commitment to "citizen plus" provides a framework for keeping Canadians together as a country. The concept of citizen plus emphasizes how aboriginal peoples have the rights and responsibilities of Canadians but also additional rights and responsibilities flowing from their historical and treaty rights (Hawks, 2000). For Cairns, the concept of citizen plus provides a middle ground that recognizes both aboriginal differences (thus rejecting assimilation) and the need for connection to, involvement with, and participation in, Canadian society (2000: 86). As far as Cairns is concerned, aboriginal self-determination and self-government as the third order of government cannot be about exclusion but about inclusion in Canadian society—it is about "getting in" rather than "getting out" in hopes of completing the "circle of confederation" as the Inuit framed it in the Royal Commission on Aboriginal Affairs (Hawkes 2000: 142). A plea for realism also incorporates the interests of those aboriginal individuals in urban areas who too often are shunted aside in debates over nation-to-nation relations and autonomous self-governments (Cairn, 2003).

In light of these competing discourses, the prospect for solving the so-called Indian Problem is indeed formidable. Aboriginal peoples must work within a framework that not only reflects an unequal distribution of political influence with central authorities but also reinforces an historical interpretation of aboriginal peoples as if they didn't matter (Green, 2003). Yet shifts are discernible: There is increasing awareness that solutions must be situated within the broader context of Canadian society. Any proposed solutions must acknowledge the structural framework that created the problem in the first place. Canada's colonialistic project established a relationship that stripped people of their land and resources; undermined the traditional authority and culture; imposed structures and values of dominance that denied and excluded; created a system of institutionalized tutelage that defused efforts at self-determination (Dyck, 1991); dismissed aboriginal cultures as irrelevant or inferior, and sought to transform aboriginal peoples into "civilized clones" (Adams, 1999). A rethinking of the Indian Problem is clearly in order. The question is not whether aboriginal peoples "are" or "have" problems. Rather, we should ask: What is it about Canada that is so problematic for the First Nations; how so; and what must be done to realign the status of aboriginal peoples from people with problems to people with *rights* (Venne, 1999)?

A mindset shift is overdue: The Indian problem should be rethought as a "Canada problem." The ongoing colonization of aboriginal peoples continues to impose a context that creates, reinforces, and amplifies the problems that plague aboriginal individuals and communities (Green, 2003). A new constitutional discourse is required that provides a postcolonial political contract for living together differently in the 21st century (Gibbins and LaForest, 1998). Patterns of governance and political institutions must be redesigned in a way that reflects a loosely organized Canada of relatively autonomous yet interdependent nations within the context of partnership and power-sharing. Two questions prevail in constructing a new social contract for solving social problems. What do aboriginal peoples want? And what is the government willing to concede? One thing is certain: throwing money at the problem will not solve anything; if anything, it may have had the effect of creating more problems. An impression may be created that poverty and powerlessness will disappear with better opportunities or enlightened attitudes, meanwhile ignoring the structural changes required of a system that remains anchored in the foundational principles of a colonial constitutional order. In that a new social contract implies a rethinking of the foundational principles that govern aboriginal people–state relations, the challenge in shifting from paternalism to partnership will prove formidable.

Aboriginal Solutions: A New Social Contract

Indigenous peoples throughout the world are casting for ways to disengage from the colonialisms of the past (Ivison et al., 2000; Stasiulis and Yuval-Davis, 1995; Havemann, 1999; Maaka and Fleras, 2004). Such a commitment is understandable for as others have noted: "What is more humiliating than being ruled by foreigners and being treated by them as inferiors in your own country?"(John Plamenatz, 1960: 146). Proposed instead is an innovative model for living together differently based on a social contract that acknowledges aboriginal peoples (and their descendents) as the original occupants whose rights and entitlements have not been extinguished but remain in effect as grounds for defining "who gets what." Energies and strategies are focused on reconstructing their relationship with settler societies in a manner that sharply curtails state jurisdictions while securing aboriginal models of self-determining autonomy over jurisdictions pertaining to land, identity, and political voice (Alfred, 1999). However progressive sounding, promises are one thing, practice has proven another, given the resistance of entrenched interests and colonialist agendas.

A parallel dynamic exists in Canada where the politics of aboriginality resonate with references to "self-governance," "aboriginal and treaty rights," "jurisdictions," and "nation-to-nation" relations. Canada's aboriginal peoples share much in common with colonized indigenous peoples around the world. They, too, have survived the colonial onslaught, with its overt commitment to (a) forcibly divest aboriginal peoples of their resources under now discarded rationales such as terra nullius; (b) strip them of their language and culture to secure control; (c) discredit their status as original occupants with corresponding rights; (d) deem their rights expendable because of "national interests" or developmental projects; and (d) absorb them into society in hopes of delegitimizing their claims to land and resources (Barnsley, 2001). But aboriginal peoples are emerging from a "long and terrible nightmare" (Christie, 2002:192). In awakening from this nightmare, there is growing awareness that government aboriginal policy never intended to do what it promised. Rather the intent lay in controlling and transforming aboriginal peoples by requiring that they think and act like the colonizers (Green, 2003).

Canada's aboriginal peoples are rethinking their options outside a colonial framework (Christie, 2002). Aboriginal peoples have taken the initiative in exploring the constitutional implications of their recently recognized status as self-ruling peoples with an "inherent right to self-government." Such an admission confirms the possibility of aboriginal claims to self-governance as one of three orders of government in Canada, alongside the provincial and federal, each of which is autonomous in its own right, yet each jointly shares in Canada's sovereignty (Royal Commission, 1996). To be sure, this upheaval of the status quo clashes with the foundational principles of a colonial constitutional order. Pressure is mounting to establish a new social contract for living together differently by balancing the pre-existing rights of aboriginal peoples with the regulatory rights of the Crown, without eroding national unity in the process.

Aboriginal Self-Governance

Aboriginal peoples increasingly claim to be relatively autonomous political communities with an inherent right to self-determining autonomy. The principle of inherent self-governance acknowledges the unique ethnicity of aboriginal nationhood in securing the rewards and recognition that flow from aboriginal people's status as original occupants. With the 1997 Statement of Reconciliation, the government has vowed to create a new partnership that ensures full aboriginal participation without loss of identity (Cassidy, 2003). Yet federal and aboriginal authorities appear to be gridlocked over a proposed realignment of aboriginal peoples–Crown relations. Lip service to partnership and self-determination is offset by colonial habits that die hard. No assurances exist as to when Crown engagement with aboriginal peoples will congeal into a new social contract. Much ultimately depends on whether Canada's political agenda can absorb a paradigm shift that invokes the principle of aboriginality for rethinking national unity.

The politics of aboriginality revolve about the key issue of self-determination—or more accurately, aboriginal models of self-determining autonomy. Nowhere is this claim more patently manifest than with reference to the principle of aboriginal governance and aboriginal self-government (Russell, 2000). Yet these concepts are far from self-evident. Within policy circles, most agree that aboriginal peoples possess a right to self-governance.

Disagreements revolve around its scope and source, and whether this self-governing right (rights equals entitlements with immunity from normal applications of the law) is inherent or conditional (Cassidy, 2003). Unanswered questions persist, including: (1) what do we mean by aboriginal self-government in principle and in practice; (2) do aboriginal peoples and the government mean the same thing with reference to aboriginal self-government; (3) what does aboriginal self-government propose to accomplish; (4) is there a distinction between self-government and self-governance; and (5) what kind of outcome is anticipated by implementation of self-governing initiatives (Asch, 2002)? Is self-governance a recipe for a national unity disaster or does it herald the onset of a new social contract for living together differently? The dearth of consensus provides a lively environment for debate and discussion. The challenge of righting historical rights is also sharpened.

Did You Know?

The concept of governance is not synonymous with government. Governance is a broader concept than government since it encompasses the relationship of governments with other sectors of society, such as citizens or business. Governance is concerned with those structures, processes, and traditions that determine how decisions are taken in society, how power is allocated, how citizens become involved, and how decision-makers are held accountable (Plimptree, 1999). Government can be defined as those powers and initiatives that enable a community to govern a territory and its occupants by setting goals and acting upon these goals without fear of external interference (Asch, 2002). Canada itself is a territory-based governance involving an intricate web of separate yet concurrent jurisdictions, and this division of jurisdictions is being played out at the level of federal and provincial governments. Similarly, aboriginal self-governance pertains to the distribution of power within aboriginal communities and with central authorities. By contrast, aboriginal self-government refers to specific structures for putting governance into practice. The principle of aboriginal self-governance is widely accepted within policy circles (Newhouse, 2002). Less agreement prevails over its practice or implementation with respect to content, scope, and jurisdiction.

Few should be surprised by the primacy of self-governance in advancing the debate over aboriginal peoples–state relations (Fleras, 1999). Canada is predisposed to governance talk: References to divided sovereignty and concurrent jurisdictions are already implicit within the federal system. Canada is a federalism that embraces a structural relationship involving two orders of government with a corresponding division of power, authority, and jurisdiction. Aboriginal self-government promises to create a third and distinct order of governance in Canada, with each order sovereign in its own right yet sharing sovereignty in others by way of multiple yet overlapping jurisdictions (Royal Commission, 1996). By virtue of a 1995 federal policy document, the government has declared conditional support for the principle of inherent self-governance through negotiated agreements within a federal framework (Augustine, 2000). Restrictions apply: Inherent self-government is based on contingent rather than sovereign rights, that is, aboriginal self-governments must operate within the Canadian federal system, be in harmony with other governments, be consistent with the Canadian Charter of Human Rights and Freedoms, and *enhance the participation of aboriginal peoples in Canadian society*. As well, the government appears to be back-pedalling in its commitment to the principle of inherent self-government (Kulchyski, 2003). Negotiations based on principle of mutual consent are giving way to consultations that uphold the Crown paramountcy over aboriginal peoples (Cassidy, 2003).

The principles and practice of aboriginal self-governance are an emergent and contested reality in Canada (Hylton, 1994; 1999). Proposals for self-governance models are varied, with differences reflecting contextual rather than categorical distinctions, involving diverse levels of development, and adjusted to community needs and resources (Royal Commission, 1996). Some models will seek integration within the existing federal framework but with greater control over the provision of key services in health or education. This is, in part, because aboriginal communities lack any viable indigenous political alternatives. Others will demand the creation of an entirely new constitutional framework based on a fundamental restructuring of aboriginal peoples–Canada relationship within a truly confederal Canada (Hogg and Turpel, 1995). Still others want to revive traditional structures by adapting them for modern situations as the basis for self-governance (Alfred, 1995; 1999). Yet other aboriginal self-governments will revolve around an indigenized administration (Kulchyski, 2003): that is, they will consist of negotiated agreements between the Crown and aboriginal peoples that are mostly administrative in nature, insofar as they entail a delegation of government resources to manage local service programs.

Four self-governance possibilities prevail: First, statehood, with complete political independence, both internal and externally; second, nationhood, with retention of authority and jurisdiction over all internal matters; third, municipality, with control over delivery of services by way of parallel institutions; and fourth, institutional, with meaningful decision-making through representation and involvement in mainstream institutions. Generally speaking, aboriginal claims for self-government are consistent with the model of "domestic dependent nations" in the United States. American First Nations do not possess external sovereignty (for example, they cannot raise an army). Nevertheless, these "domestic dependent nations" retain considerable control ("sovereignty") over those internal jurisdictions not preempted by federal and state authority. To date, the Canadian government has conceded the possibility of self-governing powers that go beyond a municipality status but less than the powers of a nation or province. Aboriginal leaders publicly endorse a model somewhere between nationhood/provinces and statehood but appear willing to compromise depending on particular circumstances. To be sure, not all aboriginal communities possess the jurisdictional capacity to fully engage in self-government because of costs and economies of scale (Tanner, 2001). But many do have the capability, and these communities are casting for ways to establish arrangements that will secure a new constitutional order for defining aboriginal peoples–state relations.

The concept of jurisdiction is central to debates over aboriginal self-governance. Patterns of jurisdiction under self-governing arrangements are open to negotiations depending on historical and social context, levels of government funding, and willingness of parties to compromise (Isaac, 2000). Debates over jurisdiction invariably involve questions about what is "mine," what is "yours," and what is "ours." A proposed division of jurisdiction establishes domains that (a) are exclusive to aboriginal jurisdiction; (b) shared arrangements that must be negotiated; and (c) are exclusive to federal and provincial authorities (Doerr, 1997). For example, the organic model of self-governance proposed by the Royal Commission (1996) endorses the principle of shared and exclusive jurisdiction over key areas. Exclusive aboriginal jurisdictions entail those matters of vital political, economic, cultural, and social concern to aboriginal peoples; do not have a major impact on adjacent jurisdictions; and can be exercised without interference from federal or provincial authorities. Jurisdictional matters are expected to vary from band to band, but most likely will include (a) control over the delivery of social services such as policing, education, and health and welfare ("institutional autonomy"); (b) control over resources and use of land for economic regeneration; (c) control over the means to protect distinct cultures and languages; (d) control over band membership and entitlements; and (e) control over federal expenditures according to aboriginal priorities rather than those of government or bureaucracy. Aboriginal jurisdictionality applies to all individuals and business on settlement land regardless of race and ethnicity except for issues under exclusive federal jurisdiction. In cases of conflict and inconsistency with aboriginal laws and Canadian laws, aboriginal law will take precedence except in domains that are exclusively federal.

No less controversial are the proposed units of aboriginal self-government. The challenge lies in creating a political framework large enough to be viable and have clout, yet sufficiently small to be responsive to local concerns. The Royal Commission on Aboriginal Peoples has proposed a compromise that vests government in aboriginal nations rather than communities. These aboriginal nations would be comprised of a sizable body of aboriginal peoples with a shared sense of national identity that constitutes a predominant population in a certain territory (Royal Commission, 1996). Between 60–80 aboriginal historically-based nations can be categorized from the 1000 or so aboriginal communities, thus reviving a political order that once organized aboriginal tribes. However the logistics of aggregating aboriginal communities into a cohesive and consensual political unit may prove formidable (Cairns, 2002). Even more perplexing will be decisions around who controls what, and on what grounds, as the next case study reveals.

CASE 11-1	Nisga'a Self-Governance: Dismantle Canada Or Live Together Differently?

The challenges and politics of establishing aboriginal models of self-governance have been put to the test in the interior of British Columbia. A landmark "treaty" in which enabling legislation embraces a kind of aboriginal sovereignty has finally put to rest an historical fiction: namely, that aboriginal claims to self-government were extinguished at Confederation when all legislative powers were divided between federal and provincial authorities. The Preamble to the "treaty" acknowledges instead "… a relationship to be based on a new approach to mutual recognition and sharing … by agreeing on rights, rather than extinguishment of rights." There is much to commend in advancing a new social contract based on the principle of rights, respect, recognition, and reconciliation. The question is whether a rethinking of the political relationship that governs aboriginal peoples–state relations will erode national unity or enhance a living together differently in a deeply divided society?

Nisga'a Self-Government

The Nisga'a Final Settlement, which came into effect in May 2000, was the

(continued on next page)

first negotiated comprehensive settlement in British Columbia since the mid-19th century. Generally, the Final Settlement provides for a type of land-based self-government within a constitutionally protected treaty framework (Isaac, 2000). Specifically the settlement secures a degree of exclusive and paramount jurisdiction over tribal land and citizens that virtually amounted to a third tier of governance alongside the federal and provincial. The terms of the settlement provide the 5500 band members who live 800 km north of Vancouver a land base of 1900 square kilometres (a fraction of the amount originally proposed); control of forest and fishery resources; $200 million in cash (but much more wealth if timber and mining rights are included); release from Indian Act provisions; a municipal level of government including control over policing, education, community services, and taxes; and the eventual elimination of on-reserve tax exemptions (including sales and income tax) (Matas, 1998). Self government will revolve around a central Nisga'a Lisums government, including four village governments, with a constitution that establishes the rules and procedures for a functioning democratic government (Isaac, 2000).

To pay for this culture and jurisdictional control, Nisga'a will receive forest and timber cutting rights; access to oil and mineral resources; a 26 percent share of the salmon fishery, plus $21.5 million to purchase boats and equipment; and a fishery-conservation trust. It is expected that this transfer in wealth and control will help to alleviate the social problems in the Nisga'a community, including high levels of unemployement, criminal offending, and derelict housing. Under Section 35 of the Constitution Act, Nisga'a will also have the constitutional right to protect and promote their language, culture, and society in areas such as marriage or adoption. Finally, Nisga'a self-government is statutorily protected—reflecting a significant shift in government policy in recognizing self-governing agreements as an inherent right (Dufraiment, 2002).

The settlement terms also define the jurisdictional basis of Nisga'a governance. The Nisga'a governance model is best described as a hybrid model that combines different levels of governance within Canada's constitutional framework. Additional new powers that transcend both the Indian Act and municipal authority have been incorporated as well, including those related to post-secondary education, environment assessment, and wills and estates (Isaac, 2000). Nisga'a self-governing powers will be consistent with those of a municipality, including control over policing, education, taxes, and community services. As well, a few provincial type powers have been incorporated, in addition to several provisions beyond the reach of federal or provincial governments. The settlement is worded to protect federal jurisdictions in criminal law, Canadian citizenship, and the Charter. However, Nisga'a laws will also apply, creating overlapping laws rather than watertight compartments, with both orders of government enjoying concurrent and exclusive jurisdictions (Gosnell, 2000).

The Reality of Nisga'a: Substance or Illusion?

Reaction to Nisga'a self-governing powers is varied. For some, Nisga'a powers are circumscribed (a super municipality) and considerably less than

(continued on next page)

those implied by federal recognition of Canada's aboriginal tribes as "peoples" with an "inherent right to self-government." Yes, Nisga'a are accorded the right to be different and apart, but this differentness and apartness cannot violate the laws of the land, infringe on the rights of others, or compromise the fundamental values of society such as gender equality. The Nisga'a do not have absolute or sovereign authority since federal laws will generally prevail when key jurisdictions collide. The Nisga'a will have full policing services on Nisga'a land, but provincial standards will continue to apply to police training, conduct, and qualifications (Isaac, 2000). And while the Nisga'a have the right to fish, they must adhere to conservation measures contained in the Agreement. In other words, Nisga'a self-government may provide a degree of relative autonomy but the structure remains firmly locked into the framework of Canadian society (Asch, 2002).

For others, Nisga'a powers should not be underestimated: The Agreement clearly reveals the continuity of Nisga'a aboriginal rights rather than extinguishing these rights as others have argued, (Rynard, 2001) including ancestral entitlements of the Nisga'a Nation such as the right to self-government (Dufraimont, 2002). To be sure, matters related to health, education, and child-welfare services must meet provincial standards. But the Nisga'a will have exclusive jurisdiction in matters related to language and culture in addition to membership and property—even when these conflict with federal/provincial laws (Asch, 2002). More generally, Nisga'a reflects a fundamental shift in Canadian society-building. Instead of an essentially monolithic exercise designed to remove all impediments in creating a singular culture and identity, Nisga'a constitutes a spatial invention that transcends the linear nature of power in constructing a post-colonial Canada (Saul, 2003).

Not everyone agrees with this assessment or is pleased with this arrangement. According to critics, an "extraordinary agreement" has "raised the spectre of racially separate development across Canada" that runs counter to a core Canadian value: that is, each person is equal before the law, with the same rights and obligations that precludes special treatment. The settlement is perceived to confer constitutional rights and benefits unavailable to other Canadians based solely on culture or race. In turn, non-Nisga'a are prohibited from voting for the region's administration, thus disenfranchising local residents from input into matters of taxation (although a consultation process will be put into place).

> The Nisga'a people, indeed all aboriginal people, should have the same rights, responsibilities, and entitlements as all other Canadians. This includes equality under the law, property rights, and accountable government. That is not currently the case with the current Nisga'a government (O'Neill, 1999: 10).

Others are concerned that self-government arrangements clear the way for declarations of sovereignty, which will then be used to confer citizenship to foreigners, grant immunity from Canadian laws, and engage in activities deemed harmful or illegal (Duffy, 2002). Canadian unity is likely to implode under such conditions.

Aboriginal leaders have also questioned the terms of the agreement. Many are upset with a political settlement that extinguishes aboriginal rights and claims

(continued on next page)

over land while further absorbing aboriginal people into mainstream institutions and values (Union of British Columbia Chiefs, 2002). Involvement in state-determined models often reinforces the very structures that aboriginal peoples are struggling to escape—in the process obscuring their history, curtailing their rights, and denying options for aboriginal models of self-determination. According to Taiaiake Alfred, Director of the University of Victoria's Program of Indigenous Governance, (Ha, 2000), aboriginal governments such as Nisga'a are little more than a charade that estranges aboriginal peoples from their own governing structures in exchange for dubious concessions. The manipulative agreement not only legitimizes Canada's occupation of aboriginal land by imposing a "final solution" to colonial exploitation. Their assimilation, surrender, and control over the future are secured as well.

The most vociferous critics are those who believe aboriginal difference should not be the basis for reward, recognition, or relationship. Singling out aboriginal peoples for special treatment is not only contrary to Canadian values of equality before the law, but also detrimental to any aboriginal empowerment. Others suggest the critics have it wrong: Nisga'a is not about race or racially separate development by restricting the rights of other "races" (Dufraimont, 2002: 471). The Nisga'a

Nation is a political community holding rights to land and self-government whose rights are based on membership in the Nisga'a community. Nisga'a is about *aboriginal rights* and the right of aboriginal peoples to construct aboriginal models of self-determining autonomy over jurisdictions of land, identity, and political voice. It is about the rights of six generations of Nisga'a who since 1887 have tried to achieve self-government by establishing native title to ancestral land that had never been surrendered to European powers. In the final analysis, Nisga'a may well promote a new kind of national unity based on the principle of "living together differently" rather than imposing a monolithic uniformity (Saul, 2003).

Case Study Questions

1 Some argue that forcing aboriginal peoples to be "more like us" will be best for all in the long run. Others say that aboriginal people's survival depends on being "less like us" by using their difference to "customize" aboriginal models of self-determining autonomy. In light of this debate, how does the Nisga'a Final Agreement contribute to or detract from Canada's national unity?

2 Aboriginal self governance is largely about jurisdiction in defining who owns (or controls) what. With respect to the Nisga'a Final Settlement, how is jurisdiction divided between the Nisga'a and federal/provincial authorities?

There is growing criticism of Nisga'a, in particular, and aboriginal self-governance, in general. Concerns are raised over costs, feasibility, effectiveness, jurisdiction, potential for corruption or abuse, and lack of community legitimacy (Cairns, 2000; Christie, 2002) Some see aboriginal self-government as a "recipe" for social disaster and disunity; others query the soundness of a system anchored around separate status and race-based entitlements; and still others express concerns over the implementation, costs, and jurisdictions (Flanagan, 1999). Yet others criticize the principle of aboriginal self-government as a quick-fix solution to a complex problem endorsed by aboriginal elites who are out of touch with urban realities and local needs. Its appropriateness has come under fire as well. The concept of aboriginal self-governance may be relevant for remote northern and land-based communities, even though the capacity will be limited by size and availability of resources. But such an initiative may ignore those who live off reserve and in urban areas (Cairns, 2002). Dangers over a new aboriginal bureaucracy and increased dependency on federal transfers are no less worrisome to critics.

Of particular concern for many critics is the spectre of dismembering Canada into incoherent bits. Critics envision a Canada that is little more than a "Swiss cheese" confederacy of fractious yet autonomous aboriginal nations with no coherent centre. But a sense of perspective is required. Aboriginal proposals for self-governance are not interested in making a total break with Canadian society. With few exceptions, aboriginal demands for self-governing sovereignty rarely extend to calls for political independence or territorial secession. Proposed instead is a new relationship that dismantles the colonialism of the past, in exchange for a new social contract in which constituent principles include respect, recognition, and reconciliation. This excerpt from the Royal Commission (1996: xi) should allay alarmist fears:

> To say that Aboriginal peoples are nations is not to say that they are nation–states seeking independence from Canada. They are collectivities with a long shared history, a right to govern themselves and, in general, a strong desire to do it in partnership with Canada.

In other words, claims to inherent aboriginal self-governance are not the same as absolute sovereignty (Asch, 2002). As the original occupants whose inalienable rights have never been extinguished by treaty or conquest, aboriginal peoples do not seek sovereignty per se. Proposed instead of *de jure* sovereignty is *de facto* autonomy where First Nations are treated *as if sovereign* for purposes of entitlement and engagement. Such an arrangement does not advocate secession. Nor is it intended to demolish Canada or dismantle its sovereignty; after all, such a wholesale destruction would not be in the best interests of aboriginal peoples. Outright demolition is neither politically feasible nor economically viable in a world where size does matter. Rather, aboriginal demands want to dismantle those structures that have precluded them from their rightful place as the founding peoples of Canada (Borrows and Rotman, 1997).

THE POLITICS OF CHANGE: REFORM, RESISTANCE, AND REACTION

Aboriginal peoples are not looking to turn back the clock. Nor are they attempting to build separatist enclaves at the expense of Canada's political integrity. Their aim is to repatriate their spiritual, economic, and cultural homeland that has been unlawfully taken from them. A collective and inherent right to self-determining autonomy is endorsed on the basis of indigeneity (ancestral occupation) rather than need, disadvantage, or compensation. Admittedly, the principle of aboriginal self-governance will mean little without some limitation on the rights and powers of existing states to preclude unnecessary interference (Young, 2001). Moreover, not all aboriginal communities are anxious to implement the right to sovereign self-governance since they are insufficiently prepared. But many are, and national unity crises are looming because of federal resistance to acknowledge the legitimacy of this right in principle and practice.

Aboriginal Challenge and Resistance

What do aboriginal peoples want? The most direct response is: The same things as all Canadian citizens. All aboriginal peoples want to live in a just and equal society wherein (a) their cultural lifestyles and language are protected from assimilationist pressures; (b) select elements of the cultural past can be incorporated into the realities of the present; (c) bureaucratic interference within their lives is kept to a minimum; (d) they are not victimized by either public racism or political indifference; (e) there is reliable and culturally safe delivery of government services; (f) collective access to power and resources is assured; and (g) they retain meaningful involvement over issues of immediate concern. These objectives and interests do not appear altogether different than those espoused by Canadians at large.

Aboriginal peoples have also expressed a desire to be different by having their difference recognized as a basis for engagement and entitlement (Fontaine, 2003). Many want to transcend the constraints of formal citizen status by expanding the scope of Canadian citizenship as grounds for belonging, recognition, and reward. Recognition of their unique status as different is paramount; without it, aboriginal peoples lose their leverage in negotiating for power. Insofar as the assertion of their difference underpins all aboriginal aspirations, equality before the law may be necessary, but ultimately insufficient, since the promotion of mathematical equality in unequal contexts is tantamount to freezing the status quo. Treating everyone the same may simply entrench the prevailing distribution of power, privilege, and property. In the belief that equal standards cannot be applied to unequal situations without perpetuating the inequality, aboriginal leaders have reinforced the commitment to unique status and equivalent treatment. In other words, aboriginal peoples have claimed the right to be different as well as the right to be the same—a kind of "citizen-plus" status that explores a middle way between assimilation and sovereignty (Cairns, 2000).

Aboriginal responses to redefining their relationship to society are varied. Responses will vary by gender, age, location, legal status, and socio-economic standing. First, proposals for a new social contract span the spectrum from "radical" to "moderate," with emphasis on the middle way in striking a balance between extremes. Aboriginal peoples don't want to separate from Canada in the territorial sense but want enough of their territory to allow institutional sovereignty (Erasmus and Sanders, 2002). As George Manuel puts it, aboriginal peoples want to cooperate with Canada rather than destroy it; they want to participate not assimilate; and they want to retain their distinct identities as one of the many identities that make Canada a unique human community (Miller, 2000: 410). Second, few want to preserve their cultural lifestyle in aspic for the edification of purists or tourists. Nor do they want to abandon their language and culture in exchange for an alien and incompatible set of Eurocentric values and beliefs. Preferred instead is the forging of relevant elements from the past with the realities of the present for advance into the future (Alfred, 1995). In other words, aboriginal peoples want to be modern, even postmodern but not at the expense of what makes them traditional. Third, aboriginal peoples are pragmatists who wish to achieve a working balance between the cultural and spiritual values of the past without rejecting the technological benefits of modern society. Fourth, achievement of political and economic power is viewed as critical for rebuilding communities into flourishing centres of meaningful activity. Yet political and economic successes may be deemed unacceptable if attained at the cost of undermining their social obligations, collective and community rights, and cultural/spiritual values.

Generally speaking, aboriginal leaders prefer to press for change through conventional channels of dialogue, consultation, and persuasion with central policy structures. Tactics include recourse to parliament, the existing court system, public opinion polls, and special interest/lobby groups such as the Assembly of First Nations. Courts are seen as valued venues for exerting pressure on the government to honour constitutional obligations. By providing a forum for resolving complex aboriginal issues that politicians prefer to deny or avoid (Mofina, 2001), courts have been particularly helpful in bringing provinces to the bargaining table. The BC government has acted upon self-government in response to the Delgamuukw decision; New Brunswick has awakened to the ramifications of the Marshall Ruling in 1999, and Ontario continues to explore the implications of Metis hunting and fishing rights as constitutionally entrenched aboriginal rights (Augustine, 2000). Constitutional forums have been employed for redress of historical inequities and promotion of collective interests. Aboriginal leaders have also relied on international bodies and agencies for assistance. They have gone to the United Nations, to Britain, and to the Vatican in hopes of putting international pressure on the Canadian government to address broken promises, miscarriages of justices, and pervasive paternalism. These tactics have attained a measure of success, partly because of Canada's sensitivity to international criticism for betraying lofty standards. Finally, a variety of activist measures have been advocated, ranging from acts of civil disobedience and threats of militancy to theatrically staged protests for mass media consumption. Occasional threats to employ violence, if necessary, have also reaped benefits in drawing both government and media attention to aboriginal grievances. With few exceptions such as Oka, Ipperwash, and Burnt Church, however, the threat of violence has not moved beyond rhetoric. How long this truce can be maintained will depend on curbing youth anger over broken government promises.

Political Reaction: Cautious Or Colonialist?

Governments exercise remarkable power and day-to-day control over aboriginal peoples (Frideres, 1998). They can set budgets, determine how money will be spent, and possess the plenary power to do almost anything they want in shaping political agendas. But few politicians can afford to cavalierly dismiss aboriginality or deny the existence of aboriginal rights. Political authorities appear receptive to aboriginal claims for righting historical wrongs—if only to avert a crisis of legitimacy while restoring some semblance of political tranquillity. Support is mounting to recognize the distinctiveness of aboriginal peoples in terms of self-governing arrangements, unless such moves involve a substantial change in power structures or redistribution of resources. Canadian politicians and policy-makers rarely dispute the validity of aboriginal arguments for self-determining rights. The principle of aboriginal self-determination through self-government is generally endorsed, even if there are grave reservations about its exercise when self-governance proves costly or inconvenient (Newhouse, 2002). Instead, debate increasingly revolves around the magnitude of these rights rather than their legitimacy. The challenge lies in finding a working balance between aboriginal rights to self-determining autonomy with Canada's rights to impose rule of law in advancing national interests.

Central authorities for the most part have stumbled in responding to the politics of aboriginality. Promises of lofty rhetoric notwithstanding, there remains a noticeable lack of political enthusiasm for implementing much of this agenda (Weaver, 1993; Macklem, 1993). Governments may have discarded the paternalism that once informed aboriginal policy and aboriginal peoples–state relations. But central authorities lack the nerve to embrace an unconventional aboriginal policy paradigm anchored around indigenous rights, political sovereignty, and constitutional legitimacy preferring, instead, to compress aboriginal demands into the imperatives of capitalism, liberal democracy, and national interests (Scott, 2001; Green, 2003). Both federal and provincial authorities tend to see aboriginal peoples as just another special-interest group to be controlled, appeased, and administered. Government officials prefer to endorse aboriginal self-government as a political concession, both contingent ("qualified") and delegated on a band-to-band basis, with accountability to parliament and the constitution, rather than as an inherent right derived from common law. Policy officials are understandably wary of dissolving once-habitual patterns of domination for uncharted waters of aboriginal nationhood or sovereignty (Levin, 1993). They are fearful of moving too quickly for fear of an electoral backlash or dismemberment of Canada.

At the core of this impasse is failure to appreciate the politics of aboriginality as a politicized ideology for radical change. Aboriginality is political in that choices about who gets what are politicized and out in public for debate. The discourse is political as well because aboriginal demands constitute grievances against the state. Initiatives that once focused on cultural preservation and formal equality before the law are now channelled into politicized struggles for jurisdictional control of power and wealth. The contrasts could not be more striking: To one side, aboriginal peoples are looking to challenge, resist, and transform; to the other side, the government is willing to accommodate, consent, and reform. Barriers to productive communication, interaction, and social change could not be more forcefully articulated.

RETHINKING THE "INDIAN" PROBLEM: SHIFTS HAPPEN

How times have changed. As recently as 1969 and the tabling of the White Paper, aboriginal peoples were on the brink of constitutional extinction. The demise of the White Paper not only signalled the end of assimilation as official government policy, but also the emergence of an aboriginal nationalism—a politicized reality that authorities are still trying to grapple with (Cairns, 2003). In the past, many believed aboriginal peoples were destined to disappear, thus reinforcing their status as irrelevant and inferior. At present, aboriginal peoples increasingly are regarded as one of Canada's founding peoples with an inherent right to self-government within a federal framework. A generation ago, most Canadians would have been ashamed to discover aboriginal ancestry; at present, Canadians are scouring their closets in hopes of finding an aboriginal ancestor they can claim (Kulchyski, 2003). Not long ago, Canadian society believed it had progress on its side; nowadays, it is aboriginal peoples who sense the possibility that the historical moment is in their hands because they now hug the moral high ground once occupied by those who justified their superiority by claims to civilization (Cairns, 2003).

Yet steps forward are not always what they seem. Aboriginal cultures are no longer excluded from Canadian society, although the tendency towards cultural appropriation remains, rather than towards authenticity. The land claims policy remains rooted in the principle of certainty—not in the sense of advancing justice in our time but to facilitate transnational resource extraction. Not unexpectedly, the relationship between aboriginal peoples and the Canadian state is so fraught with complexity, confusion, and contestation that many recoil at the prospect of tiptoeing through the minefield. The prospect of a sustainable solution is more daunting still. The key challenge lies in the creation of a new social contract for living together differently. But this challenge is compromised by Crown refusal to take aboriginal difference seriously. Stereotypes that portray aboriginal peoples as slaves to customs or hapless welfare dependents reinforce a blaming-the-victim syndrome.

Aboriginal peoples have struggled to counteract the vicious cycle of exclusion and dependency that historically entrapped them (Dyck, 1991; Salée, 1995). Collectively and individually, aboriginal peoples have looked for ways to reclaim their rightful place in society without abdicating uniqueness and entitlements.

Aboriginal peoples have taken the initiative in demanding a radical restructuring of society along constitutional lines. Resistance has shifted from a focus on survival and consolidation, to challenging the distribution of power within a reconstitutionalized state (Kulchyski, 2003). Many Canadians understandably are alarmed by the seemingly radical nature of aboriginal proposals. Political authorities, ever fearful of losing power or control, have responded with an arsenal of delaying or defusing tactics. Contrary to popular belief, however, aboriginal demands are not radical in the conventional sense. Few actively espouse either the dismemberment of Canadian society or the imposition of aboriginal cultural values on society at large. Proposed, instead, is a radical redistribution of power and resources in the hope of advancing a new social contract for living together differently.

Granted, aboriginal demands may be perceived as a threat to Canadian unity or vested interests. But consider the alternatives if these demands appear threatening to Canada or if they seem unrealistic in light of contemporary realities. A continuation of ineffectual government interference and paternalistic handouts is not the answer. Nor is there much to be gained by a commitment to a business-as-usual mentality. Even less helpful is throwing more money at the problem by expanding the legion of experts in hopes of fostering assimilation through self-sufficiency. Put bluntly, the costs of repriming the constitutional agenda may be formidable: However, even more prohibitive will be the costs of doing nothing by carrying on as before.

DISCUSSION QUESTIONS

1   What are some of the key issues that must be addressed if we are to better understand the so-called "Indian Problem"?

2   What are the major social, economic, and cultural problems that confront aboriginal communities?

3   It is argued that the key dynamic in aboriginal peoples–Canada relations revolves around a central argument. To one side are those who believe the solution to the Indian Problem lies in becoming more like "us"; to the other side are those who endorse the need to take aboriginal differences seriously. Explain.

4   What solutions are proposed by aboriginal leaders to solve the Indian Problem? How do aboriginal solutions differ from mainstream political proposals?

5   By reference to the Nisga'a Settlement, demonstrate whether an aboriginal right to self-governance by way of self-government is a solution to the Indian problem or more of a problem?

 ## WEBLINKS

Indian Affairs and Northern Development.   **www.ainc-inac.gc.ca**

Assembly of First Nations.   **www.afn.ca**

Royal Commission on Aboriginal Affairs.   **www.ainc-inac.gc.ca/ch/rcap**

chapter twelve

Immigration and Multiculturalism

FRAMING THE PROBLEM

A central irony of the human condition can be rephrased as a paradox. The very concerns that lie at the root of our pride and identity—culture and colour—tend to be the very issues—ethnicity and race—that sometimes breed divisiveness and conflict (Macionis and Gerber, 2004). This paradox is played out in Canada's engagement with diversity. The politics of diversity have proven both a sore point and a source of pride, resulting in initiatives for engaging with differences that have drawn both criticism and praise. Of Canada's many contributions to the global coexistence, few have attained as much notice—or notoriety—as the principles and practices of official multiculturalism. The concept of multiculturalism has evolved from relative obscurity to a position of prominence and popularity in Canada (Hutcheon, 1990). Inception of multiculturalism as official government policy in 1971 has also elicited international praise as an enlightened tool for "managing" race and ethnic relations. Yet public reaction to Canada's official multiculturalism remains mixed. Acceptance and rejection intermingle with indifference or ambivalence, thus complicating any overall assessment (Kymlicka, 2001; Zwicker, 2001).

To one side, most Canadians would agree that multiculturalism is a defining feature of Canada (Fleras, 2001). Canadians embrace the principle of multiculturalism as a unifying symbol of national identity rather than a divisive force (Bricker and Greenspon, 2001). With multiculturalism, a distinctive "diversity talk" has emerged that is gradually changing how Canadians define themselves in relationship to the world around them. Official multiculturalism secures a uniquely Canadian way for engaging diversity as different yet equal without eroding Canada's social fabric. Recourse to multiculturalism not only empowers minorities with leverage to pursue the dual goals of equality and participation. The protective canopy of multiculturalism also creates cultural space for minorities, in the process defusing the threat of interethnic strife. Multiculturalism has proven its worth on the economic front as well. A combination of immigrant enthusiasm with ethnic entrepreneurs and international linkages continues to reap economic dividends.

To the other side, multiculturalism is not without critical scrutiny (Abu-Laban, 2003; Saunders and Haljan, 2003). For some, multiculturalism is a problem because it encourages too much diversity at the expense of national unity. A multicultural commitment to embrace diversity may be laudable according to this line of argument; nevertheless, cultural practices contrary to Canadian core values may prove disruptive. For others, multiculturalism is deemed a problem because it promotes too much unity at the expense of diversity. The "pretend pluralism" of an official multiculturalism cannot connect with those who want their differences to be "taken seriously." Worse still, multiculturalism condones a hegemonic strategy of control that reduces ("depoliticizes") differences to levels of celebration or commodity (Bannerji, 2003). The end result is a no-win situation: Multiculturalism is subject to criticism for doing "too much" despite reassuring words that everything is alright (a kind of "wolf in sheep's clothing") or for doing "too little," despite bold claims to transform Canadian society (a kind of "sheep in wolf's clothing").

Such a cacophony of opinions is not altogether surprising (Li, 2000). The politics of diversity complicate the prospect for living together with differences at a time of demographic change. Questions arise that unsettle the very concept of Canada-building: Can a society be constructed around the coexistence of many (multi-) cultures at odds with widely accepted norms and values? Or does the reckless promotion of diversity undermine the integrity of the centre, to the detriment of the whole? Is it possible to build a society around the primacy of group-based difference? Or should our similarities as individuals secure the basis for cooperative coexistence? How much unity does Canada really require? How much diversity can it tolerate before self-destructing?

Answers to these questions are hotly debated, no more so than in controversies over immigration and multiculturalism. To say that Canada is a multicultural society of immigrants is patently obvious. A complex set of protocols and programs are in place that regulates who gets in, why, from where, and how. Yet Canadians display a marked ambivalence toward immigration and immigrants. Some see immigrants as a group of rich folk who buy their way into Canada; others see them as poor people who have fled misery in search of opportunity; and still others as a burden or asset depending on the criteria (Kazemipur and Halli, 2003). This ambiguity is organized around competing discourses: On the one hand, immigration is endorsed as a solution to problems created by an ageing population, a nation-wide skills shortage, and multicultural expertise in a global economy. On the other hand, immigrants are defined as a problem: As problem people, they come with problems in need of costly solutions or they create problems that disrupt, erode, or destroy (Collacott, 2003). Such a love-hate relation toward immigration and immigrants does not bode well for Canada's future. In that official multiculturalism has been enlisted as a tool to counteract this negativity, the politics of pluralism will rarely yield consensus or cooperation.

Many have said that the worth of a society should be measured not by the problems it confronts but by how it confronts its problems. This playful inversion is nicely captured in the tension between multiculturalism and immigration within the context of Canada-building. This chapter focuses on how immigration and multiculturalism contribute to, yet detract from Canada's national interests in ways mutually reinforcing yet sometimes contradictory. The linking of immigration with multiculturalism is deliberately pursued: Immigration provides the rationale for multiculturalism; multiculturalism, in turn, secures a receptive social climate for immigrant settlement (also Burstein, 2003). Consider this editorial in making the connection:

> Generations of immigrants have successfully built what has come to be known internationally as the Canadian model. These immigrants and refugees are drawn to a society continually ranked as a destination of choice, a society that values their contributions not simply in the economic sphere, but in a social and cultural context as well. If this nation has not always been at ease with its multicultural heritage, it has nevertheless sought to make diversity a key feature of everyday Canadian life. Today this social investment is paying dividends (Editor, *Horizons*: 2002: 1).

Put bluntly, Canada has many needs related to society-building. Relying on multiculturalism and immigration to address these needs produces benefits; by the same token, however, costs are involved. Neither immigration nor multiculturalism can be reduced to either problem or solution. Rather, they are both: Both immigration and multiculturalism may be interpreted as two-edged swords that solve problems even as they create new ones. Solutions lead to additional problems while benefits may prove costly—depending on criteria, consequences, or context. Two social problem themes prevail in this chapter: First, proposed solutions to social problems often trigger unanticipated consequences. Solving one problem may generate new problems even with the best of intentions. Second, defining problems or solutions is highly contested. What some define as a problem is perceived by others as a solution because of differing perspectives, and vice versa. Complicating the assessment is the possibility that the impact of immigration and multiculturalism is concurrently positive and negative rather than mutually exclusive.

This chapter begins by looking at immigration policies, patterns, and programs. Immigration is explored at different levels, including: (a) who gets in and why; (b) the challenges of fitting in and settling down; and (c) the perceived costs and benefits. A balanced approach that avoids either extreme yields surprising results. The chapter concludes by focusing on the politics of official multiculturalism: What is Canada's official multiculturalism intended to do, and why? Can it be judged as a success or failure in embracing the challenge of immigration? And on what grounds can a judgment be made? Inasmuch as official multiculturalism originated to address the challenges of immigration and diversity, this chapter will begin with a brief overview of "who are Canadians" and "how did we become this way?"

ETHNIC DIVERSITY IN CANADA: POCKETS OF DIVERSITY, STRETCHES OF UNIFORMITY

Canada embraces an astonishing diversity of immigrants and refugees from different parts of the world. The first of many movements was inaugurated by East Asian populations across the Bering Strait as far back as 50 000 years ago. Their descendents are thought to constitute Canada's indigenous (or aboriginal) peoples. Both French and English traders/adventurers/explorers constituted the second wave of immigrants. These colonizers eventually displaced the aboriginal populations by unilaterally proclaiming official status as Canada's founding ("charter") members. The third wave consisted of a mosaic of European immigrants who arrived during the 20th century as part of Canada's society-building commitments. A fourth wave is securely in place: The magnitude and nature of immigration has shifted significantly to include a kaleidoscope of immigrants from Asia, Africa, and South and Central America. Canada's demographic profile has been profoundly altered because of this revolutionary change, especially in major urban centres, thus posing new challenges for living together.

Since 1867, more than 14 million people have immigrated to Canada, initially from Europe and then from around the world, gradually expanding Canada's demographic diversity (Canadian Heritage, 2003). Nearly all (92 percent) of Canada's population was of British or French ancestry at the time of confederation (Palmer, 1975). Between 1896 and 1914, the balance tilted when up to 3 million immigrants from Central and Eastern Europe arrived to domesticate the west. Immigration increased substantially prior to and just after World War I, reaching a peak of over 400 000 in 1913. Another wave of Eastern European immigrants during the 1920s brought the non-British, non-French proportion up to 18 percent. The post-World War II period resulted in streams of refugees and immigrants from the war-torn European theatre. Immigration since the 1980s has originated from so-called non-conventional countries, thus displacing Europe and the United States as prime sources. The 1990s saw a continuation in numbers and composition: More immigrants came to Canada than in any other decade during the past century. Immigration sources continue to be dominated by Asia and the Middle East, accounting for 58 percent of the total between 1991 and 2001. The growing number of immigrants of colour has not only contributed to a more vibrant and cosmopolitan Canada; controversy over the direction of Canada's immigration policies and programs has been rekindled as well.

Ethnic Composition

The demographic impact of immigration on Canada confirms an old cliché: Things are not what they seem to be when assessing the status of diversity in Canada. From afar, Canada looks extremely diverse. Its population is divided into First Nations, the descendents of the original charter groups and European migrants, and the new multicultural minorities. Up close, however, the picture differs. Canada is not nearly as diverse as perceptions suggest. Wide swathes of uniformity encapsulate pockets of intense ethnic diversity, giving Canada a decidedly uneven mosaic.

Appearances are deceiving in yet another way. Over 40 percent of Canadians may have some non-British, non-French, and non-aboriginal origins. And yes, at 13.4 percent of the population, visible minorities constitute nearly one out of seven Canadians. Nevertheless, Canada remains a predominantly European society. According to the most recent Census data involving total responses (single plus multiple responses) to ethnic origins, the top ten ethnic origins in Canada are Canadian 39.4 percent, followed by English at 20.2 percent, French 15.8 percent, Scottish 14.0 percent, Irish 12.9 percent, German, 9.3 percent, Italian, 4.3 percent; Chinese 3.7 percent, Ukrainian, 3.6 percent, and aboriginal, 3.4 percent. With the exception of Quebec and Ontario, where Italian-Canadians prevail, those of German descent are the most frequently reported non-British, non-French ethnic origin in the other provinces. A closer look at "Canadian" as an ethnic origin category revealed that most of the respondents were of British or French ancestry or spoke English and French as their first language. This Canadian category, and the fact that more and more Canadians are identifying themselves as having multiple ancestries (38 percent), has made it increasingly futile to divide Canadians into a limited number of distinct ethnic groupings (CRIC, 2003).

Foreign-Born Canadians

Canada is home to approximately 6 million foreign-born Canadians. At 18 percent, the proportion of immigrants relative to the population at large is at its highest in 70 years, putting Canada just behind Australia with its 22 percent. Sources of immigration have shifted as well: Immigrants from Europe predominated before 1961: Of the top five countries of foreign birth in Canada, the United Kingdom prevailed at 24.3 percent, followed by Italy (16.5 percent), Germany (10.8 percent), Netherlands (8.9 percent), and Poland (5 percent). Between 1991 and 2001 immigrant sources shifted dramatically. The top five countries included China, 10.8 percent; followed by India, 8.5 percent; the Philippines, 6.7 percent; Hong Kong, 6.5 percent; and Sri Lanka, 3.4 percent. If both Taiwan at 2.9 percent and Hong Kong are factored in, the Chinese component stands at 20.2 percent.

Regional and municipal variations are noticeable (Driedger, 2003). Ontario is home to nearly 60 percent of Canada's foreign-born population. This industrial heartland continues to attract the largest number of immigrants, with well over half of the new arrivals. Next in line are British Columbia, Alberta, and Quebec. The Atlantic provinces have negligible totals. Immigrants also gravitate to large urban regions. Both absolute numbers and relative percentages make Montreal, Toronto, and Vancouver more diverse than provincial or national averages. Nearly 94 percent of all immigrants lived in census metropolitan areas. Toronto, Vancouver, and Montreal accounted for about three-quarters of all arrivals. Nearly 44 percent of Toronto's census metropolitan population is foreign-born, followed by Vancouver at 37.5 percent; Hamilton, 23.6 percent; Windsor, 22.3 percent; and Kitchener, 22.1 percent. Toronto's ratio of foreign-born residents exceeds that of Miami, 40 percent; Sydney and Los Angeles, 31 percent; and New York, 24 percent, thus making it one of the world's most ethnically diverse cities.

Crude figures can be misleading: Consider the immigrant situation in the census metropolitan area of Kitchener (which includes Kitchener, Waterloo, and Cambridge) as a case in point. Between 1996 and 2001, the four leading countries of immigration into the city of Kitchener included Yugoslavia, Bosnia, Romania, and Croatia. In Waterloo, the four leading sources were China, India, South Korea, and Pakistan. In Cambridge, the figures were India, Pakistan, United Kingdom, and the United States. These figures are consistent with public perceptions: Kitchener is usually regarded as a working-class city that attracts the less skilled. By contrast, Waterloo attracts the more skilled because of its two universities and a robust information technology sector.

Visible Minorities

An increasing percentage of new Canadians are visible minorities. (The term "visible minority" refers to an official government category of native- and foreign-born, non-White, non-Caucasoid individuals, including Blacks, Chinese, Japanese, Koreans, Filipinos, Indo-Pakistanis, West Asians and Arabs, Southeast Asians, Latin Americans, and Pacific Islanders. Almost 4 million visible minorities live in Canada, comprising 13.4 percent of the population and reflecting a threefold increase from 4.7 percent in 1981. Nearly 60 percent of immigrants between 1991 and 2001 arrived from Asia or the Middle East, while another 20 percent were from the Caribbean, and Central and South America. Less than 20 percent of Canada's immigrants migrated from Europe or the United States. Those of Chinese origin are the most populous visible minority, with a total of 1 million persons, or about 30 percent of the visible minority population. South Asians follow next with 671 000, or 21.0 percent, and Blacks with 574 000, or 17.9 percent.

The distribution of visible minorities by province is uneven. Ontario, British Columbia, Alberta, and Quebec continue to attract the largest number of visible minorities. Visible minorities remain predominantly an urban phenomenon. They are attracted to major metropolitan centres because of opportunity, excitement, support, and acceptance. A growing critical mass proves irresistible as a magnet for the next wave of immigrants and refugees. The numbers say it all: In 1971, less than 1 percent of Toronto's population was a visible minority. By 2001, the percentage of Toronto's population by census metropolitan area who are visible minorities stood at 38.6 percent. The figures are equally impressive elsewhere: Visible minorities comprise about 37 percent of the population in Vancouver, while Montreal is close to the national average with 13.4 percent. Each of these census centres is dwarfed by the proportion of visible minorities in other Canadian cities, namely, Richmond, British Columbia at 59 percent or Markham, Ontario at 55.5 percent. Other parts of Canada appear less appealing to visible minorities. Visible minorities in outliers such as Trois Rivieres, Quebec and Chicoutami-Jonquiere, Quebec are less than 1 percent of the city populations.

To sum up: Immigration and diversity are predominantly a regional and urban growth industry. Both foreign-born and Canadian-born visible minorities tend to gravitate to four regions: Montreal, southern Ontario, the Edmonton–Calgary corridor, and south mainland British Columbia and south Vancouver Island. Such a demographic reality will have a profound impact on living together with our differences. Not surprisingly, the government is looking for ways to redistribute new immigrants across Canada in hopes of alleviating strain on existing services while addressing a rural labour shortage. However well intentioned if impractical, such an initiative exposes the obvious: Canada can best be described as an uneven mosaic. Relatively concentrated pockets of urban multicultural diversity are interspersed with vast stretches of ethnically monochromatic hinterland.

CANADA AND IMMIGRATION

The "have" countries are waking up to a new reality: The politics of immigration are more salient than ever in this era of human uprootedness. The workforce in many industrialized countries has begun to shrink because of declining birth rates and an ageing population— resulting in a high priority for the recruitment of skilled workers. Many countries are signatories to international obligations for protecting those seeking refugee status (Janigan, 2002). Yet immigration remains an awkward and sometimes disturbing experience for both immigrants and the host country as well as for the sending nation. Too many countries take a narrowly reactive approach to immigration. There is little concern for coordinating goals with respect to: (a) orderly migration, (b) rational calculation of numbers and absorptive capacity; (c) transforming migration into an instrument of sustained economic growth; (d) safeguarding immigrant rights; (e) reducing conflict with native-born populations; and (f) improving settlement and integration of immigrants (Castles, 2000). In proving an exception to this rule, Canada continues to garner international acclaim as a model for the 21st century by the prime minister of France who explained:

The 21st century has made its decisions. It imposes on us protection of the environment; it imposes decentralization, integration, cultural diversity. It has made its choice for new technology, for controlled immigration. The values of the 21st century are already there; the 21st century has already chosen its first country: Canada (Fraser, 2003: A-20).

Did You Know?

Humans are a people on the move. According to the UN (2002), an estimated 175 million people lived outside their country of birth in the year 2000. Most of the migrants resided in Europe (56 million), Asia (50 million) and North America (41 million). As a result, one in ten persons living in the more developed regions is a migrant, compared with about one in 70 in developing countries. Of the 175 million migrants, about 159 million are deemed international immigrants in search of economic opportunity or family reunification, while up to 20 million are refugees fleeing a well-founded fear of persecution because of who they are, including 9 million refugees in Asia followed by 4 million in Africa. Another 1 million are asylum seekers in search of political freedom. In addition there are between 20 to 25 million internally displaced persons within their own countries who are primed to seek their fortunes elsewhere. The plight of people on the move—refugees, asylum seekers, and economic and environmental immigrants—has evolved into a major social problem as major threats to national security/sovereignty and global stability in the post "9/11" era (Wilkinson, 2003).

Canada: An Immigrant Society

Canada is frequently praised—and pilloried—as a society of immigrants. It is one of the few jurisdictions in the world that is defined as an official immigration country (Ucarer, 1997). United States and Australia are two notable immigration countries, so too are Brazil and Argentina, several Latin American countries and, most recently, New Zealand. Three characteristics distinguish immigration countries: First, proactive programs are in place for regulating the quantity and quality of immigrants into the country. Second, initiatives have been implemented to assist in the integration of migrants. This settlement process not only includes social and material adjustment; immigrants also receive all civil and political rights associated with citizenship in that country. Third, immigration is viewed as central to society-building. A social contract is implied: Immigrants are expected to promote building society by taking up jobs, filling in underpopulated areas, contributing to population growth, working hard, and obeying the law. Governments, in turn, are expected to reciprocate with guarantees of equal opportunity, public safety, and citizenship rights.

Compare this inclusiveness with non-immigration countries. Non-immigrant countries or "complete societies" (Castles and Miller, 1998) are relatively stable and established, culturally and socially speaking, and have been that way for centuries. The population is composed primarily of the descendents of the original settlers with a long history on the land (Li, 2003: 9). Immigration in so-called "complete" societies does not fit into the long-term plans related to national identity or societal unity. For example, so-called complete societies such as Germany discourage immigration or deny its legitimacy in society-building. Instead of pro-immigration, initiatives are immigrant-dampening policies that deter inflows, limit long-term stays, discourage permanent residences, label immigrants as guest workers, and penalize them accordingly by withholding citizenship and attendant rights (Ucarer, 1997). Those of German parentage are automatically granted citizenship because of kinship ("bloodlines"); by contrast, foreigners and their children are generally excluded from citizenship regardless of birthplace.

The situation differs markedly in Canada. Settler societies such as Canada have relied on immigration to populate, displace, domesticate, extract, or manufacture. Canada's immigration policies were reformulated over time to attract agricultural settlers, then to encourage those with technical skills and professional expertise, and more recently those with substantial investment portfolios (Li, 2003). Canada remains a country of choice for those migrants who hope to improve fortunes, reunite with family and relatives, seek adventure and challenge, and escape political repression (Halli and Driedger, 1999; Hiebert, 1999). In that the foreign-born have played a pivotal role in Canada's national development, and will continue to do so in the foreseeable future, Canada's claims to the status of an immigration society are well founded.

On the whole, Canada has become a more vibrant and dynamic society because of immigrants. Immigrants have contributed to Canada's cultural diversity and economic prosperity without unravelling its social fabric or national identity. With immigration, the image of Canada as a British outpost in the North Atlantic has morphed into a cosmopolitan mosaic of different cultures and languages (Dyer, 1998). In the space of a generation, immigration has transformed the demographic and cultural face of urban Canada. Once stodgy provincial cities like Vancouver and Toronto are now regarded as first class cosmopolitan centres whose strength is drawn from diversity. But reaction to this demographic and cultural revolution remains mixed. Yes, many Canadians have embraced immigration with the kind of civility that is becoming a trademark of an inclusive society (Siddiqui, 1998). Yet an undercurrent of concern or resentment persists. Concerns over national unity and identity are routinely raised amidst fears that Canada has lost control of its borders (Bissett, 2003). So too is the spectre of immigrants as a threat to internal security, especially in light of September 11th. Canada's loose regulations and lax enforcement are accused of fostering a haven for terrorist groups, enabling them to launch forays from within or fund conflicts from without (Bell, 2003). In other words, its status as an immigrant society, notwithstanding, Canada remains a "reluctant host" that appears welcoming at times, but obstructionist at other times, but whose ambivalence—even hostility—toward certain foreign-born is palpable beneath a veneer of tolerance.

Many agree that Canada requires immigration to maintain its standard of living. Disagreement tends to revolve around the issue of "how many," "where from," and "what kind." But debates over immigration must go beyond the question of costs and benefits. For in the final analysis, the very notion of Canada as a distinct society is inseparable from immigration. As deftly put by a former Minister of Immigration when linking national identity with immigration: "Immigration is fundamentally about nation-building—about deciding who we are as Canadians and who we want to become.... We need a clear and practical vision of the kind of nation we want to build." (Sergio Marchi, Annual Report, 1994: iii). Or consider this glowing passage by Michel Dorais, Deputy Minister of Citizenship and Immigration Canada (2002: 4), "Immigration is one of the most visible expressions of many of the values that underpin our collective identity as Canadians: incorporation of differences, recognition of cultural diversity, building of communities based on mutual respect, and bringing the world inside our borders." The link between identity and immigration is captured by questions:

- What does it mean to be a Canadian in an age of migration?
- What kind of Canada is envisaged for the future?
- What is Canada's perception of itself in relationship to the world at large?
- What core values must be protected? Which values are open for negotiation?
- How do immigrants contribute to or detract from a preferred vision of Canada?

Answers to these questions require careful deliberation beyond the realm of political slogan or public posturing. Analysis must focus on the future of society and how immigrants can contribute to the kind of society we value and envision. Such analysis is inseparable from immigration debates regarding "who gets in," "why," and "how."

Immigration Program: Who Gets In?

It is one thing to acknowledge Canada's commitment to immigration-based society-building. It is quite another to acknowledge the racism—both personal and structural—to have infiltrated Canada's immigration program (Li, 2003; Driedger, 2003). Immigrants to Canada have long experienced exclusion because of race or national origin (Avery, 2000). Preference for British and northern European immigrants created a hostile reception for those deemed to be incapable of assimilation or dangerous (Walker, 1998). For example, Chinese were explicitly denied entry into Canada between 1923 and 1947. Others such as Jews did not fare much better as expressed upfront in the title of a book *None Is Too Many* (Abella and Troper, 1982). It was not until the 1960s that Canada discarded its discriminatory immigration program. Immigrants were subsequently accepted on the basis of skills or compassion rather than race or national origins.

Passage of the 1978 Immigration Act produced a uniquely Canadian way for handling immigration. Four elements underscored the program: a rational basis for immigrant numbers; a balancing of social, economic, and humanitarian concerns in the selection process; a commitment to public safety; and fostering immigrant integration through settlement programs (which stood at $366 million in 1999/2000). Four objectives were defined including (a) social—to reunify families through sponsorship; (b) economic—to foster a strong economy through a skilled workforce; (c) humanitarian—to fulfill Canada's international obligations by providing safe refuge for those seeking asylum; and (d) security—to ensure safety of Canadians by managing the risks associated with immigration.

The Act also consolidated the range of admissible immigrants. Entry conditions for admission into Canada were organized into three categories: sponsored, independent, and nominated. Close relatives could be sponsored for immigration if family members were willing to support them; entry as independents depended on accumulating sufficient points (see page 335); and nominated immigrants had to rely on points but could earn up to 30 points for having relatives in Canada (Driedger, 2003). Current immigrant entry is classified into the landing categories of family, economic, and refugee categories. The breakdown of these categories is listed in Table 12.1, in addition to numbers in each level and a percentage of the total. A temporary residents' category is also shown.

TABLE 12.1	Persons Admitted to Canada by Category, 2001

Immigrants: Family Class

- Immediate family
- Parents and grandparents
- Others·

Total family class = 66 646 (26.6 % of total)

Immigrants: Economic

- Skilled workers + dependents
- Business (including investors, entrepreneurs, and self-employed) + dependents
- Provincial nominees

(58 860 (applicant) + 78 259 (dependents)
(4082 + 10 498)

(1274)

Total = 152 973 (61.09% of total)

Refugees

- Government assisted — 8693
- Privately sponsored — 3570
- In Canada (IRB approved) — 11 891
- Dependents abroad — 3740

Total = 27 894

TOTAL IMMIGRANTS & REFUGEES — 250 346 (12.3% of total)

Temporary Residents

- Foreign students admitted in 2001 — 73 979
- Foreign workers admitted in 2001 — 93 083
- Refugee claimants — 44 608

Emigration to the U.S. — 30 203

Citizenship grants — 167 353

Adapted from Statistics Canada, 2003; also the Department of Citizenship and Immigration Canada. Available at http://cicnet.ci.gc.ca.

Family Reunification Class Canada recognizes the need for families to stay together, if only to facilitate the process of integration. Immediate members of the family, namely a spouse and dependent children under 21, are automatically allowed into Canada, provided they are of good health and without a criminal record. Parents and grandparents are also included but more distant relatives must "top-up" with "points" for admission into Canada (see page 336). Currently, the family reunification category accounts for about 26 percent of all immigration to Canada, a figure that has dropped sharply in recent years.

Economic ("Independent") Class Canada is increasingly dependent on skilled immigrants for economic growth. The foreign-born now comprise 19.9 percent of the labour force, with future projections pointing to immigrants as 70 percent of new wage earners. The economic (or independent) class includes skilled workers and business (including entrepreneurs, self-employed, and investors). Skilled workers are assessed under a new point system that emphasizes their flexibility in skills, adaptability to changing economic conditions, especially education levels, official language proficiency, ties to Canada, and employment experience (Tolley, 2003). The principal applicant requires 67 points for entry into Canada while dependents are exempt from the point grid. Nevertheless, both the principal applicant and their dependents must pass the usual health and security clearances. It should be noted that the new rules have come under attack as "unfair" or "too tough" by immigrant groups and immigration lawyers. Also criticized is the government decision to retroactively apply the new rules to those already in the pipeline (Thompson, 2003). A class action suit is now in the courts regarding the legality of the government's actions.

TABLE 12.2	Skilled Worker Selection Criteria, 2002
Factor	Points Allotted
Education	25 (5 points for high school degree; 25 for MA or PhD)
Language	24 (4 points each for fluency in speaking, listening, and reading/writing first official language; 2 points each for second official language
Experience	21 (15 points for one year experience for skilled worker in listed occupation; 21 points for 4 years experience)
Age	10 (10 points for those aged 21 to 54; 0 points for those less than 17 or more than 55)
Arranged Employment	10 (10 points for guaranteed job in Canada)
Adaptability	10 (up to 5 points each for education of partner, having studied in Canada, having worked in Canada
TOTAL	100
Additional Employment Points	
Investor and Entrepreneur	35 points based on level of experience, previous trips to Canada, and participation in business immigration initiatives
Self-Employed	35 points based on level of experience

Adapted from Immigration and Refugee Protection Act, *Canadian Gazette,* Vol 136 (9), 14 June, 2003

A subcategory of the economic class is known as the "business class." Entry on business class entails a transfer of capital as the price of admission into Canada. Immigrants are selected based on their ability to invest, to be self-employed, or to establish entrepreneurships (CIC, 2003). Under the investment program, applicants must demonstrate business experience, a minimum net worth of CDN$800 000, and a willingness to invest CDN$400 000 in Canada. The entrepreneur program seeks to attract experienced persons who will own and actively manage businesses in Canada that will generate employment opportunities for Canadians. They are expected to have a minimum net worth of CDN$300 000. Self-employed persons must demonstrate an intention and capacity to create their own jobs, for example, by purchasing a farm. The program has been criticized as unfair by allowing some to "buy" their way into Canada. It is also plagued by abuse and mismanagement. Plans are in place to transfer more responsibility to the provinces for the monitoring of investment funds.

Refugee Class   Refugees are the third and perhaps most controversial of Canada's immigrant categories. While immigrants are defined as those who have voluntarily left their countries and who intend to settle permanently in Canada, refugees are defined as those who have fled their countries of origins and cannot return because of well-founded fears of persecution based on race or national origins (George, 2003). Refugees are accepted as part of Canada's humanitarian commitments and legal obligations to the world community. Canada has performed admirably compared to those countries that perfunctorily deny refugee acceptance. Since World War II, Canada has officially admitted over half a million refugees, with recent annual intakes in the 20 000–35 000 range. Canada's apparent generosity and support of international refugee programs has been amply documented, most notably with receipt of the Nansen Medal in 1986—the first country ever to be bestowed such an honour by the United Nations.

Two categories of refugees are recognized, neither of whom require points for entry. One category includes sponsored refugees. Sponsored refugees are preselected abroad by government officials, others by private agencies, individuals, clubs, or church groups. Both government and privately sponsored refugees receive landed immigrant status before arriving in Canada. Private sponsors are obligated to provide support for up to ten years. Additional assistance is furnished through government programs once the sponsored arrive. A second category of refugees consists of those claimants who arrive unannounced by foot, boat, or plane, often without documentation such as passports, and claim refugee status upon arrival in Canada. A series of court rulings has enshrined a system that allows access to Canada's refugee pipeline for virtually anyone who sets foot on this country, and utters the magic words, "I want asylum"—a situation that can be abused by the unscrupulous (Thompson, 2003). If a refugee claim is not disqualified within 72 hours on grounds of a terrorist or security threat, refugee claimants are provided with housing, food, medical care, and legal counsel to plead their case before the Immigration and Refugee Board (IRB). In 2001, the IRB recognized nearly 12 000 in-Canada refugees by granting them permanent resident/landed immigrant status.

Temporary Residents   Temporary residents consist of students and foreign workers. The number of temporary residents in December 2001 stood at 273 662, thus exceeding the immigrant and refugee numbers. This includes 15 000 seasonal workers under the Agricultural Worker Program, in addition to nearly 8000 women who work in Canada under the Live-in Caregiver Program (Bagnall, 2003). Temporary residents also include asylum seekers who arrive unannounced to claim refugee status and are waiting for a decision on their status. In 2001, 44 000 refugees claims were made, resulting in a processing bottleneck, with 52 761 cases in the pipeline at the end of 2002. Of the claims finalized by the IRB in 2002, about 47 percent were granted refugee status, about the same number as the year before (Thompson, 2003). Much of the debate over Canada's refugee determination process revolves around four key questions: who is a refugee; how can we find out; is the system working; and is the system fair?

To sum up: Canada's immigration program remains as robust as ever. A total of 228 575 new immigrants came to Canada in 2002, a slight drop from the 251 000 in 2001 (CIC, 2003). China was the leading source country accounting for 33 000 migrants or 15 percent of the total. India and Pakistan followed. Economic immigrants accounted for 60 percent of the total (or 138 226 new migrants), while the family class stood at 29 percent (or 65 087 new migrants). Nearly half of all new migrants (49 percent) were destined for Toronto upon arrival. The long-term objective of the government's immigration program remains in tact: to expand immigration levels to approximately one percent (300 000) of Canada's population, while bearing in mind the need for supports to attract skilled labour, strengthen the social fabric, and enhance cultural diversity (CIC, 2002).

In June 2002, the Immigration and Refugee Protection Act replaced the 1978 Immigration Act. The new Act addressed four areas of concern, including, immigration to Canada; refugee protection; enforcement; and the IRB. The Act provided only a legislation framework for establishing principles as guidelines; the specifics, practicalities, and regulations would be handled by government decree and directives. Under terms of the Act, measures are in place to (a) ensure the best interests of children; (b) liberalize admission criteria; (c) speed-up the processing of applications; and (d) expand the circle of close relatives for family reunification. Despite relaxing some restrictions, however, the Act conveys a negative tone. Rather than welcoming and fostering the integration of immigrants and refugees, the Act appears defensive in seeking to *protect* Canada by highlighting control, containment, and regulations (Jimenez and Crepeau, 2002). The dangers of such defensiveness are palpable: Immigrants and refugees may become labelled as little more than scapegoats for Canada's insecurities.

IMMIGRANT EXPERIENCES: FITTING IN, SETTLING DOWN

Getting in is one thing. Settling down and fitting in have proven equally challenging. Immigrants and refugees come to Canada with the best intentions to adapt and succeed. Upon arrival, immigrants begin the process of adjustment into the mainstream hierarchy, without necessarily severing links to tradition (Isajiw, 1999). Yet Canada has not always proven the haven that many had expected. Formidable obstacles persist in a society whose welcome mat may be revoked at the slightest provocation. Talk of social contract notwithstanding, immigrants tend to be seen as guests in Canada who had better behave or pay the price. The price of admission into Canada is steep: Immigrants may not be second-class citizens under the law but remain so in public perception and national discourses (Siddiqui, 2000).

On paper, government policies and programs have facilitated the process of integration (Halli and Driedger, 1999). Emphasis is directed at improving immigrant social capital by building bridges through participation and bonding through shared values and norms (Kunz, 2003; Duncan, 2003; Frith, 2003). And, yes, entrenchment of official multiculturalism has established a collective platform for enhancing levels of social inclusion and social capital (Bourhis and Montreuil, 2003). But Canada's immigrant minorities are rarely in positions of power to take advantage of such opportunities. A unity of purpose remains elusive because of geographic dispersal, cultural heterogeneity, political powerlessness, public unease, and general lack of economic clout. Of course, not all is downside: most new Canadians appear relatively satisfied with the quality of life in Canada. Many appreciate the opportunities and services available to them and their children, the promise of human freedom, and sufficient market transparency to succeed (Li, 2003). As movingly put by Myrta Rivera, Executive Director of KW Multicultural Centre (*Kitchener–Waterloo Record*, 30 June, 2003).

> I came to Canada in search of a feeling, not a place. I sought justice, respect, acceptance. I found it. I feel safe here, respected. I am in Canada. This is home.

Still, some will confront a series of problems that have accompanied them into Canada or encounter problems during settlement. Problems arise not only because of personal shortcomings related to culture shock, lack of political power, loss of economic well-being, and personal isolation but also because of discriminatory barriers that preclude entry or acceptance.

Concerns: Fitting In

Fitting in and settling down involves a three-stage process: Initially new immigrants require basic services related to shelter, language training, and access to social services. In the second phase, emphasis shifts to the pursuit of self-sufficiency and productivity through jobs. In the third phase, immigrants want opportunities to participate fully in the social and civic life of their community (Goar, 2003). Generally speaking, the primary concerns of immigrant-Canadians are practical, success-oriented, and survival-related. Compared with the highly politicized demands of Canada's aboriginal peoples for self-determining autonomy, the concerns of immigrants and refugees are focused on equality, participation, and freedom (Fleras, 2001). Foremost is the desire to "put down roots" by "fitting in" to Canadian society yet retaining a link with the past. More specifically, immigrants' needs can be itemized as follows:

1   The elimination of all forms of discrimination, racism (including stereotyping), and exploitation in the workplace.

2   The expansion of opportunities in the labour and education markets as well as ease of access to services in housing, government institutions, and mass media.

3   Conferral of full citizenship rights, including the right to pursue interests and activities without undue bureaucratic interference or central surveillance.

4   Access to the best that Canada has to offer without diminishing their children's sense of cultural identity.

5   The right to express themselves in terms of their identity without foreclosing equal opportunity.

6   Respect for their difference and public acceptance of immigrants as a legitimate and valued part of society (Parekh, 1997).

Taken together, immigrant-Canadians desire the best that both worlds have to offer. They want to be treated as individuals by being accepted for what they do rather than who they are. Conversely, they also want others to appreciate them for who they culturally are without sacrificing meaningful involvement in society. Immigrant women and men are anxious to participate in the modern without forsaking the traditional. Full citizenship rights are important but so too is recognition of their cultural worth, without enduring taunts of being less Canadian. In other words, abandoning a cultural identity as a condition of acceptance may not be acceptable for many. Identities are integral to people's sense of who they are (Frideres, 2002). A sense of community and continuity is instilled that secures the resourcefulness to adapt and flourish (Kymlicka, 2001; Parekh, 1997).

Settling Down: "The Best of Times, the Worst of Times"

What immigrants want is not necessarily what they get. Immigrants find themselves in new social contexts that are confusing, frustrating, and challenging because of their newcomer status (Frideres, 2002). Their visible status may preclude a smooth transition into Canadian society, while public reaction to their physical visibility and cultural differences has also complicated the settlement process. Many have endured racial discrimination in the fields of employment, education, housing, and government services (Pendakur, 2000). Licensed occupations, including medicine and dentistry, continue to impose restrictions and deny accreditation that blocks the employment of immigrants with foreign experience or credentials. Refusal to recognize or the tendency to undervalue foreign credentials does not come cheaply. Foreign-trained professionals may experience downward social mobility because of these institutional barriers (Basran and Zong, 1999). Canadians also suffer from failure to take advantage of the potential brain gain. For example, the Regional Municipality of Waterloo is home to nearly 100 foreign-trained doctors who cannot practice; yet up to 20 000 residents do not have access to a physician.

Recent immigrants have not performed as well as those who arrived earlier (Jackson and Smith, 2002). Unlike previous immigrants, claims Michael Walker of the Vancouver-based Fraser Institute (2003), new immigrants are now likely to have lower incomes, slower rates of integration, higher welfare dependency, and more utilization of social programs than both the resident population and previous immigrants. They earn less on entering the labour market than a decade earlier (Chui and Zietsma, 2003), although immigrants will soon account for all net labour force growth in Canada (Biles and Burstein, 2003). Both skilled and unskilled new Canadians find themselves segregated in menial occupations with little in the way of security or prospects for promotion, despite evidence they are better educated—22 percent of recent immigrants have a university degree compared to about 17 percent of Canadian-born. Immigrants also have a higher percentage with less than high school education than those born in Canada (18 percent versus 16 percent). A Catch-22 is a constant: Without Canadian experience, many cannot get certified even with extensive retraining; alternatively, without a job, they cannot get the Canadian experience to gain a toehold (Van Rijn, 1999). Such an anomaly suggests an inherent unfairness—not to mention a colossal waste of human resources. Highly skilled immigrants are invited to Canada, yet many are left to virtually fend for themselves without adequate supports or programs (Thompson, 2003). Not surprisingly, perhaps, the top five jobs for recent male arrivals with university degrees include hospitality services, transportation (from limos to taxis to trucks), and janitorial work—jobs that pay close to minimum wage, which in Ontario has remained unchanged at $6.85 since 1995 (raised to $7.15 in late 2003) despite a 20 percent loss of purchasing power.

Income differences provide additional insight. Evidence from Statistics Canada also indicates a drop in the incomes of highly qualified immigrants compared to similarly qualified Canadian-born workers (Canadian Press, 2003). In 2000, male immigrants earned 79.8¢ compared to a Canadian-born worker's dollar, in contrast to over 90¢ in 1990 and dollar-for-dollar in 1980. Female immigrants earned 87.3¢ in 2000, compared to 93.3¢ in 1990 and $1.03 in 1980. A lengthening catch-up period is evident as well: The foreign-born take longer to match average rates of employment, earnings, and family income. Principal applicants who landed in Canada in 1980 under the skilled/economic category had earnings 23 percent above the Canadian average one year after arrival (Thompson and Kunz, 2002). By the late 1980s, the premium disappeared. By the mid-1990s economic principal applicants suffered a 20 percent deficit one year after landing, relative to the Canadian average. The reasons behind this discrepancy remain unclear (Biles and

Burnstein, 2003; Ruddick, 2003): Possibilities include the following: the overall economic climate including punishing unemployment rates in the early 1990s; relatively high number of family reunification immigrants without immediately employable skills; continued non-recognition or underevaluation of foreign education or expertise; professional qualifications but limited language proficiency; and possibly racism. Such outcomes should come as no surprise if we factor in the combination of reduced government spending and declining income supports and social services with economic restructuring and public-sector downsizing, resulting in less good jobs and flat wages (Hyndman, 2003).

Poverty is increasingly a major problem. A study by Statistics Canada indicated that in the year 2000, 35.8 percent of immigrants who arrived in the previous five years were living below the low income cut-off line, a measure of relative poverty. The increase held true regardless of education levels, age groups, family types, or fluency in either of the official languages. This rate has been rising steadily since 1980 when it stood at 24.6 percent for recent immigrants. By contrast, the poverty rate for Canadian-born households has declined, from 17.2 percent in 1980 to 14.3 percent in 2000, with improvements even for the most vulnerable such as the elderly or single parents (Kazemipur and Halli, 2003; Carey, 2003; Dunphy, 2003). As a result, according to the director of research for the Canadian Council for Social Development, two kinds of Canadians can be discerned for poverty measurement—those who were born here and those who weren't (Carey, 2003). The implications are disturbing: The convergence of poverty with race and entry, in addition to immigrant anger and frustration, creates a "lethal cocktail" that cannot be ignored (Biles and Burnstein, 2003).

The situation is especially grim for refugees (Wilkinson, 2003). Traumatized by emotional and psychological abuses en route to Canada, refugees are expected to adapt to the unique social, cultural, and geographic climate with only minimal social assistance. The impact of cultural shock may be debilitating because of exposure to radically different lifestyles, mixed messages and conflicting expectations, rapid social change, and an inhospitable climate. The transitional stresses that accompany refugee claimants are compounded by their language difficulties, shame at their inability to find employment, and low self-esteem due to loss of control over their destiny. Refugees with gainful employment still suffer from lack of Canadian experience, are vulnerable to recession or restructuring in the workplace, encounter discrimination at work, and must cope with language and culture barriers. Even those who appear to have "made it" may remain marginalized. Many continue to feel undervalued and underappreciated, looked down upon by the dominant sector yet torn between the sometimes conflicting pressures of affirming their distinctiveness while negotiating mainstream norms.

Immigrant and refugee school children are subject to a host of conflicting demands and pressures. Some may perform poorly because of racial stereotyping, low teacher expectations, curricula and textbook content at odds with minority experiences, and lack of positive role models among school staff. Others experience a sense of social dislocation; elders drift apart from the junior generation, younger women chafe over traditional roles and pervasive paternalism, and educated elites become estranged from the community at large. Obedience, deference to authority, and loyalty to family are valued. But too much deference may culminate in conflicts as parents and offspring struggle to find a workable balance between the permissiveness of contemporary society versus culturally-steeped and religiously-infused traditions (Fleras, 2002). Insofar as young people may find themselves caught between cultures, yet fully accepted by neither, the challenge of adaptation is rendered more complex and painful (also Handa, 2003; Anisef and Kilbride, 2003).

Immigrant women encounter additional problems because of gender (Bannerji, 2000; Fleras and Elliott, 2003). Abuses are confronted across all phases of the migratory process: Women and children are often denied access to health and education, subjected to abuse and violence, prevented from reuniting with families, detained or deported in conditions that violate international standards, vulnerable to smuggling networks, and confronted by discrimination both explicit and systemic (Annan, 2002). They find themselves restricted to the lower echelons of the Canadian labour force because of low-paying job ghettoes such as manufacturing, service industries, and domestic work. Domestic workers on two-year probationary periods are particularly vulnerable to exploitation and abuse (Macklin, 1999). For immigrant women, immigration comes with costs. Canada may be a land of opportunity and freedom for some but an entrapment for others. The loneliness stemming from isolation has the effect of leaving immigrant women both vulnerable and depressed. Many are penalized as well because of limited language skills, lack of training opportunities, child-rearing and school-related problems, racial prejudice, underemployment, lack of "Canadian experience," and limited support services. Such a marginalization reinforces what many already know: That it is women who often bear the costs of settling into Canada (Rose et al., 2002).

IMMIGRATION: COSTS OR BENEFITS?

All indicators suggest a continuation of Canada as a favourite destination for those fleeing political oppression, ethnic conflicts, demographic pressure, environmental disasters, and economic stagnation. Immigrants and refugees are not only "pushed" from their homeland, but also "pulled" to Canada because of opportunity and freedom (Castles and Miller, 1998). By world standards, Canada is a desirable destination (Li, 2003). Canada remains a country of choice for many immigrants because of its high standard of living, productive economy, publicly funded health and education systems, rights to citizenship, and the protections of multiculturalism. Canadians, in turn, have reacted to immigrants and immigration in different ways, ranging from enthusiasm and endorsement on one hand, to resentment on the other, with a combination of indifference, resignation, or indecision in between.

National polls expose the conflicting messages. A survey by Environics involving six focus groups and 2003 Canadians in late November 2002 confirmed high levels of tolerance in Canada (Marcoux, 2002). Most (92 percent) feel comfortable with people from other races in social situations while 83 percent believe diversity enriches Canadian culture. Yet 36 percent of the respondents believe there are too many immigrants in Canada, albeit down from 46 percent in January 1996. Equally mixed messages are expressed in a survey of 1701 Canadians 18 years of age and over commissioned by the Association for Canadian Studies (2002) and carried out in August of 2002. According to Jack Jedwab who analyzed the survey, 40 percent of the respondents thought there was too much immigration into Canada while 39 percent believed the number was just right and 14 percent thought the figure was too low. These figures are consistent with those of CRIC (2003) whose surveys also indicate a high level of support for immigration concurrent with substantial displays of concern.

Ambivalent attitudes toward immigrants and immigration cannot be dismissed. Many are supportive of immigrants as hard-working and positive contributors to society. But others see it differently: Canadians as a rule may accept the necessity or inevitability of immigrants but bristle at legislative loopholes and unscrupulous stakeholders that make a mockery of Canada's generosity, compromise Canadian borders, and imply the entire system is out of control (Stoffman, 2002; Francis, 2002). Some criticize what they see as excessively generous concessions to immigrants at a time of relentless cutbacks in services and benefits. Others take exception to settlement and language costs. Still others are concerned about the "problems" that immigrants bring with them to Canada. Allegations abound that immigrants are using their ties abroad to establish illegal international distribution systems for contraband drugs, extortion rackets, loan sharking, prostitution, and smuggling of illegal aliens into Canada. Palpable as well is the growing fear that immigrants are undermining Canadian identity, as are perceptions that immigrants are refusing to integrate and, preferring instead, to insulate themselves into ethnic enclaves. Timing is everything: Canadians may not be unduly upset over immigration when the economy is booming. Concerns mount when the economy cools and (a) competition intensifies for good jobs and scarce resources; (b) immigrant labour becomes a permanent underclass; and (c) imbalances appear in education, welfare and service demands, and income distribution (Goldsborough, 2000). Finally, Canadians may be comfortable with immigrants who look poor, appear to be grateful for new opportunities, are culturally compatible, willing to start at the bottom of the socioeconomic ladder, and who see their entry into Canada as a privilege, not a right. But there appears more resentment toward immigrants who are "uppity," affluent, confident, assertive, and are unwilling to put up with racial slurs as the price of admission into Canada (Siddiqui, 1999).

Why do Canadians exhibit such ambivalent attitudes toward immigrants and immigration? After all, other than those who claim aboriginal ancestry, all Canadians are immigrants or descendents of immigrants. Responses reflect diverse perceptions of immigrants as a problem or a solution because of perceived benefits and costs. For some, immigrants may be seen as helpful but hardly indispensable to Canada's prosperity—of marginal rather than central importance to its future (Li, 2003: 11). For others, immigrants are seen as a costly luxury that Canada can ill afford if there is no justifiable reason (Stoffman, 2002). Still others don't know or don't care to define the role of immigrants in building Canada. The immigration debate ultimately boils down to one key question: "Do immigrants create a net benefit or cost for Canada?" (Li, 2003: 13).

Benefits

Canada is a land of immigrants in which prosperity and identity are dependent on the perpetual movement of people. Studies in other parts of the world, such as Australia, New Zealand, and the United States confirm how, on balance, immigrants are a net contributor to "frontier societies" demographically, socially, culturally, and economically (Spoonley and Fleras, 1999). Initial periods of settlement are heavily dependent on immigrants; they continue to be an important source of labour during phases of rapid industrial expansion (Bolaria and Li, 1988). Immigration pluses outrank the minuses especially in those developed countries where fertility rates have dropped below the replacement level, while high levels of emigration bolster the value of working-aged skilled migrants (Gamble and Cumming, 2002).

The same conclusions apply to Canada. Immigrants enhance Canada's ability to compete in the global economy, in part because Canada itself is a global society by virtue of its multicultural character, both domestically and globally (Augustine, 2003). Immigrants create more jobs than they take; as consumers they provide markets for Canadian goods; they are more likely to start businesses than other Canadians; are better qualified in terms of education; and pay more in taxes than they receive in health and social services. Immigrants not only ease labour shortages during phases of capitalist expansion; they toil in jobs that other Canadians dislike. A taps-on, taps-off mentality that treats immigration as a source of labour has been replaced by a model of sustained economic growth with immigrants providing a permanent and critical mass of producers and consumers. The demographics of Canada also work in favour of increased immigration. An aging population pyramid with declining birth rate totals (1.7 children per family, which is below the replacement rate of 2.1; and a growth rate of 2.3) puts the onus on younger immigrants for future support of social programs. Rather than hurting an economy, in other words, immigrants are prone to provide a much-needed kick-start.

In general, then, immigrants have had a positive impact on Canada despite the inevitability of costs along the way (Li, 2003; Sweetman, 2003).The vast majority of immigrants get jobs, are not on welfare, and contribute to the economy (Corcoran, 2003). In addition to their roles as producers and consumers, immigrants tend to possess drive and vitality, with boundless energy and optimism, and a willingness to take entrepreneurial risks by capitalizing on international links to improve Canada's competitive position in a global economy. No wonder there are those who argue that Canada needs immigrants more than they need "us." Or that immigrants are doing "us" a favour by coming here, rather than the reverse, in the process confirming that immigrants are more of a solution to Canada's problems rather than a problem per se.

Costs

Many Canadians are critical of immigrants and immigration. Immigration policy itself is accused of being driven by well-intentioned "warm fuzzies" to assist others less fortunate, together with an implicit yet possibly mistaken belief that making Canada bigger will make it better (Collacott, 2002). Not only are immigrants perceived as threats to Canada's economy and cultural identity but also are criticized as "unwelcome guests" who steal jobs, housing, and education; who undermine moralities and foster crime; and who swamp access to increasingly scarce services. Others deplore immigrants for making unreasonable demands on Canadian society when it should be Canadians who call the shots based on realistic assessments of Canada's absorptive capacities (Campbell, 2000). With possibly up to 200 000 illegal immigrants in Canada, security worries are rampant. Finally, Canada may be criticized for draining highly trained human capital from those parts of the developing world that have borne the cost of training much needed professionals.

The refugee determination process has come in for scathing criticism (Stoffman, 2002; Jimenez, 2003). By UN standards, Canada's refugee determination process is regarded as one of the world's best, despite disagreement from refugee lawyers and advocacy groups who believe the system is too tough on refugees. Others tend to think the system is too lax: With an acceptance rate of about 55 percent historically (currently, 47 percent but nearly 89 percent as recently as 1989), Canada admits refugee claimants at six times the international norm, including refugee claims from citizens of democratic societies such as Israel, the United Kingdom, and the United States. The top five refugee-producing countries in

2003—Pakistan, Mexico, Columbia, China, and Costa Rica—are countries better known for their economic difficulties than civil unrest (*The Globe and Mail*, 12 June, 2003). And concerns continue to mount about the wisdom of releasing refugees into the community rather than a detention centre, especially for those without proper identification. While immigrants are required to pass tough selection criteria and rigid medical and criminal standards prior to entry into Canada, refugees may enter fraudulently, few are detained, even fewer are deported, and serious criminals remain at large—in effect rewarding illegal behaviour and eroding respect for the law (Bissett, 2003). Still others criticize the logic behind the very notion of a refugee. The UN convention was created to reflect the realities of the Cold War with its corresponding influx of refugees in the aftermath of World War II, according to Sergio Karas an immigration lawyer based in Toronto (Humphreys, 11 March, 2003). But a mechanism established to cope with the post-war tide of displaced people in Europe may no longer be effective in dealing with mass movements of people who confront famine, civil war, and catastrophe rather than persecution based on nationality.

What is wrong with the refugee determination system? "Everything," says Daniel Stoffman (2002). Canada spends too much on refugee claimants but not enough on conventional refugees in camps. Instead of selecting needy and deserving refugees from camps, Canada prefers to focus on those asylum seekers who claim refugee status upon arrival here. Not only is it expensive when dealing with refugee determination and integration, costing millions each year, including expenditures on legal aid and health care, but the process creates a pull factor, according to Stoffman. Others are enticed to claim refugee status because Canada is increasingly seen as a "patsy" that accepts most claimants, even those from NATO countries and stable holiday destinations such as Costa Rica. A reluctance to deport those who are rejected reinforces this "powder-puff" image. With nearly 36 000 deportees unaccounted for over the past six years, not only is the integrity of the overall system in jeopardy, but the incentive for illegal entry is also increased as well (Curry and McIntosh, 2003). The solution is simple enough: more government sponsored refugees. Pre-selected refugees are more cost-efficient since they have achieved official status before arrival and do not require costly lawyers or IRB hearings.

Burden and Opportunities

Canada's ambivalence toward immigration and refugees is puzzling (Li, 2003). The same sentiments that make Canada a safe migration alternative also reveal a mean and self-serving streak. To be sure, few Canadians are entirely pro-immigration or anti-immigration, although most tend to underestimate the relevance of newcomers to Canada's vitality, prosperity, and evolution (Li, 2003). Nevertheless, polls confirm that many believe there is too much immigration of the wrong kind from the wrong place. Canadians may value diversity in principle but draw the line over those immigrant demands that challenge core Canadian values, are critical of mainstream institutions, or promote the goal of separate ethnic enclaves (Hiebert, 2003). Consider the ambiguities: Canadians do not want Canada to be a haven for terrorists because of misplaced generosity, but they also squirm at the thought of deporting people back to misery or death. Canadians do not like the idea of being duped, but they also don't want to seem callous and indifferent to the plight of those less fortunate. Canadians may resent immigrants and refugees who prove a social cost or medical burden, but what right do we have to play "God"?

These ambiguities point to an improbable conclusion: Perhaps the ambivalence stems from ignorance. There is still much yet unknown about the impact of immigration in terms of costs and benefits, both real and perceived, that can be assessed objectively and rationally. Or perhaps the problem lies in assessing immigration in terms of an either-or contest when both costs and benefits are intertwined in ways that cannot be sharply distinguished or quickly assessed. Immigrants provide opportunities that have yet to be fully realized; they also impose a burden that should not be lightly downplayed. In that critics and supporters tend to align themselves with one position to the exclusion of others, a polarized view is conveyed that glosses over the complexity of reality out there. The next case study explores the logic behind these debates.

CASE 12-1	"Talking Past Each Other:" Debating the Debate over Immigration

Canada rests on a curious contradiction. To one side, Canada is a society of immigrants whose resources and resourcefulness have transformed it into one of the world's best countries to live in. Immigrants have contributed substantially to Canada's economic growth and population increase, cultural enrichment, and urban vitality. To the other side, Canada comes across as a politely xenophobic society that dislikes immigrants. Poll after poll indicates what many intuitively know: There is a substantial antipathy toward immigrants and immigration because of preconceived notions of "how many," "where from," and "what kind." Accusations flow fast and furious in this conflicted context. Those who criticize the system are denounced as thinly veiled bigots whose hidden agenda is racist-driven rather than based on genuine concerns. By contrast, those who defend the system are seen as dupes or cowards whose sympathies have been hijacked by powerful immigration lobbies.

Many Canadians understandably are bewildered by this cacophony of yeahs and nays. Critics contend that a continuation of current immigration practices is contrary to Canadian society. Supporters believe that any curtailment in immigration is detrimental to Canada's national and international interests. Critics tend to focus almost entirely on the costs of immigration (Stoffman, 2002; Collacott, 2002; Francis, 2003). As far as they are concerned, there is no logic or rationale that justifies Canada's immigration policy with respect to numbers, origins, or qualifications. Furthermore, they argue, most of the purported social, demographic, and economic benefits can be shown to be illusory or mired in political correctness. Canada is accused of having one of the world's most misguided and muddled immigration policies because of flawed assumptions regarding economic benefits and Canada's ageing population (Stoffman, 2002). Conversely, supporters dwell on the positive benefits of immigration (Li, 2003). A two-pronged approach is generally pursued. The economic benefits from immigrants are touted, as are the social and cultural contributions. Immigrants are shown to be more law-abiding, socially-integrated in terms of stronger family ties, to pay more into taxes than they receive in benefits, and are less likely to rely on health and welfare services.

(continued on next page)

Admittedly, immigration critics are not nearly as anti-immigrant as rhetoric sometimes implies. Few reject immigration that is controlled, conforms with Canadian laws, offers tangible benefits to the Canadian economy, does not jeopardize Canada's national security, and advances Canada's national interests. Criticism is directed at those categories of immigrants that do little for Canada, yet pose problems of dependency or unproductivity. Criticized as well are those immigrants who appear to treat Canada as simply a stepping stone before going to the States or returning home— a situation exacerbated by a multicultural policy that allegedly encourages traditional cultural ties at the expense of emotional connections to Canada (Blatchford, 2003). Criticism is also projected at partisan politics: Both major federal parties are anxious to increase the number of immigrant voters in electorally rich urban centres (Stoffman, 2002). Too many immigration plans go against the grain of Canadian society while extracting maximum electoral advantage at odds with Canada's common good. Also taken to task are immigrant lawyers and consultants, in addition to immigrant service providers, whose livelihood varies with immigrant number.

In short, the debate boils down to a battle between the pragmatists (critics) and the altruists (supporters). One wants less, the other wants more, and both are anxious to defend their position to the hilt even if this means invalidating the legitimate concerns of their opponents. The immigration debate reflects an inability for both sides to meet on common grounds since each endorses as a strength what the other side regards as weakness. In responding to the question of whether immigrants create an economic burden or opportunity, critics say no (for the most part), supporters say yes (in general, despite some short-term adjustment problems), and each tweaks the data accordingly to advance their position at the expense of others. Consider, for example, the concept of "benefits." Debates over the "benefits" of immigrants are marred by ambiguities over "operationalizing" the terms (assigning a measurable value to abstract concepts). Most models are limited to assessing net economic benefits based on quantifiable calculations such as earnings. Intangible contributions such as unpaid labour are rarely taken into account. Such a definitional gap may create conditions for talking past each other.

Who is right or wrong? On what grounds can we make a decision? Put bluntly, critics and supporters are both right and wrong. Immigration is far too complex and contradictory for reduction into two mutually opposed categories; after all, immigration is as much a problem as a solution, depending on the context or criteria. Outcomes are not distributed equally: Some provinces and urban areas receive a disproportionate share of benefits while other regions are relatively unaffected. Some 49 percent or 111 339 immigrants came to Toronto in 2001, compared with 1.15 percent or 2611 for the four Atlantic provinces. Some sectors of society derive benefits, others suffer, and still others are generally immune to any impact. Some Canadians, such as unskilled workers, may be penalized by immigration; others, such as immigration lawyers, may prosper; the vast majority of Canadians are only marginally affected (Stoffman, 1998). Businesses that cater to immigrants may flourish, but taxpayers must defray the social

(continued on next page)

costs of expanding existing social services (Smith, 1997). Some classes of immigrants (such as economic) may provide immediate benefits; some may not (refugees), and still others may do so indirectly or eventually (family).

In short, the benefits and costs of immigration are concurrent. Both benefits and costs impact simultaneously so that Canadians are drawing benefits while simultaneously absorbing costs. Immigration may create congestion and exert pressure on limited institutional resources; yet the same immigration may also prove a boon to real estate agents or car dealers because of a larger market for pitching consumer products. Children may have to cope with more crowded classrooms and overworked teachers. Yet they also have the benefit of coming into contact with diversity on a meaningful basis. Diversity enriches our lives, yet an ethnic mix can also create friction, fragmentation, or fallout. Refugee claimants may be criticized for jumping the queue; nonetheless, many Canadians thrive on the cheap labour they provide in factories, restaurants, motels, and homes.

The American author, Joel Millman (1997), makes an interesting observation. He argues that no person, no matter how opposed to immigration in principle or practice, is without some sympathy for the plight of the world's poorest. Similarly, even the most enthusiastic booster is sufficiently concerned about opening the floodgates, and demands some kind of restrictions. That makes it doubly important to acknowledge the validity of arguments, both for and against. Neither criticism nor praise are either entirely right or entirely wrong, but both right and wrong, depending on the context, criteria, and consequences. Few solutions to immigration questions are either-or, but rather of a both-and variety. Inflated claims on either side of the debate often conceal both one's own weaknesses and the opponents' strengths. A sense of proportion is helpful in assessing the immigration benefits and costs. Costs are inevitable if benefits are to be anticipated. A country cannot expect to have an immigration-driven policy of sustained economic growth without some social and economic repercussions. In other words, if Canadians value the cultural and economic benefits associated with immigration, they must be prepared to absorb the costs and inconvenience. One without the other is unrealistic.

Case Study Questions

1   As noted by the sociologist Peter Li (2003), the immigrant debate revolves around a central question: Do immigrants create a net benefit or net cost in the minds of "mainstream" Canadians, and how can we find out by means of objective criteria? Demonstrate the arguments both for and against immigration.

2   Assume you are Minister of Immigration with powerful decision-making capacities. How would you go about creating an immigration program that addressed the competing arguments of the pro-immigration and anti-immigration lobbies?

Canadians are generally a pragmatic lot. Few want a complete halt to all immigration, given the demands of a globalizing and interconnected world. By the same token, few would condone an open welcome mat with no restrictions on entry. Preference is for an agenda that lies in between these extremes. But such a preference raises the question of "how many" (on what grounds do we justify a figure); "where from" (how much control does Canada have over who wants to get in); and "what kind" (should skilled class or family reunification class prevail? This assessment also confirms the necessity of ensuring that immigration remains a legitimate subject for debate, especially if Canada is to avoid the kind of racist violence that engulfs "fortress" Europe as it copes with the challenges—and paradoxes—of becoming more multicultural in response to the immigration crisis.

OFFICIAL MULTICULTURALISM: PROBLEM-SOLVING OR PROBLEM-MAKING?

Immigrant societies confront a dilemma in living together with differences: how to make society safe "for" diversity, yet safe "from" diversity (Schlesinger Jr., 1992). Is it possible for a society of many ("multi-") cultures to survive without cleaving into warring camps? The challenge is fairly straightforward: A social and political framework is required that can engage with differences as different yet equal, without eroding a corresponding commitment to national unity or individual rights. Settler societies such as Australia and New Zealand have endorsed multicultural principles as a framework for accommodating immigrant minorities (Vasta and Castles, 1996; Pearson, 2001). But endorsement is not the same as implementation or enforcement. Inasmuch as multiculturalism engages with diversity by challenging society to move over and make space, its contribution to society-building is widely acknowledged. Insofar as the promotion of diversity without a unifying vision may unravel or disperse, a commitment to multiculturalism should not be lightly taken.

Multiculturalism has proven a victim of its own success. The centrality of multiculturalism to contemporary discourses has yielded such an array of meanings that many despair of any clarity, consistency, or consensus (Saunders and Haljan, 2003). Both championed yet maligned, idealized as well as demonized, multiculturalism can mean everything, yet nothing, depending on context or criteria (Pieterse, 2003). Such flexibility can be helpful at times: Needless misunderstanding prevails at other times as people grope about for a common ground to communicate concerns or aspirations. Broadly speaking, multiculturalism can be defined as a commitment to engage diversity as different yet equal (Fleras, 2001). It consists of a doctrine that promotes the ideal of a society of many cultures in a state of cooperative coexistence provided, of course, that measures are taken to advance cultural diversity without sacrificing social justice and national unity. More specifically, especially in a Canadian context, multiculturalism consists of an official doctrine, along with a corresponding set of policies and practices, for advancing the mutually related but analytically separate goals of cultural differences, social equality, societal integration, and national unity (Wilson, 1995).

To say that Canada is officially multicultural is stating the obvious: Official multiculturalism originated in 1971 when Canada became the world's first country to adopt a formal commitment. Endorsement of multiculturalism as government policy acknowledged that a society of many (multi-) cultures was possible provided people's cultural differences didn't interfere with the attainment of full citizenship and democratic rights. The challenge lay in creating as neutral an environment as possible to preclude ethnic entanglements from getting in the way of equal participation. The status of official multiculturalism was further secured with its constitutional entrenchment in the Charter of Rights and Freedoms in 1982. Enshrinement of multiculturalism made it obligatory to interpret the Charter of Rights and Freedoms in a manner consistent with Canada's multicultural heritage. Passage of the 1988 Multiculturalism Act further embedded official multiculturalism within the legal framework of Canada. The government was expected to promote multiculturalism by making the public service more representative of and responsive to the diversity it serves (CIC, 2003). The dismantling of the short-lived Department of Multiculturalism in 1993 ended the golden era of official multiculturalism, followed by increasing political indifference to the principles, practices, and funding of multicultural policies—a decline that has yet to abate.

The origins and development of an official multiculturalism make it abundantly clear. Official multiculturalism is a pragmatic exercise in conflict management. As a political program to achieve political goals in a politically acceptable manner (Peter, 1978), multiculturalism drew its inspiration from the quest for Canada-building. Its inception sought to (a) defuse the tension created by Quebecois separatism; (b) placate the "other ethnics" who objected to the simplistic bicultural view of Canada; and (c) provide Canada with a buffer against American cultural encroachment (Zwicker, 2001). In each case, the goal was directed at managing diversity in advancing a distinctive yet cohesive Canada, both safe from ethnicity, and safe for ethnicity. This logic persists into the present: Only the means for managing diversity have evolved in response to demographic shifts and political developments. Multiculturalism has evolved from a focus on European ethnicity and preserving identities to an emphasis on visible minorities with corresponding attention to racism and racial discrimination; cross-cultural understanding, promotion of shared citizenship, and underrepresentation of historically disadvantaged minorities (Augustine, 2003). Since the mid-1990s, the notion of shared citizenship, institutional participation, and belonging has crept into the lexicon of official multiculturalism.

Despite its formal status and general acceptance, Canada's official multiculturalism remains widely misunderstood. Contrary to popular perception, official multiculturalism is not about celebrating differences or promoting ethnicity. Cultural diversity is tolerated under an official multiculturalism to the extent that individuals may identify with the cultural tradition of their choice provided this affiliation does not interfere with the rights of others, break the law, or violate key values and institutions. The focal point of an official multiculturalism is *disadvantage and inclusion,* not differences and exclusion. The removal of disadvantages because of prejudice and discrimination in advancing institutional inclusion remains the driving force behind Canada's multiculturalism policy (Fleras, 2001). To the extent that cultural differences are acknowledged, they are predicated on the liberal-universalist principle that our commonalities as individuals supersede our differences as group members. With the "pretend pluralism" of an official multiculturalism, cultural differences are deemed to be superficial, relatively unimportant in defining who you are or what you should get, and best restricted to the private or personal domain. More importantly, differences related to ethnicity, race, or nationality cannot be used to preclude full participation, democratic rights, or equal citizenship. In that an official multiculturalism is more concerned with our similarities than our differences, its role in building a Canada of many immigrant cultures cannot be easily refuted.

PUTTING MULTICULTURALISM TO THE TEST: THE GOOD, THE BAD, AND THE UGLY

Framing multiculturalism as a solution to the "problem" of immigration has drawn its share of criticism (Zwicker, 2001). Multiculturalism is criticized for doing too much or too little, depending on how people envision the future of Canada and the role of multiculturalism in achieving this anticipated vision. For some, multiculturalism is deemed a threat to Canada despite reassurances to the contrary ("a wolf in sheep's clothing"); for others, multiculturalism comes across as a toothless tiger despite promises of change and accommodation ("a sheep in wolf's clothing"). With varying visions of Canada as a society of many cultures, criticism is inevitable, largely because of disagreements over responses to the following questions: (a) what Canadians think multiculturalism does; (b) what they think it ought to do; (c) what multiculturalism really sets out to do; and (d) what realistically can be accomplished in light of political realities. Criticism also stems from failure to separate different levels of meaning implicit within the concept. References to multiculturalism can include multiculturalism as fact (ethnic diversity in Canada), as ideology (endorsing the ideals of tolerance), as policy (official initiatives to achieve goals), as practice (its manipulation by politicians and minority leaders), and as challenge (as a critique of monocultural society) (Fleras, 2001). Also contributing to criticism and confusion is a failure to distinguish the pragmatism of Canada's official multiculturalism from more freewheeling popular multiculturalisms found in the United States and Europe (Goldberg, 1994; also Pieterse, 2003).

To say that Canadians are divided over multiculturalism is surely an understatement. Multiculturalism is endorsed by some as a solution to the "problem" of living together with differences. Others, however, criticize multiculturalism as more of a problem than a solution. For purposes of analysis, critical reaction to multiculturalism can be classified into three categories (1) multiculturalism as "divisive," since it undermines Canadian society; (2) multiculturalism as "regressive," since it defuses minority aspirations and needs; (3) multiculturalism as "irrelevant," since it promises more diversity or equality than it can deliver. Each of these criticisms will be analyzed and assessed to determine their validity or value. Each criticism will then be criticized in turn to yield an alternative perspective. An oppositional reading suggests a more positive spin, reinforcing the notion that, like immigration, both benefits and costs interweave with burdens and opportunities. In this way multiculturalism will be revealed for what it is: an imperfect but innovative social experiment for living together with differences that is workable, necessary, and fair.

Is Multiculturalism Divisive?

To what extent does multiculturalism divide? Does it contribute to or undermine the possibility of a united Canada? Multiculturalism is widely denounced as an irritant to the goals of national unity and identity. The promotion of multiculturalism runs the risk of "Balkanizing" Canada by encouraging the creation of relatively separate ethnic communities with little in common for living together. Construction of a national identity is next to impossible when minorities are encouraged to pursue ethnic "tribalisms" at the expense of their duties as citizens (Bissoondath, 1994). Worse still, the possibility of ethnic conflict is intensified without a unifying vision for connecting the parts. And with continuing immigration from cultures whose values differ sharply from the mainstream, the risk of ethnic entanglements is significantly increased.

A close analysis of these arguments suggests an alternative view. Official multiculturalism originated and continues to exist as a pragmatic instrument for promoting unity— even uniformity—rather than diversity. Multiculturalism is not about celebrating diversity per se, as demonstrated in a careful reading of the Multiculturalism Act of 1988 (or of Trudeau's multiculturalism speech in 1971). Stated simply, the logic behind an official multiculturalism is clearly inclusive: to create a progressive and prosperous Canada that incorporates diversity as integral and legitimate without undermining either the interconnectedness of the whole or distinctiveness of the parts in the process. Multiculturalism rejects the promotion of self-sufficient ethnic groups with separate institutions and parallel power bases. It does not encourage an "anything goes" mentality. Emphasized instead is the right of individuals to identify with the ethno-cultural tradition of their choice provided this affiliation does not break laws, violate rights, or challenge core values and institutions.

Official multiculturalism is not about Canada-bashing. It is about Canada-building by integrating (not assimilating) minorities into society through removal of individual or institutional impediments. A "playful inversion" helps to put everything into perspective. An official multiculturalism is not what divides Canada or encourages ethnic enclaves. More accurately, it is the imposition of "monoculturalism" that creates the real problem in a changing and diverse society because of its potential to exclude or deny those who fall outside a preferred orbit. Furthermore, multiculturalism is not divisive in the same sense as the cultural politics of Quebec or First Nations. Most immigrant-Canadians are not anxious to dismantle Canada; rather, they have a vested interest in strengthening the country of their choice. The divisiveness within multiculturalism—where it does exist—arises from its manipulation by opportunistic politicians and minority leaders that have sabotaged multicultural principles for monocultural motives.

What about Canadian identity? Does multiculturalism foster a "visionless coexistence" through the mindless promotion of endless diversity where anything goes (Bibby, 1990)? On the contrary, multiculturalism enhances a perception of Canadians as a community of communities who are bound together by the one thing they share in common: their multiculturalism (CRIC, 2003). This commitment to multiculturalism (within a bilingual framework) is one of the definitive characteristics that distinguishes Canadians from Americans. Rather than undermining a sense of Canadianness, in other words, multiculturalism encourages a shared identity that secures the foundation for forging Canadians into a moral community (Canada Heritage, 2002). Or as put by Jean Chrétien, former prime minister of Canada, when challenged about the prospects of an identity crisis in light of high immigration levels and a proactive multicultural policy: "Multicultural!" is Canada's identity, explained Chrétien, "its identity is multicultural" (Lloyd, 2003).

Is Multiculturalism Regressive?

Multiculturalism has been criticized as a regressive tool that hinders rather than helps minority women and men. Official multiculturalism is dismissed as a policy of containment that is powerless in discrediting the cultural hegemony of the dominant sector (Henry and Tator, 2000; Bannerji, 2000). It also has the effect of controlling ethnicity by reinforcing those very structures that marginalized minorities in the first place. Consider how multiculturalism was accused not only of selling out to tighter security measures but also of failing to protect Arabs and Muslim Canadians because of heightened security concerns in the aftermath of "9/11" (Khouri, 2003). In failing to secure access to the corridors of power and resources, multiculturalism has also had the effect of creating ethnic ghettos that exclude and deny (Bissoondath, 1994). This exclusion may foster an underclass of minorities who have no say or stake in the system, with corresponding detriment to society at large (James, 1999). Such a critique involves two dimensions: Can cultural solutions be applied to structural problems involving the removal of systemic barriers (Bannerji, 2003)?

Can a policy directed at reforming society possibly address the root cause of social problems, or do we have yet another case of applying a quick-fix solution to a complex problem? In that multiculturalism is dismissed for not rising to the challenge of righting the wrongs, its dismissal as little more than hegemonic eyewash is assured.

There is an element of truth in criticizing multiculturalism as more problem than solution. Some minorities remain locked into low-paying ghettos without much prospect for escape (Kunz et al., 2001). New Canadians are not doing as well as earlier immigrants along a variety of fronts (Chui and Zietsma, 2003). Canadians such as African-Canadians and aboriginal peoples continue to perform poorly on many socio-economic indicators. Yet their exclusion and exploitation long predated the appearance of official multiculturalism. Moreover, there is no evidence to indict official multiculturalism for neglect of duty. To the contrary, the explicit intent of multiculturalism is the removal of discriminatory barriers to equality. Canada's multicultural policies have focused on dismantling the cultural fences that block ethnic involvement in Canadian society. The current anti-racist thrust of contemporary multiculturalism continues in this vein with its focus on full and equal participation. Consequently, programs and initiatives for righting past wrongs have been directed towards removing institutional barriers to improve institutional inclusion.

The conclusion seems inescapable. Multicultural objectives are concerned with integrating minorities into society rather than celebrating differences (Kymlicka, 1999). According to the logic of multiculturalism, diversity per se is not the problem, rather it is both public perceptions and socio-economic structures that define differences as problematic and disable minorities by excluding them from social space and social interaction. Multiculturalism is about removing minority disadvantage by ensuring that diversity markers are not used to deny, exclude, or exploit. With multiculturalism, everyone should be treated the same by ensuring that no is denied or excluded because of their differences. Reference to institutional inclusiveness looms heavily in this equation. In the past, immigrants and minorities were expected to fit into the existing institutional framework as part of the adjustment process. At present, however, institutions also are expected to move over and accommodate by rooting out systemic biases related to recruitment, hiring, promotion, and training.

Admittedly, there is no conclusive proof that an official multiculturalism improves minority socio-economic status. Its impact is indirect rather than explicit or measurable. Implementation of an official multiculturalism secures a supportive environment that fosters an equality of opportunity for all Canadians regardless of race or heritage. Multiculturalism provides a morally authoritative framework for managing intergroup tensions, capitalizing on opportunities created by diversity, improving integration by establishing settlement programs, and advancing access to equality and inclusion (Burnstein, 2003). Finally, an official multiculturalism equips minorities with an official platform for articulating their grievances by holding governments accountable for actions at odds with multicultural principles. In sum, an official multiculturalism serves to advance the interests of minorities, albeit within the framework of national interests—at least in principle if not always in practice.

Is Multiculturalism Irrelevant?

Manoly Lupul (1983) once remarked that multiculturalism is not taken seriously by anyone who is a somebody. There is a sliver of truth in this indictment (Jaworski, 1979).

Multiculturalism comes across as little more than a frivolous political diversion in which currency is symbolic rather than substantial. Much was promised in advancing high faluting multicultural principles, but little was delivered, except the illusion of transformation. Not unexpectedly, Canada's multiculturalism continues to be accused of covertly promoting assimilation (Bannerji, 2000). With multiculturalism, ethnic cultures are rigidified into frozen museum pieces rather than living and lived-in realities. Under multiculturalism, the centre continues to define what counts as difference, and what differences count. This "monocultural" commitment to a "pretend pluralism" rather than a commitment to "take difference seriously" has done little to disturb the prevailing distribution of power and privilege (also Macklem, 2001).

The consequences of promising much but delivering little exposes the moral bankruptcy of multiculturalism. Put bluntly, multiculturalism is dismissed as a relic from a bygone era. Canada is accused of coasting on a 30-year reputation in that an official multiculturalism no longer resonates with the realities of the 21st century (Goar, 2003). Multiculturalism was devised by well-established groups of Whites (French speaking, English speaking, and Europeans such as Italians, Germans, and Ukrainians). It was also introduced at a time when immigrants did not require much support in fitting in or settling down. Jobs were readily available in manufacturing and construction even for those with little English and limited schooling. But breaking into today's labour market and securing high-paying jobs is much more difficult, critics say, and failure of multiculturalism to address this challenge cannot be lightly brushed aside

Here the critics get it right—albeit for the wrong reason. There is no question that multiculturalism embraces an integrative and often conservative agenda. And, yes, multiculturalism is more about the symbols than the substance of change. But dismissing the symbolic value of multiculturalism may be premature. Symbols have the power to move mountains, and the symbol of Canada as multiculturalism secures the moral authority to bring about change. Moreover, such criticism simply chides multiculturalism for something it was never intended to do or was capable of doing in a diverse and changing Canada. An official multiculturalism never set out to challenge or transform the status quo. Goals were much more modest and practical: to advance the concept of a society of many cultures through the integration of immigrant Canadians regardless of colour or origins. Instead of a politicized diversity that challenged Canada's foundational structures, multiculturalism sought to "neuter" ethnicity by making it symbolic, situational, and safe—and unlikely to foster ethnic entanglements in the competition for scarce resources. Multiculturally speaking, minorities are entitled to identify and affiliate with the cultural tradition of their choice without sacrificing involvement in Canada. Canada, in turn, benefits from such symbolic attachments by creating a context in which all Canadians can live together with their differences by ensuring their differences don't get in the way of being Canadian.

ASSESSING MULTICULTURALISM: DOING WHAT IS WORKABLE, NECESSARY, AND FAIR

How does one assess 33 years of official multiculturalism? Has it been worth it? On balance, yes. Compared to the past, Canada is a much more tolerant and inclusive society. Compared to other societies, Canada's official multiculturalism stands as a paragon of virtue in the art of living together with differences. A package of policies and programs promises to advance minority concerns without compromising Canada's interests. To be sure, Canada's official multiculturalism is deeply flawed and deserving of constructive criticism. Canada may be an official multiculturalism; however, its multiculturalism is built on quicksand, not bedrock—with the result that public support can be described as a mile wide but only an inch thick (also Klute, 2001). Too much of what passes for official multiculturalism consists of platitudinous clichés rather than an honest appraisal of what is workable, necessary, and fair. Both public and political support of official multiculturalism tends toward the tepid. Multiculturalism commitments may prove little more than a polite political fiction—tolerable during peace or prosperity but revoked when costly or in an emergency.

A sense of proportion and perspective is required. However valid and valuable, criticism of multiculturalism is largely one-sided and polemical, and often misreads both intent or capacities. The contributions of official multiculturalism in advancing a cooperative coexistence should not be judged against unrealistic standards. Just as multiculturalism cannot be blamed for everything that is wrong in Canada, so too should we avoid excessive praise. The nature of its impact and implications hovers somewhere between the poles of unblemished good and unabashed evil. Multiculturalism is neither the root of all Canada's social problems nor the all-encompassing solution to problems that rightfully belong to political or economic domains. It is but one component—however imperfect—for engaging immigrant diversity by balancing the competing demands of national unity and individual rights with the concerns of minority women and men (Kallen, 2003). The multidimensionality of multiculturalism is deftly captured in this passage from the Department of Canadian Heritage (2003):

> What sets Canada apart from most other countries is how differences within the population have not only been accepted, but are recognized as a source of strength. Canada's ethnocultural diversity generates a rich and productive mix of different ideas and perspectives that promotes creativity, innovation, and "global thinking." The many different ethnic origins and nationalities within the Canadian population mean that, as a trading nation in the global economy, we have invaluable ties to all parts of the world. But it is in building a peaceful, harmonious society that diversity plays its most dynamic role. It challenges us to adapt and relate to one another *despite* our differences, which encourages understanding, flexibility, and compromise. This makes us resilient— able to accommodate different points of view and see different ways to solve problems. It is one reason why Canada has distinguished itself on the world stage as a successful mediator in the promotion of international peace and human security.

Multiculturalism has done much to re-contour Canada's political landscape. From a monocultural colony and Anglocentric outpost, Canada has evolved into one of the world's most cosmopolitan societies. Multiculturalism has also bolstered Canada's much ballyhooed status as a trailblazer in creating a society both diverse yet cohesive, equitable yet inclusive (Li, 2003). The notion that a society of many cultures can exist by emphasizing unity and uniformity rather than diversity may not appeal to those with unrealistically high expectations for multicultural coexistence. But options are limited for constructively engaging diversity in a capitalist, liberal-democratic Canada. Under the circumstances, it is not a question of whether Canada can afford multiculturalism. More to the point, Canada cannot afford *not* to embrace multiculturalism in advancing the ideals of national unity and cultural diversity without sacrificing economic prosperity and international repute.

DISCUSSION QUESTIONS

1   On the basis of material in this chapter, what is (are) the problem(s) that Canada's official multiculturalism is trying to solve? Has multiculturalism proven more of a solution or a problem in advancing Canada-building?

2   In what ways is immigration in Canada both a cost and a benefit? Do public and critical perceptions of immigration add to or detract from our understanding of immigration?

3   Critics of Canada's immigration program tend to organize their criticism around the questions of "how many," "where from," and "what class." Indicate the nature of the debate with respect to these questions.

4   What are the major concerns and goals of immigrants in Canada? What barriers preclude attainment of these concerns and goals?

5   Account for why immigrants who arrived in the 1990s are not doing as well in catching up to their Canadian counterparts as immigrants who arrived in the 1970s.

 ## WEBLINKS

Canada's official site for multiculturalism under the auspices of the Department of Canadian Heritage.   **www.pch.gc.ca**

Canada's official site that addresses a host of immigrant issues, especially in relation to citizenship.   **http://cicnet.ci.gc.ca**

Additional information about Canadian immigration issues.   **www.info-Canada.com**

part five

Globalization and Global Problems

G*lobalization*. Rarely has a concept leapt into ordinary discourse with such intensity and scale, alarming some, reassuring others, and bewildering most (Brawley, 2003). As the dominant force in the last decade of the 20th century, globalization entails a convergence of relationships that transcend national boundaries, including policy shifts to promote economic efficiency through trade liberalization and the deregulation of national markets through removal of impediments to a freewheeling market economy. A commitment to "lean and mean" in a global economy has proven a bonus for some: The economy is booming, stock markets are soaring, corporate profits are escalating, inflation is dead, and shareholders are clutching hefty returns on their investments. The forces of globalization are proving capable of generating new freedoms and material affluence by unlocking dormant potentials. Awareness of a shared human experience on a planetary scale is expanding under globalization, thus reinforcing a belief that what we have in common as achievement-oriented individuals is more important than what divides us as members of different groups.

Yet the "insatiable restlessness" of global capitalism comes with a price tag (Skidelsky, 1998). Many are disturbed by this global ideological shift toward open borders and financial deregulation (Watson, 1999). Economic benefits are in evidence, to be sure, but for whom and at what costs to individual security, social cohesion, and political survival—in effect, reminding critics of a 1950s observation by a Brazilian general when commenting on the health of his country's economy: "The economy is doing great, but unfortunately the people in it aren't" (Hargrove, 1998: 3).Three questions come to mind: first, how to ensure that globalization and economic integration do not lead to domestic social disintegration; second, how to foster social cohesiveness not only in the sense of shared values pertaining to mutual commitment, trust, and reciprocity but also through the distribution of benefits; and third, to find a working balance between intrusive government intervention and unfettered market forces (Standing Senate Committee on Social Affairs, *Toronto Star* 1999).

We may all share a single planet, but we live in radically different worlds of the haves and the have-nots. To one side are those lucky enough to be born in the right time and the right place; to the other side are those held captive by cruel circumstances (Traverse, 2003). For those born "lucky" the last decade has proven a boom; for others, including the inhabitants of over 50 countries, many in Africa, they are poorer and hungrier than they were in 1990. Those who bear a disproportionate share of the burdens and risks associated with growth but with few of the benefits will not passively accept their fate. Without a stake in the system and economic growth, the excluded may withdraw support for policies and programs that endorse open economies. Others may try to tear down the system with violence, if necessary, to procure a more equitable state of society. As Ralph Peters (1999: 41) writes in a millennial essay for *Maclean's* magazine:

> The paradox of the next century is that it will be one of fabulous wealth for us, but of bitter poverty for billions of others. The world will "come together" but already has begun to divide anew between open and tradition-bound societies, between rule-of-law states and lawless territories with flags, and between brilliant postmodern economies and cultures utterly unequipped for global competition. We will be envied and hated by those without a formula to win.

Contemporary social problems are increasingly expressed as global problems. Global problems related to overpopulation, environmental deterioration, sprawling urbanization, global monoculturalism, ethnic nationalism, and gaping inequalities are as much a problem of the developed world as the developing world, but each of these appears to be most acutely manifested in developing world contexts. The challenge for the new millennium because of these formidable problems is fourfold: The first is that of peace. This prospect is complicated by the existence of countries at war or emerging from conflicts involving genocide and intercommunal massacres. The second is poverty and inequality, a situation in which the rich and the poor live side by side at both national and international levels. The third is focused on sustainable development and the management of the global environment that ensures a future for generations to come. Fourth and finally is the need to overcome the more disorienting aspects of globalization, namely, the loss of those maps and compasses by which a society can control a destiny consistent with its priorities and agenda. And herein is the quintessential dilemma of the millennium: the challenge is not to stop the expansion of globalization with its free flow of money and ideas, although a system that privileges profits over people may prove problematic if allowed to career out of control. Rather, the trick is in negotiating "bottoms-up" rules for preserving the advantages of global markets and competition without discarding those human, environmental, and community resources that enhance the quality of life on our increasingly fragile yet beleaguered planet.

chapter thirteen

Globalization and Global Problems

FRAMING THE PROBLEM

The world we inhabit appears to be in disarray. The global drive for growth is laying waste to a planet that cannot possibly sustain a consumer-driven lifestyle without self-imploding (Suzuki, 1999). Images of emaciated refugees or mangled corpses have become so commonplace as to lose all shock value. Lip service to democratic ideals is routinely betrayed by the authoritarianism of despots, military juntas, tribal cleansings, and religion-based fanaticism. The social fabric of society is further shredded by a proliferation of hatred and hostilities but a shortage of good will and political will (Worldwatch Institute, 2003). The scope of poverty is staggering: According to the UN Human Development Report, about one-quarter of the world's population (or around 1.5 billion people) live on less than one American dollar a day. Nearly a billion are illiterate; another billion go hungry; and about one-third of the population in the developing countries will not survive to 40—half of the average life expectancy in Canada (Leisinger et al., 2002). To the consternation of many, this gulf between rich and poor is drifting towards a kind of "global apartheid." Extremes of power and wealth are compressed into geographically segregated zones to create an "apartness" every bit as punitive and pervasive as apartheid once was in South Africa (Richmond, 1994).

No one should underestimate the cumulative impact of these unruly forces. Developing countries appear to be hopelessly mired in an endless cycle of crisis, conflict, corruption, and catastrophe, with no solution in sight. Contradictions prevail, and are captured in this scathing indictment of a three-tiered world—those that spend money to keep their weight down, those who eat to live, and those who don't know where their next meal will come from (Kawachi and Kennedy, 2002). Or consider this disparity: The Internet may be transforming how we work, relate, and communicate in a global world, but half of the world's population has yet to make its first phone call (Leigh, 2001). A conflict of interest is inevitable: The developing world craves the material trappings of a modern society, with a comparable standard of living. Yet it appears incapable of paying the price for economic progress. Instead of pulling together for national unity and the common good, the prognosis is yet more tribalism, xenophobia, and ethnic chauvinism. To add insult to injury, efforts to help may hinder (Rieff, 2002): Many developing countries are recipients of foreign aid assistance or favourable trade arrangement but developmental opportunities are squandered because of corruption, expediency, miscalculation, or gross incompetence—on both sides of the give-and-take ledger.

Who is responsible for the social problems of the developing world? Should the local inhabitants take responsibility for poverty and impoverishment that infuse their daily lives? Or does responsibility rest with external forces? Centuries of exploitation under colonialism have proven pivotal in shaping negative outcomes. Many developing countries have been ruthlessly stripped of the very resources they require for recovery. Both direct and indirect rule have sapped entire communities of the resourcefulness for addressing local problems. Patterns of dependency and underdevelopment are no less debilitating. Direct colonial rule is no longer the case, having given way to indirect rule (or neocolonialism), with its nominal political independence but continued economic control and dependency. However, a corporate global market model known as globalization may well represent the latest incarnation of colonialism by another name.

Globalization has emerged as one of the most politically charged battlegrounds of our era (Clark, 2003; Atasoy and Carroll, 2003). Much of the debate touches on the nature and scope of globalization—either as a benign force for prosperity or as a ruthless engine of injustice (Legrain, 2003). For some, globalization symbolizes a catalyst for universal progress; for others, a race to the bottom for the poor of this world; and for still others, free market penetration across the globe with some costly side effects. The benefits of globalization are widely proclaimed, but many don't like what is happening to society or their personal lives (Goar, 2003; Bricker and Greenspon, 2003; Renner and O'Sheehan, 2003). Who can blame them? The triumph of globalization has culminated in an integrated global system that differentially incorporates societies into a vast productive loop that transcends time and space (Bricker and Greenspon, 2001). But cross-border flows of capital and money markets continue to play havoc with national performance over needs, growth, identity, and competitiveness (Chan and Scarritt, 2002). Cultural diversity, social security, and ecologically sensitive practices are increasingly displaced by a global governance that extols commercialism, consumerism, and a culture of disenchantment (Hahnel, 1999; Rajee, 2000). Not surprisingly, the emergence of globalization as the prevailing economic paradigm of our era is not without criticism, especially when short-term profits take priority over long-term prosperity (Kelsey, 2002). Critics rip into globalization as:

... a system fuelled by the belief that a single global economy with universal rules set by global corporations and financial markets .... Everything is for sale even those areas of life once considered sacred. Increasingly, these services and resources are controlled by a handful of transnational corporations that shape national and international law to suit their interests. At the heart of this transformation is an all-out assault on virtually every public sphere of life .... The most important tool in this assault has been the creation of international trade agreements whose tribunals and enforcements supersede the legal systems of nation-states ... (Barlow, 1999).

Such bleakness does not bode well for a functioning world order, and this chapter takes a cue from this scenario by exploring global problems from a social problem perspective. A raft of global problems is discussed by situating them within the context of globalization as a promise and a peril. The chapter begins appropriately enough by looking at the concept of globalization as a powerful social force with a double-edged capacity to enrich or disempower—depending on the context, criteria, or consequences. The focus then shifts to a host of global problems that engulf the planet at present; namely, overpopulation, urbanization, poverty, global monoculture, and ethnic conflicts, with particular attention to disfigurements to the environment. This chapter emphasizes the importance of uncovering those root causes that are largely responsible for global problems. Proposed solutions are shown to be sharply contested and deeply flawed. For some, the developing world must become more modern by discarding those social and cultural dimensions that preclude progress. For others, the path to salvation lies in severing the bonds of dependency and underdevelopment by becoming less Western while pursuing a relatively independent course of action. The politics of foreign aid and (under)development provide insight into the promises and perils of "helping others." Good intentions notwithstanding, foreign-aid programs have proven more of a problem than a solution because of hidden agendas, faulty assumptions, and unforeseen consequences. Emergence of a human rights agenda as a basis for living together promises an innovative blueprint for a new global governance.

A word of caution before proceeding. Placement of global problems in this section is not meant to blame the developing world. Developing world countries are no more the architects of their own misfortunes than poor Canadians are wholly responsible for their poverty. Structural forces and government policies that perpetuate patterns of dependency and underdevelopment must shoulder the blame. That makes it doubly important for Canadians to connect their pampered lifestyle with an unjust profit-oriented process, the exploitative nature of which is globalized (Bigelow and Peterson, 2002). To do otherwise, that is, by holding the victims entirely accountable for forces largely beyond their control, is too simplistic in a world where an Indonesian worker earns a couple of bucks a day making Nikes that retail for $150 in Canada. Nor should we expect the developing countries to make disproportionate sacrifices for a solution. On the contrary, global problems are arguably Western problems; the responsibility for solutions must be allocated accordingly. In other words, the Western world must reposition itself as a solution to the global problems that it created in the first place. Finally, global problems are not exclusive to the developing world. Canada too has its share of problems related to poverty, overpopulation, urbanization, ethnic conflicts, and environmental degradation. Academia, however, dictates a discussion of these global problems where they are most acutely manifest and most in need of solutions.

GLOBALIZATION: PROBLEM OR SOLUTION?

use

The world is full of contradictions, conflict, and change. Whether we approve or disapprove, broad historical forces are disrupting the routine and familiar to the dismay of many. For some, the greatest danger comes from those religiously inspired or state-sponsored terrorist groups that have no qualms about using weapons of mass destruction against civilian targets (Dershowitz, 2002). For others, the major threat is the "systemic terrorism" of global market forces, including transnational corporations and the structural adjustments advocated by the World Trade Organization and International Monetary Fund (Kelsey, 2002). With globalization, a new constitutional framework is envisaged that promises to redefine the rules and institutions by which to govern society and a world order. This new global governance is not simply a reorganization of widgets around a computer-based economy. A revolutionary shift in "doing business" is now taking place, in effect offering an opportunity for some, marginalization for others, and confusion for still others (Shiva, 2002). Just as the Industrial Revolution signified a radical break with its feudal predecessors, so too has an information-driven, post-industrialism established a fundamentally different way of creating, defining, and distributing wealth. The transformative dimension of globalization is captured by Jane Fraser and Jeremy Oppenheim in a 1997 issue of *The McKinsey Quarterly*:

> We are on the brink of a major, long term transformation of the world economy from a series of local industries locked in closed national economies to a system of integrated global markets contested by global players (Davies, 1999).

gyrate
cacophony

With globalization, the ground rules are changing. So too is the game itself, as players and strategies realign themselves accordingly. The globalization game board has no boundaries, the rules of the game are up for grabs, the number of players increases exponentially, occasionally the owners will pick up the ball and move away when the financial tap dries up, and every so often the playing field may tilt and gyrate wildly out of control (Davies, 1999). Such a cacophony of contradictions is as disruptive as it is opportunistic as people struggle to make sense of the world by integrating seeming opposites into a liveable blueprint (also Manji, 2003/04).

The term "globalization" is one of those nebulous turns of phrases with a fathomless capacity to infuriate, confuse, or enlighten. As an inexact term for a wild assortment of activities and processes, globalization is often hailed as the defining historical moment of our times, despite suffering from overuse as the prevailing mantra of business, politics, and culture (Scholte, 1997). People read different meanings into globalization (Doran, 2002; Hall, 2002): Some focus on the rapid and unfettered flow of capital through international trade and movement of capital (from currencies to stocks); others emphasize the integration of national economic systems with the emergence of a global division of labour; still others focus on the expanding communication networks that organize people's lives around a global village so that political or cultural events in one part of the world quickly come to have significance for people in other parts of the world; and yet others point to non-state actors such as transnational corporations who are heralding a paradigm shift in world politics and global economics because of advances in communication, transportation, and information technologies (Hall, 2002; Lagon, 2003; Legrain, 2003). Even the ontological status of globalization is up for grabs. Globalization is acknowledged by some as a real and profoundly transformative force that is here to stay (Hall, 2002). Opposed are those skeptics who regard this diagnosis as highly exaggerated (Held and McGrew, 2002; Atasoy, 2003).

References to the inevitability of globalization are dismissed as little more than a smokescreen or scapegoat that politicians or CEOs invoke to justify unpleasant decisions ("beyond our control") such as cuts in social spending or factory closures.

Reactions to Globalization

The mantra of globalization is widely approved, but there is an underbelly to globalization that rankles and provokes (Friedman, 2003). Globalization not only symbolizes a lightening rod that captures public unease over a rapidly changing world; it also provokes strong reactions (from protests to terrorism) because of disruptions to the economy and concerns over cultural influences, writes Ian Linden in his book *A New Map of the World* (Geographical Dossier, 2003). New vulnerabilities are exposed or created by globalization: Criminal elements take advantage of the technology to traffic in drugs or arms; international pedophiles exchange information; terrorist groups take advantage of more porous borders; and diseases travel more quickly than before (Hall, 2002). Foremost among these concerns are fears over unbridled American power, the might of big business, the pace of economic change, the growing divide between rich and poor, the sense of powerlessness, and a hollowing out of state regulatory powers by market fundamentalism (Legrain, 2003). Globalization is accused of intensifying inequities as regions and states compete for corporate investment, in the process lowering wages, eroding environmental standards, and compromising human rights protections (Worldwatch Institute, 2003). Financial transactions under globalization are deemed a recipe for chaos or crisis. The vast sums that are traded daily on the financial markets do little to enhance national economic performance since any wheeling and dealing is divorced from trade or production (Legrain, 2003; also Plender, 2002). Even corporate mergers do not result in productive gains. Rising stock prices simply provide corporations with more cash to buy up competitors (Hurtig, 2002). The result? All citizens, institutions, and values are increasingly squeezed into an ideological framework that defines the quality of something by its market value. Furthermore, the globalization of culture may amplify global uniformity around the free market values of individualism, rationality, and progress (Ritzer, 2000). Finally, globalization is associated with threats of insecurity through high technology or proliferation of weapons of mass destruction or criminality ranging from trafficking (including humans) to the piracy of intellectual property (Lagon, 2003).

No less evident is support for globalization. The anticipated benefits of globalization are fourfold: an expanded pie vision so that everyone's lot is improving; information penetration which will undermine elite control while creating a real-time information economy; a universal solvent vision that washes away autocratic regimes through trade liberalization and foreign investment; and a "peace dividend" by weaving interdependencies between nation-states (Lagon, 2003). For supporters, globalization is viewed as a catalyst for national prosperity through the elimination of artificial barriers to free enterprise. A borderless world of boundless prosperity is envisaged, anchored around the promotion of global consumerism and the demise of market-meddling state institutions (Capling, 1997). According to Johan Norberg, author of *In Defence of Globalization*, worldwide living standards under globalization are rising because of increased productivity and wages. For example, the number of those living on less than a dollar a day declined from 28 percent in 1990 to 23 percent in 1998. The number of "democratic" regimes grew from 44 to 82 between 1985 and 2000, while the number of authoritarian regimes dwindled from 67 to 26

(Legrain, 2003). Investments in developing countries by transnational corporations provide new technology, new management skills, a larger market, and more educated workers. Freer trade reduces poverty and increases wealth—although many Western countries do not always practice what they preach when imposing tariffs and anti-dumping legislation that effectively blocks trade with poorer nations (Canadian Press, 30 April, 2003).

An intermediate position acknowledges both benefits and costs, often simultaneously (Brooks, 2003). Put bluntly, globalization is not some rigidly scripted unfolding with uniform effects across a variety of societies but a complex process involving multiple flows of ideas and goods with different impacts in diverse contexts (Chan and Scarritt, 2002). A dialectical line of thinking interprets globalization as a problem and an opportunity regardless of the criteria employed. For cosmopolitan elites, the cultural hybridity and instantaneous flows of information and communication associated with globalization are empowering; for locals in developing countries, the impact is yet more impoverishment (Richmond, 2002). Globalization offers economic growth for some; others are discarded as little more than disposable labour; information can liberate but also impose more sophisticated forms of surveillance and control; and growing interconnectedness through information sharing can intensify animosities and fuel reactionary politics as is amply demonstrated in the ongoing tensions between Israel and Palestinian Authority (Held and McGrew, 2002; Lagon, 2003). The promise of universal harmony through a single global economy is contradicted by a fear of anarchic global forces that propel vested interests into more dangerous rivalries (Gray, 1997). Some lament a globalization that erodes national sovereignty to the point of paralysis. Others take comfort in a process that is exposing human rights violations while taming the lawlessness that hides behind the cloak of national sovereignty. In some cases, benefits create costs. The primary objectives of modern globalization—namely, scale, access, speed, efficiency, predictability, and control—may enhance people's ability to control their lives (Naim, 2003). Yet increased interconnectedness leaves humankind more vulnerable to unforeseen risks—a situation graphically brought home by the May 2000 "love bug" virus that infected government, business, and personal computers around the world costing billions in damage and lost productivity. In the words of Hedley (2002: 3) in acknowledging risks when globalization strips away the insulating effects of a delayed response:

> The love bug incident reveals an interesting paradox about control in the global age. On the one hand, interconnected real-time global networks are created to increase predictability and control. Yet on the other hand, their very structure makes them highly susceptible to massively disrupting chain reactions which are threats to control. Consequently, the price ... is higher environmental risk.

It is this two-edged character of globalization—connectedness as control or out of control—that generates much of the concern, criticism, and controversy. Not everyone is against globalization per se; what is resented is a globalization imposed "from above" by greedy corporate interests rather than a "bottoms-up" globalization that puts people ahead of profits (Star and Adams, 2003).

On the surface, there is nothing radically new about globalization as a powerful force that integrates societies into a worldwide web of trade and investments. Globalization is not distinguished by the volume of international trade which, only now, is approaching pre-1914 levels of free trade (Leigh, 2001; Atasoy, 2003). What is new is the striking speed and sweep of this transformation (Richmond, 2002; Coleman, 2002). Globalization is innovative in matching communication and information technologies with an ideological frame-work that extols the virtues of unregulated free market dynamics, free trade as a catalyst for growth, elimination of import substitution economies and protective tariffs, privatiza-tion of public enterprises, and an aggressive consumerism (Mander and Goldstein, 1996). Its novelty extends to relationships increasingly organized around linkages that *transcend* national boundaries rather than simply between them to exchange goods or services. Thanks to the gravity-defying, leapfrogging ease of computer-driven communications, the world is differently structured under globalization: The forces of production, distribution/transmission, and consumption of goods and services are globally organized rather than managed at local or national levels (Hedley, 2002). Global flows that both con-flate yet transcend time and space ensure a truly global economy—one big domestic mar-ket—with export trade as primary rather than residual.

conflate

Globalization is redefining the established world order. In conceding that the terrain in which these processes operate is global rather than national or local, that is, across rather than between borders, the world of sharply bounded trading units dissolves into a loosely integrated world order involving novel patterns of human organization, wealth creation, and social action (Albrow, 1996; Supiot, 2003). Under globalization, national economies are reorganized around an integrated system of production. Gone are Fordist models of production with their emphasis on mass and standardized production, vertical integration, economies of scale, and deskilled labour (Holly, 1996). A post-Fordist model of wealth creation is embraced instead around the primacy of export trade rather than domestic con-sumption. Inefficient industries are abandoned in favour of more flexible systems for pro-ducing varied and specialized goods and services, while foreign investment and onshore jobs are vigorously pursued through creation of "business-friendly" environments. This reorganization of production into global loops of cost-effective sites compels economies to specialize or perish in the competition for markets, investments, and jobs (Laxer, 1991). In global trade parlance, this specialization conforms to the law of comparative advantage; that is, prosperity is best achieved when each economy specializes in what it does best, and trades accordingly (Clegg, 1996).

Conceptualizing Globalization

Albert Einstein once said that categories are not inherent in phenomena. A similar line of reasoning applies to defining globalization. There is no one correct definition of global-ization but many different meanings depending on who is defining and in what context (Hedley, 2002). The term globalization encompasses everything from downsizing and deregulation, to the freer movement of goods, ideas, and capital across rather than between borders, with information highways thrown in for good measure. Related processes are encompassed as well, including the interconnectedness associated with a global village, with the growing perception that people are enjoying the same food and drink, watching the same movies, and driving the same cars as everyone else. The multidimensional nature of globalization is clearly evident, namely, globalization as economic phenomenon (reduced trade barriers, high volumes of international commerce and investment, world-wide competition, and mobility of production to cheaper sites); as well as political (a diminishing of state sovereignty because of international agencies, transnational corpora-tions, and regulatory bodies); cultural (potential to homogenize cultures because of market forces that disrupt local conventions); social (disruption to community patterns); and communicative (new and rapid information networks) (Chan and Scarritt, 2002).

Defining globalization depends on how people frame it—positively or negatively. To one side, are optimists: Globalization is defined as a process of change in which the local and the national are amalgamated with the global into a single, integrated world system that transcends national borders. A relatively free exchange of goods and services is generated through the elimination of barriers, opening local markets to global capital flows of everything from money and markets to people and ideas that move swiftly and smoothly across national boundaries. For Ian Linden, author of *A New Map of the World*, globalization refers to the global integration of the economy involving two main features: the vast volume of cross-border world trade (70 percent) by transnational corporations; the shift in the world economy from physical commodities to money exchanges in the form of derivatives or foreign investment—daily financial flows in the late 1990s stood at $1.5 trillion per day thanks to the instantaneous transfer of money and information, up from $200 million per day (Geographical Dossier, 2003). To facilitate the flow of finance capital, the World Trade Organization insists that (a) goods sourced in another country must receive the same treatment as domestic goods (i.e., governments cannot discriminate in favour of local interests); (b) the best treatment that governments give to any one member must be extended to all members; and (c) governments must continue to dismantle barriers that preclude free trade (Kelsey, 2002). The compression of "space-time" profoundly influences the unprecedented speed of transactions in the global marketplace (Atasoy, 2003). Such insight is aptly articulated by Held and McGrew (2002: 1):

> Globalization, simply put, denotes the expanding scale, growing magnitude, speeding up and deepening impact of transcontinental flows and patterns of social interaction. It refers to a shift or transformation in the scale of human organization that links distant communities and expands the reach of power relations across the world's regions and continents.

Note: globalization and globalism differ. Globalization involves a process of transformation, whereas globalism refers to a neoliberal market ideology that endows globalization with the following values and norms: primacy of economic growth, importance of free trade for prosperity, unrestricted free market, individual choice, reduced government intervention, and a modernization model of economic development (Steger, 2002).

To the other side of the definitional divide are the critics. Globalization is defined as the geographic penetration of capitalist market relations into new sites of production in the relentless quest of profits, markets, and shares (Barlow and Clarke, 1996). The driving imperative of economic globalization is maximizing profit for capitalist classes by creating a global free market in which capital and investment can move freely to secure the highest return with the least impediment (Kelsey, 2002). Some equate globalization to an exercise in "soft hegemony," that is, a tool by rich societies to gain disproportionate advantage (Chan and Scarritt, 2002). Others are less sanguine: In a strongly worded critique, William Robinson (1996) couches globalization in apocalyptic terms as a planetary struggle between the cosmopolitan rich and the parochial poor from which there is no escape. The impact of globalization on human and environmental worlds is comparable in predatory scale to the ravages of 19th century colonialism. In that corporate globalization is simply an extension of a colonialism and capitalism with its commitment to exploit cheap labour under international agencies and transnational corporations, it's business as usual (Nagra, 2003).

Four implications follow from these definitions: First, globalization constitutes an international system of exchange with its own set of rules, logic, structures, and procedures. As an economic process, globalization involves a significant increase in cross-national flows of trade, investment, and technology that reflects and reinforces a global division of labour (Steger, 2002). It also involves an integration of markets, nation-states, and information technologies into one productive loop. Second, globalization goes beyond a simple economic shift created by the cross-border exchanges of high technology, instantaneous communication, investment, reduced subsidies, and free trade. The globalization of business has prompted a reorganization of products, markets, and finances of unprecedented magnitude and scope, in effect creating interdependencies that could not have existed in the past. No economy is left untouched in the ruthless compulsion to displace protectionism with export-oriented trade. Yet the resulting interdependency is uneven and fragmented, with gross disparities in control over power, resources, and status. Societies and sectors differ in their degree of vulnerability and ability to take advantage of opportunities (Chan and Scarritt, 2002). While some benefit, many are excluded, thereby reinforcing patterns of segregation in an interconnected globe (Held and McGrew, 2002). Globalization also entails a shift in values: Cultural alternatives are under threat from a singular hegemony revolving around commercialism, consumerism, and discontent. Third, the ascendancy of globalization has compelled a rethinking of what society is for. Borders have become increasingly porous with the advent of microchip technologies, while the salience of the nation-state as a relatively autonomous unit of political economy is challenged by the unimpeded flow of capital and investment. Questions arise: Does society exist to enhance the well-being of its community members through state intervention? Or is its prime purpose to create economic-friendly conditions by unfettering markets? What is the role of the market versus the state in creating and distributing wealth? As Marx predicted a century and a half ago, a solution ("answer") has yet to be found to this problem ("question"). Fourth, the interplay of world economic markets and globalization has undermined conventional thinking about national sovereignty. People increasingly see the world as a single place they call home, with a corresponding reorientation of social awareness and social imagination in people's perception of citizenship, identity, community, and democracy (Geographical Dossier, 2003). The once exclusive authority of the sovereign state is diminished further when stateless corporations, known as transnational corporations, replace domestic production as engines for wealth creation.

| CASE 13-1 | Transnational Corporations: Engines of Injustice Or Catalysts for Growth? |

The cumulative effect of centuries of capitalist expansion cannot be underestimated. All countries are now absorbed into a capitalist world system in which free market principles define, organize, and design the production and distribution of goods and services. National economies are inextricably linked with a free-flowing international division of labour. Competition for markets, jobs, and resources is increasingly conducted without much interference from the regulatory mechanisms of national boundaries. The result? Affluent countries

(continued on next page)

enrich themselves at the expense of the poor by taking unfair advantage through the control of investment, bank loans, hedge-fund speculation, trade and tariffs, and industrial dependency. The engines behind this reorganization in the production and consumption of goods with a corresponding uneven development and imbalanced international division of labour are transnational (or multinational) corporations (Randall and Theobald, 1998).

Few will dispute the impact of transnational corporations in transforming the world along global lines (Clegg, 1996). Once reviled in capitalist and communist countries alike because of their predatory instincts, transnationals are now eagerly courted as the embodiment of modernity and progress, with governments around the world lining up to attract these money-making machines (Emmott, 1993). They are the foremost actors on the global stage, straddling national boundaries and generating sales in automobiles, oil, electronics, computers, and banking that often exceed the aggregate (GNP) output of most countries (Carnoy, 1996). The incursion of huge transnational corporations into genetically modified crops confers enormous power over the world's food supply through increased dependency on agrochemicals (Simms, 1999). Their spectacular growth in recent years can be attributed to different factors, including government failure to regulate overseas investment, rapid telecommunication and transport systems, reduction of tariffs and trade duties, and the softening up of domestic markets for international trade. With capital more mobile than at any time in history, all countries are competing for a share of this investment (Bricker and Greenspon, 2001). Transnationals have taken advantage of largely American-driven moves to expand the investment market by exploiting wage and cost differentials among different regimes in the world (Palat, 1996). The ultimate goal is an integrated global production system in which individual countries constitute but one link in a vast production chain of transnationally controlled "stateless corporations."

Transnational corporations can be defined as multi-tiered networks that include parent companies, foreign affiliates, alliances with other companies, and contractual agreements that enhance control over the entire production process. This control extends from research and development to transport, assembly, marketing, and finance. The scale of transnationals is staggering. Globalization is being driven by about 60 000 transnational corporations with more than half a million overseas affiliates, accounting for about one-quarter of total global output, the most lucrative source of foreign investment for developing countries, and a key conduit for the introduction of advanced technologies (Edwards, 1999). Currently, the world's largest transnationals include Wal-Mart Stores with revenues in 2002 of $219.8 billion or approximately the same volume as the GDP in Sweden, followed by Exxon Mobil at $191.6 (larger than Turkey), General Motors, BP, Ford Motor, Enron, DaimlerChrysler, Royal Dutch Shell, General Electronic (which was number one in 1998), and Toyota Motors (*Fortune Magazine*, 26 July, 2002). Only three Canadian companies rank in the world's top 100 transnationals: Seagrams at 23rd, BCE (the telecommunications company) at 49th, and Thomson (printing and publishing) at 52nd (Edwards, 1999). By the late 1990s,

(continued on next page)

51 of the top 100 economies in the world were transnational corporations: Mitsubishi was bigger than the fourth most populous country in the world (Indonesia), GM was larger than Denmark or Norway, and Daimler-Chrysler outpaced both South Africa and Saudi Arabia. The combined revenue of the 200 largest corporations is greater than that of the 182 nation-states that have responsibility for the livelihood of 80 percent of humanity (Clarke, 1999). Only ten industrialized countries export more than the world's ten biggest transnationals, according to the *UNESCO Courier* (July/August, 1999). Canada, of course, is not immune to this corporatization: Foreign corporate holdings of Canadian companies stood at $217 billion in 1998, up from $148 billion in 1990 (MacKinnon, 1999). Of the 12 725 foreign-owned corporations in Canada in 1998 with revenues of $15 million or assets of $10 million, 53.6 percent were American-owned, and 26.6 percent were from the European Union, according to Statistics Canada, with chemical, transportation equipment, and electrical products the sectors with the highest degree of foreign control in 1996.

The global economic power harnessed by the transnational mobility of these stateless conglomerates is impressive. Unfettered as they are by national boundaries or state loyalties, transnationals can move to whatever part of the globe that promises the best return on their investment. They operate in a global context that does not as yet have an adequate framework for regulating these dynamos. Both wealth creation and the means of production have been redesigned in response to the logic of transnationalism. Consider the protectionism of the past: the Import

Substitution Model was directed at erecting high tariffs to attract capital, thus taking advantage of protection from external competition to ensure local prosperity (Bricker and Greenspon, 2001; Doran, 2002). But the strategy is no longer viable: Global systems of production involve components and assembly in different countries, with a new international division of labour on the basis of product location (Crane, 1996). The capacity of a transnational to outsource production is matched only by an ability to market internationally. The home office of Nokia cell phones may be Finland, but parts and labour are linked with Japan, Thailand, Taiwan, and the United States (Doran, 2002). The transformation of the world into a global loop of cost-effective production sites makes a mockery of the moniker: "Made in country X."

The role of transnationals in advancing global systems is self-evident. Yet the integrity of sovereign states is under challenge. These stateless corporations now wield more economic and political clout than many national governments. Transnationals can shift production from one location to another because of increased capital mobility. One country can be played off against another by moving labour-intensive operations offshore to take advantage of cheaper labour and tax breaks (Marchak, 1991). These changing production patterns impose new and frightening realities for workers (Balakrishnan, 2002). The cost of a pair of Nike Air Siroccos (US$120), coupled with Phil Knight's stock value in Nike ($4.5 billion) and millions paid for high-profile sponsors certainly dwarfs the daily wage of workers in Indonesia ($1.10); China ($2.00); and Vietnam ($1.60) (Bigelow and Peterson, 2002). As bluntly stated

(continued on next page)

by Adam Zimmerman, chairman of Noranda, "If you are in a business that can move, why bother with the hassles of staying in Canada?" (Hurtig, 1991). What is the point of doing business in a country where industrial wages average around $15/h while people in developing countries are willing to work for $15 a day, with few worker benefits and even fewer workplace protections?

Impoverished countries are even more susceptible to transnational blackmail. In order to maintain reserves of foreign or "hard" currency for servicing their debts, developing countries must exchange subsistence agriculture for cash crop production, with the simultaneous loss of livelihood for its people and of self-sufficiency for society at large (Goldenberg, 1997). Transnational investment in resource industries culminates in the growth of capital-intensive resource extraction at the expense of a sustainable subsistence base. Existing companies may be crowded out because of competition, while nascent industries may never gain a foothold because of economies of scale (Edwards, 1999). Farmers are thrown off their land and compelled to pursue wage labour, in effect embedding once self-sufficient subsistence earners into a global system of dependency and underdevelopment.

There is nothing inherently *bad* about such an economic process. Problems arise from the loss of self-determination when corporate demands supersede national interests. Transnationals have shown a disdain for countries that maintain barriers to investment or trade. Monetary policies that are market-unfriendly are shunned, including those that promote higher levels of direct taxation, extensive labour and environment rights, and generous social benefits. The best the government can do is to smooth the way for business by deregulating the economy, controlling public spending, and securing a pliant labour force. Central governments will become little more than glorified local authorities whose sovereignty is more apparent than real. Or, in the border-busting words of the US head of IBM World Corp: "The boundary separating your nation from mine is no more meaningful than the equator—a line on maps, void of meaning."

Put bluntly, transnational corporations are in the economic driver's seat. As stateless transients in pursuit of profit in a global market economy, transnationals eschew national allegiance or loyalty, often putting their own interests ahead of local or national interests (Hitchcock, 1997). Transnational global capital can flee and flow anywhere with the click of a mouse, in the process creating its own rules behind the cover of the global economy (Eisenstein, 1996). Transnationals can shuffle factories around the world in search of cheap labour and governments that wink at taxes, environmental laws, and safety regulations. The globalization of transnationals is rapidly transcending political borders, but also regulatory systems, since the greater the internationalization, the easier it is to slip between the cracks of national regulation (Gwyn, 1998). Of particular concern is the corporate takeover of democratic life, as transnationals transform social priorities such as health that once was the responsibility of the state into a for-profit commodity (Clarke, 1999). The shift in power and wealth from states to transnationals raises an important question: What is the role of the state and society in the new global order (Richmond, 2002)?

(continued on next page)

> *Case Study Questions*
>
> 1 Indicate how and why transnational corporations are at the cutting edge in advancing a global market economy.
>
> 2 Are transnational corporations a force for good (catalyst for productive change) or a force for exploitation (engine of injustice)?

Globalization, Anti-Globalization, Neo-Globalization?

There is little doubt that corporate globalization has redefined how business is done. Advances in telecommunications and transportation have compressed the world into a globally integrated production loop of cost-effective sites. The worldwide reorganization of markets has dismantled trade barriers while "rationalizing" ("restructuring") domestic markets in the scramble for global advantage (Tepperman and Blain, 1999). On paper, the economic benefits of globalization are too tempting to dismiss. Taken as a whole, global market integration is a desirable process in improving living standards (Mandle, 2003). There is much to commend in a logic that correlates national wealth with the removal of pesky tariffs for international trade, improving productivity through competition, enhancing the climate for jobs and investment, and reducing unwarranted government intervention and lavish social spending. Freeing up global economies through the discipline of the market is thought to increase choice, reward risk, unleash creativity, and eliminate waste—provided, of course, the government adopts measures that cushion the blows for those most vulnerable to the winds of change (Mandle, 2003). Business elites have welcomed the prospects of fostering a global market economy. They want the right to invest and divest with minimal restriction, to establish their businesses without unnecessary barriers, and to apply universal standards to ensure harmonization between countries (Drache and Gertler, 1991). In short, a fundamental restructuring in the relationship between society and the economy is taking place under globalization (Atasoy, 2003). Those with the resources and resourcefulness to take advantage of the opportunities have been amply rewarded.

Others are not so lucky. The promises associated with globalization have not unfolded as many had hoped. Evidence points to a growing gap between developing and developed economies that mirrors the divide between the privileged and disadvantaged classes (Chan and Scarritt, 2002). Critics remind us that market-motivated philosophies can throw people out of work and dissolve social service access, in effect foreclosing choices, widening disparities, diminishing diversity, and eroding national identity (Held and McGrew, 2002). People feel betrayed or disillusioned because of threats to national and cultural sovereignty, worker rights, and the environment (Derber, 2002). Transfer of economic control from an interventionist state to the unfettered market may inflict collateral costs. A more competitive money market has enriched a few, yet the pressure for profit amplification has dampened employment prospects for those without the resources to profit from a freewheeling global economy. Trade liberalization has been a bonus to some nation-states but disruptive for those whose goods and services incur a "value-added tax" because of higher environmental, social, and labour costs. Not surprisingly, Canadians remain divided over the impact of the North American Free Trade Agreement on its tenth anniversary (January 1, 2004), with supporters emphasizing benefits, while opponents claim the agreement has thrown thousands out of work, widened the gap between rich and poor, and superseded national sovereignty over issues of worker rights and the environment (Associated Press, 31 December, 2003).

The challenge for the 21ˢᵗ century is clearly before us: To create an open and democratic society in which market freedom advances the priorities of social justice and ecological sustainability. New rules and institutions will be needed. On the assumption that economic globalization and global integration are inevitable and beneficial, argues Paehlke (2003), global political institutions must be established that ensure maximum benefits with minimum costs. A working balance between markets (globalization) and society (intervention) is central to this governance; that is, how to unleash the creative energies of globalization without eroding the cooperative basis of human social existence, including the promotion of democracy, human rights, community development, and a sustainable environment (Chan and Scarritt, 2002). The solution is not to discard globalization but to create a "people's" (humanistic) globalization in lieu of a corporate globalization.

Consider the possibility of a humanistic globalization: A people-driven globalization prioritizes human needs and concerns within the framework of a differently managed globalization—one that spreads the benefits and wealth more equitably rather than enriching the few at the expense of many. A humanistic globalization is about conserving communities, about providing children with a sustainable future, about renewing relationships with the natural world, about trade that privileges people's needs over profits, employing resources that are locally available, and about encouraging diversity by escaping the clutches of a conformist global monoculture and the Americanization of culture. To attain this goal, emphasis is shifted toward (a) reorienting of economies from production for export to production for local markets; (b) becoming less dependent on foreign investments and markets; (c) carrying out income distribution to create a more vibrant internal market; (d) de-emphasizing growth to ensure environmental sustainability; (e) subjecting the private sector to monitoring by civil society; and (f) encouraging production at community and national levels to preserve the integrity of society (Chan and Scarritt, 2002). The UN Development Report captures a sense of the challenge:

> The challenge of globalization in the new century is not to stop the expansion of global markets. The challenge is to find the rules and institutions for stronger governance—local, national, regional, and global—to preserve the advantages of global markets and competition, but also to provide enough space for human community and environmental resources to ensure that globalization works for people, not just for profits (UN Development Report, 1999).

Nowhere is this challenge more pressing than in Canada where Canadians are at the crossroads of globalization: More of the same? Rejection? Or modification? There is much to commend in rejecting a market-driven globalization for that of a people's globalization with its promise of local sufficiency at political, economic, and cultural levels (Starr and Adams, 2003). Otherwise, as critics such as Mel Hurtig (2001) argue, Canada could well become a colony of the United States judging by the number of American takeovers of Canadian businesses (of the 10 000 foreign takeovers between 1985 and 2002, 6437 were American interests), costing Canada billions in lost taxes that could have been used to promote social goals (Burtt, 2003). To be sure, Canada's options are limited. In a society where 43 percent of its GDP is export related, Canada is hardly in a position to revert to an inward-looking world of closed borders, protective tariffs, and national production (Doran, 2002). For Canada, it is not a case of either-or, that is, globalization or no globalization. Rather the question is what *kind* of globalization do we want? Do we want a top-down globalization that is driven by transnational corporations primarily for the benefit of corporate elites? Or a "bottoms-up" neoglobalization that ensures benefits are equitably distributed, is protective of Canada's political autonomy, ensures some degree of progress and prosperity, and promotes a market economy without reducing Canada to a market society where everything is measured and evaluated around the bottom line. A people's globalization may prove a viable alternative that not only advances the interests of all Canadians, but such an alternative may also prove an antidote in addressing a host of global problems that Canada ignores at its own peril.

GLOBAL PROBLEMS

In a world that is convulsed by conflicts and contradictions, there is hardly a shortage of global problems for study. The refrain is strangely familiar: Too many people exist, too many of them live in the wrong places, with too many problems and not enough resources to curb the crisis. While there is no consensus regarding which problems to select for analysis, certain conditions are of such magnitude and consequence that they practically beg for inclusion. Foremost are the issues of overpopulation, urbanization, poverty, global monoculturalism, ethnic conflicts, and ecological trauma. Each of these problems has the potential to terminate planetary existence if left unchecked.

Consider the situation in Africa. Here is a country that occupies 20 percent of the world's land, is home to 818 million people, and sits on enormous reserves of wealth (Ross, 2003). Yet Africa is wracked with poverty, violence, pestilence, vast disparities in wealth, spotty governance, non-existent infrastructures, and stupefying levels of oppression. Statistics confirm the worst. African countries occupy nine of the bottom ten positions in the United Nations' Human Development Index. Forty percent of adult Africans remain functionally illiterate, 40 million are suffering through a hunger crisis, AIDS is decimating the population, and life expectancy remains stuck at 52 years (Kleiss, 2003). Resources continue to be depleted at alarming rates, giving rise to further cycles of starvation, disease, or pestilence. The economic situation continues its freefall: Africa's contribution to global productivity has shrunk by 50 percent since 1970; its debt is now equivalent to its GNP, having multiplied twentyfold in recent years; food production in the sub-Sahara is about 15–20 percent lower than in the late 1970s; and per capita income has plunged by 25 percent from 1987 (Parris, 1997). Petroleum export revenues may have earned Nigeria $200 billion during the past decade; yet per capita income remains unchanged from 30 years ago (Leisinger et al., 2002). The poorest country in the world, Sierra Leone, is so destitute that at $410 per person per year it is poorer in real terms of GDP than the poorest country in 1820, namely China (Kawachi and Kennedy, 2002).

No less dismaying are the human costs. The brutalities in Rwanda or Somalia clearly reveal an Africa in the throes of a demoralizing round of random violence so stunning in its savagery and amorality that many are questioning the very nature of humanity as essentially good (Ignatieff, 1993; Jung, 2003). Parts of Africa continue to be engulfed by lawlessness of such unprecedented cruelty in the struggle for survival that perhaps Thomas Hobbes was right: Human life is nasty, brutish, and short without the Leviathan to impose order (Kaplan, 2000). Interethnic killings and deaths in refugee camps because of starvation or disease continue to mount, including a mind-boggling 4 million Congolese in the Ituri province (O'Reilly, 2003). A combination of droughts, ethnic and clan killings, and armed conflicts under military juntas has created a refugee pool of upwards to 13 million people. Compounding the anarchy is the utter chaos that the HIV/AIDS epidemic is wreaking on the continent (Herzberg, 1999). Let's not mince words: The plight of Africa could well emerge as the world's most pressing social problem in the 21st century.

Did You Know?

Killing because of hate is one thing. Dying from love is, paradoxically, cruel. The AIDS epidemic has struck Africa with a vengeance, particularly in sub-Saharan Africa, accounting for 83 percent of all AIDS deaths since the inception of the epidemic here (Englund, 1999). An estimated 34 million people in this region have been infected, of whom 11.5 million have died, a quarter of them children. By comparison, there are around 890 000 people living with AIDS/HIV in Canada and the United States. Poverty intensifies the suffering: While the United States spent $880 million combating 40 000 new HIV infections, about $165 million was spent in Africa to offset some 4 million new infections (Schiller, 1999). The poverty of the people makes it difficult to get those medicines that can prolong health and life, especially the AIDS cocktail (anti-retroviral regime), which can cost up to $60 000 a year to administer. Much of what passes for medical care consists of a cot, a couple of aspirins, and a towel for a victim's forehead. Also contributing to these figures is the stigma associated with AIDS. The shame associated with AIDS is so powerful a deterrent that people will refuse treatment since acceptance implies acknowledgement or ostracism. In some areas, between 20 and 50 percent of the women have been found to be infected. A third of these women will transmit the virus to their children. Yet these same women risk being beaten and thrown out of the house if implicated, even if infected by their husbands. Not surprisingly, women are unlikely to force the issue of condoms or question partners about fidelity for fear of abuse or abandonment (Schiller, 1999).

How valid are these perceptions of Africa as a living hell? Of course, there's an element of truth to these observations. Who could deny the pervasiveness of poverty, despotic rule, crowded living conditions, interethnic and religious rivalries, and the threat of natural catastrophes? This is not the entire story, however, and a sense of proportion is badly needed—without dismissing the severity of the problem. First, not all developing countries in Africa are economic basket cases. Economic growth is substantial in certain areas; life expectancies are inching upwards as are school enrolments and rates of adult literacy; infant mortalities have halved since 1965; and democratic institutions are gradually displacing once authoritarian regimes (Worldwatch Institute, 2003). This observation is consistent with other studies in arguing that humankind in general has experienced unprecedented improvement in almost every welfare indicator in the past 50 years, including health, wealth, freedom, and literacy (Lomborg, 2001). Second, poverty, crowding, despotism, conflict, and disasters may be pervasive, but neither Canada nor the United States are exempt from such indictment. Consider the status of Canada's First Nations whose living conditions on some reserves dip below developing world standards. Besides, any civilization that spawned two world wars and continues to supply small arms and land mines for ongoing conflicts can hardly claim the moral high ground. Third, Africans cannot assume all of the responsibility for their plight. The political and economic legacy of colonialism continues to disrupt or destroy, despite attainment of nominal political independence (Kaplan, 1994). A hodgepodge of countries exists with no logic or reason and the borders and demographics of which reflect European rather than African interests (Ejiogu, 2001). The possibilities for confrontation are endless under these circumstances.

Fourth and finally, too much of our understanding of African life as "nasty, brutish, and short" reflects a media preoccupation with "triggers" such as Algeria (religious conflicts); Ethiopia (mass starvation); Somalia (clan killings); Congo (genocide); and South Africa (post-apartheid difficulties). Media coverage remains superficial in conveying images of evil, horror, and backwardness. Or as David Rieff (2002: 32) puts it, "… television news, even at its best, seems like reality doled out with an eyedropper for someone assumed to have the attention span of a gnat," thus making it difficult to say something original, explain in depth, or write outside clichés that rob incidents of their specificity. But not all developing world countries are patterned after these media hot spots. Many are relatively peaceful and reasonably well-adjusted to the surrounding environment. Moreover, fixation on the sensational tends to overlook the routines of daily life—the cooperation, consensus, and regulation—that must surely exist for basic human survival (Ross, 2003). Failure to balance the good with the bad does a disservice by reinforcing a predominantly one-sided view of the developing world as the breeding ground for the downward spiral.

Overpopulation

Sociologists have a saying: "The rich get richer, the poor get children." Despite its mocking tone, the expression latches onto a popular perception of the developing world as one that is teeming with people with neither the resources nor the space to make a go of it. There is some truth to this perception. The world is experiencing a population explosion that is unprecedented in human history. From 1804, when the world population reached the 1 billion mark, it took 123 years to reach 2 billion, but only 12 years to go from 5 billion in 1987 to 6 billion on October 12th, 1999, in effect doubling in less than 40 years, with projections of 9 to 10 billion by 2050 if current growth of about 80 million per year continues. Virtually all of the growth stems from the poorest of developing countries despite countless activities in family health and family planning (Leisinger et al., 2002). Sixty percent of the world's population increase is concentrated in ten countries, with India, at 16 percent and China, at 11.4 percent, leading the way. Not surprisingly, many people are alarmed and for good reason. By the time you have finished reading this paragraph, yet another 50 people will be added to this burgeoning total (Leisinger et al., 2002).

Why this demographic explosion? Why, indeed, given that half of the world's married women rely on family-planning techniques, with the result that in 61 countries, women's fertility rates have dropped below the replacement level of 2.1 children per woman (*Los Angeles Times*, 11 October, 1999). Skyrocketing rates reflect the 1 billion teenagers that are entering their reproductive years, including 45 percent of the sub-Saharan population that is less than 15 years of age (Leisinger et al., 2002). Longer life spans are another obvious answer. Life expectancies have increased substantially, while infant mortality rates have declined because of improved medical care, the eradication of certain fatal diseases, and advances in technology. Poverty may also be a contributing factor. Family sizes tend to expand in reaction to unstable or marginal environments. Larger families provide a margin of safety for survival in environments of grinding poverty, economic emergencies, and the lack of any safety net for the aged or unemployed. But parents with more children tend to invest less in health and education for each child, thus making it more difficult for children to escape poverty (Leisinger et al., 2002). In other words, what is often defined as a global problem (that is, large families) may provide a short-term solution for survival when lacking alternatives or security.

The politics of population is proving vexing. Yes, life expectancy in the developing world has crept up to 63 years (compared with an average of 75 in the industrialized world). Much of this increase can be attributed to longer survival rates among children because of improved immunization programs. Yet the downside is inescapable. Increases in life expectancy may compound the problem of overpopulation in many developing world countries, resulting in corresponding demands on diminishing resources and sprawling urban processes. Yes, control of diseases and death rates is a positive goal. Yet this creates additional pressure on existing social services that already are stretched to the limit. Local environments are especially vulnerable to escalating demands. The depletion of basic necessities, coupled with the proliferation of waste, are worrying in their own right. Satisfying the food needs of 80 million additional persons each year will pose new challenges, including conflicts over scarce resources, with a corresponding erosion of social order and security (Homer-Dixon, 1999; Kaplan, 2000). To be sure, human ingenuity in the form of agricultural biotechnology can expand the limits of the earth's carrying capacity, despite predictions by population pessimists of a catastrophic depletion of natural resources. Yet advances in food production have not translated into a world free of hunger or malnutrition. Spectacular changes in food yields, including a doubling of grain harvests and tripling of livestock production since the early 1960s, should provide sustainable food supply—if equitably distributed—to meet the basic needs of all of Earth's inhabitants. But more than 800 million remain food-deprived, that is, they cannot produce or procure enough food at all times to lead healthy and productive lives (Leisinger et al., 2002). And those most affected by low rations are children whose nutritional deficiencies may doom them to permanent deformities. Worse still, a new face of African famine is emerging. Unlike the intense and short-lived emergencies in the past because of bad weather that were solved through humanitarian efforts, a slow-burning humanitarian crisis reflects a hunger and malnutrition that may become a permanent feature of African societies such as Ethiopia (*Guardian Weekly*, 23 May, 2003).

Urbanization

Half of the world's population of 6 billion people are estimated to live in cities. In the developing world, the figure stands at about 23 percent of the population, up from 13 percent in 1950. Africa and East Asia have the lowest rates, while 71 percent of the Latin American population is urban (including 86 percent in Argentina). The rates in Canada and the United States are about 80 percent at present. Singapore and Hong Kong are almost entirely urban. Yet even in areas with low urban-to-rural ratios, the presence of sprawling urban agglomerations is the rule, not the exception (see Table 13.1). Projected figures are no less astonishing in their scale, with an estimated 30 million in Mexico City by 2020, thus confirming a shift in the world's largest urban areas.

The drawbacks of urbanization in the developing world needs little introduction. The inequalities of power, wealth, opportunity, and survival that hobble humanity have a way of crystallizing in cities (Sheehan, 2003). Most "instant" cities were not built for such volumes. Even more daunting is the prospect of rapid growth in "infrastructureless" cities whose inhabitants must survive without garbage collection and waste-water treatment. The only constant is the ever-present threat of diseases such as bubonic plague or malaria.

TABLE 13.1	World's Largest Urban Areas		
World's Largest Urban Areas in 1900 by Population (millions)		World's Largest Urban Areas in 2001 by Population (millions)	
London	6.5	Tokyo	26.5
New York	4.2	Sao Paulo	18.3
Paris	3.3	Mexico City	18.3
Berlin	2.7	New York	16.8
Chicago	1.7	Mumbai (Bombay)	16.5
Vienna	1.7	Los Angeles	13.3
Tokyo	1.5	Calcutta	13.3
St Petersburg	1.4	Daka	13.2
Manchester	1.4	Delhi	13.0
Philadelphia	1.4	Shanghai	12.8

Adapted from Sheehan, 2003.

According to a UN study on global urban conditions, nearly 1 billion people (the vast majority from the developing world) live in squalid, unhealthy areas that lack water, sanitation, public services, or legal security (Vidal, 2003). A context is created that is conducive to antisocial behaviour and a proliferation of social problems.

Nevertheless, many people continue to be attracted to the city because of "push-and-pull" factors. Migrants are pushed out of rural communities because of unemployment, limited land resources, lack of opportunity and employment, boredom, and dislike of political factionalism. Peasants have had to abandon their farms and communities in contexts where powerful crime syndicates battle opposing guerilla and paramilitary groups for control of lucrative drug trade (Spindler, 2003). Migrants are pulled into cities to escape these reasons. For some, safety and economic survival for themselves and their children is a compelling reason; for others, the lure is the glamour, excitement, and sophistication; for still others, a move to cities is but one step in emigrating to a far away land. Laissez-faire globalization and structural adjustment policies (from privatization to removal of subsidies) imposed on the poor countries by global institutions such as the World Trade Organization have also reinforced an urban relocation (Vidal, 2003). The decision to uproot is not always productive. Subsistence employment in fields is exchanged for low-paying urban jobs, often supplemented by proceeds from scavenging and involvement in the invisible economy

In theory, many developing countries profess to discouraging urban migration, citing problems related to employment, sanitation, limited transportation and traffic snarls, pollution, access to services, and crime. Yet many countries gear public policy towards urban residents in hopes of keeping them contented, distracted, and subservient. Only lip service is paid to bolstering rural economies and social services. Resources are diverted to sustain the activities of people in cities with consumerist consumption habits (Honey, 1999). National pride is often at stake as well. Cities are viewed as symbols of progress in advancing industry, wealth, and prestige, despite the prevalence of poverty, homelessness, and slums. Slums themselves are paradoxical (Shaheen, 2003): They reveal the ingenuity of people in desperate circumstances while exposing the failure of government to take advantage of human resources. The informality of slums provides urban dwellers with a tenuous toehold on the employment front, yet prevents people from securing long-lasting economic improvements. What makes slums so inexpensive is the lack of government services, yet slum residents may end up paying more for essential services from private sources while the government provides relatively cheap services in more affluent and stable neighbourhoods.

In short, developing world urbanism would appear to qualify as a *bona fide* social problem. Potential damage to society and the environment are but two problems associated with developing world urbanization. Yet inhabitants of these cities may not see urban life as a cost. Even the inconveniences and dangers of city life are a small price to pay for its opportunities and excitement. Besides, there is not much point in returning to resource-depleted rural environments that offer little in the way of opportunities or options.

Poverty

Many concede the pervasiveness of poverty as a major global problem. They have seen too many media images of the poor and the starving in developing countries to think otherwise. What most do not recognize is the magnitude of this problem, the reasons why it exists, and why eradication is a formidable task. The globalization of world economies rarely confers equal access to the benefits of commercial success. Some prosper, others become increasingly impoverished, with glaring disparities in wealth, power, and status between the haves and the have-nots (Chan and Scarritt, 2002). Consider, for example, the doubling of the disparity gap in per capita income between the world's richest 20 countries and the world's poorest countries from 1960 to 1995. Lesser incomes not only translate into poorer health and shortened life expectancy (Renner and O'Sheehan, 2003), but an unequal society is also more prone to political instability, increased crime, reduced productivity, and dysfunctional institutions (Sarin, 2003).

Defining global poverty can be a problem. Many inhabitants of the developing world are absolutely poor when compared with North American standards or measured by GNP per person. The most common figure suggests that about one-quarter of the world lives on less than one American dollar per day, while nearly one-half of the world's population subsists on less than two American dollars per day. Admittedly, emphasizing economic factors cannot tell the whole story of the developing world where a dollar goes much farther. Economic criteria overlook improvements in the general standard of living related to health or education. Measurements often ignore how costs of living are difficult to compare because of reduced needs, cheaper infrastructures, smaller tax bases, and diminished expectations. Also ignored is how community networks and an informal economy can bolster standards of living, although this may not show up in the national ledger. Still, poverty is real, and bites deeply for those without the resources and resourcefulness to succeed.

Why does developing-world poverty exist? Overpopulation is widely regarded as a primary cause of developing-world poverty. The reverse may also be true; poverty causes overpopulation. For example, poverty contributes to overpopulation by encouraging large families as a survival tactic (Leisinger et al., 2002). The fact that the poorest countries continue to be the fastest growing lends support to this argument. Equally important as contributing factors are structural factors, including: unequal economic distribution, the lack of political will to correct this, and the legacy of colonialism with its reinforcement of dependency and underdevelopment. With most of the developing world population relying on agriculture for a living, the prognosis looks bleak. Many farmers will continue to suffer in poverty without a fair price for their exported commodities, especially in those rich countries that extol the virtues of freer trade but continue with agricultural subsidies and anti-dumping legislation (Barr, 2003). Lastly, the structural adjustments programs imposed on poorer countries by the World Bank or the International Monetary Fund (IMF) directives disproportionately impact on the poorest of the poor (namely, women and children) because of cutbacks in services or subsidies. Still, proposals to combat poverty continue to embrace a host of private sector tools, including title to property, foreign investment, individual entrepreneurship, and profit-oriented development (Lanoszka, 2003).

Expressions and causes of poverty vary from rural to urban regions. For urbanites, poverty is directly related to the lack of jobs. The most obvious markers are squalid housing arrangements, a lack of sanitation or waste disposal, and the constant danger of violence. For farmers and peasants, poverty stems from inadequate prices for goods produced for export. International prices fluctuate wildly, or the demand for agricultural products or raw materials may collapse in the face of synthetics and substitutes. The presence of poverty in the midst of high expectations can create problems. The chronically poor may rebel by channelling their perceived deprivation into religious movements at odds with secular rule. Others prefer to protest via terrorism or mass insurrection. The irony is sadly tragic: As the Special Report in the 24 May, 2003 issue of *The Economist* notes, the world's poorest countries are disproportionately likely to be at war. Poverty fosters conflict, conflict further impoverishes, thus reinforcing the observation that poverty is political.

Global Monoculturalism

The cultural dimension of globalization is no less ambiguous in impact and implications. As noted, the ideological principles of the global economy are not new (Supiot, 2003). Only now they are being applied globally, with the result that all human cultures are expected to comply with a global game, the rules of which include aggressive consumerism, replacement of import-substitution economic models for export-oriented models, primacy of free trade and unregulated investment, privatization of public enterprises, and obsession with exponential economic growth (Mander, 1996). Needless to say, modern technology has prolonged human life spans and comfort zones in ways that could hardly be imagined even a generation ago. But in reflecting a Western corporate vision, a globalizing technology also has the potential to destroy the diversity of human cultures (which may be defined as maps of meaning by which realities are negotiated).

The world appears to be in the throes of a worldwide transformation of cultures. The pressure to conform to the expectations of global and consumerist monoculture is eroding regional difference and cultural identities. Developing world exposure to media views of Western society, with its sophistication, fast cars, designer clothes, and shiny white teeth, is not without consequence. Such a one-dimensional fantasy world can make people ashamed of those traditions that lack glamour, entail hard work, frugality, and involve sacrifices. Corporations may not plan the destruction of diversity, often lacking an awareness of the consequences of decisions and structures on real people in other parts of the world. Nevertheless, a collateral weakening of cultural diversity appears inevitable under the circumstances (Suzuki, 1999). In castigating globalization as a step toward homogenous consumption, with a corresponding diminishment of self-sufficiency and dismantling of local traditions, Helena Norberg-Hodge (1996: 20) makes a similar point:

> The myth of globalization is that we no longer need to be connected to a place on the earth. Our every need can be supplied by distant institutions and machines. Our contact with other people can be through electronic media. Globalization is creating a way of life that denies our natural instincts by severing our connection to others and to nature. And—because it is erasing both biological and cultural diversity—it is destined to fail.

However pervasive the lure of globalization, a global monoculture is not inevitable. People do not have an innate or automatic craving for the West (Norberg-Hodge, 1999). Only select aspects are desirable, namely, entertainment, material goods, or fast foods, while dimensions such as values and beliefs are less acceptable. Moreover, fears of global uniformity may be exaggerated. The very opposite may be in evidence, despite concerns over a cultural cloning that pollutes, assaults, and flattens every cultural space into one upsized McWorld, especially among teenagers with money to spend in fulfilling their cravings for novelty and things American.

In short, cultures and the people who live in them are proving to be much more resilient, resourceful, and unpredictable. Instead of a global monoculture is an evolving hybrid of expressions in which the new and old are precariously juxtaposed, mutually transformed, or syncretically reinterpreted (Zwingle, 1999). Rejection of a standardized, one-size-fits-all mentality may bolster the distinctiveness of local and regional differences. As a result, two apparently contradictory trends are unfolding in the new millennium: To one side, societies are converging because of globalization and consumerism; to the other side, is a growing divergence because of cultural pride in providing a competitive edge and oases of tranquility in times of turmoil. Playing one off against the other may not necessarily yield disarray but provide an opportunity for creative growth. As Mahatma Ghandi said last century in defending the balancing of the local with the global, "I do not want my house to be walled in on all sides and my windows to be stuffed. I want the cultures of all the lands to be blown about my house as freely as possible. But I refuse to be blown off my feet by any."

Ethnic Conflict

A paradox is upon us: The integration of human societies into a global system is counterbalanced by an equally powerful surge of separatist-leaning ethnic nationalism (Beisner, 2000). Just as there are growing fears of a convergence toward a single global monoculture, given the influences of transnational corporations, globetrotting media, and rampant consumerism, so too is there evidence of a divergence based on tribal loyalties and ethnic attachments. In a globalizing world of standardization and homogeneity, people cling even more fiercely to whatever local customs impart distinctiveness, in some cases pushing the primacy of these differences to the brink of conflict. A new dynamic is at play: In a post-Cold War world, people do not divide themselves along ideologically slanted economic lines, as Samuel Huntington points out in his book *The Clash of Civilizations*. World politics are being realigned along cultural or religious lines, especially in the aftermath of September 11th, resulting in new patterns of conflict or cooperation that transcend the bipolar politics of the Cold War. As the traditional nation-state recoils from the challenges of capital mobility and international trade, ethnic nationalisms may flourish to fill the void created by these gaps.

The disruptiveness of this reconfiguration is of growing concern. The politics of ethnicity are proving the catalyst behind a new world (dis)order. Ethnic conflicts pose a major problem in deeply divided societies because of the potential to destroy social cohesion and national unity (Byrne and Irvin, 2000). According to Dietrich Jung (2003), 90 percent of the 218 wars between 1945 and 2001 involve ethnic or civil conflicts, have taken place in the developing world, tend to last longer than conventional inter-state wars, have proven more difficult to end by political means, often involve mobilized militia or "warlords," and the population is routinely exposed to years of violent terror (Renner, 2003). The imploding effect created by this "clash of barbarisms" (Achcar, 2002) threatens to divide even established democracies into squabbling factions. The end result is catastrophic: Nation-states may relinquish both legitimacy and self-determining autonomy to act on behalf of their citizens.

If the 20th century was heralded as the age of ideological nationalism (for example, capitalism or communism), the 21st century may well be defined or destroyed by the dynamics of ethnic nationalism. Reactions to this transformation are varied: For many, ethnicity (defined as a shared awareness of perceived ancestral differences as a basis for reward, recognition, or relationships) is not a social problem. Those who embrace ethnicity endorse it as a solution to many contemporary problems, both social and personal (Solomos and Black, 1996). A commitment to ethnicity allows an escape from feelings of irrelevance, powerlessness, alienation, and impersonality. Appeals to ethnicity foster a sense of continuity, belonging, and security, especially for those at the margins of society without alternate channels for coping with societal stress. Ethnicity constitutes an oasis of meaning and commitment—even relaxation and enjoyment—in an increasingly complex urban-technological environment. The pooling of combined resources allows ethnic minorities to compete more effectively in crowded contexts. Under the banner of ethnicity, members of a group seek to maximize their social and economic advantages in a rational and calculated manner. Nowhere is this more evident than with indigenous peoples. Indigenous peoples are demanding levels of political autonomy that reflect their status as the original occupants whose collective rights to self-determining autonomy over jurisdictions from political voice to land and identity have never been extinguished but remain intact as the basis for a new social contract in living together differently (Maaka and Fleras, 2004).

What some see as an opportunity, however, others define as a problem. Critics have denounced the surge in ethno-cultural assertiveness as divisive, backward-looking, and wasteful (Fleras and Elliott, 2003). Ethnically-based nationalisms have been singled out as major contributors to international conflicts as well as a threat to societal integrity, whereas state-based (or civic) nationalisms seek cultural uniformity, ethnic (or cultural) nationalisms endorse cultural uniqueness, to the detriment of social cohesion (Gans, 2003). Aggressive ethnic attachments are rebuked as atavistic survival mechanisms at odds with the dynamics of globalization, cultural rationality, and national integration. Radical ethnicity is condemned as an inexcusable reversion to tribalism in which blind conformity to the collective and an obsession to avenge past wrongs is contrary to cooperative coexistence. A robust ethnicity also clashes with the principles of liberal-universalism that underpin globalization; that is, a belief that what we have in common as rights-bearing, profit-seeking, and freedom-loving individuals is more important than what divides us as members of groups; that what we do as individuals is more important than who we are; that the content of character is more important than the colour of skin; and that reason prevails over emotion as a basis for thinking and doing. Instead of a shared humanity and common values, an insurgent ethnicity emphasizes a dislike of others and a refusal to cooperate in exploring ways for living together with differences.

For still others, the question of ethnicity goes beyond the notion of good or bad. Like it or not, they say, ethnicity is here to stay as a formidable dynamic in human affairs. Under what conditions does ethnicity become the basis for collective action related to identity, community, or social movements (Fenton, 2003)? Two scenarios are possible in an ethnicized era: First, local attachments are likely to intensify under a globalization that fosters homogenization, centralizes power, destroys livelihoods, creates displacement, and degrades environment (Shiva, 1999). Or, alternatively, the universalizing and centralizing forces of globalization may erode the distinctiveness of local cultures. Second, the relationship between ethnicity and globalization remains uncertain. The politics of globalization may inflame existing ethnic tensions (some of which were suppressed by superpower hegemony). Or a lively ethnic mixture may blunt the freewheeling incursions of global market activity (Randall and Theobald, 1998). In either case, the challenge of making society not only safe *for* ethnicity but also safe *from* ethnicity may well emerge as the key global challenge for the new millennium (Schlesinger, 1992). Even more daunting a challenge is the prospect of making ethnicity safe *for* society as well as safe *from* society.

Environmental Crisis: The Fragile Planet

The natural environment is critical in shaping each country's global agenda. Consider the ways in which environmental politics could influence government policy or public perceptions: a shortage of raw materials, drought and crop failure, deforestation in the tropics, and pollution ranging from waste mismanagement and noxious emissions, to global warming and ozone depletion. The worst case scenario assumes a direct link between environmental scarcity and violence (Kaplan, 2000; Homer-Dixon, 1999). Others reject such a causal link, arguing that it is not scarcity per se that is the problem but power relations that determine who gets what (Peluso and Watts, 1999). The world produces enough food to provide every man, woman, and child with about 3600 calories per day, but the greed and excesses of the industrial world create large pockets of hunger (Kawachi and Kennedy, 2002). In other words, it is not shortages that trigger conflicts associated with environmental scarcity. Abundance is the problem.

Efforts to do something about this pending ecological crisis are often lost in a haze of platitudes, rarely leading to concerted or coordinated cooperation. In 1992, for example, 150 leaders gathered in Rio de Janeiro, Brazil, and raised righteous concern over the deteriorating environment. The Rio Declaration promised that "[s]tates shall cooperate in a spirit of global partnership to conserve, protect, and restore the health and integrity of the Earth's ecosystem." A document was signed by more than 1600 senior scientists, including over half of all Nobel Prize winners. Five years later, a follow-up summit of more than 60 leaders learned that, lofty rhetoric notwithstanding, the global environmental crisis had deepened in terms of forest destruction, fresh water shortages, worldwide overfishing, and mass extinction of species (Schoon, 1997). The gap between the rich and poor nations had intensified, as had the division between rich and poor within societies. The effects on the environment have proven calamitous: The poor of the world strip forests for warmth and cooking, while the rich install more air conditioning. Emissions of fossil fuels by rich nations have risen to the point where artificially contrived climatic shifts are a real possibility with the build-up of greenhouse gases. Not surprisingly, the Canadian Institute for Business and the Environment has pinned a "C−" on Canada for its lack of progress since the Rio Declaration. And the 2002 World Summit on Sustainable Development confirmed the cliché: *plus ça change, plus c'est la même chose*—the more things change, the more they stay the same (Worldwatch Institute, 2003). The world still has a long way to go before achieving the admittedly ambitious goals of the 1992 Rio treaties (Middleton and O'Keefe, 2003). Moreover the sheer complexity and scale of environmental problems have reached the point where individual countries cannot solve them alone. Only cross-national solutions can possibly cope with the crisis.

The world now confronts a global eco-crisis of sobering proportions (Hunter, 2001). Many believe that we are nearing the outer limits of the earth's capacity to support its inhabitants. Population, pollution, and production have been accelerating at exponential rates to create social and ecological problems of such magnitudes that the pattern cannot be sustained much longer without apocalyptic catastrophe (Haller, 2002). Disruptions include: (1) a world where increasing numbers lack access to a decent living; (2) the dangers of pollution that disturbs global chemical cycles that, in turn, regulate ecosystem processes; (3) risks associated with toxic chemicals; (4) ecological decline in which diversity diminishes as species disappear; and (5) perils of biotic mixing that allows a SARS-like scenario of microorganisms to travel or proliferate (Bright, 2003). In a devastating indictment of the future of the human race, a UN-based report entitled "Global Environment Outlook 2000" specified the main threats to human survival were posed by water shortages, global warming, depleted stocks, and nitrogen pollution. Global catastrophe, it concluded, could only be averted through political will and ongoing citizen choices. However, proposed solutions lack any consensus. The rich countries say that environmental degradation such as global warming is a global problem, and that all countries must pitch in to ratify any deals. The poor countries counter by affixing blame to the rich, claiming that the latter should be the ones to fix this environmental mess, not those who can least afford to do so. To expect the poor to make more concessions and compromises is to sentence millions to yet more poverty.

Admittedly, chronic environmental degradation threatens the lives and life chances of the rich and poor alike. A sense of perspective must acknowledge two different types of environmental destruction. The wealthy impose the heaviest toll on the planet by virtue of their pollution-laden and materials-intensive consumerism. The poor not only live with some of the worst environmental conditions imaginable but also eke out a living by taxing an already impoverished environment to the limit (Renner and O'Sheehan, 2003). Blaming the developing world for ecological woes is common enough. Yet many of the world's environmental problems stem from Western consumption patterns, obscene levels of waste and wastefulness, and an obsession with the cult of more or bigger. For example, the export of prawns and shrimp to the richest countries has grown into a major industry (US$9.5 billion in prawns alone) (Barnett and Wasley, 2003). Prawning and shrimping have also destroyed massive areas of coastal mangrove forests to accommodate crustacean farms (Goldsmith, 1999; Shanahan, 2003). Environmental violence—ranging from human rights abuses, rampant corruption, illegal land appropriation, and intimidation leading to violence and death—often accompanies the enclosure or loss of common pool resources (Stonick and Vandergeest, 2001). Or think of the environmental havoc because of our fixation on coffee. Modern plantation-grown coffee (unlike coffee that naturally grows in shade) requires huge amounts of chemicals, and can lead to deforestation and reduced habitat for natural species of birds and animals (Mittelstaedt, 1999). And in both cases, local farmers lose their self-sufficiency. Arable lands are converted into cash-crop holdings, thus intensifying peasant dependence on wage labour. Or these lands are forcibly appropriated by local elites to expand their holdings. Paradoxically, however, the developing world is expected to disproportionately contribute to the protection of the global environment—even if this means curbing local consumption or curtailing regional economic growth.

Canada is no exception to this assault on the environment. Canada's environment has deteriorated dramatically in terms of air and water pollution, loss of wetlands, waste and nuclear disposal, and chemical poisons in soil and the food chain (Hrynyshyn, 2003). These assaults on Canada's environment may be attributed to a host of causes, including global warming, automobile traffic, nitrates in rivers, reliance on pesticides, deforestation, toxic substances, and depletion of otherwise sustainable resources. Environmentalists have criticized Ottawa for reneging on a promise made in 1995 to reduce noxious emissions to a pre-1990 level. Instead, greenhouse gases have risen by 13 percent, prompting the Montreal-based Commission for Environmental Cooperation to single out Ontario as the continent's third worst jurisdiction for controlling hazardous emissions, just ahead of Texas and Ohio in the discharge of industrial pollutants (Mittelstaedt, 2003). Treatment of waste is a national disgrace, as well, says the Sierra Legal Defence Fund (Mittlestaedt, 1999). Major Canadian cities on both coasts are accused of using the environment as a dumping ground for untreated sewage and excrement. The virtual collapse of the cod fishing industry in the Atlantic provinces, coupled with widespread lay-offs in west coast fishing, attest to the damage that can be inflicted by greed, carelessness, or indifference.

In theory, Canadians put a premium on protecting the environment over promoting economic growth (McArthur, 1997). In reality, most vote with their pocketbook since "thinking green" may entail inconvenience or costs. Politicians in Canada continue to prattle on about jobs and deficits as if a resource-depleted world can readily yield workable solutions to these problems (Suzuki, 1998). And yet the natural environment remains under siege not because Canada lacks resources to defuse the crisis, but rather because there is a lack of political will, despite repeated government efforts to turn it around, especially at the level of air pollution, water quality, the wetlands extent, forest cover, greenhouse gases, and bio-diversity (Hawaleshka, 2003). A growing reliance on global free trade is unlikely to enhance environmental concerns; after all, a commitment to profit bites too deeply to expect otherwise. Time will tell whether the profit-motivated private sector can possibly protect the "ecological capital" that sustains all planetary life.

Proposals to address environmental issues must be couched as global social problems. We are all in this together, and together we have to make changes, with the rich assuming the major role in the clean up. A mindset shift of monumental proportions is required. First of all a wake-up call: The very idea of an environmental crisis or shortage is perceived by many Canadians as a contradiction in terms, given Canada's material abundance. To the contrary: Canada is not a sprawling swath of unlimited landscape and resources. Yes, Canada remains a site of astonishing environmental wealth: 20 percent of the world's undeveloped areas; 25 percent of remaining wetlands, 20 percent of freshwater holdings, and 10 percent of the outstanding forests (Hawaleshka, 2003). But these resources are finite, under stress, and are gradually being whittled away by greed or misdeed. The combination of industrial scale agriculture, road and dam building, aquaculture and excessive fishing, urbanization, forestry and mining, and gas and oil exploration should further disabuse Canadians of any complacency or smugness. Or consider the largely unprecedented yet extreme climatic disruptions in 2003, ranging from salmon suffocating in warm British Columbia streams to a Newfoundland town entombed in ice, from the 2500 wildfires that engulfed the interior of British Columbia and forced the evacuation of 50 000 residents to the once-in-a-lifetime hurricane (Juan) that swamped Halifax (Mitchell, 2003). Second, the natural world does not exist in isolation from human communities. One billion people live in unprecedented prosperity; another billion live in abject destitution. According to Durning (1991), both rich and poor engage in consumption patterns (one from greed, the other from need) that exert pressure on existing resources such as water, land, forests, and atmosphere. There is much to commend in balancing production and human needs with the environment, but this line of reasoning is flawed. Human needs and a healthy environment are not opposing claims that must be balanced, writes Jared Diamond (2003), but inexorably linked since there is no such thing as human survival without a functioning environment.

FOREIGN AID AND (MIS-) DEVELOPMENT: SOLVING GLOBAL PROBLEMS?

The global integration of national and transnational economies is an established fact. The magnitude and scope of this convergence cannot be overestimated. Nor can there be any doubt about the unevenness of this process. These imbalances in the global process are especially evident by observing post-war trends in international assistance. Since World War II, affluent countries have transferred billions of dollars of assistance to the poorer, developing world. The rationale behind these transfers is quite simple. Is it possible for people to live together globally when those from Switzerland and the United States have a median income of between $34 000 and $36 000, while the median income of $400 is the norm for the poorest 50 countries? Not only are these extremes morally awkward for many, but such a disparity also has the potential to disrupt the international status quo, with long-term repercussions for global survival. Only a reduction in this gap can stave off the threat of global confrontations or deter the movement of asylum-seekers in search of economic opportunity.

One strategy for achieving this goal has focused on expanding initiatives in foreign aid and development. A package of short- and long-term programs has been implemented in hopes of bolstering the living standards of developing countries. Foreign aid is justified as an investment in global security and international peace, rather than as an act of charity or chivalry (Culpepper, 1993). A reduction in local inequalities may forestall global tension, defuse ethnically-driven conflicts, avert massive migration, and deter environmental destruction. But after 40 years of development and assistance, the track record is mixed at best. Criticism is mounting over the use of foreign aid to bring about renewal and reform, instead of relying on liberalizing trade, the discipline of the market, or structural adjustments, and private sector reforms. The moral underpinnings of foreign aid pose an awkward dilemma. Foreign aid may conjure up images of endless bags of food, selfless doctors, inoculation campaigns to protect children, and American actors making late night pitches to sponsor needy children. The reality is a foreign aid program that may unwittingly (a) secure a political and economic power base for local dictators; (b) encourage ethnic factions who perpetuate conflict by withholding food for political ends; (c) foster increased dependency on Western goods, services, and expertise; (d) be hijacked by powerful charities and agricultural interests to promote their goals; and (e) perpetuate the last refuge of Western colonialism (Maren, 1997). The effectiveness of foreign assistance is also being questioned because of unacceptably slow or nonexistent rates of progress in coping with global social problems.

Conceptualizing Foreign Aid

Foreign aid is based on the concept of improving a country's economy by modernizing its services and production facilities. The philosophical underpinnings of developmental assistance reflect the success of the Marshall Plan, which provided for the reconstruction of war-ravaged Europe through massive airlifts of supplies and the provision of technical assistance. The plan was so successful that a blueprint for all future assistance strategies was secured. The less fortunate (the South) receive assistance from the privileged (the North) through the transfer of wealth (resources, skills, expertise) in hopes of improving the gross national product (GNP) through economic development.

Foreign aid programs assume different forms. At one end of the transfer continuum are donations of emergency assistance when countries experience natural catastrophes such as floods or famines. At the other end are long-term investments, which can include donations of foodstuffs or finished products, investment and expertise for sustainable community development, bilateral trade exchanges, and infrastructure development related to roads, communication links, and hospitals. In recent years, the focus and scope of foreign aid and development have taken a new direction. An earlier commitment to throwing money and experts at a problem has given way to the principle of locally-driven, sustainable development (best encapsulated in the aphorism "give people fish, and they will eat for a day; teach them how to fish and they will eat for a lifetime"). But what happens when the local fishing place becomes polluted or stocks are depleted?

Canada is widely admired as a generous contributor to the international scene. Under the auspices of the Canadian International Development Agency (CIDA), developing nations have been the recipients of billions of dollars in assistance. Funding has been funnelled into a variety of programs, both in the short term (emergencies) or long term, and ranging in scale from megaprojects to locally-driven sustainable development. However, Canada's commitments do not match reality. At a proposed $3 billion for 2004/05 Canada's foreign aid spending will return to its 1992/93 levels, but as a percentage of the GNP still below that of a decade ago, and, at 0.28 percent of the GNP in 2002, far below the 0.7 percent that Canada once promised (*Toronto Star,* 19 February, 2003). With the possible exception of the Netherlands and the Scandinavian countries (for example, Denmark's contribution in 2001 equalled 0.97 percent of its GNP, up from 0.09 percent in 1960), a comparable downward trend is evident elsewhere: Foreign aid, once a key component of American foreign policy, continues its free fall from 0.53 percent in 1960 to a paltry 0.12 percent of the GNP in 2002. World totals have plummeted as well, with Japan, the United States, Canada, and Australia the lowest contributors of the 21 richest countries, although totals have rebounded to $58 billion, a comparable figure to spending in 1995 (CDG/FP, 2003). Pakistan, India, Indonesia, China, and Vietnam are the main recipients (*National Post Business*, December, 2003).

Even these miserly sums are deceiving: Canada's efforts are dismissed as the proverbial drop in the bucket. In the withering words of a development expert about CIDA: "The traditional thing, Canadian aid, is about saying, 'Oh my God, there's four billion starving out there, lets go and make a difference among 10 million of them' ... You're going around giving a little bit of microcredit, you're putting some Band-Aids here, you're washing a little bit of children there, its nothing new" (Cash, 2003). Canada's insistence on strings-attached bilateral trade arrangements ensures that nearly two-thirds of every foreign aid dollar makes it way back to Canada. Recipients of Canada's foreign aid rarely fit an expected profile: Less than 20 percent of Canada's foreign aid is directed at the neediest and poorest countries, with many Eastern European countries such as Poland in receipt of comparably larger sums. Taken together, 33 percent of all aid is directed at "geographic programs" (including everything from infrastructure to lines of credit), 16 percent consists of cash transfers to international financial agencies (such as the International Monetary Fund), 12 percent is for food, 9 percent matches funds from other agencies (such as Oxfam), and 6 percent is for administration.

Perils and Pitfalls: Foreign Aid As a Trojan Horse?

The result of nearly a half century of foreign aid assistance has proven inconclusive. Many have concluded that billions in foreign aid spending have had little impact on reducing global inequality. Egypt may have been the largest single national recipient of CIDA bilateral aid between 1994 and 1999 but with little appreciable difference in the lives of ordinary Egyptians (Cash, 2003). Nor has it had much effect on the economic policies of the developing world, despite the use of foreign aid as an incentive to modernize along capitalist lines. How do we account for this singular lack of success? Does the problem reflect the fact that foreign aid has more to do with politics and commerce than with poverty or powerlessness? Can a band-aid solution get at root causes? Can a quick-fix solution address fundamental issues related to structure and system? Are target populations adequate to the task of assisting in their own development? Is the problem one of expediency; that is, is the transfer of wealth from the rich to the poor, and back again? Is foreign assistance a tool for encouraging independence and growth, or little more than a welfare and dependency trap? To what extent, then, can foreign aid be interpreted as a problem as much as a solution?

On the surface, there is much to be said for the commitment to help others to eventually help themselves. In reality, too much foreign aid is concerned with politics or the economy rather than with poverty eradication or people empowerment. Consider the following flaws in design and execution of foreign aid programs (Goldsmith, 1999).

First, the rationale behind foreign aid has historically focused on political leverage for helping "allies." Political calculations dictated that enemies (communist countries) would be overlooked regardless of need or duress. Foreign assistance was rationalized on the grounds of stabilizing—and rewarding—countries that were friendly to the West, thus allowing capitalist expansion without fear of unnecessary unrest or unwelcome takeovers. The fact that the bulk of American foreign aid continues to be siphoned into Israel and Egypt confirms the centrality of politics in the post Cold War era.

Second, most aid could not be separated from economic considerations. Foreign aid often materialized as a disguised export subsidy for the donor country, with strings attached because of "bilateral" political or economic concessions. Under "tied" assistance, currently accounting for about 40 percent of total international aid flow, countries would receive benefits provided they purchased donor-made goods in return (CGD/FP, 2003). Such an arrangement is of obvious benefit to donor countries like Canada. But developing countries are forced to purchase unnecessary goods at often uncompetitive prices as a precondition to qualify for foreign assistance. Not surprisingly, the strings-attached mentality further ensnared the host country in the workings of a global economy. Other aid is contingent on making punishing structural adjustments to induce higher productivity in industry or agriculture through free-market pricing, private ownership, inflation reduction, stripped-down government expenditures, elimination of food subsidies, and reduced social services. These austerity measures may please World Bank donors but do little to alleviate human misery.

Third, the bulk of foreign aid is of an expedient nature rather than humanitarian-driven. Generous offers of emergency assistance are often an excuse to discard surplus commodities without depressing international commodity markets. This has happened in the past. The fact that disaster relief may intensify the suffering of the victims (for example, sending powdered milk to relief victims who cannot comfortably digest milk enzymes) is unconscionable. That the government can get away with offloading embarrassing and subsidized stockpiles of milk powder, butter, and wheat—and still look good in the process—is called "politics."

Fourth is poor program design and implementation. Projects continue to be poorly planned by technical experts out of touch with the particular needs of a country. Efforts are sabotaged by poor delivery systems and a lack of communication with local experts about how best to modify Western-style programs for local conditions. Experts may be inclined by training to design computer-based irrigation technologies when all the local community really needs is a handheld well pump. Megaprojects like superhighways or international airports are often counterproductive because of their adverse effect on local economies and the environment. Lastly, problems of maintenance are rarely addressed. Sophisticated technology may require expensive upkeep and constant repairs, thus further alienating the masses from participation or benefit.

The Problem with Solutions

The string of foreign aid failures is now legendary. Many see foreign aid and development as a superficial solution that never gets to the root of the problem. The poor become poorer, partly because developmental programs deal with symptoms rather than causes, ignore the broader social and cultural context, and disregard the interconnectedness of society and the environment. A short-term solution may induce a long-term problem. For example, it is one thing to feed people during emergencies; it is quite another to furnish them with the tools to feed themselves; it is still another to appreciate the need for bottom-up infrastructural and institutional changes (Cash, 2003; Lanoszka, 2003). Such short-sightedness may not drive foreign aid; nevertheless, the consequences of assistance actions are such that, despite good intentions, they inadvertently harm those who need it most. Too much, they say, is spent on building bridges and roads but not enough on helping the poor since only a miniscule percent of foreign aid budgets are earmarked for health or education (Knox, 1996).

Developmental assistance has been criticized for fattening political elites and spawning a global array of non-governmental organizations but doing little to improve living standards. Public reaction to foreign aid remains as vocal as ever, especially by those who denounce the exercise as morally dubious, politically odious, and economically retrograde. Foreign aid is perceived as wastefully tossing money into a bottomless pit. As the former editor of the *New Internationalist* sarcastically put it, foreign aid "transfers money from the poor people of the rich country to the rich people of the poor countries" (Nicholson-Lord, 1992). Not surprisingly, then, the richest countries such as Japan and the United States tend to score poorly on the CGD/FP Commitment to Development Index. And Canada's eroding commitment to an engaged internationalism as an honest broker and helpful fixer continues to slide (Cohen, 2003). Even more galling is an awareness that foreign aid may unwittingly abet conflict or suffering by propping up murderous regimes (Unland, 1996). Famines in parts of Africa are not caused by droughts but by civil war, according to this line of thinking, and pouring in more relief intensifies the fighting (Toolis, 1998). That foreign aid may end up doing more harm than good is a stunning admission that even well-intentioned solutions may make a bad situation even worse.

That doubts over foreign aid are escalating should come as no surprise. Such an indictment is no reason to blame individual fieldworkers for glitches in the process. There is even less reason to accuse the recipients of being lazy or corrupt. Rather, failure is often built into the principles and practices of foreign aid because of political, economic, and cultural factors. Nevertheless, a backlash against foreign aid is inevitable as the donor countries wrestle with their own fiscal demons. Resentment smoulders when governments are seen as helping those overseas while ignoring the plight of the domestic poor. Public perceptions are playing a key role in cutbacks. Many believe developing countries are responsible for the predicament in which they find themselves. The developing world is criticized for not doing enough to reduce inequities, defuse ethnic animosities or religious strife, or curtail military spending that consumes scarce resources at the expense of productive potential. Response to this criticism has brought about a rethinking of developmental assistance in recent years. The shift to more human-centred assistance (focused on health, education, and ameliorating poverty) is widely touted, as is the emphasis on sustainability (locally-owned development) and proactive initiatives (with an emphasis on prevention rather than cure). According to Hernando de Soto of Peru's Institute for Liberty and Democracy, bottom-up changes can include the following: improving schools, hospitals, and plumbing; enforcing the rule of law, including elimination of local crime lords and extortion rackets; creating a framework for property rights, enforceable contracts and investment environment; and establishing access to legal structures that tap into people's hidden wealth and entrepreneurship. Increasingly, attention and funding are directed towards cooperative programs, often involving women in collectives, as catalysts for change. Still, questions remain about whether foreign aid reduces or magnifies the problems of the developing world.

What to do? The solution is not to discontinue foreign aid and development; after all, people need assistance to survive regardless of our moral qualms. The goal is to examine the problem in global terms and to apply local solutions that transcend dependencies and foster meaningful local development. This is accomplished in part by taking foreign aid out of official hands and putting it to use as directly as possible for those truly destitute. Agencies such as CIDA have revised their mission to include sustainable development and community-based growth. Partnerships are being forged that focus on local projects and areas of poverty, with women increasingly being targeted as the beneficiaries. There has also been a move to decentralize and deregulate the procedures by which programs and projects are designed and delivered. Local involvement is critical: For if there is one thing we have learned, it is that social problems are rarely solved by telling others what to do or by doing it for them. Problems are even less likely to be solved if solutions fail to come from within the community, fail to focus on the structures that created the problem in the first place, and fail to provide a level of assistance that is consistent with that community's level of development. Without principles and a principled approach, solutions become problems by another name.

ROOT CAUSES/STRUCTURAL SOLUTIONS: GLOBALIZATION AND GLOBAL PROBLEMS

The media have failed to connect the dots and show how many of today's international crises have their roots in globalization (*The Ecologist*, Vol 29, No 3, 1999).

The world of today is inundated by an avalanche of deepening crises and open conflicts. Such a candid admission may seem counterintuitive, given the glowing praises and promises of globalization, but does acknowledge the double-edged character of global development. The growing interdependence of world peoples through shrinking borders, compressed time-space, and instant communication has the potential to create or preclude opportunities, to generate benefits as well as political, economic, social, and ecological insecurities, and to foster divisions alongside increased integration. The contradictions of globalization are conveyed by the UN Human Development Report, 1999 (the full text of the report is available on the Internet at: www.undp.org/hdro).

> This 10th Human Development Report—like the first and all the others—is about the growing interdependence of people in today's globalizing world. This era of globalization is opening many opportunities for millions of people. Increased trade, new technologies, foreign investments, expanding media, and Internet connections are fueling economic growth and human advance.... We have more wealth and technology—and more commitment to a global community—than ever before.

> But today's globalization is being driven by market expansion—opening national borders to trade, capital, information—outpacing governance of these markets and their repercussions for people.... When the market goes too far in dominating social and political outcomes, the opportunities and rewards of globalization spread unequally and inequitably—concentrating power and wealth in a select group of people, nations and corporations, marginalizing the others ...

This duality in outcomes is clearly evident: Globalization and global capitalism have the potential to deliver billions from poverty, create opportunities for choice and personal development, and reinforce democracies around the world. They also have the potency to deny, exclude, or exploit. Critics and supporters align themselves accordingly: On one side are concerns about global warming and the extinction of species; on the other are worries about the onset of a global monoculture, ethnic conflicts, and intensifying levels of poverty. If these problems and paradoxes are perceived as isolated from each other, the challenge of solution seems insurmountable. If interpreted as diverse symptoms of the same root cause, however, the situation appears amenable to reform (Editorial, *The Ecologist*, 1999).

At the heart of most global problems is an economic system that separates producers from consumers in a way that enriches some at the expense of others, estranges people from nature, and removes local decision-making from large institutions. The dominance of a global market economy has had the effect of dividing both people and nations, with winners reaping the rewards while victims cope with the effects. According to the UN Development Report:

> In the globalizing world of shrinking time, shrinking space, and disappearing borders, people are confronting new threats to human security—sudden and hurtful disruptions in the pattern of daily life. In both poor and rich countries, dislocations from economic and corporate restructuring and from dismantling the institutions of social protection, have meant greater insecurity in jobs and incomes. The pressures of global competition have led countries and employers to adopt more flexible labour policies with more precarious work arrangements.

Unrestricted global trade and imposition of Western developmental models are exacerbating environmental problems: Forests are depleted, seas overfished, water awash with pollutants, and croplands seriously degraded (Goldsmith, 1999). Globalization of markets fosters a rampant competition in which countries compete to create the most attractive conditions for industry, even if this means running roughshod over environmental concerns or social regulations. A global economy also requires the conversion of yet untapped inhabitants into consumers, with corresponding pressure on already depleted resources. The construction of transportation infrastructures from highways to airports, often at public expense, may be justified as a convenience for citizens but is often tailored to the needs of the largest corporations and their vision of the world: one in which every society is dependent on a single, high-tech, energy-intensive consumer economy under the control of a small number of transnationals (Gorelick, 1999). In other words, Edward Goldsmith writes, freewheeling development and global capitalism are more of a problem rather than a solution for those in the developing world. Moreover, this global dynamic may be eroding those very things that individuals and communities require in order to survive; that is, clean air, safe water, a unifying vision, and a sense of security and community.

Empowerment stems from understanding the economic roots of global social and environmental problems. More importantly, an optimism is fostered because the concept of global problems is rendered more manageable by the recognition of their prime cause (Editorial, 1999). The forces of global capitalism are not immutable or irreversible, with no alternatives to consumerism, free trade, or economic growth (Chan and Scarritt, 2002). Rather, these global forces are socially constructed, rather than natural, normal, or inevitable. They consist of conventions created by vested interests to put profit before people. The challenge is to undo the exploitative by creating a more humane globalization anchored around the principles and practices of human rights.

HUMAN RIGHTS: TOWARDS A NEW GLOBAL GOVERNANCE

There is much that is perplexing about the state of the world at present. Problems are appearing out of nowhere, and appear to be overwhelming the finite resources and resourcefulness at our disposal, while solutions appear hopelessly inadequate to do anything of substance. Global and domestic poverty intensify even as productivity increases; environmental concerns rank high, but we appear powerless to halt its destruction; and people have access to new technologies and automation yet are working harder than ever (Paehlke, 2003; Goar, 2003). New diseases such as SARS, West Nile Virus, and Mad Cow Disease are creating scenarios as frightening as those of the bubonic-plagued Middle Ages; intertribal violence has transformed the Congo into the most lethal killing fields since World War II; Palestinian–Israeli tensions are consumed by violence so coldly premeditated that any hope for reconciliation vanishes in the haze of Palestinian suicide bombers and Israeli bullets; financial markets can unleash fiscal chaos with the click of a mouse; and environmental degradation, particularly in the tropics, continues to spin madly out of control. Yet there are flickers of hope that things are not as bad as they seem to be, and that solutions can be implemented as situations arise. Nowhere is this optimism more brimming than in the emergence of human rights as a global issue, with profound implications for living together with differences (Fields, 2003). Putting human rights at the forefront of global governance may prove a turning point for the 21st century (UN Development, 1999; Teeple, 2001).

The international legal framework for human rights originated with the Universal Declaration of Human Rights by the UN General Assembly in 1948. Article One declared that "All humans are born free and equal in dignity and in rights. They are endowed with reason and conscience and should act towards one another in a spirit of brotherhood." The declaration articulated a vision of the world in which all states would endorse the protection of all human rights (civil, political, economic, social, and cultural) under a rule of law anchored in the principle of equality and non-discrimination. Such an initiative stood in sharp contrast to a world when (a) self-determination was denied to colonized people throughout the world; (b) indigenous peoples had yet to challenge their status; and (c) racial discrimination remained legally entrenched in Canada and the United States. The International Bill of Rights was strengthened by the adoption of the International Covenant on Civil and Political Rights and Economic, Social, and Cultural Rights in 1966. Specialized human rights treaties by the UN included the prohibition of discrimination (1966), discrimination against women (1979), torture (1984), and the violation of children's rights in 1989. A high commissioner for human rights has been appointed. To atone for the 120 million people who have perished in wars, political persecution, genocide, and ideologically engineered famine, Canada and 120 countries are laying the foundation for an international criminal court, with jurisdiction over genocide, crimes against humanity, war crimes, and aggression (UN Development, 1999).

The significance of this human rights movement cannot be lightly dismissed. As a result of these humanitarian initiatives, most of which have been ratified by numerous states, the post-World War II era has seen an expansion of constitutionally protected rights from a few states to a near universal appreciation (Chinkin, 1999). Fifty-five years after its proclamation, the UN Declaration of Rights has been called the "sacred text" and a major article of faith in framing international politics and policies; a yardstick by which human progress is measured; and the foundational document that subsumes all other creeds directing human behaviour (Ignatieff, 1999). The commemoration of the Declaration is a reminder that human rights constitute political and civil rights, as well as economic and social rights. We also are reminded that the basic principles upon which human rights are based are universal, and, although the mechanisms that infuse life into them are shaped by features specific to each society, there is no justification for citing cultural relativism or respect for cultural identity as an excuse for violation of human rights (Mayor, 1999). In a postmodern world that holds nothing to be true, except the truth that remains trapped within us, Michael Ignatieff writes, the emergence of universal human rights over the primacy of state sovereignty is nothing short of astonishing.

Put simply, the world is developing a conscience. In a world of satellite television and the Internet, news of mass murder and atrocities travels quickly. A sense of human solidarity is fostered that transcends national boundaries and ethnic differences. In consolidating this international discourse that all human beings have basic rights and liberties, the concept of state sovereignty is being challenged: States are increasingly seen as instruments at the service of their citizens, rather than vice versa, with the result that states can no longer justify mistreatment of citizens as "internal matters." In the words of the UN Secretary-General, Kofi Annan (1999), "Strictly traditional notions of sovereignty can no longer do justice to the aspirations of people everywhere to attain their fundamental freedoms. Massive and systematic violations of human rights—wherever they may take place—should not be allowed to stand." In other words, state sovereignty is contingent on nation-state respect of individual rights—an idea that was introduced by the Nuremberg Trials when it was proclaimed that a society's human rights violations were subject to international prosecution. These aspirations were never implemented because of Cold War politics. Nevertheless, the thaw has resulted in an assault on national sovereignty, no more so than on March 24th, 1999, when NATO began bombing Serbia, the first multinational attack designed largely to curb violations of human rights within a country's borders

(Rosenberg, 1999). A similar line of reasoning was applied by the United States in justifying a coalition-led invasion of Iraq in 2003, despite the lack of official UN backing.

This interventionism on behalf of human rights is not without problems. The impunity of human rights violators throughout the world continues to mock the vision of the Declaration. Violations continue to be committed in the name of religion, custom, tradition, or ethnicity. Admittedly, human rights abuses at present differ from those of the Cold War era. According to Michael Ignatieff, in his article "Intervention and State Failure," Cold War abuses originated with strong totalitarian states, whereas post Cold War violations stem from weak or collapsing states. Non-state actors, including transnational corporations, may also compromise human rights through corporate decisions that deny, exclude, or exploit (Chinkin, 1999). Rights discourses too often dwell on people's negative rights (to be free from oppression or constraints) rather than on positive rights (to have full and equal participation in society) (Chan and Scarritt, 2002). Fundamental freedoms will remain fragile as long as poverty, exclusion, and inequality persist, and the role of government is restricted to mediator and security rather than protector of the general interest (Mayor, 1999).

Even the concept of human rights is not self-evident despite its emergence (alongside democracy and the free market) as the normative standard of our time (Fields, 2003). And the debate over the universality of human rights remains unabated with critics dismissing the existing package as a reflection of Western values (such as individuals, freedom, equality, and democracy) and cover for advancing national interests. Proposed instead are genuinely universal human rights that reflect the values of all cultures, including collective rights of indigenous peoples to self-determining autonomy (Freeman, 2003; Supiot, 2003). In short, as Christine Chinkin explains, the ideal of human rights standards has been achieved in principle. Now the really hard work begins with respect to implementation and enforcement as an ongoing social practice rooted in a people's struggle against political and economic domination (Fields, 2003). Putting this principle into practice will prove the definitive challenge for the 21st century.

DISCUSSION QUESTIONS

1   Define globalization in a way that captures its many dimensions, including political, economic, social, and cultural.

2   Discuss the benefits and costs of globalization as they might apply to Canada.

3   Who or what are largely responsible for global problems. Defend your answer.

4   Indicate why foreign aid as a form of development is likely to fail.

5   What are the key issues that define the debate over human rights?

 ## WEBLINKS

Globalization.   **www.encarta.msn.com**

Canadian International Development Agency.   **www.acdi-cida.gc.ca**

Global Problems Research.   **www.kn.pacbell.com**

References

ABC Canada Literacy Foundation (2001). "Who Wants to Learn?" Available at www.abc-canada.org.

Abel, Sue (1997). "Shaping the News." *Waitangi Day on Television.* Auckland University Press.

Abella, Irving and Harold Troper (1982). *None is Too Many. Canada and the Jews in Europe 1933–1948.* Toronto: Lester and Orpen Dennys Ltd.

Abella, Rosalie (2003). "Indifference is Injustice's Incubator." Excerpt from an acceptance speech upon receipt of the Canadian Council of Christians and Jews human relations award. Printed in the *Toronto Star.* November 28.

Abercrombie, Nichalas (1995). *Television and Society.* London: Polity Press.

Aboriginal Healing Foundation Research Series (2002). *Aboriginal Sex Offending in Canada.* Written by John H. Hylton. Ottawa.

Abraham, Carolyn and Lisa Priest (2003). "Cutbacks fed SARS calamity, critics say." *Toronto Star.* May 1.

Abu-Laban, Y. (1998). "Welcome/STAY OUT: the Contradiction of Canadian Integration and Immigration Policies at the Millenium." *Canadian Ethnic Studies* XXX(3): 190–211.

Abu-Laban, Yasmeen (2003). "For Export: Multiculturalism and Globalization." In K. Pryke and W. Soderland (Eds.), *Profiles of Canada* (pp. 249–278). Toronto: Canadian Scholars Press.

Abu-Laban, Yasmeen and Daiva K. Stasiulis (1992). "Ethnic Pluralism Under Siege. Popular and Partisan Opposition to Multiculturalism." *Canadian Public Policy* 18(4): 365–386.

Abwunza, Judith (1997). *Women's Voices, Women's Power. Dialogues of Resistance from East Africa.* Peterborough: Broadview Press.

Achcar, Gilbert (2002). The Clash of Barbarisms. September 11 and the Making of the New World Disorder. New York: Monthly Review Press.

Adair, Vivyan and Sandra Dahlberg (Eds.) (2003). *Reclaiming Class. Women, Poverty, and the Promise of Higher Education in America.* Philadelphia: Temple University Press.

Adams, Howard (1999). *A Tortured People.* Penticton, British Columbia: Theytus Press.

Adams, Michael (2003). *Fire and Ice. The United States, Canada, and the Myth of Converging Values.* Toronto: Penguin.

Agocs, Carol and Monica Boyd (1993). "Ethnicity and Ethnic Inequality." In Jim Curtis, Ed Grab, and Neil Guppy (Eds.), *Social Inequality in Canada,* 2nd ed. (pp. 330–352). Toronto, Ontario: Prentice Hall.

Aijmer, Goran and Jon Abbink (2000). *Meanings of Violence. A Cross Cultural Perspective.* New York: Berg.

Akin, David (2003). "Study highlights a new kind of gender gap." *The Globe and Mail.* June 24.

Albo, Gregory and Jane Jenson (1996). "Remapping Canada: The State in the Era of Globalization." In J. Littleton (Ed.), *Clash of Identities.* Toronto: Prentice Hall.

Albrow, Martin (1996). *The Global Age.* London: Polity Press.

Alfred, Gerald Robert (1995). *Heeding the Voices of Our Ancestors: Kahnawake Mohawk Politics and the Rise of Native Nationalism in Canada.* Toronto: Oxford University Press.

Alfred, Taiaiake (Gerald Robert) (1999). *Peace, Power, Righteousness.* Toronto: Oxford University Press.

Alfred, Taiaiake (Gerald Robert) (2000). "Solving the Indian Problem." *Windspeaker.* February.

Alia, Valerie (1999). *Un/Covering the North. News, Media, and Aboriginal People.* Vancouver: UBC Press.

Altheide, David L. (2002). *Creating Fear. News and the Construction of Crisis.* New York: Aldine de Gruyter.

Alvi, S., W. DeKeseredy, and D. Ellis (2000). *Contemporary Social Problems in North American Society.* Toronto: Addison-Wesley.

Amato, Paul R. et al. (2003). "Continuity and Change in Marital Equality between 1980 and 2000." *Journal of Marriage and Family* 65(February): 122.

American Press (2003). "Wal-Mart Charged With Racketeering." Reprinted in *The Globe and Mail.* November 12.

Andersen, Robin (1996). *Consumer Culture and TV Programming.* Boulder, Colorado: Westview Press.

Anderssen, Erin and Michael Valpy (2003). "Face the Nation: Canada Remade." *The Globe and Mail.* June 7.

Andresen, Martin A., Greg W. Jenion, and Michelle L. Jenion (2003). "Conventional Calculations of Homicide Rates Leads to Inaccurate Reflection of Canadian Trends." *Canadian Journal of Criminology and Criminal Justice.* January 1–14.

Andrews, Corbin (1999) "A License to Parent?" *National Post.* February 22.

Anisef, Paul and Kenise Murphy Kilbride (Eds.) (2003). Managing Two Worlds: The Experiences and Concerns of Immigrant Youth in Ontario. Toronto: Canadian Scholars Press.

Annan, Kofi (1999). "Two Concepts of Sovereignty." *The Economist.* September 18: 49–50.

Annan, Kofi (2002). "Immigrants, Refugees Must Not be Seen as a Burden." Message on the occasion of International Migrants Day. December 18.

Apple, Michael W. (1996). *Cultural Politics and Education.* Buckingham: Open University Press.

Armstrong, Natalie (1999). "Ontario Named Continent's No. 2 Industrial Polluter." *National Post.* August 11.

Armstrong, Pat and Hugh Armstrong (2001). The Context for Health Care Reform in Canada. In P. Armstrong et al. (Eds.), *Exposing Privatization: Women and Health Care Reform in Canada* (pp. 11–48). Aurora, Ontario: Garamond.

Arnold, Tom (1999). "Parents Lack Basic Knowledge of Child-Rearing, Survey Finds." *National Post.* April 22.

Arnold, Tom (2003). "Ferndale inmates play golf, order pizza, watch cable TV." *National Post.* February 11.

Arnold, Tom (2003). "Ontario gets third private hospital." *National Post.* February 18.

Arnold, Tom (2003). "Two-parent households are waning.' *National Post.* October 23.

Asbury, Kathryn E. (1989). "Innovative Policing: Foot Patrol in 31 Division, Metropolitan Toronto." *Canadian Police College Journal* 13(3): 165–181.

Asch, Michael (Ed.) (1997). *Aboriginal and Treaty Rights in Canada: Essays on Law, Equity, and Respect for Difference*. Vancouver: UBC Press.

Asch, Michael (2002). "Self-Government in the Millenium". In J. Bird et al. (Eds.), *Nation to Nation* (pp. 65–73). Toronto: Irwin Publishing.

Ash, Stacey (2001). "Gender gap board worried." *Kitchener-Waterloo Record.* December 11.

Ashini, Napes (2002). "Niassinam: Cariboo and F 16s." In J. Bird et al. (Eds.), *Nation to Nation.* Toronto: Irwin Publishing.

Associated Press (2002). "U.S. Violent Crime Rate Hits New Low." Reprinted in the *National Post.* September 10.

Associated Press (2003). "10 years later, free trade still being hotly debated." Printed in the *Kitchener-Waterloo Record.* December 31.

Association for Canadian Studies. (2002). "September 11th —Aftermath and Impact on Canada and Canadians." Analysis by Jack Jedwab.

Atasoy, Yildiz (2002). "Explaining Globalization." In Y. Atasoy and W. Carroll (Eds.), *Global Shaping and its Alternatives* (pp. 1–9). Aurora: Garamond Press.

Atasoy, Yildiz and William K. Carroll (Eds.) (2002). *Global Shaping and Its Alternatives*. Aurora: Garamond Press.

Atkinson, Joe (1994). "The State, the Media, and Thin Democracy." In Andrew Sharp (Ed.), *Leap into the Dark. The Changing Role of the State in New Zealand since 1984* (pp. 146–177). Auckland: Auckland University Press.

Attalah, Paul and Leslie Shade (2002). *Mediascapes. News Patterns in Canadian Communications.* Toronto: Nelson.

Augoustinos, Martha and Katherine J. Reynolds (Eds.) (2001). *Understanding Prejudice, Racism and Social Conflict.* Thousand Oaks, California: Sage.

Augustine, Jean (2003). "Interview." *Canadian Issues.* April: 7–9.

Augustine, Noah (2000). "Sovereignty key issue for Aboriginals." *Toronto Star*. January 11.

Babcock, Linda, Sarah Laschever, Michele Gelfand, and Deborah Small (2003). "Why Women Earn Less." *National Post.* October 8.

Backhouse, Constance (1999). *Colour-Coded: A Legal History of Racism in Canada. 1900–1950.* Toronto: University of Toronto Press.

Bagnall, Janet (2003). "Women of the House." *Montreal Gazette.* March 7.

Baker-Said, Stephanie (2003). "Sexism in the City." *Markets* 12(11): 28–36.

Balmer, Brice (2003). "Let's Break the Poverty Cycle." *Kitchener-Waterloo Record.* November 20.

Banaji, Mahazir (2003). "Colour blind?" *THIS.* January/February: 44.

Bannerji, Himani (2000). The Dark Side of the Moon. Toronto: Canadian Scholars Press.

Bannerji, Himani (2003). "Multiple Multiculturalisms and Charles Taylor's Politics of Recognition." In D. Saunders and D. Haljan (Eds.), *Whither Multiculturalism* (pp. 35–46). Leuven University Press.

Banton, Michael (1987). *Racial Theories*. London: Cambridge University Press.

Barer, Morris L., Steve Morgan, and Robert G. Evans (2002). "Of course we can afford it." *Toronto Star*. December 16.

Barlow, Maude and Bruce Campbell (1996). *Straight Through the Heart. How the Liberals Abandoned the Just Society*. Toronto: HarperCollins.

Barlow, Maude and Heather-Jane Robertson (1993). *Class Warfare: The Assault on Canadian Schools*. Toronto: Key Porter.

Barnett, Antony and Andrew Wamsley (2003). "Brutal Bangladeshi gangs feed off Britain's taste for prawns*." Guardian Weekly,* May 13.

Barnsley, Paul (2001). "Native Youth Remain in Distress." *Windspeaker*. January.

Barr, Gerry (2003). "Canada must not backpedal at Cancun." *National Post*. June 2.

Barrett, Stanley (1994). *Paradise. Class, Commuters, and Ethnicity in Rural Ontario*. Toronto: University of Toronto Press.

Barrett, Stanley (2002). *When Culture Meets Power*. Westport, Colorado: Praeger.

Barrett, Stanley R. (1987). *Is God a Racist? The Right Wing in Canada*. Toronto: University of Toronto Press.

Barro, Robert J. (2003). "Medicare: Forget the Drug Benefit and Face Up to Real Reforms." *Business Week*. July 14: 28.

Beauchesne, Eric (2002). "University to cost $125 000, bank predicts." *National Post*. November 24.

Becker, H. (1963). *Outsiders*. New York: Free Press.

Bell, Stewart (2003). "Canada Terrorist Haven: Global Risk Consultant." *National Post*. November 12.

Benecki, Leslie (2003). "Family medicine needs a new treatment." *Kitchener-Waterloo Record*. March 26.

Bennett, Tony and Diane Watson (Eds.) (2003). *Understanding Everyday Life*. Cambridge, Massachusetts: The Open University/Blackwell.

Benwell, B. (Ed.) (2003). Masculinity and Men's Lifestyle. Oxford UK: Blackwell.

Bercuson, David, Robert and J. L. Granastein (1997). *Petrified Campus: The Crisis in Canadian Universities*. Toronto: Random House.

Berezin, Alexander A. (2003). "Pseudo-problem." Letter to *University Affairs*. October.

Berry, John W. and Rudolf Kalin (1993). "Multiculturalism and Ethnic Attitudes in Canada. An Overview of the 1991 National Survey." Paper presented to the Canadian Psychological Association Annual Meetings, Montreal, Quebec. May.

Berton, Pierre (1975). *Hollywood's Canada*. Toronto: McClelland & Stewart.

Best, Joel (1995). *Images of Issues: Typifying Contemporary Social Problems*, 2nd ed. Hawthorne, New York: Aldine de Gruyter.

Best, Joel (2000). "Constructing Children's Problems." In D. Dunn and D. Waller (Eds.) *Analyzing Social Problems* (pp. 154–160). Engelwood Cliffs, New Jersey: Prentice Hall.

Best, Joel (Ed.) (2001). *How Claims Spread. A Cross-National Diffusion of Social Problems*. New York: Aldine de Gruyter.

Bibby, Reginald W. (1990). *Mosaic Madness. The Potential and Poverty of Canadian Life.* Toronto: Stoddart.

Biles, John and Meyer Burstein (2003). "Immigration: Economics and More." *Canadian Issues.* April 13–15.

Bird, John, Lorraine Land, and Murray Macadam (2002). *Nation to Nation. Aboriginal Sovereignty and the Future of Canada.* New Edition. Toronto: Irwin Publishing.

Bissett, James (2003). "Amnesty Betrays Legal Immigrants." *National Post.* December 5.

Bissoondath, Neil (1994). *Selling Illusions: The Cult of Multiculturalism in Canada.* Toronto: Penguin.

Blackwell, Tom (2002). "Gender conflict a suicide trigger for teen girls." *National Post.* July 4.

Blackwell, Tom (2003). "Youth law likely to reduce crime rate." *National Post.* May 27.

Blatchford, C. (2003). "From the Hearts of New Canadians." *National Post.* April 4.

Blythe, Martin (1994). *Naming the Other. Images of the Maori in New Zealand Film and Television.* Metuchen, New Jersey: Scarecrow Press.

Bolaria, B. Singh and Peter Li (1988). *Racial Oppression in Canada*, 2nd ed. Toronto: Garamond.

Boldt, Menno (1993). *Surviving as Indians. The Challenge for Self-Government.* Toronto: University of Toronto Press.

Bonilla-Silva, Eduardo (1996). "Rethinking Racism: Towards a Structural Integration." *American Sociological Review,* 62: 465–480.

Borcea, Dana (2003). "Chief Blasts Justice System in Teen Slaying." *National Post.* December 11.

Borrows, John and Leonard Rotman (1997). "The Sui Generis Nature of Aboriginal Rights: Does It Make a Difference?" *Alberta Law Review,* 36: 9–45.

Bourhis, Richard and Annie Montreuil (2003). "Exploring Receiving Society Attitudes Toward Immigration and Ethnocultural Diversity." *Canadian Issues.* April: 39–41.

Boyle, Theresa (2003). "In Ontario, they call it private health by stealth." *Toronto Star.* April 12.

Brawley, Mark R. (2003). *The Politics of Globalization. Gaining Perspectives, Assessing Consequences.* Peterborough, Ontario: Broadview Press.

Brazier, Chris (1999). "The Radical Twentieth Century." *New Internationalist.* No. 309. January/February.

Brennan, Richard (2003). "Public pays for Tory propaganda, critics say." *Toronto Star.* May 12.

Breton, Raymond (1998). "Ethnicity and Race in Social Organizations: Recent Developments in Canadian Society. In R. Helmes-Hayes and J. Curtis (Eds.), *The Vertical Mosaic Revisited.* Toronto: University of Toronto Press.

Bricker, Darrell and Edward Greenspon (2001). *Searching for Certainty. Inside the New Canadian Mindset.* Toronto: Doubleday.

Bright, Chris (2003). "A History of Our Future." In Worldwatch Institute (Ed.), *State of the World 2003* (pp. 3–13). New York: WW Norton.

Brodie, Janine (1997). "The New Political Economy of Region." In W. Clement (Ed.), *Understanding Canada. Building on the New Canadian Political Economy.* Montreal/Kingston: McGill-Queen's University Press.

Brooks, Stephen (1998). *Public Policy in Canada. An Introduction.* Toronto: Oxford University Press.

Brooks, Stephen (2003). "Globalization and its Consequences in Canada." In K. Pryke and W. Soderland (Eds.), in *Profiles of Canada* (pp. 223–248). Toronto: Canadian Scholars Press.

Brown, Richard Harvey and J. Daniel Schubert (2002). *Introduction. The Contested Academy.* American Behavioral Scientist, 45 (7): 1051–1060.

Brown, Tony N. (2003). "There's No Race on the Playing Field." *Journal of Sport & Social Issues.* 27(2): 162–183.

Browning, D. S. and G.G. Rodriguez (2002). *Reweaving the Social Tapestry.* New York: W.W. Norton.

Bruser, David (2003). "Middle-income Students Pinched." *Toronto Star.* October 4.

Buckley, Helen (1992). *From Wooden Plows to Welfare: Why Indian Policy Failed in the Prairie Provinces.* Toronto: McMillan Collier.

Burgess, Michael (1996). "Ethnicity, Nationalism and Identity in Canada–Quebec Relations: The Case of Quebec's Distinct Society." *Journal of Commonwealth & Comparative Politics,* 34(2): 46–64.

Burke, Mike and Susan Silver (2003). "Universal Health Care: Current Challenges to Normative Legacies." In A. Westhues (Ed.), *Canadian Social Policy* (pp. 164–181). Waterloo: Wilfrid Laurier Press.

Burstein, Meyer (2003). "Consistency and Precision in Public Policy." In D. Saunders and D. Haljan (Eds.), *Whither Multiculturalism* (pp. 289–299). Leuven University Press.

Burtt, Bob (2003). "U.S. Control of Canada Growing, Author Says." *Kitchener-Waterloo Record.* November 1.

Byers, Michele (2003) "Buffy the Vampire Slayer. The Next Generation of Television." In R. Dicker and A. Piepmeier (Eds.), *Catching a Wave* (pp. 171–187). Boston: Northeastern University Press.

Cairns, Alan (2003). "Aboriginal Peoples in the Twenty-first Century. A Plea for Realism." In C. Gaffield and K.L. Gould (Eds.), *The Canadian Distinctiveness into the XXIst Century* (pp. 135–166). Ottawa: University of Ottawa Press.

Campbell, Charles M. (2000). *Betrayal & Deceit.* West Vancouver: Jasmine Books.

Campbell, Murray (1996). "Work in Progress. A Century of Change." A Six-Part Series. *The Globe and Mail.* November 28.

Canadian Council of Social Development (2003). Census Analysis. Census Shows Growing Polarization of Income in Canada. www.ccsd.ca/pr/2003/censusincome.htm

Canadian Health Network (2003). www.canadian-health-network.ca

Canadian Heritage (2003). Multiculturalism: Strength through Unity. http://www.pch.gc.ca/progs/multi/reports

Canadian Labour Congress (2003). *Aboriginal Rights Resource Tool Kit.* Ottawa.

Canadian Press (2003). "Ottawa to revamp its hiring practices." Reprinted in the *Toronto Star.* February 7.

Canadian Press (2003). "Surgery Waits Equal for Rich or Poor, Canadian Study Finds." Printed in the *Toronto Star,* February 18.

Canadian Press (2003). "KW to get private MRI clinic." Printed in the *Kitchener-Waterloo Record.* February 22.

Canadian Press (2003). "Gender gap narrows—to 30% less for women." Reprinted in the *Kitchener-Waterloo Record.* March 3.

Canadian Press (2003). "Innovative workplace practices by manufacturers don't improve staff loyalty, Statistics Canada finds." Printed in the *Kitchener-Waterloo Record.* March 26.

Canadian Press (2003). "Profiling defined in court ruling." Reprinted in the *Toronto Star.* April 20.

Canadian Press (2003). "Fewer Boys Opting for University." Reprinted in the *Kitchener–Waterloo Record.* June 2.

Canadian Press (2003). "Region's crime rate falling." Printed in the *Kitchener-Waterloo Record* by Liz Monteiro. July 25.

Canadian Press (2003). "White Journalist Dressed as Black Man Experiences Racism in Montreal." Reprinted in the *Kitchener-Waterloo Record.* October 3.

Canadian Press (2003). "French Immersion Linked to Truancy." Reprinted in the *Toronto Star.* October 16.

Canadian Press (2003). "Attacks on Teens Show Increases in Brutality." Reprinted in the *Kitchener-Waterloo Record.* December 8.

Caragata, Lea (2003). "Housing and Homelessness." In A. Westhues (Ed.), *Canadian Social Policy* (pp. 67–89). Waterloo: Wilfrid Laurier Press.

Carey, Elaine (2003). "Canada's workforce is most educated." *Toronto Star.* March 12.

Carey, Elaine (2003). "Gender gap in earnings staying stubbornly high." *Toronto Star.* March 12.

Carey, Elaine (2003). "Canadians less satisfied with health care: Poll." *Toronto Star.* May 6.

Carey, Elaine (2003). "Income gap growing between immigrants, native-born." *Toronto Star.* June 20.

Carey, Elaine (2003). "Male-female wage gap traced to employers." *Toronto Star.* June 22.

Carey, Elaine (2003). "Domestic abuse rates still rising." *Toronto Star.* June 24.

Carey, Elaine (2003). "Child poverty spreading fast in GTA: Report." *Toronto Star.* June 30.

Carey, Elaine (2003). "Internet Helps Reading Skills, Study Finds." *Toronto Star.* July 29.

Carey, Elaine (2003). "Cancer Care Failing: Probe." *Toronto Star.* October 18.

Carrington, Peter (1999). "UW Researcher Finds Little Change in Canada's Youth Crime Rate." *UW Gazette.* April 28.

Carter, Cindy and C. Kay Weaver (2003). *Violence and the Media.* Philadelphia: Open University Press.

Case, Charles (2000). "Racist and Egalitarian Ideologies in Modern American Culture." In D. Dunn and D. Waller (Eds.), *Analyzing Social Problems* (pp. 81–88). Engelwood Cliffs, New Jersey: Prentice Hall.

Cash, Colby (2003). "What is this money in aid of?" *National Post.* August 28.

Cassidy, Frank (2003). "First Nations Governance Act: A Legacy Lost." *Policy Options,* 24(04): 46–50.

Castles, Stephen (2000). *International Migration at the Beginning of the Twenty-First Century: Global Trends and Issues.* UNESCO. Oxford, UK: Blackwell.

CDG/FP Commitment to Development Index (2003). "Ranking the Rich." *Foreign Policy* May/June: 19–28.

Centre for Research and Information on Canada (CRIC) (2003). *A Changing People: Being Canadian in a New Century*. The CRIC Papers. April.

Chan, Janet B.L. (1997). *Changing Police Culture. Policing in a Multicultural Society.* Cambridge, UK: Cambridge University Press.

Chan, Steve and James R. Scarritt (2002). "Globalization, Soft Hegemony, and Democratization: Their Sources and Effects." Pp. 1–33 in *Coping with Globalization.*

Cheal, David (2003). "Aging and Demographic Change in Canadian Context.*" Horizons*, 6(2): 21–23.

Cheal, David (Ed.) (2002). "Introduction: Contextualizing Demographic Concerns." In D. Cheal (Ed.), *Aging and Demographic Change in Canadian Context* (pp. 3–21). Toronto: University of Toronto Press.

Chennells, David (2001). *The Politics of Nationalism in Canada. Cultural Conflict Since 1760.* Toronto: University of Toronto Press.

Chic, Jacquie and John Fraser (2003). "Why are the poor getting poorer." *Toronto Star*. May 20.

Chomsky, Noam (2003). Hegemony or Survival? America's Quest for Global Dominance. New York: Henry Holt & Co.

Christian, William (2003). "Rocky road between Ottawa and Quebec City won't end" *Kitchener-Waterloo Record*. April 19.

Christie, Gordon (2000). "The Nature of Delgamuukw." *Windspeaker*. August.

Chui, Tina and Danielle Zietsma (2003). "Earnings of Immigrants in the 1990s." *Canadian Social Trends,* No. 78 (Autumn): 24–28.

Churchill, Ward (2003). *Perversions of Justice. Indigenous Peoples and Angloamerican Law.* San Francisco: City Lights.

CIC (2002). *Pursuing Canada's Commitment to Immigration—Citizenship and Immigration Canada.* Ottawa: Minister of Public Works and Government Services.

CIC (2002). "Who is a Business Immigrant." http://cicnet.ci.gc.ca/english/business/index

Clairmont, Don (1988). *Community-Based Policing and Organizational Change. Occasional Papers.* Halifax: Atlantic Institute of Criminology.

Clarke, John (2001). "Social Problems: Sociological Perspectives." In M. May et al. (Eds.), *Understanding Social Problems* (pp. 3–15). Malden, Massachusetts: Blackwell.

Cleaver, Frances (Ed.) (2002). *Masculinities Matter. Men, Gender, and Development*. New York: Zed Books.

Coady, Tony (2000). *Why Universities Matter: A Conversation about Values, Means, and Directions.* St. Leonards, New South Wells: Allen & Unwin.

Cogan, Jeanine and Amy Marcus-Newhall (2002). "Introduction." *American Behavioral Scientist,* 46 (1): 8–13.

Cole, Johnella Betsch and Beverly Guy-Sheffall (2003). *Gender Talk. The Struggle for Women's Equality in African American Communities.* New York: Ballantine Publishing.

Coleman, William D. (2002). "The Politics of Globalization." In R.Dyck (Ed.), *Studying Politics* (pp. 389–406). Toronto: Nelson.

Collacott, Martin (2002). *Canada's Immigration Policy. The Need for Major Reform. A Fraser Institute Occasional Paper.* No. 64. Vancouver.

Consedine, Jim (2003). "The Third Millenium—Restorative Justice or More Crime and Prisons?" Paper Presented to the Foundation of Indigenous Research, Science, and Technology. Wellington. Available at www.firstfound.org

Conway, John Frederick (2001). *The Canadian Family in Crisis,* 4th ed. Toronto: James Lorimer & Co.

Coon Come, Mathew (1999). "Cree Chief Slams Gathering Strength." *Windspeaker.* January.

Coontz, Stephanie (1992). *The Way We Never Were: American Families and the Nostalgia Trap.* New York: Basic Books.

Corak, Miles (2003). "University degrees still have dollar value in Canada." *Kitchener-Waterloo Record.* March 12.

Corcoran, Terence (2003). "Immigration Debate Takes Troubling Turn." *National Post.* November 27.

Coren, Michael (2003). "The genuine meaning of marriage is lost." *National Post.* June 19.

Covell, Katherine and R. Brian Howe (2001). *The Challenge of Children's Rights for Canada.* Waterloo: Wilfrid Laurier Press.

Cowan, Tyler (1999). "Cashing in on the Cultural Free Trade." *National Post.* April 24.

Coyle, Jim (2003). "Invisible enemy shakes faith in science." *Toronto Star.* March 29.

Coyne, Andrew (2003). "We lost our place." *The Globe and Mail.* May 15.

CRIC (2003). *Health Care: A System Under Strain.* Published by the Centre for Research and Information on Canada. www.cric.ca

CRIC (2003). "Canadians' Priorities: More Money for Health Care, Education, and Improved Federal Provincial Cooperation." Media Release by the Centre for Research and Information on Canada. www.cric.ca

Crook, Marion (2003). *Out of the Darkness: Teens Talk About Suicide.* Vancouver, BC: Arsenal Pulp Press.

Croteau, David and William Hoynes (2000). *Media/Society. Industries, Images, and Societies,* 2nd ed. Thousand Oaks, California: Sage.

Crowley, Kevin (2003). "Business acceptance an uphill battle." *Kitchener-Waterloo Record.* February 22.

Cryderman, Brian, Christopher O'Toole, and Augie Fleras (1998). *Policing in a Multicultural Society: A Handbook for the Police Services.* Markham: Butterworths.

Curry, Bill and Andrew McIntosh (2003). "Ottawa loses track of 36,000 deportees." *National Post.* April 9.

Curtis, James, Edward Grab, and Neil Guppy (Eds). (2004). *Social Inequality in Canada. Patterns, Problems, and Policies.* Toronto: Pearson Education.

Day, Richard and Tonio Sadik (2002). "The B.C. Land Question, Liberal Multiculturalism, and the Spectre of Aboriginal Nationhood." *BC Studies,* 134: 5–34.

Dei, George Sefa (2000). "Contesting the Future: Anti-Racism and Canadian Diversity." In S. Nancoo (Ed.), *21st Century Canadian Diversity* (pp. 295–319). Toronto: Canadian Scholars Press.

DeKeseredy, Walter S., Shahid Alvi, Martin D. Schwartz, and E. Andreas Tomaszewski (2003). *Under Seige. Poverty and Crime in a Public Housing Community.* Lanham MD: Lexington Books.

Derber, Charles (2002). *People Before Profit: The New Globalisation in an Age of Terror, Big Money, and Economic Crisis.* Souvenir Press.

Dershowitz, Alan (2002). *Why Terrorism Works?* Princeton: Yale University Press.

Desai, Sabra and Sangeeta Subramanian (2003). "Colour, Culture, and Dual Consciousness: Issues Identified by South Asian Immigrant Youth in the Greater Toronto Area." In P. Ansif and K.M. Kilbride (Eds.), *Managing Two Worlds* (pp. 118–161). Toronto: Canadian Scholars Press.

Devereaux, P. J. (2003). "A Systematic Review and Meta-Analysis of Studies Comparing Mortality in Private For-Profit and Private Not-for-Profit Hospitals." *Horizons,* 5(2).

Diamond, Jack (1997). "Provinces are Archaic. More Power to the Cities." *The Globe and Mail.* May 26.

Diamond, Jared (2003). "The Last Americans. Environmental Collapse and the End of Civilization." *Alternatives Journal,* 29(1): 43–47.

Dicker, Rory and Alison Piepmeier, (Eds.) (2003). *Catching a Wave. Reclaiming Feminism for the 21st Century.* Boston: Northeastern University Press.

Diebel, Linda (2003). "Ten questions for a SARS inquiry." *Toronto Star.* June 8.

DiManno, Rosie (2003). "You call that a pestilence? That's not a real pestilence." *Toronto Star.* May 26.

Doerr, Audrey (1997). "Building New Orders of Government: The Future of Aboriginal Self-Government." *Canadian Public Administration,* 40(2): 274–289.

Doherty-Delorme, Denise and Erika Shaker (2003). "Missing Pieces." *Kitchener-Waterloo Record.* May 19.

Donnelly, Fred (2003). "Faculty's Place in the Corporate World." Book Review of The University in a Corporate Culture. *University Affairs.* October.

Donnison, David (2001). "The Changing Face of Poverty." In M. May et al. (Eds.), In *Understanding Social Problems* (pp. 87–106). Malden, Massachusetts: Blackwell.

Doob, Anthony and Carla Cesaroni (2003). *Responding To Youth Crime in Canada.* Toronto: University of Toronto Press.

Dorais, Michel (2002). "Immigration and Integration through a Social Cohesion Perspective." *Horizons,* 5(2): 4–5.

Doran, Charles F. (2002). "What Canada and the United States Stand for ... in the Age of Globalization." *Canadian Issues.* September: 6–11.

Dosman, Edgar (1972). *Indians. The Urban Dilemma.* Toronto: McClelland & Stewart.

Douglas, Edward Te Kohu (2003). "Indigenous Peoples and Justice—A Foreward." Paper presented to the Foundation for Indigenous Research, Science, and Technology. Wellington, New Zealand. Available at www.firstfound.org

Douglas, Shirley (2003). "Romanow: The Prognosis." *The Globe and Mail.* November 28.

Dow, Steve (2003). "Racism caught in the Net." www.smh.com.au, March 25.

Doward, Jamie (2003). "Too old at 35 as job ageism starts earlier." *Guardian Weekly.* June 26–July 2.

Doyle, Aaron (2003). *Arresting Images. Crime and Policing in Front of the Television Camera.* Toronto: University of Toronto Press.

Doyle, John (2003). "SARS coverage fuels fear instead of calming it." *The Globe and Mail.* April 28.

Driedger, Leo and Shiva S. Halli (2000). *Race and Racism. Canada's Challenge.* Ottawa: Carleton University Press.

Driedger, Leo (2003). *Race and Ethnicity. Finding Identities and Equalities.* Toronto: Oxford University Press.

Drost, Herman, Brian Lee Crowley, and Richard Schwindt (1995). *Marketing Solutions for Native Poverty.* Toronto: C.D. Howe Institute.

Dua, Enakshi and Angela Robertson (Eds.) (1999). *Scratching the Surface: Canadian Anti-Racist Feminist Thought.* Toronto: Women's Press.

Dubuc, Alain (2002). "Presentation." In E. R. Griffiths (Ed.), the *LaFontaine Baldwin Lectures. Dialogue on Democracy in Canada* (pp. 55–86). Toronto: Penguin.

Duff, Joel (2003). "Tackling Student Debt a Priority." *Toronto Star.* May 26.

Duffy, Andrew (2002). "Chief creates state, adopts his citizens." *National Post.* May 16.

Dufraiment, Lisa (2002). "Continuity and Modification of Aboriginal Rights in the Nisga'a Treaty." *UBC Law Review,* 35(2): 455–457.

Duncan, Howard (2003). "Social Inclusion, Social Capital, and Immigration." *Canadian Issues,* April: 30–32.

Duncanson, John, Dale Anne Freed, and Chris Sorensen (2003). "There's racism all over the place." *Toronto Star.* February 26.

Dunn, Dana and David Waller (2000). *Analyzing Social Problems. Issues and Approaches.* Englewood Cliffs, New Jersey: Prentice Hall.

Dunphy, Bill (2003). "Immigrant poverty rate soaring. Rate has risen from 24.6 percent in 1980 to 35.8 percent in 2000." *Hamilton Spectator.* June 20.

Durban, Jonathan (2003). "Fear Factory." *Maclean's.* June 9: 24–25.

Durst, Douglas (2003). "Aboriginal Persons with Disabilities. A Public Policy Gap." *Saskatchewan Institute of Public Policy Newsletter.* No. 7, September: 6.

Duxbury, Linda and Chris Higgins (2002). *2001 National Work-Life Conflict Study. Report One.* Ottawa: Health Canada.

Dyck, Noel (1991). *What Is the Indian Problem?* St. John's, Nfld.: Memorial University.

Ecologist (1999). "Beyond the Monoculture: Shifting From Global to Local," 29(3).

Editorial (1999). "Introduction." *Ecologist,* 29(3): 153.

Editorial, (2002). "Why Young People Kill to Belong." *The Globe and Mail.* October 10.

Editorial, (2003). "Justice is blind, not colour-blind." *Toronto Star.* April 2.

Editorial (2003). "'Brutal' Don jail an Embarrassment." *Toronto Star.* May 8.

Editorial, (2003). "Policies encourage growing inequality." *Toronto Star.* May 17.

Editorial (2003). "The freedom to choose for-profit care." *National Post.* May 26.

Editorial, (2003). "Whites needn't apply." *National Post*. May 29.

Editorial (2003). "No better time to be Canadian." *Kitchener-Waterloo Record*. June 30.

Editorial (2003). "Positive models." *Guardian Weekly*. July 2–9.

Editorial (2003). "U.S. Health No Bargain." *Toronto Star.* August 24.

Editorial (2003). "Being Male, Being Female." *Christchurch Press.* September 20.

Editorial (2003). "Better Homes for Natives." *National Post*. November 1.

Edwards, David and David Cromwell (2003). "It Wasn't Just Blair; the Media Also Duped Us." *New Statesman*. June 9: 21.

Edwards, Steven (2003). "UN Agency Scolds Canada for Allowing Spanking." *National Post.* October 8.

Egelman, William (2004). *Understanding Families. Critical Thinking and Analysis.* Toronto: Pearson.

Ejiogu, E.C. (2001). "The Roots of Political Instability in an Artificial 'Nation-State': The Case of Nigeria. *IJCS,* xlii: 3–18.

EKOS Research Associates (2003). "Making Ends Meet. The 2001–2002 Student Financial Survey." Montreal: Canadian Millenium Scholarship Foundation.

Elmasry, Mohamed (1999). "Framing Islam." *Kitchener-Waterloo Record*. December 16.

Engstrom, Erika (2003). "Hegemony in reality-based TV programming: the world according to A Wedding Story." *Media Report to Women* (Winter): 10–14.

Erasmus, Georges (2002). "Presentation. In R. Griffiths (Ed.), *The LaFontaine-Baldwin Lectures. Dialogue on Democracy in Canada. Second Annual* (pp. 99–126). Toronto: Penguin.

Erasmus, Georges and Joe Sanders (2002). "Canadian History: An Aboriginal Perspective." In J. Bird et al. (Eds.), *Nation to Nation* (pp. 3–11). Toronto: Irwin.

Faludi, Susan (1999). *Stiffed. The Betrayal of the American Man*. New York: William Morrow.

Fenlon, Brodie (2002). "Suicide still the top killer." *Toronto Sun.* December 5.

Fenton, Steve (2003). Ethnicity. Cambridge, UK: Polity Press.

Fields, A Beldon (2003). *Rethinking Human Rights for the New Millenium*. New York: Palgrave Macmillan.

Fiorito, Joe (2003). "John, You Should Have Known Better." *Toronto Star*. May 18.

Fish, Stanley (1997). "Boutique Multiculturalism, or Why Liberals Are Incapable of Thinking About Hate Speech." *Critical Inquiry* (Winter): 378–395.

Flanagan, Tom (1999). *First Nations? Second Thoughts*. Vancouver: UBC Press.

Fleras, Augie (1996). "The Politics of Jurisdiction." In David Long and Olive Dickason (Eds.), *Visions of the Heart* (pp. 178–211). Toronto: Harcourt Brace.

Fleras, Augie (1999). "Politicizing Indigeneity: Ethnopolitics in White Settler Dominions." In Paul Havemann (Ed.), *Indigenous People's Rights* (pp. 187–234). Auckland: Oxford University Press.

Fleras, Augie (2001). *Social Problems in Canada: Constructions, Conditions, and Challenges,* 3rd ed. Toronto: Pearson.

Fleras, Augie (2002). *Engaging Diversity. Multiculturalism in Canada.* Toronto: Nelson ITP.

Fleras, Augie (2003). *Mass Media Communication in Canada.* Toronto: Nelson ITP.

Fleras, Augie and Jean Leonard Elliott (1991). *The Nations Within.* Toronto: Oxford University Press.

Fleras, Augie and Jean Leonard Elliott (2003). *Unequal Relations: An Introduction to Race and Ethnic Dynamics in Canada*, 4th ed. Toronto: Prentice Hall.

Fleras, Augie and Jean Lock Kunz (2001). *Representing Diversity. Media and Minorities in a Multicultural Canada.* Toronto: Thompson Publishing.

Fleras, Augie and Paul Spoonley (1999). *Recalling Aotearoa: Indigenous Politics and Ethnic Relations in New Zealand.* Melbourne: Oxford University Press.

Fleras, Augie and Roger Maaka (2004). *The Politics of Indigeneity.* Dunedin, New Zealand: Otago University Press.

Fontaine, Nahanni (2002). "Aboriginal Women's Perspective on Self-Government." *Canadian Dimension.* November/December: 9–10.

Fontaine, Phil (2003). "Native Status Not an Obstacle." Letter to *National Post.* November 3.

Fortune Magazine (2002). "Fortune Global 500." http://fortune.com/lists/G500

Foss, Krista (2002). "Men as likely to face abuse from partner, Statscan says." *The Globe and Mail.* June 27.

Fournier, Suzanne (1999). "Native Women Fight Male Councils in Land Battle." *National Post.* April 26.

Francis, Daniel (1992). *The Imaginary Indian: The Image of the Indian in Canadian Culture.* Vancouver: Arsenal Pulp Press.

Francis, Diane (2002). *Immigration. The Economic Case.* Toronto: Key Porter Books.

Francis, Diane (2003). "We Haven't Come That Far After All." *National Post.* November 1.

Francis, Diane (2003) "$27 billion doesn't go far these days." *National Post.* February 2.

Fraser, Graham (2003). "Canada praised as model for 21st century." *Toronto Star.* May 22.

Fraser, Graham (2003). "Survivor guilt sets in as journalists jettisoned." *Toronto Star.* May 15.

Fraser, Graham (2003). "Liberal vote total dropped." *Toronto Star.* April 19.

Frederickson, George (2002). *Racism. A Short History.* Princeton University Press.

Freeze, Colin (2003). "City suffers 'exponential' rise in obesity, Basrur says." *The Globe and Mail.* June 7.

Frideres, James (1998). *Native Peoples in Canada: Contemporary Conflicts*, 5th ed. Toronto: Prentice.

Frideres, James (2002). "Immigrants, Integration, and the Intersection of Identities." Paper prepared for the Intersection of Identities Conference. Canadian Heritage. Niagara Falls. April 25–26.

Friedan, Betty (1963). *The Feminine Mystique.* New York: W. W. Norton.

Friedman, Jonathan (2003). *Globalization, the State and Violence.* Lanham, Maryland: Rowman and Littlefield.

Friedman, Thomas L. (1999). *The Lexus and the Olive Tree: Understanding Globalization.* Farrar, Straus, and Giroux.

Friesen, Henry (2003). "Growing the asset." *Toronto Star.* April 18.

Friscolanti, Michael (2003). "The North wrestles multiple problems." *National Post.* June 17.

Friscolanti, Michael (2003). "Indian Act Shields Corruption: Study." *National Post.* October 29.

Frith, Rosaline (2003). "Integration." *Canadian Issues.* April: 35–36.

Frizzell, Alan and Jon H. Pammett (Eds.) (1996). *Social Inequality in Canada.* Ottawa: Carleton University Press.

Fulford, Robert (2003). "The irresponsible damage of separatism." *National Post.* April 19.

Fullan, Michael (2003). "Schools failing grades." *The Globe and Mail.* May 19.

Gaffield, Chad (2003). "Perspectives on the Canadian Distinctiveness into the XXIst Century. In C. Gaffield, and K.L. Gould (Eds.), *The Canadian Distinctiveness into the XX1st Century* (pp. 3–12). Ottawa: University of Ottawa Press.

Gaines, Patricia (2002). "Healing the Wounds of Crime. Restorative Justice Programs Offer Emotional support to both victims and offenders." *Utne.* November/December: 76 80.

Galloway, Gloria (2003). "Too Much TV Impairs Reading, Study Suggests." *The Globe and Mail.* October 29.

Galt, Virginia (2002). "Huge wage gap tied to race: CLC." *The Globe and Mail.* November 29.

Galt, Virginia (2003). "Statscan studies workplace stress." *The Globe and Mail.* June 26.

Gamble, Warren and Geoff Cumming (2002). "Immigration: The Numbers Game." *New Zealand Herald.* November 30.

Ganahl, Dennis J., K. Kim and S. B. Netzley (2003). "Longitudinal analysis of network commercials. How advertisers portray gender." *Media Report to Women* (Spring): 11–13.

Gans, Chaim (2003). *The Limits of Nationalism.* New York: Cambridge University Press.

Gans, Herbert (2003). *Democracy and the News.* New York: Oxford University Press.

Gatehouse, Jonathan (2003). "The Good News about the Bad News." *Maclean's.* June 9.

Gauld, Robin (2003). *Continuity Amid Chaos. The Context of Health Care Management and Delivery in New Zealand.* Dunedin: Otago University Press.

Geographical Dossier (2003). "What is Globalization?" *Geographical.* October: 44–47. Available at www.geographical.co.uk

George, Lianne (2003). "This ain't OshKosh B'Gosh." *National Post.* April 19.

George, Usha (2003). "Immigration and Refugee Policy in Canada: Past, Present, and Future." In A. Westhues (Ed.), *Canadian Social Policy* (pp. 145–163). Waterloo: Wilfrid Laurier Press.

Gibbins, Roger and Guy Laforest (Eds.) (1998*). Beyond the Impasse: Toward Reconciliation.* Montreal: Institute of Research for Public Policy.

Gillespie, Marie (1996). *Television, Ethnicity, and Cultural Change.* London: Routledge.

Gillespie, Kerry (2003). "Visible Homeless Small Part of the Total." *Toronto Star.* September 14.

Girard, Daniel (2003). "Fontaine steers to the mainstream." *Toronto Star.* July 19.

Giroux, Henry A. (1996). *Fugitive Cultures: Race, Violence, and Youth.* New York: Routledge.

Giroux, Henry A. (1996). "Insurgent Multiculturalism as the Promise of Pedagogy." In D.T. Goldberg (Ed*.), Multiculturalism: A Critical Reader* (pp. 325–343). Oxford: Blackwell.

Giroux, Henry A. (2003). *The Abandonned Generation. Democracy Beyond the Culture of Fear.* New York: Palgrave Macmillan.

Gleckman, Howard (2003). "The Medicare Reform is No Cure." *Business Week.* July 14: 36.

Glover, Ian and Mohamed Bronine (2001). "Introduction: The Challenge of Longer and Healthier Lives." In I. Glover and M. Bronine (Eds.), *Ageism in Work and Employment* (pp. 3–23). Aldershot, UK: Ashgate Publishing.

Goar, Carol (2003). "Trapped behind a stereotype." *Toronto Star.* February 24.

Goar, Carol (2003). "A woman's place is in politics." *Toronto Star.* March 5.

Goar, Carol (2003). "Welcome Mat Needs Mending." *Toronto Star*. Jan 31.

Goar, Carol (2003). "Time to Tame Globalization." *Toronto Star.* September 8.

Goddard, John (2003). "Spanking case opens in Supreme Court." *Toronto Star.* June 6.

Goldberg, David Theo (1994). "Introduction: Multicultural Conditions." In T. Goldberg (Ed.), *Multiculturalism: A Critical Reader* (pp. 1–44). Cambridge: Basil Blackwell.

Goodfellow, Cathy Lane (2003). "Meaningful Consequences." *Law Now*, October/November.

Gordon, Mary (2003). "Audit points to bias in student hiring." *Toronto Star.* July 4.

Gorrie, Peter (2003). "SARS just one part of a global puzzle." *Toronto Star*. March 24.

Gosine, Andil (2003). "Myths of Diversity." *Alternatives Journal,* 29(1): 1–4.

Gosnell, Joseph (2000). "Nisga'a Treaty Opens Economic Doors for Everyone." Speech to the Canadian Club. May 15. Reprinted in *Canadian Speeches,* 14(4): 10–14.

Grab, Edward G. (2002). *Theories of Social Inequality*, 4th ed. Toronto: Harcourt.

Graham, Katherine (1999). "Urban Aboriginal Governance in Canada: Paradigms and Prospects." In J. Hylton, (Ed.), *Aboriginal Government in Canada. Current Trends and Issues* (pp. 377–391). Saskatoon: Purich Publishing.

Gray, Jeff (2003). "Life-expectancy gap narrows." *The Globe and Mail*. April 2.

Gray, John (1997). *False Dawn. Delusions of Global Capitalism*. London: Granta Books.

Gray-Rosendale, Laura and Gil Harootunian (Eds.) (2003). *Fractured Feminisms. Rhetoric, Context, and Contestation.* Albany: State University of New York Press.

Graydon, Shari (2001). "The Portrayal of Women in the Media: The Good, the Bad, and the Beautiful." In C. McKie and B. Singer (Eds.), *Communications in Canadian Society*, 5th ed. (pp. 179–195). Toronto: Thompson Publishing.

Green, Joyce (2003). "From Oppression, Towards Liberation." *Canadian Dimension* November/December: 30–32.

Greenspon, Edward (2003). "Letter from the Editor." *The Globe and Mail.* June 7.

Greenspon, Edward (2003). "What passes for normal in news." *The Globe and Mail.* May 10.

Greenway, Norma (2002). "As funding falls, student tuition climbs." *National Post.* September 17.

Greer, Germaine (1999). *The Whole Woman*. New York: A.A.Knopf.

Gregg, Allan R. (2003). "SARS and the fear factor." *Maclean's*. May 5.

Griggs, Barbara (1997). *Green Pharmacy. The History and Evolution of Western Herbal Medicine.* Rochester Vermont: Healing Arts Press.

Grob, Gerald N. (2002). The *Deadly Truth. A History of Disease in Americ*a. Cambridge MA: Harvard University Press.

Guardian Weekly (2003). "Forgotten Famine." May.

Guppy, Neil and Scot Davies (1998). *Education in Canada. Recent Trends and Future Challenges.* Ottawa: Statistics Canada.

Gwyn, Richard (1998). "Maybe National Unity Problem Not Meant to be Solved." *Toronto Star*. June 10.

Gwyn, Richard (2000). "Welcome to the New World of Corporatism." *Toronto Star.* April 28.

Gwyn, Richard (2004). "White collar workers lose out to corporate greed." *KW Record.* January 7.

Ha, Tu Thanh (2000). "Ottawa violates Native Rights, U.N. told." *The Globe and Mail.* July 28.

Hacker, Helen Mayer (1951). "Women as a Minority Group." *Social Forces:* 60–69.

Hall, Nigel (2002). "Globalisation and Third World Poverty." *Social Work Review.* Summer: 3–5.

Halli, Shiva and Leo Driedger (Eds.) (1999). *Immigrant Canada. Demographic, Economic, and Social Challenges.* Toronto: University of Toronto Press.

Hammersmith, Bernice (2002). "Restoring Women's Value". In J. Bird (Ed.), *Nation to Nation* (pp. 120–130). Toronto: Irwin.

Hanrahan, Maura (2003). "Water Rights or Wrongs." *Alternatives Journal,* 29(1): 14–17.

Hargrove, Buzz and Wayne Skene (1998). *Labour of Love: The Fight to Create a More Humane Canada.* Toronto: Macfarlane Walter and Ross.

Harries, Kate (2003). "When spanking is unacceptable: Judge*." Toronto Star.* April 3.

Harris, David (2002). *Profiles in Injustice: Why Racial Profiling Cannot Work.* New York: New Press.

Harris, Michael (1998). *Lament for an Ocean. The Collapse of the Atlantic Cod Fishery: A True Crime Story.* Toronto: McClelland & Stewart.

Harris, Roma and Manjunath Pendakur (2002). *Competing Visions: The Social Impact of Information and Communications Technology.* Toronto: Garamond.

Harter, Bruce and Ted Hall (2003). "From the Blame Game to Accountability in Health Care." *Policy Options* 24, (10): 49–54.

Harvey, Robert (2003). *Global Disorder. American and the Threat of World Conflict.* New York: Carroll and Graf Publishers.

Havemann, Paul (Ed.) (1999). *Indigenous Peoples' Rights in Australia, Canada, and New Zealand.* Auckland: Oxford University Press.

Hawaleshka, Danylo (2003). "Nature Under Seige." *Maclean's.* June 2: 24–35.

Hawkes, David (2000). "Review of Citizens Plus." *Isuma* (Autumn): 141–142.

Hawkins, Darnell F. (2003). *Violent Crime: Assessing Race and Ethnic Differences.* New York: CUP.

Health Canada (1994). *Strategies for Population Health: Investing in the Health of Canadians.* Ottawa: Health Canada.

Heath, Joseph (2001). *The Efficient Society: Why Canada is as Close to Utopia as it Gets.* Toronto: Penguin.

Heilbrun, Carolyn G. (1999). *Women's Lives: The View from the Threshold.* Toronto: University of Toronto Press.

Held, David and Anthony McGrew (2002). *Globalization/Anti-Globalization.* Cambridge, UK: Polity Press.

Helmes-Hayes, Rick and Jim Curtis (Eds.) (1998). *The Vertical Mosaic Revisited.* Toronto: University of Toronto Press.

Henderson, Helen (2003). "Promised increase is meager in disability support." *Toronto Star.* June 14.

Henry, Frances and Carol Tator (2002). *Discourses of Domination: Racial Bias in Canadian English-language Press.* Toronto: University of Toronto Press.

Henry, Frances, Carol Tator, Winston Mattis and Tim Rees (1999). *The Colour of Democracy,* 2nd ed. Toronto: Harcourt Brace.

Henry III, William A. (1994). "In Defence of Elitism." *Time,* August 29.

Herman, Edward S. and Noam Chomsky (1988). *Manufacturing Consent: The Political Economy of the Mass Media.* New York: Pantheon Books.

Heyding, Christina (2003). "Annika's giant step." Letter to the editor. *Toronto Star.* May 26.

Hicks, Peter (2003). "The policy implications of aging." *Horizons,* 6(2): 12–16.

Hiebert, Daniel (2003). Immigration and Minority Enclaves. Canadian Issues. April 27–29.

Hiller, Susanne (2002). "CAS calls for mandatory parenting classes." *National Post.* September 17.

Hochschild, A. (1989). *The Second Shift: Working Parents and the Revolution at Home.* New York: Viking.

Hockey, Jenny and Allison James (2003). *Social Identities Across the Life Course.* New York: Palgrave Macmillan.

Holford, Patrick (2003). "Food for Thought." *The Ecologist*: 20–23.

Holstein, James A. and Gale Miller (Eds.) (2003). *Challenges & Choices. Constructionist Perspectives on Social Problems.* New York: Aldine de Gruyter.

Holtzman, Linda (2000). *Media Messages: What Film, Television, and Popular Music Teach Us about Race, Class, Gender and Sexual Orientation.* Armonk, New York: M.E. Sharpe.

Honey, Kim (1999). "Cities Getting Too Big for the Planet, Professor Says." *The Globe and Mail.* January 26.

Hooks, Bell (2003). *Rock my Soul.* New York: Atria Books.

Houpt, Simon (2003). "U.S. got lucky, experts agree." *The Globe and Mail.* June 13.

Howes, Carol (2001). "The New Native Economy." *National Post.* January 27.

Hrynynshyn, James (2003). "Poisoned Ground." *THIS* magazine. November/December: 20–23.

Humphries, Adrian (2003). "Censorship reduces students to reading 'pap', study says." *National Post.* May 5.

Humphries, Adrian and Stewart Bell (2003). "Organized Crime Widespread." *National Post.* October 28.

Hunter, Garson (2003). "The Problem of Child Poverty in Canada." In A. Westhues (Ed.), *Canadian Social Policy,* 3rd ed. (pp. 29–49). Waterloo: Wilfrid Laurier Press.

Hurtig, Mel (2002). *The Vanishing Country. Is It Too Late to Save Canada?* Toronto: McClelland & Stewart.

Hutsul, Christopher (2003). "Marriage limbo." *Toronto Star.* June 25.

Hylton, John (1994; 1999). *Aboriginal Self-Government in Canada. Current Trends and Issues,* 2nd ed. Saskatoon: Purich Publishing.

Hyndman, Jennifer (2003). "Immigrants are not a problem*." The Globe and Mail.* July 4.

Ignatieff, Michael (1993). *Blood and Belonging. Journeys into the New Nationalism.* New York: Viking.

Ignatieff, Michael (1999). "Human Rights: The Middle Crisis." *The New York Times Review.* May 20.

Ignatieff, Michael (2001). "The Hate Stops Here." *The Globe and Mail.* October 25.

Infantry, Ashante (1999). "Opportunity Knocks ... But Not for All. Beyond 2000. Home to the World." *Toronto Star.* May 2.

Inglehart, Ronald and Pippa Norris (2003). "The True Clash of Civilizations." *Foreign Policy.* March/April: 63–71.

Isaac, Thomas (2000). *Aboriginal Law: Cases, Materials, and Commentary*, 2nd ed. Saskatoon: Purich Publishing.

Isajiw, Wsevolod (Ed.) (1997). *Multiculturalism in North America and Europe: Comparative Perspectives on Interethnic Relations and Social Incorporation.* Toronto: Canadian Scholars Press.

Isbister, John (2003). *Promises Not Kept. Poverty and the Betrayal of Third World Development.* Bloomfield, Connecticut: Kumarian Press.

Ivison, Duncan, Paul Patton, and Will Sanders (Eds.) (2000). *Political Theory and the Rights of Indigenous Peoples.* Oakleigh Victoria: Cambridge University Press.

Jack, Ian (2003). "Feds target white-collar criminals." *National Post.* June 13.

Jackson, Andrew and Ekuwa Smith (2002). "Does a Rising Tide Lift All Boats? Recent Immigrants in Economic Recovery." *Horizons,* 5(2): 22–24.

Jackson, Michael (2002). *Justice Behind the Walls: Human Rights in Canadian Prisons.* Vancouver: Douglas & McIntyre.

James, Carl E. (1996). *Perspectives on Racism and the Human Services Sector.* Toronto: University of Toronto Press.

James, Carl E. (2003). *Seeing Ourselves. Exploring Race, Ethnicity, and Culture,* 3rd ed. Toronto: Thompson Education.

Janigan, Mary (2002). "Immigrants. Who Should Get In?" *Maclean's.* December 16: 20–26.

Jaworski, John (1979). *A Case Study of Canadian Federal Government's Multicultural Policies.* Unpublished MA thesis, Political Science Department, Ottawa: Carleton University.

Jedwab, Jack (2003). "Tolerance, Stereotypes, and Identity in Canada. An Analysis of Canadian Public Opinion." Prepared for the Association of Canadian Studies. March/April.

Jenson, Jane (1996). "Quebec: Which Minority?" *Dissent* (Summer): 43–49.

Jimenez, E. and F. Crepeau (2002). "The Immigration and Refugee Protection Act." *Horizons,* 5(2): 18–20.

Jimenez, Marina (2003)."HIV lurks undetected in Black communities." *National Post.* July 14.

Jimenez, Marina (2003). "Twice Deported, Twice a Killer." *National Post.* November 11.

Jobb, Dean (2003). "Who's Responsible?" *Canadian Business.* March 3: 39–43.

Johnson, Laura C. (2003). *The Co-Workplace. Teleworking in the Neighborhood.* Vancouver: UBC Press.

Jonas, George (2003). "Racism and sexism? That's an affirmative." *National Post.* June 25.

Jones, Beryl Mae (2000). "Multiculturalism and Citizenship: The Status of 'Visible Minorities' in Canada." *Canadian Ethnic Studies,* 32(1): 111–124.

Jones, Helen (2001). "Health Inequities." In M. May et al. (Eds.), *Understanding Social Problems* (pp. 149–162). Malden, Massachusetts: Blackwell.

Jung, Dietrich (2003). "Introduction. Towards a Global Civil War?" In D. Jung (Ed.), *Shadow Globalization, Ethnic Conflicts, and New Wars. A Political Economy of Intra-State War* (pp. 1–6). London: Routledge.

Kallen, Evelyn (2003). *Ethnicity and Human Rights in Canada. A Human Rights Perspective on Ethnicity, Race, and Systemic Inequality.* Don Mills: Oxford University Press.

Kanter, Rosabeth Moss (1977). *Men and Women of the Corporation.* New York: Viking.

Kaplan, Robert D. (1994). "The Coming Anarchy." *The Atlantic Monthly.* February: 44–76.

Kaplan, Robert D. (1999). *The Coming Anarchy.* New York: Random House.

Kaplan, Robert D. (2002). *Warrior Politics. Why Leadership Demands a Pagan Ethos.* New York: Random House.

Kaplan, William (Ed.) (1993). *Belonging. The Meaning and Sense of Citizenship in Canada.* Montreal/Kingston: McGill-Queen's University Press.

Kawachi, Ichiro and Bruce P. Kennedy (2002). *The Health of Nations. Why Inequality is Harmful to Your Health.* New York: The New Press.

Kazemipur, A. and Shiva S. Halli (2003). "Poverty Experiences of Immigrants: Some Reflections." *Canadian Issues.* April 18–20.

Keahy, Deborah and Deborah Schnitzer (2003). *The Madwoman in the Academy. 43 Women Boldly Take on the Ivory Tower.* Calgary: University of Calgary Press.

Keith, W. J. (1997). "The Crisis in Contemporary Education." *Queen's Quarterly,* 94: 511–520.

Kelleher, David (2001). "Problematic Identities and Health." In M. May et al. (Eds.), *Understanding Social Problems* (pp. 175–184). Malden, Massachusetts: Blackwell.

Kelsey, Jane (1997). *The New Zealand Experience*, 2nd ed. Auckland: Auckland University Press.

Kennedy, Mark (2002). "Health care mismanaged, poll suggests." *National Post.* December 30.

Kenny, Sr. Nuala (2002). "Justice and Compassion in Canadian Health Reform." Talk presented at St. Jerome's University, Waterloo, Ontario. November 2002.

Keung, N. (2003). "Gay Bashing Homophobia Still Escalating, Many Say." *Toronto Star.* June 29.

Khouri, Raja (2003). "Canada's Security Agenda a Threat to Multiculturalism." Speech to the RCMP, Ottawa, February 27. Reprinted in *Canadian Speeches,* 17(1): 42–44.

Kilbourne, Jean (1999). *Deadly Persuasion: Why Women and Girls Must Fight Against the Addictive Powers of Advertising.* New York: Free Press.

Kim, Claire Jean (2002). "Managing the Racial Breach. Clinton, Black–White Polarization, and the Race Initiative." *Political Science Quarterly,* 55.

Kimmel, Michael (2000). *The Gendered Society.* New York: Oxford University Press.

Kimmel, Michael S. and Abby L. Ferber (Eds.) (2001). *Privilege. A Reader.* Boulder, Colorado: Westview Press.

Kingston, Anne (2002). "Aloneness becomes normal." *National Post.* October 23.

Kingston, Anne (2003). "Today's Y Chromosome Muddle." *National Post.* September 23.

Kinsella, Warren (2001). *Web of Hate: Inside Canada's Far Right Network.* Revised and Updated. Toronto: HarperCollins Books.

Kishan, Daya and Des Freedman (2003). *War and the Media.* Thousand Oaks, California: Sage.

Klein, Naomi (1999). *No Logo. Taking Aim at the Branding Bullies.* New York: Picador.

Klein, Naomi (2002). *Fences and Windows. Dispatches from the Front Lines of the Globalization Debate.* Toronto: Vintage.

Kleiss, Karen (2003). "Facts of African Life." *Toronto Star.* May 25.

Kleiss, Karen (2003). "AIDS Sparks Orphan Crisis in Africa." *Toronto Star.* November 27.

Knapp, Caroline (2003). *Appetites: What Women Want.* Counterpoint.

Kobayashi, Audrey (1999). "Multiculturalism and Making a Difference: Comments on the State of Multiculturalism Policy in Canada." *Australian–Canadian Studies,* 17(2): 33–39.

Kostash, Myrna (2000). *The Next Canada. In Search of Our Future Nation.* Toronto: McClelland & Stewart.

Krahn, Harvey and Graham Lowe (1994). *Work, Industry, and Canadian Society,* 2nd ed. Toronto: Prentice Hall.

Kuitenbrouwer, Peter (2003). "More women holding top jobs, study finds." *National Post.* March 13.

Kulchyski, Peter (2003). "40 Years in Indian Country." *Canadian Dimension.* November/December: 33–36.

Kunz, Jean Lock (2003). "Social Capital: A Key Dimension of Social Integration." *Canadian Issues.* April 33–34.

Kunz, Jean Lock and Augie Fleras (1998). "Women of Colour in Mainstream Advertising: Distorted Mirror or Looking Glass?" *Atlantis,* 13: 48–73.

Kurthen, Hermann (1997). "The Canadian Experience with Multiculturalism and Employment Equity: Lessons for Europe." *New Community,* 23(2): 249–270.

Kymlicka, Will (1995). *Multiculturalism and Citizenship. A Liberal Theory of Minority Rights.* Oxford: Clarendon Press.

Kymlicka, Will (2000). "Paddling on a Parallel Course." *The Globe and Mail.* June 10.

Kymlicka, Will (2001). *Politics of the Vernacular.* Toronto, Ontario: Oxford University Press.

Laab, Jennifer (1996). "Change." *Personnel Journal.* July.

Laghi, Brian (2003). "Manley pumps billions into health care." *The Globe and Mail.* February 19.

Laghi, Brian (2003). "Ontario Accuses Ottawa of Two-Tier Health Care." *The Globe and Mail.* March 22.

Laghi, Brian (2003). "Female, seeking public office? Better try Sweden." *The Globe and Mail.* March 7.

Lagon, Mark P. (2003). "Visions of Globalization: Pretexts for Prefabricated Prescriptions Band Some Antidotes." *World Affairs,* 165(3): 142–148.

Lambertus, Sandra (2004). *Wartime Images, Peacetime Wounds. The Media and the Gustafson Lake Standoff.* Toronto: University of Toronto Press.

Land, Lorraine (2002). "Gathering Dust or Gathering Strength: What Should Canada Do with the Report of the Royal Commission on Aboriginal Peoples." In J. Bird et al. (Eds.), *Nation to Nation* (pp. 131–138). Toronto: Irwin

Langlois, Stephanie and Peter Morrison (2002). "Suicide Deaths and Attempts." *Canadian Social Trends* (Autumn): 20–25.

Lankin, Frances (2003). "Opinion." *Toronto Star.* September 23.

Lanoszka, Anna (2003). "Cutting Through the Development Barriers." *The Globe and Mail.* August 12.

LaPrairie, Carol (1997). "Reconstructing Theory: Explaining Aboriginal Over-Representation in the Criminal Justice System in Canada." *The Australian and New Zealand Journal of Criminology,* 30(1): 39–54.

Lasch-Quinn, Elisabeth (2002). "Loving and Leaving." *The New Republic.* May 6: 42–46.

Lauder, Matthew (2002). "News Media Perpetuation of Racism in a Democratic Society." Cancon Articles. Available at www.canadiancontent.ca/articles/071502mediaracism.html

Lauder, Matthew (2003). "False Perceptions of an Inclusive Society: A Century of Racism and Hate in Canada." Amnesty International. Available at www.canadiancontent.ca/articles/121801racism.html

Laurance, Jeremy (2002). "UN Releases Staggering Figures on Global Violence." *New Zealand Herald.* March 10.

Lauziere Marcel (2003). "Welcome to Canada: They lied about the opportunities." *The Globe and Mail.* May 26.

Lawton, Valerie (2003). "Chretien Resumes an Old Battle." *Toronto Star.* May 10.

Lawton, Valerie (2003). "Ottawa hails child benefit for drop in poverty rates." *Toronto Star.* July 5.

Lawton, Valerie (2003). "Food Bank Ranks Swelling." *Toronto Star.* October 16.

Layton-Henry, Zig and Czarina Wilpert (Eds.) (2003). *Challenging Racism in Britain and Germany.* New York: Palgrave Macmillan.

Leadbetter, Charles (2002). *Up the Down Escalator: Why the Global Pessimists are Wrong.* New York: Viking.

Lee, Simon (2003). *Uneasy Ethics.* London: Pimlico.

Leenaars, Antoon A., E. de Wilde, S. Wenckstern, and M. Kral (2001). "Suicide Notes of Adolescents: A Life-Span Comparison." *Canadian Journal of Behavioural Science,* 33(1): 47–57.

Legrain, Philippe (2003). "The Delusion of World Capitalism." *Newstatesman.* April 21: 48–49.

Leigh, Andrew (2001). "Globalisation and Deglobalisation." *A.Q. (Australian Quarterly).* January–February: 6–10.

Leisinger, Klaus M., Karin M. Schmitt, and Rajul Pandya-Lorch (2002). *Six Billion and Counting. Population and Food Security in the 21st Century.* Washington. International Food Policy Research Institute.

Leithwood, Kenneth, Michael Fullan, and Nancy Watson (2003). "Saving our public schools." *Toronto Star.* February 25. Also available at "Our Schools We Need." http://schoolsweneed.oise.utoronto.ca

Lemel, Yannick and Heinz-Herbert Noll (Eds.) (2002). *Changing Structures of Inequality: A Comparative Perspective.* Montreal/Kingston: McGill-Queen's University Press.

Lemieux, Denise and Marion Mohle (2003). "Gender Inequality in Five Modern Societies." In Y. Lemel and H-H. Noll (Eds.), *Changing Structures of Inequality. Comparative Perspectives* (pp. 333–368). Montreal/Kingston: McGill Queen's University Press.

Leong, Melissa (2003). "Tough-chick chic." *Toronto Star.* June 1.

Lester, Paul Martin and Susan Dente Ross (2003). *Images That Injure, Pictorial Stereotypes in the Media.* Westport, CT: Praeger.

Levin, Jack and Jack McDevitt (2002). *Hate Crimes Revisited: America's War on Those Who Are Different.* Boulder, Colorado: Westview Press.

Levin, Michael (Ed.) (1993). *Ethnicity and Aboriginality: Case Studies in Ethnonationalism.* Toronto: University of Toronto Press.

Levitt, Cyril (1997). The Morality of Race in Canada." *Society.* July/August: 32–37.

Ley, David and Daniel Hiebert (2001). "Immigration Policy as Population Policy." The *Canadian Geographer,* 45(1): 120–125.

Li, Peter S. (2003). *Destination Canada. Immigration Debates and Issues.* Toronto: OUP.

Li, Peter S. (2003). "Understanding Economic Performances of Immigrants." *Canadian Issues.* April: 25–26.

Li, Peter S. (2003). "Visible Minorities in Canadian Society: Challenges of Racial Diversity." In D. Juteau (Ed.), *Social Differentiation. Patterns and Processes* (pp. 117–154). Toronto: University of Toronto Press.

Lian, Jason and Ralph David Matthews (1998). "Does the Vertical Mosaic Still Exist? Ethnicity and Income in Canada 1991." *Canadian Review of Sociology and Anthropology,* 35(4): 461–477.

Liddiard Mark (2001). "Homelessness" In M. May et al. (Eds.), *Understanding Social Problems* (pp. 118–129). Malden, Massachusetts: Blackwell.

Little, Bruce (2004). "Most job creation last year was in low-pay categories." *The Globe and Mail.* February 2.

Livingston, D.W. and Peter H. Sawchuk (2003). *Hidden Knowledge. Organized Labour in the Information Age.* Garamond Press.

Lloyd, John (2003). "Fortress Europe Prepares to Repel Immigrants." *The Globe and Mail.* January 24.

Lomborg, Bjorn (2001). *The Skeptical Environmentalist*. Cambridge University Press.

Long, David and Olive Dickason (1996/2000). *Visions of the Heart*. Toronto: Harcourt Brace.

Lorber, Judith (1998). *Gender Inequality: Feminist Theories and Politics*. Los Angeles: Roxbury.

Loseke, Donileen R. (2003). *Thinking about Social Problems*, 2nd ed. New York: Aldine de Gruyter.

Lowe, Graham (2003). "Trust Eases Stress." *The Globe and Mail*. October 22.

Maaka, Roger and Augie Fleras (2004). *The Politics of Indigeneity. New Zealand and Canada Perspectives*. Dunedin, New Zealand: Otago University Press.

MacIntyre, Nicole (2003). "Income has the biggest impact on health, professor says." *Kitchener-Waterloo Record*. April 10.

MacIvor, Heather (2003). "Women in Canada: Two Steps Forward, One Step Back." In K. Pryke and W. Soderland (Eds.), *Profiles of Canada* (pp. 145–178). Toronto: Canadian Scholars Press.

Mackey, Eva (1999). *The House of Difference. Cultural Politics and National Identity in Canada*. London: Routledge.

Macklem, Katherine (2003). "The New View from TV Land." *Maclean's*. May 5.

Macklem, Patrick (1993). "Ethnonationalism, Aboriginal Identities, and the Law." In M.Levin (Ed.), *Ethnicity and Aboriginality* (pp. 9–28). Toronto: University of Toronto Press.

Macklem, Patrick (2001). *Indigenous Difference and the Constitution in Canada*. Toronto: University of Toronto Press.

Maclean, Eleanor (1981). *Between the Lines: How to Detect Bias and Propaganda in the Press and Everyday Life*. Montreal: Black Rose Books.

MacNamara, Kate (2002). "Women gain 'slow and steady' ground in Canada's boardrooms." *National Post*. March 27.

Mahtani, Minelle (2001). "Mapping the Meanings of 'Racism' and 'Feminism' Among Women Television Broadcast Journalists in Canada." In F. W. Twine and K. Blee (Eds.), *Feminism and Racism: International Struggles* (pp. 349–366). New York: Free Press.

Mahtani, Minelle (2002) "Representing Minorities: Canadian Media and Minority Identities." *Canadian Ethnic Studies* xxxiii(3): 99–131.

Maioni, Antonia (2003). "Canadian Health Care" In K. Pryke and W. Soderland (Eds.), *Profiles of Canada* (pp. 307–326). Toronto: Canadian Scholars Press.

Malvaux, Julianne (1999). "Women at Work." *In These Times*. November 28: 14–15.

Mander, Jerry (1996). "The Dark Side of Globalization." *The Nation*. July 15/22.

Mander, Jerry (1999). "How Cyber Culture Deletes Nature." *The Ecologist,* 29(3): 171–172.

Mander, Jerry and E. Goldstein (1996). *The Case Against the Global Economy and for a Turn toward the Local*. San Francisco: Sierra Club Books.

Mandle, Jay R. (2003). *Globalization and the Poor*. New York: Cambridge University Press.

Manji, Irshad (2003/2004). "The Strange Case of Liberal Canada." *Time*. December 29–January 5: 70–71.

Maracle, Brian (1996). "One More Whining Indian Tilting at Windmills." In J. Littleton (Ed.), *Clash of Identities* (pp. 15–20). Toronto: Prentice Hall.

Marchak, Pat (1991). *The Integrated Circus. The New Right and the Restructuring of Global Markets*. Montreal/Kingston: McGill/Queen's University Press.

Marchand, Philip (2003). "New meaning for ad infinity." *Toronto Star*. May 3.

Marchildon, Gregory P. (2003). "A Single Payer, Universal Health System? Current U.S. Proposals and the Canadian Model." Published by the Canadian Institute at the Woodrow Wilson International Centre for Scholars. www.wilsoncentre.org

Marcoux, Laurent (2002). "Communication and Social Cohesion in a Post September 11th World." *Horizons,* 5(2): 14.

Marshall, James, Eve Coxon, Kuni Jenkins, and Alison Jones (2000). *Politics, Policy, Pedagogy: An Introduction*. Palmerston North, New Zealand: Dunmore Publishing.

Martinuk, Susan (1999). "Blubber About Whales." *National Post*. May 20.

Mascoll, Philip (2002). "Undergrad tuition fees up 135% over 11 years." *Toronto Star*. August 22.

Mascoll, Philip (2003). "Radical' New Ideas Sought to Fight Urban Poverty." *Toronto Star*. May 24.

Mascoll, Philip (2003). "New light on poverty yardsticks." *Toronto Star*. May 28.

Mascoll, Philip and Elaine Carey (2003). "New poverty gauge out today." *Toronto Star*. May 27.

Mathews, K. and W. Wacker (2002). *The Deviant's Advantage: Fringe Ideas to Create Mass Markets. New York: Three Rivers Press.*

Matthews, Roy (1983). The Creation of Regional Dependencies. Toronto: University of Toronto Press.

May, Margaret, Robert Page, and Edward Brunson (Eds.) (2001). *Understanding Social Problems. Issues in Social Policy*. Malden, Massachusetts: Blackwell.

Mayor, Frederico (1999). "All Human Rights for All." *UNESCO Courier*. November: 9.

McCabe, Aileen (2003). "Women Still Living Longer, StatsCan Finds*." National Post*. September 26.

McClelland, Susan (2003). "Institutional Correction." *Maclean's*. June 9: 45–48.

McDaniel, Susan A. (2002). "Intergenerational Linkages: Public, Family, and Work." In D. Cheal (Ed.), *Aging and Demographic Change in Canadian Context* (pp. 22–71). Toronto: University of Toronto Press.

McFarland, Janet (2003). "Pay Tied More to Performance, Survey Finds." *The Globe and Mail*. October 28.

McGinn, Anne Platt (2003). "Combating Malaria." In Worldwatch Institute (Ed.), *State of the World 2003* (pp. 62–84). New York: WW Norton.

McGregor, Judy (Ed.) (1996). *Dangerous Democracy. News Media Politics in New Zealand*. Palmerston North: Dunmore.

McLaughlin, Eugene et al. (2003). "Introduction. Justice in the Round—Contextualizing Restorative Justice." In E. McLaughlin et al. (Eds.), *Restorative Justice: Critical Issues* (pp. 1–18). Thousand Oaks Calicornia: Sage.

McMurtry, John (2003). "Corporate interests infiltrate schools." *Kitchener-Waterloo Record*. January 6.

McQuail, Dennis (2000). *McQuail's Mass Communication Theory*. Thousand Oaks, California: Sage.

McQueen, Ken (2003). "Boy vs Girl." *Maclean's*. May 26: 27–32.

McRoberts, Kenneth (1997). *Misconceiving Canada. The Struggle for National Unity.* Toronto: Oxford University Press.

Mendelsohn, Matthew (2003). "Listen up, Canada." *The Globe and Mail.* July 2.

Mendelsohn, Matthew (2003). "Birth of a new ethnicity." *The Globe and Mail.* June 9.

Menon, Vinay (2003). "Battling For Truth in War Reports." *Toronto Star.* November 12.

Menon, Vinay (2003). "Television is good for you." *Toronto Star.* June 14.

Michelman, Kate (2003). "Women's Equality Under Attack." *The Humanist.* 63(6): 10–13.

Mickey, Thomas J. (2003). *Deconstructing Public Relations.* Mahwah, New Jersey: Lawrence Erlbaum Associates.

Middleton, Neil and Phil O'Keefe (2003). *Rio Plus Ten. Politics, Poverty and the Environment.* London: Pluto Press.

Miller, John (1998). *Yesterday's News: Why Canada''s Daily Newspapers are Failing Us.* Halifax: Fernwood.

Miller, John (2000). *Skyscrapers Hide the Heavens. A History of Indian–White Relations in Canada,* 3rd ed. Toronto: University of Toronto Press.

Miller, John (2003). "Covering Diversity. Diversity Watch—Ryerson School of Journalism." Available at Diversitywatch.ryerson.ca/course/

Miller, John (2003). "What Newspapers Need to Do." *Innoversity Newsletter* 2(3). Available at www.innoversity.com/newsletter/volume2/issue3/newspapers/html

Mills, Nicolaus and Kira Brunner (Eds.) (2002). *The New Killing Fields. Massacre and the Politics of Intervention.* New York: Basic Books.

Mintz, Susannah B. (2003). "In a Word, Baywatch." In R. Dicker and A. Piepmeier (Eds.), *Catching a Wave* (pp. 57–80). Boston: Northeastern University Press.

Mitchell, Alanna (2003). "Environment Canada's Annual Roundup Reveals that Climate Change Hit Hard in 2003, Making it …" *The Globe and Mail.* December 29.

Mittelstaedt, Martin (2003). "Canadian polluters worse than in the U.S., report says." *The Globe and Mail.* April 17.

Moeller, Susan D. (1998). *Compassion Fatigue: How the Media Sell Disease, Famine, War, & Death.* New York: Routledge.

Mofina, Rick (2001). "Natives say they are driven to court." *National Post.* January 16.

Monteiro, Liz (2003). "Violent crimes rates down in region, statistics show." *Kitchener-Waterloo Record.* May 15.

Monture-Angus, Patricia A. (2003). "Organizing Against Oppression: Aboriginal Women, Law, and Feminism." In K. Pryke and W.Soderland (Eds.), *Profiles of Canada* (pp. 279–306). Toronto: Canadian Scholars Press.

Mooney, Linda, David Knox, Caroline Schacht, and Adie Nelson (2004). *Understanding Social Problems,* 2nd Canadian edition. Toronto, Ontario: Nelson.

Moore, Oliver (2003). "Diabetes Soaring in Native Population." *The Globe and Mail.* September 24.

Morgan, Gareth (1986). *Images of Organization.* Toronto: Oxford University Press.

Morgenson, Donald (2003). "Make room for Socrates." *Kitchener-Waterloo Record.* January 6.

Morgenson, Donald (2003). "The world's leaders ignore Cinderella." *Kitchener-Waterloo Record.* July 6.

Morreale, Joanne (Ed.) (2003*). Critiquing the Sitcom.* Syracuse University Press.

Morrow, Raymond A. (1998). "Mass-Mediated Culture, Leisure, And Consumption: Having Fun as a Social Problem." In Les Samuelson and W. Antony (Eds.), *Power and Resistance* (pp. 283–309). Halifax: Fernwood.

Mosley, Paul and Anne Booth (2003). "Introduction and Context." In A. Booth and P. Mosely (Eds), *The New Poverty Strategies* (pp. 3–20). New York: Palgrave Macmillan.

Muro-Ruiz, Diego (2002). "The Logic of Violence." *Politics,* 22(2): 109–117.

Murray, Jaqueline (2003). "Same-sex unions: The final frontier of marriage evolution." *The Globe and Mail.* June 27.

Nadeau, Richard and Thierry Giasson (2003). "Canada's Democratic Malaise: Are the Media to Blame? Choices. Stengthening Canadian Democracy." *IRPP,* 9(1) 1–32.

Nadeau, Richard et al. (1997). "Why public support is so low for aboriginal spending." *The Globe and Mail.* February 23.

Nagra, Narine (2003). "Whiteness in Seattle." *Alternatives Journal,* 29(1): 23–25.

Naim, Moises (2003). "An Indigenous World." *Foreign Policy.* November/December: 95–96.

Nakata, M. (Ed.) (2001). *Indigenous Peoples, Racism, and the United Nations.* Sydney: Common Grounds Publishing.

Napran, Laura (2003). "Don't 'dumb down' liberal arts." *Kitchener-Waterloo Record* Jan 3.

Nares, Peter (2003). "Creating assets for poorest among us." *Toronto Star.* June 20.

Neill, Rosemary (2003). "White-Out/Black-Out." *Australian Canadian Studies,* 21(1): 7–16.

Nelson, Adie and Augie Fleras (1998). *Social Problems in Canada,* 2nd ed. Toronto: Prentice Hall.

Nelson, Adie and Barrie Robinson (2000). *Gender in Canada,* 2nd ed. Toronto: Prentice Hall.

Nett, Gina (2001). "Super Highway or the Same Old Spot?" *Utne Reader.* May/June P. 74–76.

Newhouse, David (2002). "Emerging from the Shadows: The Evolution of Aboriginal Governance in Canada from 1969 to 2002." Paper presented to the Reconfiguring Aboriginal–State Relations Conference. Queens University, Kingston,Ontario. November 1–2.

New Statesman (2003). "How Fat Became a Political Issue." August 18.

Neysmith, Sheila (2003). "Caring and Aging: Exposing Policy Issues." In A. Westhues (Ed.), *Canadian Social Policy* (pp. 182–199). Waterloo: Wilfrid Laurier Press.

Nikiforuk, Andrew (2003). "The past plagues are in vogue." *The Globe and Mail.* April 26.

Nikiforuk, Andrew (2003). "Keeping the biotech genie in the bottle." Book Review. *Globe and Mail.* May 3.

Nikiforuk, Andrew (2003). "Why hospitals can be bad for your health." *Toronto Star.* May 6.

Nurse, Andrew (2003). "A Profile of Canadian Regionalism." In K. Pryke and W. Soderland (Eds.), *Profiles of Canada* (pp. 35-62). Toronto: Canadian Scholars Press.

O'Keefe, Tracy and Katrina Fox (Eds) (2003). *Finding the Real Me. True Tales of Sex and Gender Diversity.* San Francisco: Jossey Bass.

Olive, David (2003). "Values Outsourced." *Toronto Star.* October 18.

Olsen, Gregg M. (2002). *The Politics of the Welfare State: Canada, Sweden, and the United States.* Toronto, Onario: Oxford University Press.

Ominayak, Bernard and Ed Bianchi (2002). "Lubicon Cree: Still No Settlement after All These Years." In J. Bird et al. (Eds.), *Nation to Nation* (pp. 163–174). Toronto: Irwin.

Ontario Human Rights Commission. (2003). "Paying the Price: The Cost of Racial Profiling." Available at http://www.ohrc.on.ca/english/consultations/racial-profiling-report_3.shtml

O'Reilly, Finbar (2003). "Congo death tolls 2 500 per day." *Toronto Star.* May 25.

Osborne, Ken (1999). *Education: A Guide to the Canadian School Debate—Or Who Wants What and Why.* Toronto: Penguin.

Owens, Anne Marie (2002). "Separating the boys from the girls." *National Post.* June 26.

Owens, Anne Marie (2003). "Boys brains from Mars.*"National Post.* May 10.

Paehlke, Robert (2003). *Democracy's Dilemma. Environment, Social Equity, and the Global Economy.* Cambridge, Massachusetts: MIT Press.

Pal, Leslie A. and R. Kent Weaver (Eds.) (2003). *The Government Taketh Away. The Politics of Pain in the United States and Canada.* Washington DC: Georgetown University Press.

Papp, Leslie (2003). "Treating cancer's no cure: Experts." *Toronto Star.* April 12.

Parmelee, Lisa Ferraro (2003). "To Your Health." *Public Perspective.* May/June: 1.

Parsons, Margaret and Marie Chen (2003). "In a world of inequality, can judges stay colour blind?" *Toronto Star.* March 3.

Peart, Joseph and Jim Mcnamara (1996). *The New Zealand Public Relations Handbook.* Palmerston North, New Zealand: Dunmore Publishing.

Peluso, Nancy Lee and Michael Watts (Eds.) (2001). *Violent Environments.* Ithaca: Cornell University Press.

Pendakur, Krishna and Ravi Pendakur (1995). "Earning Differentials among Ethnic Groups in Canada." Ref. SRA-24. Social Research Group. Hull: Department of Canadian Heritage.

Pendakur, M. and R. Harris (2002). *Citizenship and Participation in the Information Age.* Toronto: Garamond.

Pendakur, Ravi (2000). *Immigrants and the Labour Force: Policy, Regulation, and Impact.* Montreal/Kingston: McGill-Queen's University Press.

Perry, Ann (2003). "Women making slow inroads into Canada's corporate ranks." *Toronto Star.* March 13.

Perse, Elizabeth M. (2001). *Media Effects on Society.* Mahwah, New Jersey: Lawrence Erlbaum Associates.

Peter, Karl (1978). "Multi-Cultural Politics, Money, and the Conduct of Canadian Ethnic Studies." *Canadian Ethnic Studies Bulletin,* 5: 2–3.

Peters, Evelyn (2001). "Geographies of Aboriginal Peoples in Canada." *The Canadian Geographer,* 45(1): 138–144.

Philp, Margaret (2000). "Aboriginal languages near extinction, experts say." *The Globe and Mail*. May 13.

Philp, Margaret (2003). "Gay Parent, Gay Child: Into the Mainstream." *The Globe and Mail*. June 10.

Picard, Andre (2003). "Native drug users hardest hit by HIV." *The Globe and Mail*. January 7.

Picard, Andre (2003). "Canada Ranked Fourth in Health Spending." *The Globe and Mail*. December 18.

Pickering, Michael (2001). *Stereotypes. The Politics of Representation*. New York: Palgrave Macmillan.

Pieterse, Jan Nederveen (2003). "The Many Doors to Multiculturalism." In B. Saunders and D. Haljan (Eds.), *Whither Multiculturalism?* (pp. 21–34). Leuven University Press.

Pincus, Fred L. (2003). *Reverse Discrimination*. Boulder, CO: Lynne Rienner Publishing.

Pinderhughes, Howard (1997). *Race in the Hood. Conflict and Violence among Urban Youth*. Minneapolis: University of Minneapolis Press.

Plamenatz, John (1960). *On Alien Rule and Self-Government*. London: Longmans.

Plender, John (2002). *Going off the Rails: Global Capital and the Crisis of Legitimacy*. John Wiley & Sons.

Plimptre, Tim (1999). "Governance and the Trends." *Horizon,* 2(6): 12.

Pocklington, Tom and Allan Tupper (2002). *No Place to Learn: Why Universities aren't Working*. Vancouver: UBC Press.

Ponting, J. Rick and Roger Gibbins (1980). *Out of Irrelevance: A Socio-Political Introduction to Indian Affairs in Canada*. Toronto: Butterworths.

Porter, John (1965). *The Vertical Mosaic*. Toronto: University of Toronto Press.

Postman, Neil (1985). *Amusing Ourselves to Death*. New York: Pantheon.

Powell, Betsy (2002). "Let punishment fit corporate crime: Police." *Toronto Star*. December 19.

Powell, Betsy (2003a). "White collar crime lament." *Toronto Star*. March 31.

Powell, Betsy (2003b). "Court cheers as stockbroker jailed." *Toronto Star*. April 1.

Pozner, Jennifer L. (2003). "The 'Big Lie': False Feminist Death Syndrome, Profit, and the Media." In R. Dicker and A. Piepmeier (Eds.), *Catching a Wave* (pp. 31–56). Boston: Northeastern University Press.

Proulx, Craig (2003). *Reclaiming Aboriginal Justice, Identity and Community. Saskatoon:* Purich Publishing.

Pyatt, Graham (2003). "Poverty versus the Poor." In A. Booth and P. Mosely (Eds.), *The New Poverty Strategies* (pp. 91–119). New York: Palgrave Macmillan.

Qadeer, M.A. (1997). "Pakistan Broke Ground for Minority Nationalism." *Toronto Star*. August 14.

Quaid, Maeve (2002). *Workfare: Why Good Social Policy Ideas Go Bad*. Toronto: University of Toronto Press.

Qualter, Terence H. (1991). "Propaganda in Canadian Society." In Benjamin D. Singer (Ed.), *Communications in Canadian Society* (pp. 200–212). Toronto: Nelson.

Rajagopal, Indhu (2002). *Hidden Academics. Contract Faculty in Canadian Universities.* Toronto: University of Toronto Press.

Ramcharan, Subhas (1989). Social Problems and Issues. A Canadian Perspective. Toronto: Nelson.

Raza, Raheel (2003). Presentation at the Jihad in the Newsroom Session. Innoversity Creative Summit Conference. Toronto. May 22.

Razack, Sherene (1994). "What Is to Be Gained by Looking White People in the Eye? Culture, Race, and Gender in Cases of Sexual Violence." *Signs* (Summer): 894–922.

Reaney, Patricia (2003). "Obesity widening problem: expert." *Toronto Star*. May 30.

Reiter, Ester (1992/1996). *Making Fast Food. From the Frying Pan into the Fryer.* Montreal: McGill-Queens University Press.

Reitz, Jeffrey and Raymond Breton (1994). *The Illusion of Difference: Realities of Ethnicity in Canada and the United States.* Toronto: C.D. Howe Institute.

Rekai, Peter (2002). "The Terrorist's Path of Least Resistance." *National Post*. November 14.

Renner, Michael and Molly O'Sheehan (2003). "Overview. Poverty and Inequality Block Progress." In *Vital Signs 2003–2004*. Worldwide Institute. London Earthscan Publications.

Rholinger, Deana A. (2002). "Framing the Abortion Debate. Organizational Resources, Media Strategies, and Movement–Countermovement Dynamics." *The Sociological Quarterly,* 43(4): 479–507.

Richards, John (2000). "Urban Aboriginals Are Failed and Forgotten in Treaty Settlements." *Canadian Speeches,* 14(4): 39–40.

Richmond, Anthony (1994). *Global Apartheid: Refugees, Racism, and the New World Order.* Toronto: Oxford University Press.

Richmond, Anthony (2002). "Globalization: Implications for Refugees and Immigrants." *Ethnic and Racial Studies,* 25(5): 707–727.

Rieff, David (1999). "Burnt Out on Suffering." *National Post*. April 10.

Rieff, David (2002). *A Bed for the Night. Humanitarianism in Crisis.* New York: Simon and Schuster.

Rifkin, Jeremy (1995). "Work: A Blueprint for Social Harmony in a World Without Jobs." *Utne Reader.* May/June: 53–62.

Rifkin, Jeremy (1996). "Civil Society in the Information Age." *The Nation.* February 26.

Ritzer, George (2000). *The McDonaldization of Society. The New Century Edition.* Newbury Park, California: Pine Forge Press.

Ritzer, George (2002). in C. Derber (Ed.), *The Wilding of America. Greed, Violence, and the American Dream,* 2nd ed. ("Foreward"). New York: Worth Publishing.

Robinson, Paul (2003). "Canada's example proves there is a 'third' way." *National Post.* June 6.

Robson, W. M. (2003). "For health care, jurisdictions matter." National Post. February 25.

Rose, Damaris, Valerie Preston, and Isabel Dyck (2002). "Women, Gender, and Immigration. Perspectives and Challenges." *Horizons* 5(2):12–13.

Ross, Oakland (2003). "Into Africa." *Toronto Star.* May 25.

Roth, Benita (2004). *Separate Roads of Feminism.* Thousand Oaks, CA: Sage.

Rowlingson, Karen (2001). "Child Poverty and the Policy Response." In M. May et al. (Eds.), *Understanding Social Problems* (pp. 107–117). Malden, Massachusetts: Blackwell.

Royal Commission on Aboriginal Peoples (1996). *Looking Forward, Looking Backward.* Volume 1. Ottawa: Ministry of Supplies and Services.

Ruddick, Elizabeth (2003). "Immigrant Economic Performance. A New Paradigm in a Changing Labour Market." *Canadian Issues.* April 16–17.

Rudin, Jonathan (2003). "Justice, race, and time." *Toronto Star.* February 17.

Russell, Peter (2004). *Recovering Terra Nullius: Mabo and Indigenous Colonization.* Toronto: University of Toronto Press.

Saguy, Abigail Cope (2003). *What is Sexual Harassment. From Capital Hill to the Sorbonne. Berkeley:* University of California Press.

Salee, Daniel (1995). "Identities in Conflict: The Aboriginal Question and the Politics of Recognition." *Racial and Ethnic Studies,* 18(2): 277–314.

Salee, Daniel and William D. Coleman (1997). "The Challenges of the Quebec Question: Paradigm, Counter-Paradigm, and Sovereignty." In W. Clement (Ed.), *Understanding Canada* (pp. 262–282). Montreal/Kingston: McGill-Queen's University Press.

Saloojee, Riad (2003). Presentation at the Jihad in the Newsroom Session. Innoversity Creative Summit Conference. Toronto: May 22.

Samson, Colin (2000). "Ontario Native's Suicide Rate among the World's Highest." Canadian Press. Reprinted in the *Kitchener-Waterloo Record.* November 21.

Samson, Colin (2003). *A Way of Life that Does Not Exist.* St. John's, Newfoundland: Institute for Social and Economic Research, Memorial University.

Samuel, John (1997). *Report on Visible Minorities and the Public Service in Canada.* Ottawa: Canadian Human Rights Commission.

Sandler, Jeremy (2003). "Showing their true colours." *National Post.* March 15.

Sapurji, Sunaya and Raju Muhhar (2003). "Hockey's race disgrace." *Toronto Star.* March 22.

Sarin, R. (2003). "Rich-Poor Divide Growing." In *Vital Signs 2003–2004.* Worldwide Institute. London Earthscan Publications.

Satzewich, Vic (Ed.) (1998). *Racism and Social Inequality in Canada.* Toronto: Thompson Publishing.

Saul, John Ralston (2003). "The Inclusive Shape of Complexity". In G. Gaffield and K.L. Gould (Eds.), *The Canadian Distinctiveness into the XXIst Century* (pp. 13–28). Ottawa: University of Ottawa Press.

Saunders Barbara and David Haljan (Eds.) (2003). *Whither Multiculturalism? A Politics of Dissensus.* Leuven: Leuven University Press.

Schissel, Bernard and Terry Wotherspoon (2003). *The Legacy of School for Aboriginal People. Education, Oppression, and Emancipation.* Toronto: Oxford University Press.

Schlesinger, Arthur M. Jr. (1992). *The Disuniting of America: Reflections on a Multicultural Society.* New York: W.W. Norton.

Schlesinger, Joe (2003). "War Stories: The Fog of Journalism. The Dalton Camp Lecture." *Toronto Star.* November 7.

Schmidt, Sarah (2002). "The under-30s are choosing common-law." *National Post.* July 12.

Schmidt, Sarah (2003). "Dream Degree U.S.A." *National Post*. October 15.

Scott, Colin H. (2001). "On Autonomy and Development." In C. Scott (Ed.), *Aboriginal Autonomy and Development in Northern Quebec and Labrador* (pp. 3–20). Vancouver: UBC Press.

Scott, James C. (1998). *Seeing Like a State. How Certain Schemes to Improve Human Condition Have Failed*. Yale University Press.

Scrivener, Leslie (2003). "Sharp increase seen in anti-semitic hate." *Toronto Star*. March 7.

Seagrave, Karen (1997). *Introduction to Policing in Canada*. Toronto: Prentice Hall.

Seale, Clive (2002). *Media & Health*. London: Sage.

Sears, Alan (2003). *Retooling the Mind Factory. Education in a Lean State*. Garamond.

Seiler, Tamara Palmer (2002). "Thirty Years Later: Reflections on the Evolution and Future Prospects for Multiculturalism." *Canadian Studies*. February: 6–8.

Sharmarke, Ali (2003). "The Media Vital In Places Like Somalia." *Toronto Star*. November 29.

Sher, Julian and William Marsden (2003). *The Road to Hell: How the Biker Gangs are Conquering Canada*. Knopf Canada.

Shiva, Vandana (2002). "Terrorism as Cannibalism." Available at Znet Daily Commentaries. www.zmag.org/sustainers/content/2002-01/23shiva.cfm

Shkilnyk, Anastasia (1985). *Poison Stronger Than Love*. New Haven: Yale University Press.

Shusta, R.M. et al. (1995). *Multicultural Law Enforcement: Strategies for Peacekeeping in a Diverse Society*. Englewood Cliffs, NJ: Prentice Hall.

Siddiqui, Haroon (1996). "Multiculturalism and the Media." In J. Littleton (Ed.). *Clash of Identities* (pp. 113–118). Toronto: Prentice Hall.

Simpson, Jeffrey (1999). "The Politics of Immigration" *The Globe and Mail*. November 23.

Singer, Benjamin (1986). *Advertising and Society*. Toronto: Addison-Wesley.

Smith, Dorothy (2003). "Whatever Happened to the Woman's Movement?" *Canadian Dimension*. September/October: 24–26.

Smith, Graeme (2003). "Teens see police as threat." *The Globe and Mail*. January 16.

Smith, Linda Tuhiwai (1998). *Decolonising Methodologies*. Dunedin, NZ: University of Otago Press.

Smith, Terry (2003). "Everyday Indignities. Race, Retaliation, and the Promise of Title VII." *Columbia Human Rights Law Review*. 34(3): 529–574.

Smyth, Julie (2003). "Women managers up 40%." *National Post*. February 12.

Sokoloff, Heather (2002). "Women awarded only 15% of federal research chairs." *National Post*. May 29.

Sokoloff, Heather (2002). "University enrolment to jump 30%." *National Post* October 15.

Sokoloff, Heather (2003). "Ottawa biased against female professors: group." *National Post*. March 19.

Sokoloff, Heather (2003). "The good, the bad, and the ugly." *National Post*. June 17.

Solomon, Norman (2003). "Media and the Politics of Empathy." *Media Beat*. www.fair.org/media-beat

Solomon, Norman (2002). "Media Bias." *New Political Science* 24(2).

Solomos, John and Les Back (1996). *Racism and Society*. London: Macmillan.

Spector, Malcolm and John I. Kitsuse (1987). *Constructing Social Problems,* 2nd ed. Menlo Park, California: Cummins.

Spender, Dale (1997). "The Revolution is Being Digitalised." *NZ Education Review.* Interview by Andrea Hotere. October 8.

Spindler, William (2003). "Columbia's Indigenous and Poor People Bear the Brunt of Conflict." *Refugees.* December: 24–26.

Starowicz, Mark (2003). "Strangling Canadian TV." *Toronto Star.* May 1.

Starr, Amory and Jason Adams (2003). "Anti-Globalization: The Global Fight for Local Autonomy." *New Political Science.* 25(1): 1–18.

Stasiulis, Daiva (1997). "The Political Economy of Race, Ethnicity, and Migration." In W. Clement (Ed.), *Understanding Canada: Building on the New Canadian Political Economy* (pp. 141–164). Montreal/Kingston: McGill-Queen's University Press.

Stasiulis, Daiva and Nira Yuval-Davis (Eds.) (1995). *Unsettling Settler Societies.* Thousand Oaks, California: Sage.

Stasiulis, Daiva K. (2000). "Feminist Intesectional Theorizing." In P. Li (Ed.), *Race and Ethnic Relations in Canada,* 2nd ed. (pp. 347–397). Toronto: Oxford University Press.

Statistics Canada (1999). "Crime Statistics in Canada." Juristat. Canadian Centre for Justice Statistics. Ottawa: Catalogue Number 85-002-XIE, Vol. 19 No. 9.

Statistics Canada (2003). *2001 Census: Analysis Series. Income of Canadian Families*. Ottawa: Minister of Industry.

Statistics Canada (2003) Aboriginal Peoples Survey: Health. No. 89 589 XIE.

Statistics Canada (2003). "Persons Charged by Type of Offence." CANSIM table 252–0014. Last modified December 22, 2003.

Statistics Canada (2004). "Crimes by Type of Offence." CANSIM table 252–0013. Last modified January 16, 2004.

St Denis, Stephen (2003). "Fighting deadliest diseases." *Toronto Star.* July 15.

Stea, David and Ben Wisner (Eds.) (1984). "The Fourth World: A Geography of Indigenous Struggles." *Antipodes: A Radical Journal of Geography,* 16(2).

Steger, Manfred B. (2002). *Globalism: the New Market Ideology.* Lanham MD: Rowman and Littlefield.

Sternbergh, Adam (2003). "Get your honky groove on." *National Post.* April 12.

Stoffman, Daniel (2002). *Who Gets In? What's Wrong with Canada's Immigration Program and How to Fix it.* Toronto: MacFarlane Waller and Ross.

Stoffman, Daniel (2002). "Fixing the Refugee Mess." *Maclean's.* December 16: 26–27.

Stoffman, Daniel (2003). "The Mystery of Canada's High Immigration Levels." *Canadian Issues.* April 23–24.

Stonach, Susan C and Peter Vandergeest (2001). "Violence, Environment, and Shrimp Farming." In N.L. Peluso and M. Watts (Eds.), *Violent Environments* (pp. 261–286). Ithaca: Cornell University Press.

Stone, Sharon D. (1993). "Getting the Message Out: Feminists, the Press, and Violence Against Women." *Canadian Review of Sociology and Anthropology,* 30(3): 377–400.

Strasburger, Victor C. and Barbara J. Wilson (2002). *Children, Adolescents, & the Media.* Thousand Oaks, California: Sage.

Sullivan, Terrence and Patricia M. Baranek (2002). *First Do No Harm. Making Sense of Canadian Health Reform.* Vancouver: UBC Press.

Sunday Star-Times (2003). "The Future is Female." September 28.

Supiot, Alain (2003). "The Labyrinth of Human Rights. Credo or Common Sense?" *New Left Review* 21. May/June: 118–133.

Suzuki, David (1998). *The Sacred Balance: Rediscovering Our Place in Nature.* Amherst, NY: Prometheus Books.

Sweetman, Arthur (2003). "Immigration and the New Economy." *Canadian Issues.* April 21–22.

Switzer, Maurice (1997). "Indians are Not Red. They are Invisible." *Media* (Spring): 21–22.

Taheri, Amir (2003). "Why we keep getting the Arab world wrong." *National Post.* May 2.

Tannen, Deborah (2003). "Deciding Who Should Speak on Campus." *The Responsive Community* 13: 4–11.

Tanner, Adrian (2001). "The Double Bind of Aboriginal Self-Government." In C. Scott (Ed.), *Aboriginal Autonomy and Development in Northern Quebec and Labrador* (pp. 201–227). Vancouver: UBC Press.

Taras, David (1991). *The Newsmakers. The Media's Influence on Canadian Politics.* Toronto: Nelson.

Taras, David (2001). *Power & Betrayal in the Canadian Media.* Peterborough: Broadview.

Taslitz, Andrew E. (2003). "Foreword. The Political Geography of Race Data in the Criminal Justice System." *Law and Contemporary Problems.* 66 (3): 1–18.

Taylor, Charles (1994). *Reconsidering the Solitudes. Essays in Canadian Federalism and Nationalism.* Montreal/Kingston: McGill-Queen's University Press.

Taylor, K-Y (2003). "Racism in America Today." *International Socialist Review,* 32. November/December: 26–35.

Tepper, Elliot (1988). "Changing Canada. The Institutional Response to Polyethnicity." The Review of Demography and its Implications for Economic and Social Policy. Ottawa: Carleton.

The Economist (2003). "The Shape of Things to Come." December 13.

Theobold, Steven (2003). "Wanted: more long weekends." *Toronto Star.* June 28.

Thobani, Sunera (2000). "Closing Ranks: Racism and Sexism in Canada's Immigration Policy." *Race & Class,* 42(1): 35–55.

Thompson, Allan (2003). "Refugee Board Backlog Despite Large Drop." *Toronto Star.* January 27.

Thompson, Allan (2003). "Critics Say Government Making It Harder to Get In." *Toronto Star.* March 15.

Thompson, Allan (2003). "Zundel haunts us." *Toronto Star.* April 19.

Thompson, Allan (2003). "Highly skilled immigrants left in lurch: Report." *Toronto Star.* June 6.

Thompson, Eden and Jean Lock Kunz (2002). "Facilitating the Labour Market Integration of Immigrants to Canada." *Horizons,* 5(2): 25–26.

Thorpe, Jacqueline (2003). "Canada mints more millionaires than U.S." *National Post.* June 12.

Tierney, William G. (2001). "Academic Freedom and Organisational Identity." *Australian Universities Review*: 7–11.

Toronto Star (2003). "Disabled often can't afford drugs they need: Study." May 20.

Toughill, Kelly (2000). "Burnt Church Natives Reject Lobster Deal." *Toronto Star*. August 10.

Townsend, Peter (2002). "Poverty, Social Exclusion, and Social Polarisation: the Need to Construct an International Welfare State." In P. Townsend and D. Gordon (Eds.), *World Poverty* (pp. 3–24). Bristol: Policy Press.

Townsend, Peter and David Gordon (Eds.) (2002). *World Poverty: New Policies to Defeat an Old Enemy.* Bristol: Policy Press.

Travers, James (2003). "Martin must focus on the poor." *Kitchener-Waterloo Record*. July 24.

Tremblay, Manon and Caroline Andrew (Eds.) (1998). *Women and Political Representation in Canada.* Ottawa: University of Ottawa Press.

Trichur, Rita (2001). "Young women shun feminist label but may still be feminist in principle." Canadian Press. Reprinted in the *Kitchener-Waterloo Record*. October 18.

Trimble, Linda and Jane Arscott (2003). *Still Counting. Women in Politics Across Canada.* Peterborough: Broadview Press.

Turner, Jonathan H. (2000). "Inequality and Stratification." In D. Dunn and D. Waller (Eds.), *Analyzing Social Problems* (pp. 62–70). Engelwood Cliffs, New Jersey: Prentice Hall.

Turow, Joseph (1992). *Media Style in Society. Understanding Initiatives/Strategies/Power.* White Plains, New York: Longman.

Turpel-Lafond, Mary Ellen (1996). "Oui the People? Conflicting Visions of Self-Determination in Quebec." *Public,* 14: 118–133.

Tyler, Tracey (2003). "Avoiding the jailhouse." *Toronto Star*. February 17.

Tyler, Tracey (2003). "Clarkson urges more women lawyers." *Toronto Star.* February 28.

Tyler, Tracey (2003). "More Inmates Serving Full Sentences." *Toronto Star.* September 27.

Vallis, Mary (2003). "Quality of care varies, report says." *National Post*. May 29.

Valpy, Michael (2003). "Men Were the Ones Who Gave You Wedgies." *The Globe and Mail.* October 4.

Valpy, Michael and Erin Anderssen (2003). "10 ways the 20s will change us." *The Globe and Mail.* July 1.

Venne, Michael and R. Chodos (Eds.) (2000). *Vive Quebec. New Thinking and New Approaches to the Quebec Question.* Toronto: James Lorimer.

Venne, Sharon (1999). *Our Elders Understand Our Rights. Evolving International Law Regarding Indigenous Peoples.* Penticton, British Columbia: Theytus Press.

Venne, Sharon (2003). "The Creator Knows Their Lies and So Should We." In W. Churchill (Ed.), *Perversions of Justice* (pp. 111–128). San Francisco: City Lights.

Vidal, John (2002). "A Third of Humanity will be Slum Dwellers by 2033." *Guardian Weekly.* October 9–15.

Vipond, Mary (2000). *The Mass Media in Canada.* Toronto: Lorimer

Vivian, John (1997). *The Media of Mass Communication.* Needham Heights, Massachusetts: Allyn Bacon.

Walker, James St. G. (1998). *"Race": Rights and the Law in the Supreme Court of Canada.* Waterloo: Wilfrid Laurier Press.

Walker, Michael (2003). "Corcoran's Immigration Mess." *National Post.* December 2.

Walkom, Thomas (2003). "Still Waiting." *The Globe and Mail.* November 29.

Wang, Xiaoyun (2003). "Harmony in our Diverse Workplace." *National Post.* October 20.

Waterfall, Barbara (2003). "Native Peoples and the Social Work Profession: A Critical Analysis of Colonizing Problematics and the Development of Decolonized Thought." In A. Westhues (Ed.), *Canadian Social Policy* (pp. 50–66). Waterloo: Wilfrid Laurier Press.

Watson, William (2003). "Poverty abolished in Canada!" Editorial. *National Post.* July 8.

Wax, Emily (2003). "Brutal Legacy of War in Congo." *Guardian Weekly.* November 6–12.

Weaver, C. Kay (2003). "Violence." Available at www.marketmag.co.nz

Webber, Jeremy (1994). *Reimaging Canada: Language, Culture, Community and the Canadian Constitution.* Montreal/Kingston: McGill-Queen's University Press.

Weber, Terry (2003). "Canada's economy 'robust'." *The Globe and Mail.* March 7.

Weinfeld, Morton (2001). *Like Everyone Else But Different: The Paradoxical Success of Canadian Jews.* Toronto: McClelland & Stewart.

Weintraub, Arlene (2003). "For-Profit Hospitals Coming up Lame." *Business Week.* July 14: 8.

Welsh, Moira (2003). "Inspired, Selfless: Heroes Who Care." *Toronto Star.* December 11.

Wente, Margaret (2003). "Fuzzy math, innumerate kids." *The Globe and Mail.* March 18.

Wente, Margaret (2003). "Whites need not apply." *The Globe and Mail.* May 29.

Werbner, Pnina (2002). *Imagined Diasporas among Manchester Muslims: The Public Performance of Pakistani Transnational Identity Politics.* Oxford, UK: James Curry Publishers.

Werbner, Pnina (2003). "The Politics of Multiculturalism in the New Europe." In B. Saunders and D. Haljan (Eds.). *Whither Multiculturalism* (pp. 47–60). Leuven University Press.

Westhead, Rich (2003). "Network Scores Revenue Touchdown." *Toronto Star.* November 14.

Westhues, Anne (2003). "An Overview of Social Policy." In A.Westhues (Ed.), *Canadian Social Policy* (pp. 5–24). Waterloo: Wilfrid Laurier Press.

Weston, Mary Ann (1996). *Native Americans in the News: Images of Indians in the Twentieth Century Press.* Westport, Connecticut: Greenwood Press.

Weston, Mary Ann (2003). "Journalists and Indians: The Clash of Cultures." Keynote speech. Symposium on American Indian Issues in the California Press. February 21. University of California at Los Angeles. Downloaded from bluecorncomics.com/weston.htm

Whitaker, Reg (1996). "Sovereign Division: Quebec's Nationalism between Liberalism and Ethnicity." In J. Littleton (Ed.), *Clash of Identities* (pp. 73–88). Toronto: Prentice Hall.

Widdowson, Frances and Albert Howard (2002). "The Disaster in Nunavut." In J. Bird et al. (eds.), *Nation to Nation*. Toronto: Irwin.

Wilkinson, Ray (2003). "Old Problems … New Realities." *Refugees*. December 5–10.

Williams, Cara (2003). "Stress at Work." *Canadian Social Trends*. Autumn: 7–10.

Williams, Mary E. (2003). *Race Relations: Opposing Viewpoints*. Thousand Oaks, California: Sage.

Willis, Andrew and Gayle MacDonald (2003). "The gap between rich and rich." *The Globe and Mail*. July 5.

Wilson, Clint II, Felix Gutierrez, and Lena M. Chao (2003). *Racism, Sexism, and the Media*. Thousand Oaks, California: Sage.

Wilson-Smith, Anthony (2002). "The kids are *really* all right." *Maclean's*. September 30.

Winter, James (1997). *Democracy's Oxygen. How Corporations Control the News*. Montreal: Black Rose Books.

Winter, James (2002). *Media Think*. Montreal: Black Rose Books.

Wise, Tim (2002). "Racial Profiling and Its Apologists." *Z Magazine*. March.

Wiwa, Ken (2003). "The fusion generation." *The Globe and Mail*. June 12.

Wolf, Naomi (1991). *The Beauty Myth*. Toronto: Random House.

Won, Shirley (2003). "Canada Faces Boomer Conundrum." *The Globe and Mail*. October 7.

Wong, Jan (1997). "Preston Manning Reforms from Geek to Sleek." *The Globe and Mail*. May 22.

Wong, Jan (2003). "The doctor is not in." *The Globe and Mail*. April 12.

Wong, Tony (2003) "Lakeside Luxury." *Toronto Star*. August 17.

Worldwatch Institute (2003). *State of the World 2003. A Worldwatch Institute Report on Progress Toward a Sustainable Society*. New York: WW Norton & Co.

Wortley, Scot (2003). "Civilian governance and Policing in a Multicultural Society. A Discussion Paper." Commissioned by the Department of Canadian Heritage for the National Forum on Policing in a Multicultural Society. February.

Wotherspoon, Terry and Vic Satzewich (1993). *First Nations: Race, Class, and Gender Relations*. Toronto: Nelson.

Wotherspoon, Terry (2003). "Aboriginal People, Public Policy, and Social Differentiation in Canada." In D. Juteau (Ed.), *Social Differentiation: Patterns and Processes* (pp. 155–197). Toronto: University of Toronto Press.

Yunus, Muhammad (2003). "Halving Poverty by 2015—We Can Actually Make it Happen." Lecture delivered to the Commonwealth Institute, London. March 11.

Zwicker, Heather (2001). "Multiculturalism: Pied Piper of Canadian Nationalism (and Joy Kagawa's Ambivalent Antiphony." *ARIEL*, 32(4): 147–175.

Index